Sabbath Diagnosis

A Diagnostic History and Physical Examination of the Biblical Day of Rest

Gary Hullquist, MD

TEACH Service, Inc.
www.tsibooks.com

ISBN 1-57258-262-6
Library of Congress Control Number: 2003110042

Published by

TEACH Services, Inc.
254 Donovan Road
Brushton, New York 12916

Organization of the Patient Chart

SABBATH DIAGNOSIS is a comprehensive examination of the seventh day and its modern clone from a clinical perspective.

Part 1: Historical Record

Previous diagnoses, medications, Surgical, Family and Social history all contribute to the differential diagnosis.

Part 2: Physical Examination

Examination of the physical evidence and diagnostic studies are reviewed to rule out unsupported diagnoses.

Rx: Medical Management

Therapeutic intervention is made on evidence-based multi-center controlled clinical trials.

Letter of Referral

September, 2003
RE: Sabbath Day

I am referring this patient to you in consultation for your professional opinion and recommendations regarding future management. Please perform a complete health status evaluation and address the long term prognosis. In light of previous reports, I am deferring a final decision on the patient's disposition pending your assessment.

Please find enclosed a summary of the clinical history, most recent physical exam and all lab findings.

I eagerly await your report,

M.D.C.

Make an Appointment

Our task, as spiritual clinicians, is to evaluate the health of the Biblical Sabbath. We may enlist the aid of specialty consultants if necessary because, like most patients, there is real potential for missing an important diagnosis or making a wrong one.

This case is being referred for a second opinion, a confirmatory consultation, because previous physicians have assessed the patient as either beyond hope, malnourished or even expired. The reports of some who have already seen this patient read like a post-mortem autopsy summary. They have consigned this corpse to the morgue. But wait, not so fast! There's a pulse, a full code has been called, and there are encouraging signs that the patient can be resuscitated. After being defibbed, the true original rhythm has been restored. A growing number of medical staff even predict that at the end of the day there will be a full recovery.

With the initial triage out of the way, our plan is to stabilize the patient and then admit for further workup. Our clinical investigation will involve the use of numerous problem solving skills. The patient's health is at stake and keen diagnostic analysis depends on integrating multiple sources of information and data. Pitfalls in this diagnostic process can occur from missing a vital piece of the patient's medical history (the subjective data) or failure to perform a complete physical examination or obtaining a pertinent diagnostic study (the objective data).

Workup Strategy
The patient's reported symptoms as well as the physical and laboratory findings must be coupled with a knowledge of disease pathogenesis (how the problem began), etiology (where it came from) and physiologic abnormalities (how it affects normal health) before a correct diagnosis can be made. Only then can effective treatment be prescribed.

The Diagnostic Process
Approaching the Sabbath subject can be very similar to the paradigm of arriving at a proper clinical diagnosis in the practice of medicine. Solving puzzles, putting the pieces together, is all part of the diagnostic process. Part 1 of our Report will consider the present, past, family and social history of the Sabbath.

The symptoms can be collected (most Christians worship once a week, only a minority observe a day of rest) and a chief complaint identified, most commonly expressed in the words of the patient ("I've needed rest for a very long time").

Past disease and surgical history must be obtained (Christians initially observed the seventh day of the week, but the 4th commandment, and in some cases all ten, has been excised through surgical removal).

Important family history can be elicited (Patriarchs and Church Fathers experienced related symptoms). Ancestral history also contributes to a body of important subjective data.

Then a detailed and comprehensive physical examination (inspection, auscultation, palpation—looking, listening, feeling the body of Scripture) as well as specific investigative studies (archeology, linguistics, and chronology) can be performed to produce a wealth of important objective data. This will be conducted in Part 2.

Now, your final diagnosis awaits you.

Historical Record

Chief Complaint
"I've been this way for a long time."

Every medical history must begin with a chief complaint, usually expressed in the patient's own words. "I feel tired all the time," "I've had a headache for the past six days," "My back hurts." This becomes the focus of the initial interview and inquiry. Our patient states the problem in concise terms: "I've been noticed by many people for a long time." Not so much a complaint as an observation.

History of the Present Illness
Taking our lead from the patient's chief complaint, we will pursue a series of leading questions related to not only the duration, but the quality, location, intensity, context, timing, modifying factors and associated symptoms. When did it begin? What kind of day is it? Where is it in the weekly cycle? How important is it? What was happening when it first started? How has it changed over time? What makes it better? What makes it worse? And what else have you noticed or experienced?

Duration: When did it begin?
Asking about duration is very important but surprisingly often bypassed in many clinical histories. The difference between an acute and chronic problem can be vital to both patient and physician response. Delay in addressing an acute process can be disastrous; impetuous interventions for a chronic condition may be equally devastating.

Although the Sabbath is nearly universally identified as a Jewish holy day, most Christians today believe it did not originate with the ancient Abraham, father of the Jews, but rather through the rather more modern Moses who lived some 500 years later. The original etiology of the Sabbath, however, can be traced much earlier than even Abraham. That, however, must wait for our next section, when we will review the details of the Sabbath's onset in the book of Genesis.

The historical ancestry and heritage of the Semitic peoples is recorded in the ancient Hebrew Scriptures where the descendants of Shem, one of the three sons of Noah, are listed. From our knowledge of Biblical anatomy, we know that later the Hebrew people originated with the patriarch Abraham, though there is some suggestion that the term itself may be derived from Eber, third after Shem and sixth before Abraham. Note that Noah was the 10th patriarch and Abram the 20th:

Shem, Arphaxad, Salah, **Eber**, Peleg, Reu, Serug, Nahor, Terah, **Abram**

Hebrew, which means "one who crossed over" (in the case of Abraham, the Euphrates river) is a term describing the language, culture and ethnic qualities of Abraham's descendents through Isaac (and especially his grandson Judah) whose decendants came to be more commonly referred to as Jews. Yet, evidence that the Sabbath was inherited through the line of Shem is the fact that the Semitic (Shemitic) people were the most responsible protectors of the Sabbath legacy and continue to be so today.

The Jews are the world's preeminent Sabbath keepers. But there are other, non-Biblical sources of Sabbath observance and its impact on many other cultures throughout the world. Part 1, the Historical Record, will trace this fascinating story through history, archeology and anthropology.

Close Relatives and Associated Symptoms

Besides Shem the other two progenitors of the post-diluvian world, Ham and Japheth, also bequeathed a sense of the seventh day and its significance to their descendants as well. Anthropological and archeological discoveries over the past centuries have uncovered a wide-spread representation of weekly religious observance indicating a distant awareness of the ancient Sabbath and its relation to the seventh day.

- **Egyptians** employed a seven note musical scale, a seven-day week and recognized seven planets (*Egyptian Rhythm*, Tehuti Research, p. 23).
- Ancient **Brahmins** placed special significance on the number seven and later Thomas Christians in **India** kept the Sabbath for centuries.
- **China** hosted Sabbath-keeping Christians for many hundreds of years.
- Almost a thousand years BC, **Homer** wrote of "the seventh day which is sacred or holy." **Hesiod** and **Plato** also referred to the seventh day. (Aristobulus, quoted in Eusebius *Praep. Evang.* 13:12,13).
- The **Romans** replaced their initial seven day week with the *nundinae*, a nine day week of seven days plus two market days. They did, however, end the year with a seven day feast called the *Saturnalia*.
- **Waldenses** and **Celts** preserved the seventh day in the Dark Ages.
- **Saxons, Britons, Norsmen, Gauls** and **Germans** all possessed a seven day week.

Sabbatarians were in significant numbers during the Reformation, promoted in Moravia, Silesia and Bohemia by Anabaptists led by former Catholic Priests Oswald Glait and Andreas Fisher. Other groups were reported in Poland, Holland, Germany, France, Hungary, Russia, Turkey, Finland and Sweden. In section 2, Family History, we will examine in detail the source of these hereditary characteristics. For now, only the immediate familial relationships will be explored.

Babylonian Pedigree or Contact?

There is some question as to whether the Babylonian Culture contributed to the genetic inheritance of the Sabbath or whether it was merely infected through contact with the Hebrew carrier. Closely related to, and in later years associated with the Jewish people, the ancient Babylonians called the seventh day the "day of completion."

> "The Sabbath-rest was a Babylonian, as well as a Hebrew, institution. Its origin went back to pre-Semitic days, and the very name, *Sabbat*, by which it was known in Hebrew, was of Babylonian origin. In the cuneiform tablets of the *Sabattu* is described as a 'day of rest for the soul,' and in spite of the fact that the word was of genuinely Semitic origin, it was derived by the Assyrian scribes from two Sumerian or pre-Semitic words, *sa* and *bat*, which meant respectively 'heart' and 'ceasing.' The Sabbath was also known, at all events in Accadian times, as a 'dies nefastus,' a day on which certain work was to be done, and an old list of Babylonian festivals and fast-days tells us that on the seventh, fourteenth, nineteenth, twenty-first, and twenty-eighth days each month the Sabbath-rest had to be observed." Sayce, A.H., *The Higher Criticism and the Monuments*, p. 74, 1895

They also shared a similar flood story, *The Gilgamish Epic*, best known of the Sumerian traditions, which tells of the Great Flood of Enlil. Gilgamish describes a hero named Utnapashti who, like Noah, built a large ship. But there the similarities fade. Utnapashti's boat has seven levels of compartments (instead of Noah's three), endured rain and wind that lasted only six days (versus 40) and then subsided on the seventh. But after that he, like Noah, offered sacrifices on the mountain top: "seven and seven did I lay the vessels" (XI:155) for which he was granted everlasting life.

In 1869 George Smith, pioneer Assyriologist, discovered among the cuneiform tablet archives of the British Museum "a curious religious calendar of the Assyrians, in which every month is divided into four weeks, and the seventh days or 'Sabbaths,' are marked out as days on which *no work* should be undertaken." Six years later Sir Henry Rawlinson published the calendar.

"It appears to be a transcript of a much more ancient Babylonian original, possibly belonging to the age of Hammurabi, which had been made by order of Asshurbanipal and placed in his royal library at Nineveh. The calendar, which is complete for the thirteenth or inter-calary month, called Elul II, and for Markheshwan, the eighth month of the Babylonian year, takes up the thirty days in succession and indicates the deity to which each day is sacred and what sacrifices or precautionary measures are necessary for each day." Henry Rawlinson, *Rest Days: A Study in Early Law and Morality*. New York: The Macmillan Company, 1916, P. 223.

Because the Babylonian calendar was a lunar calendar, and since the length of one lunar orbit is about 29.53 days, it alternated between 29 and 30 day months. This appears to have been inherited from ante-diluvian practices. A comparison of the chronological details of Noah's flood also indicate a pattern of alternating 29 and 30 day months. (See Epidemiology)

For the Babylonians there were certain restrictions assigned to every seventh rest day and the monthly dark days:

"Asurbanipal in the seventh century promulgated a calendar with a definite scheme of a seven-day week, a regulation of the month by which all men were to rest on days 7, 14, 19, 21, 28. The old menology of Nisan made the two days of the dark of the moon, 29, 30, rest-days, so that each lunar month had 9 rest-days, on which neither the sick could be cured nor a man in difficulty consult a prophet; none might travel and fasting was enforced." Langdon, S., *Babylonian Menologies and the Semitic Calendars*, London: Oxford University Press, 1935, p. 86.

Especially identified were the 7th, 14th, 19th, 21st and 28th days of the month.

Day	Significance
1	first visible crescent
7	waxing half moon
14	full moon
19	dedicated to an offended goddess
21	waning half moon
28	last visible crescent
29,30	invisible moon, dark days

The 19th was important because it is in fact the 49th (7x7) day from the first day of the previous month. The seventh day, though, was singled out as the day of rest: priests couldn't cook with fire that day or change their clothes, which must be white on the seventh day. The king couldn't drive a chariot or issue any royal decrees. Soothsayers couldn't mutter; the sick couldn't take any medicine. This degraded form of the Sabbath, like the perverted one in Christ's day burdened by hundreds of trivial prohibitions, at least demonstrates a shared and common source with the original Sabbath of creation, preserved through Noah's three sons and propagated to all civilizations after the dispersion at the tower of Babel. Shem then preserved the Sabbath through Abraham's ancestors and ultimately the Jewish nation.

The Hebrew word **shabbat** and **shabbata** (from which the English *sabbath* is translated) is applied in its verb form, **shabath**, in Genesis chapter 2:

> "And on the seventh day God ended his work which he had made; and he **shabath** on the **sh'biy**... and God blessed the seventh day, and sanctified it..." Genesis 2:2,3

Since Hebrew does not contain any vowels in the original consonantal roots, all these words are exactly the same: s-b-t or shin-bet-tav triad.

The influence of this Hebrew word on the name for the seventh day of the week used by hundreds of other languages, Semitic and Indo-European, testifies to the antiquity and pervasive nature of the Sabbath. A partial list of the languages, ancient and modern, that have incorporated this root into the seventh day designation is listed below:

SEMITIC LANGUAGES (descendants of Noah's son, Shem)

- Hebrew, Ancient and Modern:
    okhad be Shab-bath   **Shabbath**
    ("one into the Sabbath")   ("Sabbath")
- Ancient Syriac
    khad be Shab-bo   **Shabbatho**
    ("one into the Sabbath")   ("Sabbath")
- Chaldee Syriac (Kurdistan and Urumia, Persia)
    khad be Shab-ba   **Shaptu/Shapta**
    ("one into the Sabbath")   ("Sabbath")
- Babylonian (dating back to 3800 B.C.)
    Makh-ru   **Sabatu**
    ("first")   ("Sabbath")
- Arabic (western Asia, northern and western Africa)
    al Ahad   **as Sabt**
    ("the one")   ("the Sabbath")
- Maltese (Malta)
    h'Add   **is Sibt**
    ("one")   ("the Sabbath")
- Ethiopic (Abyssinia)
    e Hud   **Sanbat**
    ("one")   ("Sabbath")

HAMITIC LANGUAGES (descendants of Noah's son, Ham)

- Coptic (Egypt, a dead language for 300 years)
    pi Ehoou emmah a ouai   **pi Sabbaton**
    ("the first day")   ("the Sabbath")
- Tamashek (Atlas mountains, Africa)
    ahai Iyen   **ahal es Sabt**
    ("first day")   ("the Sabbath")
- Kabyle (North Africa, Ancient Numidan)
    ghas al Ahad   **ghas as Sebt**
    ("day the one")   ("the Sabbath day")
- Hausa (Central Africa)
    Lahade   **as Sebatu**
    ("the one, or first")   ("the Sabbath")

JAPHETIC LANGUAGES (Noah's son, Japheth)

- Hindustani (Muhammadan and Hindu, India)
    yek Shamba   **Shamba**
    ("one to the Sabbath")   ("Sabbath")

- Pasto (Afghanistan)
  yek Shamba   **Shamba**
  ("one to the Sabbath")   ("Sabbath")
- Pahlivi (ancient Persian)   **Shambid**
  Mittira ("sun")   ("pleasantest day of the week")
- Persian (Persia)   **Shambah**
  yek Shambi ("one to the Sabbath")   ("Sabbath")
- Armenian (Armenia)
  mia Shapti   **Shapat**
  ("one to the Sabbath")   ("Sabbath")
- Kurdish (Kurdistan)
  yek-shamba   **shamba**
  ("one to the Sabbath")   ("Sabbath")
- Brahuiky (Beluchistan)
  yek-shambe   **shembe**
  ("one to the Sabbath")   ("Sabbath")

MIDDLE AGES LANGUAGES

- Georgian (Caucasus)   **Shabati**
  Kvira ("lordly")   ("Sabbath")
- Suanian (Caucasus)
  Moushladh'h   **Sammtyn**
  ("day one")   ("Sabbath")
- Ingoush (Caucasus)
  Kyrynda   **Shatt**
  ("lordly")   ("Sabbath"
- Malayan (Malaya, Sumatra)
  Hari ahad   **hari Sabtu**
  ("day one")   ("day Sabbath")
- Javanese (Java)
  Dina ahad   **Saptoe** or **Saptu**
  ("day one")   ("Sabbath")
- Dayak (Borneo)
  Andau ahat   **Sabtu**
  ("day one")   ("Sabbath")
- Makassar (southern Celebes and Salayer islands)
  Aha   **Sattu**
  ("one")   ("Sabbath")
- Malagassy (Madagascar)
  Alahady   **al Sabotsy**
  ("the one")   ("the Sabbath")
- Swahili (east equatorial Africa)
  al Ahad   **as Sabt**
  ("the one")   ("the Sabbath")

- Mandingo (west Africa, south of Senegal)
    al Lahaddo **Sibiti**
    ("the one") ("Sabbath")
- Teda (central Africa)
    Lahadu **es Sebdu**
    ("the one") ("the Sabbath")
- Bornu (central Africa)
    Lade **Sibda**
    ("the one") ("Sabbath")
- Fulfulde (central Africa)
    Lahade **as Sebdu**
    ("the one") ("the Sabbath")
- Logone (central Africa)
    sel Lade **se Sibde**
    ("the one") ("the Sabbath")
- Bagrimma (central Africa)
    Lahadi **Sibbedi**
    ("the one") ("Sabbath")
- Maba (central Africa)
    Ahad **Sab**
    ("one") ("Sabbath")
- Permian (Russian)
    Vovzem, Kresene **Subota**
- Votiak (Russian)
    zuc-arna, arna-nunal **Subbota**

LANGUAGES USING FIRST DAY AS A BUSINESS DAY

- Arabic (very old names)
    au-had **Shi-yar**
    ("business day") ("chief or rejoicing day")
- Osmanlian (Turkey)
    bazaar-guni **yom es Sabt**
    ("market day") ("day of the Sabbath")
- Kazani-Tartar (east Russia)
    atna kone **Subbota**
    ("market day") ("Sabbath")
- Circassian (Circissia)
    mouy-isht-kha-maf **Mafizaka**
    ("market day") ("morrow after assembly")

MIDDLE AGES with FIRST DAY RELIGIOUS CONCEPTS

These relatively modern languages show the influence of Christian
    missionaries applying variations of Latin "Dominicus" or
    "Dominus" (Lord's Day) to the first day of the week.

- Orma (south of Abyssiania)
      Gifti   **Zambada**
      ("lady," "Virgin Mary day")   ("Sabbath")
- Congo (west equatorial Africa)
      Sumingo (Domingo)   **Sabbado** or **Kiansbula**
      ("second market day")   ("Sabbath")
- Wolof (Senegambia, west Africa)
      Dibar   **Alere asser**
      (Diamanche)   ("last day Sabbath")
- Norman French (10th and 11th centuries)
      Diemane   **sabbedi**
      ("Sabbath day")
- D'oc. French (ancient and modern)
      Dimenche   **Dissata**
      ("day dominical")   ("day Sabbath")
- Ecclesiastical Roman
      Dominica   **Sabbatum**
      ("Sabbath")
- Latin (Italy)
      dies solis ("day of the sun")   **Sabbatum**
      Dies Dominicus ("day of the Lord")   ("Sabbath")
- Italian (Italy)
      Demenica   **Sabato, Sabbato**
      ("Sabbath")
- Spanish (Spain)
      Domingo   **Sabado**
      ("Sabbath")
- Portugese (Portugal)
      Domingo   **Sabbado**
      ("Sabbath")
- French (France)
      Diamanche   **Samedi**
      ("day dominical")   ("Sabbath day")
- Roman (Sapin, Catalonia)
      Diumenge   **Dissapte**
      ("day Sabbath")
- Wallachian (Roumania or Wallachia)
      Duminica   **Sambata**
      ("Sabbath")

- German
  - Sonntag
    ("sun day")
  - **Samstag**
    ("Sabbath day")
- Swedish
  - Söndag
    ("sun day")
  - **Lördag**
    ("Lord's day")
- Danish
  - Søndag
    ("sun day")
  - **Lørdag**
    ("Lord's day")
- Norwegian
  - Søndag
    ("sun day")
  - **Lørdag**
    ("Lord's day")
- Finnish
  - Sunnuntai
    ("sun day")
  - **Lauantai**
    ("Lord's day")
- Dutch
  - Zondag
    ("sun day")
  - **Zaterdag**
    ("Saturday")
- Russian
  - Voskresenje
    ("Sabbath")
  - **Subbota**
- Hungarian
  - Vasarnap
    ("Sabbath")
  - **Szombat**
- Romanian
  - Duminica
    ("Sabbath")
  - **Simbata**
- Illyrian (Dalmatia, Serbia)
  - Nedjelja
    ("Sabbath")
  - **Subota**
- New Slovenian (Illyria, in Austria)
  - Nedela
  - **Sobota** ("Sabbath")
- Bulgarian (Bulgaria)
  - Nedjelja
    ("Sabbath")
  - **Subbota**
- Polish (Poland)
  - Niedziela
  - **Sobota** ("Sabbath")
- Bohemian
  - Nedele
  - **Sobota** ("Sabbath")
- Lusatian (Saxony)
  - Njedzela
  - **Sobota** ("Sabbath")
- Prussian (Prussia)
  - Nadele
  - **Sabatico**

This list was originally organized by William Meade Jones in his *Chart of the Week* and subsequently entered into the Library of Congress in 1886.

Notice the Scandinavian use of "Lord's Day" for the seventh day is indication of the strong historical influence on this language group.

Many have noted how far reaching the Sabbath impacted the many peoples and civilizations throughout history.

> "The fact that the celebration of such a day existed fairly universally, and that the nearer one approaches the heart of Asia, the more this day tends towards the seventh day, points to a common origin of this custom, which can only be explained by an original unity of usage amongst the first children of men." Abraham Kuyper, *Tractaat van den Sabbath* (Treatise on the Sabbath), Wormser, Amsterdam, 1890, p. 18

> "Echoes of this seventh creation day of rest persist regularly and rhythmically down through the ages." Frances Nigel Lee, *The Everlasting Covenant Sabbath*, doctoral thesis.

Jewish historian Josephus also attributes the creation week to the origin of the Jewish Sabbath:

> "Moses says that in just six days the world and all that is therein was made. And that the seventh day was a rest and a release from the labour of such operations. WHENCE it is that we celebrate a rest from our labour on that day, and call it the Sabbath; which word denotes rest in the Hebrew tongue." Josephus, *Antiquities of the Jews,* Book 1, Chapter 1, Section 1

The Sabbath is a well-established ancient observence.

Associated Symptoms
Once the presenting problem is identified, then an exploration of related systems and their symptoms is made. When someone complains of feeling "tired," of being "restless," having "no energy," or give a history of having "chronic fatigue," then it's obvious that such patients need rest. It is generally appreciated that "one week without God makes one weak." Once this is identified, we can obtain more detail by asking specific questions about associated symptoms:

1. When do you have these feelings? "at the end of a busy week"
   Then read Exodus 20:8-12.

2. What makes it worse?
   "carrying a burden of guilt," "fearing the future"
   Then read Matthew 11:28.

3. What makes it better?
   "forgetting about the past," "taking a day off"
   Then join the Creator on the day of re-creation.

4. What else do you notice when you feel this way?
   Do you feel hungry?
   Do you have an empty feeling?
   Are you unfulfilled?
   Then read Matthew 5:6.

5. Do you feel dizzy? Like you're losing your balance?
   Can't tell which way's up?
   Then read John 14:6.

Now we can explore the origins and initial causes.

Etiology

The cause, the source, the origin of any clinical condition is known as the etiology of that process. Frequently both the etiology and the diagnosis are made simultaneously. For example, a specific identifiable organism may be responsible for a patient's infection; an environmental toxin may be deemed the underlying cause of an allergic reaction or malignant change. The etiology of a condition, the mechanism, how it started, where it came from, is an important component of determining diagnosis. In arriving at the Sabbath Diagnosis, etiology is a crucial factor in our evaluation.

Big Bang Beginning

Both the Genesis account of creation and that embraced by modern astrophysics describe a unique event, a one-time singularity that began from nothing with the production of light and plenty of it. This interesting convergence between theology ("God said, Let there be light") and cosmology began with Edwin Hubble in the 1920s with his description of an expanding universe. Astronomers soon began to ponder how this cosmic expansion started in the first place. George Gamow, a nuclear physicist who worked on the atomic bomb project during World War II, imagined the very first thermonuclear reaction of cosmic proportions beginning as an infinitely dense sea of stupendously hot neutrons inside the mother of all pressure cookers blowing its top in a flash of pure energy. This primordial inferno, Gamow suggested, produced all the elemental atomic particles of the universe in approximately 30 minutes.

Gamow excelled at persuasive writing and released his first book, *One, Two, Three, Infinity,* in 1947. Presenting his A-bomb universe as an accepted fact and in such a vivid, plausible way, quickly made his theory immensely popular among the lay readers and gained immediate reception by the scientific community. Sir Fred Hoyle, whose competing theory of thermonuclear neogenesis failed on technical grounds, sarcastically referred to Gamow's scheme as nothing more than a "big bang." Ironically, the term stuck. Soon, everyone seemed to be jumping on the Bang Wagon.

While Einstein had favored a spatially finite universe, Gamow succeeded in also making it finite in the realm of time as well. While this idea was fascinating it was also shocking. To some it seemed to be an insult to common sense. To others it was a welcome return to the Biblical universe—having a definite origin, created in an instant, by a process no longer in operation, beyond examination, and nonreproducible. The philosophical consequences were slow in coming, but twenty years later questions were being asked. What caused the Big Bang? What came before it? Many rejoiced over this theory that invited the hypothesis of supernatural power.

Creation Sabbath

"In the beginning God created the heaven and the earth.
And the earth was without form, and void;
and darkness was upon the face of the deep.
And the Spirit of God moved upon the face of the waters.
And God said, Let there be light: and there was light.
And God saw the light, that it was good:
and God divided the light from the darkness.
And God called the light Day, and the darkness he called Night.
And the evening and the morning were the first day." Genesis 1:1-5

In the beginning, God created our planet home in six days and rested the seventh. Genesis, the book of beginnings, tells the story. The very first week on Earth set the pattern, and Man has marked time ever since by that original seven day formula. Life is bound to the creation connection. Our Creator set the pace for the human race as a cycle of time stamped with His own divine signature. Seven days kick-started this world with a reoccurring theme that pervades not only Biblical Scriptures but the distant memory of every culture and life form. This is where the story of the Sabbath begins.

Day 1 He said, "Let there be light"
** 2 He divided the waters with the atmospheric heaven**
** 3 He formed dry land and green vegetation**
** 4 He created the sun, moon and stars**
** 5 He fashioned creatures for the air and water**
** 6 He designed all land animals and the first humans**

Six days. Oh, God could have done it in far less. However, the story of Genesis "is not about power, but about people. It is not about science, but about serenity." Des Cummings captured these thoughts in his captivating book, *Original Love*, (Hart Books, 2001). Many more excerpts are to follow.

Creation Triplets

Elohim, the plural Creator God, based creation on multiples of three. For three days He spoke into existence the primal habitats and environments. Then for three days He commanded the objects and life forms to inhabit them. Notice the pattern in these events:

Day	Environments	Day	Occupants
1	**LIGHT**	4	**LIGHT** bodies
2	**WATER-AIR**	5	**WATER-AIR** creatures
3	**LAND**	6	**LAND** creatures

The first three days of creation provided this world with three different environments: outer space, fluid space and solid space. The next three days provided an array of objects and life forms for each environment. Genesis even lists them in groups of three:

Three Heavenly Lights:	sun, moon, stars
Three Times:	days, months, years
Three Kinds of Plants:	grass, herbs, trees
Three Sea-Air Forms:	birds, whales, water creatures
Three Land Forms:	Cattle, creeping things, beasts

Each of the first six days has its mate. And just as Adam realized he was alone after his arrival on day six, so the Sabbath is unmatched, alone, unique. And just as God provided Adam with a perfect mate, so God provided one for the Sabbath: Himself in the bonds of holy matrimony with the human race.

> God is our husband, (Isaiah 54:5)
> we are His bride, (Revelation 21:2, Ephesians 5:25)
> the Sabbath is our wedding chapel (Cummings)

At the end of the sixth day, after preparing the perfect home for His children, God did not simply speak man into existence as He did for the rest of creation; Jesus, our Creator, bent down and personally formed Adam and Eve with His very own hands.

Seventh Day: God's Day and Man's First
The world's first Sabbath was inaugurated just hours after Adam and Eve's creation on the sixth day. Unfallen man began existance observing the Sabbath. It was their first full day of life. And it was God's wedding gift to the first human couple. The Sabbath was their honeymoon, and God provided everything to make it the most romantic, the most perfect celebration of life and love.

As Des Cummings, Jr. so artfully writes,

"In six days God created Life;
        on the seventh He created Love."
He put "creatures of choice" in "a garden of love."

"On the sixth day God unites Adam and Eve in marriage...
        "they become one flesh"
"On the seventh day God unites humanity and divinity...
        "together they become one spirit"

"Life without love is existence,
but life filled with love is Sabbath."

Sabbath Trinity

There is no question that the seventh day received special recognition from God at the time of creation. Notice the Sabbath trinity:

> "And on the seventh day God ended his work which he had made; and he **rested** on the seventh day... and God **blessed** the seventh day, and **sanctified** it..." Genesis 2:2,3

These three acts of God on the seventh day infused the Sabbath with three fundamental qualities: Rest, Blessing and Sanctification. Des Cummings, Jr. calls them the primary colors of love."

Could "rest" be green? "Blessing" blue? "Sanctification" white? Just a thought. But whatever the tri-color banner might be, Eden's three-fold benediction is a perfectly parallel compliment to the fourth commandment in Exodus chapter 20:

> "For in six days the LORD made heaven and earth, the sea, and all that in them is, and **rested** the seventh day: wherefore the LORD **blessed** the Sabbath day, and **hallowed** it." Exodus 20:11

While God spoke once at the end of the first five days and three times on the sixth day, on the seventh day He didn't say anything, instead He did three things: He rested on it, He blessed it, and He sanctified it—made it holy. Even the angels follow this pattern of three as they cry continuously about His throne, "Holy, holy, holy." Isaiah 6: 3; Revelation 4:8.

Let's take a closer look at the Sabbath trinity.
On the seventh day God

- **Rested** from His work- Hebrew Word *shabat* or Sabbath.
  It means to cease from work or activity.
- **Blessed** the seventh day- Hebrew Word *barak*
  It means to kneel in adoration, to bless, to benefit.
- **Sanctified** it- Hebrew word *qadosh*
  He made it holy, clean, consecrated, dedicated, set apart for a
  special purpose.

1. Holy Time: "He Sanctified It"

Abraham Joshua Heschel, in his famous book *The Sabbath*, observes
that this word *qadosh/kadesh*, wrapped in "the mystery and majesty
of the divine," has many shades of meaning. Besides sanctified, it can
be rendered as hallowed, made holy, separated, separate from others,
different from the common, cut out from the ordinary, or a cut above
the rest, transcendent.

The first holy object in history, he observes, was not a holy mountain,
it wasn't a holy altar or a shrine or a holy place. The first time this
word *qadosh* (holy) appears in the Bible it is applied to a *day* in *time*.
"God blessed the seventh *day* and made it *holy*."

Then, nearly 2500 years later, at Sinai God called for "holiness in man: "Thou shalt be unto me a *holy* people, a *holy* nation, a royal priesthood." It wasn't until after this that God directed Moses to build a sanctuary with a holy *place*.

Space-Time
Time was sanctified by God on the seventh day.
Man was pronounced holy at Sinai.
Space was consecrated in the tabernacle.

Sanctity of time came first,
Sanctity of man came second,
Sanctity of space came last.

Samuele Bacchiocchi also recognizes the special time-focused aspect of the Sabbath:

> "Of all the commandments, the Sabbath offers us the most concrete opportunity to show our love to God because it invites us to consecrate our time to Him. Time is the essence of our life. The way we use our time is indicative of our priorities." *Sabbath in the Crossfire*, Chapter 3, Part 2B.

Des Cummings makes a similar connection between space and time:
> "God is love in person,
> Sabbath is love in time,
> Church is love in place"

But Heschel especially compares and contrasts the six days of space with the seventh day of time:

Space On the six days of labor:	Time On the seventh day of rest:
we build things in space	we build a sanctuary in time
we belong to space/body	we sample eternity
we wrestle with the world	we nurture the seeds of eternity
we dominate the world	we try to dominate the self
we struggle for existence	we call a truce with all conflict
we ponder and worry	we abstain from strain
we hope for redemption	we experience redemption
the results of creation	the mystery of creation
the world of creation	the creation of the world
the tyranny of things	holiness in time
the world has our hands	our soul belongs to Someone else
the earth is our mother	God is our Father
a world of things	a world of Spirit
time is money	time is life

Man is self-centered; the Sabbath is God-centered.
We prefer pleasure and profit; the Sabbath gives us the peace and presence of God. Samuele Bacchiocchi, *Crossfire*, Chap 3, Part 2B.

Whereas the focus of every human religion is on a special *place* (a temple, a shrine, a holy mountain), God seeks the worship of His creatures in a special *time* that uniquely identifies Him as their Creator. While we as humans tend to think of the creation of *things*, God is known for His creation of events in *time*. As Heschel points out, a thing can possess only a single exclusive space in the universe and can occupy only one location at a time, but an instant of time is shared equally by every thing in the universe simultaneously and no one thing can possess it exclusively.

Holy Presence
In Exodus 3 Moses encountered the presence of God in a burning bush. And "when the LORD saw that he turned aside to look," He said to him, "Do not draw near this place. Take your sandals off your feet, for the place where you stand is holy ground." Why was it holy? God was there. Only the presence of God can make something holy.

When God came down on mount Sinai to speak to His chosen people, His presence made not only the mountain but the people holy. When the holy people entered the promised land, their presence and God's Shechinah glory made it the Holy Land. When our holy God meets with His creatures on the seventh day, His presence transforms it into the Holy Sabbath day. God sanctified the Sabbath for the purpose of bringing union and communion between Himself and His creation.

Holy Proclamation
In addidtion to God's presence, an object is sanctified by His proclamation. At Sinai, God instructed Moses to "Set bounds about the mount, and sanctify it" Exodus 19:23. To set it apart, to sanctify it meant to announce and proclaim its holiness to the people "saying, Take heed to yourselves, that you go not up into the mount or touch the border of it." God told Moses to sanctify the mountain; Moses then told the people not to touch it; it was off limits, out of bounds, holy. Because the mountain was sanctified, they were to treat it as holy as God Himself.

Holy Appointment
And not only does sanctifying involve holy presence and holy proclamation, it also includes the idea of appointment. When the cities of refuge were established, Joshua wrote that "they *appointed* Kedesh in Galilee" as the first of six cities. This word 'appointed' in Hebrew is *qadash* which, being the same root means "to appoint, bid, consecrate, dedicate, hallow, be or keep holy, keep, prepare, proclaim, purify, and sanctify (according to Strong's entry 6942).

The cities of refuge were appointed by a public announcement or proclamation that they be set apart for a special purpose. This same word is used to "*Sanctify* a fast, call a solemn assembly, gather the elders and all the inhabitants of the land into the house of the Lord." Joel 1:14. "Blow the trumpet in Zion, *sanctify* a fast, call a solemn assembly." Joel 2:15 Likewise, when God set apart the Seventh day He sanctified it by His *presence*, He *appointed* the Sabbath as His day of rest and He *proclaimed* it holy to His newly created children.

Amos 3:3 says "Can two walk together unless they are agreed?" When we agree to keep our weekly appointment with God we are in step with creation and our Creator.

The Sabbath is holy, not because we keep it, but because God set it apart. And it was set apart by God, not man. The Sabbath continues to be sanctified, it continues to be holy whether men observe it or not. God's act, not man's, determined that fact in the beginning.

2. "He Blessed It"

> "Blessed is the man that does this, and the son of man that lays hold on it; that keeps the Sabbath." Isaiah 56:2.

One day in seven, every individual shares the same freedom, breathes the same air of liberty. It reminds us that there are limits to the exploitation of natural resources. The 18th century Rabbi Levi Yitzhak of Berdichev once said, "Sabbath is the time when we stand still and let our blessings catch up with us." Moses told Aaron to bless the children of Israel with these words:

> "The Lord bless you, and keep you;
> The Lord make His face to shine upon you, and be gracious unto you;
> The Lord lift up His countenance upon you, and give you peace."
> Numbers 6:24-26

Aaron's blessing captures the three-fold Sabbath formula enacted by God on the seventh day of Creation:

The Lord bless thee	He blessed it
And keep thee (make His face to shine upon thee)	He Sanctified it
And give thee peace.	He rested on it

The Sabbath is not only a time but a state of mind. Those who dwell within its atmosphere discover a realm where there is no room for strife, no fighting, fear or distrust. God is present and "He leads us beside the *still* waters." That brings rest.

3. "He Rested On It"
"For he spake in a certain place of the seventh *day* on this wise, and God did rest the seventh day from all his works." Hebrews 4:4.

After working those first six magnificent days of explosive creativity, God chose to rest on the seventh. Why rest? He certainly didn't need to. "He that keepeth Israel shall neither slumber nor sleep." Psalm 121:4. And "the everlasting God, the Lord, the Creator of the ends of the earth, fainteth not, neither is weary" Isaiah 40:28. He was not tired from six days of hard labor. He simply paused, reflected on the results of His creative energy and enjoyed what He had accomplished. "On the seventh day he rested, and was refreshed." Exodus 31:17. "God saw every thing that he had made, and behold, it was very good." Genesis 1:31. "The morning stars sang together, and all the sons of God shouted for joy." Job 38:7.

Genesis tells us that on the seventh day God "finished His work." We would naturally think that He finished His work on the sixth day and rested the seventh. But, in fact, He created one more thing on the seventh day: rest, tranquility, peace, stillness, harmony, serenity, repose, happiness. According to Des Cummings, "The universe was incomplete without it."

Sabbath rest invites us to let God do His work for us and in us. When Egyptian armies threatened Israel at the water's edge, God said:

"Fear not, stand *still*, and see the salvation of the Lord; The Lord shall fight for you, and you shall hold your *peace*." Exodus 14:13,14 Was this a Sabbath day? It certainly was a Sabbath experience of rescue and redemption, peace and protection.   See Appendix A

David said, "Rest in the Lord, and wait patiently for him" Psalm 37:7. Sabbath teaches man the vital lesson of leaving the business of salvation up to God. It is the final rest, the ultimate rest from sin that God desires for us to enter. "For we which have believed do enter into rest...Let us labor therefore to enter into that rest." Hebrews 4:3, 11. Sabbath rest is a pledge of mutual fidelity and commitment, an external and visible bond that unites believers.

Sabbath, as the rest at the end of each week, became a prelude to the final Sabbath of rest from sin at the end of time, a model for the time when man will once again experience

- "peaceful habitation" "in quiet resting places"
  Deut. 12:9; 25:19; Isaiah 14:3; 32:18.
- "rest from all enemies" 2 Samuel 7:1.

and God will find His "resting place" among His people and in His temple (2 Chron. 6:41; 1 Chron. 23:25; Psalm 132:8, 13, 14; Isaiah 66:1).

The seventh day is thus distinguished from the other six:
Sabbath is a day of rest and peace, liberty and release.
Sabbath is a blessed day, and we who enter it are blessed as well.
Sabbath is a holy day, and God sanctifies us and cleanses us and makes us holy on His day so He can present us to Himself, so He can bless us.

Original Seven Day Week
With the first five days God pronounced each one "Good." On the sixth day He pronounced it "Very good." And yet He wasn't through. One more thing was needed. On the seventh day God paused to reflect on the magic and beauty of that special, once in a lifetime moment—and He created the Sabbath.

The first seven days thus became the prototype for all following weeks. For six days He fashioned the perfect planet; then He paused for one more day to enjoy His work of art. This pattern of seven is seen repeatedly throughout the scripture record.

Cosmic Sanctuary Week
An interesting example of the seven day week motif is seen in a parallel found in the last chapter of Exodus where Moses recounts how the sanctuary was organized. The same sequence in the same

order is also listed in chapter 35:11-16. But here in Exodus 40, like the "evening and the morning" formula used in Genesis 1, each item ends with a standard phrase: "as the Lord commanded Moses." Notice each particular component of the sanctuary as they are listed. There are seven in all.

1 Verse 19 "He spread abroad...the **covering** of the tent above upon it." "as the Lord commanded Moses."
2 Verse 21 "and set up the **veil** of the covering and covered the ark." "as the Lord commanded Moses."
3 Verse 23 "He set the **bread** in order upon it before the Lord." "as the Lord commanded Moses."
4 Verse 25 "He lighted the **lamps** before the Lord." "as the Lord commanded Moses."
5 Verse 27 "He put the golden **altar**...and he burnt sweet **incense**" "as the Lord commanded Moses."
6 Verse 29 " He put the **altar** of burnt **offering** by the door" "as the Lord commanded Moses."
7 Verse 30 "He set the **laver**...and put water there to **wash** *withal*." "as the Lord commanded Moses."

Now notice how the concepts associated with these seven symbols are directly parallel to and correspond with the seven days of creation:

1	LIGHT	"divided light from the darkness"	covering
2	WATER-AIR	"divided waters under from above"	veil
3	LAND	"earth brings forth seed and fruit"	bread
4	LIGHT	"Let there be lights in the firmament"	lamps
5	WATER-AIR	"fly above the earth in the open air"	incense
6	LAND	"cattle, creeping thing, and beast"	sacrifices
7	SABBATH	"washed, purified, cleansed"	laver

This is a broad picture of the cosmic sanctuary. The vastness of space is its covering "above upon it" as "darkness was upon the face of the deep. And the Spirit of God moved upon the face of the waters" (Genesis 1:2). The veil between the holy and most holy places is represented by the division of the two firmaments (1:6). The dry land brings forth vegetation and grain from which bread is prepared. "Bread comes out of the earth" (Job 28:5). The sun, moon and stars become the lampstand. Birds fly in the sky as living incense ascends to heaven. Land animals serve as sacrifices for the altar.

When we come to the Sabbath, the emphasis in this part of the parallel sanctuary comparison is on sanctification and holiness. Paul, speaking of the Church, said that Christ so loved it, He "gave himself for it: that he might *sanctify* and *cleanse* it with the *washing* of *water* by the word." (Ephesians 5:25, 26). On the Sabbath, God wants to wash away the dirt of our labor, to cleanse our tired bodies, and purify our weary hearts., "that he might present it to himself a glorious church, not having spot, or wrinkle, or any such thing; but that it should be *holy* and without blemish." (Verse 27).

The seventh day also is linked to cleansing in the purification ceremony of the Red Heifer sacrifice. If anyone should ever touch a dead body, a bone or a grave they were declared "unclean for seven days." Numbers 19:16. But there was a remedy. The ashes of the red heifer could be mixed with water and sprinkled on them with hyssop on the third and seventh days. "And on the seventh day he shall purify himself, and wash his clothes, and bathe himself in water, and shall be clean at even." Num 19:19. Failure to do this would bring the severe consequences of being "cut off from among the congregation, because he has defiled the sanctuary of the Lord: the water of purification has not been sprinkled upon him; he is unclean."

Water of separation, water of purification, sanctifying water. This is the Sabbath water of the laver, cleaning us from sin and death.

The apostle John, in his visionary journey through the heavenly sanctuary, began in the holy place where he saw Christ walking among the candlesticks. His next stop, in chapter 4, was in a vast area before the throne of God.

> "A throne was set in heaven... and there were seven lamps of fire burning before the throne... and before the throne there was a **sea of glass** like unto crystal." Revelation 4:2,5,6.

This passage give us a glimpse of how immense the heavenly sanctuary really is compared to the earthly model. Instead of the brass basin fashioned by Moses or even the multiple lavers provided by Solomon, here the heavenly laver is a sea! Its mention indicates that John is now in a Sabbath environment. Notice the themes of holiness, time and creation in the surrounding verses.

> "And the four beasts...rest not day and night, saying, **Holy, holy, holy,** Lord God Almighty, which **was, and is, and is to come**." Rev. 4:8

This is a reference to God's timelessness, and time is a prime aspect of Sabbath holiness. Then the Sabbath focus turns to worship and the Creator.

> "The 24 elders fall down before him that sat on the throne, and **worship** him that liveth for ever and ever, and cast their crowns before the throne, saying, Thou art worthy, O Lord, to receive glory

and honor and power: for thou hast **created** all things, and for thy pleasure they are and were **created**." Revelation 4:10, 11.

Worship Worthy

Worship takes place with the proclamation of God's creatorship. It is this very link to creation that authorizes worship on the seventh day Sabbath.

> "O come, **let us worship** and bow down: let us kneel before **the Lord our maker**" Psalm 95:6

True worship is conducted by grateful creatures in honor of, and in grateful loyalty to, their Creator-Redeemer. The primary issue throughout the book of Revelation is worship. It will also be the final factor determining loyalty to God at the end of time. The last message of warning to the world, just before Christ returns to this earth, is a call to worship:

> "And I saw another angel flying in the midst of heaven having the everlasting gospel to them that dwell on earth, to every kindred and tongue and people; crying with a loud voice, saying, Fear God and give glory to Him, for the hour of His judgment is come, and *worship Him who made the heavens and the earth and the fountains of water*." Revelation 14:6-8

This is nearly identical to the Sabbath language of Exodus 20 where God declares Himself the One who "made heaven and earth, the sea and all that in them is." In the final moments of time, just before Christ appears in the clouds with sickle in hand, ready to harvest the earth, the last call to the entire world is given to worship the Creator. Sabbath symbolism is strongly portrayed in these verses.

Seven-part Genesis

The seven day pattern of the creation story also shows up in a segmented sequence involving the entire book of Genesis as seven identifiable sections that correspond to each day of the week. Again the seventh section demonstrates distinct Sabbath qualities. This has been described by both James B. Jordan (Basileans lectures, 1990) and Gordon J. Wenham (*Word Biblical Commentary: Genesis 1-15*, Waco, Texas: Word Books, 1987).

Jeremy Holmes has further noted that each section is separated by the reoccurring phrase "these are the generations," similar to the patterns used in Exodus 40 and Genesis 1. This distinctive expression is used six times following the creation story to introduce six additional sections to Moses' Book of Beginnings.

The Seven Sections of Genesis

1 The **Creation** of heaven and earth
   Gen 2:4 "These are the generations of the heavens and of the earth"
2 The **Fall**: separation of waters above and below
   Gen 5: 1 "This is the book of the generations of Adam"
3 The **Flood: waters gathered,** dry land & plants appear
   Gen 10:1 "These are the generations of the sons of Noah"
4 The **Call of Abram** to take the light of God to the world
   Gen 11:10 "These are the generations of Shem" and v. 27 "Terah"
5 The **Life of Abraham** who offers the incense of prayer
   Gen 25:12 "These are the generations of Ishmael" and v. 19 "Isaac"
6 The **Life of Isaac** who was offered on an altar of sacrifice
   Gen 36:1 "These are the generations of Esau"
7 The **Story of Jacob and Joseph** and rest in Goshen

Immediately following the seventh day of creation, Genesis 2:4 records the first occurance of the reocurring phrase by stating "These are the generations of the heavens and of the earth."

This is followed by the story of the Fall of Man and his separation from God which sin brings. This story clearly parallels the theme of the second day of creation when the waters above were *separated* from the waters below and the further parallel of Exodus 40 where the veil in the sanctuary *separates* the Holy from the Most Holy place.

Probably the clearest parallel is drawn between the third day of creation, when the waters are gathered and the dry land appears, and the third Genesis division which deals with the story of Noah and the Flood where the ark emerges from a world of water in the mountains of Ararat as dry land first appears.

But it is unquestionably significant that Genesis ends with the Sabbath themes of reconciliation and rest that are captured in the story of Jacob and Joseph. God's people are finally reconciled with each other, they find rest in the land of Goshen and are at peace with their Gentile neighbors who have experienced the blessings of God through Joseph's Divinely inspired food management program during the seven years of agricultural abundance and another seven of global famine.

Seventh Sabbath Generation

The Sabbath essence of seventhness is also seen in the parallel generations of Adam's descendents. Seven generations from Adam ends with Enoch through the line of Shem and with an ungodly Lamech through the line of Cain. After introducing both of these characters, their lives are detailed in a matching pair of interlude passages.

Lamech the ungodly was the world's first polygamist and the second known murderer who boasts of killing another man. While God promised Cain a seven-fold retribution on anyone who might kill him (Gen 4:15 a symbol of God's perfect mercy), this Lamech blasphemously claims he will be avenged 77 times, a symbol of complete or perfect vengeance. Contrast this with the grandson of Enoch who was also named Lamech. This godly Lamech lives 777 years, an expanded multiple of seven and symbol of complete or perfect righteousness.

Enoch, seventh from Adam, experiences perfect rest in God's presence by not seeing death. Only three individuals are listed in the great faith chapter of Hebrews 11 as representatives of those who lived before the flood: Abel who was martyred, Noah who lived through great tribulation, and Enoch who was translated right into heavenly rest without dying. At the time when this occurred, only one person had died of natural causes among the sons of God: Adam. Seth was still alive at age 896. Now the second non-violent departure from this life had taken place.

But Sabbath rest and deliverance is promised through the son of the Lamech who lived 777 years. He gives to this son the sabbatical name of Noah, "rest." Lamech explains: "He will comfort us in the labor and painful toil of our hands."

The Creator's Day
The fact that Moses records the special blessing placed on the seventh day, is indication that he received this fact as part of the oral tradition recounting Adam's original experience. Martin Luther recognized this when he said,

> "If Adam had stood in his innocency, yet he should have kept the seventh day holy, that is, on that day he should have taught his children, and children's children, what was the will of God, and wherein his worship did consist; he should have praised God, given thanks, and offered." Quoted by William Twisse (1578-1646) in *Morality of the Fourth Commandments Still in Force to Binde Christians delivered by way of Answer to the translator of Doctor Prideaux his Lecture, Concerning the Doctrine of the Sabbath,* London, 1641, pp. 56, 57.

If Adam would have told his children, then God would clearly have informed the first man about the first Sabbath because

"The Sabbath was made for man" Mark 2:27

The word "made" used here is *egeneto* from *ginomai*, meaning "to create." In other words, the Sabbath was *created* for man *after* man was created. It was added as a benefit to the human race. Because of its Creation week origin, the Sabbath is therefore one of God's created works, and the quintessential symbol of creation. It is not surprising, then, that God identifies Himself as the Creator throughout the Bible:

> "Lift up your eyes on high, and behold who hath **created** these things" "The everlasting God, the Lord, **the Creator** of the ends of the earth" Isaiah 40:26, 28
>
> "When I consider Thy heavens, **the work of Thy fingers**, the moon and the stars, which Thou hast **ordained**" Psalm 8:3
>
> "The heavens declare the glory of God; and the firmament showeth His **handiwork**." Psalm 19:1
>
> "He has **made** His wonderful works to be remembered" Ps. 111:4
>
> He "laid the foundations of the earth...when the morning stars sang together and all the sons of God shouted for joy" Job 38:4, 7
>
> "By the word of the Lord were the heavens **made**; and all the host of them by the breath of His mouth" "For He spake, and it was done; He commanded, and it stood fast." Psalm 33:6, 9
>
> "By the word of God the heavens were of old, and the earth standing out of the water" 2 Peter 3:5
>
> He is "the living God, which **made** heaven and earth, and the sea, and all things that are therein" Acts 14:15.
>
> "For in six days the Lord **made** heaven and earth, the sea, and all that in them is." Exodus 20:11
>
> "The invisible things of Him from **the creation of the world** are clearly seen, being understood by the things that are **made**, even His eternal power and Godhead" Romans 1:20
>
> "God that **made** the world and all things therein, seeing that He is Lord of heaven and earth...has **made** of one blood all nations of men for to dwell on all the face of the earth" Acts 17:24, 26

He Who made all nations of men did not say "the Sabbath was made for Jews" but "for man," *anthropos,* mankind, and originally for the first man. Adam was not a Jew. Abraham, the father of the Jews, was not born for another 2000 years.

After stating that the Sabbath was made for man's benefit. Jesus identified Himself as "Lord of the Sabbath" (verse 28). Why is He Lord of the Sabbath?

> "Through faith we understand that **the worlds were framed by the word of God**." Hebrews 11:3.

> "**By the word of the Lord were the heavens made**; and all the host of them by the breath of His mouth." "For He spake, and it was done; he commanded, and it stood fast." Psalm 33:6,9

> "In the beginning was **the Word...all things were made by Him**...And the Word was made flesh, and dwelt among us" John 1:1,3,14

> "God...has in these last days spoken unto us by **his Son...by whom also he made the worlds**" Hebrews 1:1,2

> "...his dear Son...who is the image of the invisible God...for **by him were all things created** that are in the heaven, and that are in earth." Colossians 1:13,15,16.

> "**He has made** his wonderful works **to be remembered**" Psalm 111:4

> "**Remember the Sabbath** day to keep it holy...the seventh day is **the Sabbath of the LORD** thy God... For in six days the LORD made heaven and earth, the sea, and all that in them is." Exodus 20:8, 10, 11

Lord's Day
Of course Christ is Lord of the Sabbath, He created it, He blessed it, it's His day—the real Lord's Day—eternal symbol of His creative and re-creative power.

It is, therefore, not surprising that belief in creation is under attack in our day. At the very time when Sabbath appreciation was reaching global awareness in the mid 1800s (see Family History), the theory of Darwinian evolution began sweeping the world. Diametrically opposed ideologies arising simultaneously has tremendous prophetic significance. "In the beginning God" was competing directly with "conditions and processes continue over billions of years." Peter predicted as much:

> "There shall come in the last days scoffers, walking after their own lusts, saying, Where is the promise of His coming? For since the fathers fell asleep, all things continue as they were from the beginning of the creation." 2 Peter 3:3,4.

The seventh day Sabbath, along with Marriage and Labor, are three institutions rooted in Creation, established from the foundation of the world for all of mankind, before sin, before a Jew, before Moses.

It is significant that never does Scripture refer to the seventh day as "the Jewish Sabbath" or "the Sabbath of Moses." The Creator claims the Sabbath as His own consistently throughout the Bible record:

> "The Sabbath of the Lord thy God" Exodus 20:10; Leviticus 23:3
> "Keep **my** Sabbaths: I *am* the Lord your God." Leviticus 19:3
> "Ye shall keep **my** Sabbaths" Leviticus 19:30
> "**My** holy day...the Sabbath" Isaiah 58:13
> "I gave them **my** Sabbaths" Ezekiel 20:12
> "**My** Sabbaths they greatly polluted" Ezekiel 20:13
> "They polluted **my** Sabbaths" Ezekiel 20:16, 21, 24; 22:8
> "Hallow **my** Sabbaths" Ezekiel 20:20

But He does make a distinction between His Sabbaths and the Sabbaths of Israel:

> "***her*** feast days, ***her*** New Moons, ***her*** sabbaths" Hosea 2:11
> "new moons and sabbaths...**your** appointed feasts" Isa 1:13, 14
> "it is a day of atonement...**your** sabbath" Leviticus 23:28, 32
> "then shall the land enjoy her sabbaths...because it did not rest in **your** sabbaths" Leviticus 26:34, 35
> "the adversaries saw her and did mock at **her** sabbaths" Lam 1:7

Sabbath Exception

The Genesis account of creation week teaches another important Biblical concept. Each day in chapter 1 follows a repetitive sequence where each day concludes with the pronouncement: "And the evening and the morning were the first day..., second day...," etc. This follows the Biblical convention of starting a new day at sunset. The sunset-to-sunset practice is more explicitly stated in Leviticus 23:26-32 when providing details for observing one of the annual ceremonial Sabbaths—in this case, the Day of Atonement.

However, this pattern of pronouncing an "evening and morning" benediction is not extended to the seventh day. Some have concluded that this made the seventh day of creation not a literal day after all, but a spiritual essence of divine rest that continues uninterrupted ever since creation and that no longer applies to man.

The Sabbath Age
A clever attempt to restart the clock of time was popularized in the early 1900s. Maurice Logan, writing for the Lord's Day Alliance, considered the possibility that the first six days were not 24-hour periods.

For support of his position, Genesis 2:4 is quoted: "These are the generations of the heavens and of the earth when they were created, in the day that the Lord God made the earth and the heavens." This shows, he claimed, that the word "day" does not always mean a 24-hour period. This is clearly true in this passage since the word for day, *yom*, appears without an accompanying number.

> "But, if the creation days were indefinite periods, as is now most generally accepted, they cannot be counted as a part of time; the time, of necessity, began with the first time measured day of man. In which case, God rested on the first day of the first week of time." Logan, Maurice S. *Sabbath Theology*, Lord's Day Alliance, 1913, p. 19.

Logan prefers to begin the week with man's appearance rather than God's creation. Then to further emphasize the unlimiting aspect of time from God's perspective Peter's analogy is cited: "One day is with the Lord as a thousand years, and a thousand years as one day." 2 Peter 3:8.

But the story of creation identifies each day with a number and a definitive phrase that indicates the effects of planetary rotation: "and the evening and the morning were the first day," etc. The fact that the weekly cycle continues to our present time as a seven day repeating sequence confirms the Genesis creation account. Unlike the lunar month and solar year, there is no corresponding astronomical cycle associated with the week. It exists only because the Creator deliberately chose to create for six days and rest for one.

Notice that the "evening and the morning" pattern was used to separate each of the previous six days of creation from the following day. On the other hand, the seventh day was the end of creation week, there were no more days to follow it. Therefore, the formula was not required.

The Genesis account does not identify the seventh day as different from the previous six. All seven days are described with the standard Hebrew designation: *yom* (day) accompanied by a preceding number. Throughout the Hebrew scriptures, this construction consistently refers to a normal 24-hour day.

The Sabbath rest by God on the seventh day "means completion, it means the perfection and peace in which the world rests." Dietrich

Bonhoeffer, *Creation and Fall. A Theological Interpretation of Genesis 1-3* (New York, 1964), p. 40. No further creation was needed.

> "...on the seventh day God, the Creator, completed His work by 'resting.' This simply means that He did not go on with the work of creation as such. He set both Himself and His creation a limit. He was content to be the Creator of this particular creation—to glory, as the Creator, in this particular work. He had no occasion to proceed to further creations. He needed no further creations." Karl Barth, *Church Dogmatics,* ET (Edinburgh, 1956), vol. 3, part 2, p. 51.

> "When creation ended with man, having found its climax and meaning in the actualization of man, God rested on the seventh day from all the work that He had done. It was to this that He looked in the recognition that everything was very good and therefore did not need to be extended or supplemented." *Ibid*, Part 1, p. 213.

The seventh day is, therefore, both commemorative and prophetic—reminding us of our roots and predicting our future.

> "Humanistic philosophers teach that life is but a prelude to death; but the Sabbath is a prelude to life on an infinitely higher, spiritual level." Heschel.

Creation Continues
The Sabbath had no mentioned "evening and morning" applied to it in Genesis 2 to symbolize that God, in a sense, is *still* creating. In that sense, God created the Sabbath on the seventh day. And in a continuous sense, God is forever creating moments of time we call the present. Jesus confirmed this in John 5:17, when a dispute arose over how to keep the Sabbath. He replied, "My Father has been working until now, and I have been working."

The Present
Each moment of time is a gift from God. That's why we call it the 'present.' But man has a tendency to spend most of his time either in the future or in the past. So many of our human emotions involve our preoccupation with these two extremes of time. We worry about the future; we grieve over the past. We're anxious about tomorrow's threats; we're depressed about yesterday's losses. Paul said, "This one thing I do, forgetting those things which are behind, and reaching forth unto those things which are before, I press toward the mark for the prize of the high calling of God in Christ Jesus." Phil. 3:13,14.

This is the essence of real Sabbath-keeping. When fully realized Sabbath with friends and family, Creator and creation, becomes a liberating spiritual adventure. "All other time is a passage away from the past and a groping toward the future; but the Sabbath is pure present." David Neff, "Fallow Time," *Christianity Today*, November 3, 2003; reprinted from *The Midas Trap*, 1990.

God finished the physical part of creation at the end of the sixth day. The spiritual phase began with the creation of the Sabbath. God deliberately memorialized the most enduring thing known to man: time. And the creation of time continues to this very moment.

God created, not only the Sabbath, but the week of seven days—for man. His interest in identifying with us (and His desire that we also identify with Him) is the reason for these two fundamental creation ordinances. Samuele Bacchiocchi makes this connection quite clear:

> "...as we work during the six days and rest on the seventh day, we are doing in a small scale what God has done on a much larger scale. God's willingness to enter into the limitations of human time at creation in order to enable us to identify with Him is a marvelous revelation of His willingness to enter into human flesh at the incarnation in order to become Emmanuel, God with us."
> *God's Festivals in Scripture and History*, part 3.

Though the actual word *Shabbat* does not appear in the creation account, the emphasis on the seventh day and rest (*shabat*) is striking. The fact that a very similar word, *shabbatu*, existed in ancient Mesopotamia may explain why Moses, under inspiration, avoided this term which was associated with the worship of the full moon. God wanted to make it clear that the Sabbath was not to be linked to any astrological cycles, but rather observed every seventh day in recognition of Elohim's creation week.

Day of Lights
The Sabbath also symbolizes the ultimate Sabbath of heaven's rest. This theme has been recognized from the earliest rabbinical histories. The seventh day, they taught, lacked the description of "evening and morning" because it points forward to the time when "there will be no night."

> " 'For the Sabbath day,' that is, for the day which darkness did not attend. You find that it is written of other days 'And there was evening and there was morning, one day' but the words 'There was evening' are not written of the Sabbath... The Sabbath light continued throughout thirty-six hours." *The Midrash on Psalms*, translated by William G. Braude (New Haven, 1959), vol. 2, p. 112.

Thus, Jewish tradition has made it the "day of lights" when the woman of the house inaugurates the Sabbath's arrival and honors its departure with the lighting of lamps. This is why "there were much lights" in the upper room at Troas when Paul preached through the night in Acts chapter 20. They were celebrating the Sabbath closing ceremonies.

Augustine also noticed the missing reference to "evening and morning" and attributed this to "the Sabbath of eternal life."

> "O Lord God, grant Thy peace unto us... the peace of rest, the peace of the Sabbath which has no evening. For all this most beautiful order of things, 'very good'... is to pass away, for in them there was **morning and evening**. But the seventh day is **without any evening**, nor hath it any setting, because Thou hast sanctified it to an everlasting continuance;... that we also after our works... may repose in Thee also in the Sabbath of eternal life." Augustine, *Confessions* 13, 24, 25, Nicene and Post-Nicene Fathers of the Christian Church (Grand Rapids, 1979), vol. 1, p. 207.

Light Restored
Isaiah described conditions when all things will be restored in terms of light and Creation.

> "Moreover the light of the moon will be as the light of the sun, and the light of the sun will be sevenfold, as the light of the seven days" Isaiah 30:26.

According to an ancient Midrash, this text teaches that all seven days of Creation were originally bathed in an extraordinary supernatural light seven times brighter than our current sun. (Bereshith Rabbah 3:6; 11:2. Louis Ginzberg, *Legends of the Jews,* Philadelphia, 1946, vol. 5, p. 8, n. 19). Because of sin, this world has been plunged into gross darkness (Isaiah 60:2). As the Sabbath symbolizes original creation it also is prophetic of this world's re-creation and restoration to its original brilliant condition.

The "seven days" of Isaiah 30 directly refers to the original light that pervaded the entire Creation week and climaxed in the Sabbath blessing, when God and the first Man entered communion on the first Sabbath, when the Lord made "His face to shine upon" Adam and Eve in their perfect Eden home.

Memorials of Creation
The convention of dividing calendars into seven day weekly intervals continues uninterrupted to the present age as a permanent ordinance in time. Marriage continues to be called Holy Matrimony, a permanent bond between husband and wife, since "what God has put together, no man should put asunder." When the question of divorce was raised, Jesus referred to the Edenic origins of the Marriage Institution: "From the beginning it was not so" Matt. 19:8. Likewise, the seventh day also stems "from the beginning" and remains a

memorial of creation, the world's oldest festival, and a perpetual reminder of our roots from the hands of our Creator.

Yet, the Bible does not speak of a Sabbath Institution; only the Sabbath day. There was no institution apart from the day. The seventh day is the Sabbath and the Sabbath is the seventh day. Sabbath is forever tied to time, bound to the day God rested. God united rest, blessing, holiness in the seventh day. No one can put it asunder.

A little piece of Paradise

Of the three Creation institutions (Sabbath, Marriage, and Labor) only the Sabbath remains unblemished by the curse of sin. Holy Matrimony has been marred by divorce, even though "since the beginning it was not so" but added "because of the hardness" of man's heart. Satisfying, productive labor in tending Eden's garden was turned into a dirty four-letter word: WORK. Man now toils "by the sweat of his brow" to survive in a world of thistles and thorns.

> "The Sabbath is not affected by any curse resulting from the Fall. Unlike the other two Creation institutions, the Sabbath remains **a little piece of Paradise**. As such, its value is enhanced by the deterioration around it. Now that work is exhausting, ceasing from labor on the Sabbath provides needed rest. More importantly, now that human beings are cut off from direct access to God, they need a reminder of His lordship even more than they did before the Fall." Roy Gane, *Sabbath and the New Covenant*, Paper presented at a consultation with the Worldwide Church of God (1997), pp.5-6. Quoted in Bacchiocchi, chapter 2, part 3.

After sin,
"Marriage would remain...
"to call couples to the commitment of love"
"to procreate children and experience family"
So also,
"Sabbath would remain...
"to call them back to God"
and to "recreate original love"

Eden Sabbath Restored

Adam and Eve lived in peace and harmony with the animal world on creation's first Sabbath. When this world is re-created after the millennial Sabbath, Eden's harmony will once again be restored. Isaiah foretells this restoration of the original creation unity when he writes that "the wolf shall dwell with the lamb and the leopard shall lie down with the kid, and the calf and the lion and the fatling together, and a little child shall lead them." Isaiah 11:6. Eden's first Sabbath is the epitome of the final rest for which creation even now still "groans."   The primordial Sabbath that blessed Adam's first home is the paradigm of heaven.

> Know that the Lord, He is God;
> It is He who has made us, and not we ourselves;
> We are His people, and the sheep of His pasture.
> Psalm 100:3,4.

No other day
Des Cummings, Jr. sums up the etiology of the Sabbath with these thoughts: God's Sabbath gift of "original love" is "the antidote for original sin" "If the Sabbath was vital to love in a perfect world, it [is] even more critical in a fallen world." No other day sets us apart from the world like the seventh day Sabbath. If God created the Sabbath only because we need to rest physically, "any old time would do;" if we want to be in God's presence in this special way, "no other day will do."

God has made a tremendous investment in executing two great acts of love that introduce both Testaments: the creation of this world *and* the death of His Son. The Sabbath is God's palace in time where He protects His investment by enhancing and protecting our relationship with Him. It is a witness to God, to ourselves and to the world, giving us time to connect with God, to develop the spiritual side of life and experience a foretaste of eternity.

Chronobiology
Finally, the seven day legacy of creation has also surfaced in the nacent field of chronobiology. Recent developments in that emerging discipline support growing evidence that most biological organisms exhibit cyclic periods involving seven days or multiples of seven days. These circaseptan and circasemi-septan (3½ day) intervals cross cultural and geo-graphical boundaries while affecting a wide range of molecular and metabolic functions. These vestiges of creation appear to support even a genetic basis for the seventh day Sabbath.

The Creation theme continues throughout the New Testament and is intimately tied to Sabbath symbolism. As we explore the influence of the creation story and Earth's first week in the earliest portions of Scripture, the seventh day will be rediscovered in every age. As we trace the successive development of the Everlasting Covenant, the original sign of creation will surface at every turn.

Why does this world still follow the ancient seven day week?
See Appendix D for a further discussion of Chronobiology.

Epidemiology

The spread of a communicable disease through various populations and communities falls under the domain of epidemiologists. These public health specialists are part pathologist and part crime scene investigator. They track down the source of the latest epidemic; they trace contacts and carriers, vectors and reservoirs in their search to understand how infective agents are transmitted.

Sabbath epidemiology is an ancient craft. The record of its spread and the location of its ground zero are shrouded behind the misty pages of the primordial past. But enough evidence exists to plot a fairly reliable course.

Sabbath Genesis
It is easy to demonstrate that there is no explicit record of Adam and Eve (nor any other patriarch) being commanded or even instructed to rest on the Sabbath. The earliest mention of the seventh day as a day of rest occurs near the beginning of the book of beginnings, Genesis. Then it disappears from the Biblical landscape like an encysted spore and seems to lie dormant for some 25 centuries before reverting back into an active form once again.

But unlike Exodus, Genesis is not a legal document featuring laws and detailed instructions concerning them. Genesis deals with origins. Since specific mention is not made of any other commandment, the silence regarding the Sabbath precept is not exceptional.   Yet there is considerable evidence that the weekly observance of God's creation Sabbath influenced the life of man at seven day intervals well before the time of Moses.

For example, the frequent use of the seven-day week (Hebrew **shebah**) in early portions of the Scriptures implies the existence of the Sabbath as well. The following periods of seven days are mentioned:

- four times in the account of the Flood (Gen. 7:4, 10; 8:10, 12)
- as the duration of Jacob's nuptial festivities (Gen. 29:27)
- Laban's persuit of Jacob (Gen. 31:23, 24)
- for the duration of mourning at his death (Gen. 50:10), and
- Job's friends' period of condolence (Job 2:13).

Sabbath Years
In addition to the connection between Sabbath and the seven day creation week in the book of Genesis, there are also significant periods of seven years associated with

- the twin dowries that Jacob labored for Laban's daughters
- the seven years of plenty and famine during Joseph's reign

Notice the interesting pattern seen here in the lives of Jacob and Joseph. Jacob worked seven years for Leah and another seven for Rachael. The first seven years were marked by the remarkable fertility of Leah with her abundance of sons, and the startling barrenness of Rachael who bore only two of Jacob's twelve. In the end, Leah enjoyed a 6:1 blessing over her rival sister. Jacob had his seven years of plenty and a comparative seven years of fecundal famine.

God appears to be establishing His policy of providing physical blessing *in anticipation* of the spiritual blessing associated with sabbatical time frames. This was later demonstrated in the double supply of manna on the day before each Sabbath, the double blessing of the pre-sabbatical year bumper crop, and the twice double blessing pronounced on the pre-sabbatical-pre-Jubilee year harvest.

Noah's Week
Going back ten generations from Abraham, this essence of Sabbath seventhness shows up again during the events of Earth's first destruction by water in Genesis chapter 7. God announced the coming of the flood rains in "seven days" (vs 4 and 10). Then, as the flood waters abated, Noah tested for the appearance of dry land by sending birds out at seven day intervals (Gen. 8:10, 12).

These references to the seven day week establish the fact that this division of time was known and practiced from the earliest of times. With its recorded introduction at the end of creation week, the probability is high that the weekly Sabbath observance was also practiced.

Frances Nigel Lee identifies 9 events during the Flood chronology that appear to synchronize with weekly events. In fact, perfect synchronism is demonstrated by using a calendar based on alternating months of 30 and 29 days, a common arrangement used by the most ancient cultures because it just about perfectly averages out the 29 ½ day lunar cycle.

The Flood comes near the beginning of Noah's 600th year of life. It lasts exactly one year. Although allignment with the seventh day cannot be proven, Noah does begins his seventh Sabbath century in a new world.

600th Year of Noah

1st month							
			1	2	3	4	5
	6	7	8	9	10	11	12
	13	14	15	16	17	18	19
	20	21	22	23	24	25	26
	27	28	29	30			

2nd month								
					1	2	3		Door shut Genesis 7:4
	4	5	6	7	8	9	(10)	Rains begin Genesis 7:11
	11	12	13	14	15	16	(17)
	18	19	20	21	22	23	24
	25	26	27	28	29		

3rd month								
						1	2
	3	4	5	6	7	8	9
	10	11	12	13	14	15	16
	17	18	19	20	21	22	23
	24	25	26	(27)	28	29	30		Rains stop after 40 days

4th month							
	1	2	3	4	5	6	7
	8	9	10	11	12	13	14
	15	16	17	18	19	20	21
	22	23	24	25	26	27	28
	29						

5th month							
		1	2	3	4	5	6
	7	8	9	10	11	12	13
	14	15	16	17	18	19	20
	21	22	23	24	25	26	27
	28	29	30				

6th month							
				1	2	3	4
	5	6	7	8	9	10	11
	12	13	14	15	16	17	18
	19	20	21	22	23	24	25
	26	27	28	29			

7th month								
					1	2	3
	4	5	6	7	8	9	10		Ark Rests on Ararat
	11	12	13	14	15	16	(17)		21st (3x7) week
	18	19	20	21	22	23	24		Genesis 8:4
	25	26	27	28	29	30	

8th month							
							1
	2	3	4	5	6	7	8
	9	10	11	12	13	14	15
	16	17	18	19	20	21	22
	23	24	25	26	27	28	29

9th month							
	1	2	3	4	5	6	7
	8	9	10	11	12	13	14
	15	16	17	18	19	20	21
	22	23	24	25	26	27	28
	29	30					

10th month			(1)	2	3	4	5	Mountain tops seen
	6	7	8	9	10	11	12	Genesis 8:5
	13	14	15	16	17	18	19	
	20	21	22	23	24	25	26	
	27	28	29					40 days later = 29+11
11th month				1	2	3	4	
	5	6	7	8	9	10	(11)	Raven sent Genesis 8:6,7
	12	13	14	15	16	17	(18)	Dove sent Genesis 8:8
	19	20	21	22	23	24	(25)	Dove sent Genesis 8:10
	26	27	28	29	30			
12th month						1	(2)	Dove sent Genesis 8:12
	3	4	5	6	7	8	9	
	10	11	12	13	14	15	16	
	17	18	19	20	21	22	23	
601st Year	24	25	26	27	28	29		
1st month							(1)	Covering removed
	2	3	4	5	6	7	8	Genesis 8:13
	9	10	11	12	13	14	15	
	16	17	18	19	20	21	22	
	23	24	25	26	27	28	29	
	30							
2nd month		1	2	3	4	5	6	
	7	8	9	10	11	12	13	
	14	15	16	17	18	19	20	
	21	22	23	24	25	26	(27)	Exit & sacrifice, 52nd wk
	28	29						Genesis 8:14-20

From the possible Sabbath that Noah was shut within the ark until the Sabbath that he and the *seven* others with him were released was exactly 52 weeks or one year. Shutting the ark's door on a Sabbath would also parallel closing Jerusalem's gates on Sabbath by Nehemiah. The remnant passengers began their deliverance on a Sabbath and were released from their confinement on a Sabbath. What more appropriate day could have been chosen? As Noah (whose name means "rest") *entered* into the ark on a Sabbath, so also "he that is *entered* into His rest, he also ceased from his own works, as God did from His." Heb. 4:9-11.

Then the week of the Flood mirrored creation week, only in reverse. As God spent six days in preparing a perfect home for all life and then ended His work on the Sabbath, so after six days of preparation, God ended "every living thing that I have *made*" on the *seventh* day (Gen 7:4). The Sabbath at the Flood was a day of judgment. So also when Christ fulfilled the judgment against our sins in His own body, He died "as the Sabbath drew on" (Luke 23:54; John 19:30-1). He will also execute judgment at His second coming which He tells us will be "as it was in the days of Noah" (Matthew 24:20, 37).

"The Lord shut him in" (Gen. 7:16). Noah couldn't do it himself, it was a divine act that separated him from the rest of the world. So, too, Sabbath-keepers are shut away from the influence of the world, separate and sanctified.

The ark itself experienced the Sabbath in the timing of its voyage. On the twenty-first (7 x 3) Sabbath, "the ark *rested* in the *seventh* month, on the *seven*teenth day of the month, upon the mountains of Ararat"—the ark came to rest on the day of rest.

When Noah "opened the window" on the Sabbath days, so did God "open the windows of heaven" on the first Sabbath of the Flood. (Gen. 8:6; 7:11). When Noah released the second bird, a dove, it returned because "the dove found no *rest* for the sole of her foot." (Gen. 8:9). This parallels the experience of Jesus because "the Son of Man had nowhere to lay His head" (Matthew 8:20).

> "The repetition of Noah's act after each sacred interval plainly lifts that act to the level of faith . . . he waited for the return of that one day of the seven which, all through this story, is the hallowed day." George S. Gray, *Eight Studies of the Lord's Day*: Houghton Muffin and Co. Boston, 1885? p. 107.

Finally, as the first Noah was instructed to "go forth and multiply upon the earth," so too the Second Noah instructed His followers to "Go into all the word and preach the gospel to every creature" (Mark 16:15).

Father Abraham

Abraham's direct connection through the ancestry of Shem exposed him to the purest form of worship to survive the Flood. Following the Babel dispersement, Abraham remained very close to the post-flood cultural center in the Chaldean city of Ur. The sacrificial worship rituals, previously associated with the Sabbath offerings of Cain, Abel and Noah, were practiced by the patriarch as recorded at least six times in Shechem, Bethel, Mamre and Moriah. Abraham also practiced the payment of tithe as demonstrated during his encounter with Melchizedec, who lived contemporaneously with and may, in fact, have been the patriarch Shem, as some have suggested.

Again the symbolic significance of the number seven occurs during the covenant that Abraham makes with Abimelech when they each offer *seven* ewe lambs in sacrifice as they swear (Hebrew *nishba*, a derivative of *sheba*, seven) at a place called *Beersheba* "well of the seven-fold oath." That this ceremony had religious implications is confirmed by the statement that there Abraham "called upon the name of the Lord." Gen. 21:28.

Abraham was a pilgrim his entire life. As Hebrews 11 reports, "he sojourned in the land of promise, as in a foreign land." He "died in faith" never having found the city "whose builder and maker is God." This is why the hall of faith nominees are listed in this summary chapter. While resting in the hope of the Sabbath promise throughout their lives, they never personally realized it. "There therefore remaineth a rest to the people of God." Hebrews 4:9.

Like Father Like Son

Abraham was the friend of God and would certainly have shared what he knew about Him with his son Isaac. God was confident that he would. "I know him, that he will command his *children* and his household after him, and *they* shall keep the way of the Lord," Gen 18:19. We know that Isaac faithfully carried the torch of true worship to the God of heaven because Jehovah later reaffirmed the covenant with him: "I will be with thee, and bless *thee*, because that Abraham obeyed My voice, and kept My charge, My commandments." Gen. 26:1-5. Isaac, like his father, also offered sacrifices and "called upon the Name of the Lord," was circumcised, and swore holy oaths (Genesis 26:3,28-31).

Jacob, as well, offered sacrifices, gave tithes (Gen. 28:32), called upon the Name of the Lord (Gen. 32:9-12), and swore oaths (Gen. 25:33; 31:53). But Jacob experienced the influence of the Sabbath in the seven year dowries (Gen. 29:20, 27) that he paid for each of his two wives. Jacob and Laban must certainly have been aware of the Sabbatical climax implied by the seventh day legacy from creation when the appeal was made, "Give me my wife, for my days are fulfilled." Gen. 29:21. Further evidence is the seven day "marriage week" honeymoon during which he celebrated his nuptial covenants. Gen. 29:20-28. There was apparently no need to explain this commonly observed custom. However, Laban finds it necessary to defend his reasons for substituting the first-born Leah for Jacob's first love Rachel, apparently because it was a local custom. This episode is clear indication that the patriarchs knew of the week and the Sabbath that marked it.

When Jacob finally left his uncle and set out for Canaan after 20 years in Haran, Rachel ran off with the family idols. It took Laban three days to discover the theft and seven days before he could catch up with Jacob's party. Gen 31:23-24. The night before reaching them, Laban had a dream from God warning him not to cause any trouble. The next day he met Jacob and they both made a covenant of peace, Jacob swore a holy oath (*nishba* related to *sheba*, seven) and offered sacrifices. Thus after Jacob spent a week fleeing and Laban toiled all week pursuing, they both rested in peace and covenant. Whether these seven days coincided with a weekly cycle and ended on a seventh-day Sabbath cannot be determined with certainty, but the Sabbath relationship is unquestionable.

Joseph and the Sabbath

When Jacob's favorite son, Joseph, ended up in Egypt, he eventually caught the attention of Pharaoh himself because of his success in interpreting dreams. Pharaoh's was quite unusual. He was standing by the river Nile, when out of the water stepped seven fat cows. But this was only the beginning. Then seven scrawny ones came up and ate up the fat ones but they still looked just as skinny as before. Pharaoh woke up in a sweat from his nightmare. But after drifting back to sleep he dreamed again. This time he saw seven huge plump ears of corn that got devoured by seven withered ears. This time Pharaoh knew he had been given an important omen. But what was the message?

The dreams completely stumped the best fortunetellers in Egypt. Seven just didn't click with the Egyptian mind at that time in history. Some have claimed that Moses picked up his fascination with the number seven while he was in Egypt, but if so this is where it came from. Joseph easily identified the seven cows and seven ears appearing in sequential order as events transpiring over seven years: seven years of plenty followed by seven years of famine. He naturally abstracted the seven physical objects into seven concrete periods of time. Of course, Joseph had the advantage of being the son of Jacob and Isaac and Abraham, knowing of the creation story, the seven day week and acquainted with the Sabbatical time periods. Seven to the Hebrew mind was inextricably linked to the realm of time.

During the seven years of famine, Jacob and his family of *seventy* members moved down to be with Joseph in Egypt. Gen. 46:27; Ex. 1:5. Jacob lived an additional 17 years in Egypt. Gen. 47:28. Just before his death he blessed his sons beginning with the combined tribe of Ephraim-Manasseh, then Reuben, Simeon, Levi, Judah, Zebulun and the seventh, Issachar. Of him, he includes the Sabbatical symbols of burden and rest:

> "Issachar is a strong ass couching down between two *burdens*: and he saw that *rest* was good, and the land that it was pleasant; and bowed his shoulder to bear, and became a servant unto tribute." Gen 49:14, 15.

He continues with Dan, Gad, Asher, Naphtali, Joseph and Benjamin. Finally when Jacob died, even the "Egyptians wept for him *seventy* days." Gen. 50:3. Then Joseph took his father's body back to Canaan where he buried him and mourned for *seven* days. Gen. 50:10.

Silence Before and After Moses

Sabbath concepts and strong sabbatical references, as we have seen, were a prominent feature within the lives of the patriarchs. The apparent Sabbath silence (in that the word "Sabbath" is not actually mentioned) between Adam and Moses, however, is not unique. A similar period spanning over 400 years also exists between the books of Deuteronomy and 2 Kings. No one argues that the Sabbath did not exist during this period of the Mosaic dispensation just because it was not mentioned in six books covering that period. One book, covering 2400 years of redemptive history, details the origin of the seventh day rest of God and yet some attempt to prove that the Sabbath did not yet exist because the English word does not appear within its pages. But six consecutive books (Joshua, Judges, Ruth, 1 Samuel, 2 Samuel, 1 Kings) while also containing no occurrence of the word "Sabbath," are not used to prove that the Sabbath did not exist for even 500 years of time transpiring between their pages. These six cannot prove that there *were* Sabbath-keepers between the days of Moses and David any more than one book proves that there were *none* between Adam and Moses.

And when the silence finally is broken in 2 Kings 4:23 the reference casually and incidentally describes the accepted custom of visiting prophets on the Sabbath. The Shunemite woman's journey to Elisha received comment from her husband because it was *not* a Sabbath. Similar associations of the Sabbath with prophetic visits were made on three other occasions: Isa. 66:23; Eze. 46:1; Amos 8:5. Chronologically, the first mention of the Sabbath after the time of Moses is made approximately 150 years earlier in 1 Chronicles 9:32 where David assigns to the Kohathites the responsibility of keeping fresh showbread in the temple each Sabbath. Again, the incident is mentioned in a matter of fact fashion. Thus, the post-Mosaic silence demonstrates that Sabbath observance was customary albeit undocumented during long chronological spans of Scripture. And when the silence of Genesis is broken, again the Sabbath is introduced incidentally with the giving of the manna.

Genesis and the six books mentioned above are not the only Old Testament books without mention of the word "Sabbath." Ezra, Esther, Job, Proverbs, Ecclesiastes, Song of Songs, Daniel, Joel, Obadiah, Nahum, Habbakuk, Zephaniah, Haggai, Zechariah, and Malachi all lack the word. Of course, this does not in any way prove that the Sabbath did not exist during the period in which these books were written.

The argument from silence could just as well be applied to the other commandments. Genesis 6:5 tells us that at the time of Noah, "the wickedness of man was great in the earth and that every imagination of the thoughts of his heart was only evil continually." Details are not provided, but the fact that "the earth was filled with violence" might suggest that at least the 6th commandment existed. At the time of Moses' birth, the Hebrew midwives refused to dispose of male newborns because "they feared God." Exodus 1:17. Otherwise, we have no record that any other commandment existed as a rule of morality. This certainly does not prove that God's law did not at that time exist. Wickedness was appreciated, it was recognized and it was punished.

Sabbath in Egypt

The apocryphal Book of Jasher, mentioned in Joshua 10 and 2 Samuel 1, provides an expanded account of Exodus 2:11 where Moses as a young man first "went out unto his brethren and looked on their burdens." Moses approached Pharaoh Melol about the matter and he treats the Israelites with favor at the request of Moses to re-institute the Sabbath:

> "And the day arrived when Moses went to Goshen to see his brethren that he saw the children of Israel in their burdens and hard labour, and Moses was grieved on their account. And Moses returned to Egypt and came to the house of Pharaoh, and came before the king, and Moses bowed down before the king. And Moses said unto Pharaoh, I pray thee, my lord, I have come to seek a small request from thee, turn not away my face empty; and Pharaoh said unto him, Speak. And Moses said unto Pharaoh, Let there be given unto thy servants the children of Israel who are in Goshen, one day to rest therein from their labour. And the king answered Moses and said, Behold I have lifted up thy face in this thing to grant thy request. And Pharaoh ordered a proclamation to be issued throughout Egypt and Goshen, saying, To you, all the children of Israel, thus says the king, for **six days you shall do your work** and labour, but on **the seventh day you shall rest**, and shall not perform any work: thus shall you do in all the days, as the king and Moses the son of Bathia have commanded. And Moses rejoiced at this thing which the king had granted to him, and all the children of Israel did as Moses ordered them. For this thing was from the Lord to the children of Israel, for the Lord had begun to remember the children of Israel to save them for the sake of their fathers. And the Lord was with Moses, and his fame went throughout Egypt. And Moses became great in the eyes of all the Egyptians, and in the eyes of all the children of Israel, seeking good for his people Israel, and speaking words of peace regarding them to the king." *Book of Jasher* 70:41-51.

But after Moses slew an Egyptian taskmaster and fled into exile, Melol dies and his son, Adikam assumed the throne and reversed the policy of his father concerning the Hebrew work schedule.

> "...he exceeded his father and all the preceding kings in wickedness, and he increased his yoke over the children of Israel. And he went

with his servants to Goshen to the children of Israel, and he strengthened the labour over them, and he said unto them, Complete your work, each day's task, and let not your hands slacken from our work from this day forward as you did in the days of my father." *The Book of Jasher* 77:21. M.M. Noah and A.S. Gould, New York, 1840.

This is essentially the same account provided by Moses suggesting that the Hebrews were resting or "slacking" from their work on a routine basis.

Forty years later when Moses returned to Egypt at God's bidding, he went directly to the leaders of Israel before going to Pharaoh. "Afterward they went to Pharaoh." Exodus 5:1.

Why did Moses go first to the leaders? He and Aaron advised the people to get themselves ready, to sanctify themselves, to return to the laws of God—one of which was the Sabbath. It is evident that this instruction regarding the Sabbath was indeed included in their pep talk because of Pharaoh's reaction: "You make them rest from their burdens!" Exodus 5:5. That word "rest" in this verse is **shabath**. You're making them keep Sabbath. Naturally, Pharaoh didn't want to let them go; they were building his cities. But suddenly they are working only six days a week.

Moses is a type of Christ, coming to lead them away from their life of rigorous labor in Egypt to their Sabbath rest in Canaan. Christ was not only the second Adam, He was also the second Moses. "Come unto me all ye that labor and are heavy laden and I will give you rest." Matt 11:28. Like Moses, Christ also returned to set His people free—free from the slavery of sin. In that sense Pharaoh, at least Pharaoh Adikam, who refused to let them keep Sabbath, was a type of Satan. Neither does the devil want us to think about eternity; he preoccupies our time with work. In Exodus 5:10,11 Pharaoh got tough: "No more straw, get your own." He increased the work load, "so they do not regard vain words." Don't think about all this promised land talk, just work.

Sabbath Before Sinai

When they were finally free of Egypt, God resumed His efforts to instruct Israel. After just a few days in the wilderness, they began to cry: you're "starving us to death!" So God gave them manna. It appeared on the ground each morning for six days, there was twice as much on Friday and none on the Sabbath. In Exodus 16 when the people attempted to gather manna on the seventh day, God said "How long will you refuse to keep my laws?" But it was not until weeks later following these instructions for the gathering of a double portion of manna on the sixth day that the formal giving of the law at Sinai took place.

This presupposes a preexisting knowledge of Sabbath significance.

> "Thou camest down also upon mount Sinai, and spakest with them from heaven, and gavest them right judgments, and true laws, good statutes and commandments: And **madest known unto them thy holy Sabbath**, and commandest them precepts, statutes, and laws, by the hand of Moses thy servant:" Nehemiah 9:13,14

This demonstrates the preexistence of the Sabbath prior to Sinai. There is even evidence to suggest that the Sabbath pre-existed this world. In Genesis 1 before the first day was created, the Spirit is described as "brooding" over the face of the deep. The Talmud recognized this as the lingering presence of God from the seventh day that had just ended. Now God begins a week of creation for *this* planet.

Law Before Sinai

Knowledge of God's Law, including His Sabbath blessing, is evidenced by several references in the Scriptural record *long* before the written Law was given to Moses on Mt Sinai. Genesis 26:5 records God's endorsement that "Abraham obeyed my voice, and kept my charge, my commandments, my statutes, and my laws." This was stated hundreds of years before the Ten Commandments were written by the finger of God.

Paul says in Galatians 3 that Abraham believed and obeyed his covenant with God 430 years before the law appeared, which was "added because of sin, till the Seed should come to whom the promise was made" verses 17, 19. Paul does not distinguish between the Ten Commandment law and the ceremonial laws of sacrifice or the civil laws of Moses. But he says it was "added." Added to what?

- If the Law did not exist before Sinai, then *adding* the law seems an illogical choice of words.
- If the Law *did* exist before Sinai, then the law that was added must be different from that which preexisted.

The law that Paul speaks of would endure "till the Seed should come." Of course, the Seed is Christ...the Seed promised in Genesis 3:15. Christ was the ultimate Sacrifice. His death ended the sacrificial system and the detailed body of law and ritualistic regulations related to it.

Notice that the command to build a sanctuary and initiate a body of ceremonial ritual laws pertaining to a sacrificial system was made only *after* the Israelites sinned against the commands of the Decalogue.

"It was only after the people had succumbed to ... worshipping a thing, a golden calf, that the erection of a Tabernacle, of holiness in *space,* was commanded." Heschel, page 9.

It appears that God would have initially preferred to reserve man's adoration and respect for holiness to the dimension of time. But when the people demonstrated their fixation on the tangible, physical nature of things in only 3-dimensional space, He made provision for their human limitations with the introduction of holy *things* and holy *places* and laws concerning them.

The fundamental Law of God, however, existed since the beginning. God "commanded" Adam and Eve to take dominion of the world, maintain and "keep" the garden of Eden, and not to touch one particular tree. Their disobedience of this last command was called sin because "sin is the transgression of the law" 1 John 3:4. And sin changed everything.

"Fear, shame and blame are the primary colors of sin," Des Cummings, Jr tells us. In place of rest, fear; instead of blessing, shame; holiness turns to blame. This was the experience of Adam and Eve when they sinned. They hid in fear, they covered their bodies in shame, and then they took turns blaming God and each other for the results of their disobedience.

"Where **no law** is, there is no transgression" Romans 4:15, because
  "**Sin** is the transgression of the Law" 1 John 3:4
But "**Death reigned** from Adam to Moses" Romans 5:14 because
  "The **wages of sin** is death" Romans 6:23

Thus, sin reigned, because God's law existed "From Adam to Moses."
When Abimelech took Sarah innocently in Genesis 20 he was faced
with the prospect of death for sinning against God (verses 3-9).

Cain was warned by God to be careful with his anger because "sin lay
at the door" Genesis 4:7. Did Cain know about God's Law? How
could he be held accountable and punished for his "sin?" Indeed,
how could his murderous act even *be* sin without a body of legal code
defining human conduct. The evidence is quite clear that the human
race was very much aware of God's Law from the very beginning of
creation and long before it was formally provided in written form at
Sinai.

Gospel Before Christ
Unfortunately, the focus on Law in the Old Testament has caused
many to limit the experience of God's people in that era to merely a
legalistic religion devoid of grace and love. This Christian arrogance
seems to ignore the existence of the Everlasting Gospel (Rev. 14:6).
Besides the richly symbolic sacrificial laws that spoke of Christ's
future death and atonement, God also provided powerful lessons of
the gospel in the very lives of those who lived before the Messiah.
Jesus said, "Abraham saw my day and rejoiced" John 8:56.

- **Abraham**, like Christ, left his home to go where God sent him.
- **Isaac**, like Christ, climbed a mountain, carrying his own wood to be a
  willing sacrifice.
- **Jacob**, like Christ, wrestled all night in anguish under the burden of guilt.
- **Joseph**, like Christ, came to his own and his own received him not, but
  hated him and plotting against him, sold him for pieces of silver. Joseph,
  like Christ, was delivered to his enemies, taken down into Egypt, falsely
  accused and placed between two prisoners. Joseph, like Christ, came up
  out of prison to be honored, providing bread to the world, forgiving his
  malefactors, and inviting them to "come unto me."
- **Moses**, like Christ, interceded his own life for the life of his people.
- **Joshua,** like Christ, led the children of Israel into the promised land.
  Joshua is the Hebrew version of the Greek name Jesus. Joshua was the
  son of Nun (eternal). Jesus is the Son of the eternal God.
- **Samson**, like Christ, destroyed his enemies through his own death.
- **Boaz**, like Christ, purchased the lost inheritance of a poor alien.
- **David**, like Christ, slayed a giant and gave victory to all his people.

The everlasting gospel of Christ and the eternal law of God were born
in the heart of our Creator from the foundation of the world and will

remain as long as He remains ruler of the Universe. Attempts to prove that the gospel of grace did not exist before the cross and that the law (together with the Sabbath) is abolished after it, are inconsistent with the story of God's undying love and eternal nature.

And not only Jewish tradition, but Christian authorities have recognized the dominance of the seventh day Sabbath in Biblical writings:

> "In the old testament, reference is made 126 times to the Sabbath, and all these texts conspire, harmoniously in voicing the will of God commanded the seventh day to be kept, because God Himself first kept it, making it obligatory on all as 'a perpetual covenant.' Nor can we imagine any one foolhardy enough to question the identity of Saturday with the Sabbath or seventh day, seeing that the people of Israel have been keeping the Saturday from the giving of the law, A.M. 2514."

These words were not written by a pro-Saturday sabbatarian, but appeared in *The Catholic Mirror*, in 1893. To learn more about why an official Catholic Church publication would affirm Saturday as the seventh-day Sabbath turn to Social History p. 139.

Sabbath After Moses

A strange amalgam of Sunday *and* Saturday sabbatarianism has recently emerged that proposes to identify two kinds of Sabbaths used by God during redemptive history. One is the original, permanent and eternal Adamic-Edenic Sabbath. Though declared in Genesis to have occurred on the seventh day, it becomes one with the New Covenant first day resurrection re-creation Sabbath. Both are claimed to be eternal and associated with creative events: creation of the world and creation of the church.

But this hybrid also distinguishes a temporary, transient Mosaic Sabbath that pertained only to the Jewish people, had symbolic value, but no lasting substance, was perverted by the Jews, and ultimately abolished, along with all the other Mosaic laws and rituals at the cross.

This parody of antinomianism is surprisingly legalistic. It embraces and defends the seventh-day Sabbath of creation and its faithful observance by all the patriarchs (making it deceptively attractive and biblical) but then applies the seventh-day Sabbath to the new first day sabbath, still one day in seven, that must be kept by Christians this side of the cross. While critical of those who separate the ceremonial and moral law to explain what was nailed to the cross and what law was abolished, this schizophrenic version of Sabbatarianism also separates the ceremonial sabbaths from the eternal

Sabbath but lumps the seventh-day Sabbath in with the ceremonial sabbaths as both being of Mosaic origin and then honors seventh-day Sabbaths before Moses and even some after him as permanent and eternal. The sense of logical consistency is effortlessly discarded.

Joshua at Jericho

After the death of Moses, Joshua took the helm, received the blessing of God and was encouraged to remain faithful to the law. He then tells the people to prepare themselves "for within three days" (Joshua 1:11) because "The Lord your God has given you *rest*, and has given you this land" Joshua 1:13. The Sabbath rest awaited them just across the river Jordan. Just as Moses told the people to "be ready against the third day" (Exodus 19:11) because "the Lord will come down in the sight of all the people" at Sinai amidst "the voice of the trumpet exceeding loud" Exodus 19:16, so Joshua would lead the people into the land of rest on the third day, they would march around Jericho for seven days, led by seven priests with seven trumpets, who blew them after encircling the city seven times on the seventh day.

Mount Sinai	Jericho
Exodus 19	Joshua 1-6
Be ready third day	Cross Jordan in 3 days (1:11, 2:16)
"We will do"	"We will do" (1:16)
Death to disobedient	Death to disobedient (1:18)
Sanctify, wash clothes	Sanctify your clothes (3:5)
Set bounds around mountain	Wall fell down flat (6:20)
Trumpet exceeding loud	Trumpets each day
People trembled	People shouted a great shout
Law given by God	Observe all the law (1:7,8)

Notice the striking similarities, the close parallel between the sentinel event in the life of Moses and that of Joshua. Some feature the fact that Israel marched for seven days around Jericho, they must have "broke" the Sabbath on at least one of those days. However, we notice that all the marching was performed by the direct command of God as a religious procession led by the priests and the ark of the covenant. Whichever day in that seven was the Sabbath we are not told, but when they marched they were not doing their work, but God's. The Sabbath commandment prohibited them from doing "all thy work." The siege of Jericho was not "servile work" but the work of God.

Joshua further told the people that God would give them a sign "that the living God is among you" because he would drive out *seven* groups of people: Canaanites, Hittites, Hivites, Perizzites, Girgashites, Amorites, Jebusites. Joshua 3:10.

Further parallels in the life of Joshua feature the Sabbath:
> They cross Jordan on dry ground on 10th day of first month.
> The Passover lamb was selected that day.
> 12 stones were set in middle of the river as a memorial.
> The men were circumcised the second time.
> They kept Passover on the 14th day.

"On the morrow after the Passover" (15th) they ate unleavened cakes. Manna ceased "on morrow after" they ate "the old corn," (16th). Joshua's conquests of Canaan ended and "the land **rested** from war." Joshua 11:23; 21:44.

Samson's Sabbath

Samson had a *seven* day marriage feast. Judges 14:15, 17, 18. He posed a riddle to the Philistines which was due by the end of the marriage feast on the *seventh* day. They got his wife to dig it out of him just in time "on the seventh day before the sun went down." This incident again demonstrates that sundown was the end of one day and the beginning of the next.

Ruth's Sabbath

Ruth the Moabitess was touched by the Sabbath concept. After she covenants with Naomi her famous pledge of dedication, to go where she goes, to lodge where she lodges, to be one with her people and one with her God, Ruth attracts the attention of Boaz. Naomi recognizes the opportunity and asks "Shall I not seek *rest* for thee?" Ruth 3:1. Wise mother-in-law that she was, Naomi instructs Ruth how to endear herself to her kinsman redeemer. Ruth executes the customary gesture perfectly and Boaz sends her home with a sign: six measures of barley. Ruth 3:15.

When Ruth returned home with her gift, Naomi immediately reads the significance of her barley bag. "The man will not rest, until he have finished the thing this day." Ruth 3:18. Ruth recognized six as an incomplete number linked to the labor of man. "Six days shalt thou labor and do all thy work." Only by reaching the full compliment of seven would Boaz find rest.

When Ruth and Boaz tied the knot and had their first son, Obed (David's grandfather), the women of Bethlehem came to Naomi and blessed her saying, "He shall be unto you a restorer of your life, and a nourisher of your old age: for your daughter-in-law which loves you, which is better to you than *seven* sons, has born him." Seven was the accepted number of completeness.

Saul's Sabbaths

Samuel told Saul to wait for him "*seven* days" in Gilgal after his anointing. 1 Samuel 10:8. After the seven days, Saul receives "another heart" from God and "the spirit of God came upon him, and he prophesied among them." Verses 9, 10.

Two years later, Samuel once again tells Saul to wait for him "*seven* days" 1 Sam 13:8. Again Saul is at Gilgal. But this time the circumstances were much different. The pressure was on. The vastly outnumbered army of Israel was facing battle against the Philistines who arrayed themselves with 30,000 chariots, 6,000 horsemen and foot soldiers "as the sand which is on the seashore." Verse 5. "But Samuel came not to Gilgal." So Saul took things into his own hands, and offered the sacrifices that Samuel was supposed to perform. But, because of his disobedience, instead of experiencing the Sabbath rest of deliverance, Saul tasted the defeat of rejection.

The men of Jabesh Gilead asked for a seven-day reprieve from the threats of Nahash the Ammonite. Saul roused out of his low-profile non-king role and came to their rescue with 330,000 recruits and completely annihilated the Ammonites. At the end of his reign, after his suicidal death and the shameful display of his beheaded corpse, the men of Jabesh Gilead retrieved his body, gave him a decent burial "under a tree at Jabesh, and fasted seven days." 1 Samuel 31:13.

Solomon's Sabbath

Solomon, "a man of rest," (1 Chron 22:9) built the temple "a house of rest" (1 Chron 28:2) for the ark of the covenant. God gave him "rest on every side" (1 Kings 5:3). Solomon dedicated the finished temple in the *seventh* month, followed by a *seven* day feast (2 Chron 7:8) with a solemn assembly in the eighth day. Then they kept the dedication of the altar another *seven* days, "and the feast seven days." Verse 9.

1	2	3	4	5	6	7
8	**9**	**10**	11	12	13	14
15	**16**	17	18	19	20	21
22	**23**					

If the temple was dedicated the 9th day of the seventh month, it would be ready to conduct the Day of Atonement festivities the following day, the 10th day of the seventh month as scheduled. Seven days counting the 9th would extend through the 15th, the beginning of the Feast of Tabernacles. This feast lasted for eight days and a reference to this is made in verse 9. The eighth day would then be the 23rd. Verse 10 says that Solomon "sent the people away" on the 23rd day of the seventh month.

Sabbaths After Solomon

Psalm 95 praises the Creator, warns against hard hearts.
God swares "nishba" that they should not enter His rest.
Psalm 116, Psalm 118, Psalm 92, all speak of the Sabbath.

King Asa had "**rest**" during his reign. 2 Chronicles 14:7.
Jehoshaphat's reign was "quiet" because God gave him "**rest.**"
2 Chron. 20:30.

"Where is the place of My **rest**?...but to this man will I look, even to him that is poor and of a contrite spirit." Isaiah 66:1,2.

"This is the **rest** wherewith you may cause the weary to **rest**: and this is the refreshing: yet they would not hear. But the word of the Lord was unto them precept upon precept, precept upon precept; line upon line, line upon line; here a little, and there a little." Isaiah 28:12, 13.

God promised His people through the prophet Jeremiah, that

> "if ye diligently hearken unto me, saith the Lord, to bring in no burden through the gates of this city on the Sabbath day, but hallow the Sabbath day, to do no work therein; then shall there enter into the gates of this city kings and princes sitting upon the throne of David, riding in chariots and on horses, they, and their princes, the men of Judah, and the inhabitants of Jerusalem; and this city shall remain forever." Jeremiah 17:24, 25

But Jeremiah also warned them that the abuse of the Sabbath evidenced by the commercial trade conducted at the gates of Jerusalem would bring a Sabbath curse of "unquenchable fire" (Jer 17:27) and an exile in Babylon for 70 years (7 x 10). The armies of Nebuchadnezzar finally sacked the city of David and destroyed Solomon's temple in 586 BC

> "to fulfill the word of the Lord by the mouth of Jeremiah, until the land had enjoyed her sabbaths: for as long as she lay desolate she kept Sabbath, to fulfill 70 years." 2 Chronicles 36:21.

Jeremiah, in his Lamentations, observed that God had "caused the solemn feasts and sabbaths to be forgotten in Zion." (Lamentations 2:6) The "adversaries [of Jerusalem] saw her and laughed at her sabbaths." Lamentations 1:7.

While Jeremiah remained behind in desolate Judea, Ezekiel was carried off to Babylon. When God called him from the role of priest to prophet, he "sat and remained there astonished among them seven days." Ezekiel 3:15. Ezekiel focused on the Sabbath as God's sign, the source of Israel's peace and prosperity, and the source of her decline and punishment. They had ceased "to put no difference between the holy and the profane" Ezekiel 22:26. God said they had "hid their eyes from My Sabbaths" verse 31.

Persian Sabbaths

Allusions to the Sabbath surface again in the Book of Esther. The opening scene reports a protracted royal party that king Ahasurerus threw for a full six months—exactly six months, to the day. After 180 days, the king tops things off with a seven day "festival." On the final seventh day, he decides to show off his trophy wife, Queen Vashti, to his seven princes and seven chamberlains "for she was fair to look on" Esther 1:11. He specifically asks her to come in wearing the royal crown, but her highness refuses. The decree, after a brief consult-ation, is made: "Let the king give her royal estate unto another that is better than she." Esther 1:19.

The parallels in this story are striking when compared to the Jewish festival calendar. It is exactly 180 days from the first feast of the year, Passover (14th day of the first month), to the last one, the Feast of Tabernacles or Ingathering, which began on the 15th day of the seventh month. This feast lasted seven days, just like the one in Esther. Jesus "stood up" on the seventh day "in the last day, that great day of the feast" of tabernacles in John 7:37 and also made an invitation.

A woman in Bible symbology represents the church, God's people. In the time of Jesus, this was the Jewish nation. "If any man thirst, let him come unto me and drink." Jesus was ready to "Gather In" His people. But they, like Vashti, refused. Then Jesus delivers nearly the same pronouncement to the rebellious Hebrew queen, "The kingdom of God shall be taken from you, and given to a nation bringing forth the fruits thereof." Matthew 21:43.

The Menorah

Jewish tradition has preserved the seven-branched candelabra first described as one of the three articles of furniture in the holy place of the Old Testament sanctuary. The seven candles represent the seven days of creation. The candles are arranged so that the middle candle is the tallest and represents the Sabbath, the pinnacle of creation and the central focus of every week. This leaves three candles on either side: three leading up to the Sabbath and three following it. The first three days of the week (Sunday, Monday, Tuesday) continue the blessings and fond memories of the Sabbath past; the next three days (Wednesday, Thursday, Friday) are lived in anticipation and preparation of the Sabbath to come.

The original menorah was constructed by Moses for the wilderness sanctuary. It was a seven-branched candlestick as described in Exodus 25:31-40 fueled by olive oil and representing the "Light of the world." Jesus applied it to Himself as He did the shewbread, the "Bread of life" come down from heaven. Jesus instructed His followers to "let your light so shine that men might see your good works and glorify your Father which is in heaven." Israel was to be "a light to the nations" Isaiah 42:6, a witness of God's character to the world. The Sabbath is God's menorah light of witness to His creative, sanctifying, transforming power.

WED THU FRI **SABBATH** SUN MON TUE

Light is not a violent force; so, too, God's people are to perform their mission of witness by setting an example, not by the use of force. When Zechariah saw the menorah in chapter 4, he heard God declare, "Not by might, nor by power, but by My Spirit."

The menorahs in both the first and second temples consisted of seven branches. But after the temple's destruction in AD 70 there was a determination to never again construct any temple furniture. Later the menorah was revived as a six-branched version. The festival of Hannakah (Chanakah) changed the original seven-branch Menorah to 8 candles because of the legendary miracle of one day's supply of oil lasting eight days.

For many centuries it has been customary for Jewish homes to end the Sabbath with the lighting of candles. This practice was gradually changed to the commencement of Sabbath on Friday evening by the slighting of two candles, each representing the two versions of the Sabbath commandment. One candle is called זכור (Zachor, remember) in commemoration of the Exodus 20 version and the other שמור (Shamor, observe) in remembrance of the account in Deuteronomy 5.

The Sabbath thus became the primary light to beam the knowledge of God around the world often with surprising connections.

Celtic Sabbath Keepers

Ireland and Scotland, as well as the other British Isles, claim an extensive religious history reaching back to the time of the Judean kings. Popular tales surface yet today about their noble heritage as descendants from at least some of the lost tribes of Israel. Part of this legacy is the Stone of Destiny or the Stone of Scone, the most sacred of Scottish treasures that came to Scotland from Ireland in the 5th century. This holy relic had originally been carried to Ireland from Judah shortly after the Babylonian destruction of Jerusalem and Solomon's temple in 586 BC. It was said to be the venerated Stone of the Covenant, Jacob's Pillow, on which he laid his head and saw the ladder reaching up to Heaven at Bethel (Gen. 28:18-22).

"Princess Tamar (Teamhair) gave her name to Tara, the seat of the High Kings of Ireland, and she married Ard Ri (High King) Eochaid, ancestor of Ugaine Mar (Ugaine the Great). Subsequently, over a millennium, Eochaid's successors were crowned in the presence of the sacred Stone. The Irish heritage then progressed to Scotland, where the relic of Judah became synonymous with the Kings of Dalriada. King Kenneth (MacAlpin (844-859) later moved the Stone to Scone Abbey when he united the Scots and the Picts. By the time of William the Lion (d. 1214), the Stone of Destiny bore witness to nearly a hundred coronations in sovereign descent from King Zedekiah." Laurence Gardner, *Bloodline Of The Holy Grail, "The Stone Of Destiny,"* Element Books, 1996, p. 299

"In its organization, then, in its use of certain texts, in many of its outward aspects, the Celtic Church circumvented the Church of Rome and functioned as a repository for elements of Nazarean tradition transmitted from Egypt, Syria, and Asia Minor." *The Messianic Legacy,* Michael Biagent, Richard Leigh & Henry Lincoln, Dell Publishing, 1986, p. 120.

"Early Celtic Christianity was the closest of all religious teachings to the original doctrines of Jesus, and it had emerged within a few years of the Crucifixion as the foremost Church of the Christian world. Christians of the Celtic Church were recorded in Ireland in the latter reign of Emperor Tiberius (AD 14-37), long before St Peter went to Rome. Given that Jesus' own teachings formed the basis of the faith, the Mosaic structure of the Old Testament was duly incorporated. Judaic marriage laws were observed, together with the celebrations of the Sabbath and Passover, while Easter was correctly held as the traditional feast-day of the Spring goddess, Eostre, long before the Roman Church foisted a new significance on the old Celtic festival at the Synod of Whitby in 644." Prince Michael Stewart, *The Forgotten Monarchy of Scotland*, Element Books, 1998, p. 30.

"A unique and indigenous culture thus developed in the form of Celtic Christianity. It derived primarily from Egypt, Syria and Mesopotamia, and its precepts were distinctly Nazarene. The liturgy was largely Alexandrian and, because Jesus' own teachings formed the basis of the faith, the Mosaic content of the Old Testament was duly retained. The old Jewish marriage laws were observed, together with the celebration of the Sabbath and Passover, while the divinity of Jesus and the Roman dogma of the Trinity played no part in the doctrine." Laurence Gardner, *Bloodline Of The Holy Grail, "The Stone Of Destiny,"* Element Books, 1996, p. 189.

"The purity and simplicity of Christian doctrine, as professed and taught by the Culdees, appears to have been in full harmony with their character, habits, and mode of life. Their Christianity had little connection with that of Rome; and when Roman innovations in doctrine and ceremonial began to increase, these found in the Culdees their most determined opponents. Instead of the Western church, they seem to have rather followed the Eastern, as established by St. John and his disciples...This is indicated by the Venerable Bede, where, while he speaks of them as schismatists because they followed uncertain rules in the observation of the great festival (Easter), he also declares that 'they only practice such works of charity and piety as they could learn from the prophetical, evangelical, and apostolic writings.' This strict adherence indeed to the written word, and utter abnegation of all other authority in religion, was the head and front of their offending." Thomas Thomson, *A History of the Scottish People from the Earliest Times*, Gresham Publishing Co., London, 1887, Vol. 1, p. 64

"The Culdees rejected the doctrine of the necessity of auricular confession, and consequently that of penance and priestly absolution. They did not believe in the existence of the real presence in the sacrament, but regarded the eucharist as a solemn act of religious commemoration. They rejected the worship of saints and angels, and on this account they dedicated their churches to the Holy Trinity alone." Thomas Thomson, *A History of the Scottish People from the Earliest Times*, Gresham Publishing Co., London, 1887, Vol. 1, p. 141

"The Culdees rejected the doctrine of works of supererogation, hoping for salvation not in the merit of themselves or others, but only in the mercy of God through faith in Jesus Christ. While refusing to pray to dead men, the Culdees also rejected prayers for the dead...They were opposed to all traditions of the church—and in this is to be found the summary of their errors and their guilt according to the views of Rome." *Ibid* p. 142

When Pope Celestine in the 5th century sent Palladius as a missionary to Scotland, he "...according to Bede, 'sent him to the Scots who believed in Christ as their first bishop.' It would appear from this circumstance that Christianity had previously prevailed among the Scoto-Irish, and that at their emigration into Scotland they had brought it with them as an essential part of their national polity." Thomas Thomson, *A History of the Scottish People from the Earliest Times*, Gresham Publishing Co., London, 1887, Vol. 1, p. 62.

Patrick of Ireland c. 360-460AD

Although different writers have claimed Britain, Ireland and France as his fatherland, Patrick was from the Celtic race, born at Kilpatrick, Scotland. He was a follower of the Christianity that came to Ireland from Syria. (Neander, *General History of the Christian Religion and Church*, vol. 1, sec. 1, pp. 85, 86; Moore, *The Culdee Church*, pp. 15-20.) The Celts are descended from Gomer, the grandson of Noah. In past ages they were known as Cimmerians. The Welsh still call themselves Cymry. Celtic Christianity included British, Gallic (French), and Galatian forms.

> "A large number of this Keltic community (Lyons, A.D. 177)—colonists from Asia Minor—who escaped, migrated to Ireland (Erin) and laid the foundations of the pre-Patrick church." Thomas Yeates, *East Indian Church History,* 1921, p 226.

Patrick is thought to have been born in Strathclyde, a Scottish kingdom just northwest of England (Neander, vol. 2, pp. 146-149). He was born about 360 AD. Two of his works survive: *Confession* and *Letter* (addressed to the British king Coroticus). In his *Letter* he describes his faith:

> "I am a servant in Christ delivered to a foreign nation on account of the unspeakable glory of an everlasting life which is in Christ Jesus our Lord."

This refers to his experience at the age of sixteen being taken captive to Ireland by pirates. More detail is given in his *Confession*:

> "I, Patrick, a sinner, the rudest and least of all the faithful, and most contemptible to great numbers, had Calpurnius for my father, a deacon, son of the late Potitus, the presbyter, who dwelt in the village of Banavan, Tiberniae, for he had a small farm at hand with the place where I was captured. I was then almost sixteen years of age. I did not know the true God; and was taken to Ireland in captivity with many thousand men in accordance with our deserts, because we walked at a distance from God and did not observe His commandments."

Obviously, celibacy was not being practiced at this time by the early British clergy. Though Patrick's father was a deacon, his grandfather was a presbyter or bishop. But Christianity was beginning to suffer from new dangers. After surviving the pagan persecutions under Diocletian, the church suddenly found itself in favor with Constantine. Now competing doctrines were threatening to enter the church through compromise. In the east Theodore of Mopsuestia was refuting oriental doctrines like Mithraism; Patrick was leading the charge in the West.

We know from his brief history that he escaped from his Irish slavery, but nothing is documented about this period of his life. When he returned to begin his ministry to the Irish, he preached and taught from the authority of the Bible, giving credit to no other authority or creed or council. He founded several Bible training centers which later grew into colleges and eventually universities. Notable graduates included Columba who took Christ to Scotland, Aidan who converted pagan England, and Columbanus who took the gospel and the Bible to Europe. Patrick closed his Letter with these words:

> "I testify before God and His angels that it shall be so as He has intimated to my ignorance. These are not my words, but of God, and of the apostles and prophets, which I have written in Latin, who have never lied."

The Latin used by Patrick was an earlier version of the Scriptures known as the Itala; it was not the translation of Jerome's Vulgate. It would be 900 years before the Vulgate encroached into the Emerald Isle. He did not rely on human tradition, the writings of men, but the word of God, the Bible, not church authority. In this he differed significantly from the policy of Rome. At this time, nearly fifty church councils and decretals were building a growing body of ecclesiastical cannon law. He makes no mention of a claimed commission by Pope Celestine. He only credits his apostleship to a divine command.

The life of Patrick "is so surrounded by legends, many of them too fabulous to be considered, that many details cannot be presented as facts," but rather that of a "miraculous hero of the fanatical fiction." Wilkinson, Benjamin G., *Truth Triumphant,* p. 85, 86.

One account purports that Patrick threw his portable stone altar into the sea where it floated next to his boat, so a poor leper could voyage with his partner all the way to Ireland. Another alleges that he went to Rome and cast a spell of sleep on the inhabitants so that he could carry off 365 sacred relics including a blood stained burial shroud of Christ and even some hair of the Virgin Mary.

When the Goths sacked Rome in 410, imperial legions left England to defend the fatherland. Patrick must have written his works before this time, because the term "Britains" was no longer used. With the Romans gone, the Anglo-Saxon invaders erased that designation from use.

For centuries the Roman church made repeated efforts to destroy the church Patrick founded. Two hundred years after his death, Boniface complained that the Scottish-Irish church allowed their "priests to marry." Michelet, *History of France,* vol 1, p. 74; vol 1, p. 134, 1844.

But most offensive was the continued observance of the seventh day Sabbath within the Celtic, Gothic, Waldensian, Armenian, and Syrian churches.

> "The Celts used a Latin Bible unlike the Vulgate, and kept Saturday as a day of rest, with special religious services on Sunday." Flick, A.C, *The Rise of the Medieval Church*, New York, 1909, p. 237.

It is clear that this practice also influenced the Scots through Columba, a student of Patrick.

> "In this matter the Scots had perhaps kept up the traditional usage of the ancient Irish Church which observed Saturday instead of Sunday as the day of rest." Barnett, T. Ratcliffe, *Margaret of Scotland: Queen and Saint*, Edinburgh: Oliver & Boyd, 1926, p. 97.

Columba 521-597 AD

Born on December 7, 521 at Garen in the county of Donegal, the Irish apostle Columba was baptized Colum, "the Dove." He is reputed to have founded some 30 collages and communities in Northern Ireland—Kells, Swords, Druncolum, Drumcliff, Screen, Kilglass, Drumhome and many more—all before the age of 42.

He was a descendant of Gathelus who was from the tribe of Judah, whose son Eremon arrived in Ireland from Egypt shortly after the Exodus. His father, Feidlimid, was chieftain of Tir-Conaill, putting Columba in succession to the Irish royal throne. But Columba studied under Finian of Clonard and, in 551, was ordained a priest of the Celtic Church which was founded directly upon the teachings of the apostles of Christ who reached Britain shortly after his death.

"His father, Feidhlimidh, or Phelim, was a grandson of Neill, of the nine hostages, head of the great house of O'Neill, and King of Ireland; and he bore the same relation in the female line to Lorn, son of Erc, one of the three leaders of the Dulriadic colony. His mother, Eithne, was the daughter of a Leinster chief connected with the royal family of Ireland." James Taylor D.D., *The Pictorial History of Scotland*, Virtue and Co., London, Vol. 1, p. 59.

In 563, at the age of 42, Columba sailed from his native Ireland as a missionary to the northern Picts of Scotland. Traveling in a small wicker frame boat covered with hides, he landed at Iona. There he established the Celtic Church.

> "Rome looked to Peter as its founder while the Celtic Church cited the authority of John. The Celtic Sabbath was celebrated on a Saturday and had more in common with the Greek service than the Latin." (*Celtic Inheritance*, Peter Berresford Ellis, Dorset Press, N.Y. 1992).

They began Sabbath at sunset each Friday. "The Sabbath was held to be a day of blessing in Wales as well as in Ireland and other Celtic lands" (*The Celtic Church in Britain*, Leslie Hardinge, p.82). The foot-washing ceremony instituted by Christ in John 13 was also carried out.

This is confirmed by the Roman Catholic historian, Bellesheim:

> "The Scots in this matter had no doubt kept up the traditional practice of the ancient monastic Church of Ireland, which observed Saturday rather than Sunday as a day of rest." Alphons Bellesheim, *History of the Catholic Church of Scotland*, Edinburgh, 1887, vol. 1, p. 250.

As well as other sources:

> "They [the Celtic Church] worked on Sunday, but kept Saturday in a sabbatical manner." Lang, Andrew, *A History of Scotland*, 1900-1907, vol. 1, p. 96.

> "It seems to have been customary in the Celtic churches of early time in Ireland as well as Scotland, to keep Saturday the Jewish Sabbath, as a day of rest from labor. They obeyed the fourth commandment literally upon the seventh day of the week." James C. Moffat, *The Church in Scotland*, Philadelphia, 1882, p. 140.

Even in Wales the Celtic Church flourished in independence:

> "There is much evidence that the Sabbath prevailed in Wales universally until A.D. 1115, when the first Roman bishop was seated at St. David's. The old Welsh Sabbath-keeping churches did not even then altogether bow the knee to Rome, but fled to their hiding places 'where the ordinances of the gospel to this day have been administered in their primitive mode without being adulterated by the corrupt Church of Rome.'" A. H. Lewis, *Seventh Day Baptists in Europe and America*, 1910, vol. 1. p. 29.

The island became one of the great centers of the Celtic Church spreading its influence well into the 11th Century. Nine years after Columba arrived in Iona with the Coronation Stone, Conal, king of western Scotland, passed away and Aidan succeeded him to the throne. Columba was selected to perform the inauguration ceremony for the new king. 1390 years later the same Coronation Stone of Destiny was used for the coronation of Queen Elizabeth II in Westminster Abbey where the stone now resides. Tradition claims it was the stone that Jacob used for a pillow after fleeing from home.

From Iona the truth about God's Sabbath was spread into the communities of western Scotland where it continued to be observed long after the church in England and Ireland had fallen under the spell of Rome and the day of the Sun.

"Having continued his labours in Scotland thirty-four years, [Columba] clearly and openly foretold this, and on Saturday the ninth of June said to his disciple Diermit: 'This day is called the Sabbath, that is, the day of rest and such will it truly be for me; for it will put an end to my labours'" Butler's *Lives of the Fathers, Martyrs, and Principle Saints,* Art. St. Colombo, A.D. 597.

When Augustine of Canterbury (not Hippo) with his 40 monks arrived in England to convert the Anglo-Saxons, he began by attacking the Celtic Church in Wales. When they refused to acknowledge the authority of Rome, he threatened them with the sword. In the end, 1200 British Christians were slaughtered. In 664 the Synod of Whitby ruled the exile of the Celtic Church from northern England. But time has reversed history.

"Strange that a people who owed Rome nothing in connection with their conversion to Christ, and who long struggled against her pretensions, should be now ranked among her most devoted adherents." Machuchlan, *Early Scottish Church*, pp. 97,98;

By the time of the Norman conquest of England in 1066 and Malcolm's rise to the Scottish throne 8 years earlier, Rome finally was able to suppress the faithful Celts through Margret Queen of Scotland. Through Sunday legislation the Culdees were ordered to conform or depart. Their property was confiscated and in 1130 they were finally expelled. But they resurfaced again in other lands.

The Cathari in the 12th century:

"He lays down also as one of their opinions, that the law of Moses is to be kept according to the letter, and that the keeping of the Sabbath, circumcision, and other legal observations, ought to take place. They hold also that Christ the Son of God is not equal with the Father, and that the Father, Son, and Holy Ghost, these three persons, are not one God and one substance; and as a surplus to these their errors, they judge and condemn all the doctors of the Church, and universally the whole Roman church" (Socrates Scholasticus, *Ecclesiastical History,* 1860 edition, Oxford, Volume 2, pp. 168, 169).

The Albigenses, Paulicians or Passaginian of France and Waldenses of Italy and Hussites of Bohemia (Bulgaria) all flourished in the 12th century and shared a common heritage:

"Like the other sects already mentioned, they had the utmost aversion to the dominion and discipline of the church of Rome; but they were, at the same time, distinguished by two religious tenets, which were peculiar to themselves. The first was a notion that the observation of the law of Moses, in everything except the offering of sacrifices, was obligatory upon Christians, in consequence of which they circumcised their followers, abstained from those meats, the use of which was prohibited under the Mosaic economy, and celebrated the Jewish Sabbath." (*Ibid*, p. 273).

Benedict suspected that the charge of circumcision was unfounded but resulted from their observance of the "Jewish" Sabbath.

"The history of the Armenian church is very interesting. Of all the Christians in Central Asia, they have preserved themselves most free from Mohammedan and Papal corruptions..."

"The Armenians in Hindoostan...have preserved the Bible in its purity, and their doctrines are, as far as the author knows, the doctrines of the Bible. Besides, they maintain the solemn observance of Christian worship throughout our empire on the seventh day; and they have as many spires pointing to heaven among the Hindoos as ourselves. Are such people then entitled to no acknowledgement on our part, as fellow Christians? Are they forever to be ranked by us with the Jews, Mohammedans, and Hindoos?" Claudius Buchannan, D.D., *Researches in Asia,* Philadelphia, 1813, p. 206.

Nestorian Christians

Nestorius (c. 382-451 AD) was Archbishop of Constantinople. When Anastasius preached a sermon on Theotokos, "Mother of god," and applied it to the Virgin Mary, Nestorius countered with a sermon of his own. Nestorius believed that Christ was two beings, one human, one divine, sharing the same body; and that Christ's divine nature was derived from God and not Mary. He was finally deposed in 431 AD following the Council of Ephesus. Nestorius was banished from the Byzantine empire and his followers were persecuted. So, Nestorian Christianity moved eastward and flourished for several hundred years in Persia, India and China. Historical records exist which describe the arrival of silkworm eggs from China brought by Nestorian missionaries to Constantinople in 551 AD. Separated from the mainstream Western Church of Rome, the Nestorians retained many elements of the original apostolic teachings. They became known as the Protestants of the East.

Evidence of the Sabbath and its influence on the peoples of the Orient is found throughout the history and heritage of many eastern countries:

- **China** originally observed the seventh day, they believed in seven material souls of man, and constructed many seven storied pagodas. This is a drawing of the Asoka pagoda in Ningbo of Zhejiang province built in the Tang Dynasty.

Among the gilt bronze statuettes of the Six and Tang Dynasties which found their way to Japan there is a kind called edabotoke, a group of seven Buddhistic statuettes—seven signifying the belief in Kako Shichibutsu—perched on seven branches of a tree. The Kako Shichibutsu (the Seven Buddhas of the Past) is a term applied to the group of Seven Buddhas who successively lived from the earliest days down to the arrival of Sakya.

Aryans of India followed a seven-day week and originated the Opasatha, a lunar-weekly rest day observed in Buddhist lands. (Parise, Frank. *The Book of Calendars*, New York: Facts on File, Inc. p. 172)

- **Brahmins** of the Ganges region in India knew the seventh day and featured the number seven prominently in their mythology and architecture. An example of just how profuse is this passage: "And so the Great Steward, at the end of the seven days, shaved off his hair and beard, donned yellow robes and went forth from the household life into homelessness. And with him went the seven anointed Khattiya kings, the seven wealthy and distinguished Brahmins with their seven hundred advanced pupils..." *Mahagovinda Sutta, Digha Nikaya* discourse 19.

- Ancient **Persians** also knew of the seventh day. Their creation story includes seven "stages": sky, ocean, earth, plants, animals, man and woman on the sixth stage. The seventh creation was fire and sun. They observe seven important festivals. The New Year ritual involves setting a special table with seven items symbolizing the seven creations and the seven immortals protecting them.

Sabbath in Persia
The Sabbath-keeping Churches in Persia underwent forty years of persecution under Shapur II, from 335-375 specifically, because they were Sabbath-keeping.

> "They despise our sun-god. Did not Zoroaster, the sainted founder of our divine beliefs, institute Sunday one thousand years ago in honour of the sun and supplant the Sabbath of the Old Testament. Yet these Christians have divine services on Saturday." (De Lacy O'Leary *The Syriac Church and Fathers*, 1909, pp. 83-84)

Near the end of the fourth century, Museus (Moses), the bishop of the Sabbath-keeping Abyssinian Church visited China. Ambrose of Milan stated that Museus had traveled extensively throughout Seres (China). (Ambrose, *De Moribus,* Brachmanorium Opera Omnia, 1132, found in Migne, *Patriologia Latina,* Vol. 17, pp. 1131-1132). Mingana maintained that the Abyssinian Museus traveled to Arabia, Persia, India and China in 370 AD.

Sabbath in India
Eusebius of Caesarea, the early Church historian, wrote in the 4th century that Pantaenus, "one of the most eminent teachers of his day" and head of the catechitical school in Alexandria late in the second century, had been "appointed to preach the gospel of Christ to the peoples of the East, and traveled as far as India."

In the fourth century, the Metropolitan Bishop of Edessa reportedly had a vision in which the apostle Thomas asked him to help his Indian flock. So the Catholicos of Seleucia-Ctesiphon, head of the Christian church in Mesopotamia and Persia, sent a group of some three hundred families from Jerusalem, Baghdad, and Nineveh as missionaries to India. Leading the group was a merchant known as Thomas of Cana. Though tradition teaches that the disciple Thomas went to India and evangelized that part of the world, some believe it was this later Thomas for whom the Thomas Christians are named.

The introduction of Sabbath-keeping to India caused an uproar in Buddhism about 220 AD. According to Lloyd (*The Creed of Half Japan,* p. 23) the Kushan Dynasty of North India, called a council of Buddhist priests at Vaisalia, to bring uniformity among the Buddhist monks on the observance of their weekly Sabbath. They had been so impressed by the Old Testament writings that they had begun to keep the seventh-day.

Sidonius, a historian wrote during the reign of Theodoric (454-526 AD):

> "It is a fact that it was formerly the custom in the East to keep the Sabbath in the same manner as the Lord's day and to hold sacred assemblies: while on the other hand, the people of the West, contending for the Lord's day have neglected the celebration of the Sabbath." (*Apollinaris Sidonii Epistolæ,* lib. 1,2; Migne, 57).

When I visited Andhra Pradesh, in southeastern India, in 1998, I was amazed at the strong Christian presence in this part of the Indian continent. About 70 percent of the indigenous population and 30 percent of the total population is Christian. Everywhere there are churches and Bible schools. And I frequently heard the proud story that Christianity was brought here by the disciple Thomas.

More interestingly, however, is the connection between Hebrew and the local dialect, Telegu. A comparative philological study of Hebrew and Telugu, suggests that Hebrew is the source of many words in proto-Telugu, a Dravidian language that anteceded Sanskrit. Sadly, and ironically, the small Jewish Indian community in this district suffers from anti-Semitic religious intolerance by the local Christian clergy who owe a great debt to the legacy of their Jewish neighbors.

Sabbath in China

Hebrews arrived in the Orient as early as the 5th century BC as part of the Assyrian and Babylonian dispersion. When Cyrus authorized the second Jewish exodus from captivity, Jewish beliefs and practices began a global distribution of enlightenment to the entire world. The effect of this can be seen in the influence Jews had on acceptance around the world of the seven day week and in many areas, according to Thomas M'Clatchie, the Sabbath:

Zend-Avesta: the God Ormuzd created the world at six different intervals lasting a whole year; man was created in the sixth period.

Etrurians: God created the world in six thousand years; man alone was created in the sixth millennium. (Suidas)

Eusebius, Hesiod, Homer, Callimachus and Linus mention the seventh day as having special importance.

Porphyry reported that the Phoenicians dedicated one day in seven to their god Cronus (Saturn).

Aulus Gellius: some philosophers attend temples on the seventh day.

Lucian of Antioch c. 250-312 : the seventh day is a holiday.

Ancient Arabians observed a Sabbath before the era of Mohammed.

Seven day week prevailed among the Indians, the Egyptians, the Celts, the Sclavonians, the Greeks and the Romans.

Josephus: "there is not any city of the Grecians, nor any of the barbarians, nor any nation whatsoever, whither our custom of resting on the seventh day hath not come."

Theophilus of Antioch: the seventh day was everywhere considered sacred.

Philo: the seventh day is a festival, not of this or of that city, but of the universe.

The St. Thomas Christians of India remained isolated from Rome. They were Sabbath-keepers, along with other groups who broke off communion with Rome after the Council of Chalcedon, including the Abyssinian, the Jacobites, the Maronites, the Armenians and the Kurds. They kept the food laws, rejected oral confession and the doctrine of purgatory. (Schaff-Herzog *The New Encyclopædia of Religious Knowledge*, art. *Nestorians* and *Nestorianer*. Funk & Wagnalls, New York & London, 1910, 12 volumes).

Isaiah prophesied that God's people, the Hebrews, would take the gospel to the world and even specified the land of "Sinim."

> "…to raise up the tribes of Jacob, and to restore the preserved of Israel: I will also give thee for a light to the Gentiles, that thou mayest be my salvation unto the end of the earth.

> "and I will preserve thee, and give thee for a covenant of the people, to establish the earth, to cause to inherit the desolate heritages; That thou mayest say to the prisoners, Go forth; to them that are in darkness, Shew yourselves.

> "Behold, these shall come from far: and, lo, these from the north and from the west; and these from the land of Sinim." Isaiah 49:6, 8, 9, 12

The land of Sinim was China. We still use Sino- in reference to that race. Jews, carried not only knowledge of the Chaldean civilization from the Tigris and Euphrates valleys but also the elements of God's Gospel including His day of rest on the seventh day. (Lacouperie, *Western Origin of Early Chinese Civilisation*, pp. 9, 12.) Through Turkestan to the Wei River of northwestern China these missionaries truly were a light and salvation to that end of the earth. (Pott, *A Sketch of Chinese History*, 3d ed., p. 2.) In *Spring and Autumn*, compiled in 481 BC, Confucius records the frequent arrival of "the white foreigners" to China.

The effect here was just as impressive. Confucius said, "The ancient kings on this culminating day (i.e., the seventh) closed their gates, the merchants did not travel and the princes did not inspect their domains." (M'Clatchie, *A Translation of the Confucian Classic of Change*, p. 118)

The Jewish immigrants remained true in their new Oriental homes. Even after a thousand years, investigators could still report that "They keep the Sabbath quite as strictly as do the Jews in Europe." (Finn, James. *The Jews in China*, B. Wertheim, London, 1843, p. 23)

Daniel's Messianic prophecies were taken to every nation planting hope of a coming Restorer everywhere it went. Within 100 years of Daniel's death there was an explosion of new religious ideologies within every major civilization. Greece produced the philosophy of Pythagorus, Persia had Zoroaster, India spawned Buddah, and China gave birth to Confucius, who was 14 years old when Daniel died. (Monier-Williams, *Indian Wisdom*, p. 49)   Each of these new religions made a remarkable departure from the previous ones: they all taught the existence of a single chief deity and a coming Prophet. Buddah predicted:

> "Five hundred years after my death, a Prophet will arise who will found His teaching upon the fountain of all the Buddhas. When that One comes, believe in Him, and you shall receive incalculable blessings!" E. A. Gordon, *World Healers or Lotus Gospel and its Bodhisattvas*, South Asia Books, 1993, pp. 31, 32, 229.

Confusius prophesied:

> "a saint should be born in the West who would restore to China the lost knowledge of the sacred tripod." *Ibid* p. 27.

It really shouldn't be surprising that when Daniel's prophecy was about to be fulfilled, Magi came from the *east* to seek the Promised One.

Later, Christian missionaries established an extensive network of churches and schools throughout China in the early centuries AD. Tradition among the St. Thomas Christians of eastern India claims that Thomas later evangelized the Yellow River region of China.

Arnobius, one of the Ante-Nicene Fathers writing about 300 AD, said that in his day the church had already been established in China. (Arnobius, *Against the Heathen*, found in *Ante-Nicene Fathers*, vol. 6, p. 438)

T'ang Dynasty 8th Century

By the 8th century the Eastern Church, sometimes called the Assyrian Church (though misnamed the Nestorian Church) was at the height of its influence and extent. Christianity's success was paralleled by the development of the Chinese culture under the Imperial T'ang Dynasty (AD 618-907) which at this time had reached heroic dimensions. This was the most advanced, progressive and liberal of all Chinese dynasties. (Saeki, *The Nestorgan Monument in China*, pp. 54, 171, 231,265; also, E. A. Gordon, *"World Healers,"* pp. 134, 181-183, 285,476)

Everything was conducted on a stupendous scale. For example, Emperor Sui's capital was constructed by two million construction workers. His fleet of pleasure boats were towed along the Yellow River by a crew of 80,000 men. On excursions his Imperial Caravan stretched for 300 miles. He maintained 3,000 concubines. And the anthology he ordered consisted of 17,000 chapters. Sansom, G. B. *Japan,* Cresset Press, London, 1932, pp. 81-84.

Close-up of the head piece, measuring approximately 1 meter wide, depicts two creatures called "Kumbhira" holding a large pearl. The Thomas Cross, similar to the one on the apostle's tomb at Meliapor, India, can be seen just below the apex of the triangular canopy sheltering the nine large Chinese characters. This engraved title is translated as "The Monument Commemorating the Propagation of the Ta-Ch'in [Judean] Illustrious Religion in the Middle Kingdom."

Sino-Syriac Christian Monument
In 781 the China Monument (shown above) a.k.a. the Ta-ch'in-ching-chiao-pei was created from a large ten foot high 3.3 foot wide two ton black marble slab to record the phenomenal growth of Christianity in China during the 8th century. The Sino-Syrian inscription was erected in the ancient capitol city of Ch'angan which is transliterated by various sources as Sian, Hsian, Chi'an or Xi'an and later known as Hsingan-fu during the 14th century Ming Dynasty. The city is situated about 1500 miles inland in the northern province of Shensi at Latitude 34° 12´ or 17´ North and Longitude 108° 5´ or 109° 30´ East (depending on the source). Its discovery ranks up there with the

Rosetta stone in importance and consists of nearly 2000 Chinese characters and 50 words plus 70 names in Syriac, the church language of Eastern Asia during Medieval times.

A copy of the monument now resides in the Pei Lin, *Forest of Tablets* or *Forest of Steles* Museum, in Xi'an. (Huc, *Christianity in China, Tartary, and Thibet,* vol. 1, pp. 45, 46.) The artifact has been mistakenly called the Nestorian Monument; it does not make any reference at all to Nestotius or his sect.

Many of these steles are mounted on the backs of marble tortoises which makes their height even more imposing. The Syriac text lists 75 names of elders, "monks," a bishop and then the following inscription:

> "In the days of the Father of Fathers, Mar Ananjesu [Khnanisho], the catholicos [universal] and patriarch, when Adam, priest, was vicar, bishop and metropolitan, of China, in the year 1092 of the era of the Greeks, Mar Jazedbuzid, priest and chrepiscopus of Kumdan the Royal city, son of Millis of blessed memory, a priest from Balkh, a city of Tachuristan, erected this marble tablet on which are inscribed the redemption of our Saviour and of the preaching of our fathers to the kings of China. Adam, deacon, son of Jazedbuzid the chorespiscopus: Mar Sergius, priest and chorespiscopus; Sabarjesu priest: Gabriel, priest and archdeacon, church rulers of the cities of Kumdan and Sarag."

The monument mentions the name of "Adam, director of the Assyrian Church" who is noted to have been intimately acquainted with:

- the Chinese emperor who ordered the stone monument
- Duke Kuo-Tzu, mighty general and secretary of state
- Dr. Issu, Assyrian clergyman
- Prajna, renowned Buddhist leader
- Kobo Daishi, greatest intellect in Japanese history, Prajna's student
- Lu Yen, founder of a powerful Chinese religious sect

"In the day of our Father of Fathers, My Lord Hananisho, Catholicos, Patriarch.... In the year one thousand and ninety-two of the Greeks." This establishes the date of the monument since the Greek empire began in 311BC, 1092-311= AD 781.   Saeki, P.Y. *The Nestorian Monument in China.* 1916. London, p. 175.

The term "Catholicos" simply means the universal leader or administrator. It is frequently translated as Universal Patriarch. It is not referring to Roman Catholicism which did not send missionaries to China until the 1500's when Portuguese explorers first brought Jesuits to the Orient.

The inscription continues:

> "my Lord Yesbuzid, Pastor and chorepiscopos of Kumdan, the Royal city, son of the departed Milis, Pastor from Balkh, a city of Tehuristan, erected this Monument, wherein is written the Law of Him, our Savior, the Preaching of our forefathers to the Rulers of the Chinese." (Saeki, *The Nestorian Monument in China*, p. 175)

Some idea of just how developed the church in China was at this time became clearer in 1908 when 35 books were discovered in a cave in northwestern China. They were a collection of church literature and included the Apostles' Creed in Chinese, a beautiful baptismal hymn in Chinese, a book on the incarnation and one on the doctrine of the cross. (Saeki, *The Nestorian Monument in China*, pp. 70, 71)

Another portion of the inscription reads:

> **"On the seventh day we offer sacrifices**, after having purified our hearts, and received absolution for our sins. This religion, so perfect and so excellent, is difficult to name, but it enlightens darkness by its brilliant precepts." M. l'Abbe Hue, *Christianity in China*, Vol. I, Ch. 2, pp. 48-49.

This segment is taken from the Syriac version of the dual language inscription. It paints a remarkable picture of the religious climate and liberties that these Chinese Christians enjoyed in the east while at the same time Charlemagne was destroying the Celtic church in France with the promise that he would be crowned Emperor of the new Holy Roman Empire. The western pope performed the coronation on Christmas day in 800 AD as his reward.

Buried Monument

In 845 religious persecution broke out against western religions under the rule of Emperor Wu-Tsung. The Christian believers in Changan buried their monument to prevent its destruction. Shortly thereafter, the T'ang Dynasty fell and general anarchy followed. But the Christian presence in China remained strong. Favor toward Christians revived during the Yuan Dynasty when the Mongols ruled China. In 1009 the leader of the northwestern Persian church sent news to Baghdad that 200,000 Turks and Mongols had accepted Christ. (Mingana, "Early Spread of Christianity," *Bulletin of John Ryland's Library*, vol. 9, pp. 308-310)

Then in 1020 a report came that there was a new Christian king of the Tartars named Pester John.

In Kirghiztan two Christian cemeteries were discovered at Semiryechensk with inscriptions on the tombstones were written both in Syriac and Turkish. There lay, side by side, 'Terim the Chinese', 'Banus the Uigurian', 'Sazik the Indian', 'Kiamata of Kashgar', 'Tatt the Mongol', and 'Shah Malison of George of Tus'. People from China, India, East and West Turkestan, Mongolia, Manchuria, Siberia and Persia. The inscriptions mentioned their occupations: "Zuma, priest, general and famous amir; Shliha the celebrated commentator and teacher, who illuminated all the monasteries with light; Pesoha the renowned exegetist and preacher; the charming maiden Julia, the betrothed of the bishop Johanan; Sabrisho, the archdeacon, the blessed old man and the perfect priest."

One stone gives evidence that here, too, the Sabbath was known and used in common time reference. Its inscription reads:

"This is the grave of Chorepiscopus Ama. In the year 1566, (or 1255 according to our time), he departed from this world in the month of July on **Sabbath**. May our Lord unite his spirit with those of the pious and upright. Amen."

(Mingana, Bulletin of the John Rylands Library, Vol. 9, no. 2, pp. 39-42. Yohannon, *Death of a Nation*, p. 102. See also Aziz Atiya, Eastern Christianity, pp. 260, 261. Stewart, *Nestorian Missionary Enterprise*, pp. 198-213).

These findings are mute testimonies to a once-flourishing Christian Church. Edward Gibbon concluded that "The Christianity of China, between the seventh and the thirteenth century, is invincibly proved by the consent of Chinese, Arabian, Syriac, and Latin evidence." (Edward Gibbon, *Decline and Fall of the Roman Empire*, ch. 47, note 118)

13th Century

Marco Polo traveled to China in the 13th century. He also encountered the original Christian Church of the East and noted how different it was from the Catholicism of his native Italy:

"Mosul is a large province inhabited by various descriptions of people, one class of whom pay reverence to Mahomet, and are called Arabians. The others profess the Christian faith, but not according to the canons of the church, which they depart from in many instances, and are denominated Nestorians, Jacobites, and Armenians. They have a patriarch whom they call Jacolit, and by him archbishops, bishops, and abbots are consecrated and sent to all parts of India, to Baudas (Baghdad), or to Cathay (China), just as the pope of Rome does in Latin countries." Komroff, *The Travels of Marco Polo*, p. 29.

Then in the 16th century, Jesuits under Francis Xavier brought the Portuguese Inquisition to the Orient after establishing a presence in India. Xavier then sailed for Japan in 1549. There he built his first church at Yamaguchi in 1552 incorporating Buddhist philosophy into his papal teaching just like the Western Church had done throughout its history.

"He utilized, also, the altar vessels, lights, incense, and some of the images found in their temples—differing as they do so little from those of the Catholic Church." E. A. Gordon, *World Healers or The Lotus Gospel and Its Bodhisattvas Compared With Early Christianity*, London, 1912. p. 481.

In 1601 another Jesuit priest from Portugal, Matteo Ricci, established Catholicism in Peking. Huc, M. L'Abbe, Evariste Regis. *Christianity in China, Tartary, and Thibet*, in 3 vols., Longmans, Brown, Green, Longmans, and Roberts, London, 1857, vol. 2, chs. 3, 4.

Father Ricci was also adopting the local customs like ancestral worship and baptizing those who still practiced them. The Jesuits were split over Ricci's policy. Sure, the Chinese were worshiping the spirits of their dead ancestors, and offering prayers and burning incense for the dead, but this wasn't any different from what the Catholics were practicing in their prayers to the dead saints and burning candles, use of images in worship, etc.

The educated Chinese were attracted to the Jesuits' knowledge of mathematics, engineering, astronomy. In 1615 China commissioned the translation of all the best European books into Chinese. And the Jesuits, because of their mastery of both languages, were given the assignment. *Ibid.*Huc, vol. 2, pp. 265, 266.

When the 8th century monument was accidentally discovered in 1625, suddenly everyone was interested. Both the Chinese and the Jesuits wanted to replace the original stone with a newer, improved, updated version. The Chinese were alarmed that they could not read the ancient characters which was embarrasing because they had long boasted that their language had remained unchanged for thousands of years. So it was their policy, when finding ancient artifacts with old Chinese inscriptions, to replace them with new copies featuring the more modern and readable Mandrin characters. Wall, Charles William. *Ancient Orthography of the Jews*, 4 vols., Whittaker and Company, London, 1840, vol. 2, p. 162.

Furthermore, the inscription indicated that there were millions of Christians in China during the 8th century Syrian expansion. The Jesuits found evidence of a strong Christian community that had existed long before they arrived. This was damaging to Rome's claim that their brand of Christianity was the first and dominant one. So the Jesuits promoted an official explanation that the replica was necessary because the Chinese characters were "badly damaged" when the original monument was unearthed. So the original stone, threatening to both the Chinese and the Catholic missionaries, was conveniently destroyed.

Martin Martini, a Jesuit missionary in China around 1655 wrote:

> "The governor was no sooner apprised of the discovery of the monument than by a curiosity natural to the Chinese, he betook himself to the place and as soon as he examined the tokens of its venerable antiquity, he first composed a book in honor of the monument and ordered that a stone of the same size be made, on which he had engraved the contents of the other and had inscribed point-by-point the same characters and the same letters which had been impressed on the original." Kircher, *La Chine*, pp. 10, 11; also Wall, Charles William. *Ancient Orthography of the Jews*, 4 vols., Whittaker and Company, London, 1840, vol. 2, p. 160.

Two other Jesuit priests, Boim and Samedus, also mentioned that a second stone was prepared with the same dimensions and a replacement inscription. Wall, Charles William. *Ancient Orthography of the Jews*, 4 vols., Whittaker and Company, London, 1840, vol. 2, p. 163.

The Jesuits were very interested in the marble stone's inscription because it clearly detailed the emergence and growth of the Church in China, its acceptance by the T'ang Dynasty, and the tremendous influence it had in China, despite the fact that this same Eastern Christian Church had been excommunicated by the Bishop of Rome some 500 years earlier. The kind of Christianity described by the monument, differed dramatically and embarrassingly with the flavor offered by Rome.

Compared to the Syriac inscription, the revised Chinese message included liberal embellishment and glaring omission. There are additional doctrinal references to images and prayers for the dead but no mention of Christ ("Him who was our Redeemer" in the Syriac), His miracles, His death, resurrection, and ascension. All these were part of the Syriac text. The Chinese revision also failed to provide additional important data which is found in the Syriac: the year of the stone's creation, the name of the Chinese Church director and the Eastern Church leadership

Charles William Wall in the early 1800s made a comparative analysis of the Syriac and Chinese inscriptions with their respective usage in previous historical ages. His evidence is convincing proof of the Chinese counterfeit. Wall, Charles William. *Ancient Orthography of the Jews*, 4 vols., Whittaker and Company, London, 1840, Vol. 2, pp. 200-245.

The Jesuits clearly assisted in the translation process. But neither they nor the Chinese could understand seventh century Syriac. So they left it alone.

After its discovery in 1625 the massive tablet was just left standing where it had been found. For nearly three centuries it sat outside near a Buddhist monastery along with other "worthless" stone relics. Then in the early 1900's Dr. Fritz von Holm attempted to purchase the stone monument for the British Museum. The Chinese recognized how valuable it was and decided to keep it. So Fritz made a replica, took it to New York in 1908. There, additional reproductions were made from casts and distributed to various museums around the world including the Gimet Museum in Paris, France, the Lateran Museum of Rome, the Metropolitan Museum of Art in New York, and atop Mt. Koya at the Kobo Daishi monastery of Kongo-buji. At the urging of European Christians the 10 foot high monument at Xi'an was finally given a place inside the present enclosure in 1907.

Five years later, the first President of the Chinese Republic, Dr. Sun Yat Sen, referred to the Nestorian Inscription on January 5, 1912 as proof that "this Chinese Christendom was a daughter of the Assyrian Church which claimed descent from the Apostle Thomas and his immediate disciples."

The complete text of the monument:

> The true Lord is without origin, profound, invisible, and unchangeable;
> With power and capacity to perfect and transform,
> He raised up the earth and established the heavens.
> Divided in nature, he entered the world to save and to help without bounds;
> The sun arose, and darkness was dispelled, all bearing witness to his true original.
> The glorious and resplendent, accomplished Emperor,
> Whose principles embraced those of preceding monarchs,
> Taking advantage of the occasion, suppressed turbulence;
> Heaven was spread out and the earth was enlarged.
> When the pure, bright Illustrious Religion was introduced to our Tang Dynasty,
> **The Scriptures were translated, and churches built,**
> And the vessel set in motion for the living and the dead;
> Every kind of blessing was then obtained,
> and all the kingdoms enjoyed a state of peace.

When Kau-tsung succeeded to his ancestral estate, he rebuilt the edifices of purity;
Palaces of concord, large and light, Covered the length and breadth of the land.
The true doctrine was clearly announced,
Overseers of the church were appointed in due form;
The people enjoyed happiness and peace,
While all creatures were exempt from calamity and distress.
When Hiuen-tsung commenced his sacred career,
He applied himself to the cultivation of truth and rectitude;
His imperial tablets shot forth their effulgence,
And the celestial writings mutually reflected their splendors.
The imperial domain was rich and luxuriant,
While the whole land rendered exalted homage;
Every business was flourishing throughout, and the people all enjoyed prosperity.
Then came Suh-tsung, who commenced anew,
And celestial dignity marked the Imperial movements.
Sacred as the moon's unsullied expanse,
while felicity was wafted like nocturnal gales.
Happiness reverted to the Imperial household,
The autumnal influences were long removed;
Ebullitions were allayed, and risings suppressed
and thus our dynasty was firmly built up.
Tai-tsung the filial and just Combined in virtue with heaven and earth;
By his liberal bequests the living were satisfied,
And property formed the channel of imparting succor.
By fragrant mementoes he rewarded the meritorious,
With benevolence he dispensed his donations;
The solar concave appeared in dignity,
and the lunar retreat was decorated to extreme.
When Kien-chung succeeded to the throne,
he began the cultivation of intelligent virtue;
His military vigilance extended to the four seas,
And his accomplished purity influenced all lands.
His light penetrated the secrecies of men,
And to him the diversities of objects were seen as in a mirror;
He shed a vivifying influence through the whole realm of nature,
And all outer nations took him for example.
The true doctrine, how expansive! Its responses are minute;
How difficult to name it! To elucidate **the three in one.**
The sovereign has the power to act!
While the ministers record; we raise this noble monument!
To the praise of great felicity.

This was erected in the 2d year of Kien-chung, of the Tang
Dynasty [A.D. 781], on the 7th day of the 1st month, being
Sunday. Written by Lu Siu-yen, Secretary to Council, formerly
Military Superintendent for Tai-chau;
while the Bishop Ning-shu had the charge of the congregations
of the Illustrious in the East.

[Two lines of Syriac text are included on the stone in the strange character set arranged down the left and right sides of the Chinese text. Kircher translates them as follows:]
"Adam, Deacon, Vicar-episcopal and Father of China. In the time of the Father of Fathers, the Lord John Joshua, the Universal Patriarch."

[Syriac at the foot of the stone, again according to Kircher:]
"In the year of the Greeks one thousand and ninety-two, the Lord Jazedbuzid, Priest and Vicar-episcopal of Cumdan the royal city, son of the enlightened Mailas, Priest of Balkh a city of Turkestan, set up this tablet, whereon is inscribed the Dispensation of our Redeemer, and the preaching of **the apostolic missionaries to the King of China.**"

[After this, in Chinese characters:]
"The Priest Lingpau."

[Then again in Syriac:]
"Adam the Deacon, son of Jazedbuzid, Vicar-episcopal.
The Lord Sergius, Priest and Vicar-episcopal.
Sabar Jesus, Priest.
Gabriel, Priest, Archdeacon, and Ecclesiarch of Cumdan and Sarag."

[The following subscription is appended in Chinese :]
"Assistant Examiner: the High Statesman of the Sacred rites, the Imperially conferred purple-gown Chief Presbyter and Priest Yi-li."

[On the left-hand edge are the Syriac names of sixty-seven priests, and sixty-one are given in Chinese.]

Inscription of the Nestorian Monument, Alexander Wykue, *Tablet Eulogizing the Propagation of the Illustrious Religion in China, With a Preface; Composed by King-Tsing,A Priest of the Syrian Church.* Published in The Open Court Magazine, Devoted to the Science of Religion, the Religion of Science, and the Extension of the Religious Parliament Idea. Volume XXIII, CHICAGO, THE OPEN COURT PUBLISHING COMPANY, 1909, p. 35 .

Po-sz', "Persians." This name was well known to the Chinese at that time, being the designation of an extensive sect then located in the Empire, and the name of a nation with which they had held commercial and political intercourse for several centuries. The statement here is in admirable harmony with the general tradition of the early Church, that the Magi or wise men mentioned in Matthew's Gospel were no other than philosophers of the Parsee sect. The "three constant principles" may perhaps mean faith, hope, and charity.

Charles F. Horne, ed., *The Sacred Books and Early Literature of the East*, (New York: Parke, Austin, & Lipscomb, 1917), Vol. XII, *Medieval China*, pp. 381-392.

Another very interesting source of medieval Sabbath keepers is a document recording the travels of two Nestorian Christians from China to Europe. The account has been preserved in E.A. Wallis Budge's Budge, *The Monk of Kublai Khan, Emperor of China; or The History of the Life and Travels of Rabban Sawma, Envoy and Plenipotentiary of the Mongol Khans to the Kings of Europe and Markos who as Yahbh-Allaha III Became Patriarch of the Nestorian Church in Asia.* London: The Religious Track Society, 1928.

TRANSLATED FROM THE SYRIAC BY SIR E. A. WALLIS BUDGE, KT.
M.A., LITT.D. (CAMBRIDGE), M.A., D.LITT. (OXFORD)
D.LIT. (DURHAM), F.S.A.
Sometime Keeper of Egyptian and Assyrian Antiquities, British Museum, Corresponding Member of the Academy of Sciences Lisbon; and Corresponding Member of the Philosophical Society of America With 16 plates and 6 illustrations in the text,
LONDON, THE RELIGIOUS TRACT SOCIETY,
Manchester, TORONTO, Madrid LISBON, BUDAPEST,
First published in 1928, Printed *by Harrison & Sons, Ltd., St. Martin's Lane, London, W.C. 2*

Section 156
"This laying on of hands took place in the month of the second Teshri, on the first Sunday of the 'Consecration of the Church,' in the year one thousand five hundred and ninety-three of the Greeks [i.e. in November, I28I], in the seven and thirtieth year of his age."

"Now it happened that in the winter of that year King ABHGHA came down to BAGHDAD, and MAR YAHBH-ALLAHA, the Catholicus, went to him **on the Sabbath** which came before the Lord's Fast (i.e. Lent). And he explained to him the affairs of the Christians [i.e. their actual condition], and found mercy (i.e. sympathy) in his sight."

Section 182
They "did not fast during **the first Sabbath of Lent**. And when they asked them, "Wherefore do ye do thus, and **separate yourselves from all [other] Christians**" (68), they replied, "This is our custom. When we were first taught the Gospel our fathers in the Faith were weakly and were unable to fast. Those who taught them the Gospel commanded them to fast forty days only."

Section 194
"And on **the day of the Sabbath of Light** MAR PAPA went to the church, and **they read the Books of the Prophets**, and the prophecies concerning the Messiah."

Chinese-Bible Characters

There seems to be a strong tie between quite a few Kanji Chinese characters and the Bible teaching, without which it's simply difficult to explain the component parts that make up the characters. Some of these words are listed in the following together with illustration of their ties with the Bible.

Creation is comprised of the following components:

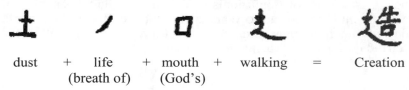

| dust | + | life (breath of) | + | mouth (God's) | + | walking | = | Creation |

Only by reading Genesis 2:7 is it possible to understand how Kanji could have come up with this character.

> The Lord formed the man from the **dust** of the **ground** and **breathed** into his nostrils the breath of **life** and the man became a **living being**.

Forbidden is comprised of the following components

| tree (of knowledge) | + | tree (of life) | + | command (from God) | = | Forbidden |

Once again the compound character makes sense only after reading the following verses:

> "And the Lord commanded the man, 'You are free to eat from any tree in the garden, but you must not eat from the tree of the knowledge of good and evil, for when you eat of it you will certainly die.' " Genesis 2:16,17

> "After he drove the man out, he placed on the east side of the Garden of Eden Cherubim and a flaming sword flashing back and forth to guard the way to the tree of life." Genesis 3:24

Ship is comprised of the following components:

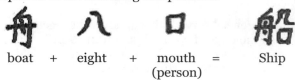

| boat | + | eight | + | mouth (person) | = | Ship |

The origin of this word becomes more meaningful after reading the following verse.

> "And Noah and his sons [Ham, Shem, and Japheth] and his wife and his sons' wives with him, went into the ark, to escape the waters of the flood." Genesis 7:7.

Ancient chinese ideography is dated to 2500 BC and identifies an original monotheism untainted by mythology or idolatry. The polytheistic cults of Confusionism, Taoism and Buddhism did not emerge until another 2000 years later. But even today the seventh day of the first lunar month in the Chinese year is called the "birthday of mankind" using the characters

literally: man's   day

The residents of Linqu in Shandong Province wear gourds on this day in the shape of the Chinese character for "human". In Singapore on this same day it is tranditional to not eat meat but rather raw fish and seven types of vegetables called *Yu Sheng* in commemoration of the "Day of Mankind" or the "birthday of humans." The seventh day has apprarently been long recognized as the memorial of creation.

C.H. Kang and Ethel R. Nelson, *The Discovery of Genesis - How the Truths of Genesis Were Found Hidden in the Chinese Language*, Concordia Press, 1979.

African Sabbath keepers

> "When Israel was a child, then I loved him, and called my son out of Egypt" Hosea 11:1
> "Princes shall come out of Egypt; Ethiopia shall soon stretch out her hands unto God." Psalm 68:31
> "From beyond the rivers of Ethiopia my suppliants, even the daughter of my dispersed, shall bring mine offering" Zephaniah 3:10

It is interesting, though not surprising, that Zephaniah should speak of Ethiopia—twice (2:12; 3:10). This Biblical author has the longest genealogical list of names of any prophet, and the list includes the name of Cush.

Sabbath has been observed throughout the recorded history of Ethiopia since the days of Nimrod, about 2140 B.C. Nimrod was the son of Cush, grandson of Noah. Genesis 10:8, 9. This places him some 700 years before the birth of Moses.

Tradition includes the story of the Queen of Sheba who brought a knowledge and worship of the Hebrew God to Ethiopia. Africanus wrote in Latin and this Old English translation survives:

> "The Iewes who have bene dispersed by God throughout the whole world, to confirme us in the holie faith, entered into Ethiopia in the Queen of Sabas daies, in companie of a son that Salomon had by her, to the number (as the Abassins affirme) of twelve thousand, and there multiplied their generation exceedingly. In that they not onely filled Abassia, but spred themselves likewise all over the neighbour provinces. So that at this day also the Abassins affirme, that upon Nilus towards the west, there inhabiteth a most populous nation of the Iewish stock, under a mighty K[ing]. And some of our moderne Cosmographers set downe a province in those quarters, which they call the land of the Hebrewes, placed as it were under the equinoctiall, in certaine unknowne mountaines, betweene the confines of Abassia, and Congo. And likewise on the north part of the kingdome of Goiame, and the southerly quarter of the kingdome of Gorham there are certaine mountaines, peopled with Iewes, who there maintaine themselves free, and absolute, through the inaccessible situations of the same. For in truth by this means, the inhabitants of the mountaines (speaking generally) are the most ancient, and freest people: in that the strong situation of their native soile secureth them from the incursions of forraine nations, and the violence of their neighbours." Leo Africanus, *The History and Description of Africa* , p. 1004.

Notice that Africanus calls her the "Queen of Sabas daies" which fully translated is "Queen of Sabbath days."
The Sabbath was kept in Egypt according to the Oxyrhynchus Papyrus which was written between 200-250 AD:

> "Except ye make the sabbath a real sabbath [Gr. sabbatize the Sabbath], ye shall not see the Father." (*The Oxyrhynchus Papyri*, Pt. 1, p. 3, Logion 2, verso 4-11, London: Offices of the Egyptian Exploration Fund, 1898).

North Africa produced such notable Christians as Augustine, Athanasius, Origin, Clement of Alexandria. But Christianity had its most indelible impact in the land of Ethiopia. It is quite interesting to discover the pervasive influence of seventh day observance in this region of Africa.

> "In the Chanaian context, and especially within the people forming the Ashanti or Akan nation, Saturday has been a traditionally accepted holy day, a day for worship of God." Nortey, Jacob J. "Independent African Churches—Are They Genuinely Christian?" *Spectrum*, Dec. 1989, p. 30.

> "Among the Yoruba people [Nigeria], the seventh day of the week is a day when no work, no marriage, no festivities, should be performed. It is

known as the forbidden day." Awoniwi, Joel. *Sabbath in Yoruba Land Before Christianity*, 2nd ed. (Ile Ife, Nigeria, n.d.), p. 17.

Ethiopian emperor Galawdewos (AD 1540-1559) quoted from Bekele Heye:

> "We do celebrate the Sabbath, because God, after He had finished the Creation of the World, rested thereon: Which day, as God would have it called the Holy of Holies, so that not celebrating thereof with great honor and devotion, seems to be plainly, contrary to God's will and precept, who will suffer heaven and earth to pass away sooner than His Word; and that especially, since Christ came not to dissolve the law but to fulfill it. It is not therefore in imitation of the Jews, but in obedience to Christ, and His holy apostles, that we observe that day."

> "Oral traditions and modern scholars and research into Akan traditions and customs affirm Saturday as Onyamee Kwaame's special day in Akanland."Owusa-Mensa, Kofi "Onyamee Kwamee (The Akan Saturday God of Saturday)" unpublished paper, p. 17.

Writing in the early twenties, Rattray, the British anthropologist, discovered that the Ashante name for God is Onyamee or Onyankopon Kwamee "whose day of service is a Saturday" adding that, "this Ashante God is the same as the Jehovah of the Israelites, whom they worshiped on the Sabbath or Saturday." Rattray, R.S., *The Ashanti*, Oxford University Press, London, 1923, p. 80.

> "The Ashanti believe that in the beginning man acted by natural law, but sin quickly obscured the natural light of reason, and it became necessary that the same precepts and prohibitions should be given to man in clearly defined terms, that he might not plead ignorance as an excuse for transgression. That is precisely what...God did on Mount Sinai in giving us the Ten Commandments." Peebles, James, *American Heritage Study Bible*, 1994, p. 119.

> "Jahn says: 'The Egyptians consecrated to Saturn the seventh day of the week.' Pauw was of the opinion that 'the Egyptians seem to have observed it very regularly.' Bunsen, speaking of Set, adds, 'He is the god of the Semitic tribes, who rested on the seventh day.' Hesiod, Herodotus, Philostratus, etc., mention that day. Homer, Callimachus, and other ancient writers call the seventh day the holy one, Eusebius confesses its observance by 'almost all the philosophers and poets.' Lucian notes that it was given to schoolboys for a holiday...On the seventh day he appointed a holy day, and to cease from all business he commanded." Bonwick, James, Egyptian Belief and Modern Thought: African Publication Society, London, 1983, pp. 412, 413.

> "In 1449 the Emperor of Ethiopia, Zara Ya'iqob, assembled a church council in the monastery at Dabra Mitmaq in Shoa...The Emperor, surrounded by his wives, his bishops, his abbots, his generals, was resolved to settle once and for all the problem of the Sabbath."

Hastings, Adrian. *The Church in Africa: 1450-1950. Oxford History of the Christian Church.* New York: Oxford University, 1994.

"The Abyssinian (Ethiopian) is a truer Sabbatarian than the Seventh Day Baptist...He observes the Jewish Sabbath as well as the Christian Sunday." Noble, Frederic Perry, *The Redemption of Africa: A Story of Civilization,* Revell: Chicago, 1899, p. 192.

"The church in Africa [recognized] that the resurrection of Christ in no way nullified the fact that 'in six days the Lord made heaven and earth.'...Even though the power of the Western papal legacy has made some indelible indentations on the churches of Africa, to this day they have refused to fully succumb. Many members of the Ethiopian Orthodox Church still observe the day which the Lord has made for all people to worship Him, and Coptic law stipulates that the seventh-day Sabbath, along with Sunday, be continuously regarded as a festal day for religious celebration." Burton, Keith A. "Western European Imperialism and the Literary Suppression of the African Fidelity to the Biblical Sabbath." Sabbath in Africa Project, 1993.

"According to the Kebra Negast, the Ethiopian book of kings, when the queen of Sheba returned from her visit to hear Solomon's wisdom, she returned home to bear his child...Although Solomon was enamored of the lad, he finally gave him permission to return, commissioning the brightest of Israelite young men to accompany his son." Bradford, Charles E. Sabbath Roots: the African Connection, L. Brown & Sons, Vermont 19991, p. 89

One group of Ethiopians believe they are the descendents of Solomon. These are the Sabbath-keeping Falasha, known as Black African Jews, they number about 90,000 with the large majority of them still in Ethiopia. They "call themselves the House of Israel ...[and] know only the Pentateuch, not the Talmud, and do not speak Hebrew." Isichei, Elizabeth A. *A History of Christianity in Africa,* Eerdmans, Grand Rapids, 1995, p. 50.

Sabbath keeping African churches:

> African Apostolic Church in Sabbath
> African Sabbath Mission Church
> African Seventh Church of God
> African Seventh-Day Adventists
> African Seventh Day Zulu Shaka Church of Christ
> Apostolic Jerusalem Church in Sabbath
> Baptist Church of the Seventh-day Adventists of Africa
> Baptist of the Seventh-day Adventists
> Christian Church Saturday
> Free Sabbatarian Mission of the Seventh-Day Observers
> Nazareth Baptist Church of South Africa in Sabbath
> New Jerusalem Sabbath Apostolic Church in Zion

Sabbath Church in Zion of South Africa
Sabbath Christian Apostolic Church in Zion
Seventh Day Adventists
Seventh Day Church of God
Seventh Day Baptist Church of Christ
South African Seventh Church of God
Sundkler, Bengt G. *Bantu Prophets in South Africa*, Oxford
University Press, New York, 1961, pp. 354-374.

The **Abyssinian Church in Ethiopia** remained Sabbath keeping despite the efforts of Jesuits to convert them to Roman Catholicism. In 1534 the Abyssinian legate before the court of Lisbon, denied any Jewish influence for their observance of the seventh day, rather he stated that they did so in obedience to Christ and the Apostles

> "Because God, after he had finished the creation of the world, rested thereon; which day, as God would have it called the holy of holies, so the not celebrating thereof with great honour and devotion, seems to be plainly contrary to God's will and precept, who will suffer heaven and earth to pass away sooner than his word; and that especially, since Christ came not to destroy the law, but to fulfil it. It is not therefore in imitation of the Jews, but in obedience to Christ and his holy apostles, that we observe that day." Geddes, *Church History of Ethiopia*, pp. 87-88

In 1604 the Jesuits finally pressured king Zadenghel into submitting to the Papacy and prohibiting Sabbath worship under severe penalty. After years of fierce struggle Rome's tyranny was broken and ultimately banished from Ethiopia. Immediately the country rejoiced as the ancient faith was once again restored. (Geddes, ibid., p. 311 and also Gibbons *Decline and Fall of the Roman Empire*, Ch. 47 "The Abyssinians were enjoined to work and to play on the Sabbath.")

Our patient's family history is highly significant and most remarkable. Attention to this important aspect of our clinical history will now be correlated to the third component of taking a patient's past history: the contribution of social factors.

Los Lunas Commandment Stone

Named after Los Lunas (ungrammatical Spanish but the actual name of the nearby town) the Commandment Stone is dated anywhere from 500 AD to 1000 BC. It consists of a large 4 x 6 foot boulder inscribed with strange characters chiseled on the volcanic basalt rock. These characters have been identified as a form of early Hebrew or Northern Canaanite-Phoenician and are important to us because they contain a reference to the Sabbath.

The stone is located in the Hidden or Mystery Mountains of New Mexico, just west of Los Lunas off Highway 25, about 35 miles south of Albuquerque. It has been known since the early 1800s but was indecipherable until paleo-Hebrew was discovered in the following century. It was only then that it could be read. We now know that the inscription is actually a short form of the Ten Commandment Decalogue contained in Exodus 20. This sequence of history is strong support for the authenticity of the stone's inscription.

My brother had the opportunity to visit and photograph this amazing artifact in 2003. The following pictures give you some idea of its size and approximate location.

The following interlinear translation was made by Stan Fox in 1999. The Hebrew text is read from right to left beginning with the top line:

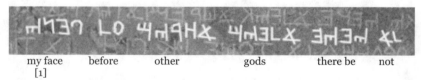

out of the land	has taken you	who	your God	Jehovah	I (am)

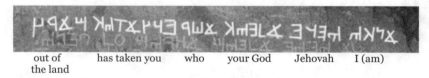

my face [1]	before	other	gods	there be	not

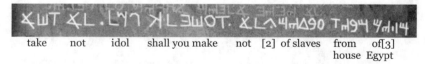

take	not	idol	shall you make	not [2]	of slaves	from house Egypt	of[3]

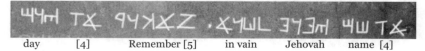

day	[4]	Remember [5]	in vain	Jehovah	name [4]

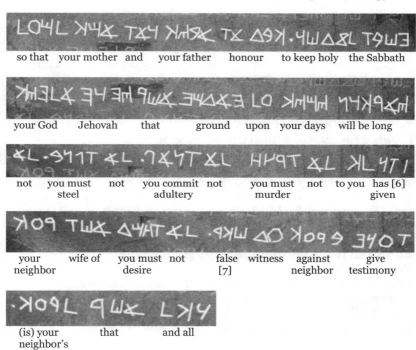

| so that | your mother | and | your father | honour | to keep holy | the Sabbath |

| your God | Jehovah | that | | ground | upon | your days | will be long |

| not | you must steel | not | you commit adultery | not | you must murder | not | to you | has [6] given |

| your neighbor | wife of | you must desire | not | false [7] | witness | against neighbor | give testimony |

| (is) your neighbor's | that | and all |

Commentary:
[1] Normal Hebrew spelling does not include the HE character
[2] Probably an insertion mark for the aberrant second line
[3] Right 3 characters are broken off
[4] Right character is broken off
[5] Normal Hebrew spelling does not include the Aleph character
[6] Right character is damaged by a surface crack
[7] Normal Hebrew spelling is QOPH instead of KAPH

The writer apparently skipped the first commandment when making the original inscription and later inserted it between the first two lines. This is why the text is so crowded in this area of the rock. This also explains why the train of thought skips when reading the lines in their current order. The end of line one begins the phrase "out of the land..." which obviously should be followed by "of Egypt..." but instead continues with "Not there be god other before my face." The scribe realizing the omission squeezed it in and made an indication in line three [2] where it should rightfully be located.

The Epigraphical Society renders the inscription in a more logical and corrected version:

I (Am) **Jehovah** [the Eternal] **Eloah** [your God] **who brought you out of the land of Mitsrayim** [Mizraim or the two Egypts] **out of the house of bondages.**
You shall not have other [foreign **gods in place of** (me).
You shall not make for yourself
molded (or carved) **idols** [graven images].
You shall not lift up your voice
to connect the name of Jehovah in hate.
Remember you (the) **Sabbath to make it holy.**
Honor your father and your mother to make long your existence upon the land which Jehovah Eloah [the Eternal your God] **gave to you.**
You shall not murder.
You shall not commit adultery (or idolatry).
You shall not steal (or deceive).
You shall not bear witness against your neighbor, testimony for a bribe.
You shall not covet (the) **wife of your neighbor and all which belongs to your neighbor.**

Cyrus Gordon proposed in 1995 that the stone is in fact a Samaritan mezuzah, typically a large flat stone placed at the entrance of a synagogue bearing the words of the Decalogue. Samaritan ship owners are known to have lived in Greek communities during the time of Theodosius I around 390 AD and could have been responsible for the Greek character influence.

However, the Los Lunas Decalogue actually follows the Masoretic text in expressing the phrase "*remember* the Sabbath day" rather than the expression "*preserve* the Sabbath day" which typically appears on Samaritan mezuzahs.

Others have observed that the inscription uses Greek letters *tau, zeta, delta*, and a reversed *kappa* in place of the Hebrew counterparts *taw, zayin, daleth*, and *kaph*. This indicates a post-Alexandrian Greek influence, even though the *aleph* is a rather archaic form. On the other hand, according to Lidzbarski (1902), Purvis (1968) the letters *yodh, qoph*, and the flat-bottomed *sin/shin* are distinctively Samaritan in form.

	Los Lunas Hebrew	Phonecian
Aleph	𝔛	𝔛
Beth	𝟿	ᕦ
Gimel	1	1
Daleth	△	◁
He	⧖	⧖
Waw	Ч	Y
Zayin	Z	Z
Heth	H	B
Yod	ꟼ	𝟏 or ⤳
Kaph	𝕏	𝕏
Lamed	L	∠
Mem	ꟺ	ꟺ
Nun	𝟏	𝟓
Ayin	O	O
Pe	ꓶ	7
Sade	ꓑ	ꓦ
Qoph	𝕏	Φ or ⤳
Resh	ᑫ	◁
Sin	Ⴞ	W
Taw	T	✝

The old Hebrew alphabet was virtually identical with the mid-Phoenician alphabet from the tenth to sixth century BC. After the Jewish return from the Babylonian exile in 538 BC, scribes began to develop their unique square-Hebrew characters.

Phoenicians are known to have sailed throughout the Mediterranean (middle earth) Sea establishing colonies at Tarshish in Spain and Carthage, North Africa. Greek historian Herodotus confirmed that Carthaginians engaged in cross-Atlantic trips during their trading excursions.

Eskimo Sabbath-keepers

An alternate source of American Sabbath activity could have come from the west. Northwestern Alaska, the cradle of Eskimo civilization, is also home to a legendary Inupiat/Ieupiaq First Nations prophet born around 1800 and known variously as Maniilaq, Maneelok, Maniixaq and Maniixauraq. At a time when Alaskan people endured a life of paralyzing fear under powerful shaman-medicine men who called up spirits from below, Maniilaq was known for his superior power from above that he called the Great Intelligence, his grandfather, "Abba". Maniilaq erected a pole wherever he lodged, placing a badger skin on its top every seventh day when he would rest and prophecy to the people. He spoke of a book and white people who would come from the east with canoes that run by themselves across the water and through the air. He broke the super-stitious power of the many taboos, speaking of a time when women would be free and a brilliant place too wonderful to describe where suffering and disease did not exist. Maniilaq lived until 1890.

When a National Endowment for the Humanities Grant became available in 1975 for the tape recording of oral history, many Eskimo interviews referred to Maniilaq's practice of resting every seventh day. Nora Paanikaaluk Norton reported the comments of an elder named Aqsivaabruk who also observed Maniixauraq resting on the seventh day Sabbath. Nora continued,

> "When Christianity was in its early stages in this area, people rested on the Sabbath, which was understood to be Saturday. Later we went along with those that changed their Sabbath to Sunday. As it was, it is said that Maniixauraq rested on the seventh of every seven days. He did not work on that day. People often said to him, 'Why are you resting? You are just lazy, that is why you are not doing anything.' He replied that he lived by the commandments of his grandfather."

Knowledge of the original Sabbath in the pre-colonial North American continent is not surprising when the oriental connection between the Nestorian and Thomas Christians in East Asia is considered. The spread of apostolic Christianity from west to east took a period of nearly eight centuries. Migration from China to Alaska is readily appreciated by way of the Bearing Strait land bridge.

Family History

For simple, superficial and trivial problems, family history is usually not important. Who needs to know whether your great aunt had palpitations when all you've got is poison ivy? Seems irrelevant. But when something attacks you down deep inside, and a vital organ is in trouble, it can be very important to know of any weak links in your genes. Hereditary background must not be ignored when obtaining a comprehensive clinical history. Our ancestral roots are a part of us. We better pay attention.

The Early Church Fathers
60 – 500 AD

> "For I know this, that after my departing shall grievous wolves enter in among you, not sparing the flock. Also of your own selves shall men arise, speaking perverse things, to **draw away disciples** after them." Acts 20: 29, 30

> "Let no man deceive you by any means; for that day shall not come, except there come **a falling away** first, and that man of sin be revealed, the son of perdition; who opposeth and exalteth himself above all that is called God, or that is worshipped; so that he as God sitteth in the temple of God, showing himself that he is God." 2 Thessalonians 2:3,4

> "For the time will come when they will not endure sound doctrine; but after their own lusts shall they heap to themselves teachers, having itching ears; and **they shall turn away** their ears from the truth, and shall be turned unto fables." 2 Timothy 2:2-4

History records the gradual development of alien worship practices; a "falling away" took place during the early centuries of the Christian era. The original apostolic church commonly known as the Nazarene sect were Sabbath-keeping Christians. Though they were first known as Nazarenes, they were also known down through the ages as Cerinthians, Hypsistari, Vadois, Cathari, Toulousians, Petrobrussians, Passagians, Waldenses... We'll encounter them later.

Jerome, about 404 AD, in a letter to Augustine, said, "They believe in Christ, the Son of God, born of Mary the Virgin, and they say about him that he suffered under Pontius Pilate and rose again." Jerome also records that the Jewish Nazarenes, or followers of Jesus of Nazareth were cursed in the synagogues "by the Pharisees," and that they mixed faith in Christ with the keeping of the Law. (Ray A. Pritz, *Nazarene Jewish Christianity: From the end of the New Testament Period until its disappearance in the Fourth Century*, The Magnes Press, Hebrew University, Jerusalem, c.1992 p.55).

Nazarenes in Pella

Epiphanius, Bishop of Salmis who lived in the 4th century, explained that the Nazarenes were direct descendants of the Christian community in Jerusalem. They migrated to Pella just prior to the Roman destruction of 70 AD. The Nazarenes were different from the predominately Gentile Christian congregations because they "fulfill till now such Jewish rites as the circumcision and the Sabbath." Epiphanius, c. 315-403 AD, *Adversus Haereses* 29, 7, *Patrologia Graeca* 42, 402.

The Nazarenes:
1. Used both Old and New Testaments.
2. Believed in the resurrection of the dead.
3. Had a good knowledge of Hebrew and read the Old Testament.
4. Believed God is the creator of all things.
5. Believed in one God and his son Jesus Christ.
6. Observed the Law of Moses.
7. Had a high respect for the writings of the apostle Paul.

These differences between Jewish and Gentile Christians included a growing respect for the day of Christ's resurrection.

"While the Jewish Christians of Palestine, who kept the whole Jewish law, celebrated of course all the Jewish festivals, the heathen converts observed only the Sabbath, and, in remembrance of the closing scenes of our Saviour's life, the Passover, though without the Jewish superstitions. Besides these, the Sunday, as the day of our Saviour's resurrection, was devoted to religious worship." Gieseler, Johann Karl Ludwig (1792-1854) *Church History,* Apostolic Age to A.D. 70, Section 29.

"The first Christian church established at Jerusalem by apostolic authority became in its doctrine and practice a model for the greater part of those founded in the first century.... These Judaizing Christians were first known by the outside world as 'Nazarenes'... All Christians agreed in celebrating the seventh day of the week in conformity to the Jewish converts." Hugh Smith, *History of the Christian Church,* 1837 pp. 50, 51, 69.

The earliest references clearly show the primary observance of the seventh day with a slow but growing acceptance of the first day.

"Yet, for some hundred years in the primitive church, not the Lord's-day only, but the seventh day also, was religiously observed, not by Ebion and Cerinthus only, but by pious Christians also, as Baronius writeth, and Gomarus confesseth, and Rivert also." William Twisse, *The Morality of the Fourth Commandment,* p. 9, London, 1641.

Now let's review what was written by these "Early Church Fathers" concerning these two days.

Philo of Alexandria 20BC – 50 AD

Philo was a Jew who lived in Alexandria, Egypt and a contemporary of both Jesus and Paul. He wrote extensively in explaining the Mosaic Scriptures. Here he describes the universal acceptance of the Sabbath:

> "For what man is there who does not honour that **sacred seventh day**, granting in consequence a relief and relaxation from labour, for himself and for all those who are near to him, and that not to free men only, but also to slaves, and even to beasts of burden; for the holiday extends even to every description of animal, and to every beast whatever which performs service to man, like slaves obeying their natural master, and it affects even every species of plant and tree; for there is no shoot, and no branch, and no leaf even which it is allowed to cut or to pluck on that day, nor any fruit which it is lawful to gather; but **everything is at liberty and in safety** on that day, and enjoys, as it were, **perfect freedom**, no one ever touching them, in obedience to **a universal proclamation**." Philo, *The Life of Moses* (De Vita Mosis) LCL, 6:273-595.

Critics may discount Philo's statement of universal seventh day observance as the delusional fantasy of a Jewish writer, but the abundant collaboration of other authors in recording the widespread acceptance of the Sabbath during the apostolic period must admit the possibility that his account is indeed factual.

Didache 60-100 AD

The *Didache* or *"The Teaching of the Lord to the Gentiles by the Twelve Apostles"* is estimated to have been written sometime between AD 60 and AD 100. It is composed of 16 sections or chapters. The first six are regarded as truly apostolic; the last ten are merely the opinion of the collection's compiler. Yet the *Didache* is still considered a valuable description of the prevailing thinking of the apostolic time period. In Section 8 a comment on fast days is made:

> "And let not your fastings be with the hypocrites, for they fast on the second and the fifth day of the week; but do ye keep your fast on the fourth and on the preparation (the sixth) day."

Notice the preparation day is identified as the sixth day or Friday. This, the crucifixion day, and Wednesday, the fourth day were treated with respect. Wednesday of Passion Week is traditionally thought to have been the day that Judas made his pact with the Jewish leaders to betray Christ.

Section 14 has a reference to "the Lord's day":

> **"And on the Lord's own day gather yourselves together and break bread and give thanks,** first confessing your transgressions,

that your sacrifice may be pure. And let no man, having his dispute with his fellow, join your assembly until they have been reconciled, that your sacrifice may not be defiled; for this sacrifice it is that was spoken of by the Lord; In every place and at every time offer Me a pure sacrifice; for I am a great king, saith the Lord, and My name is wonderful among the nations."

The passage, however, does not indicate which day of the week it is referring to, only that the term "Lord's own day" was in use at that time. But time would soon make dramatic changes in the thinking of the "Fathers."

> "For fifty years after St. Paul's life, a curtain hangs over the church, through which we vainly strive to look; and when at last the curtain rises, about A.D. 120, with the writings of the earliest Church Fathers, we find a church in many aspects very different from that in the days of St. Peter and St. Paul." Hurlbut Jesse L., *The Story of the Christian Church*, Zondervan, 1967 p. 41.

Pliny 62-113 AD

The noted Latin author, Pliny the Younger, served as Roman consul for the Emperor Trajan around 100 AD and for the next three years as governor of Bithynia in Asia Minor. One of the earliest references to Christian practices was written by him:

> "They were in the habit of meeting on **a certain fixed day** before it was light, when they sang in alternate verses a hymn to Christ, as to a god, and bound themselves by a solemn oath, not to do any wicked deeds, but never to commit any fraud, theft or adultery, never to falsify their word, nor deny a trust when they should be called upon to deliver it up after which it was their custom to separate, and then reassemble to partake of food—but food of an ordinary and innocent kind." Pliny the Younger, *Letters*, book 10, Letter 96. Loeb ed., vol. 2, pp. 402-405.

Some have used this to support the early Christian practice of assembling on the first day of the week. But again the document does not specify any particular day, only that it was fixed. However, there is considerable indication that these early Christians respected the binding obligation of the Ten Commandment law.

Tertullian, who wrote around AD 200, also referred to this very statement of Pliny:

> "He found in their religious services nothing but meetings at early morning for singing hymns to Christ and God, and sealing home their way of life by a united pledge to be faithful to their religion, forbidding murder, adultery, dishonesty, and other crimes." Tertullian's *Apology*, sect. 2.

Other commentators have been just as unable to find any evidence in Pliny's indefinite statement for first-day observance:

"This statement is evidence that these Christians kept a day as holy time, but whether it was the last or the first day of the week, does not appear." Coleman, *Ancient Christianity Exemplified*, chap. 26, sect. 2.

"These persons declare that their whole crime, if they are guilty, consists in this: that on certain days they assemble before sunrise to sing alternately the praises of Christ as of God." *Buck's Theological Dictionary*, art. Christians.

"As the Sabbath day appears to have been quite as commonly observed at this date as the sun's day (if not even more so), it is just as probable that this 'stated day' referred to by Pliny was the seventh day, as that it was the first day; though the latter is generally taken for granted." Taylor, W.B., *Obligation of the Sabbath*, p. 300.

Taking for granted the very point that should be proved, is meager evidence in support of first-day observance. More reasonable is the fact that Pliny's testimony was written only a few years after the time of the apostles. It relates to a church which probably had been founded by the apostle Peter (1 Peter 1:1. *Clarke's Commentary*, preface to the epistles of Peter). It is certainly far more probable that this church, only forty years after the death of Peter, was keeping the fourth commandment, than observing a day never recorded in Scripture with divine authority. This vague and indefinite testimony from Pliny proves nothing in support of Sunday or Saturday observance; for it does not designate any particular day of the week.

Ignatius of Antioch 69-115 AD

Ignatius, Bishop of Antioch, allegedly wrote the following account of Christ's death shortly before his own martyrdom in Rome:

"...On the day of the preparation, then, at the third hour, He received the sentence from Pilate, the Father permitting that to happen; at the sixth hour He was crucified; at the ninth hour He gave up the ghost; and before sunset He was buried. During **the Sabbath** He continued under the earth in the tomb in which Joseph of Arimathaea had laid Him. At the dawning of **the Lord's day** He arose from the dead, according to what was spoken by Himself, "As Jonah was three days and three nights in the whale's belly, so shall the Son of man also be three days and three nights in the heart of the earth." The day of the preparation, then, comprises the passion; **the Sabbath** embraces the burial; **the Lord's day** contains the resurrection." *Epistle of Ignatius to the Trallians*, Chapter IX.

This is one of the earliest alleged uses of the term "Lord's day" to reference the resurrection—if it is considered reliable. Eusebius listed only seven letters written by Ignatius, but fifteen have subsequently been attributed to him. During the 17th century much debate arose over the authenticity of these extra eight letters. Some manuscripts were discovered that showed significant embellishments and additions compared to earlier copies. These became known as the Long versions. The shorter and older forms were generally accepted as more authentic.

Then in the mid 1800s a Syriac text was discovered that contained only three letters of even briefer length addressed to Polycarp, the Ephesians and the Romans. They were disappointing because none mentioned either Sabbath or Sunday.

> "The deficiencies of the Armenian version are in part supplied by the abridged recension in the original Syriac. This abridgment contains the three genuine letters to the Ephesians, the Romans, and to Polycarp." *The Catholic Encyclopedia*, Vol. VII, 1910, Art. "St. Ignatius of Antioch"

What is equally significant is that even if this work was not written by Ignatius, the coexisting term "the Sabbath" indicates that both days were still commanding attention *after* the early second century. Ignatius also mentioned fast days, in the disputed letter to the Philippians, together with a tinge of anti-Semitism:

> "... Do not lightly esteem the festivals. Despise not the period of forty days, for it comprises an imitation of the conduct of the Lord. After the week of the passion, do not neglect to fast on the fourth and sixth days, distributing at the same time of thine abundance to the poor. If any one fasts on the Lord's Day or on the Sabbath, except on the paschal Sabbath only, he is a murderer of Christ." *Epistle of Ignatius to the Philippians*, Chapter XIII.

He repeats the same sentiment in the next chapter as well:

> "If any one celebrates the Passover along with the Jews, or receives the emblems of their feast, he is a partaker with those that killed the Lord and His apostles." *Epistle of Ignatius to the Philippians*, Chapter XIV.

The epistles of Ignatius, so often quoted in behalf of first-day observance, are illustrated by this excerpt:

> "Wherefore if they who are brought up in these ancient laws came nevertheless to the newness of hope; **no longer observing sabbaths**, but **keeping the Lord's day**, in which also our life is sprung up by him, and through his death, whom yet some deny (by which mystery we have been brought to believe, and therefore wait that we may be found the disciples of Jesus Christ, our only master): how shall we be able to live different from him; whose disciples the very prophets themselves being, did by the Spirit expect him as their master." *Ignatius to the Magnesians*, 3:3-5; some place this in chapter 9.

But this letter to the Magnesians is widely acknowledged to be spurious. (See Appendix E for further details).

The epistle of Barnabas   c. 130 AD

Because the Epistle of Barnabas is purported to have been written during the time of the apostles by no less than a peer of Paul, it has been vigorously debated and frequently cited by supporters of the proposition that first-day observance was established by Christ and the apostles.

> "Lastly he saith unto them, Your new-moons and your sabbaths I cannot bear them. Consider what he means by it; the sabbaths, says he, which ye now keep, are not acceptable unto me, but those which I have made; when resting from all things, I shall begin the eighth day, that is, the beginning of the other world; for which cause we observe the eighth day with gladness, in which Jesus arose from the dead, and having manifested himself to his disciples, ascended into Heaven." *Epistle of Barnabas* 13:9, 10; or chapter 15 in some versions.

But historian Mosheim frankly acknowledges that this epistle is a fabrication.

> "The epistle of Barnabas was **the production of some Jew**, who, most probably, lived in this century, and whose mean abilities and superstitious attachment to Jewish fables, show, notwithstanding the uprightness of his intentions, that he must have been a very different person from the true Barnabas, who was St. Paul's companion." Mosheim, *Ecclesiastical History*, century 1, part ii. chap. ii. sect. 21.

> "As to what is suggested by some, of its having been written by that Barnabas who was the friend and companion of St. Paul, the **futility of such a notion** is easily to be made apparent from the letter itself; several of the opinions and interpretations of Scripture which it contains, having in them so little of either truth, dignity or force, as to render it impossible that they could ever have proceeded from the pen of a man divinely instructed." Mosheim, *Historical Commentaries*, century 1, sect. 53.

See Appendix E for additional historians who have also commented on the questionable authenticity of this document.

Eighth Day and the Great Shabbat

The early church clearly considered the passion week to be related to the days of creation. They were also eighth day millennialists. According to this Jewish belief the world will exist in its present form for six thousand years, and then followed by a millennium of rest: the Great Shabbat. Following that, the eighth millennium will begin with God's recreation of a new heaven and new earth. The following quotations are from the two works which we have already identified as sources of questionable authenticity. Nevertheless, here they are.

"He finished in six days. This implieth that the Lord will finish all things in six thousand years, for a day is with Him a thousand years. And He Himself testifieth, saying, 'Behold, today will be as a thousand years.' Therefore, my children, in six days, that is, in six thousand years, all things will be finished. 'And He rested on **the seventh day**.' This meaneth: when His Son, coming [again], shall destroy the time of the wicked man, and judge the ungodly, and change the sun, and the moon, and the stars, then shall He truly rest on **the seventh day**." *Epistle of Barnabas*, Chapter XV.

This demonstrates a sense of respect for both the Sabbath rest and the resurrection joy.

"Let us therefore no longer keep the Sabbath after the Jewish manner, and rejoice in days of idleness; for "he that does not work, let him not eat." For say the [holy] oracles, "In the sweat of thy face shalt thou eat thy bread." But let every one of you keep the Sabbath after a spiritual manner, rejoicing in meditation on the law, not in relaxation of the body, admiring the workmanship of God, and not eating things prepared the day before, nor using lukewarm drinks, and walking within a prescribed space, nor finding delight in dancing and plaudits which have no sense in them. And after the observance of the Sabbath, let every friend of Christ keep the Lord's Day as a festival, the resurrection-day, the queen and chief of all the days [of the week]. Looking forward to this, the prophet declared, "To the end, for the eighth day," on which our life both sprang up again, and the victory over death was obtained in Christ." *Epistle of Ignatius to the Magnesians*, Chapter IX.

The number eight had a spiritual significance, becoming the number of the resurrection over time, and has been used in reference to the eight people in Noah's Ark (see 1 Peter 3:20). There are seven days in the week, and the eighth day is then the first day of the next week. The day of resurrection is likened to the first day of creation, and also the first thousand years of the new heaven and new earth. But eight had also been adopted by those who apostasized from the true worship of Jehovah such as Jeroboam and his eighth month Feast. See Surgical History, Alternative Worship.

Justin Martyr 100-165 AD

The first documented and undisputed reference to Sunday as a day of worship was made in the middle of the second century. Sunday, already a recognized festival in the Gentile world, was welcomed by the growing numbers of Gentile Christians as a convenient refuge in distinguishing themselves from any further association with the increasingly unpopular Jews of the Roman Empire. Justin was a Greek thinker who accepted Christianity around age 30 for its superior ethics and philosophical attractiveness, but who still retained much of his "heathen" preferences. Notice how he uses the pagan names of the week days in this letter to the Roman Emperor

Antoninus Pius (about 150 AD), an apologetic attempt to demonstrate how much Christianity had in common with the non-Christian world:

> "And **on the day called Sunday,** all who live in cities or in the country gather together to one place, and the memoirs of the apostles or the writings of the prophets are read, as long as time permits; then, when the reader has ceased, the president verbally instructs, and exhorts to the imitation of these good things. Then we all rise together and pray, and, as we before said, when our prayer is ended, bread and wine and water are brought, and the president in like manner offers prayers and thanksgiving, according to his ability, and the people assent, saying Amen... Sunday is the day on which we all hold our common assembly, because it is the first day on which God, having wrought a change in the darkness and matter, made the world; and **Jesus Christ our Saviour on the same day rose from the dead. For he was crucified on the day before that of Saturn, and on the day after that of Saturn, which is the day of the Sun,** having appeared to His apostles and disciples, He taught them these things, which we have submitted to you also for your consideration." *The First Apology of Justin*, chapter 67. Ante-Nicene Christian Library, Vol. 2, pp. 65, 66.

Justin Martyr is the first to suggest that the Sabbath is no longer kept on a particular day, but rather becomes spiritualized into "resting" from bad behavior on *every* day of the week:

> "**The new law requires you to keep perpetual Sabbath,** and you, because you are idle for one day, suppose you are pious, not discerning why this has been commanded you; and if you eat unleavened bread, you say the will of God has been fulfilled. The Lord our God does not take pleasure in such observances: **if there is any** perjured person or a **thief among you, let him cease to be so**; if any adulterer, let him **repent; then he has kept the sweet and true Sabbaths of God.**" Ante-Nicene Christian Library, Vol. 2. Dialogue with Trypho, chap. 12, p. 101.

Justin goes even further by proudly asserting that Christians "differ in nothing from the heathen in their manner of living, because they neither observe festivals, nor Sabbaths, nor the rite of circumcision." *Dialogue*, chapter 10. Thus, Justin's testimony establishes the fact that by the middle of the second century, some Christians at least were meeting on Sunday but it was not being kept as a day of rest.

Prior to that time, Sunday, the Day of the Sun, was associated with the first day of the creation-week because that was the day when light was created. Justin gave this as the reason in his *Apology* to the Emperor Antoninus Pius (about 150 AD). He reported that Christians assembled on the day of the Sun to commemorate the first day of creation "on which God, transforming the darkness and prime matter, created the world." (67, 7).

Jerome confessed: "If it is called the Day of the Sun by the pagans, we most willingly acknowledge it as such, since it is on this day that the light of the world appeared and on this day the Sun of Justice has risen" (*Die dominica Paschae homilia* , Corpus Christianorum Series Latina 78, 550, 1, 52).

The "falling away" that Paul spoke of (Acts 20:29, 30; 2 Thessalonians 2:1-7) was most certainly in full swing now.

Irenaeus   125-202 AD

Irenaeus was Bishop of Lyons, Southern France, from 177-202. He was a disciple of Polycarp, who was in turn a disciple of John the Apostle.

> "There is nothing now remaining of Irenaeus besides his five books against heresies, and fragments of some other pieces; and those five books, which were written by him in Greek, are extant only in an ancient Latin version, excepting some fragments preserved by Eusebius, and other Greek writers who have quoted them." Lardner, *Credibility of the Gospel History*, Vol. 2, pp. 292, 293. London, 1847.

In his fifth book he gives the following speculation on Christ's death (occurring on Friday) and its relationship to the Sabbath:

> "...the Lord suffered death, in obedience to His Father, upon that day on which Adam died while he disobeyed God. Now he died on the same day in which he did eat. For God said, 'In that day on which ye shall eat of it, ye shall die by death.' The Lord, therefore, recapitulating in Himself this day, underwent His sufferings upon **the day preceding the Sabbath**, that is, the sixth day of the creation, on which day man was created; thus granting him a second creation by means of His passion, which is that [creation] out of death. And there are some, again, who relegate the death of Adam to the thousandth year; for since 'a day of the Lord is as a thousand years,' he did not overstep the thousand years, but died within them, thus bearing out the sentence of his sin." Irenaeus *Against Heresies*, Book V, Chap. XXIII

And in book four he describes in considerable detail a defense for Christ's healing on the Sabbath as being completely in harmony with the law:

> "It is clear, therefore, that he loosed and vivified those who believe in him as Abraham did, **doing nothing contrary to the law when he healed upon the Sabbath-day**. For the law did not prohibit men from being healed upon the Sabbaths; [on the contrary] it even circumcised them upon that day, and gave command that the offices should be performed by the priests for the people; yea, it did not disallow the healing even of dumb animals. Both at Siloam and on frequent subsequent occasions, did he perform cures upon the Sabbath; and for this reason many used to resort to him on the Sabbath-days. **For the law commanded them** to abstain from every servile work, that is,

from all grasping after wealth which is procured by trading and by other worldly business; but it exhorted them **to attend to the exercises of the soul, which consist in reflection, and to addresses of a beneficial kind for their neighbor's benefit**. And therefore the Lord reproved those who unjustly blamed him for having healed upon the Sabbath-days. **For he did not make void, but fulfilled the law,** by performing the offices of the high priest, propitiating God for men, and cleansing the lepers, healing the sick, and himself suffering death that exiled man might go forth from condemnation, and might return without fear to his own inheritance. And again, **the law did not forbid those who were hungry on the Sabbath-days to take food lying ready at hand:** it did, however, forbid them to reap and to gather into the barn." *Against Heresies*, Library of the Fathers, B. 4, chap. 8; Ante-Nicene Christian Library, Vol. 5, pp. 397, 398.

Irenaeus also spoke of the binding nature of the Decalogue:

"They (the Jews) had therefore a law, a course of discipline, and a prophecy of future things. For God at the first, indeed warning them by means of natural precepts, which **from the beginning he had implanted in mankind, that is, by means of the Decalogue (which if any one does not observe, he has no salvation)** did then demand nothing more of them." *Against Heresies*, B. 4, chap. 15. Anti-Nicene Christian Library, Vol. 5, p. 419.

Sabbath in the third century was also being kept in Egypt as documented in the Oxyrhynchus Papyrus (c. 200-250 AD):

"Except ye make the sabbath a real sabbath [Gr. sabbatize the Sabbath], ye shall not see the Father" *The Oxyrhynchus Papyri*, Pt. 1, p. 3, Logion 2, verso 4-11, London: Offices of the Egyptian Exploration Fund, 1898.

Tertullian 160-240? AD

Quintus Septimus Florens Tertullianus was probably born at Carthage, son of a centurian. He wrote extensively about every aspect of the Christian faith which he accepted after becoming a Roman lawyer. His Gentile roots displayed in strong contrast a theology directly opposite to that of Iraneus. The following excerpt contains the essential arguments against Sabbath keeping that are still used today:

"It follows, accordingly, that, in so far as the abolition of carnal circumcision and of the old law is being demonstrated as having been consummated at its specific times, so also the observance of the Sabbath is being demonstrated to have been temporary.

"For the Jews say, that from the beginning God sanctified the seventh day, by resting on it from all His works which He made; and that thence it was, likewise, that Moses said to the people: 'Remember the day of the Sabbaths, to sanctify it: every servile work ye shall not do therein, except what pertaineth to life.' Whence [we Christians] understand that we still more ought to observe a Sabbath from all 'servile work' always, and not only every seventh day, but through all time. And through this arises the question for us, what Sabbath God willed us to keep? For the Scriptures point to a Sabbath eternal and a Sabbath temporal. For Isaiah the prophet says, '*Your* Sabbaths my soul hateth;' and in another place he says, '*My* Sabbaths ye have profaned.' Whence we discern that the temporal Sabbath is human, and the eternal Sabbath is accounted divine; concerning which He predicts through Isaiah: 'And there shall be,' He says, 'month after month, and day after day, and Sabbath after Sabbath, and all flesh shall come to adore in Jerusalem, saith the Lord;' which we understand to have been fulfilled in the times of Christ, when 'all flesh' – that is, every nation – 'came to adore in Jerusalem' God the Father, through Jesus Christ His Son, as was predicted through the prophet; 'Behold, proselytes through me shall go unto Thee.' Thus, therefore, before this temporal Sabbath, there was withal an eternal Sabbath foreshown and foretold; just as before the carnal circumcision there was withal a spiritual circumcision foreshown. In short, let them teach us [as we have already premised] that Adam observed the Sabbath; or that Abel, when offering to God a holy victim, pleased Him by a religious reverence for the Sabbath; or that Enoch, when translated, had been a keeper of the Sabbath; or that Noah the ark-builder observed, on account of the deluge, an immense Sabbath; or that Abraham, in observance of the Sabbath, offered Isaac his son; or that Melchizedek in his priesthood received the law of the Sabbath.

"But the Jews are sure to say, that ever since this precept was given through Moses, the observance has been binding. Manifest accordingly it is, that the precept was not eternal nor spiritual, but temporal, which would one day cease. In short, so true is it that it is not in the exemption from work of the Sabbath – that is, of the seventh day – that the celebration of this solemnity is to consist, that Joshua, the son of Nun, at the time that he was reducing the city of Jericho by war, stated that he had received from God a precept to order the people that priests should carry the ark of the testament of God seven days, making the circuit of the city; and thus, when the seventh day's circuit had been performed, the walls of the city would spontaneously fall. Which was so done; and when the space of the seventh day was finished, just as was predicted, down fell the walls of the city. Whence it is manifestly shown, that in the number of those seven days there intervened a Sabbath-day. For seven days, whencesoever they may have commenced, must necessarily include within them a Sabbath-day; on which day not only must the priests have worked, but the city must have been made a prey by the edge of the sword by all the people of Israel. Nor is it doubtful that they 'wrought servile work,' when in obedience to God's precept, they drave the preys of war. For in the times of the Maccabees, too, they did bravery in fighting on the Sabbaths, and routed their foreign foes, and recalled the law of their fathers to the primitive style of life by fighting on the Sabbaths. Nor should I think it was any other law which they [thus] vindicated, than the one in which they remembered the existence of the prescript touching 'the day of the Sabbaths.'

"Whence it is manifest that the force of such precepts was temporary, and respected the necessity of present circumstances; and that it was not with a view to its observance in perpetuity that God formerly gave them such a law." Tertullian, *An Answer to the Jews*, chapter 4. Ante-Nicene Christian Library, Vol. 18, pp. 211-213.

He speaks from experience as a "heathen" and even boasts that Christians have more opportunity to "grant indulgence to the flesh" because they have more festive days, "every eighth day" in fact:

"By us to whom Sabbaths are strange, and the new moons and festivals formally beloved by God, **the Saturnalia and New Year's and Midwinter's festivals and Matronalia are frequented – presents come and go – New Year's gifts – games join their noise – banquets join their din**. Oh, better fidelity of the nations to their own sect, which claims no solemnity of the Christians for itself. **Not the Lord's-day, not Pentecost, even if they had known them, would they have shared with us; for they would fear lest they should seem to be Christians. We are not apprehensive lest we seem to be heathens.** If any indulgence is to be granted to the flesh, you have it. I will not say your own days, but more too; for to the *heathens* each festive day occurs but once annually; you have a festive day every eighth day. Call out the individual solemnities of the nations, and set them out in a row, they will not be able to make up a Pentecost." *Tertullian on Idolatry*, chapter 14. Ante-Nicene Christian Library, Vol. II, pp. 162, 163.

He tries to defend the Christian use of the sun day, praying toward the east, by blaming the pagans for adopting it into the calendar's week and then resting on it and following the example of (Jewish) strangers.

"Others, with greater regard to good manners, it must be confessed, suppose that the sun is the God of the Christians, because it is a well-known fact that we pray toward the east, or because we make Sunday a day of festivity. What then? Do you do less than this? Do not many among you, with an affectation of sometimes worshiping the heavenly bodies likewise move your lips in the direction of the sunrise? It is you, at all events, who have even admitted the sun into the calendar of the week; and you have selected its day [Sunday) in preference to the preceding day, as the most suitable in the week for either an entire abstinence from the bath, or for its postponement until the evening, or for taking rest and for banqueting. By resorting to these customs, you deliberately deviate from your own religious rites to those of strangers." *Ad Nationes,* i. 13, in The Ante-Nicene Fathers, Vol. III, p. 123.

But Tertullian often contradicted himself, reversing previous positions and presenting a confusion of thought. This may have been the result of his later apostasy from the Church when he founded his own sect about 212 AD.

> "He had a fund of great and multifarious knowledge, but it was confusedly heaped up in his mind without scientific arrangement. His depth of thought was not united with logical clearness and judgment; a warm ungoverned imagination that dwelt in sensuous images was his ruling power." Neander, *Church History*, First Three Centuries, p. 425.

> "This writer contradicts himself in the most extraordinary manner concerning the Sabbath and the law of God. He asserts that the Sabbath was abolished by Christ, and elsewhere emphatically declares that he did not abolish it. He says that Joshua violated the Sabbath, and then expressly declares that he did not violate it. He says that Christ broke the Sabbath, and then shows that he never did this. He represents the eighth day as more honorable than the seventh, and elsewhere states just the reverse. He asserts that the law is abolished, and in other places affirms its perpetual obligation. He speaks of the Lord's-day as the eighth day, and is the second of the early writers who makes an application of this term to Sunday, if we allow Clement to have really spoken of it. But though he thus uses the term like Clement he also like him teaches a perpetual Lord's-day, or, like Justin Martyr, a perpetual Sabbath in the observance of every day. And with the observance of Sunday as the Lord's-day he brings in "offerings for the dead" and the perpetual use of the sign of the cross. But he expressly affirms that these things rest, not upon the authority of the Scriptures, but wholly, upon that of tradition and custom." J.N. Andrews, *Testimony of the Fathers*, pp. 63, 64.

"Every eighth day" may refer to Sunday, but most likely included Saturday as well because he defends the seventh-day Sabbath especially in *Against Marcion*, book 2, chapter 21. Ante-Nicene Christian Library, Vol. 7, pp. 100, 101. This quote from Bishop Kaye summarizes his position:

> "From incidental notices scattered over Tertullian's works, we collect that Sunday, or the Lord's-day, was regarded by the primitive Christians as a day of rejoicing and that to fast upon it was unlawful. The word **Sabbatum is** always used to designate, not the first, but **the seventh day of the week, which appears in Tertullian's time to have been also kept as a day of rejoicing... The custom of observing every Saturday as a fast, which became general throughout the Western church, does not appear to have existed in Tertullian's time."** Kaye, *Ecclesiastical History of the Second and Third Centuries, Illustrated from the writings of Tertullian*, p. 388. London, 1845

Tertullian displays a strange mix of truth and error, light and darkness, because he lived close enough to the time of the apostles to have access to glimmers of truth, yet far enough away from them to be caught in the deepening shadows of the Dark Ages. Yet it appears that both Sabbath and Sunday were celebrated as joyous festivals in the vicinity and time of Tertullian.

Cyprian c.200 -258 AD
Also from Carthage, Cyprian was a student of Tertullian. He was likewise influenced by his "master" to find hidden meaning in ceremonies, numbers and days.

> "For in respect of the observance of **the eighth day** in the **Jewish circumcision** of the flesh, a sacrament was given beforehand in shadow and in usage; but when Christ came it was fulfilled in truth. For because the eighth day, that is, **the first day after the Sabbath**, was to be that on which the Lord should rise again, and should quicken us, and give us **circumcision of the spirit**, the eighth day, that is, the first day after the Sabbath, and **the Lord's-day**, went before in the figure; which figure ceased when by and by the truth came, and spiritual circumcision was given to us." Cyprian, Epistle 58, section 4. *Ante-Nicene Christian Library,* Vol. 8, p. 198.

Clement of Alexandria c. 150-215 AD
Titus Falvius Clemens. Very little of his writings remain, only fragments called *Stromata, Miscellaneous Discourses.* The sample here applies the rest of the seventh day as preparation for the "Primal Day" in which light was first created, another version of transference to the first day.

> "And the fourth word is that which intimates that the world was created by God, and that he gave us the seventh day as a rest, on account of the trouble that there is in life. For God is incapable of weariness, and suffering, and want. But we who bear flesh need rest. The seventh day, therefore, is proclaimed a rest - abstraction from ills – preparing for the Primal Day, our true rest; which, in truth, is the first creation of light, in which all things are viewed and possessed. From this day the first wisdom and knowledge illuminate us. For the light of truth, a light true, casting no shadow, is the Spirit of God indivisibly divided to all, who are sanctified by faith, holding the place of a luminary, in order to the knowledge of real existences."

But then he becomes even more mystical in an attempt to turn Sunday into Saturday and Friday into Sabbath:

> "For the eighth may possibly turn out to be properly the seventh, and the seventh manifestly the sixth, and the latter properly the Sabbath, and the seventh a day of work. For the creation of the world was concluded in six days. For the motion of the sun from solstice to solstice is completed in six months in the course of which, at one time the leaves fall, and at another plants bud and seeds come to maturity. And they say that the embryo is perfected exactly in the sixth month, that is in one hundred and eighty days in addition to the two and a half as Polybus,

the physician, relates in his book 'On the Eighth Month,' and Aristotle, the philosopher, in his book: 'On Nature.' Hence the Pythagoreans, as I think, reckon six the perfect number, from the creation of the world, according to the prophet, and call it Meseuthys and Marriage, from its being the middle of the even numbers, that is of ten and two. For it is manifestly at an equal distance from both." Clement of Alexandria, *The Miscellanies*, Book 6, chapter 16. *Ante-Nicene Christian Library,* Vol. 12, p. 386.

Such were the extremes to which men who go to avoid the seventh day of the Jews. And, like Justin Martyr, Clement shares the same no-Sabbath conviction, worshiping God on all days:

"Now we are commanded to reverence and to honor the same one, being persuaded that he is Word, Saviour and Leader, and by him, the Father, not on special days, as some others, but doing this continually in our whole life, and in every way." Clement of Alexandria, "The Miscellanies," Book 7, chapter 7. *Ante-Nicene Christian Library*, Vol. 12, p. 431.

Origin 185-253 AD

Origin was a pupil of Clement whose influence is clearly seen in the writings of Origin. Unfortunately, most of his works were transcribed from his orations by reporters and the accuracy is questionable.

"Leaving the Jewish observances of the Sabbath, let us see how the Sabbath ought to be observed by a Christian. On the Sabbath-day all worldly labors ought to be abstained from. If, therefore, you cease from all secular works, and execute nothing worldly, but give yourselves up to spiritual exercises, repairing to church, attending to sacred reading and instruction, thinking of celestial things, solicitous for the future, placing the judgment to come before your eyes, not looking to things present and visible but to those which are future and invisible, this is the observance of the Christian Sabbath." Origin, *Twenty-Third Homily on Numbers*, Tome ii., p. 358.

The "Christian Sabbath" is only different, according to Origen, in the manner in which it is observed, for he also prescribed Sabbath-keeping:

"After the festival of the unceasing sacrifice [the crucifixion] is put the second festival of the Sabbath, and it is fitting for whoever is righteous among the saints to keep also the festival of the Sabbath. There remaineth therefore a sabbatismus, that is, a keeping of the Sabbath, to the people of God." Origen, *Homily on Numbers 23*, para. 4, in Migne, *Patrologia Græca*, Vol. 12, cols. 749, 750.

But he also perpetuated the no-Sabbath theory inherited from his master. Every day is the Lord's day, no particular day is the Sabbath; no specific time is sacred, rather all time is sacred:

"...to the perfect Christian, who is ever in his thoughts, words and deeds serving his natural Lord, God the Word, all his days are the Lord's, and he is always keeping the Lord's-day." *Origen against Celsus*, Book 8, chapter 22. *Ante-Nicene Christian Library*, Vol. 23, p. 509.

Eusebius 260-340 AD
Bishop of Caesarea but best known for his historical record.

"Then comes Eusebius the Historian, and he makes it good that the Religion of the Patriarchs before Moses' Law was nothing different from the Christian; and how proves he that? They were not circumcised, no more are we; they kept not any Sabbath, no more do we: they were not bound to abstinence from sundry kinds of meats, which are prohibited by Moses; nor are we neither. Where still observe how constantly these several Fathers rank Circumcision and the Sabbath in one rank or order, which shows that they thought them both of the same condition." Peter Heylyn; *The History of the Sabbath*, The Second Edition, Revised. London, 1636. p. 44.

It is Eusebius who makes the first reference to Sunday as "the day of the resurrection" well into the fourth century AD. (Eusebius of Caesarea, *Commentary on Psalm 91, Patrologia Graeca* 23, 1168; *Apostolic Constitutions* 2, 59, 3).

When in Rome
Ambrose of Milan is said to have kept Sabbath while in Milan and Sunday in Rome, giving rise to the saying *when in Rome do as the Romans do* (Peter Heylyn, *op. cit.*, 1612). The Church in Milan was the center of Sabbath-keeping in the West during the 4th century (*ibid.*, part 2, para 5, pp. 73-74). The Sabbatati had their school there. When Peter Waldo joined them the Sabbath had been observed in Italy for centuries. But the Council of Friaul (c. 791) condemned its observance by the peasants in canon 13:

"We command all Christians to observe the Lord's day to be held not in honour of the past Sabbath, but on account of that holy night of the first of the week called the Lord's day. When speaking of that Sabbath which the Jews observe, the last day of the week and which our peasants observe." (A. Mansi, *Sacrorum Conciliorum Nova et Amplissima Collectio*, vol 13, p. 851).

Christians frequently asked themselves why they kept the first day of the week and offered many reasons for doing so, but none gave the rationale that Christ had changed the day or that the apostles received such a command from Christ. Not until Constantine did such reasoning appear.

"they give sundry other reasons of their own, fanciful in most cases, and ridiculous in some." Robert Cox, *Sabbath Literature*, Vol. 1, p. 353.

Anti-Nicean Fathers

The 4th century collection of eight books purporting to be written by the apostles but compiled by a Clement of Rome "are today of the highest value as an historical document, revealing the moral and religious conditions and the liturgical observances of the third and fourth centuries." *The Catholic Encyclopedia* Vol 1. Article Apostolic Constitutions. 1907, 1999 *Nihil Obstat,* Remy Lafort, S.T.D., Censor *Imprimatur+*, John Cardinal Farley, Archbishop of New York.

> "Have before thine eyes the fear of God, and always remember the ten commandments of God, to love the one and only Lord God with all thy strength; to give no heed to idols, or any other beings, as being lifeless gods, or irrational beings or demons. Consider the manifold workmanship of God, which received its beginning through Christ. **Thou shalt observe the Sabbath, on account of Him who ceased from His work of creation**, but ceased not from His work of providence; it is a rest for meditation of the law, not for the idleness of the hands." Apostolic Constitutions (*Ante-Nicene Fathers,* Volume 7, p. 413, 1951 edition).

> "He therefore charged us Himself to fast these six days on account of the impiety and transgression of the Jews, commanding us withal to bewail over them, and lament for their perdition. For even He Himself 'wept over them, because they knew not the time of their visitation.' But He commanded us to fast on the fourth and sixth days of the week; the former on account of His being betrayed, and the latter on account of His passion. But **He appointed us to break our fast on the seventh day at the cock-crowing, but to fast on the Sabbath-day. Not that the Sabbath-day is a day of fasting, being the rest from the creation, but because we ought to fast on this one Sabbath only**, while on this day the Creator was under the earth." *Apostolic Constitutions,* Book V, section XV.

Anti-Nicene Fathers, Vol. I, The Epistle of Mathetes to Diognetus

Considered to be "a sequel to the Clementine Epistle" dated at AD 130.

Chapter III – Superstitions of the Jews

> For He that made heaven and earth, and all that is therein, and gives to us all the things of which we stand in need, certainly requires none of those things which He Himself bestows on such as think of furnishing them to Him. But those who imagine that, by means of blood, and the smoke of sacrifices and burnt-offerings, they offer sacrifices [acceptable] to Him, and that by such honours they show Him respect,—these, by supposing that they can give anything to Him who stands in need of nothing...

Chapter IV – The Other Observances of the Jews.

But as to their scrupulosity concerning meats, and **their superstition as respects the Sabbaths,** and their boasting about circumcision, and their fancies about fasting and the new moons, which are utterly ridiculous and unworthy of notice,—I do not think that you require to learn anything from me. For, to accept some of those things which have been formed by God for the use of men as properly formed, and to reject others as useless and redundant—how can this be lawful? And to speak falsely of God, as if He forbade us **to do what is good on the Sabbath-days**—how is not this impious?

During the reign of Theodoric (454-526 AD) Sidonius wrote:

"It is a fact that it was formerly the custom in the East to keep the Sabbath in the same manner as the Lord's day and to hold sacred assemblies: while on the other hand, the people of the West, contending for the Lord's day have neglected the celebration of the Sabbath." Sidonius, *Apollinaris Sidonii Epistolæ*, lib. 1,2; Migne, 57.

Summary:

No trace of Sunday observance is found until about the middle of the second century. It first appears in Justin Martyr's First Apology where he makes a mystical interpretation of certain Scriptures referring to the millennium. The resurrection of Christ on that day is mentioned only incidentally as a secondary reason. Near the close of the second century, the idea of commemorating the resurrection by the observance of the Sunday begins to grow, and the term "Lord's day" appears.

During the third century, no-law-no-Sabbath theory develops. Writers of that century teach there is no sacred time under the gospel dispensation. No days are holy, no observance of specific times are religiously binding. Sabbath consists in rest from sin. Cyprian fancies circumcision as a type of the eighth day.

Sunday observance at this time was not sabbatic. It consisted of public religious instruction and prayers. In the third century the celebration of the Lord's Supper on Sunday became common. But it was also celebrated regularly on the Sabbath. Many Christians continued to observe the Bible Sabbath in spite of persistent efforts to discourage keeping the seventh day.

Social History

Spouses, children, work status, personal health habits, exposure to high risk activities—these are important elements of the clinical record. This is the patient's social history and is an important description of one's health and health risks. In today's world of AIDS and STDs, Hepatitis and second-hand smoke, industrial chemicals and radiation, social history is extremely important. You may not be able to do a thing about your heredity, but you *can* prevent a slew of debilitating and deadly lifestyle diseases.

As we continue to collect valuable history in our clinical evaluation of the Sabbath, exposure to high risk behaviors, work status, and intimate relationships will be of utmost importance. We'll begin with exposure—to the sun and the risk for sun worshippers.

Sunday Tradition

From the most ancient of times, earth's nearest star has been the object of wonder and worship. The oldest book of Scripture recognized the perversion of sun worship. Beholding "the sun when it shined, or the moon walking in brightness" was considered an iniquity because it denied "the God that is above." *Job 31:26*

The Chinese Temple of Heaven in Peking has an altar to the sun. It is oriented precisely in line with the rising sun on the December 21 winter solstice.

- The Hindu god *Indra* means "the day brought by the sun."
- The cult of Mithra involved worship of *sol invictus*.
- In Babylon, the sun god was *Shamash*.
- The Aztecs of the new world worshipped *Tonatiuh*, a solar diety.

The Incas offered still beating hearts from human sacrifices to their sun god *Inti* and also placed dead rulers in the sun temple of Cuzco.

- In Japan emperors were worshipped as descendants of the sun-goddess *Amaterasu.*
- Egypt revered *Ra,* the sun god of *Heliopolis* (sun city), and worshipped their Pharaohs as the sons of *Ra.*

Stonehenge, a sun temple of neolithic England, is exactly oriented toward the rising sun at the summer solstice.

Roman basilicas of Constantine and St. Peter's were both arranged according to the solar equinoxes.

Abraham the Astronomer

Josephus quotes the Chaldean historian Berosus for his comments on Abraham and his legendary knowledge of astronomical behavior: "In the tenth generation after the Flood, there was among the Chaldeans a man [Abraham] righteous and great, and skilful in the celestial science" (Josephus, *Antiquities of the Jews*). But Abraham distinguished himself by *not* worshipping the celestial bodies. In Abraham's day the city of Ur had become steeped in Babylonian idolatry and the worship of its patron moon-god Sin. In contrast, Abraham was a lone believer in the God of creation who ordered life around the seven day week.

> "He [Abraham] was a person of great sagacity, both for understanding all things and persuading his hearers, and not mistaken in his opinions; for which reason he began to have higher notions of virtue than others had, and he determined to renew and to change the opinions all men happened then to have concerning God; for he was the first that ventured to publish this notion, that there was but one God, the Creator of the universe; and that, as to other [gods], if they contributed anything to the happiness of men, that each of them afforded it only according to his appointment, and not by their own power." Josephus, *Antiquities of the Jews*, book I, chapter VII, verse 1.

> "This his opinion was derived from the irregular phenomena that were visible both at land and sea, as well as those that happen to the sun and moon, and all the heavenly bodies, thus:- 'If [said he] these bodies had power of their own, they would certainly take care of their own regular motions; but since they do not preserve such regularity, they made it plain, that in so far as they co-operate to our advantage, they do it not of their own abilities, but as they are

subservient to Him that commands them; to whom alone we ought justly to offer our honour and thanksgiving.' " (*ibid.*).

The citizens of Ur revolted against such monotheistic notions. "For which doctrines, when the Chaldeans and other people of Mesopotamia raised a tumult against him, he thought fit to leave that country; and at the command, and by the assistance of God, he came and lived in the land of Canaan." Josephus, *Antiquities of the Jews*, book I, chapter VII, verse 1.

Generations later, in Deuteronomy 4:19 God provided Abraham's descendants with "statutes and judgments" and instructed Moses to teach them "Lest thou lift up thine eyes unto heaven, and when thou seest *the sun, the moon, and the stars*, even all the host of heaven, shouldest be driven to worship them." The second commandment of the Decalogue specifically prohibits the worship of images and other gods. Unfortunately, the Bible record mentions numerous references to sun worship and its practice among even God's professed people.

Israel soon "worshipped all *the host of heaven*, and served Baal." 2Kings 17:16 In chapter 21:3-6 Manasseh "worshipped all *the host of heaven*, and served them." "And he built altars for all *the host of heaven* in the two courts of the house of the Lord. And he made his son pass through the fire, and observed times." Holy days were assigned to commemorate important celestial celebrities, the sun receiving preeminent attention.

In Zephaniah 1:5 God's people are described as worshiping *the host of heaven* upon their housetops.

2 Kings 23:11 records how good king Josiah, as part of his reform policy, "took away the horses that the kings of Judah had given to *the sun*, at the entering in of the house of the Lord." And he "burned the *chariots of the sun* with fire." Ancient Persian, Greek, and Roman customs depicted the sun as a divine charioteer who daily drove his steeds across the sky.

Ezekiel 8:16 depicts a group of 25 men sitting in the temple doorway between the porch and altar with their backs turned toward the temple while their faces looked eastward. "And they *worshipped the sun* toward the east," an unspeakable abomination and insult to God.

Nimrod

Here the story of Nimrod deserves special inspection. Josephus, in his *Antiquities Book 1 Chapter 4,* describes Nimrod, the great grandson of Noah, as having "great strength." He was the driving force behind the tower of Babel project in defiance of God's promise to never again destroy the world by flood. This agrees with Genesis 10:9,10 where Nimrod, "a mighty one in the earth" and "a mighty hunter before (against) the Lord," is said to have established the first kingdom on earth. This was centered in Babel and later extended to Erech (or Uruk, named after the first city built before the flood, Enoch), Akkad, Nineveh and Calah—all in the land of Shinar or Sumer of archeological fame and today's Persian Gulf. He single-handedly built the original Babylonian Empire and distinguished himself as "the first man to rule the whole world." The *Encyclopedia Judaica* further indicates that he was "the first to eat meat and make war on other people." (Keter Publishing House Ltd., Jerusalem, Israel, 1971, vol. 12, p. 1167)

Jewish tradition also credits Nimrod with wearing the original animal skins that Adam and Eve were provided at their fall by the hand of God. At the pinnacle of his success, he inaugurated the practice of emperor-worship, leading the world of his time to "pay divine homage to him" as the one responsible for making the Sun to shine and life to spring from the earth. Extra-biblical accounts mention his order to kill all male children during the time of Abram's birth in a preview of both Pharoah and Herod. This animosity with "the Friend of God" later surfaces in the figure of Amraphel when he and three other buddies unknowingly cross the path of an adult Abraham.

Amraphel, according to the Talmud, is identified as Nimrod (cf *Targum Yonathan; Eruvin* 53a; Rashi) especially since he also is called the king of Shinar (Genesis 14:1). This would be theoretically possible, since his immediate contemporaries were reported to live over 400 years and he would have been only a little over 300 at the time of Lot's capture. Consider, for example, Salah (the grandson of Shem and second cousin to Nimrod) was also still alive during Abraham's lifetime.

Genesis 10 is a post-flood genealogy which places Nimrod in relation to his contemporaries. The arrangement is depicted in the following table displayed on the following page. Although we are not given the ages for Ham and Cush, we can assume that they would be comparable to those in the line of Shem. This would make Nimrod about 265 years old at the time of Abraham's birth (adding the generational ages of the patriarchs from Eber to Terah).

Noah
Shem
Arphaxad (born 2 years after the flood, lived a total of 456 yrs)
(53yrs)   Salah (433 years total)
          (30yrs)   Eber
                    (34yrs)   Peleg   104
                              ((30yrs)   Reu   136
                                        (32yrs)   Serug   166
                                                  (30yrs)   Nahor   195
Ham   (29yrs)   Terah   265
          Cush   (70 yrs) Abram
                Nimrod (only 265 years old at Abram's birth

If this is true, then Nimrod, now in his declining years and A.K.A. Amraphel, had the poor judgment of sacking Sodom and Gomorrah and then leaving with Lot. When the news reached Abraham, he went into rescue mode, pursued after his abducted nephew and ultimately "slaughtered" the marauding kings in the valley of Shaveh at night in a four-prong attack with only 318 men (a strategy that Gideon would later employ against the Mideanites).

It is here that the legendary Semiramis enters the picture. Her name is the Hellenized form of Sumerian "Sammuramat", or "gift of the sea." Various historical references to this mysterious woman of antiquity tend to collaborate a common theme: she was a beautiful, shrewd and powerful ruler of ancient Sumer. Both famed as the wife and mother of Nimrod by different sources, the apparent conflict can be better understood when the entire story is considered. Semiramis was originally Nimrod's wife, Queen of Shinar and ruler of a vast religious hierarchy of priests and priestesses. She was the real agent behind Nimrod's divine status which she strengthened even more after his death. While he was away on military exploits, she conceived an illegitimate son. Some accounts tell of Nimrod's return and threat to depose her; others that she arranged his death. But all agree that she explained the "miracle birth" as the result of an immaculate conception by Nimrod's returning spirit and that the newborn child was, in fact, Nimrod reincarnated.

The child was named Damu, or Dammuzi (in later Chaldean), and known as Tammuz in Hebrew, Adonis in Greek. Soon Tammuz became accepted as divine and became widely worshipped as the god of flocks and pastures, the heavenly shepherd. In many localities he was considered the god of springtime, raised to life again like his father Nimrod. As annual celebrations were established, the onset of summer heat and its withering effect of crops inspired the story that Tammuz was killed by a wild boar: spring had died. His death at the summer solstice was celebrated by national weeping and his name honored in the 4th month of the Babylonian calendar.

The custom of the Yule log also signified the death of Nimrod/Tammuz ("Yule" being the Chaldean word for "infant"). Cut down by his enemies and burned in a fire, he would reappear the following day as the splendid Christmas tree, risen triumphant from the ashes like the Phoenix.

Queen of Heaven

Semiramis consequently deified herself as the mother of the god Damu (since only a god can beget a god) , and installed herself as "The Queen of Heaven." She became the model for all subsequent goddesses, while Tammuz became the antitypical Father-Son figure adopted by every civilization since.

Jeremiah 44:18 reports the people of Israel burning "incense to **the queen of heaven**." This was *Ishtar*, the mother goddess of the Assyro-Babylonian culture. Cuneiform scripts from Mesopotamia describe her in the most remarkable flattery:

> 'I pray to thee, O Lady of ladies, goddess of goddesses...O gleaming one, Ishtar, assembler of the host...Where thou dost look, one who is dead lives; One who is sick rises up, the erring one who sees thy face goes aright...Faithfully look upon me and hear my supplication. Promise my forgiveness and let thy spirit be appeased.' *Babylon, Albert Champdor, Eleck Books Ltd., 1958, p. 151*

She was *Ashtoreth*, the goddess of fertility, maternity and sexual love in Palestine. In Ephesus she was the many-breasted *Diana* or *Artemis*. In Rome she was *Venus*, the goddess of love and death. In Asia she was *Atargatis*, the "Great Mother." She was the Italian *Madonna, Belitini,* "Our Lady," the morning and evening star.

The Queen of Heaven, long used by the worshipers of Jehovah to reference the Sabbath, was adopted as the title for the Sun King's widow, who was now also mother to Tammuz. This Mother-Son symbol is recognized in many cultures under numerous titles. Likewise, Nimrod/Tammuz, the Father-Son relationship is equally important. Both were diabolical corruptions of the original plan laid before the foundation of the world.

Apollo, "child of the sun," is usually depicted with a halo, nimbus, solar disk or luminous circle enshrouding his head. *Circe*, "daughter of the Sun," was illustrated in a Pompeii mosaic with the same halo.

The following table demonstrates the wide-spread representation of the mother-son theme across many language-culture groups.

Christianity:	God the Father	Christ	Mary, Madonna
Hindu:	Brahma	Krishna	Queen of Heaven
India:	Iswara	Isi, Parvati	
Egypt:	Seb	Horus/Osiris	Isis, Minerva
Rome:	Jove	Jupiter	Fortuna
		Bacchus	Mae Domina (My Lady)
Scandinavia:	Odin	Balder	Frigga
Ephesus			Diana
Greece:		Plutus	Ceres
		Adonis	Venus
			Ammas (ama "mother")
Babylon:	Baal	Tammuz	Baalti
Assyria:	Bel	Nimrod	Semiramis

Alexander Hislop comments further on this nearly universal use of the sun disk.

> "Near the small town of Babain, in Upper Egypt, there still exists in a grotto, a representation of a sacrifice to the sun, where two priests are seen worshipping the sun's image... In the same temple of Babylon, the golden image of the Sun was exhibited for the worship of the Babylonians, In the temple of Cuzco, in Peru, the disk of the sun was fixed up in flaming gold upon the wall, that all who entered might bow down before it. The Pæonians of Thrace were sun-worshippers; and in their worship they adored an image of the sun in the form of a disk at the top of a long pole." Hislop, *The Two Babylons*, p. 162.

Apis, Egyptian bull god with sun disk.

Isis with sun disk holding Horace.

In Arabia the moon is held in higher esteem than the sun as the supreme symbol of divinity. This is why the crescent moon is so widely employed in Arabian symbols, art, flags, and heraldry. According to their calendars, Lord Moon was born on the 24th of December. Elsewhere, as Plutarch recorded in his *De Iside*, vol. II, sec. 52, p. 372, the observance of sun worship at the end of the winter solstice (December 25) celebrated the appearance of "God incarnate." This coincided with the "reappearance" of the sun which thereafter would begin to once again ascend higher in the sky as days became longer in length.

The Roman Catholic mass places special importance on the roundness of the eucharistic wafer-disk because it symbolizes the solar disk, emblem of the Son and Seed of the woman. Seeds were also depicted as a circle in ancient times. *Zer*, our zero, was the term for seed. *Zero-ashta* "seed of the woman (Ashtarath)" became *Zoroaster*, head of the fire-worshipers. In the *Orphic Hymns* (Hymn xliv. 1) *Bacchus* (Zoroaster) is referred to as *Pyrisporus* (fire-born) *Pyr*—fire as in pyromaniac, *sporus*-seed as in spore.

The first century in the Roman Empire was marked by the spread of new religions: Egyptian Isis cult, Zoroastrian Mithras worship, and Christianity. Toleration was shown by Rome to the first two, but this was not extended to the Christians. Rome saw little difference between Christians and Jews—both refused to acknowledge the emperor as divine.

But it was Jewish revolts that resulted in frequent and severe massacres. Caligula ordered his statue placed in the Most Holy place of the temple in Jerusalem. Tiberius deported 4000 Jews from Rome to rid the city of their menace. Then Titus conducted one of the most terrible sieges in history, captured Jerusalem in A.D. 70, destroyed the Temple and slaughtered as many as a million Jews. In spite of this, or because of it, Jewish revolts and rebellions continued under Trajan and Hadrian.   Half-crazy rulers like Nero and Domitian ordered general persecution under the pretext that national calamaties (barbarian invasions and pestilences) were clearly the anger of the gods against the offensive Judeo-Christian doctrines.

Dies Solis
The first day of the Roman Calendar was called *dies solis*, 'Day of the Sun,' because it was dedicated to Earth's closet star. Our Monday is actually Moon Day or *dies lunas*, dedicated to Earth's satellite. Each day had its honorary celestial deity. But Sunday was preeminent among the pagan culture and quickly adopted as a safe policy by Christians.

"Sunday, the first day of the week, was adopted by the early Christians as a day of worship...It was called the 'Lord's Day'...no regulations for its observance are laid down in the New Testament, nor indeed, is its observance even enjoined...." (*The Schaff-Herzog Encyclopedia of Religious Knowledge*, under the word "Sunday," Vol.IV, pp.2259-60).

Constantine

Flavius Valerius Constantinus, a.k.a. Constantine, was born at Nis on Feb. 27, 280, in what is now Serbia, son of the commander Constantius Chlorus (later Constantius I) and Helena a Balkan barmaid. Constantine became co-emperor in 305.

Following the example of his father and earlier 3rd-century emperors, Constantine was a solar henotheist, believing that the Roman sun god, *Sol*, was the visible manifestation of an invisible "Highest God" (*summus deus*), who was the principle behind the universe and companion of the Roman emperors. Constantine's adherence to this faith is evident from his claim of having had a vision of the sun god in 310 while in a grove of Apollo in Gaul, France. At that time Christianity was exploding throughout the Roman Empire causing earlier Emperors to regard Christians as a threat to the empire because they refused to acknowledge the divinity of the Caesars.

In 312 Constantine prepared for battle against Maxentius, his rival in Italy. On the eve of the impending battle, and greatly outnumbered by his opponent's army, Constantine reportedly received a dream. He claimed to have seen Christ who told him to inscribe the first two letters of his name ΧΡΙΣΤΟΣ on his troops' shields and banners.

The next day he reported seeing another vision in the sky of a cross superimposed on the sun and emblazoned with the words *in hoc signo cruces vinces,* "in the sign of the cross you will be the victor." Constantine immediately adopted the cross as his emblem and had it put on troops and banners. The following day Constantine defeated Maxentius in the battle of Milvian Bridge. A fresco in the Vatican, (The Sala di Constantino, Palazzi Vaticani, Rome) painted by Raffaello (c. 1509 A.D.) depicts the moment that Emperor

Constantine saw the cross in the sky. In the fresco a banner displays a winged serpent or dragon, the symbol of ancient Pagan Rome.

Coins minted from this period depict Constantine's symbol.

Constantine then defeated Maxentius at the Battle of Milvian Bridge, near Rome. The Senate hailed the victor as savior of the Roman people. Thus, Constantine, who had been a pagan solar worshiper, now looked upon the Christian deity as a bringer of victory.

Persecution of the Christians was ended, and Constantine's co-emperor, Licinius, joined him in issuing the Edict of Milan (313), which mandated toleration of Christians in the Roman Empire. As guardian of Constantine's favored religion, the church was then given legal rights and large financial donations.

> "But it was during the rule of Constantine the Great that the cult of *Deus Sol Invictus* reached extraordinary heights, so that his reign was even spoken of as a Sun Emperorship. Constantine was the personification of *Deus Sol Invictus* on earth, and could consider the statue of the sun in the Forum bearing his name as a statue of himself" (Gaston H. Halsberghe, *The Cult of Sol Invictus*, 1972, p. 167)

In 325, he presided over the Council of Nicaea which changed the time of the Lord's Resurrection from the day following Passover to the Sunday following Passover. For three centuries Passover and the associated anniversary of the resurrection had in many churches been observed according to the original Biblical specification linked to lunar cycles and thus would land on a different day of the week each year. But Constantine's adherence to Sol arranged to fix the date to an annual Sunday. This was to coincide with the old Roman festival of Easter which usually fell about a week after Passover when the moon rose after midnight.

Dies Natalis Invicti or the birthday of the Unconquered Sun (Dec. 25) was the principal day for this cult which had its roots laid in common with the Nimrod-Tammuz-Semirimis cults. It was on this day of the winter solstice that the sun began its ascent in the sky, the days began to get longer. This was interpreted as the resurrection of the solar deity. Constantine called this day the birthday of Christ.

The Decree of Constantine was immortalized in the Codex of Justinian:

> "On the venerable day of the sun [Sunday] let the magistrates and people residing in cities rest, and let all workshops be closed." (Codex Justinianus, lib.3, tit.12:3; translated by Phillip Schaff in *History of the Christian Church*, 1864, Vol.III, p.380).

Constantine set up a new Capital about 1,000 miles to the east of Rome and named it after himself: Constantinople. Now Istanbul, it has remained the center of the "Orthodox" church to this day. Thus Rome and Constantinople became two new rival "church" headquarters in opposition to Jerusalem.

This paralleled the experience of Apostate Israel, the northern kingdom spawned by Jeroboam following the reign of Solomon. Jeroboam also set up two rival worship centers: one in Dan, and one in Bethel. Both had golden calf altars competing with the worship of Jehovah in Jerusalem.

Constantine is best known for his Sunday Law, but his motivation was not primarilly based on Christian theology.

> "The devotion of Constantine was more peculiarly directed to the genius of the sun, the Apollo of Greek and Roman mythology; and he was pleased to be represented with the symbols of the god of light and poetry. The unerring shafts of that deity, the brightness of his eyes, his laurel wreath, immortal beauty, and elegant accomplishments, seem to point him out as the patron of a young hero. The altars of Apollo were crowned with the votive offerings of Constantine; and the credulous multitude were taught to believe that the emperor was permitted to behold with mortal eyes the visible majesty of their tutelar deity; and that, either waking or in a vision, he was blessed with the auspicious omens of a long and victorious reign. The sun was universally celebrated as the invincible

guide and protector of Constantine." (Edward Gibbon, *Decline and Fall of the Roman Empire*, Chapter 20, par. 3.)

"This legislation by Constantine probably bore no relation to Christianity; it appears, on the contrary, that the emperor, in his capacity as Pontifex Maximus, was only adding the day of the sun, the worship of which was then firmly established in the Roman Empire, to the other festival days of the sacred calendar." (Hutton Webster, Ph.D., *Rest Days: The Christian Sunday, The Jewish Sabbath, And Their Historical and Anthropological Prototypes*, 1916, pp. 122, 123)

"What began as a pagan ordinance, ended as a religious regulation."

386 Gratian, Valentinian, and Theodosius decreed that all litigation and business should cease on Sunday

416 Pope Innocent I decrees Saturday be observed as a fast day

425 Theodosius the Younger ruled no Sunday circus or theatricals

538 Council of Orleans ordained that plowing, cutting, reaping, threshing, tilling, and hedging should be avoided that people might more conveniently attend church.

590 Pope Gregory denounced those who do not work on the seventh day as the prophets of Antichrist.

About 150 years after Constantine, the western part of the Empire went into captivity to the Gothic barbarians and the world entered the long night of the Dark Ages. But there was light at the end of this tunnel. As prophesied by Daniel and John, the Reform-ation arose 1260 years later to strike a deadly wound through the sword of God's Word bringing light to an ignorant world made available by the invention of the printing press.

Easter Origins

Catholicism has a long history of taking credit for the establishment of Sunday as the Christian day of worship. This was accomplished by emphasizing Easter while ruling against the Sabbath. We'll focus on three of the many councils convened over the centuries.

Eusebius, the early church historian who lived in the fourth century, relates that Bishop Sixtus of Rome was the first *not* to observe the Passover, and began observing Easter Sunday in its place (between AD 116-126). This was during the reign of Emperor Hadrian (AD 117-138), who adopted a Roman policy of radical repression of Jewish rites and customs.

Early Christians in most places observed the Jewish Passover, up until 135 AD and the second Roman conquest of Jerusalem, when the headquarters of the Jewish Church was finally closed, and Jews were banished from the city. The new Greek bishops appointed by the

Romans to oversee the new Gentile Christian church in Jerusalem, observed the Roman "Easter," thus provoking the controversy into sharp focus after 135 AD. By this time the "Easter" tradition was strong enough to challenge the authentic Passover truth of the apostles and their successors.

The first recorded attempt of the bishop at Rome to extend his rule over the entire Christian church was an edict regarding Sunday. All Christian churches celebrated Passover, but while the eastern churches observed it as God had instructed, upon the fourteenth day of the first Hebrew month regardless of which day of the week it might fall on (Quartodecimans), the western churches, following Rome's lead, kept it upon the Sunday following Good Friday (Quintadecimans).

About 154 AD **Polycarp** of Smyrna, who had observed the Passover with the apostle John and other original apostles, traveled to Rome to discuss the growing controversy arising between the church at Rome observing Easter, claiming Christ arose from the dead on that day, and the churches in the East which observed the apostolic tradition of Passover. The meeting with Anicetus ended in a deadlock, neither persuading the other to change.

Polycrates 130-196 AD
Later, in the days of Victor, Bishop of Rome (189-199 AD), the dispute became very severe. In AD 196 Victor imposed this custom upon all churches, compelling them to keep Passover on Sunday at the threat of excommunication. *Schaff-Herzog Encyclo-paedia of Religious Knowledge.* Christians who continued to observe communion on Passover were labeled "Quartodecimans," meaning those who observed the "fourteenth," the day on which Passover was kept. This group, under the leadership of Polycrates, bishop of Ephesus, refused to fall into line with Rome's schedule for Easter on the Spring Equinox (in honor of the Sun's return from a wintery death).

Polycrates, representing the eastern bishops in Asia Minor, wrote to Victor, in reply to his blutsering threats. Polycrates again appealed to the practice of the apostles Philip and John, to Polycarp (John's disciple), Thraseas, and many others, who had celebrated Passover on the 14th of Nisan. He then resolved that, on the basis of Scriptures, he would not be intimidated by Rome nor would he change.

> "We observe the exact day; neither adding, nor taking away. For in Asia also great lights have fallen asleep [he speaks here of the death of many brethren], which shall rise again on the day of the Lord's coming, when He shall come with glory from heaven, and shall seek out all the saints.

Among these are Philip, one of the twelve apostles, who fell asleep in Hierapolis; and his two aged virgin daughters, and another daughter, who lived in the Holy Spirit and now rests at Ephesus; and, moreover, John, who was both a witness and a teacher, who reclined upon the bosom of the Lord, and, being a priest, wore the sacerdotal plate. He fell asleep at Ephesus. And Polycarp in Smyrna, who was a bishop and martyr; and Thraseas, bishop and martyr from Eumenia, who fell asleep in Smyrna. Why need I mention the bishop and martyr Sagaris who fell asleep in Laodicea, or the blessed Papirius, or Melito, the Eunuch who lived altogether in the Holy Spirit, and who lies in Sardis, awaiting the episcopate from heaven, when he shall rise from the dead? **All these observed the fourteenth day of the Passover according to the Gospel, deviating in no respect, but following the rule of faith.** And I also, Polycrates, the least of you all, do according to the tradition of my relatives, some of whom I have closely followed. For seven of my relatives were bishops; and I am the eighth. And **my relatives always observed the day when the people put away the leaven.** I, therefore, brethren, who have lived sixty-five years in the Lord, and have met with the brethren throughout the world, and have gone through every Holy Scripture, am not affrighted by terrifying words. For those greater than I have said 'We ought to obey God rather than man.' " Eusebius of Caesarea, *Church History*, Book V, ch. 24)

Victor immediately excommunicated the Asian bishops who refused to adopt the Easter Sunday tradition, and then for good measure he excommunicated all the churches of Asia as well.

Council of Nicea 325 AD

The controversy continued to boil in Christendom until the early fourth century. Then another heresy arose. Athanasius, a priest in Alexandria began to oppose the teachings of Arius, another priest who proposed a different nature for Christ that limited His divinity and emphasized His humanity. The fierce Arian controversy divided Christendom and eventually forced Emperor Constantine in AD 325 to call all the leading clergy of the empire to settle the dispute at the council of Nicaea, in Asia Minor.

"On the one side were **the old, historical, apostolic traditions**; on the other side, the **new, Christian, Catholic spirit**, striving to part company with its ancient Jewish birthplace. The Eastern Church, at least in part, took the former view, the Western Church, the latter view...The sight of some churches fasting on the same day when others were rejoicing, and of two Passovers in one year, was against the very idea of Christian unity. The celebration of it on the same day as was kept by the wicked race that put the Saviour to death was an impious absurdity... The Jewish practice must give way to the new innovation." Stanley *"Eastern Church"* lect. 5, p. 54

The majority of the bishops sided with Athanasius, denouncing Arius and his followers to banishment and persecution. But Constantine had another agenda: to settle the "Easter question" once and for all. At this time, the Roman Empire had become extremely anti-Semitic, or anti-Jewish. Constantine himself hated the Jews and deploring the division in the church, which he wanted to make the state religion of the Roman Empire, commanded all the bishops at the Council to embrace "the practice which is observed at once in the city of Rome, and in Africa, throughout Italy, and in Egypt." (Bacchiocchi, *From Sabbath to Sunday*, p.204).

Constantine wanted to establish a world religion totally free from all Jewish influence. Speaking about Passover, he said:

> "It appeared an unworthy thing that in the celebration of this most holy feast [Easter] we should follow the practice of the Jews, who have impiously defiled their hands with enormous sin... Let us therefore have nothing in common with the detestable Jewish crowd." Eusebius, *Life of Constantine*, NPNF, I, p.524-525.

> "Let us, then, have nothing in common with the Jews, who are our adversaries... Therefore this irregularity must be corrected, in order that we may no more have anything in common with the parricides and errs of our Lord." Bower's *History of the Popes;* Dowling's *History of Romanism*; and Boyle's *Historical View of the Council of Nicea.*

With his authority and influence, the Council decreed:

> "All the brethren in the East who formerly celebrated Easter [sic, he should have said 'Passover'] with the Jews, will henceforth keep it at the same time as the Romans, with us..."

Renown scholar J.B. Lightfoot concluded that Rome and Alexandria [symbolical of Babylon and Egypt—the two countries which God called His servants to come *out* of!] both adopted Easter-Sunday in order to avoid even resembling the Jews. He wrote:

> "In the Paschal controversy of the second century, the bishops of Jerusalem, Caesarea, Tyre and Ptolemais ranged themselves not with Asia Minor, which regulated the Easter festival by Jewish Passover, but with Rome and Alexandria, thus avoiding even the semblance of Judaism." *The Apostolic Fathers*, 1885, II, part 1, p.88.

The Jews never fasted on Sabbaths, a day that was to them a time of joy and celebration. Sabbath was a day for feasting. The apocryphal book of Judith documents this custom:

> "And she fasted all the days of her widowhood, save the eves of the sabbaths, and the sabbaths, and the eves of the new moons, and the new moons, and the feasts and joyful days of the house of Israel." *Judith* 8:6; R. H. Charles (ed.), *The Apocrypha and Pseudepigrapha of the Old Testament* (Oxford: Clarendon Press, 1913), I:256.

The book of Jubilees sternly warned against breaking the Sabbath: "And every man who does any work thereon, or goes a journey, or tills (his) farm... or whoever fasts or makes war on the Sabbaths" could face fatal consequences. *Jubilees* 50:12, 13; Charles, *op. cit.*, II, 82.

The truth of God was being buried under a growing mountain of paganism. Scriptures were being replaced by superstition. Passover was finally replaced by Easter, the spring festival of the goddess of fertility and fecundity. The pagan whore-goddess Semiramis, called "Easter," had her celebration grafted into the universal Christian Roman Catholic Church.

> "Opposition to Judaism introduced the particular festival of Sunday very early, indeed, into the place of the Sabbath." Neander, Wilhelm August Johann, *History of the Christian Religion and Church,* Rose's translation, p. 168.

> "The observance of the Sabbath among the Jewish Christians gradually ceased. Yet the Eastern Church to this day marks the seventh day of the week (excepting only the Easter Sabbath) by omitting fasting, and standing in prayer; the Latin Church, in direct opposition to Judaism, made Saturday a fast day. The controversy on this point began as early as the end of the second century." Philip Schaff, *History of the Church,* p. 372, 1864 edition; p. 205, 1952 edition.

> "Christianity did not destroy paganism; it adopted it... the Greek mysteries passed down into the impressive mystery of the Mass. Other pagan cultures contributed to the syncretist result. From Egypt came the idea of a divine Trinity... from Egypt the adoration of the Mother and Child... The Mithraic ritual so closely resembled the eucharistic sacrifice of the Mass that Christian fathers charged the Devil with inventing these similarities to mislead frail minds. Christianity was the last great creation of the ancient pagan world." Will Durant, *The Story of Civilization: Caesar and Christ*, Vol. III, p.595.

Council of Laodicea 364 AD

Strangely, those who wanted to endorse Sunday as a memorial to the resurrection also wanted to christen it with the essence of rest snatched from the Sabbath. So the Council of Laodicea, an Eastern, Greek-speaking synod, was convened in AD 364 addressing again the Sabbath controversy.

> "Canon 29. Christians ought not to Judaize, and to rest on the Sabbath, but preferring the Lord's day, should rest if possible as Christians. Wherefore if they shall be found to Judaize, let them be accursed from Christ." Hefele, Charles Joseph, *A History of the Councils of the Church,* Edinburgh: Clark, 1896, Vol II, p. 316.

The Council published several other "canon" or laws regarding what the Church considered was true and proper in regards to the issue of Sabbath versus Sunday worship.

CANON 16 - The Gospels are to be read on Sabbath, with the other Scriptures [apparently at Communion services; see canon 49, below]. CANON 49 - During Lent, the Bread must not be offered except on the Sabbath Day and on the Lord's Day only. CANON 51 - The nativities of Martyrs [actually, the death days, on which martyrs were considered to have been born to eternal life] are not to be celebrated in Lent, but commemorations of the holy Martyrs are to be made on the Sabbaths and Lord's days.

These references to both Sabbath and Lord's day clearly demonstrate that there were still many who observed the seventh day well into the 4th century. But in spite of such efforts to discourage honor for the seventh day, Sabbath observance continued to receive widespread respect and recognition throughout Christendom.

"We also find in ancient writers frequent mention made of **religious assemblies on the Saturday, or seventh day of the week**, which was the Jewish Sabbath*. It is not easy to tell the original of this practice, nor the reasons for it ... I consider it here only as a day of public divine service ... Athanasius, who is one of the first that mentions it says: **They met on the Sabbath, not that they were infected with Judaism, but to worship Jesus, the Lord of the Sabbath**... And Cassian takes notice of the Egyptian churches, that among them the service of the Lord's day and the Sabbath, was always the same;... In another place he observes that in the monasteries of Egypt and Thebes, they had no public assemblies on other days, besides morning and evening, except upon **Saturday and the Lord's day**, when they met at (three o'clock), that is, nine in the morning, to celebrate the Communion." Joseph Bingham, M.A *Antiquities of the Christian Church*, Book 13, Chapter 9, Section 3. *The term "Jewish Sabbath" is not used in Biblical Scripture.

"The ancient Christians were very careful in the observation of Saturday, or the seventh day... It is plain that all the Oriental churches, and the greatest part of the world, observed the Sabbath as a festival... Epiphanius says the same." *Ibid.*, Vol. II, Book 20, Ch. 3, Sec 1, 66. 1137, 1136.

Socrates Scholasticus (380-439) identified that both Saturday and Sunday were considered "festal days" at this period in history:

"The Arians, as we have said, held their meetings without the city. As often, therefore, as the festal days occurred — I mean Saturday [Sabbath] and the Lord's day — in each week, on which assemblies are usually held in the churches..." *(Socrates' Ecclesiastical History*, Book 6, Chapter 8, *The Nicene and Post-Nicene Fathers*, Volume 3, p. 144).

Sozomen reported that Constantine at first ordered no work be performed on both the first and fifth days:

> "He [Constantine] also enjoined the observance of the day termed the Lord's-day which the Jews call the first day of the week and which the Pagans dedicate to the sun, as likewise the day before the seventh, and commanded that no judicial or other business should be transacted on those days, but that God should be served with prayers and supplications. He honored the Lord's-day because on it Christ arose from the dead, and the day above mentioned because on it he was crucified. He regarded the cross with peculiar reverence, on account both of the power which it conveyed to him in the battles against his enemies, and also of the divine manner in which the symbol had appeared to him." Sozomen, *Ecclesiastical History*, Book 1, chap. 8, 450 AD.

The Eastern Church, centered at Constantinople, kept both Sabbath and Sunday, whereas the western Church at Rome only honored Sunday:

> "Likewise some meet both upon the Sabbath and upon the day after the Sabbath, as at Constantinople, and among almost all others. At Rome and Alexandria they do not. Among the Egyptians, likewise, in many cities and villages, there is also a sacred custom among all of meeting on the evening of the Sabbath, when the sacred mysteries are partaken of." (Ecclesiastical History of Sozomen, c 450 AD in *The Nicene and Post Nicene Fathers*, Book 7, Chapter 19).

Leaven and Lent

The apostle Paul wrote that a little leaven leavens the whole lump (1 Corinthians 5:6-7). The "leaven" of Easter began to pollute and contaminate the Church, leading the way for a host of auxiliary doctrines, dogmas, and pagan practices to infiltrate the Church, also.

For example, Alexander Hislop describes how the pagan forty-day "fast" of Lent, and Easter, were both incorporated into Church doctrine by the Roman Catholic Church, with abbot Dionysius the Little as chief instrument in the change-over. Hislop explains:

> "This change of the calendar in regard to Easter was attended with momentous consequences. It brought into the Church the grossest corruption and the rankest superstition in connection with the abstinence of Lent. Let any one only read the atrocities that were commemorated during the 'sacred fast' or Pagan Lent, as described by Arnobius and Clemens Alexandrinus, and surely he must blush for the Christianity of those who, with the full knowledge of all these abominations, 'went down to Egypt for help' to stir up the languid devotion of the degenerate church, and who could find no more excellent way to 'revive' it, than by borrowing from so polluted a source; the absurdities and abominations connected with which the early Christian writers had held up to scorn.

That Christians should ever think of introducing the Pagan abstinence of Lent was a sign of evil; it showed how low they had sunk, and it was also a cause of evil; it inevitably led to deeper degener-ation. Originally, even in Rome, Lent, with the preceding revelries of the carnival, was entirely unknown... But at last, when the worship of Astarte was rising into the ascendant, steps were taken to get the whole Chaldean Lent of six weeks, or forty days, made imperative on all within the Roman Empire of the West." Hislop, *The Two Babylons*, p.106-107.

Weeping for Tammuz

Modern Lent practices in many cultures beyond Catholicism appear to have a common Babylonian-Ishtar-Tammuz origin.

Whence, then, came this observance? The forty days abstinence of Lent was directly borrowed from the worshippers of the Babylonian goddess [Astarte / Ishtar]. Such a Lent of forty days, "in the spring of the year," is still observed by the Yezidis or Pagan Devil-worshippers of Koordistan, who have inherited it from their early masters, the Babylonians.

Such a Lent of forty days was held in spring by the Pagan Mexicans, for thus we read in Humboldt, where he gives account of Mexican observances: "Three days after the vernal equinox .... began a solemn fast of *forty days* **in the honour of the sun**." Such a Lent of forty days was observed in Egypt, as may be seen on consulting Wilkinson's *Egyptians*.

Among the Pagans this Lent seems to have been an indispensable preliminary to Tammuz, which was celebrated by alternate weeping and rejoicing, and which, in many countries, was considerably later than the Christian festival, being observed in Palestine and Assyria in June, therefore called the "month of Tammuz;" in Egypt, about the middle of May, and in Britain, some time in April. To conciliate the Pagans to nominal Christianity, Rome, pursuing its usual policy, took measures to get the Christian and Pagan festivals amalgamated, and, by a complicated but skillful adjustment of the calendar, it was found no difficult matter, in general, to get Paganism and Christianity—now far sunk in idolatry—in this as in so many other things, to shake hands. Charles Panati, *Sacred Origins of Profound Things*, the Penguin Group, 1996, page 206.

It is not clear what the original period of fasting was in the Roman Church prior to the time of the Nicene Council, but we have distinct evidence that it did not exceed three weeks for many years following it. Socrates wrote about A.D. 450 that "Those who inhabit the princely city of Rome fast together before Easter three weeks, excepting the Saturday and Lord's day."

Originally, even in Rome, Lent, with the preceding revelries of the Carnival (Mardi Gras, which is reminescent of the feasting following the Ramidan fast in muslim countries), was entirely unknown. Even when fasting before the Christian Passover (Easter) was later felt to be necessary, it was only a matter of time that it came to conform with the rituals of Paganism. The way for full acceptance of this practice was prepared by the Council held at *Aurelia* in the time of *Hormisdas,* Bishop of Rome, [514-523].

Council of Aurelia 519 AD

Lent became mandated by a council of the church held at Aurelia around 519 AD. The Council decreed that Lent should be solemnly observed *before* Easter. A few days following this decree the calendar was adjusted by Dionysius.

> "The difference, in point of time, betwixt the Christian Pasch [Passover], as observed in Britain by the native [Celtic] Christians, and the pagan Easter enforced by Rome, at the time of enforcement, was a whole month; and it was only by violence and bloodshed, at last, that the festival of the Anglo-Saxon or Chaldean goddess came to supercede that which had been held in honour of Christ.

> "Such is the history of Easter. The popular observances that still attend the period of its celebration amply confirm the testimony of history as to its Babylonian character. The hot cross buns of Good Friday, and the dyed eggs of Pasch or Easter Sunday, figured in the Chaldean rites just as they do now. The 'buns' known too by that identical name, were used in the worship of the Queen of Heaven, the goddess Easter, as early as the days of Cecrops, the founder of Athens—that is, 1500 years before the Christian era." (*ibid*, p.107-108).

Easter Today

Easter continues in our time to hold a prominent position in the theology of the worship day. Pope John Paul II's Apostolic Letter, *Dies Domini*, of May 31, 1998 is loaded with numerous references to religious festivals and holy days admittedly of human devising:

> "**Easter** which returns week by week" Sec. 1
> "The **Easter liturgy**" Sec. 1
> "Liturgy of the **Easter Vigil**" Sec. 2
> "The Church celebrates the **Easter mystery**" Sec. 3
> "Sunday is above all **an Easter celebration**" Sec. 8
> "The **weekly Easter**, The day of the Risen Lord" Sec. 18
> "A **sacrament of Easter**" Sec. 19
> "The **Easter proclamation**" Sec. 21
> "The **Easter banquet**" Sec. 44, etc.

Anyone familiar with the origins of Easter, a pagan fertility holiday derived from the ancient Babylonian sex goddess Astarte, Ishtar, Aschtar a.k.a. "queen of heaven, Light of the World, Opener of the Womb, Goddess of Goddesses, Lady of Victory, Forgiver of Sins," wonders why this list of Easter references does not include one to the

Easter Bunny. The Bible has much to say in condemning the immoral Asthoreth poles (blatant phallic symbols popular among the idolatrous Canaanites). Astarte/Ishtar was the promiscuous goddess of Sacred Prostitution. But there is no wonder in how this adopted festival became embellished over time with dietary restrictions and prescribed ceremonial ritual.

> "Preceded by a preparatory fast, celebrated in the course of a long vigil, extended into the fifty days leading to Pentecost, the feast of Easter— 'solemnity of solemnities'—became the day par excellence for the initiation of catechumens." *Dies Domini* Sec. 76

Abundant evidence exists in the New Testament Scriptures of the continued use and recognition of the original holy days given by God to His covenant people. For example, while the Ephesians were championing the fertility goddess Diana, the church at Ephesus continued to "keep the feast" 1 Corinthians 5:8,7.

Ishtar Sunrise Tablet

Many-breasted fertility
Goddess of Ephesus

Meanwhile the Western Church continued to add to its repertoire of man-made ceremonies and holy days. Again from *Dies Domini*:

> "Celebrating this annual cycle of the mysteries of Christ, the holy Church venerates with special love **the Blessed Virgin Mary**,...In a similar way, by **inserting into the annual cycle the commemoration of the martyrs and other saints** on the

occasion of their anniversaries, the Church proclaims **the Easter mystery of the saints** who suffered with Christ and with him are now glorified. When celebrated in the true spirit of the liturgy, the **commemoration of the saints** does not obscure the centrality of Christ... the **Liturgical Year,** is expressed most eloquently in the fundamental and sovereign character of Sunday as the Lord's Day. Following the season of the Liturgical Year in the Sunday observance which structures it from beginning to end." *Dies Domini,* Sec. 78

"Sunday emerges therefore as the natural model for understanding and **celebrating feast-days of the Liturgical Year,** which are of such value for the Christian Life that the Church has chosen to emphasize their importance by **making it obligatory** for the faithful to attend...they are **established in tradition** and how well they are **supported by civil legislation.** *Ibid,* Sec. 79

What better example of the commandments of men: you can't eat meat on Good Friday, you must deprive yourself of some personal pleasure during the feast of Lent, you must celebrate the feast days of the Liturgical Year, put ashes on your forehead, say so many Hail Mary's, do your penance, fiddle with rosary beads...etc., etc.

Nowhere in the Bible do we find the saints or people of God ever observing this pagan day. In fact, God commands very plainly, "Learn *not* the way of the heathen" (Jer.10:1). Jesus Christ never observed "Easter." Nor did He command His apostles or church to ever observe it. The one place the word "Easter" is found in the King James version of the New Testament (Acts 12:4), it is an obvious mistranslation of the Greek word *Pascha,* "Passover," as all modern translations accurately show.

Thomas Aquinas (d. 1274)

Aquinas was a major influence in shaping Catholic theology during the peak of the Church's dominance during the middle ages. He developed the position that day of worship was "changed" by the authority of the Church not Scripture.

"In the New Law the observance of the Lord's day took the place of the observance of the Sabbath, not by virtue of the precept, but by the institution of the Church."

1545 Council of Trent

When the Reformation reacted to such arrogance, it made equally bold statements, challenging the Church to Scriptural accountability. In response, Rome solidified its position on tradition and its regard for the Bible in matters of faith. The Reformers charged the Church with apostatizing from the truth as contained in the written word. "The Word," "Thus saith the Lord," "The Bible and the Bible only," was their motto. Scripture only, *sola scriptura*, was the proclaimed platform for the Protestants. Rome was shaken by this new threat to her authority and responded with the Council of Trent.

The Council was held from 1545-1563 in an attempt to destroy the progress of the Protestant Reformation. In the bull announcing the council, the pope offered a sale of indulgences promising "full remission of sins" to those who would attend the procession, give an alms to some pauper, or recite the Lord's prayer and angelic greeting five times. In the opening litany of the council a recital of all the angels and saints was presented as mediators, patrons, and intercessors.

In contrast, the Protestant appeal to Scripture was so compelling that a significant number of attendees urged the Council to drop their stance on tradition and adopt the same Biblical standard as the Reformers in order to eliminate their charges. But the ultra-Catholic party was determined to maintain the course and keep tradition as the basis of authority. This was the only way to defend the many non-scriptural doctrines that the Church had defended for centuries.

Finally on January 18, 1562, Archbishop Reggio D. Gaspare de Fosso of Calabra delivered the following speech as the solution to the debate at the last opening session of Trent:

> "The Protestants claim to stand upon the written word only. They profess to hold the Scripture alone as the standard of faith. They justify their revolt by the plea that the Church has apostatized from the written word and follows tradition. Now the Protestants claim, that they stand upon the written word only, is not true. Their profession of holding the Scripture alone as the standard of faith, is false. PROOF: The written word explicitly enjoins the observance of the seventh day as the Sabbath. They do not observe the seventh day, but reject it. If they do truly hold the scripture alone as their standard, they would be observing the seventh day as is enjoined in the Scripture throughout. Yet they not only reject the observance of the Sabbath enjoined in the written word, but they have adopted and do practice the observance of Sunday, for which they have only the tradition of the Church. Consequently the claim of 'Scripture alone as the standard,' *fails;* and the doctrine of 'Scripture *and tradition*' as essential, is fully established, the Protestants themselves being judges." Heinrich Julius Holzmann, *Kanon und Tradition (Canon and Tradition)*, published in Ludwigsburg, Germany, in 1859, page 263.

An Italian source also records the argument:

> "The Sabbath, the most glorious day in the law, has been changed into the Lord's day... These and other similar matters have not ceased by virtue of Christ's teaching (for He says He has come to fulfill the law, not to destroy it), but they have been changed by the authority of the church."

(Archbishop Gaspare de Fosso, *Sacrorum Conciliorum nova amplissima Collectio*, 1902, vol. 33, pp. 529,530.)

The speech is also recorded in *Nova Collectio Section 217. Session XVII. Concilium Tridentinum. Diariorum, Actorum, Epistularum, Tractuum.. Tomus Octavus. Actorum Pars Quinta.* Freiburg: B. Herder, 1919, p. 293-299. However, because this source does not mention the Sabbath-Sunday argument, some have argued that the account given by Holzmann is spurious. Regardless of this, the tone and tack of the Catholic Church for 300 years following Trent has been consistent with Reggio's oratory, apocryphal or not!

The argument was immediately seen by the Council as the answer to their dilemma. The Protestants couldn't dodge this one. Their own statement of faith—the Augsburg Confession of 1530—had clearly admitted that "the observation of the Lord's day" had been established by "the Church" alone.

The party for "Scripture alone," surrendered and the council unanimously condemned Protestantism and the whole Reformation as an unwarranted revolt from the authority of the Catholic Church. The Council then proceeded on April 8, 1546 "to the promulgation of two decrees, the first of which, enacts under anathema, that Scripture *and tradition* are to be received and venerated equally, and that the deutero-canonical [the apocryphal] books are part of the canon of Scripture. The second decree declares the Vulgate to be the sole authentic and standard Latin version, and gives it such authority as to supersede the original texts; forbids the interpretation of Scripture contrary to the sense received by the Church, 'or even contrary to the unanimous consent of the Fathers.' "

The inconsistency of the Protestant practice with their own profession gave the Catholic Church the very ground she needed to condemn the Reformers and the entire Protestant movement as only an ambitious rebellion against the Church's rightful authority.

This Council went on to deny every Reformation doctrine, including Scripture alone and grace alone. In fact, Trent hurled 125 anathemas of eternal damnation against Bible-believing Christians. Among its many declarations is again the claim to change the Sabbath. These proclamations and anathemas were fleshed out in the murderous persecutions vented upon Bible-believing Christians by Rome through its Inquisitions, and the solemn fact is that the Council of Trent has never been annulled.

The Vatican II Council of the mid-1960s referred to Trent dozens of times, quoted Trent's proclamations as authority, and reaffirmed

Trent on every hand. The New Catholic Catechism cites Trent nearly 100 times. There is not the slightest hint that the proclamations of the Council of Trent have been abrogated by Rome. At the opening of the Second Vatican Council, Pope John XXIII stated, "I do accept entirely all that has been decided and declared at the Council of Trent." Every cardinal, bishop and priest who participated in the Vatican II Council signed a document affirming Trent.

The Cathechismus Romanus was commissioned by the Council of Trent and published by the Vatican Press under orders of Pope Pius V in 1566. This Catechism may also be found in more resent sources such as *Catechism of the Council of Trent* (Donovan's translation, 1867) Part 3, chap. 4, p. 345. Slightly different wording is presented in the McHugh and Callen translation, 1937 ed. p. 402.

> "It pleased the church of God, that the religious celebration of the Sabbath day should be transferred to 'the Lord's day.' "

When the Chicago Columbia Exhibition was slated to open its doors on a Sunday, 300 years after the Council of Trent, the Protestant ministers were prominent in raising opposition to this blatant "sacriledge to the Lord's Day." Rome saw in this an opportunity to exploit the hypocracy of their estranged brethren.

VOL. XLIV. NO. 34.   BALTIMORE, SATURDAY, SEPTEMBER 2, 1893.   PRICE FIVE CENTS.

ROME'S CHALLENGE | WHY DO PROTESTANTS KEEP SUNDAY?

Produced in 1893 as an attempt to discredit Protestants, this title became a 32-page pamphlet of reprints from four editorials from *The Catholic Mirror* published on September 2, 9, 16 and 23.

"Examining the New Testament from cover to cover, critically, we find the sabbath referred to 61 times. We find, too, that the Saviour invariably selected the sabbath (Saturday) to teach in the synagogues and work miracles. The four gospels refer to the sabbath 51 times...."

"...the Redeemer refers to Himself as 'the Lord of the sabbath'...He never once hinted at a desire to change it...thus the sabbath (Saturday) [remains] from Genesis to Revelation."

"Hence the conclusion is inevitable...that of those who follow the Bible as their guide, the Israelites and Seventh-day Adventists have the exclusive weight of evidence on their side, whilst the Biblical Protestant has not a word in self-defense for his substitution of Sunday for Saturday...."

"The Bible and the Sabbath constitute the watchword of Protestantism; but we have demonstrated that it is the Bible against their Sabbath...We have shown that no greater contradiction ever existed than their theory and practice! We have proved that neither their Biblical ancestors nor themselves have ever kept one Sabbath day in their lives...."

"The Catholic Church for over 1,000 years before the existence of a Protestant, by virtue of her divine mission, changed the day from Saturday to Sunday...We say by virtue of her divine mission, because He who called Himself the 'Lord of the Sabbath' endowed her with His own power to teach, 'He that heareth you, heareth me'...and promised to be with her to the end of the world. She holds her charter from Him—a charter as infallible as perpetual...."

"The Protestant world at its birth found the Christian Sabbath (Sunday) too strongly entrenched to run counter to its existence...It was therefore placed under the necessity of acquiescing in the arrangement, thus implying the Church's right to change the day, for over 300 years...."

"The history of the world cannot present a more stupid, self-stultifying specimen of dereliction of principle than this... That immense concourse of Bible Christians, the Methodists, have declared that the Sabbath has never been abrogated, whilst the followers of the Church of England, together with her daughter, the Episcopal Church of the United States, are committed by the 20th Article of Religion that the church cannot lawfully ordain anything 'contrary to God's written Word,' yet God's written Word enjoins His worship to be observed on Saturday absolutely, repeatedly, and most emphatically...All Biblical sects occupy the same self-stultifying position which no explanation can modify, much less justify."

"They have ignored and condemned their teacher, the Bible... and they have adopted a day kept by the Catholic Church... the 'Mother of Abominations'...."

Sentinel

Saint Catherine  **Catholic Church**

1106 St. Clair Blvd · ALGONAC, MICHIGAN 48001 · (810) 794-3301

Volume 50	May 21, 1995	Number 22

Pastor's Page

Our Lord really simplified things when He said that the new law consisted in only two parts: love God and love neighbor. In the Hebrew Scriptures there were hundreds of laws that governed things in minutest detail. And the early Christians, most of whom were Jewish, had to really struggle with change. Some thought that many of the old laws should be carried over into the new Testament.

And, when we come to apply the Lord's commandments to concrete situations, we have to specify about particulars. So, the very early Church, without a long tradition, decreed that nobody should be overburdened, but idolatry, that is, taking part in pagan sacrifices, and sins against chastity are clearly against loving God and neighbor.

The Church has always had a strong sense of its own authority. "Whatever you bind on earth is bound in heaven", Jesus said.

Perhaps the boldest thing, the most revolutionary change the Church ever did, happened in the first century. The holy day, the Sabbath, was changed from Saturday to Sunday. "The Day of the Lord" (dies Dominica) was chosen, not from any directions noted in the Scriptures, but from the Church's sense of its own power. The day of resurrection, the day of Pentecost, fifty days later, came on the first day of the week. So this would be the new Sabbath. People who think that the Scriptures should be the sole authority should logically become 7th Day Adventists, and keep Saturday holy.

With a long long period of practice and reflection, Church law developed and changed with changing circumstances. It takes a fair amount of wisdom and study to know in detail the various Church laws. The latest revision of our Catholic Church law took place about 15 years ago, some time after the Vatican Council.

The law of Christ is always primary: we must love God and neighbor. Particular laws are made, not to be overly burdensome, but to apply, in particular circumstances how the law of Christ is carried out in practice.

Some people think there should be no law, no government. They are anarchists, and of course they make themselves into their own law. We witness such people bombing innocents, shooting randomly in neighborhoods, destroying property, making up convenient (for themselves) rules about life, liberty, chastity, killing the unborn, free speech.

"My yoke is easy, my burden is light "said the Lord. It takes strong faith to be able to see that in all circumstances.

Here's how to love God next Thursday: Come to Mass and participate.

CSA

If you have not yet responded to the C.S.A. drive, you will be receiving information in the mail. Please place your contribution in the basket, bring to the rectory or you may mail it to the rectory.

Ascension Thursday

May 25, 1995
Masses: 9:15 a.m. & 7:00 p.m.

Festival Meeting

There will be a festival meeting of all chairpersons and all interested parishioners, Tuesday, May 23 in the meeting room in Church. All are welcome to attend. New ideas are always appreciated.

A more modern version of the same position.

The tone today is quite different. But for many years the Church of Rome continued her appeal to authority over the Protestant world by throwing in their face the claim of establishing Sunday observance.

James Cardinal Gibbons, who presided over the *Catholic Mirror,* expressed the same view nearly twenty years earlier:

> "But you may read the Bible from Genesis to Revelation, and you will not find a single line authorizing the sanctification of Sunday.

The Scriptures enforce the religious observance of Saturday, a day which we never sanctify." *The Faith of our Fathers*, 88th ed., 1876, pp. 89

That same year another Catechism was produced reaffirming the Church's established position:

Stephen Keenan, *A Doctrinal Catechism* 3rd ed. 1876
A DOCTRINAL CATECHISM; WHEREIN DIVERS POINTS OF CATHOLIC FAITH AND PRACTICE ASSAILED BY MODERN HERETICS ARE SUSTAINED BY AN APPEAL TO THE HOLY SCRIPTURES, THE TESTIMONY OF THE ANCIENT FATHERS, AND THE DICTATES OF REASON ON THE BASIS OF SCHEFFMACHER'S CATECHISM.

THIRD AMERICAN EDITION, REVISED AND CORRECTED, CONFORMABLY TO THE DECREES OF THE COUNCIL OF THE VATICAN. IMPRIMATUR: + JOHN CARDINAL McCLOSKEY, ARCHBISHOP OF NEW YORK

P. J. KENEDY AND SONS
PUBLISHERS TO THE HOLY APOSTOLIC SEE,
3 AND 5 BARCLAY STREET NEW YORK

Page 174:

> **"Question:** Have you any other way of proving that the Church has power to institute festivals of precept?
>
> **"Answer:** Had she not such power, she could not have done that in which all modern religionists agree with her— she could not have substituted the observance of Sunday, the first day of the week, for the observance of Saturday, the seventh day, a change for which there is no Scriptural authority."

Appeal to Authority
Catholic appeal to the Mother Church's authority rather than Scripture continues into modern times:

> "All of us believe many things in regard to religion that we do not find in the Bible. For example, **nowhere in the Bible do we find that Christ or the Apostles ordered that the Sabbath be changed from Saturday to Sunday**. We have the commandment of God given to Moses to keep holy the Sabbath Day, that is the 7th day of the week, Saturday. **Today most Christians keep Sunday because it has**

been revealed to us by the Church outside the Bible." "To Tell You The Truth," *The Catholic Virginian*, Vol. 22, No. 49 (Oct. 3, 1947).

"After all, fundamentalists meet for worship on Sunday, yet there is no evidence in the Bible that corporate worship was to be made on Sundays. The Jewish Sabbath, or day of rest, was, of course, Saturday. **It was the Catholic Church that decided Sunday should be the day of worship for Christians**, in honor of the Resurrection." *Catholicism and Fundamentalism*, by Karl Keating, copyright 1988 by Ignatius Press, San Francisco, bearing the Nihil Obstat and Imprimatur of the Catholic Church, page 38.

See Appendix F for a historical review of Catholic Comments concerning Sunday observance.

See Appendix G for selected canon from the Council of Trent.

Surgical History

Prior surgical procedures can impact the diagnostic process in a number of ways. Appendicitis can be quickly eliminated from our differential diagnoses when we learn that the patient has already had a previous appendectomy. Being informed that the patient has a history of a renal transplant introduces additional potential diagnoses in a differential list. Surgery can involve repair of damaged tissue, excisional removal of disease or tumor masses, and insertion of donor tissue or mechanical devices. The Sabbath, likewise, has come under the knife and more than once. Radical excision and even transplantation has been performed on the day of days.

Removal of major segments (modified radical versectomy) has rendered the Sabbath emasculinated and abbreviated to a sparse image of itself. From the full-bodied 94 word version, the 4th commandment has in modern times undergone a reductionplasty shrinking it down to a mere four: "Remember the Sabbath day."

More devastating was the attempt at a complete organ transplant. The seventh day Sabbath was replaced with a nonhomologous substitute, a completely different day altogether. A long and rocky course followed when rejection was suppressed with powerful agents. See Doctor's Orders.

Alternative Worship

As the Sabbath signified release from slavery, so neglect and even rejection of the Sabbath resulted in a return to bondage. Ezekiel, prophet to the northern kingdom of Israel now captive in a foreign land, described the situation. When the people asked why all this was happening to them, God answered through His prophet:

> "Thus says the Lord GOD: 'Have you come to inquire of Me?'"...
> "Thus says the Lord GOD: 'On the day when I chose Israel and **lifted My hand in an oath** to the descendants of the house of Jacob, and made Myself known to them in the land of Egypt, **I lifted My hand in an oath** to them saying, 'I am the LORD your God.' On that day **I lifted My hand in an oath** to them, to bring them out of the land of Egypt into a land that I had searched out for them, flowing with milk and honey, the glory of all lands. Then I said to them, 'Each of you, **throw away the abominations** which are before his eyes, and do not defile yourselves with **the idols of Egypt**. I am the LORD your God.' **But they rebelled** against Me and would not obey Me. They did not all cast away the abominations." Ezekiel 20:3-8

Obviously, idolatry was a big part of the problem. They had forsaken the worship of the Creator God. "They worshiped the creature more than the Creator," Romans 1:25. But then God identifies the real underlying reason:

> "Moreover I also gave them **My Sabbaths**, to be a sign between them and Me, that they might know that I am the Lord who sanctifies them. Yet the house of Israel rebelled against Me in the wilderness; they did not walk in **My statutes**; they despised **My judgments,** which if a man does, he shall live by them; and they greatly defiled **My Sabbaths**. (verses 12-13)

Hebrews 4 identifies the Sabbath as fundamental to realizing the fullness of God's plan. Israel failed to enjoy freedom in the land of promise after the Exodus because they "defiled" God's Sabbaths, denying His position as their Creator, returning spiritually to the idols of Egypt, and as a result, returned physically back into captivity.

Israel's New Feasts

When Israel split into the northern and southern kingdoms Jeroboam, breakaway king of the northern capitol in Samaria, became fearful that his people would eventually reunite with the tribes of Judah and Benjamin, the southern kingdom. In order to compete with his southern rival He said to himself, "Now the kingdom may return to the house of David: If these people go up to offer sacrifice in the house of the LORD at Jerusalem, then the people will turn back to their lord, Rehoboam king of Judah, and they will kill me." 1 Kings 12:26-27.

So, to keep his subjects from flocking down to Jerusalem three times a year, he established his own brand of alternative worship with centers in Dan and Bethel where he crafted a golden calf deity for each temple, and scheduled his own festivals, feast days, Crescent Moons, and other holy days. One of these is recorded in 1 Kings 12:32, 33:

> "And Jeroboam ordained a feast in the eighth month on the fifteenth day of the month, like unto the feast that is in Judah...which he had devised of his own heart."

He created his own counterfeit Feast of Tabernacles for the people to observe in the **eighth month, not the seventh**, as God had ordained in Leviticus 23:34 (1 Kings 12:28-33). It appears that this substitution of eight for seven was extended even to the weekly Sabbath, a popular reason offered still today.

The Host of Heaven

It is clear that northern Israel's flavor of religion, though perverted, was parallel to that of Judah. When the northern ten tribes were finally hauled off into Assyrian exile, God listed the reasons for their captivity:

> "They left **all the commandments** of the Lord their God, and made them molten images, even two calves, and made a grove, and worshiped all the host of heaven, and served Baal." 2 Kings 17:16

"All the commandments" would naturally include the fourth. The host of heaven included "the sun, the moon, and the stars" that Moses had warned the children of Israel not to worship (Deuteronomy 4:19). While Judah worshiped the God of creation, Israel worshiped the creation of God. While Judah observed God's Sabbaths and God's feasts, Israel observed "her" Sabbaths and "her" feasts. Among these the sun and moon played prominent roles.

The Egyptian Connection

It should be noted that Jeroboam had spent time in Egypt (1 Kings 11:40; 12:2). Fleeing from Solomon, he sought refuge in the courts of Shishak, king of Egypt. Jeroboam would naturally have been exposed to the Egyptian gods while living there. Ra, the sun god, was the patron god of Heliopolis (Sun City) and a popular theme in hieroglyphic depictions. The title Pharaoh (pha-*ra*-oh) actually means "son of the Sun." The Pharaoh was considered not only a king but a Sun god. But the Egyptians also worshipped the moon. According to the Harris Papyrus dated to the time of Ramses III, Pharaoh Shishak's wife was Asiatic. This is an interesting connection, because throughout large portions of Asia, especially China, a long tradition of observing the mid-Autumn Moon Festival has been preserved. Since Autumn occurs during the seventh, eighth and ninth lunar months (counting from the spring equinox), the mid-Autumn harvest moon occurs exactly on the fifteenth day of the eighth lunar month. Even today, this part of the world observes the date with the baking and giving of Moon Cakes.

Judah Also

Reference to the sun and moon as objects of worship was eventually adopted by the southern kingdom, as well. In 2 Kings 21:3-6 we read that Manasseh

> "worshipped all the host of heaven and served them." "And he built altars for all the host of heaven in the two courts of the house of the Lord. And he made his son pass through the fire, and observed times."

Manasseh "observed times" by assigning Holy days to commemorate important celestial celebrities, the sun receiving preeminent attention. Again in verse 11, good king Josiah, as part of his reform policy, "took away the horses that the kings of Judah had given to the sun, at the entering in of the house of the Lord." And he "burned the chariots of the sun with fire." Ancient Persian, Greek, and Roman customs depict the sun as a divine charioteer who daily drove his steeds across the sky.

Faux Feasts Cease

200 years after Jeroboam established his faux feasts, Israel was still observing their substitute holy days and Sabbaths. God warned them in Hosea 2:11, "I will also cause all *her* mirth to cease, *her* feast days, *her* New Moons, and *her* Sabbaths—all *her* appointed feasts." Many point to this verse as evidence that God was going to discontinue the Sabbath for Israel. But remember, "Israel" here is not the Jews as a whole, but only the northern 10 tribes who had rebelled against God. Later they intermarried with the indigenous population and became known as the Samaritans.

Days of the Baals

Two verses later Hosea makes this abundantly clear: "I will visit upon her [punish her for observing] the days of Baalim [the Baals] wherein she burned incense to them." (verse 13).

What were the days of the Baals? Baal was the principal male deity of Phoenicia and Phillistia. The word Baal means 'lord.' These days of Baal were Baal's days or 'lord's days.' Substitute worship on substitute days.

The evidence is that Jeroboam made the day of Baal the national day of worship. Notice this brief summary of his actions: "Then Jeroboam drove Israel from following the LORD, and made them commit a great sin" (2 Kings 17:21). Jeroboam is the only king the Bible records to have "made Israel sin." Not only is it recorded in this verse, but also in 20 additional passages.

Finally, near the end of the southern kingdom, as Judah followed in the idolatrous footsteps of their northern brothers, the prophet Ezekiel was shown in vision a group of 25 men sitting in the temple doorway between the porch and the altar with their backs to the temple while their faces looked eastward. "And they worshipped the sun toward the east" (Ezekiel 8:16), an unspeakable abomination and insult to their Creator God.

"They worshipped the sun toward the east."

Sabbaticals and the 70 Years

The sabbatical year played a prominent role in determining God's judgment on Judah. When Nebuchadnezzar finally torched the temple and sacked the city in 586 BC, disregard for sabbatical years was given as the reason for their 70 years of Babylonian captivity.

> "To fulfill the word of the LORD by the mouth of Jeremiah, until the land had enjoyed her sabbaths: for as long as she lay desolate she kept sabbath, to fulfill threescore and ten years." 2 Chronicles 36:21

Seventy years worth of neglected land sabbaths would correspond to 490 years during which God's people failed to observe this important institution. The full limit of God's probationary time had expired and payment of the 70 year debt was due. Dates for the 70 year span appear in at least three different periods:

- The Babylonian Empire lasted 70 years (607 to 537 BC) beginning with the overthrow of the Assyrian capitol city of Nineveh and ending with its conquest by a coalition of Medes and Persians.
- The Jewish Captivity lasted exactly 70 years (604 to 534 BC) beginning with the first deportation when Daniel was taken captive and ending with the degree of Cyrus.
- The Temple also lay desolate for 70 years (586 to 515 BC).

God had promised to "heal their land" 2 Chronicles 7:14. And like the many miracles of healing performed by Christ on the Sabbath, the land was given a sabbath of decades to heal while Israel's contagion was quarantined in Babylon.

The sabbatical year was a hot issue during the reign of Zedekiah, Judah's last king. The story is found in Jeremiah 34:8-17. Zedekiah was apparently given one last chance to stay the impending judgment by making "a covenant with the people at Jerusalem" "to proclaim liberty" to their Hebrew servants that they might "go free." The princes obeyed and let their bondsmen go. But then, like Pharaoh with the original Hebrew slaves, they reversed their decision, changed their minds and "brought them into subjection" once again.

God sent a message through Jeremiah to Zedekiah reminding him of the original covenant which established the law of the Hebrew slave. "At the end of seven years" Hebrew slaves were to go free. But Israel didn't listen to God then and they weren't listening now. Because of this, God declares that they "polluted" His name by defaulting on their promise to let their servants go free in the seventh year. So now God says, "Since you didn't listen to Me in providing liberty, I proclaim liberty to you: to the sword, to pestilence and to famine." 2 Chronicles 36:17.

Idolatry, combined with Sabbath-breaking (both the weekly Sabbath and the seventh year land Sabbath), was the primary cause of their defeat and captivity (Ezekiel 20:1-24; see Nehemiah 13:15-22; 2 Kings 17:5-18). It will also be the cause of earth's final judgment at the end of time.

Untempered Mortar
Immediately before the return of Christ, God tells His people to "Cry aloud, spare not, lift up your voice like a trumpet, and show my people their transgression" Isaiah 58:1.   But the people are apparently unaware that they are sinning against God. They still "seek me daily, and delight to know my ways... they take delight in approaching to God" verse 2. Then what is "their transgression?"

Ezekiel, contemporary with Isaiah, prophesied that God's people would be led astray by some who "prophesy out of their own hearts" Ezekiel 13:2. God called them "foolish prophets" because they "have not gone up into the gaps [broken places], neither made up the hedge for the house of Israel" verses 3,5.

So, what were these gaps in the hedge? Who made them? And what was the hedge? The Bible answers these questions itself. In the story of Job Satan complained that God protected Job with a "hedge about him" Job 1:10. Job enjoyed this benefit because he obeyed God's law, he was "perfect and upright" verses 1,8. As long as we obey God, His law is a bulwark against evil; but when we disobey, we break the law, we make a breach, an opening in our wall of protection, the enemy can then come in and overthrow us.

God tells Isaiah to "write it before them in a table, and note it in a book, that it may be for the time to come [margin, 'the latter day') for ever and ever: that this is a rebellious people, lying children, children that will not hear the law of the Lord" Isaiah 30:8, 9.

This rebellious people tell the foolish prophets, "Prophesy not unto us right things, speak unto us smooth things, prophesy deceits: get you out of the way, turn aside out of the path" Isaiah 30:10,11.

In "the latter days," in "the time to come," just before Christ returns there will be those who claim to serve the Lord, but are "rebellious" because they refuse to "hear the law of the Lord." They tell their ministers to only preach "smooth things," to "turn aside out of the path" and "get out of the way." What is the path and the way?

"Blessed are the undefiled in the way, who walk in the law of the Lord" Psalm 119:1. "They also do no iniquity: they walk in His ways" verse 3. "Make me to go in the path of Your commandments" verse 35. "Stand in the ways, and see, and ask for the old paths, where is the good way, and walk therein, and you shall find rest for your souls." Jeremiah 6:16. Again, the Bible clearly explains itself. The rebellious people just before Christ's return will want to avoid walking in the path of God's commandments. Instead of finding rest in the Sabbath commandment they say, "We will not walk therein." Verse 16 last part.

Then, because of their refusal, God says, "I will bring evil upon this people, even the fruit of their thoughts, because they have not harkened unto my words, nor to my law, but rejected it" verse 19. Isaiah says the same thing. These people who desire to "turn aside out of the path" are told that "this iniquity shall be to you as a breach ready to fall, swelling out in a high wall" Isaiah 30:13. A wall, like the hedge of protection, is symbolic of God's law.

Restorers of the Breach
In the last days, one of the commandments will be removed from the wall leaving a gap. But God's faithful children will restore and repair the foundations of God's truth which were neglected and lost.

> "And they that shall be of thee shall build the old waste places: thou shalt raise up the foundations of many generations; and thou shalt be called, **The repairer of the breach, The restorer of paths to**

dwell in. If thou turn away thy foot from the Sabbath, from doing thy pleasure on my holy day; and call the Sabbath a delight, the holy of the LORD, honourable; and shalt honour him, not doing thine own ways, nor finding thine own pleasure, nor speaking thine own words: Then shalt thou delight thyself in the LORD; and I will cause thee to ride upon the high places of the earth." Isaiah 58:12-14

But the ministers who preach that the law is no longer binding show no desire to repair the damage. "Your prophets are like the foxes in the deserts. You have not gone up into the gaps, neither made up the hedge for the house of Israel to stand in the battle in the day of the Lord." Ezekiel 13:5.

The Day of Salvation is nearly over and the "Day of the Lord" is approaching yet these preachers of "smooth things" stand their ground. "They have seen vanity and lying divination, saying, 'The Lord saith': and the Lord hath not sent them: and they have made others to hope that they would confirm the word." Ezekiel 13:6. These respected leaders of the faithful claim a "Thus saith the Lord" but they have no Scripture to back it up.

God pronounces judgment on them for their deceitful practices, "Because, even because they have seduced my people, saying, Peace; and there was no peace; and one built up a wall, and, lo, others daubed it with untempered mortar" Ezekiel 13: 10.

The religious leaders then attempt to hide the breach and cover it up with a substitute wall, a different law. One of them "built up a wall" (the Roman Church changed the law) "and others" (the Protestant Churches) "daubed it with untempered mortar." While one group of shepherds actually builds the counterfeit wall, the other white-washes it with fanciful claims that "The Lord said" so.

The new wall looks good. It's been painted nice and white, but it doesn't really have any mortar to hold it together. A new law, constructed by man cannot last. God then says, "it will fall: there shall be an overflowing shower; and great hailstones shall fall" Ezekiel 13:11. He promises to "bring it down to the ground, so that the foundation thereof shall be discovered" verse 14.   Great hailstones fall during the seventh plague just before Christ's second coming. At that time the true source of the false wall will ultimately be exposed.

"Her priests have violated my law, and have profaned mine holy things: they have put no difference between the holy and profane, neither have they showed difference between the unclean and the clean, and **have hid their eyes from my Sabbaths**, and I am profaned among them. Her princes in the midst thereof are like wolves ravening the prey, to shed blood, and to destroy souls, to get dishonest gain. And **her**

prophets have daubed them with untempered mortar, seeing vanity, and divining lies unto them, saying, 'Thus saith the Lord God,' when the Lord has not spoken." Ezekiel 22:26-29.

Isaiah chapter 24 describes the final destruction of the earth at the second coming of Jesus. "The Lord makes the earth empty and makes it waste and turns it upside down" verse 1. The reason is then given: "because [the inhabitants] have transgressed the laws, changed the ordinance, broken the everlasting covenant" verse 5. Psalm 119 further explains God's "strange act" in coming to destroy planet earth: "It is time for you, Lord, to work: for they have made void Thy law" verse 126.

> And I sought for a man among them, that should make up the hedge, and stand in the gap before me for the land, that I should not destroy it: but I found none" Ezekiel 22:30

God could not find anyone among the religious leaders to make up the hedge, to stand in the gap, to repair the breach and restore His Sabbath. But a few of the faithful remnant will respond to His call to "cry aloud." They will lift up their voices like trumpets across the earth to show God's people who are honest in heart the way and the path to walk in. The reformation which begun in the 14th and 15th centuries continues even today as the foundation truths of the Everlasting Gospel are being rediscovered once again.

Reconstructive Surgery
Daniel chapter 7 anticipates a time when reconstructive surgery would be made in an attempt to alter the basic structure of God's times and God's law. The exact wording in verse 25 is that the lead surgeon would "think to change times and laws" suggesting that the procedure would not be totally successful. History bears this out.

Copies of the operative reports following these surgical interventions (catechisms) list completely different anatomy and structure than that describing the original pre-operative findings. While the second precept has been totally ablated, the only commandment dealing with time has been significantly truncated and the tenth, in order to preserve a total count of ten, has been bisected into two individual commands. The following is a side-by-side comparative analysis with before and after specimens:

Here it is: ***Original Recipe*** and less filling ***Law Lite***:

The Original LAW of God	The LAW Revised
I	**I**
Thou shalt have no other gods before Me.	Thou shalt not have strange gods before Me.
II	**II**
Thou shalt not make unto thee any graven image, or any likeness of any thing that is in heaven above, or that is in the earth beneath, or that is in the water under the earth: Thou shalt not bow down thyself to them, nor serve them: for I the Lord thy God am a jealous God, visiting the iniquity of the fathers upon the children unto the third and fourth generation of them that hate Me; and showing mercy unto thousands of them that love Me, and keep My commandments.	Thou shalt not take the name of the Lord thy God in vain.
III	**III**
Thou shalt not take the name of the Lord thy God in vain; for the Lord will not hold Him guiltless that taketh His name in vain.	Remember that thou keep holy the Sabbath day.
IV	**IV**
Remember the Sabbath day, to keep it holy. Six days shalt thou labor and do all thy work: but the seventh day is the Sabbath of the Lord thy God: in it thou shalt not do any work, thou nor thy son, nor thy daughter, thy manservant, nor thy maidservant, nor thy cattle, nor the stranger that is within thy gates: for in six days the Lord made heaven and earth, the sea and all that in them is, and rested the seventh day: wherefore the Lord blessed the Sabbath day, and hallowed it.	Honor thy father and thy mother.

"The Church, on the other hand, after changing the day of rest from the Jewish Sabbath, or seventh day of the week, to the first, made the Third Commandment refer to Sunday as the day to be kept holy as the Lord's Day. The Council of Trent (Sess. VI, can. xix) condemns those who deny that the Ten Commandments are binding on Christians." *Catholic Encyclopedia*, Article "Ten Commandments"

V	V
Honour thy father and thy mother: that thy days may be long upon the land which the Lord thy God giveth thee.	Thou shalt not kill.
VI	**VI**
Thou shalt not kill.	Thou shalt not commit adultery.
VII	**VII**
Thou shalt not commit adultery.	Thou shalt not steal.
VIII	**VIII**
Thou shalt not steal.	Thou shalt not bear false witness against thy neighbor.
IX	**IX**
Thou shalt not bear false witness against thy neighbor.	Thou shalt not covet thy neighbor's wife.
X	**X**
Thou shalt not covet thy neighbor's house; thou shalt not covet thy neighbor's wife, nor his manservant, nor his maidservant, nor his ox, nor his ass, nor anything that is thy neighbor's.	Thou shalt not covet thy neighbor's goods.

The Lord's Day
Which day is the Lord's Day? The Ten Commandments identify the seventh-day as the original day of rest enjoined by the Creator. But traditional thinking has equated the first day with not only the "Sabbath" but "the Lord's Day" as well, a designation that occurs in only one scripture.

John's gospel was written in A.D. 98, two years *after* the book of Revelation. Though his first work uses the term "Lord's day" in chapter 1, he does not employ this designation in his gospel. In John 20:1 and 19, the two verses most often considered to reference the same day, Sunday, John simply calls it "the first day of the week."

The following is a comparative analysis of this important passage as it is rendered by a number of different translations and paraphrases:

Revelation 1: 10

I was – Amplified Bible, Norlie's Simplified NT, Original New Testament, The Message, William Tyndale NT
It was – Living Bible
I came to be – Complete Jewish Bible, Concordant Literal NT, Emphasized Bible, New World Translation, The Scriptures SISR
I became – Holy Bible in Modern English
I entered into – Wuest Expanded Translation
Present – Modern Speech NT
Inspired – Holy Bible in Modern English, Phillips Revised Edition
By inspiration – New World Translation
I fell into a trance – Knox Translation, Noli NT, Twentieth Century NT
I found myself – Kleist-Lilly NT, Modern Speech NT
I knew myself – Phillips Revised Student Edition
There it was that – Cassirer NT

In the Spirit – Amplified Bible, Complete Jewish Bible, Emphasized Bible, Modern Speech NT, Norlie's Simplified NT, The Scriptures SISR, The Message
In the sphere of the spirit - Wuest Expanded Translation
In Spirit – Concordant Literal NT
By the spirit – Phillips Revised Student Edition
The Spirit took control of me – Contemporary English Version
The Spirit took possession of me – Cassirer NT
The Spirit of prophecy came upon me – Lambsa Bible
Rapt in His power – Amplified Bible
In prophetic ecstasy – Kleist-Lilly NT
Ecstatic – Original NT
A different experience – Wuest Expanded Translation

On the Lord's day – Amplified Bible, Contemporary English Version, Cassirer NT, Holy Bible in Modern English, Living Bible, Lambsa Bible, Kleist-Lilly NT, Knox Translation, Norlie's Simplified NT, Original NT, Phillips Revised Student Edition, Twentieth Century NT
In the Lord's day – Concordant Literal NT, Emphasized Bible, New World Translation
On the Day of the Lord – Complete Jewish Bible, Modern Speech New Testament
On the Day of Yahweh – The Scriptures SISR
On Sunday – Noli NT
On a Sunday – William Tyndale NT
It was Sunday – The Message
And I was worshiping – Living Bible

The Modern Speech New Testament –
Footnote: *The day of the Lord*, i.e. either the time of the Redeemer's Parousia or return to the earth, or else the interval that was to elapse before the coming of that time. That was the Seer's standpoint. In *The Teaching of the Apostles*, xiv, we read, "Every Lord's [day] of the Lord come together and break bread." Otherwise we have no reason to suppose that Sunday had yet received its present name of "the Lord's day."

New World Translation –
Footnote: [in the Lord's day].
See 1 Corinthians 1: 8 and 1 Corinthians 5: 5.

The Scriptures SISR –
Footnote: [The Day of Yahweh]. The prophetic Day, so called in at least 30 places, and referred to in 300 similar terms.

Worrell New Testament –
Footnote: On the Lord's day: or the first day of sabbaths, the day on which Christ rose from the dead, and the day on which the Holy Spirit descended at Pentecost.

> "The festival of Sunday, like all other festivals, was always only a human ordinance, and it was far from the intentions of the apostles to establish a divine command in this respect; far from them, and from the early apostolic church, to transfer the laws of the Sabbath to Sunday. Perhaps at the end of the second century a false application of this kind had begun to take place; for men appear by that time to have considered laboring on Sunday as a sin." *Neander's Church History*, translated by H.J.Rose, 1852, p. 186.

Lord of the Sabbath
Reformed Churches (Presbyterians and Dutch Reformed Church) defend the permanence of the Moral law including the fourth commandment, but consider the seventh day aspect of it ceremonial.

> As the Lord of the Sabbath, Jesus fulfills the Sabbath, creating the perfect rest by His atoning death and resurrection. That the Sabbath is now fulfilled Jesus shows by changing the Sabbath Day from the seventh day of the week to the first day of the week. Not the Church, but the Lord Jesus set the first day of the week apart as the day of rest for the New Testament people of God. The Church has no authority to change the Sabbath Day or to require believers to observe the first day of the week. The Church does not make laws; she only proclaims the will of her sovereign Lord, as that will is revealed in Holy Scripture. The Lord of the Sabbath Himself ordained the first day of the week as the day of rest for the Church come of age. He did this by rising from the dead on the first day

(Luke 24:1); by meeting with His disciples on the first day, prior to the Ascension (John 20:19; John 20:26); by coming back to the Church in the Holy Spirit on the first day (Pentecost was a Sunday); and by directing the apostles and the Apostolic Church to gather for worship on the first day (Acts 20:7; I Cor. 16:1,2).

Ignatius, disciple of John, is claimed to use the title "Lord's day" for Sunday in an alleged epistle to the Magnesians. However, dispute continues over the validity of this document, but most regard at least the so called "Long" versions to be forgeries.

So, what is the Lord's day? Many Bible commentaries state with certainty that John was in the Spirit on Sunday. Our long history of associating the English phrase makes it appear so, but the Greek text does not support such a conclusion. First, "the Lord's Day" does not appear anywhere else in Scripture. When Acts 20 is examined as an example of the early church meeting on Sunday, it describes the occasion as occurring on "the first day of the Week," not the Lord's Day.

Greek expresses the first day of the week or Sunday as either *mia sabbaton* (μια σαββατον) or *proto sabbaton* (προτο σαββατον), both expressions mean "the first from the Sabbath" (first day following the weekly Sabbath) or "the first of the Sabbaths" (meaning the first portion of the seven weeks that span from Passover to Pentecost). There is only one instance of *mia hemera sabbaton*, which explicitly says the first *day* of the sabbath (week).

The Greek for "the Lord's day" is τε Κυριακη ημερα or *te Kuriake hemera*, which is literally "the of-Lord day." Grammatically, this is the genitive (possessive) case. In English this can also be expressed as "the Day of the Lord" and is exactly equivalent to "the Lord's Day." This compares closely with the Hebrew phrase "day of the Lord," as used in Isaiah 2:12-21:

> "For **the day of the LORD** [Yehovah] of hosts *shall be* upon every *one that is* proud and lofty, and upon every *one that is* lifted up; and he shall be brought low: And upon all the cedars of Lebanon, *that are* high and lifted up, and upon all the oaks of Bashan, And upon all the high mountains, and upon all the hills *that are* lifted up, And upon every high tower, and upon every fenced wall, And upon all the ships of Tarshish, and upon all pleasant pictures. And the loftiness of man shall be bowed down, and the haughtiness of men shall be made low: and the LORD alone shall be exalted in that day. And the idols he shall utterly abolish. And they shall go into the holes of the rocks, and into the caves of the earth, for fear of the LORD, and for the glory of his majesty, when he ariseth to shake terribly the earth. In that day a man shall cast his idols of silver, and his idols of gold, which they made *each one* for himself to

worship, to the moles and to the bats; To go into the clefts of the rocks, and into the tops of the ragged rocks, for fear of the LORD, and for the glory of his majesty, when he ariseth to shake terribly the earth."

At least four points can be made from this passage:

1. The Day of the LORD will affects the entire earth.
2. Human pride will be brought low.
3. A great earthquake will shake the world.
4. People will seek to escape from the glory of the LORD.

These characteristics of "the day of the LORD" are applied to the second coming of Christ by New Testament authors:

1. Every eye will see Him. Revelation 1:7.
2. The mighty are humbled. Phil 2:10-11; Rev 6:14-15.
3. A great earthquake. Revelation 6:14.
4. They cry to the rocks and mountains. Revelation 6:15.

The day of the LORD is also known as "the great day of His wrath." Other texts such as Isaiah 13:9; Jeremiah 46:10; Joel 1:15, 16; 2 Peter 3:10, all speak of a day in which God brings judgment and destruction upon the earth. This is the setting in John's Revelation where the focus is on "those things which are shortly to come to pass," the climax of God's redemption. John, too, hears a voice sounding like a trumpet (John 4: 1; 8: 13; and 9: 14) as he is taken in the Spirit to a great day in the future, the Great and Terrible Day of the Lord which comes at the end of time just before the return of Christ. John was transported to that prophetic day by the power of the Spirit to experience it first hand and report to Christians of all ages what that day will be like, so we can be ready and waiting for its arrival.

Extreme Make-over

Such has been the extensive surgical history of the rest day. Truly, it has had little rest. Constantly under the knife, it has received an unrelentless series of staged cosmetic procedures in man's attempt at an extreme make-over of God's day. But in recent years there have been some consultants expressing a second opinion.

Dr. Ernest R. Palen, minister of New York's Middle Collegiate Church, suggested in 1966 that Christians re-unite with Jews in observing Saturday instead of Sunday. "It should not be too great a break for us," he said, "to observe the same Sabbath day that Jesus himself observed." *New York Times*, March 14, 1966.

In the same article, a spokesman for the National Council of Churches noted that "the loss of the traditional Sunday as a day of worship would not be catastrophic and might be healthy." He explained that "Sunday was picked (by early Christians) rather arbitrarily."

Ten years later, in the November 5, 1976 issue of *Christianity Today*, Editor Harold Lindsell also proposed that Saturday become a national day of rest. "For Protestants and Catholics, it should prove no theological hardship... there is nothing in Scripture that requires us to keep Sunday rather than Saturday as a holy day."

Indications for surgical repair clearly support the medical necessity for a restorative procedure. Today, the evidence confirms the clinical opinion from a growing number of breach restorers.

Review of Systems

A systematic review of each body system is necessary in order to form a complete survey of the presenting problem. For example, a chest infection can affect other body systems than merely the respiratory tract. Besides cough, chest pain and dyspnea (shortness of breath), pneumonia can generate many other symptoms:

- Fever and chills (general systemic effects of infection),
- Tachycardia (cardiovascular system),
- Headache (central nervous system),
- Dizziness (neurologic system),
- Nausea (gastrointestinal system),
- Myalgias (musculoskeletal system).

As Paul observed, when one member of the body suffers, the whole body is affected. We must, then, investigate each system of the body for the presence or absence of abnormality. The results of each inquiry is a record of what the patient directly reports. It is not second-hand information; it is not an account of past procedures or performance but what the patients feel and experience themselves.

We must examine the facts of recent history. "In testing theories and practices, the historic argument is ultimate." (A.H. Lewis, *A Critical History of the Sabbath and the Sunday in the Christian Church*, American Sabbath Tract Society, 1907). Events in time are really the decisions of God and occur by the guiding hand of His Providence. Therefore, our review of systems will begin with an inquiry into the traditional position of Protestant Churches on the validity and authority of God's Ten Commandment Law. Each system is here examined.

Baptist

"We believe the Scriptures teach that the law of God is the eternal and unchangeable rule of His moral government; that it is holy, just, and good; and that the inability which the Scriptures ascribe to fallen men to fulfill its precepts arises entirely from their love of sin; to deliver them from which, and to restore them through a Mediator to unfeigned obedience to the holy law, is one great end of the gospel, and. of the means of grace connected with the establishment of the visible church." *New Hampshire Confession of Faith*, Article 12, quoted in o. C. S. WALLACE, *What Baptists Believe* (1934), p. 79.

"To prove that the Ten Commandments are binding, let any person read them, one by one, and ask his own conscience as he reads, whether it would be any sin to break them. Is this, or any part of it, the liberty of the gospel? Every conscience that is not seared as with a hot iron must answer these questions in the negative... The lawgiver and the Saviour were one; and believers must be of one mind with the former as well as with the latter; but if we depreciate the law which Christ delighted to honor, and deny our obligations to obey it, how are we of His mind? Rather are we not of that mind which is enmity against God, which is not subject to the law of God, neither indeed can be?... If the law be not a rule of conduct to believers, and a perfect rule too, they are under no rule; or, which is the same thing, are lawless. But if so, they commit no sin; for where no law is there is no transgression; and in this case they have no sins to confess, either to God or to one another; nor do they stand in need of Christ as an advocate with the Father, nor of daily forgiveness through His blood. Thus it is, by disowning the law, men utterly subvert the gospel. Believers, therefore, instead of being freed from obligation to obey it, are under greater obligation to do so than any men in the world. To he exempt from this is to be without law, and of course without sin; in which case we might do without a Saviour, which is utterly subversive of all religion." American Baptist Publication Society, *Tract No. 64*, Pages 2-6.

Charles Spurgeon

"Jesus did not come to change the law, but He came to explain it, and that very fact shows that it remains; for there is no need to explain that which is abrogated... By thus explaining the law He confirmed it; He could not have meant to abolish it, or He would not have needed to expound it... That the Master did not come to alter the law is clear, because after having embodied it in His life, He willingly gave Himself up to bear its penalty, though He had never broken it, bearing the penalty for us, even as it is written, 'Christ hath redeemed us from the curse of the law, being made a curse for us.'... If the law had demanded more of us than it ought to have done, would the Lord Jesus have rendered to it the penalty which resulted from its too severe demands? I am sure He would not. But because the law asked only what it ought to ask, namely, perfect obedience, and exacted of the transgressor only what it ought to exact, namely, death as the penalty for sin– death under divine wrath–therefore the Saviour went to the tree, and there bore our sins, and purged them once for all." *Perpetuity of the Law of God*, Sermon May 21, 1882, Pages 4-7.

Methodists

"Although the law given from God by Moses as touching ceremonies and rites, doth not bind Christians, nor ought the civil precepts thereof of necessity be received in any commonwealth; yet, notwithstanding, no Christian whatsoever is free from the obedience of the commandments which are called moral." *Constitution of the Methodist Episcopal Church*, "Articles of Religion," Art. 6, in *Methodist Episcopal Church Doctrines and Discipline* (1928), p. 7.

John Wesley

"The moral law contained in the ten commandments, and enforced by the prophets, He [Christ) did not take away. It was not the design of His coming to revoke any part of this. This is the law which never can be broken, which 'stands fast as the faithful witness in heaven.' The moral law stands on an entirely different foundation from the ceremonial or ritual law.... Every part of the law must remain in force upon all mankind, and in all ages; as not depending either on time or place, or any other circumstances liable to change, but on the nature of God and the nature of man, and their unchangeable relation to each other." Wesley, John, *On the Sermon on the Mount*, Discourse 6, Sermons on Several Occasions (1810), pp. 75,76.

Uriah Smith & James White

"There are plainly two kinds of laws: one class binding on man before he fell, regulating his duty to God, and to his fellowmen; the other class, growing out of the changed condition of man after he had fallen and the plan of salvation had been introduced. If man had never fallen, it would have been his duty just the same to render supreme honor to God, and to deal justly with his fellowmen. But if he had never fallen, there never would have been any laws regulating ceremonies, sacrifices, offerings, baptism, the Lord's supper, etc. These all grow out of man's necessities in consequence of his fall. The first may be called original or primary laws; and they are, in the very nature of things, immutable and eternal; the others are derived, secondary or typical laws, and are temporary and changeable." *The Biblical Institute*, White, James, Smith, Uriah, 1878 reprint 2000 by TEACH Services, 352 pages, pp. 118-119.

Methodist Episcopal

"Ques. –What does God require of man?
Ans. –Obedience to His revealed will.
Ques. –What is the rule of our obedience?
Ans. –The moral law.

Ques. –Where is the moral law given?
Ans. –In the ten commandments.
Ques. –Are all Christians under obligation to keep the law?
Ans. –Yes."
Catechism Number 2, pp. 38, 43; Number 1, p. 18.

Presbyterian

"The moral law doth forever bind all, as well justified persons as others, to the obedience thereof; and that not only in regard of the matter contained in it, but also in respect of the authority of God the Creator who gave it. Neither doth Christ in the gospel in any way dissolve, but much strengthen, this obligation." *The Constitution of the Presbyterian Church in the United States of America*, Chapter 19, sec. 5, (1896), pp.88,89.

"The laws of the Jews are commonly divided into moral, ceremonial, and judicial. The moral laws are such as grow out of the nature of things, which cannot, therefore, be changed—such as the duty of loving God and His creatures. These cannot be abolished, as it can never be made right to hate God, or to hate our fellow men. Of this kind are the ten commandments; and these our Saviour has neither abolished nor superseded." Albert Barnes, *Notes, Explanatory and Practical, on the Gospels* (1860 edition), Vol. 1, p. 65.

John Calvin

"We must not imagine that the coming of Christ has freed us from the authority of the law; for it is the eternal rule of a devout and holy life, and must, therefore, be as unchangeable as the justice of God, which it embraced, is constant and uniform." *Commentary on a Harmony of the Gospels*, 1845 Translation by William Pringle, Volume I, p. 277.

"The law sustained no diminution of its authority, but ought always to receive from us the same veneration and obedience." *The Institutes of the Christian Religion*, (1536) ii. 7, sec. 15.

Congregational

"The law of God is and must of necessity be unchangeable and eternal." Dwight, Timothy, *Theology*, Vol. IV, p. 120.

"Through the atonement of Christ more honor is done to the law, and consequently the law is more established, than if the law had been literally executed, and all mankind had been condemned. Whatever tends most to the honor of the law, tends most to establish its authority." Jonathan Edwards, *Works of Jonathan*

Edwards, Edition of 1842, Vol. 11, p. 369. [president of Princeton University]

Dwight L. Moody

"Now men may cavil as much as they like about other parts of the Bible, but I have never met an honest man that found fault with the ten commandments. infidels may mock the Lawgiver and reject Him who has delivered us from the curse of the law, but they can't help admitting that the commandments are right. Renan said that they are for all nations, and will remain the commandments of God during all the centuries."

"The people must he made to understand that the ten commandments are still binding, and that there is a penalty attached to their violation." "The commandments of God given to Moses in the mount at Horeb are as binding today as ever they have been since the time when they were proclaimed in the hearing of the people. The Jews said the law was not given in Palestine (which belonged to Israel), but in the wilderness, because the law was for all nations." "Jesus never condemned the law and the prophets, but He did condemn those who did not obey Him. Because He gave new commandments, it does not follow that He abolished the old. Christ's explanation of them made them all the more searching." *Weighed and Wanting,* (Fleming H. Revell Co: New York, 1898) Pages 11, 16, 15.

Lutheran

"23. How many kinds of laws did God give in the Old Testament? Three kinds: 1. The ceremonial church law; 2. The civil !aw; 3. The moral law.

"24. Which of these laws is still in force?
The moral law, which is contained in the ten commandments.

"25. Cannot this law be abolished?
No; because it is founded on God's holy and righteous nature." Epitome of Pontoppidan's *Explanation of Martin Luther's Small Catechism* (1935), pp. 6, 7.

"I wonder exceedingly how it came to be imputed to me that I should reject the law of ten commandments.... Can anyone think that sin exists where there is no law? Whoever abrogates the law, must of necessity abrogate sin also." Luther, *Against the Antinomians,* Translated from Luther's Works (Weimar ed.), vol. 50, pp. 470,471.

"He who destroys the doctrine of the law, destroys at the same time political and social order. If you eject the law from the church, there will no longer be any sin recognized as such in the world; for the gospel only defines and punishes sin by reference to the law." Michelet, M, *Life of Luther* v. 4, Hazlitt's translation (2d edition: London, 1856), p. 315.

Protestants in more recent times continue to acknowledge the Biblical support for the seventh day Sabbath. Now let's explore a review of Sabbath observance by systems.

Anglican/Episcopal
John Milton
"The reason for which the [Sabbath] command [of Exodus 20:8-11] was originally given, —namely, as a memorial of God's having rested from the Creation of the World—cannot be transferred from the seventh day to the first; nor can any new motive be substituted in its place, whether the resurrection of our Lord or any other—without [first in Scripture receiving] the sanction of a divine commandment...

For if we under the gospel are to regulate the time of our public worship by the prescriptions of the Decalogue—it will be far safer to observe the seventh day, according to the express commandment of God, than on the authority of mere human conjecture to adopt the first day of the week]." *A Posthumous Treatise on the Christian Doctrine*, bk. 2, chap. 7 [*(1608-1674) the most famous poet of English literature, and author of Paradise Lost*]

Peter Heylyn
"Take which you will, either the Fathers or the moderns, and we shall find no Lord's Day instituted by any apostolical mandate, no Sabbath set on foot by them on the first day of the week"

"Neither did he (Jesus), or his disciples, ordain another Sabbath in the place of this, as if they had intended only to shift the day; and to transfer this honor to some other time. Their doctrine and their practise are directly contrary, to so new a fancy. It is true, that in some tract of time, the Church in honor of his resurrection, did set apart that day on the which he rose, to holy exercises: but this upon their own authority, and without warrant from above, that we can hear of; more then the general warrant which God gave his Church, that all things in it be done decently, and in comely order." *History of the Sabbath* (1636, London) Part 2, Ch.2, p.7

Isaac Williams
"And where are we told in the Scriptures that we are to keep the first day at all? We are commanded to keep the seventh; but we

are nowhere commanded to keep the first day... The reason why we keep the first day of the week holy instead of the seventh is for the same reason that we observe many other things, not because the Bible, but because the church has enjoined it." *Plain Sermons on the Catechism*, (1882) vol. 1, pp.334, 336.

Canon Richard Eyton

"There is no word, no hint, in the New Testament about abstaining from work on Sunday...into the rest of Sunday no divine law enters...The observance of Ash Wednesday or Lent stands exactly on the same footing as the observance of Sunday." *The Ten Commandments*, (1894, Westminster) pp. 52, 63, 65.

George Franklin Seymour, S.T.D., LL.D

"We have made the change from the seventh day to the first day, from Saturday to Sunday, on the authority of the one holy, catholic, apostolic Church of Christ." (Bishop 1877-1906) *Why We Keep Sunday*, Article 12.

William E. Gladstone

"The seventh day of the week has been deposed from its title to obligatory religious observance, and its prerogative has been carried over to the first under no direct precept of Scripture." *Later Gleanings*, p. 342 [*(1809-1898) leading British statesman, four times prime minister, member of Parliament for 62 years*]

Phillip Carrington

"The Bible commandment says on the seventh-day thou shalt rest. That is Saturday. Nowhere in the Bible is it laid down that worship should be done on Sunday." Toronto Daily Star, Oct 26, 1949 [*Anglican archbishop of Quebec speaking to an assembly of clergymen*]

Jeremy Taylor

"The Lord's day did not succeed in the place of the [Bible] Sabbath, but the... Lord's day was merely of ecclesiastical institution. It was not introduced by virtue of the fourth commandment, because they for almost three hundred years together kept that day which was in that commandment." *The Rule of Conscience, 1851*, pp. 456-548 [*(1613-1667) chaplain to the King of England, bishop and president of a Welsh college*]

Frederic William Farrar

"The Christian Church made no formal, but a gradual and almost unconscious transference of the day to the other." *The Voice from Sinai*, p. 167 [*(1831-1903) Anglican clergyman, dean of Canterbury*]

Hobart Church News, July 2, 1894.

"The observance of the first day instead of the seventh day rests on the testimony of the Catholic church, and the [Catholic] church alone."

Episcopal Explanation of the Catechism

"The day is now changed from the seventh to the first day...but as we meet with no Scriptural direction for the change, we may conclude it was done by the authority of the church."

Baptist

Dr. Edward T. Hiscox

"There was and is a command to keep holy the Sabbath day, but that Sabbath day was not Sunday. It will however be readily said, and with some show of triumph, that the Sabbath was transferred from the Seventh to the First day of the week, with all its duties, privileges and sanctions. Earnestly desiring information on the subject, which I have studied for many years, I ask, where can the record of such a transaction be found? Not in the New Testament—absolutely not. There is no scriptural evidence of the change of the Sabbath institution from the Seventh to the First day of the week...

"I wish to say that this Sabbath question, in this aspect of it, is the gravest and most perplexing question connected with Christian institutions which at present claims attention from Christian people; and the only reason that it is not a more disturbing element in Christian thought and in religious discussion is because the Christian world has settled down content on the conviction that somehow a transference has taken place at the beginning of Christian history.

"To me it seems unaccountable that Jesus, during three years' discussion with His disciples, often conversing with them upon the Sabbath question, discussing it in some of its various aspects, freeing it from it's false [Jewish traditional] glosses, never alluded to any transference of the day; also, that during forty days of His resurrection life, no such thing was intimated. Nor, so far as we know, did the Spirit, which was given to bring to their remembrance all things whatsoever that He had said unto them, deal with this question. Nor yet did the inspired apostles, in preaching the gospel, founding churches, counseling and instructing those founded, discuss or approach the subject.

"Of course I quite well know that Sunday did come into use in early Christian history as a religious day, as we learn from the

Christian Fathers and other sources. But what a pity that it comes branded with the mark of Paganism, and christened with the name of the sun-god, then adopted and sanctified by the Papal apostasy, and bequeathed as a sacred legacy to Protestantism." [New York ministers' conference, Nov. 13, 1893, reported in *New York Examiner* , Nov. 16, 1893]

William Owen Carver
"There was never any formal or authoritative change from the Jewish seventh-day Sabbath to the Christian first-day observance."

"There are in the New Testament no commands, no prescriptions, no rules, no liturgies applying to the observance of the Lord's Day...."

"There is no organic [no actual] connection between the Hebrew Sabbath and the Christian Lord's Day... It was only a short while until gentiles predominated in the [early church] Christian movement. They brought over the consciousness of various observances in the pagan religions, pre-eminently the worship of the sun—a sort of Sunday consciousness." *The Lord's Day in Our Day*, 1940, pp. 49, 52, 54. [*(1868-1954) professor of comparative religion at the Southern Baptist Theological Seminary, in Louisville, Kentucky*]

Joseph Judson Taylor
"Before the giving of the law from Sinai the obligation of the Sabbath was understood. When some of the people went out [four chapters before Sinai] to get manna, God said unto Moses: 'How long refuse ye to keep My Commandments and My Laws? The Lord hath given you the Sabbath, therefore He hath given you on the sixth day bread enough for two days' [Ex. 16]. Indeed, it may be questioned if the Law given through Moses on tables of stone disclosed any new truth ...The fourth commandment does not institute a Sabbath, nor does it sanctify a day; it simply writes the Sabbath among the immutable things of God."

"Not once did [the disciples] apply the Sabbath law to the first day of the week—that folly was left for a later age, nor did they pretend that the first day supplanted the seventh."

"The sacred name of the seventh day is Sabbath. This fact is too clear to require argument [Exodus 20:10, quoted]...On this point the plain teaching of the Word has been admitted in all ages..." *The Sabbatic Question*, 1914, pp. 14-17, 22, 24, 41. [*(1885-1930) vice-president of the Home Mission Board, Southern Baptist Convention*]

Congregationalist
Dr. R. W. Dale
"...it is quite clear that however rigidly or devotedly we may spend Sunday, we are not keeping the Sabbath... The Sabbath was founded on a specific Divine command. We can plead no such command for the obligation to observe Sunday... There is not a single line in the New Testament to suggest that we incur any penalty by violating the supposed sanctity of Sunday." *The Ten Commandments* (New York: Eaton & Mains), pp. 127-129 or (Hodder & Stoughton), p. 106-107.

Johnathan Edwards
"A further argument for the perpetuity of the Sabbath we have in Matthew 24:20, 'Pray ye that your flight be not in the winter, neither on the Sabbath day.' Christ is here speaking of the flight of the apostles and other Christians out of Jerusalem and Judea, just before their final destruction, as is manifest by the whole context, and especially by the 16th verse: 'Then let them which be in Judea flee into the mountains.' But the final destruction of Jerusalem was after the dissolution of the Jewish constitution, and after the Christian dispensation was fully set up. Yet it is plainly implied in these words of the Lord, that even then Christians were bound to a strict observance of the Sabbath." *The Works of President Edwards,* Worcester edition, 1844-1848, vol. IV, pp. 621-622.

Dr. Lyman Abbott
"The current notion that Christ and His apostles authoritatively substituted the first day for the seventh, is absolutely without any authority in the New Testament." *Christian Union,* June 26, 1890

Timothy Dwight
"...the Christian Sabbath [Sunday] is not in the Scriptures, and was not by the primitive Church called the Sabbath." *Theology: Explained and Defended* (1823), Sermon 107, vol. 3, p. 258. [*(1752-1817) president of Yale University 1795-1817*]

Disciples of Christ
Alexander Campbell
"Now there is no testimony in all the oracles of heaven that the Sabbath is changed, or that the Lord's Day came in the room of it." *Quoted in The Reporter, Washington, Pennsylvania, October 8, 1921*

"If it [the Ten Commandments] yet exist, let us observe it...And if it does not exist, let us abandon a mock observance of another day for it. 'But,' say some, 'it was changed from the seventh to the first day.' Where? when? and by whom?—No, it never was changed, nor could it be, unless creation was to be gone through again: for the reason assigned [in Genesis 2:1-3] must be changed before the observance or respect to the reason, can be changed. It is all old wives' fables to talk of the change of the Sabbath from the seventh to the first day. If it be changed, it was that august personage changed it who changes times and laws ex officio. I think his name is 'Doctor Antichrist.' " *The Christian Baptist,* February 2, 1824, vol. 1, no. 7

"Either the [Ten Commandment] Law remains in all its force, to the utmost extent of its literal requirements, or it is passed away with the Jewish ceremonies. If it yet exists, let us observe it according to law. And if it does not exist, let us abandon a mock observance of another day for it." *Address to the Readers of the Christian Baptists, part 1, Feb. 2, 1824, pp. 44-45*

"The first day of the week is commonly called the Sabbath. This is a mistake. The Sabbath of the Bible was the day just preceding the first day of the week. The first day of the week is never called the Sabbath anywhere in the entire Scriptures. It is also an error to talk about the change of the Sabbath from Saturday to Sunday. There is not in any place in the Bible any intimation of such a change." *First Day Observance* , pp. 17, 19. [*(1788-1866) Irish Protestant founded in America the Disciples of Christ Church also founder and president of Bethany College*]

Dr. D. H. Lucas
"There is no direct Scriptural authority for designating the first day 'the Lord's Day.' " *Christian Oracle,* January 23, 1890.

Lutheran
Martin Luther
"God blessed the Sabbath and sanctified it to Himself. It is moreover to be remarked that God did this to no other creature. God did not sanctify to Himself the heaven nor the earth nor any other creature. But God did sanctify to Himself the seventh day... The Sabbath therefore has, from the beginning of the world, been set apart for the worship of God." *Commentary on Genesis,* Vol. 1, Comment on Gen. 2:3, pp. 138-139 [*(1483-1546) leader of the great Sixteenth Century Reformation*]

"We have seen how gradually the impression of the Jewish Sabbath faded from the mind of the Christian Church, and how completely the newer thought underlying the observance of the first day took possession of the church. We have seen that the Christians of the first three centuries never confused one with the other, but for a time celebrated both." *The Sunday Problem*, (1923), p. 36, a study book of the United Lutheran Church.

Augsburg Confession of Faith

"They [Roman Catholics] refer to the Sabbath Day, as having been changed into the Lord's Day, contrary to the Decalogue, as it seems. Neither is there any example whereof they make more than concerning the changing of the Sabbath Day. Great, say they, is the power of the Church, since it has dispensed with one of the Ten Commandments." Article 28 written by Melanchthon, approved by Martin Luther, 1530; *The Book of Concord of the Evangelical Lutheran Church,* Henry Jacobs, editor (1911), p. 63. Also in Philip Schaff, *The Creeds of Christiandom*, 4th Edition, vol. 3, p. 64.

"They [the Catholics] allege the change of the Sabbath into the Lord's day, as it seemeth, to the Decalogue [the Ten Commandments]; and they have no example more in their mouths than the change of the Sabbath. They will needs have the Church's power to be very great, because it hath dispensed with a precept of the Decalogue." Part 2, Article 7 [written only thirteen years after Luther nailed up his theses to start the Reformation].

Augustus Neander

"The festival of Sunday, like all other festivals, was always only a human ordinance, and it was far from the intentions of the apostles to establish a Divine command in this respect, far from them, and from the early apostolic Church, to transfer the laws of the Sabbath to Sunday." *The History of the Christian Religion and Church,* Henry John Rose, translator (1843), p. 186.

John Theodore Mueller

"But they err in teaching that Sunday has taken the place of the Old Testament Sabbath and therefore must be kept as the seventh day had to be kept by the children of Israel... These churches err in their teaching, for Scripture has in no way ordained the first day of the week in place of the Sabbath. There is simply no law in the New Testament to that effect." *Sabbath or Sunday* , pp. 15, 16. [(1885-1949) *Professor of Saint Louis Seminary.*]

Andreas Rudolf Karlstadt

"When servants have worked six days, they should have the seventh day free. God says without distinction, 'Remember that you observe the seventh day'...Concerning Sunday it is known that men have instituted it...It is clear however, that you should celebrate the seventh day." *Concerning the Sabbath and Commanded Holidays,* 1524, chap. 4, pp. 23-24 [*(1480-1541) joined Luther at Wittenberg in 1517 when the German Reformation began and taught the Bible Sabbath*]

H. Gunkel

"The taking over of Sunday by the early Christians is, to my mind, an exceedingly important symptom that the early church was directly influenced by a spirit which does not originate in the gospel, nor in the Old Testament, but in a religious system foreign to it." *Zum Religions-geschichtl Verständnis des Neuen Testaments,* 1903 p. 76.

Lutheran Free Church
George Sverdrup

"For when there could not be produced one solitary place in the Holy Scriptures which testified that either the Lord Himself or the apostles had ordered such a transfer of the Sabbath to Sunday, then it was not easy to answer the question. Who has transferred the Sabbath, and who has had the right to do it?" *En Ny Dag (A New Day),* in *Sondagen og dens Halligholdelse (Sunday and its Observance),* 1879 [*(1848-1907) Norwegian-born founder of the Lutheran Free Church and principal of the Augsburg Seminary, Minnesota*]

Methodist
Harris Franklin Rall

"Take the matter of Sunday. There are indications in the New Testament as to how the church came to keep the first day of the week as its day of worship, but there is no passage telling Christians to keep that day, or to transfer the Jewish Sabbath to that day." *Christian Advocate,* July 2, 1942, p.26.

John Wesley

"But, the moral law contained in the ten commandments, and enforced by the prophets, he [Christ] did not take away. It was not the design of his coming to revoke any part of this. This is a law which never can be broken... Every part of this law must remain in force upon all mankind, and in all ages; as not depending either on time or place, or any other circumstances liable to change, but on the nature of God and the nature of man, and their unchangeable relation to each other." *The Works of the Rev. John Wesley, A.M.,* John Emory, ed. (New York: Eaton & Mains), Sermon 25, vol. 1, p. 221.

Adam Clarke
"There is no intimation here that the Sabbath was done away, or that its moral use superseded, by the introduction of Christianity. I have shown elsewhere that, 'Remember the Sabbath day, to keep it holy,' is a command of perpetual obligation." *The New Testament of our Lord and Saviour Jesus Christ,* Vol. 2, p. 524 [*(1760-1832) Irish Wesleyan minister, writer, and three times Methodist conference president*]

Amos Binney
"It is true that there is no positive command for infant baptism. Nor is there any for keeping holy the first day of the week. Many believe that Christ changed the Sabbath. But, from His own words, we see that He came for no such purpose. Those who believe that Jesus changed the Sabbath base it only on a supposition." *Theological Compendium,* 1902 edition, pp. 180-181, 171 [*(1802-1878), Methodist minister and presiding elder, also wrote a Methodist New Testament Commentary*]

Taylor Lewis
"If we had no other passage than of Genesis 2:3, there would be no difficulty in deducing from it a precept for the universal observance of the Sabbath to be devoted to God, as holy time, by all of that race for whom the earth and its nature were specially prepared. The first men must have known it. The words 'He hallowed it,' can have no meaning otherwise. They would be a blank unless in reference to some who were required to keep it holy." Translator's note on Gen. 2:3, in John Peter Lange's, *A Commentary: Genesis,* 1868, p. 197 [*(1802- 1877) ancient language and literature professor at Union College and NewYork City University*]

Harris Franklin Rall
"Take the matter of Sunday. There are indications in the new testament as to how the church came to keep the first day of the week as its day of worship, but there is no passage telling Christians to keep that day or to transfer the Jewish Sabbath to that day." *Christian Advocate,* July 2, 1942 p. 26

Dwight L. Moody
"The Sabbath was binding in Eden, and it has been in force ever since. This fourth commandment begins with the word 'remember,' showing that the Sabbath already existed when God Wrote the law on the tables of stone at Sinai. How can men claim that this one commandment has been done away with when they will admit that the other nine are still binding?"

"I honestly believe that this commandment [the Sabbath commandment] is just as binding today as it ever was. I have talked with men who have said that it has been abrogated [abolished], but they have never been able to point to any place in the Bible where God repealed it. When Christ was on earth, He did nothing to set it aside; He freed it from the traces under which the scribes and Pharisees had put it, and gave it its true place. 'The Sabbath was made for man, not man for the Sabbath' [Mark 2:27]. It is just as practicable and as necessary for men today as it ever was—in fact, more than ever, because we live in such an intense age." *Weighed and Wanting* (Fleming H. Revell Co.: New York), pp. 47, 48. [*(1837-1899) the most famous evangelist of his time, founder of the Moody Bible Institute*]

Presbyterian
T. C. Blake, D.D.
"The Sabbath is a part of the Decalogue—the Ten Commandments. This alone forever settles the question as to the perpetuity of the institution...Until, therefore, it can be shown that the whole moral law has been repealed, the Sabbath will stand...The teaching of Christ confirms the perpetuity of the Sabbath." *Theology Condensed*, pp.474, 475.

Dr. Archibald Hodge
"God instituted the Sabbath at the creation of man, setting apart the seventh day for that purpose, and imposed its observance as a universal and perpetual moral obligation upon the race." Tract No. 175, Presbyterian Board of Publication, pp. 3-4.

Thomas Chalmers
"For the permanency of the Sabbath, however, we might argue its place in the Decalogue, where it stands enshrined on a tablet that is immutable and everlasting." *Sermons*, 1817, vol. 1, pp. 51-52.

William Dool Killen
"In the interval between the days of the apostles and the conversion of Constantine, the Christian commonwealth changed its aspect. The Bishop of Rome—a personage unknown to the writers of the New Testament—meanwhile rose into prominence, and at length took precedence of all other churchmen. Rites and ceremonies of which neither Paul nor Peter ever heard, crept silently into use, and then claimed the rank of divine institution."

"The Great Teacher never intimated that the Sabbath was a ceremonial ordinance to cease with the Mosaic ritual. It was instituted when our first parents were in Paradise; and the precept enjoining its remembrance, being a portion of the

Decalogue, is of perpetual obligation. Hence, instead of regarding it as a merely Jewish institution, Christ declares that it was made for MAN. or, in other words, that it was designed for the benefit of the whole human family. Instead of anticipating its extinction along with the ceremonial law, He speaks of its existence after the downfall of Jerusalem [in A.D. 70, 39 years after the crucifixion]. When He announces the calamities connected with the ruin of the holy city, He instructs His followers to pray that the urgency of the catastrophe may not deprive them of the comfort of the Sabbath rest. 'Pray ye,' said He, 'that your flight be not in the winter, neither on the Sabbath-day.' " Matt. 24.201" *The Ancient Church*, 1883, xv-xvi pp. 188-189 [*professor of ecclesiastical history in the (Protestant) Irish Assembly's College in Belfast, Ireland*]

Others
Sir William Dornville
"Centuries of the Christian era passed away before Sunday was observed by the Christian church as a sabbath. History does not furnish us with a single proof or indication that it was at any time so observed previous to the sabbatical edict of Constantine in A.D. 321." *The Sabbath: or an Examination of Six Texts*, vol. 1, p. 291.

Nicholas Summerbell
"The Roman Church...reversed the Fourth Commandment by doing away with the Sabbath of God's word, and instituting Sunday as a holiday." *History of the Christian Church*, 3rd ed., 1873, p. 415 [*(1816-1889) president of Union Christian College, Indiana*]

William Prynne
"The seventh-day Sabbath was solemnized [i.e. observed] by Christ, the Apostles and the primitive Christians—until the Council of Laodicea did, in a manner, quite abolish the observance of it. The Council (A.D. 364) first settled the observance of the Lord's Day."

"It is certain that Christ Himself, His apostles, and the primitive Christians for some good space of time, did constantly observe the Seventh-day Sabbath." *"Dissertations on the Lord's Day."* page 33. [*17th century Puritan*]

Charles Buck
"Sabbath in the Hebrew language signifies rest, and is the seventh day of the week...and it must be confessed that there is no law in the New Testament concerning the first day." *A*

Theological Dictionary, art. "Sabbath," p. 403 [*(1771-1815) was a British Independent minister and author*]

Henry Morehouse Taber
"Why will not Christian people investigate and find out for themselves (which they easily can), that the keeping of Sunday as a 'holy Sabbath day,' is wholly without warrant?

"I challenge any priest or minister of the Christian religion, to show me the slightest authority for the religious observance of Sunday. And, if such cannot be shown by them, why is it that they are constantly preaching about Sunday as a holy day? Are they not open to the suspicion of imposing upon the confidence and credulity of their hearers? Surely they are deliberately and knowingly practicing deception upon those who look to them for candor and for truth, unless they can give satisfactory reasons for teaching that Sunday is a sacred day. There never was, and is not now, any such 'satisfactory reasons.' No student of the Bible has ever brought to light a single verse, line or word, which can, by any possibility, be construed into a warrant for the religious observance of Sunday." *Faith or Fact,* 1897, p. 114. [*(1825-1897) American Businessman, banker, religious liberal, and promoter of public educational buildings*]

"Quotations from the writings of the 'Church Fathers,' and others familiar with Church history, support this statement, and include the names of Tertullian, Eusebius, Ireneus, Victorinus, Theodoretus, Origen, Chrysostom, Jerome, Luther, Melanchthon, Zwingle, Knox, Tyndale, Grotius, Neander, Mosheim, Heylyn, Frith, Milton, Priestly, [and] Domville. John Calvin had so little respect for the day that he could be found playing bowls most any Sunday.

"The claim that Sunday takes the place of Saturday, and that because the Jews were supposed to be commanded to keep the SEVENTH day of the week holy, THEREFORE that the FIRST day of the week should be so kept by Christians, —is so utterly absurd as to be hardly worth considering."

"Here is the church of Christ, called out of Roman Catholicism in the sixteenth century to take its stand on "the Bible and the Bible only," professing loyalty to God's Book, loyalty to God's law, loyalty to God's Sabbath, loyalty to all God's truth, and yet still observing a day that the Bible never once commands to be kept, and altogether discarding the day the Bible declares to be holy." Haynes, Carlyle B., *From Sabbath to Sunday,* p. 37.

Historians

John Dowling

"There is scarcely anything which strikes the mind of the careful student of ancient ecclesiastical history with greater surprise than the comparatively early period at which many of the corruptions of Christianity, which are embodied in the Roman system, took their rise; yet it is not to be supposed that when the first originators of many of these unscriptural notions and practices planted those germs of corruption, they anticipated or even imagined they would ever grow into such a vast and hideous system of superstition and error as is that of popery." *History of Romanism,* 13th Edition, p. 65.

Antoine Villien

"It would be an error to attribute ['the sanctification of Sunday'] to a definite decision of the Apostles. There is no such decision mentioned in the Apostolic documents [the New Testament]." *A History of the Commandments of the Church,* 1915, p. 23.

McClintock and Strong

"It must be confessed that there is no law in the New Testament concerning the first day." *Cyclopedia of Biblical, Theological and Ecclesiastical Literature,* Vol. 9, p. 196.

William D. Killen

"Rites and ceremonies, of which neither Paul nor Peter ever heard, crept silently into use, and then claimed the rank of divine institutions. [Church] officers for whom the primitive disciples could have found no place, and titles which to them would have been altogether unintelligible, began to challenge attention, and to be named apostolic." *The Ancient Church,* p. xvi.

W. Rordorf

"Until well into the second century [a hundred years after Christ] we do not find the slightest indication in our sources that Christians marked Sunday by any kind of abstention from work." *Sunday: The History of the Day of Rest and Worship in the Earliest Centuries of the Chrisitan Church,* Philadelphia, 1968, p. 157.

Edward Brerewood

"The ancient Sabbath did remain and was observed...by the Christians of the Eastern Church [in the area near Palestine] above three hundred years after our Saviour's death." *A Learned Treatise of the Sabbath,* Oxford: 1630, p. 77.

Walter Woodburn Hyde

"Remains of the struggle [between the religion of Christianity and the religion of Mithraism] are found in two institutions adopted from its rival by Christianity in the fourth century, the two Mithraic sacred days: December 25, 'dies natalis solis' [birthday of the sun], as the birthday of Jesus,—and Sunday, 'the venerable day of the Sun,' as Constantine called it in his edict of 321." *Paganism to Christianity in the Roman Empire*, 1946, p. 60.

p. 257.

"Modern Christians who talk of keeping Sunday as a 'holy' day, as in the still extant 'Blue Laws,' of colonial America, should know that as a 'holy' day of rest and cessation from labor and amusements Sunday was unknown to Jesus...It formed no tenant [teaching] of the primitive Church and became 'sacred' only in the course of time. Outside the church its observance was legalized for the Roman Empire through a series of decrees starting with the famous one of Constantine in 321, an edict due to his political and social ideas."

p. 261.

"This [Constantine's Sunday decree of March 321] is the 'parent' Sunday law making it a day of rest and release from labor. For from that time to the present there have been decrees about the observance of Sunday which have profoundly influenced European and American society. When the Church became a part of State under the Christian emperors, Sunday observance was enforced by civil statutes, and later when the Empire was past, the Church in the hands of the papacy enforced it by ecclesiastical and also by civil enactments."

Wilhelm Augustus Johann Neander

"The festival of Sunday, like all other festivals was always only a human ordinance, and it was far from the intentions of the apostles to establish a Divine command in this respect, far from them, and from the early apostolic church, to transfer the laws of the Sabbath to Sunday." *The History of the Christian Religion and Church*, 1843, p. 186.

William L. Gildea

"The [Catholic] Church took the pagan buckler of faith against the heathen. She took the pagan Roman Pantheon [the Roman], temple to all the gods, and made it sacred to all the martyrs; so it stands to this day. She took the pagan Sunday and made it the Christian Sunday...The Sun was a foremost god with heathendom. Balder the beautiful: the White God, the old

Scandinavians called him. The sun has worshipers at this very hour in Persia and other lands...Hence the Church would seem to have said, 'Keep that old pagan name. It shall remain consecrated, sanctified.' And thus the pagan Sunday, dedicated to Balder, became the Christian Sunday, sacred to Jesus. The sun is a fitting emblem of Jesus. The Fathers often compared Jesus to the sun; as they compared Mary to the moon." "Paschale Gaudium," in *The Catholic World*, p. 58, March 1894.

Authur Weigall

"The Church made a sacred day of Sunday...largely because it was the weekly festival of the sun;—for it was a definite Christian policy to take over the pagan festivals endeared to the people by tradition, and give them a Christian significance." *The Paganism in Our Christianity*, 1928, p. 145.

M. E. Walsh

"Is it not strange that Sunday is almost universally observed when the Sacred Writings do not endorse it? Satan, the great counterfeiter, worked through the 'mystery of iniquity' to introduce a counterfeit Sabbath to take the place of the true Sabbath. Sunday stands side by side with Ash Wednesday, Palm Sunday, Holy (or Maundy) Thursday, Good Friday, Easter Sunday, Whitsunday, Corpus Christi, Assumption Day, All Soul's Day, Christmas Day, and a host of other ecclesiastical feast days too numerous to mention. This array of Roman Catholic feasts and fast days are all man made. None of them bears the divine credentials of the Author of the Inspired Word."

A. R. Fausset

"Sun worship was the earliest idolatry."
Fausset Bible Dictionary, Zondervan, 1984, p. 666.

Gaston H. Halsberge

"Sun worship was one of the oldest components of the Roman religion." *The Cult of Sol Invictus*, 1972, p. 26.

Franz F. V. M. Cummont

" 'Babylon, the mother of harlots,' derived much of her teaching from pagan Rome and thence from Babylon. Sun worship—that led her to Sunday keeping,—was one of those choice bits of paganism that sprang originally from the heathen lore of ancient Babylon: The solar theology of the 'Chaldeans' had a decisive effect upon the final development of Semitic paganism... [It led to their] seeing the sun the directing power of the cosmic system. All the Baals were thence forward turned into suns; the sun itself being the mover of the other stars—like it eternal and 'unconquerable'... Such was the final form reached by the religion of the pagan Semites, and following them, by that of the Romans... when they raised 'Sol Invictus' [the Invincible Sun] to the rank of supreme divinity in the empire." *Astrology and Religion Among the Greeks and Romans*, p. 55.

Will Durant

"When Christianity conquered Rome, the ecclesiastical structure of the pagan church, the title and the vestments of the 'pontifex maximus,' the worship to the 'Great Mother' goddess and a multitude of comforting divinities...the joy or solemnity of old festivals, and the pageantry of immemorial ceremony, passed like material blood into the new religion—and captive Rome conquered her conqueror. The reins and skills of government were handed down by a dying empire to a virile papacy." *Caesar and Christ*, p. 672.

H. G. Guiness

"The power of the Caesars lived again in the universal dominion of the popes." *Romanism and the Reformation*

Joseph Faa Di Bruno

"Like two sacred rivers flowing from paradise, the Bible and divine Tradition contain the Word of God, the precious gems of revealed truth. Though these two divine streams are in themselves, on account of their divine origin, of equal sacredness, and are both full of revealed truths, still, of the two, Tradition [the sayings of popes and councils] is to us more clear and safe." *Catholic Belief*, 1884, p. 33.

Chamber's Encyclopedia, article, "Sabbath"

"Unquestionably the first law, either ecclesiastical or civil, by which the Sabbatical observance of that day is known to have been ordained, is the edict of Constantine, A.D. 321."

Phillip Schaff

The First Sunday Law of Constantine I (reigned 306-337):

"On the Venerable Day of the Sun ['Venerable die Solis'—the sacred day of the Sun] let the magistrates and people residing in cities rest, and let all workshops be closed. In the country, however, persons engaged in agriculture may freely and lawfully continue their pursuits; because it often happens that another day is not so suitable for grain-sowing or for vine-planting; lest by neglecting the proper moment for such operations the bounty of heaven should be lost—given the 7th day of March [A.D. 321], Crispus and Constantine being consuls each of them for the second time." *Codex Justianianus*, lib. 3, tit. 12,3; trans. in *History of the Christian Church*, Vol. 3, p. 380.

James Efird
"As far as I know, there is no verse which specifies that Sunday is the day for Christians to observe the Sabbath." professor of biblical interpretation at Duke University Divinity School in North Carolina.

Vincent J. Kelly
"Constantine's decree marked the beginning of a long, though intermittent series of imperial decrees in support of Sunday rest." *Forbidden Sunday and Feast-Day Occupations*, 1943, p. 29.

H. G. Heggtveit
"Constantine labored at this time untiringly to unite the worshipers of the old and the new into one religion. All his laws and contrivances are aimed at promoting this amalgamation of means melt together a purified heathenism and a moderated Christianity... Of all his blending and melting together of Christianity and heathenism, none is more easy to see through than this making of his Sunday law: The Christians worshiped their Christ, the heathen their sun-god [so they should now be combined]." *Illustreret Kirkehistorie*, 1895, p. 202.

Pope Sylvester
"If every Sunday is to be observed by Christians on account of the resurrection, then every Sabbath on account of the burial is to be regarded in execration [cursing] of the Jews." quoted by S. R. E. Humbert, "Adversus Graecorum Calumnias," in J. P. Migne, *Patrologie*, p. 143 [*pope (314-337 AD) when Constantine I was Emperor*]

Bishop Eusebius
"All things whatsoever that were prescribed for the [Bible] Sabbath, we have transferred them to the Lord's day, as being more authoritative and more highly regarded and first in rank, and more honorable than the Jewish Sabbath." quoted in J. P. Migne, *Patrologie*, p. 23, 1169-1172 [*Eusebius of Caesarea was a high-ranking Catholic leader during Constantine's lifetime*].

E. M. Chalmers
"As we have already noted, excepting for the Roman and Alexandrian Christians, the majority of Christians were observing the seventh-day Sabbath at least as late as the middle of the fifth century [A.D. 450]. The Roman and Alexandrian

Christians were among those converted from heathenism. They began observing Sunday as a merry religious festival in honor of the Lord's resurrection, about the latter half of the second century A.D. However, they did not try to teach that the Lord or His apostles commanded it. In fact, no ecclesiastical writer before Eusebius of Caesarea in the fourth century even suggested that either Christ or His apostles instituted the observance of the first day of the week.

"These Gentile Christians of Rome and Alexandria began calling the first day of the week 'the Lord's day.' This was not difficult for the pagans of the Roman Empire who were steeped in sun worship to accept, because they [the pagans] referred to their sun-god as their 'Lord.' " *How Sunday Came into the Christian Church*, p. 3.

Socrates Scholasticus

"Although almost all churches throughout the world celebrate the sacred mysteries on the Sabbath every week, yet the Christians of Alexandria and at Rome, on account of some ancient tradition, have ceased to do this." *Ecclesiastical History*, Book 5, chap. 22 [*written shortly after A.D. 439, 100 years after Constantine's Sunday Law*]

Hermias Sozomen

"The people of Constantinople, and almost everywhere, assemble together on the Sabbath, as well as on the first day of the week, which custom is never observed at Rome or at Alexandria." *Ecclesiastical History*, vii, 19, in *A Select Library of Nicene and Post-Nicene Fathers*, 2nd Series, Vol. 2, p. 390 [*soon after A.D. 415*]

Lyman Coleman

"Down even to the fifth century the observance of the Jewish Sabbath was continued in the Christian church, but with a rigor and solemnity gradually diminishing until it was wholly discontinued." *Ancient Christianity Exemplified in the Private, Domestic, Social and Civil Life of the Primitive Church*, chap. 26, sec. 2, 1853, p. 527.

A History of the Councils of the Church, Vol. 2, p. 316.

"Contantine's [five Sunday Law] decrees marked the beginning of a long though intermittent series of imperial decrees in support of Sunday rest."

Hutton Webster
"What began, however, as a pagan ordinance, ended as a Christian regulation; and a long series of imperial decrees, during the fourth, fifth, and sixth, centuries, enjoined with increasing stringency abstinence from labor on Sunday." *Rest Days*, pp. 122-123, 270.

Council of Laodicea, c. A.D. 337, Canon 29
"Christians shall not Judaize and be idle on Saturday [in the original: 'sabbato'—shall not be idle on the Sabbath], but shall work on that day; but the Lord's day they shall especially honour, and as being Christians, shall, if possible, do no work on that day. If, however, they are found Judaizing, they shall by shut out ['anathema,' excommunicated] from Christ." quoted in C. J. Hefele, *A History of the Councils of the Church,* Vol. 2, p. 316. [*the first Sunday Law decree of a Christian council, about 16 years after Constantine's first Sunday Law of A.D. 321*]

Priest Vincent J. Kelly
"The keeping of the Sunday rest arose from the custom of the people and the constitution of the [Catholic] Church... Tertullian was probably the first to refer to a cessation of affairs on the Sun day; the Council of Laodicea issued the first counciliar legislation for that day; Constantine I issued the first civil legislation." *Forbidden Sunday and Feast-Day Occupations*, p. 203 [*a thesis presented to the Catholic University of America*].

James T. Ringgold
"About 590, Pope Gregory, in a letter to the Roman people, denounced as the prophets of Antichrist those who maintained that work ought not to be done on the seventh day." *The Law of Sunday*, p. 267.

Martin J. Scott
"Now the [Catholic] Church... instituted, by God's authority, Sunday as the day of worship. The same Church, by the same divine authority, taught the doctrine of Purgatory... We have, therefore, the same authority for Purgatory as we have for Sunday." *Things Catholics Are Asked about,* 1927, p. 236.

Apostasy
John Dowling
"There is scarcely anything which strikes the mind of the careful student of ancient ecclesiastical history with greater surprise than the comparatively early period at which many of the

corruptions of Christianity, which are embodied in the Romish system, took their rise; yet it is not to be supposed that when the first originators of many of these unscriptural notions and practices planted those germs of corruption, they anticipated or even imagined they would ever grow into such a vast and hideous system of superstition and error, as is that of popery... Each of the great corruptions of the latter ages took its rise in a manner which it would be harsh to say was deserving of strong reprehension... The worship of images, the invocation of saints, and the superstition of relics, were but expansions of the natural feelings of veneration and affection cherished toward the memory of those who had suffered and died for the truth." *History of Romanism: From the Earliest Corruptions of Christianity to the Present Time*, Book ii. chap. i. sect. 1 (Edward Walker: New York), 1845.

Whitaker, Treacher and Arnot

"In Justin Martyr's time, within fifty years of the apostolic age, the cup was mixed with water, and a portion of the elements sent to the absent. The bread, which at first was sent only to the sick, was, in the time of Tertullian and Cyprian, carried home by the people and locked up as a divine treasure for their private use. At this time, too, the ordinance of the supper was given to infants of the tenderest age, and was styled the sacrifice of the body of Christ. The custom of praying for the dead, Tertullian states, was common in the second century, and became the universal practice of the following ages; so that it came in the fourth century to be reckoned a kind of heresy to deny the efficacy of it. By this time the invocation of saints, the superstitious use of images, of the sign of the cross, and of consecrated oil, were become established practices, and pretended miracles were confidently adduced in proof of their supposed efficacy. Thus did that mystery of iniquity, which was already working in the time of the apostles, speedily after their departure, spread its corruptions among the professors of Christianity." *The Modern Sabbath Examined*, London: 1832, pp. 123, 124.

Rose's Neander p. 184.

"And yet, perhaps, religious images made their way from domestic life into the churches, as early as the end of the third century; and the walls of the churches were painted in the same way."

Roger Williams 1671
The first Sabbatarian church in America was established in Rhode
Island in 1671 by Roger Williams who had been banished from the
Massachusetts colony, in 1636. Charged with not keeping the
Sabbath, Williams observed that there was no scriptural support for
"abolishing the 7th day." Instead he indicted his critics: "You know
yourselves do not keep the Sabbath, that is the 7th day."

Williams, an outspoken antagonist of the Puritan theocracy in
Massachusetts, founded a safe haven in the wilderness, a refuge for
the oppressed of all creeds, a "shelter to persons distressed for
conscience" on land purchased from the natives which he named
"Providence."

Notably, he also introduced the Biblically based practice of baptism
by immersion. LeRoy E. Froom. *The Prophetic Faith of Our Fathers*.
The Review and Herald Publishing Association, 1946, p. 48-50.

In the past century we have witnessed a dramatic change in the
Sabbath review of systems. From a system-wide support of the
seventh-day by most protestant churches we now witness their
rejection of not only the Lord's original day of rest but the Ten
Commandment as well.

"...never before in the history of Christianity has the Sabbath been
attacked by those who previously had championed its observance."
Bacchiocchi, *The Sabbath Under Crossfire*, Chapter 3.

Physical Exam: Inspection

Identifying Landmarks

Visible Patterns: Sacred or Superstitious?

Much can be learned by a simple visual inspection of the patient. Gross deformities, missing limbs, asymmetry, discolorations, and distribution of normal features are examples of information gleaned by simply looking. From the earliest of times, man has observed certain facts from this first level of physical examination.

- The sun through our solar orbit gives us the yearly cycle.
- we get the monthly cycle from the moon and its lunar orbit.

Then why a seven day week?

There appears to be a break in the linear and logical progression of astronomical phenomena and the major units of conventional time. Is seven just a lucky number? Or is it a favorite with the Deity? It does appear that numbers in Scripture have particular significance. The number seven seems to be associated with Spiritual Perfection. In Hebrew, *sheba* (seven) means "full, satisfied." As the seventh or last in a series it marks the end or completion, and thus gives the sense of rest.

"In the beginning God created the heavens and the earth"

בְּרֵאשִׁית בָּרָא אֱלֹהִים אֵת הַשָּׁמַיִם וְאֵת הָאָרֶץ׃

The first verse in Scripture is composed of seven Hebrew words and 28 (4x7) letters. The first three Hebrew words translated "In the beginning God created" contain 14 letters (7 x 2 = 14). The last four Hebrew words "the heavens and the earth" have 14 letters. The fourth and fifth words have 7 letters. The sixth and seventh words have 7 letters. The three key words: God, heaven and earth have 14 letters. The number of letters in the four remaining words is also 14. The Hebrew numeric value of the first, middle and last letters is 133 (7 x 19). The Hebrew numeric value of the first and last letters of all seven words is 1393 (7 x 199).

Proverbs 9:1 speaks of the seven pillars of wisdom
Proverbs 26:25 seven abominations of the hypocrite's heart
Matthew 18:22 Jesus said to forgive 70 x 7 times

Revelation mentions 7 churches receiving 7 promises,
7 seals, 7 angels with 7 trumpets, 7 candlesticks, 7 stars,
7 spirits of God, 7 thunders, 7 heads, 7 crowns, 7 last plagues,
and 7 sickles.

Passover started on the 14th day (7 x 2) of the first month
  It was kept for 7 days.
7 weeks later the Feast of Pentecost/Weeks (7 x 7)
  It was celebrated for 7 days.
The Day of Atonement occurred in the 7th month
  On it the blood was sprinkled 7 times before the veil
Every seven years was a Sabbatical year of release
  Debts were canceled and the land rested.
Every seven Sabbatical years brought the year of Jubilee
  All land returned to the original owners.

7 pairs of clean animals entered the ark
7 days after Noah entered the ark, the rains began
7 days after the raven, Noah sent forth a dove
7 fat and skinny cows and ears were dreamed by Pharaoh
7 times Elijah prayed for rain on Mt Carmel
7 times Naaman dipped in the Jordan river
7 priests with 7 horns marched 7 days around Jericho
7 questions are asked of Jonah by the mariners
7 years Nebuchadnezzar lived as a beast
7 times the priest sprinkled blood on the ark on the 7th month
7 miracles are listed in the Gospel of John
7 miracles are recorded as performed on the Sabbath day
7 parables are listed in Matthew 13
7 gifts of the Spirit in Romans 12
7 characteristics of wisdom in James 3
7 deacons were chosen by the church
7 elements of unity in Ephesians 4:4-6
7 "better" things and 7 "eternal" things in Hebrews
7 graces in 2 Peter 1
7 clean pairs of animals went into the ark
7 phrases in the Lord's prayer (1st 3 relate to God, last 4 to man)
Just as in the 10 Commandments 1st 4 pertain to God, last 6 to man
7 times Christ spoke from the cross
7 hours He hung there: 6 in agony, 1 in death

Luke's genealogy lists 77 names
  with God at one end, Jesus at the other.
Lamech, grandson of Enoch the seventh patriarch, lived 777 years.

Jesus is a human who is also the perfect Son of God.
The Word became flesh, the Creator became the creature
  and entered our dimensions of time and space.
It is on the Sabbath that we enter God's time and space.
  Where His grace and truth create us anew in His image.

It certainly appears that 7 is the identifying signature of God.

Contralaterally: On the other hand

"...the seventh number is oft used in Scripture to signify the vilest and most execrable things."   Peter Heylyn; *The History of the Sabbath*, The Second Edition, Revised. London, 1636. p. 36

Heylyn lists a number of examples to prove his point:

> 7 devils were cast out of Mary Magdalene
> 7 evil spirits return to the man in Christ's parable
> 7 last plagues ravage the earth
> 7 vials of God's wrath are poured out
> 7 headed beast bears the whore
> 7 mountains are where the whore sits

This is not surprising because seven represents perfectly full, complete—not good. There can, after all, be perfect goodness *and* perfect evil.   But seven overwhelmingly dominates   the positive aspects of perfection within the realm of Biblical Scripture. And as the seventh of a series following six it uniquely identifies the sabbatical pattern of redemption, release and restoration.

Redemption, Release, Restoration

6 days God created	7th He rested
6 days Moses waits at Sinai's base	7th he climbs the mountain
6 days follow Matt 6:28	7th Jesus was transfigured
6 years Joash hid in the Temple	7th year he was crowned
6 hours Christ suffers on cross	7th hour He rests in death
6 thousand years of sin on earth	7th millennium rest

Theologically, it is valid to conclude that the seventh-day Sabbath observance is a sign of a trusting relationship with God. Of course, on a simple level, it has to do with obedience. But since the choice of 7 appears arbitrary, and the other Commandments make sense on their own standing, to honor the Sabbath must express confidence in God by faith. Actually, Sabbath keeping is the antithesis of legalism. It is the symbolic epitome of righteousness by faith, not works.

But the appeal to seven-significance extends beyond the bounds of Scripture. Though verging on mystical veneration, a number of

sources make reference to a vast array of naturally occurring phenomena that feature the number seven.

For example, many gestational periods are in multiples of seven:
- Mouse & Chicken – 21 days (7 x 3)
- Rat & Rabbit – 28 days (7 x 4)
- Duck 42 (7 x 6), Cat 56 (7 x 8), Dog 63 (7 x 9),
- Lion in 98 (7 x 7 x 2), Sheep 147 (7 x 7 x 3) days
- Humans 280 days (7 x 40)

Eggs from wasp and bee species hatch in seven half-days.
Eggs of other insect species hatch in multiples of seven whole days.

The diatonic musical scale is based on seven notes: ABCDEFG.
The octave reaches to an eighth note—a repetition of the first.
There are seven colors in the rainbow:
          Red, orange, yellow, green, blue, indigo, violet
Indian mythology features a great seven-stringed lyre the size of our
planet called the cosmic heptachord. This was considered to be a
symbol of cosmic harmony.

Both Greek and Roman cultures favored the number seven. Rome
was built on seven hills, there were seven reeds in the pipes of Pan
and seven strings in the lyre of Helios, the sun god.

In geometry, only seven circles of the same size can group perfectly
without overlap or gap:

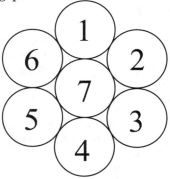

Six

Now consider the number of man: 6
Man is a carbon-based life form
(6th element, but must have 7th element, oxygen to live)
Man was created on the 6th day
6 days are given for man to labor
6th Commandment relates to the worst sin of murder
6th phrase in the Lords prayer deals with sin
6 times Jesus was asked for a sign
Noah was 600 years old when the Flood came
Israelites numbered about 600,000 men in Exodus 12:37
Pharaoh pursued them with 600 of his best chariots Exodus 14:7
6 cities of refuge (Jesus is the 7th)
6 water jugs in Jesus' first miracle were filled by men
In the 6th hour of Jesus hanging on the cross, darkness covered the land.

Human time is immersed in the number 6:
60 seconds in a minute	6 x 10
60 minutes in an hour	6 x 10
24 hours in a day	6 x 4
30 days in a month	6 x 5
12 months in a year	6 x 2

The original biblical calendar was 360 days
Circles are divided into 360 degrees
12 inches in a foot
3 feet in a yard
6 x 6 = 36 and factorial 36! (the sum of all digits between 1-36) = 666

Solomon received 666 talents of gold in one year
Goliath was 6 cubits tall, his spear weighted 600 shekels, and he wore 6 pieces of armor (Ephesians 6:14-18 lists 7 pieces for the Christian)
Nebuchadnezzar made an image 60 cubits high, 6 cubits wide.
Music for bowing to his image was played by 6 instruments.

Deut. 8:8; Numbers 11:5 list 6 foods of Egypt:
> fish, cucumbers, melons, leeks, onions, garlic

In Hosea 2:5 Israel's false lovers bring her 6 things:
> bread, water, wool, flax, oil, drink

Hosea 2:8,9 God gives His people 7 things:
> corn, silver, gold, wool, flax, oil, wine

Man alone = 6
Man + Jesus Christ = 7, complete and restored.

Contrast Study
This contrast and comparison between the numbers six and seven is a valuable tool in clinical examination. Physicians frequently will compare a symptomatic limb (either by simple visual inspection or X-ray imaging) with the opposite which serves as a "normal" control. Differences are often enhanced by taking two views, before and after using a contrast agent.

The contrast between six and seven is unmistakable. The number seven appears throughout scripture as the distinctive signature of God. Beginning with creation week, which was punctuated by a seventh-day of rest and release from labor, Sabbath becomes a dominant concept as it expands into multiple sabbatical intervals. The common motif in each is not only rest, but restoration, liberation, freedom and release.

Seventh day	**Sabbath**, release from work and labor
Seventh week	**Pentecost**, Sabbath of Sabbaths
Seventh month	**Atonement**, release from sin
Seventh year	**Land Sabbath**, release of slaves
Seventh Sabbatical	**Jubilee**, release of debt, restored estates
Seventh decade	**Lifetime**, Psalm 90:10
Seventh lifetime	**Probation**, Daniel 9:24 (7 x 70)
Seventh Millennium	**New Earth** restored, sin no more

Every seventh day was a release from work and labor.
Every seventh year slaves were released. Exodus 21:1.
Every seventh sabbatical year opened the year of Jubilee when all land was returned to the original owners and all debts were erased.

Jubilee: the Super Sabbath
The term jubilee was first used by Moses in the details he provided in his five volume epic work, the Pentateuch. The jubilee was the culmination of a trilogy of Sabbath concepts, the climax of rest, release and restoration.

Beginning in the beginning, God established the Sabbath as His holy day of rest and celebration of a perfect creation. Then when God created the Hebrew nation and gave them rest from their slavery, He instituted a Sabbath of years.

> **"When you come into the land** which I give you, **then shall the land keep a Sabbath** unto the Lord. Six years you shall sow your field, and six years you shall prune your vineyard, and gather in its fruits; but in the seventh year shall be a Sabbath of rest unto the land...you shall neither sow your field nor prune your vineyard." Leviticus 25:2.

So after every six days man would rest from his weekly labor and after every six years the land would rest or lay fallow, and man would rest from his yearly cultivating chores. But this wasn't all. After every six sabbatical years of land rest, a super Sabbath was to be celebrated.

> "You shall number **seven Sabbaths of years**...seven times seven years...**forty and nine years**. Then shall you cause the trumpet of the **jubilee** to sound (throughout all your land) on the tenth day of the seventh month, in the **day of atonement**." Leviticus 25:8.

Seven days made a week; seven years made a sabbatical year of land rest; seven sabbatical years brought the jubilee, announced by the sound of the jubilee trumpet (Hebrew *yobel*, from which jubilee is derived) in the seventh month on that most critical of all days: the day of atonement, the day of judgment. Was the jubilee also a year of judgment?

> "And you shall hallow **the fiftieth year** and **proclaim liberty** throughout all the land: it shall be **a jubilee** unto you." Leviticus 25:10.

The jubilee was to be celebrated for an entire year and it was a time of liberty. What did Jesus proclaim when He began his ministry?

Jesus "came to Nazareth...and as his custom was, he went into the synagogue on the Sabbath day" and read from Isaiah,

> "The Spirit of the Lord is upon me, because he has anointed me to preach the gospel to the poor; he has sent me to heal the broken-hearted, to preach deliverance to the captives and recovering of sight to the blind, **to set at liberty** them that are bruised, to preach **the acceptable year** of the lord." Luke 4:16, Isaiah 61:1,2.

What was Jesus saying? He was announcing His mission to "set at liberty" the bruised and battered human race. Moses described the jubilee as a time when "you shall return every man his possession and every man his family." Leviticus 25:10. Jesus came to redeem our world back to Him, to "save his people from their sins" Matthew 1:21. Is it not significant that he began his work in "the acceptable year of the Lord"?

"Jesus came into Galilee...saying, **"The time is fulfilled**, and the kingdom of God is at hand." Mark 1:14. What time was fulfilled? The prophecy of Daniel 9 certainly identified the last week of the 70 weeks "determined" upon the Jewish nation. A week of prophetic time or seven years was divided into two three and a half year periods.

Jesus was born "in the fullness of time" (Galatians 4:4) but he also began his ministry "in the fullness of time" and drew attention to "the acceptable year" because AD 27 was a sabbatical year when liberty was proclaimed "throughout all the land." It marked the beginning of the last week of the 70 weeks.

The jubilee was also noted as a second land Sabbath. Leviticus 25:11 instructed the people, "You shall not sow, neither reap...for it is the jubilee; it shall be holy unto you."

Two years of sequential land rest would have been devastating to the agricultural prosperity of Israel except for God's miraculous intervention. God said,

> "Then I will **command my blessing** upon you in the **sixth year**, and it shall bring forth **fruit for three years**. And you shall sow the eighth year, and eat yet of old fruit until the ninth year; until her fruits come in you shall eat of the old store." Leviticus 25:21.

So, every seven years a land Sabbath, and after 49 years (ending in a seventh land Sabbath) the jubilee would come as a second year land Sabbath occurring as the 50th year and also the first year of the next seven year cycle.

```
712345671234567123456712345671234567123456712345671234567...
   1       2       3       4       5       6       7J      1
   F       F       F       F       F       F      FF
```

While the land was to lay fallow once every seventh year, it was to rest for two consecutive years when a jubilee came around. This double-land Sabbath was a rare event in the Biblical record. But there is sparse evidence that Israel *did* observe the Sabbatical and Jubilee years...for a while. At least one such episode occurred during the reign of Hezekiah, king of Judah.

The Bible records this unusual event in both Isaiah 37 and 2 Kings 19, two chapters that are also unique in being virtually reproduced word for word! These two chapters are the only pair in Scripture to share this distinction. Such duplicity was not simply an editorial oversight, it was to emphasize their important significance.

These passages recount the threatened attack by Sennacherib, the king of Assyria (northern Iraq) and God's miraculous super Sabbath deliverance. The king from the north invaded Israel by pushing 185,000 of his troops across the Syrian border. The northern ten tribes fell quickly. Only Judah remained. Jerusalem was under siege and the future looked pretty grim.

Hezekiah described it as "a day of trouble" "and blasphemy." He called on Isaiah to "lift up prayer for the remnant that are left." God's people were faced with eminent annihilation. And then God speaks, "You shall eat this year such things as grow of themselves, and in the second year that which springs of the same; and in the third year sow and reap and plant...This shall be a sign unto you."

It certainly was. The Arab threat was removed overnight by an act of God. Sennacherib loses his entire army in one night (cf Passover) and retreats back to Nineveh where he is assassinated by his own sons. This is reminiscent of another "king of the north" who sets up his headquarters "between the seas" (Mediterranean, Black and Caspian seas) and yet "comes to his end, and none shall help him." Daniel 11. The last king of the north will act during the final remnant of time, when God's final remnant will again be facing the threat of death.

Sennacherib's Last Stand occurred in 702 BC a known jubilee. Notice how it fits into future 49 year jubilee anniversaries, some of which we recognize as important dates:

BC	5 jubilees					10 jubilees									**AD**
702	653	604	555	506	**457**	408	359	310	261	212	163	114	65	16	**34**

Counting 49 year intervals from 702 BC, five jubilees later falls exactly on 457 BC, the starting date for Daniel's 70 week prophecy which would last 490 years or 10 jubilees. The commandment to restore and rebuild Jerusalem was issued in 457 BC, the seventh year of Artaxerxes king of Persia as recorded in the seventh chapter of Ezra.

The jubilee decade officially ended with the stoning of Stephen. The period of grace extended to the Jewish nation as God's covenant people came to an end. Stephen in his final moments saw Christ "standing at the right hand of throne of God" to signal a critical transition in redemptive history. A similar event will occur when Christ as Michael again "stands up" to signal the end of a final probation and the commencement of the final time of trouble and eminent salvation.

Every 49 years "on the tenth day of the seventh month, in the day of atonement" Israel was to sound the trumpet of jubilee throughout the land. While the Day of Atonement was the most solemn of all the yearly feasts, the jubilee was the most joyful event in a person's lifetime. Trumpet blasts would signal another entire year of farming freedom. "And you shall hallow the fiftieth year and proclaim liberty throughout all the land." In addition, all debts were erased! Land, that had been leased out, was returned to the original owners. Real estate values jumped back to prime levels. Alien slaves were given their liberty, just as the Hebrew slaves had received theirs the year before.

As the sun set on the awesome day of Judgment, the people realized anew what God had done for them—He had forgiven and separated them from their debt of sin. Now they were prepared with grateful hearts to forgive the debts of their fellow men, to release them from servitude, to restore all to their own inheritance. Indeed, jubilee was the epitome of release, redemption and restoration.

The final significance of the Hezekiah episode, however, is that it is also the only biblical record of a double land Sabbath. Remember, Isaiah said, "Eat this year (the sabbatical year) such as groweth of itself and the second year (another land rest) such as groweth the same." Isaiah 37:30. This second year was a jubilee year, following the seventh sabbatical year.

The concept of Sabbath and jubilee have a greater significance in terms of the End Time events. The connection has been entertained since ancient times. William Hales mentions it in his *Analysis of Chronology*, Vol. 1 p. 44: "Hesiod might have been acquainted with that early tradition of six millenary ages of the world which prevailed throughout the East." Revelation 20 speaks of a millennium, a 1000 year period of rest from sin. Indeed, Biblical chronology places the age of our planet close to 6000 years. Peter points out that "a day with the Lord is as a thousand years" and visa versa (2 Peter 3:8).

This kind of thinking has captivated the imagination of Bible students since the time of Christ. *The Epistle of Barnabas*, written in the second century AD discussed this theme:

> "In six days God created the works of his hands, and finished them on the seventh day; and he rested on that day, and sanctified it... What this means is, that He is going to bring the world to an end in six thousand years, since with Him one day means a thousand years..." Staniforth, M (Translator) 1968. *Early Christian Writings*. Penguin. Great Britain. Tatford, F A 1947. Paperback edition 1969. *Prophecy's Last Word*. Pickering & Inglis. Great Britain. pp. 241, 13

The Book of Jubilees (1:29) and a fragment (11Q Melchizedek) discovered 1956 in Qumran Cave II also apply sabbatical times to the second coming. But it was the 17th century Irish scholar Bishop James Usher (1581-1656) who added up the Bible chronologies and calculated the year of creation as 4004 BC. This date has fueled much 6000 year speculation ever since. Validating this approximate date from Scripture is a relatively easy task. Here is a summary of the important figures:

Adam to Flood

Adam	130
Seth	105
Enosh	90
Kenan	70
Mahalel	65
Jared	162
Enoch	65
Methuselah	187
Lamech	182
Noah	600
1656 years	

Flood to Abram

Shem	2
Arphaxshad	35
Shelah	30
Eber	34
Peleg	30
Rue	32
Serug	30
Nahor	29
Terah	70
292 years	

Abram to Seed

100 (Gen 17:17)

Seed to Exodus
400 yrs (Gen 15:13)

Exodus to Temple
480 yrs (1 Kings 6:1)
    100
    400
    480
980 years

The Kings of Judah

Solomon 40-4=	36	Azariah (15:1)	37	Jotham (15:32)	15
Jehu (11:42)	6	Elah (16:8)	1	Joram (2 Kings 3:1)	4
Joash (12:1)	22	Zechariah (15:8)	1	Ahaz (16:1)	11
Rehoboam	17	Zimri (16:15)	4	Jehoram (8:16)	7
Jehoahaz (13:1)	14	Shallum (15:13)		Hoshea (17:1)	3
Abijam (15:1)	2	Omri (16:23)	7	Ahaziah (8:25)	1
Jehoash (13:10)	1	Menahem (15:17)	11	Hezekiah (18:1)	29
Asa (15:9)	1	Ahab (16:29)	3	Manasseh (21:1)	55
Amaziah (14:1)	14	Pekahiah (15:23)	2	Josiah (22:1)	31
Nadab (15:25)	1	Jehosaphat	16	Jehoiakim (23:36)	3
Jeroboam (14:23)	26	Pekah (15:27)	1		
Baasha (15:33)	23	Ahaziah (22:51)	1	**406 years**	

Jerusalem attacked by Nebuchadnezzar in 604, 597, 586 BC.

Adam to Flood	1656	1656	
Flood to Abram	292	1948	
Abram to Seed	100	2048	
Seed to Exodus	400	2448	
Exodus to Temple	480	2928	
Kings of Judah	406	3334	many variables here!
Exile to Christ	604	3938	approximate
		about 4000	years total

In the 1696 best-seller, *The Rise and Fall of the Papacy*, Robert Fleming, an Anglican minister in London, predicted a revolution in France in 1793, loss of power to the Vatican in 1848, and the start of the Millennium in 2000 AD. He nailed the first two. And many other year 2000 enthusiasts anxiously awaited the dawn of the third millennium with apocalyptic expectations.

Even Edward Gibbon, the respected historian, discussed this topic in his *The Decline and Fall of the Roman Empire*:

"The ancient and popular doctrine of the Millennium was intimately connected with the second coming of Christ. As the works of creation had been finished in six days, their duration in the present state, according to a tradition which was attributed to the prophet Elijah, was fixed to six thousand years. By the same analogy it was inferred that this long period of labour and contention, which was now almost elapsed, would be succeeded by a joyful Sabbath of a thousand years..." Gibbon, Edward, *The Decline And Fall Of The Roman Empire*. An Abridgement by D M Low. Penguin Great Britain, 1963. p. 158.

Accounting for the fact that there is no year zero, the end of 6000 years, would therefore be 1997 AD. But this assumed that the 6000 year period started with creation. Others have noted that Christ's death, not His birth, is the greater event on the Salvation landscape and have suggested that perhaps the 6000 years began with the fall of mankind and the introduction of sin on planet earth. If the crucifixion of Christ around 30 AD marked the time boundary between the first 4 millennia and the last 2, then the 6000 years would have begun approximately 30 years later than Ussher's calculation and would consequently push the end of the 6000 years to sometime around the year 2030.

Thus, today (while there is no Biblical proof for such speculations) there is considerable recognition and agreement that we have nearly finished the sixth millennium 'day' and a seventh millennium will be celebrated as a 1000 year long Sabbath in heaven while the earth "enjoys its Sabbath rest."

The Sabbath is intimately linked with the Second Coming. Both speak of redemption and release. As we meet with our invisible Lord on the final day of each week, so we will meet with the visible Lord of lords on the final Day of the Lord at the end of time.

Another way to view the progression of Sabbath rests is to consider that at the end of

6 days	**Man Rests**
6 years	**Land Rests**
48 years (6 x 8)	**Nations Rest**
6000 years	**Earth Rests**

Original Limits

There are 120 jubilees in 6000 years when counting 50 years for each jubilee (an alternate attribute of the jubilee when it is stated as the fiftieth year). Even when using the 49 year interval to count 120 jubilees, a second observation emerges. 49 x 120 = 5880. Not quite 6000 years, in fact, 120 years short.

120 50-year Perfect Jubilees from Creation: 6000 years

120 + 120 49-year Normal Jubilees from the fall: 5880 years

Although not explicitly stated in any canonical works, the time during which Adam and Eve enjoyed a sinless existence in the Garden of Eden may have been 120 years. This is, after all, the number God so often uses as His limit for man.

He gave the antediluvians exactly 120 years as their limit;
He allowed Moses 120 years;
He let the united kingdom of Israel reign 120 years before dividing it.

Two Floods
120 is also associated with the outpouring of the Holy Spirit.
After 120 years of warning God opened the windows of heaven and flooded the world with water and took away man's spirit.
120 priests blew trumpets "as one" at Solomon's Temple dedication when fire came down and glory filled the temple (2 Chron. 5:11-14).
120 disciples were in the upper room at Pentecost "in one accord" when the Holy Spirit appeared as tongues of fire (Acts 2) and filled human temples empowering them to be His witnesses.

After 120 jubilees another flood will cover the earth. Habakkuk 2:14 foretold a time when "The earth shall be filled with the knowledge of the glory of the Lord as the waters cover the sea." Revelation 18 describes the message delivered with a loud cry as filling the earth with God's glory.

Testing the Limits
An interesting division of 120 is 40 indicating a testing time:

> Noah waited 40 days before sending out the raven
> Flood rains fell for 40 days and 40 nights.
> Jonah warned Nineveh for 40 days
> Abraham waited 40 years for Isaac
> Spies were 40 days in Canaan; only two passed the test
> Moses was 40 days on Sinai as the people failed their test
> Christ passed His 40 day test in the wilderness cum lauda
> Moses' life was divided into three periods of 40 years
> • 40 years in Egypt's royal court
> • 40 years tending sheep in obscurity
> • 40 years leading Israel
> Daniel was over three presidents of 40 princes (120 total)
> The first three kings of united Israel, Saul, David and Solomon, each reigned for 40 years

The 120 jubilees of earth's history can also be divided into three periods of 40 jubilees (1960 years) each to produce the following:

The Flood Era	The Jewish Era	The Christian Era
Abraham	Stephen	
40 Jubilees	**40 Jubilees**	**40 Jubilees**
1960 years	**1960 years**	**1960 years**

The year 2000 is year 5757/5758 in the Jewish calendar where year 1 was the creation of Earth. This calendar, which is contracted by some 250 years, is thought to have been first devised during the reign of Solomon in the 10th century BC.

The collection of observations, inspecting for the visible appearance of the Sabbath, in this chapter are just that: observations. In its application to the end of sin on planet Earth, the Sabbath provides fascinating parallels but it should not be made to predict the end of the world. The beauty of God's timing can only be fully appreciated "when the time shall come" John 16:4.

Yet, I believe Jesus *wants* us to know when He is *about* to come so we may prepare to join Him in finishing the sin problem. Of course, no one is going to know exactly when it will be. "Of that day and hour knows no man, no not even the angels of heaven, but my Father only," Jesus said in Matthew 24:36. Mark adds, "neither the Son." But Jesus told us to "learn a lesson of the fig tree... when you see all these things, *know* that it is near, even at the doors" verse 33.

Jesus said, "Watch: for you know not what hour your Lord doth come" Matthew 24:42. He said very much the same thing to the church of Sardis: "If therefore you do not watch, I will come on thee as a thief, and you will not know what hour I will come upon you" Revelation 3:3. Let's turn this negative warning into a positive instruction: Watch therefore and you *will* know what hour I will come. "Take heed," He adds, "lest your hearts be overcharged (pre-occupied) with eating and drinking and the cares of this life, and so that day come upon you unawares" Luke 21:34. In other words, if you *do* take heed, that day will not come upon you unawares. The wisemen knew it was time for the star; they were watching and ready.

See Appendix B for additional details on the Jubilees.

Vital Signs

P.E.

Physical examination involves the use of all the special senses in a hands-on evaluation of a patient's structural integrity. We look, we listen, we touch and probe. Visual inspection, auditory auscultation and tactile palpation are the basic tools of every physical exam. We can "taste and see that the Lord is good," just as "God saw all that He had made and, behold, it was very good." Thomas put his hand into the side of Jesus and touched His wound to verify the reality of the risen Christ. "Jesus put forth His hand and touched" and healed the leper (Matt 8:3) and said, "Whosoever hears these sayings of mine and does them, will be likened unto a wise man." Matthew 7:24.

A knowledge of gross anatomy, the normal and anomalous (variations of normal) forms of the body and its multiple members, is indispensable. In diagnosing the Sabbath, we will conduct a complete, comprehensive, head-to-toe examination of the body of Scripture, the Bible.

> "The Bible, I say, the Bible only, is the religion of Protestants! ... I for my part, after a long and (as I verily believe and hope) impartial search of 'the true way to eternal happiness, I do profess plainly that I cannot find any rest for the sole of my foot but upon this rock only. I see plainly and with mine own eyes that there are popes against popes, councils against councils, some Fathers against others, the same Fathers against themselves, a consent of the Fathers of one age against a consent of the Fathers of another age.... There is no sufficient certainty but of Scripture only for any considering man to build upon. This, therefore, and this only, I have reason to believe: this I will profess; according to this I will live... Propose me anything out of this Book, and require whether I believe it or no, and seem it never so incomprehensible to human reason, I will subscribe it with hand and heart, as knowing no demonstration can be stronger than this: God hath said so, therefore it is true." Chillingworth, *The Religion of Protestants a Safe Way to Salvation* (1846), p.463.

A complete, comprehensive physical examination must begin and end with the authority of God's Word. This has been the standard of Protestant theology since the Reformers first took their stand against error. It will be our laboratory specified range of normals as well.

BP, P, R, T, Wt

The initial physical assessment begins with the recording of the patient's vital signs—basic physiologic measurements that reflect the general stability of major body systems: temperature, pulse, respiration rate and blood pressure. These are the signs of life. When there is no palpable pulse, no visible respirations and when no distinctive bruit swish can be heard below the blood pressure cuff, the patient is pronounced dead.

Simply looking at the patient and noting the overall appearance, size, shape, or even focusing on more specific parameters subject to simple inspection such as eye color, skin moisture, obvious amputations or gross deformities can provide much valuable information. But the vital signs may tell a different story.

Covenant Signs: are they vital?

Since the seventh-day Sabbath is addressed within the precepts of the Ten Commandments, its relationship to the Old Covenant, the laws of Moses and the Hebrew liturgy cannot be ignored. So,

- Is the Sabbath part and parcel of, exclusively linked to, and uniquely identified with the Old Testament dispensation?
- Or does this Edenic institution predate the time of the Jews?
- If the Old Covenant has been replaced by the New, has the Sabbath also been replaced by a new day?
- Are the Ten Commandments relevant in New Testament times?

Does the Sabbath still have a pulse? Is it in a regular rate and rhythm? Does it still beat every seventh day? Or has it skipped a beat? Does the Sabbath have a new pacemaker? To answer these questions we must understand the covenants, the laws of God, the consequences of sin, and God's solution to it; Sabbath physiology and what makes it tick.

The word covenant (Hebrew, *berith*) occurs over 250 times in the Old Testament, and more than 150 times it refers to the covenant which God made with Israel at Sinai. God often calls it "My covenant." The word itself means a bond, a compact, an agreement, a treaty or a solemn pledge. Covenants between individuals were commonly formed by neighbors in the ancient world. These were called bilateral parity covenants, or covenants between equals. "I'll do this and you'll do that." For example Abraham and Abimelech made a covenant in Genesis 21 and Jacob made one with Laban in chapter 31.

There were also unilateral covenants, popular among the Hittites, that were typically treaties between a king and his subjects. Mendenhall and Baltger, among others, classify the Sinai covenant in this category. At Horeb, the mountain of God, Israel was incorporated as a theocracy under God's direct rule. He was their King, pledging them support and protection.

Why a Covenant?

There is considerable evidence that God had a plan, long before sin ever originated, of what He would do if any of His creatures ever decided to rebel against Him. This was the very first covenant, a promise that God made to Himself. According to Scripture it was:

- "kept secret from the foundation of the world." Matt 13:35
- "prepared...from the foundation of the world." Matt 25:34
- "chosen...before the foundation of the world." Ephesians 1:4
- "foreordained before the foundation of the world." 1 Peter 1:20

The Plan

A plan to deal with sin and rebellion was formulated in the mind of God "before the foundation of the world." God decided that He would deal personally with such a crisis. "Before all things...it pleased the Father that in him [Christ] should all fullness dwell." That Jesus should take the role of "Son" and become "the head of the body, the church...the beginning, the first born from the dead; that in all things he might have the pre-eminence." Col 1:17-19. As "the image of the invisible God" Jesus would be the creative and redemptive agent of the God-head. Verse 15. "For by him were all things created, that are in heaven, and that are in earth, visible and invisible." Verse 16; John 1:3.

Then, if sin should ever arise, Christ, though "in the form of God," would make "himself of no reputation" and take "upon him the form of a servant" and become "made in the likeness of men." Phil 2:6, 7. Then "by the obedience of One" many would "be made righteous." Rom 5:19. Jesus would then humble himself and become "obedient unto death, even the death of the cross," Phil 2:8, that "through the blood of his cross" He might "reconcile all things unto himself." Col 1:20.

Thus, because He "gave himself a ransom for all," Christ would then become the "one mediator between God and men." 1 Tim. 2:5,6. This plan was "the wisdom of God in a mystery, even the hidden wisdom, which God ordained before the world." 1 Cor. 2:7.

What would God do? Allow Himself to be "despised and rejected of men," to bear "our griefs, and carry our sorrows" Isa 53:3,4, take our sins upon himself, 1Pet 2:24, then "pour out his soul unto death," making "intercession for the transgressors," making "his grave with the wicked" and become "cut off out of the land of the living." Verses 12, 10, 9, 8. He would then "raise again the third day" and "sit at the right hand of God in heaven" to be our "Advocate with the Father" being "faithful and just to forgive us our sins, and to cleanse us from all unrighteousness" 1 John 2:1;1:9.

What would man do? "Believe on the Lord Jesus Christ" "Repent and be baptized" Acts 2:38, be "crucified with Christ" Gal. 2:20, "not henceforth live unto themselves, but unto him which died for them" 2 Cor. 5:15, "receive the gift of the Holy Ghost" Acts 2:38, "cleanse ourselves from all filthiness of the flesh and spirit, perfecting holiness in the fear of God" 2 Cor. 7:1, "bringing into captivity every thought to the obedience of Christ" 2 Cor. 10:5, by resting in Him "which has begun a good work in you" "to will and to do of his good pleasure" "until the day of Jesus Christ." Phil. 1:6; 2:13.

This plan is the gospel, the "good news" of salvation from sin. It is comprised of three "R's": Ruin, Redemption, and Regeneration.

- God's original plan for man was *ruined* by sin.
- God revealed His plan to *redeem* man by dying for him.
- God *regenerates* us with His Spirit into new creatures.

This has always been His plan from before the foundation of the world. It is His Everlasting Gospel and the basis of all covenants.

The Oldest Covenant
What was the old covenant? Just how old is it? Most Christians think of Moses and the Ten Commandments given at Sinai when the subject of the Old Covenant comes up. After they escaped from Egypt, Israel promised to keep the law—"all" that God had said, and God promised to bless them, make them a "holy nation" and "a light to the Gentiles." But the Bible mentions several other covenants between God and man that were given long before Moses.

We will explore how each covenant was given an identifying sign. And, as we shall see, each inherited the signs of previous covenants. Collectively, these covenants actually represent progressive phases of the continuous Eternal Covenant, a.k.a. the Everlasting Gospel of the kingdom in the New Testament (Rev. 14:6). Although the Bible speaks of an old and a new covenant, there is a continuity of faith and a foundation of grace with each new "upgrade."

Sabbath was the vital sign for the **Creation Covenant**.
Sacrificial blood was the sign for the **Edenic Covenant**.
Rainbow was the sign for **Noah's Flood Covenant**.
Circumcision was the sign for **Abraham's Covenant**.
Law was the sign for the **Mosaic Covenant at Sinai**.
Baptism was the sign for the **Christian Covenant**.
Seal of God is the sign for the **Remnant Covenant**.

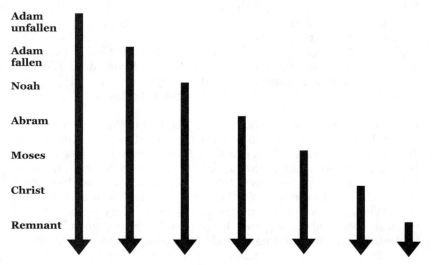

Seven Covenants with Seven Signs

Creation Covenant

> "And the Lord God took the man and put him into the garden of
> Eden to dress it and to keep it. And the Lord God commanded the
> man." Gen 2:15,16

Adam was created with a perfect, sinless disposition and placed in a
perfect unblemished world. Though no explicit written law is
recorded in the Genesis account, Adam certainly had "a law written
upon his heart" Romans 2:13-15. In addition to God's positive
instructions to manage and maintain his garden home, he was also
"commanded" in negative terms to avoid eating from one specific
forbidden tree.   This set of rules defined a contrasting balance
between activity and refrain, duty and resistance. This arrangement
implied that Adam, fashioned "in the image of God," would play out a
parallel experience as he followed His Creator's pattern of work
followed by rest.

That Adam was under obligation to keep God's commands is perfectly clear; that he observed the Sabbath every seventh day is frequently contested by the fact that there is no record of such. But a covenant with Adam is plainly stated. There was an expectation between God and man. Unending life and blessing was offered on condition of obedience. Likewise, the consequences of death were also presented.

Edenic Covenant
When Adam "transgressed the covenant" Hosea 6:7 margin, God promised the Seed of the woman to bruise the head of the serpent Genesis 3:15. The theme of the Everlasting Covenant is the Seed. This Seed was later promised to Abraham. This "Seed is Christ" Gal. 3:16. Jesus would become the Second Adam. He would one day suffer and die at the hand of the serpent's seed, that generation of vipers, who were of their father the devil, that old serpent the devil.

Adam's sin was not only against God, but also against his descendants. Hosea 6 compares his sin with that of Ephraim and Judah as "treachery, robbery, and murder" verse 9. As Adam's sin lead to the death of all mankind, he was guilty of bringing death to his offspring as well as himself (6th commandment), of robbing them (8th) and their descendents (3rd) of an eternal rest with their Creator (4th). When Eve "saw the fruit that it was good," she coveted it (10th); when she believed the serpent's lie (9th) to "become as gods," she also broke the first commandment. God had spoken His commands to the pair directly (2nd) and expected them to honor Him with respect for His authority (5th). Every aspect of the covenant was broken by their disobedience.

When Jesus made "coats of skins and clothed them" Genesis 3:21, He was demonstrating that He would one day die for us and clothe us with His righteousness. There in Eden, Jesus promised to be "the Lamb slain from the foundation of the world." Rev 13:8. The first animals were sacrificed to cover the results of Adam's sin. The last Sacrifice would take away "the sin of the world." John 1:29.

With the introduction of animal sacrifices at the time of the fall, sacrificial offerings became a regular practice of the patriarchs. This suggests that God may have instructed Adam and Eve in the need to do so. Again, no explicit record of this appears in Genesis. Yet evidence that this occurred is seen in the sacrifices offered by Cain and Abel in Genesis chapter 4.

"And in the process of time it came to pass, that Cain brought of the fruit of the ground an offering unto the Lord. And Abel, he also brought of the firstlings of his flock and of the fat thereof." Genesis 3:3,4

The phrase "in process of time" is in Hebrew *qets* "end" *yamin* "days" or literally "at the end of the days." The Sabbath is at the end of each week and would be the most appropriate time to worship and offer sacrifice. It is evident that this particular day was not involved in tilling the ground or tending the sheep. Also we know that only Abel's sheep was accepted by God. Even at this very early time, long before the Mosaic law, shedding of blood was required to atone for sin.

Genesis 3:24 indicates that there remained a visible reminder of the creation story long after Adam and Eve left the garden of Eden. Though no mention of Sabbath observance is included, Adam would have certainly recited the story of creation including the origin of God's Sabbath to many generations over his 930 year lifespan. This would have become part of the extensive oral tradition that still existed when Moses provided the first written record. Thus the

Edenic Covenant inherits the Sabbath sign of the creation covenant
and adds the sign of sacrificial blood.

Flood Covenant
Noah was still practicing sacrifices at the time of the flood. Genesis
8:20. It is highly likely that he also was aware of the Sabbath as an
inherited sign.

The flood experience for Noah was in many ways a reenactment of
creation. Notice the parallels:

Creation	Flood
3 environments are made	Noah's 3 sons are saved
3 occupants for each environment	Their 3 wives joined them
3 acts: rested, blessed, sanctified.	Ark 300 cubits long,
	30 cubits and 3 stories high
The animals passed by Adam	The animals pass by Noah

God states that the flood rains would begin within seven days.
Genesis 7:4. This is then confirmed in verse 10. Later as the flood
waters were abating, Noah waited three seven day periods between
sending various birds from the ark. The week, based on the creation
story, punctuated by the Sabbath, was apparently a regular and
recognized feature of life in Noah's day.

Before the flood, God told Noah that He would "establish My covenant; and thou shalt come into the ark." Genesis 6:18. After the flood God confirms and details the "everlasting covenant" with Noah and all of earth's creatures. Genesis 9:9-17. The rainbow is assigned as the token or sign of His covenant "between me and the earth" which God promises to "remember" when He sees the bow in the cloud.

The covenant with Noah and the earth was a unilateral agreement. There was nothing that man or creature was required to perform. God alone promises to keep the covenant. Thus Noah inherits the Sabbath, sign of creation, the sacrificial signs, and is given a new sign: the rainbow.

Abraham's Covenants
When Abram makes his covenant with God, he is in the practice of building altars and sacrifices. Genesis 12:7, 8; 13:18. "Melchizedek, king of Salem, brought forth **bread** and **wine**, and he was the priest of the most high God." Genesis 14:18. Melchizedek then blessed Abram and Abram paid him a tithe. This may very well have been a sacrificial event as well, but the bread and wine seem to be included as part of a religious ritual rather than simply a social meal.

The covenant is repeated a third time in Genesis 15:18. This time it was accompanied with instructions to offer **specific animal sacrifices** characteristic of later Mosaic regulations: a heifer 3-months-old, a she goat 3-years-old, a ram 3-years-old, a turtledove, and a young pigeon. Genesis 15:13-16.

These experiences show that Abram has also inherited the sign of sacrificial blood. As a creature of Earth, he automatically inherits the sign of the Flood covenant. But what about the Sabbath? Did Abram inherit it as well? Or had its observance been lost in obscurity by this time in history?

When "the Lord appeared unto him in the plains of Mamre" in Genesis 18:1 Abraham invites Christ, Let me "**wash your feet, and rest** yourselves under the tree." (verse 4). This is laver symbolism associated with rest, indirectly and directly referring to the Sabbath functions of holiness (cleansing) and rest.

Next, at age 99 in Genesis 17:1-14 Abram is given a fourth covenant. This one included a change in his name to Abraham and introduction of **circumcision** as the **"token" or sign** (verse 11) "for an *everlasting covenant*" (verse 7).

Circumcision is Forever
The sign of Abraham's everlasting covenant was circumcision. Why? Because it was permanent. No going back. Can't change your mind. Once circumcised, always circumcised. This was the idea God wanted to convey by using this permanent physical change to the body as the sign of His Everlasting Covenant. When Israel first broke their covenant with God, rejecting His plan for them at Kadesh, they were denied this sign for 38 years. Only when they finally crossed the Jordan river in faith and obedience was the sign again restored (Joshua 5:2-9).

Over time, however, men came to trust in the symbol instead of the commitment it represented. God pleaded with Israel, "Circumcise yourselves to me, and take away the foreskins of *your heart*" (Deuteronomy 10:16; Jeremiah 4:4). Paul repeated the same idea: "*Real* Jews are Jews because of what is inside them, not because of anything done to their external flesh; likewise, *real* circumcision is of the heart" (Romans 2:29).

New Testament Circumcision
Circumcision was a very permanent symbol of the unalterable dedication to follow the way of God and all His bidding. That's why Paul concluded, "For circumcision verily profiteth, if thou keep the law...Therefore if the uncircumcision *keep the righteousness of the law*, shall not his uncircumcision be counted for circumcision?" Romans 2:25, 26. Just as Abraham's faith was "counted to him for righteousness" so loyalty to God's law is what is really important and constitutes the true heart circumcision of the New Testament. "Circumcision is nothing, and uncircumcision is nothing, but the *keeping of the commandments* of God" 1 Corinthians 7:19.

The commitment to be loyal to God and His will for us, to be "doers and not hearers of His word" is the heart circumcision that Christ requires. "If you love me, keep my commandments." The covenant commitment goes to the very core of our being. While the marriage covenant promises "until death do us part," our magnificent God transcends death. "I have loved you with an *everlasting* love," He says. (Jeremiah 23:40). Yes, God plays for keeps.

God wanted to convey this important truth of commitment to His people by the many perpetual rules He instructed them to keep surrounding the sanctuary services:

Tabernacle lamps remained lit as "a perpetual statute" Ex. 27:21
Aaron and his sons were priests for "a perpetual statute" Ex. 29:9
The incense was offered "perpetually" Exodus 30:8

They couldn't eat fat or blood as "a perpetual statute" Leviticus 3:17
The feasts were to be "a perpetual statute" Leviticus 23

By these observances, Israel would learn that:

His *ways* are everlasting. Habakkuk 3:6.
His *mercy* endures forever. Psalm 136.
His *name,* Psalm 72:17.
His *righteousness,* Psalm 111:3.
His *judgments,* and His *truth* endure forever. Psalm 117:2.
His *throne* is forever. Psalm 45:6.
His *word* is settled forever. Psalm 119:89; 1 Peter 1:25.
He *reigns* forever (Psalm 146:10) because He *lives* forever
    (Daniel 12:7; Revelation 4:9,10; 5:14; 10:6)
    to ever make intercession for us. Hebrews 7:25.

In fact, whatever He does is done forever. Ecclesiastes 3:14.
He is the same yesterday, and today, and forever. Hebrews 13:8.

Is it any wonder then that He **remembers His covenant forever**?
(Psalm 105:8, 111:8,9). "Know therefore that the Lord your God... is
the faithful God, which **keeps covenant** and mercy with them that
love Him and keep His commandments to a thousand generations"
(Deuteronomy 7:9).

Thus Abraham inherited the Sabbath, sacrificial and rainbow signs.
He was then given a new sign: circumcision. Abraham's covenant
promises were later repeated to each of his descendants so that God
became known as "the God of Abraham, Isaac and Jacob."

Mosaic Covenant at Sinai
In preparation for their Exodus from Egypt, God instructed Moses in
the details of the Passover sacrifice and the sign of the blood that was
to be painted on the doors of every dwelling. Only those who were
circumcised could observe this ritual. In fact, Moses had to quickly
circumcise his own sons on his way from Midian to Egypt in
preparation for it himself.   Thus Israel inherited the signs of
sacrificial blood and circumcision.

When Moses reinstituted Sabbath observance among the Hebrew
slaves, Pharaoh blamed him for "making the people rest (*shabat*)."
Six weeks before reaching Sinai, God tested the people on their
compliance with His law in general and the Sabbath in particular by
giving them manna six days and none on the seventh. Thus Israel
inherited the signs of the Sabbath, sacrificial blood and circumcision.

When Moses met God on Mount Sinai, he entered into His glorious presence on the seventh day. Ex 24:15,16. There he received the Law as the sign of another covenant. God wrote this Law Himself on "Tables of stone" which were called "Tables of the testimony." Ex. 31:18, 2 Cor. 3:3. The Ten Commandments were also called "words of the covenant" (Exodus 34:28) and "tables of the covenant." Deuteronomy 9:9, 11.

At Sinai, God entered into a renewed covenant with the descendants of "Abraham, and of his oath unto Isaac; And has confirmed the same to Jacob for a law, and to Israel for an *everlasting covenant*" 1 Chronicles 16:15-17; Psalm 105:8-10. Then they were given the sign of the law. "Bind them for a **sign** upon thine **hand**...as frontlets between thine **eyes**... These words, which I command thee this day, shall be in thine **heart**." Deuteronomy 6:6-8; 11:18.

Then God asked Moses to build a sanctuary "according to all that I show thee after the pattern of the tabernacle, and the pattern of all the instruments thereof." Ex 25:9. In the tabernacle was the most holy place, and in the most holy place was the ark of the covenant, and inside the ark was placed the "tables of the covenant" written "by the finger of God," the Ten Commandments. Moses saw the original copies in heaven, and he was given a copy by God Himself.

The people of Israel promised to keep the Ten Commandments. "All that God has said we will do." This was their vow, their promise, their covenant agreement with God. In Hebrew this word for vow is *berith*. (Strong's 01285 *briyth* ber-eeth'). The terms, the oath-bound stipulations or "words" of the covenant in Hebrew is *eduth*. (Strong's 05715 `*eduwth* ay-dooth'). This word is also translated "testimony" and both words, *berith* and *eduth,* are translated "covenant," the source of much confusion.

This contract agreement or covenant was then ratified by the sprinkled blood of an ox (Exodus 24:7,8). A copy of the covenant was placed inside the earthly ark of the covenant (Heb. 9:4; 1 Ki. 8:21) just like the copy in heaven, but in the side of the ark Moses put "the book of the law" written by himself "as a witness against" them (Deut. 31:36).

It is clear that the Ten Commandment Law was the significant added sign for the covenant made at Sinai. Why did God choose this sign?

As he was there, alone with God in the mountain, Moses made an unusual request—he asked to see God's glory. What did God show him? A bright brilliant blinding radiance? Certainly Moses experienced that. So did the entire camp of Israel. The mountain appeared to be on fire. There was lightening and thunder and smoke. But like Elijah standing at the mouth of a cave on mount Horeb "the mountain of God," so too, Moses heard God's *voice* describing His glory.

"The Lord, the Lord God, merciful and gracious, long-suffering, and abundant in goodness and truth, keeping mercy for thousands, forgiving iniquity and transgression and sin, and that will by no means clear the guilty; visiting the iniquity of the fathers upon the children, and upon the children's children, unto the third and to the fourth generation." Exodus 34:6

This is God's glory: He is merciful, gracious, patient, good, true, and forgiving. These words, describing what God is like, His personality, His character, are strikingly similar to the language used in the second commandment of the Decalogue:

"I the Lord thy God am a jealous God, visiting the iniquity of the fathers upon the children unto the third and fourth generation of them that hate me: and showing mercy unto thousands [of generations] of them that love me, and keep my commandments." Exodus 20:5,6

What a compelling indication that the Ten Commandment Law represents the quintessential characteristics of its Creator—our Creator; it is a transcript of His character. Jesus, after living a perfect life, honoring and "magnifying the law" (Isaiah 42:21), said that He had "glorified" His Father (John 17). He admonished us to "let your light so shine that men might see your good works and *glorify* your Father which is in heaven" (Matthew 5:16).

Moses saw and heard God's glory, His character. Jesus demonstrated that character in His life. If we have seen him, we have seen the Father. And He invites us to display the same character in our own lives.

Notice the character, the moral principles, embodied in the Decalogue:

1 exclusive worship	6 respect life
2 direct worship	7 fidelity
3 reverent worship	8 honesty
4 loyal worship	9 truthfulness
5 respect authority	10 contentment

These Ten Words of God are eternal principles which transcend racial, linguistic, and cultural boundaries because they describe the One who "was and is and will ever be."

Now, notice these comparisons between God and His spiritual law:

God is...	The Law is...
Genesis 21:33: **everlasting**	Psalm 111:7-8: **everlasting**
Psalm 25:8: **good**	Romans 7:12: **good**
Psalm 145:17: **holy**	Romans 7:12: **holy**
Deuteronomy 32:4: **just**	Romans 7:12: **just**
I John 1:5: **light**	Proverbs 6:23: **light**
I John 4:8: **love**	Romans 13:10: **love**
Matthew 5:48: **perfect**	Psalm 19:7: **perfect**
Psalm 145:17: **righteous**	Psalm 119:172: **righteous**
John 4:24: **spiritual**	Romans 7:14: **spiritual**
Deuteronomy 32:4: **truth**	Psalm 119:142: **truth**

Thou Shalt Not

The Exodus 20 account, where God speaks His Law to Israel, begins with the recognition that they were "borne on eagle's wings" out of Egypt by Jehovah. On this basis the Ten Commandments are introduced with the explanatory phrase: therefore "Thou shalt not." *Because* God removed them from the evil empire of sin that Egypt symbolized, *because* He had saved them in a mighty display of power from the menacing Egyptian army, *because* He has met their every material need—therefore, thou shalt not need any other god. Therefore, thou shalt not need to lie, steal, kill, etc. Considered in this positive form, the Law is truly Ten Commandments instead of Two Commandments and Eight Prohibitions.

Some have mistakenly assumed that God imposed a legalistic covenant of works upon ancient Israel knowing that they would fail in order to teach them a lesson. This makes the old covenant nothing more than a divine trick, a cruel experiement in asking weak humans to keep a law that they couldn't possibly keep. Then He provides the Christian Church with a new and improved covenant of grace. What does such a theory say about the character of God?

In fact, God first delivered His people from the chains of Egypt by grace and faith alone, only then did He deliver to them His covenant law. Israel was not given the law as a way to *secure* their release from slavery, but as the *result* of their already accomplished redemption. Israel was not chosen *because* they kept God's law, but *so* they might keep it (Deut. 9:6).

The Everlasting Covenant Promised Again
After Israel and Judah broke their promises to remain true to God and his law, they were carried off into exile "Because they continued not in my covenant...saith the Lord" Heb 8:9. But still God promised to renew His everlasting covenant with them.

> "I will make an *everlasting covenant* with them" Jeremiah 32:40

> "I will remember my covenant with thee in the days of thy youth, and I will establish unto thee an *everlasting covenant.*" Ezekiel 16:60

> "I will make a covenant of peace with them; it shall be an *everlasting covenant* with them: and I will place them, and multiply them, and will set my sanctuary in the midst of them for evermore." Ezekiel 37:26

> "Behold, the days come, saith the Lord, when I will make a new covenant with the house of Israel and with the house of Judah: not according to the covenant that I made with their fathers in the day when I took them by the hand to lead them out of the land of Egypt: because they continued not in my covenant, and I regarded them not, saith the Lord.
> For this is the covenant that I will make with the house of Israel after those days, saith the Lord; I will put my laws into their mind, and write them in their hearts, and I will be to them a God, and they shall be to me a people." Hebrews 8:8-10

This covenant would be different. Not like the one at the Exodus.
That one was written on stone.
This one would be written in their hearts.

Similarities and Continuities

Under the Old Covenant people were under obligation to remain obedient to God's commandments; under the New Covenant people are saved by grace through faith in the perfect sacrifice of Jesus Christ, God's gracious provision for salvation.

Likewise under the Old Covenant people were saved by grace through faith in the promised Messiah who would one day die for their sins (John 8:56) ; and under the New Covenant Christians honor God by doing His will, keeping "the commandments of God" (Rev. 12:17) through the indwelling, transforming power of His Spirit.

SIMILARITIES	
OLD COVENANT	**NEW COVENANT**
Keep God's Commandments written on stone	Keep God's Commandments written in our hearts
Saved by grace through faith in the Lamb to be slain Hebrews 11; Rom. 4:6, 13	Saved by grace through faith in the Lamb that was slain Ephesians 2:8
Had a sanctuary on earth	Has a sanctuary in heaven
Sins forgiven by shed blood	Sins forgiven by Christ's blood
Mediated by Moses Ex 24:2,3 and a high priest	Mediated by Christ our High Priest

> "Let us therefore fear, lest a promise being left us of entering into his rest, any of you should seem to come short of it. *For unto us was the gospel preached, as well as unto them.*" Hebrews 4:1,2

Old Testament patriarchs heard the gospel, as well as us. "God... at sundry times and in divers manners spake in time past unto the fathers by the prophets." Hebrews 1:1. Jesus said, "Abraham rejoiced to see my day; and he saw it, and was glad." John 8:56. "Abraham believed God, and it was counted unto him for righteousness." Romans 4:3. Even "Noah found grace in the eyes of the Lord." Genesis 6:8.

If there was a difference between how Old and New Testament believers were saved, it would seriously question the consistency and fairness of God. Such a dichotomy between redemptive periods would imply that the basis of salvation has changed over time. At first God required strict attention to a vast array of sacrificial rules and regulations. Then later, requirements were dramatically simplified as God learned through experience that humanity simply couldn't obey the original Law.

Such an arrangement would make God fallible, inconsistent and quasi-omniscient, relying on trial and error. But scripture teaches otherwise.

- "I am the Lord, I change not" Malachi 3:6
- "Jesus Christ is the same yesterday, today, and forever" Hebrews 13:8
- "The Father of lights with whom there is no variableness, neither shadow of turning" James 1:17
- "My covenant will I not break, nor alter the thing that is gone out of my lips" Psalm 89:34
- "if we believe not, yet he abideth faithful: he cannot deny himself" 2 Timothy 2:13
- "It is impossible for God to lie" Hebrews 6:18.

The New Covenant is an extension of the Everlasting Covenant of which the Mosaic Covenant was also an earlier extension. It does not replace by elimination the Old Covenant to Israel anymore than the Covenant at Sinai replaced or eliminated the Covenant made with Abraham. Each renewed covenant *builds* on the previous.

The New Covenant brought to life the reality of the Old Covenant in the person of Jesus Christ, confirming and reaffirming all the previous covenants. The New Covenant is made with those who are "in Christ" who are considered to be "Abraham's seed and *heirs* according to the promise." Galatians 3:29.   New Testament Christians, therefore, *inherit* the promises and provisions, the signs and symbols of the previous covenants: the one made at Sinai, the one made with Abraham and the one made originally in Eden to the very first man and woman.

There are, however, some elements of the Old Covenant that clearly continue and some that clearly end at the New Testament transition:

CONTINUITIES

OLD COVENANT	NEW COVENANT
Made with Israel of old	Made with a new Israel by faith
Circumcision of the flesh	Circumcision of the heart
The Lord's Passover	The Lord's Supper
Moses lifted up serpent	Christ was lifted up
Unbelievers "cut off"	Unbelievers "cast out"
Sabbaths kept	Weekly rest day continues

TERMINATIONS

OLD COVENANT
Animals died for sinners
Shedding of blood

NEW COVENANT
Christ died once for sinners
Shedding of blood stopped

All agree with these continuities and terminations. But what about other aspects of Old Testament religious, civil, social, sanitary and health practices?

Health

Unclean foods	Medical evidence supported
Moldy dwellings destroyed	Medical evidence supported
Blood & Fat eliminated	Medical evidence supported

Sanitary

Excrement disposed outside	Modern practice approves
Disease quarantined	Germ theory confirmed
Hand-washing	Contagious diseases appreciated

Social

Incest prohibited	Still recognized as genetic risk
Adultery not tolerated	Even recognized by movie plots

Civil

Theft, Murder, Lies punished	Same standard prevails today

Old Covenant notwithstanding, both science and modern society recognize the validity of many Mosaic regulations. While some Christians argue that Peter's dream of the unclean beasts in Acts 10 permits New Testament believers to eat anything that crawls, slithers or flies, medical science now confirms the health risk of eating scavenger food sources—from allergic anaphylaxis to parasites and atherosclerosis—as well as forcing vegetarian cattle into becoming cannibalistic scavengers by feeding them recycled body parts.

Other regulations concerning body fluids, infectious diseases, environmental hazards, marital and social conduct are appreciated and respected by today's civilized nations. Only the continued value (and especially the obligation) of the Hebrew religious calendar is disputed. While the symbols of Passover have been inherited by Christianity, the timing is not preserved. And many regard the other annual festivals to be "fulfilled" in Christ and now obsolete.

Though **Passover** lives on through the Lord's Supper Communion service with newer and deeper meaning for the Christian church, there is general consensus that the other Old Testament festivals have no significance for New Testament believers. Recent studies over the past century have increasingly disputed this popular position. The spring festivals of Passover, Wave Sheaf, Unleavened Bread and Pentecost have indeed been more fully realized by the coming of Christ. But the fall festivals of Trumpets, Atonement and Tabernacles have yet to meet their final realization in the final judgment, the millennium and the second coming.

New Testament Covenant
In anticipation of the Messiah's first coming, God said,

> "Behold, I will send my messenger, and he shall prepare the way before me: and the Lord whom you seek, shall suddenly come to his temple, even the messenger of the covenant, whom you delight in: Behold, he shall come." Malachi 3:1

Jesus has always been the Messenger of the covenant. He made the first covenant in Eden after walking in the cool of the day, searching for Adam. He made the covenant with Abraham, who saw his day and rejoiced. He gave the law on mount Sinai and made the covenant with Israel. And now He was coming to give the law again in a sermon on another mount. The New Testament church witnessed the realization of all the previous covenants in the person of "Jesus, that great shepherd of the sheep, through the blood of the *everlasting covenant*" Hebrews 13:20. Isaiah 42 identifies Christ as God's Servant, His Elect, Who put His spirit upon Him and gave Him "for a covenant of the people," Verses 1-6.

The first Christians inherited all the signs of the Everlasting Covenant that had been introduced by God through Christ to past generations. For example, Jesus was circumcised the eighth day. So also, Christians, both Jews and Gentiles, were circumcised: either outwardly in the flesh, but more importantly, inwardly in the heart (Romans 2).

Christ observed Passover and the Feast of Tabernacles inheriting the sign of sacrificial blood. But in addition to Passover, Paul and other Christians are documented throughout the book of Acts as keeping Pentecost, the Feast of Tabernacles, and probably the Day of Atonement but now for a much more important reason: "Christ our Passover" is sacrificed for us; Christ is our Atonement; Christ is the Tabernacle; He is the Water of life in the laver; Christ, the Light of the world, is the golden lamp stand; He is the show Bread of life; He is the Manna come down from heaven; His flesh is the Vail; He is the Mercy Seat standing between us and the law; He is the budding Rod, symbol of a resurrected life; He *is* the Law *and* the Lawgiver. Thus Christians inherited the sign of sacrificial blood (and the entire sacrificial system!) in the Person of Jesus Christ who shed His blood for us on the cross of Calvary.

Christ kept the Ten Commandments ("Who of you convinceth me of sin?"John 8:46) and taught their observance not only to "the letter of the law" but even in its spirit. Paul taught that the Law is established by the Christian's faith in Christ. Near the end of the first century AD, John saw the temple of God "opened in heaven and there was seen in his temple the ark of the testament" (Revelation 11:19), the same original one Moses had seen long before as the pattern for the sanctuary he constructed. This same law still existed in the heavenly temple as the testament, the everlasting covenant between God and His covenant people. Thus Christ and His followers inherited the sign of God's Law now written on their hearts. Heb 8:10.

The Sign of Baptism
What, then, was the added sign of the New Covenant? As Christ realized in His life, death and resurrection all the promises of the previous covenants, He commissioned His disciples to "teach all nations, baptizing them in the name of the Father, and of the Son, and of the Holy Ghost." Matt. 28:19. Immediately Phillip baptizes the Ethiopian eunuch. Peter baptizes Cornelius and his household. Paul baptizes the jailor and his household. Everywhere the apostles were baptizing as the sign of accepting Christ, their Lord and Saviour.

The Everlasting Covenant to the Remnant

There has always been a remnant who have remained faithful to God.

Noah and his family were the remnant saved from the flood.

Abraham was the remnant saved out of Ur.

Caleb and **Joshua** were the remnant who survived the wilderness.

Elijah and seven thousand were the faithful remnant from Israel.

Zerubabel led a remnant out of Babylon.

There were only 120 remaining after Christ's ascension.

"Even so then at this present time also there is a remnant" Rom. 11:5.

At the end of time, just before Jesus returns to rescue His faithful children from the threat of certain death, the Everlasting Covenant is finalized between God and man.   The seed of the woman, while hiding from the dragon, remains loyal to God by preserving:

His Sabbath
> they worship "Him who made the heaven and earth,
> the sea and the fountain of waters." Revelation 14:8.

His sacrificial blood
> "They have washed their robes and made them white
> in the blood of the Lamb" Revelation 7:14.

His Law
> "Here are they that keep the commandments of God." Rev. 14:12.

Circumcision
> They have *circumcised their hearts* in a permanent, irrevocable commitment to follow His will in all things.

Baptism
> They have been *baptized* in the sin-cleansing waters and by the transforming Spirit.

They have preserved the *signs* of their spiritual ancestors and now they are ready to receive the identifying sign of the final covenant.

To the overcomers in the church of Philadelphia, Christ promises to "write upon him the **name** of my God, and the **name** of the city of my God, which is new Jerusalem, which cometh down out of heaven from my God: and I will write upon him my new **name**." Rev. 3:12.

Three names. What is the name of God? "The name of the Lord is a strong tower: the righteous runneth into it, and is safe." Proverbs 18:10. When Moses went back to Egypt he told the people that the "I AM" sent him. God explained to Moses: "Thus shalt thou say unto the children of Israel, The Lord God of your fathers, the God of Abraham, the God of Isaac, and the God of Jacob, has sent me unto you: this is my name for ever, and this is my memorial unto all generations." Exodus 3:15.   The God of covenants is His name. Where are these names written?

In Their Foreheads

"And I saw another angel ascending from the east having the seal of the living God: and he cried with a loud voice...Saying, Hurt not the earth...till we have sealed the servants of our God in their *foreheads*." Revelation 7:2, 3.

"And I looked, and, lo, a Lamb stood on the mount Zion, and with him a 144,000, having his *Father's name* written in their *foreheads*." Revelation 14:1.

"And they shall see his face; and *his name* shall be in their *foreheads*." Revelation 22:4

What is the Father's name? Paul said that we cry "Abba, Father" (Galatians 4:6). How is this name used in Hebrew?

> **ab** = Father [Strongs entry number 2]
> **ath** = Sign, a portent [Strongs 852, from 226 'awth']
> **awth** = Signal, omen, monument, mark [Strongs 226]

Sabbath in Hebrew is "shabath," composed of three characters: Sh - b – th. In English, the core of the word "Sabbath" is "abba": S - **abba** -th

The word Sabbath contains within its very structure components that convey the meanings: "Sign of the Father," "Mark of the Father," "Memorial or monument to the Father."

It is no wonder that after presenting the call to worship in Revelation 14:6 and the warning to those who receive a mark in their *forehead* and in their *hand*, that those who are sealed with the name of God in their *forehead* are identified:

> "Here is the patience of the saints: here are they that keep the **commandments of God**, and the **faith of Jesus**." Rev. 14:12.

The Sabbath rest and blessing is then pronounced upon them.

> "And I heard a voice from heaven saying unto me, Write, **Blessed** are the dead which die in the Lord form henceforth: Yea, Saith the Spirit, that they may **rest** from their labors; and their works do follow them." Rev 14:13.

They have accepted the "Everlasting gospel" (Rev. 14:6) that calls all men everywhere to:

1. "Fear God" and
2. "give glory to Him" and
3. "Worship Him who made heaven and earth" (verse 7)

Fear God: reverence Him, respect Him, submit to Him, obey Him.
(1 Sam. 15:22,23; Matt. 15:9; John 9:31; James 2:24,26; Eccl. 12:13)
Give Him glory: honor Him, keep His Word, manifest His
character or name (John 17:4,5; 14:13,14; 13:31,32; Exodus 33:18, 34:6,7)
Worship Him: worship the Creator, the One who made us.

But how do we worship the Creator? We do so by obeying His commandments, respecting His memorial of creation, honoring His example and giving glory to His creative works.

> "**Blessed** are they that **do his commandments**, that they may have right to the tree of life, and may enter in through the gates into the city." Revelation 22:14.

Breaking the Covenant at the End

Isaiah 24 describes the world at the end of time, after Jesus appears to redeem his faithful children, after the rejecters of His mercy are destroyed "by the brightness of His coming," 2 Thessalonians 2:8, when "the Lord makes the earth empty...and turns it upside down...*because they have transgressed the laws, changed the ordinance, broken the* **everlasting covenant**" Isaiah 24:5.

Popular concepts of the end focus on an evil antichrist figure that makes and then breaks a covenant with Israel in the middle of a seven year tribulation period. This fanciful scenario requires the unnecessary creation of a non-existent evil covenant when God's everlasting covenant already exists.

The *everlasting covenant* is the same one promised to Adam and Eve, to Abraham, to Isaac and Jacob, to the freed children of Israel at Sinai, to David, to the returning exiles through Ezra and Nehemiah, to the apostles and believers in Christ—the same presented by Moses. "All of you stand this day before the Lord your God," Moses said, "that you should enter into **covenant** with the Lord and into His oath...that He may establish you today for a people unto Himself, and that He may be to you a God, as He has said unto you and as He has sworn unto your fathers, to Abraham, Isaac, and Jacob. And not only to you do I make this covenant and this oath, but *also with those that are not here* with us this day" Deuteronomy 29:10-15. He's talking about us! God embraced the entire human family with His everlasting covenant.

> "For this is the covenant that I will make with the house of Israel after those days, saith the Lord; I will put my laws into their mind, and write them in their hearts." Hebrews 8:10

The House of Israel

God never makes a covenant with anyone except the house of Israel. We, too, must be Israelites adopted into God's spiritual family; we must be spiritual Jews, children of Abraham, "heirs of the promise"— in order to receive the New Covenant. Every one who has ever been saved, Old Testament or New, has been saved under the provisions of the Everlasting Covenant. God's conditions and provisions for salvation have always been the same: acceptance of His gift of grace through the sacrifice of His Son to "forgive us our sins and cleanse us from all unrighteousness" 1 John 1:9.

Seven Vital Covenant Signs

When all of the vital signs have been taken we can check the values for any abnormality. Fortunately, all parameters appear normal. Sabbath, the first vital sign, continues its regular rate and rhythm with each successive phase of the Everlasting Covenant. Our patient is well and stable.

God's Everlasting Covenants

Creation Covenant promised unending life in a perfect world
 sign: perpetual seventh day **Sabbath, marriage**
 man and God in union become one spirit
 Marriage Covenant promises life-long fidelity
 sign: husband and wife in union become one flesh
 Then, after sin,

Edenic Covenant promised the Seed of the woman
 Inherited signs: (Sabbath)
 Added sign: **sacrifice**

Flood Covenant promised never to destroy earth by water again
 Inherited signs: (Sabbath), sacrifice
 Added sign: **rainbow**

Abrahamic Covenant promised multiplied seed
 Inherited signs: (Sabbath), sacrifice, rainbow
 Added sign: **circumcision** (Gen 17:11)

Mosaic Covenant promised land
 Inherited Signs: Sabbath, rainbow,
 (Ex. 31:12), sacrifice (Passover Ex. 12:13;
 13:9), and circumcision
 Added sign: **Ten Commandments** (Deut 6:8)

Messianic Covenant promised redemption from sin
 Inherited Signs: Sabbath, sacrifice,
 Circumcision=keeping law, Passover=Lord's Supper
 Added sign: **Baptism** (Matt. 28:19) for resurrection
 Phillip & Ethiopian, Peter & Cornelius, Paul & Jailor, etc.

Remnant Covenant will receive all of the above promises:
 Millennial Sabbath rest, marriage of the Lamb
 Union with Christ (follow Lamb wherever He goes)
 Exodus from spiritual Egypt
 Enter the promised land of Heaven
 Sabbath Rev 22:17
 Sacrifice=Lamb is light Rev 21:23
 Circumcision=keep commandments Rev 22:14
 Feasts=Tree of Life Rev 22:2
 Baptism=River of Life Rev 22:1, Sea of Glass

 Added sign: Father's **name** in forehead, the Seal of God'

The Heart

Two vital signs are directly dependant on cardiac function. Pulse rate and blood pressure correlate with the frequency and strength of myocardial contractions. Closely related to the heart rate is rhythm. While taking our patient's pulse, we can evaluate rhythm at the same time. Is the pattern regular at rest? Pressure readings are recorded with two values: a systolic work load and diastolic rest phase. Normal values predict optimal health.

In the very heart of God's Law, a vital sign is measured. With a regular rhythm beating every seven days, marked by alternating work and rest, the Sabbath is central and vital to the health of all Creation.

Examining the heart involves auscultation of the heart sounds, listening for murmurs, gallops and rubs. Our stethoscope may reveal murmurs or complaints by some who regard the heart as outdated and no longer necessary. We must be sensitive to the galloping sounds of others who are quick to jump over the normal Sabbath rhythm, as well as the rubbing tone of friction and resistance against the original pacemaker.

God's Bridge to Man

The fourth commandment, enshrined in the very center of the law, bridges both sides of the Decalogue by respecting our loyalty to God and our duty to man. It embodies the work of Christ Who was both God and man. Christ honored God by restoring man on the Sabbath. On the cross He reconciled God and man and then rested on the Sabbath. Truly, the Sabbath is a sign between God and man. (Ezekiel 20:20). The fourth commandment is the only one that specifically includes Gentiles, "the stranger within thy gates." Even the animals are to rest.

The biological need for rest is demonstrated even at the cellular level. Dr. Sang Lee points out that only during the resting phase of cell division can DNA repair itself from damage to its nucleotide base-pair sequencing. Organisms that are denied rest deteriorate from the stress of unrelenting activity. Rest is therefore a basic requirement of life itself.

Heart of the Law

In the very center of the Ten Commandments is the center of the fourth commandment. Fifteen verses comprise the Ten Words of God as listed below with the number of words in each verse. Notice the fourth commandment, spanning verses 8-11 is by far the longest:

20:3 Thou shalt have no other gods before me. 8

20:4 Thou shalt not make unto thee any graven image, or any likeness of any thing that is in heaven above, or that is in the earth beneath, or that is in the water under the earth. 36

20:5 Thou shalt not bow down thyself to them, nor serve them: for I the LORD thy God am a jealous God, visiting the iniquity of the fathers upon the children unto the third and fourth generation of them that hate me; 41

20:6 And shewing mercy unto thousands of them that love me, and keep my commandments. 14

20:7 Thou shalt not take the name of the LORD thy God in vain; for the LORD will not hold him guiltless that taketh his name in vain. 27

20:8 Remember the sabbath day, to keep it holy. 8

20:9 Six days shalt thou labour, and do all thy work: 10

20:10 But the *seventh day is the sabbath* of the LORD thy God: in it thou shalt not do any work, thou, nor thy son, nor thy daughter, thy manservant, nor thy maidservant, nor thy cattle, nor thy stranger that is within thy gates: 43

20:11 For in six days the LORD made heaven and earth, the sea, and all that in them is, and rested the seventh day: wherefore the LORD blessed the sabbath day, and hallowed it. 33

20:12 Honour thy father and thy mother: that thy days may be long upon the land which the LORD thy God giveth thee. 22

20:13 Thou shalt not kill. 4

20:14 Thou shalt not commit adultery. 5

20:15 Thou shalt not steal. 4

20:16 Thou shalt not bear false witness against thy neighbour. 9

20:17 Thou shalt not covet thy neighbour's house, thou shalt not covet thy neighbour's wife, nor his manservant, nor his maidservant, nor his ox, nor his ass, nor any thing that is thy neighbour's.33

The middle verse, eight verses into the fifteen, is Exodus 20:10. There are 7 verses before verse 10 and 7 verses after it. There are 297 words in the King James Version of the Decalogue. The middle word is the 149th word.

There are 148 words before the middle word,
    and 148 words following it.
The first 7 words of the middle verse are:
"But the seventh day is the Sabbath"

The 149th word, the middle word of the Ten Commandments is found within this phrase taken from the middle verse which is located within the "central" fourth commandment. The middle word is "*is*", the equality function of the central formula:

seventh day = the Sabbath

Rabbinical writings have also recorded even more aspects of the peculiar seventhness found within the fourth commandment:

- It begins with the seventh letter of the Hebrew alphabet, and
- It includes the seventh verse in the Ten Commandments
- It legislates rest for seven categories of creatures
  according to Jewish sage Rabbi Jacob Ba'al ha-Turim

Other commentators also recognize the central importance of the fourth precept:

> "The Sabbath commandment explains all the other command-ments, or all the other forms of the one commandment. It is thus to be placed at the head."   Karl Barth, *Church Dogmatics*, ET (Edinburgh, 1956), vol. 3, p. 53.

God chose stone on which to write His law because of its enduring qualities. The oldest existing man-made structures—the Pyramids of Egypt—were constructed of stone. Amazing Facts' Doug Bachelor notes that the "rocks in the box," the Law in the Ark of the Covenant, speak of the permanent, unchanging, eternal nature of God and His everlasting Law.

Pathophysiology

Though Sabbath survives conceptually in the weekly worship services of all Christian churches, there are today differences of opinion as to *when* and *why* it should be observed. There are 3 Major Historical Views as to the cause of Sabbath's fate:

1. **Nonsabbatarians**
   Believe the holy rest day has been *abrogated* by Christ
   Any day will do, but Sunday is convenient.
2. **Sunday Sabbatarians**
   Believe God's holy day of rest was *transferred* to the first day
3. **Saturday Sabbatarians**
   Believe God's holy day of rest is *perpetuated* on the seventh day

Abrogating Antinomians

Nonsabbatarians are generally also antinomians. In order to eliminate the Sabbath, they propose that the Law has been abolished altogether.

Abrogation was revived during the 16th century reformation. The Augsburg Confession of 1530 demonstrated these sentiments by confessing that "since the gospel has been revealed, all the ceremonies of Moses can be omitted." Andreas Bodenstein von Karlstadt (1480-1541), Dean of theology at Wittenberg U, wanted to take the reformation even further than Luther and reject anything without direct Biblical support; Luther was determined to retain everything not expressly forbidden. Though the split initially centered over "adoration of the host" (Luther for, Karlstadt against), it also included the issue of the Law and Sabbath observance. Luther was adverse to what he considered a legalistic and Judaizing religion; Karlstadt encouraged Christians to observe the Decalogue including the fourth commandment:

> "Sabbath keeping has a double object; in obedience to God we must rest in peace and pray to God for all holiness and wait to receive it. Moses said that the Sabbath is the rest of God."

While Karlstadt went on to influence Anabaptists and Mennonites, Luther's antipathy between Law and Gospel was later adopted by Puritans, Quakers and several modern antinomian denominations.

Wily Rordorf popularized this view in his 1968 book, *Sunday: The History of the Day of Rest and Worship in the Earliest Centuries of the Christian Church*. According to Rordorf, Sabbath was originally introduced as a "social institution" at the time of the Exodus and annulled by Christ when the Jewish nation rejected Him. Rordorf appeals to Christ's "provocative acts of healing" on the Sabbath as supporting evidence.

Donald A. Carson's *"From Sabbath to Lord's Day"* 1982 proposes that Christ transcended the Sabbath by His messianic claims, providing His followers the freedom to choose a new, reinterpreted day of worship. Carson maintains, however, that the use of Sunday as the new worship day didn't occur until the end of the Apostolic age.

Transfer Theology
Those who would merely transfer solemnity away from the seventh day are not quite as drastic. They narrow their focus to simply the Sabbath commandment and eliminate it as either a Jewish tradition or an archaic, arbitrary command that is now totally optional for the Christian Church.

Appreciation of "the basic underlying unity" between the Old and New testaments gave birth to the Transference View. When Constantine decreed the first Sunday Law in 321 AD, Sabbath requirements were simply shifted over to Sunday. Later, theological support for this transfer was developed in the writings of Thomas Aquinas during the early 13th century. Aquinas proposed that the 4th commandment contains both moral and ceremonial aspects. The need for rest and an inborn desire for worship were the moral qualities of the Sabbath precept, which he saw as natural and innate within the heart of man. But the specification of the seventh day and its symbolic link to creation were, in his opinion, of only ceremonial value.

This position ultimately resulted in the removal of the Sabbath just as effectively as the first view. Two hundred years later the Council of Trent decreed that this transfer and abrogation took place at the moment of Christ's death along with all the other Jewish rituals.

Calvin later added God's work in us and the protection of dependent workers to the moral qualities list.

Baptists, Methodists, Congregationalists and Presbyterians have all subscribed to this position. Recent works supporting it include *"This is the Day"* by Robert T. Beckwith and Wilfrid Stott, 1978, and *"The Lord's Day"* by Paul K. Jewett, 1971.

These authors maintain that the change of worship day did not destroy the meaning and practice of the Sabbath, "but rather enriches those meanings by relating the festival to Christ." Beckwith-Stott p. 44. Sunday is to them the "continuation and enrichment" of the Sabbath legacy.

But how can symbolic significance be transferred without destroying the original symbol? Indeed, the original is destroyed for all practical purposes by these adherents. "Continuation" and "enrichment" is all very well as long as these qualities are shared with the progeny.

How does the resurrection of Christ change the day of worship? What is the mechanism? Does it have precedent? Where is the documented collaboration from a divine source?

Jewet's idea is that the Old Testament promise of redemption (symbolized by the seventh day rest of a complete creation) was fulfilled by Christ, rendering the seventh day Sabbath of no further pertinence. And the New Testament promise of final rest and future resurrection (symbolized by the first day celebration of initial resurrection) awaits fulfillment by the second coming.

Then, at the sound of the last trump, one might expect that the first day would likewise be fulfilled and rendered of no further value and purpose. However, this is not a popular component of Sunday theology. Additional confusion is provided by the conflicting notions of a completed creation-rest receiving fulfillment at Christ's death and an unfulfilled resurrection-hope that is sustained by the prospect of a future heavenly rest.

Ratzlaff, a Nonsabbatarian, maintains that the Sabbath was the continual sign for weekly renewing the Covenant. And so it is. It is the "perpetual sign" that renews the Eternal Covenant every week.

Each Sabbath was a return to the Edenic state where God supplied every blessing, where His people could "freely eat" and they would spend the day communing with God, freed from the responsibility of work. And this principle was applied on an ever expanding scale.

> "Each of the Sabbaths pointed them forward with hope to the next sabbatical event. The seventh-day Sabbath was a weekly reminder of the coming seasonal sabbath. The seasonal sabbaths were a reminder of the coming sabbatical year. The sabbatical year was a reminder of the coming jubilee." Ratzlaff, *Sabbath in Crisis*, 1990, p. 61

What a wonderful description of the continued value of the Sabbath as it builds in ever expanding anticipation the "shadow of good things to come." Until these future events are realized, the Sabbath remains a valid and profitable symbol, a practical and vital sign.

Eliminating the Law

In order to explore in more detail the pathophysiology of abrogating the Law, we will conduct a thorough dissection of the heart. The status of God's Law is pivotal to Sabbath acceptance, pertinence and legitimacy to Christianity. Opponents of Sabbath observance have marshaled a host of arguments in their effort to eliminate it:

1. Sabbath was a positive law, revealed only to the Jewish nation.
2. Sabbath was a ceremonial law, part of the defunct Old Covenant.
3. Sabbath was one of the Ten Commandments, now abolished.

So determined to escape God's claim for the seventh day, they are even willing to annul His Ten Commandments. It is nothing new. Wesley recognized this behavior way back in the 18th century:

> "In the highest rank of the enemies of the gospel of Christ, are they who openly and explicitly "judge the law" itself, and "speak evil of the law": who teach men to break (to dissolve, to loose, to untie the obligation of) not one only, whether of the least, but all the commandments at a stroke. The most surprising of all the circumstances that attend this strong delusion, is that they who are given up to it, really believe that they honor Christ by overthrowing his law, and that they are magnifying His office while they are destroying His doctrine! Yea, they honor Him just as Judas did when he said, "Hail, Master," and kissed Him. And He may as justly say to every one of them, "Betrayest thou the Son of Man with a kiss?" It is no other than betraying Him with a kiss, to talk of His blood, and take away His crown, to set light by any part of His law, under pretense of advancing His gospel. Nor indeed can anyone escape this charge, who preaches faith in any such manner as either directly or indirectly sets aside any branch of obedience: who preaches Christ so as to annul, or weaken in any wise, the least of the commandments of God." John Wesley, Sermon 95.

Paradoxically, while the Christian world kisses off God's Decalogue, it struggles with a great deal of ambivalence in doing so. There is an undeniable appeal within its precepts to a sense of propriety. Few take exception with it as a reasonable code of ethics and morality. This is why it has served for millennia to influence the foundation of all civilized society.

Abolished

Sadly, there are many who believe and teach that part of God's Everlasting Covenant has been nullified, abolished, done away, removed, nailed to the cross. [See ENT Exam] This is especially amazing when we read that even the angels "do his commandments, hearkening unto the voice of his word." Psalm 103:20

- The great sin of the Jewish nation was in rejecting their Creator.
- For the Christian world it is in rejecting the Creator's Law.

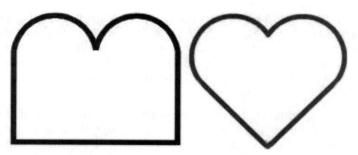

| Old covenant saints kept the law without the love behind it. They missed the blessings of love behind the sacrifices. | New covenant saints also miss the blessings of obedience to God's will by singing, "All You Need is Love." |

Because of the one commandment that asks us to remember it, many have looked for some way to forget it. While those who appeal to the Ten Commandments as the basis of Christian behavior are labeled as misguided legalists.

1. Natural, Positive and Moral Law

Theologians have sometimes identified two different classifications of law. Those that are recognized by all societies, even primitive ones, such as murder, stealing, lying, adultery are called "Natural Laws" because most people don't have to be told they are wrong. Paul referred to this innate understanding in Romans 2:

> "For when the Gentiles, which have not the law, do by nature the things contained in the law, these, having not the law, are a law unto themselves." Romans 2:14

A second category of law are those which are not "built in" such as the Sabbath commandment. Man may naturally sense the need for rest, but when to do so is not so natural. This is called "positive" law. Compared with the obvious rules of Natural law, Positive law often appears unnatural and arbitrary.

> "So which would be a greater mark of loyalty and love to God? Obeying a precept you naturally know is right, like honoring your parents? Or obeying a precept you don't naturally know is right, something you only know about because the God of heaven requested it, like keeping His Sabbath holy?" Bob Pickle in "*A Response to the Video: Seventh-day Adventism, The Spirit Behind the Church.*" Pickle Publishing Company, Halstad, Mn, 2002.

Arbitrary Laws

Adam and Eve could eat of any tree except one. How arbitrary of God to make a specified restricted access to food such a big deal—with a death penalty attached, no less! This was not a natural law. They had to be explicitly told which tree and the nature of the consequences for disobedience. This was very much a positive law. And its purpose was to test their loyalty to God.

Abraham was specifically told to circumcise the foreskin of his flesh. This was absolutely not a natural law! It wasn't obvious or plain to understand why it was necessary except that it was important for some reason to God. He explicitly asked Abraham to do it as a demonstration of his loyalty. And it had permanent implications whether he obeyed or not: either cut it off or you get cut off.

How arbitrary of God. Why foreskin? If He wanted a permanent physical alteration, why not a tattoo? Or a pierced ear? Besides, at least those markings would be an open and visible witness to one's divine allegiance and applicable to all members of the human race. God was testing Abraham's loyalty.

Sabbath is not a natural law.
It is an arbitrarily specified precept.
The day is based on the earth's rotation.
The month is based on the moon's orbit.
The year is based on the earth's orbit.
But the week is based purely on God's creative cycle of work and rest.

This may seem arbitrary of God to ask for the seventh day of our time, to keep it holy and worship the Creator. The sun rises the same on that day as on any other day. But it is this very unnatural aspect of time that also makes it an exceptionally good test of loyalty.

Bacchiocchi maintains that it was scholasticism, under the influence of classical philosophy, which fabricated the idea that the Decalogue is based on "Natural Law." Certainly the concept is not Biblical. In Scripture the Sabbath is presented as a divine revelation based on creation. It is not a natural law.

Moral and Ceremonial Law

A third division is frequently proposed in classifying the Laws of God. The Natural laws are called Moral, while the Sabbath commandment is claimed to be ceremonial. This idea is centuries old. Thomas Aquinas embraced it as far back as the 13th century:

> "The precept of the Sabbath observance is moral... in so far as it commands man to give some time to the things of God... but it is a

ceremonial precept ...as to the fixing of the time." Thomas Aquinas, *Summa Theologica,* New York, 1947, Part I-II, Q. 100, 3, p. 1039

Melanchthon, Luther's friend, also adopted the idea.

"In this commandment there are two parts, one general, which is always necessary for the Church, and one specific, which refers to a special day that pertains only to the government of Israel... For the *general* in this commandment pertains to that which is moral and natural and permanent, namely the keeping of the Church's worship; and the *specific*, which points to *the* seventh day, pertains to ceremony... it is not binding on us; therefore we have gatherings on the first day, namely on Sunday." Melanchthon, *On Christian Doctrine, Lou Communes 1555*, Clyde L. Manschreck, ed. and trans., Grand Rapids, 1965, p. 96

John Calvin likewise embraced this position. To him the Sabbath was merely "a legal ceremony shadowing forth a spiritual rest, the truth of which was manifested in Christ." (John Calvin, *Commentaries on the First Book of Moses Called Genesis*, trans. John King (Grand Rapids, 1948), p. 106).

Universal Eternal Moral Law
Some identify the Ten Commandment Decalogue as the fundamental moral standard on which the ceremonial statutes were based. Advocates of this view place the origin of the moral law in the heart of God from eternity past, as eternal as the Deity, a description of the Divine character. The Sabbath Commandment, in the heart and center of God's Ten Words, is likewise considered eternal and is believed to have been observed by all of God's creation throughout the universe even before the formation of our planetary system.

As part of God's redemptive process for recovering lost humanity and "because of transgression," He "added" (Gal. 3:19) to His already existing moral Law a more detailed body of laws (ceremonial, civil and dietary) to demonstrate before the rest of the world the appealing beauty of God's salvation, the justice of His dealing with domestic relationships, and the health advantages of His ideal lifestyle. But these are two separate laws; the Decalogue is purely moral.

Samuele Bacchiocchi asks, "How can observing a Day be moral, but observing the 7th day ceremonial? This proposition is based on the assumption that God only asks for a seventh of our time, whereas Moses picked the seventh day as a uniquely Jewish day. But is this a valid assumption?" Jesus didn't think so. He argued that if one day in seven was all that God required, the priests who worked Sabbath, the busiest day of the week for them, should have received another week day in which to rest as compensation for laboring all day Saturday.

"Is a principle from divine *example* less binding than one from divine *command*? Do not **actions** **speak louder than** **words**? What better way for God to demonstrate the Sabbath's moral qualities than to make it a rule of Divine conduct?" Bacchiocchi wonders. He then concludes:

After God rescued the children of Israel He revealed to them:

> **principles** of moral conduct and **provisions** for salvation

God gave Moses "the table of stone, with the *law* and the command-ment" (Ex 24:12) as a guide to moral conduct and behavior,
                                AND
the "pattern of the *tabernacle*" (Ex. 25:9) with its own laws to explain through symbolic examples His provision of grace and forgiveness.

...For the Jews Only
Old Covenant was made with ancient Israel only
This argument is claimed to be supported by the following text:
"The Lord made not this covenant with our fathers, but with us, even us, who are all of us here alive this day." Deut. 5:2, 3.
"Others could join the covenant community, but *only* if the males were *circumcised* and all *kept the Sabbath*." Ratzlaff p. 47

This is true. The covenant with Abraham was made only to Abraham. Likewise, the New Covenant was also promised only to "the house of Israel" and "Judah." Jeremiah 31:31. Yet the Christian church inherited the covenant by faith in allowing God to "graft them in" to the original olive tree. Romans 11:17.

But what about the Sabbath? Is it a relic of the Jewish past? "The children of Israel shall keep the sabbath" Ex. 31:16. But was the memorial to creation only made available to the Jews? If so, then is the "God of Israel" (Psalm 147:19, 20; Romans 3:1, 2; 9:4, 5) only the God of the Jews?

A Vital Heart Sign
When God renewed His covenant with Israel (Ex. 2:24) He "made known to them" His Sabbath (Neh. 9:14) saying, "My Sabbaths you shall keep, for it is a sign between Me and you" (Ex. 31:13), "I gave them My Sabbaths to be a sign between Me and them" (Eze. 20:12). Neither passage states that the Sabbath was made for Israel; it was given to them, entrusted to them. It was a sign "for in six days the Lord made heaven and earth, and on the seventh day He rested and was refreshed" (Ex. 31:17). Again, God explains the reason for the Sabbath when He rested at creation, not because manna rested on the seventh day during the wilderness wandering.

Jews Made for the Sabbath

The Sabbath was not made for the Jews, but the Jews were made for the Sabbath "that they might know that I am the Lord that sanctify them" (Eze. 20:12). But Jews have not only kept the Sabbath, the Sabbath has kept the Jews, sustaining them through exile and holocaust. By keeping it, they were sanctified, singled out, set apart from the rest of the world as His peculiar treasure, dedicated and committed to Him by their exclusive and loyal observance of His day. Yet,

> "It was not the Sabbath which had set Israel apart from all other nations, but it was the idolatry of all other nations that caused God to set the Hebrews apart for Himself." J.N. Andrews, *History of the Sabbath*.

Jehovah, His Law and His Sabbath did not become Jewish, but the Hebrew people became the chosen vessel to preserve a knowledge of God, His Law and the Sabbath in the world. God did not intend to restrict Himself or the Sabbath to only one small ethnic group. He offers to sanctify any that hallow the Creator's day.

> "Blessed is the man that does this, and the son of man that lays hold on it; that keeps the Sabbath from polluting it, and keeps his hand from doing any evil." Isaiah 56:2

He did not say "Blessed is the Jew that does this." In fact, Isaiah 56 clearly extends the invitation to "all people":

> 3 "Neither let the son of **the stranger**, that hath joined himself to Jehovah, speak, saying, Jehovah hath utterly separated me from his people.
> 4 For thus saith Jehovah unto the eunuchs that keep my Sabbaths, and choose the things that please me, and take hold of my covenant;
> 5 Even unto them will I give in mine house and within my walls a place and a name better than of sons and of daughters: I will give them an everlasting name, that shall not be cut off.
> 6 Also the sons of **the stranger**, that join themselves to Jehovah, to serve him, and to love the name of Jehovah, to be his servants, **every one** that keepeth the Sabbath from polluting it, and taketh hold of my covenant;
> 7 Even them will I bring to my holy mountain, and make them joyful in my house of prayer: their burnt offerings and their sacrifices shall be accepted upon mine altar; for mine house shall be called an house of prayer for **all people**."

The Sabbath was intended for *anyone* who has "joined himself to Jehovah" for God says that "everyone who keeps from defiling the Sabbath" will be accepted in His sight. Limiting the acceptance of worship to only certain peoples makes God guilty of favoritism and discrimination. Instead, God desires that all creation share in the union of spirit that His Sabbath provides. Instead of transferring the Sabbath to another day, God extends it to all people.

All-in-one General Purpose Jewish Commandments

Those who identify the seventh day Sabbath with Jewish religious practices maintain that it was given specifically to the Israelites at Sinai. They view the Sabbath as merely one part of an entire collection of laws and regulations that included civil, sacrificial, sanitary, dietary and moral statutes. These are then collectively and interchangeably called the "Law of God" as well as the "Law of Moses." For example:

> John 1:17 "The law was given **through Moses**, but grace and truth came through Jesus Christ"
>
> John 7:19 "Did not **Moses give you the law?**"
>
> Matthew 15:4 "**God commanded 'Honor your father and your mother;'** and 'He who curses father or mother let him be put to death.' "
>
> Mark 7:10 "**Moses said, 'Honor your father and your mother;'** and 'He who curses...' "
>
> Luke 2:22 "according to **the law of Moses**"
> Luke 2:23 "as it is written in **the law of the Lord**"

The "law of God" was also called the "law of Moses" in that Moses received it from God. Jesus said as much. "Moses therefore gave unto you circumcision; (not because it is of Moses, but of the fathers;)" John 7:22. Scripture plainly tells us that God gave circumcision to Abraham. It is credited to Moses because he, under God's direction, reinstituted it at the time of the Exodus as Israel re-inherited the signs of the covenant.

God's law plainly existed before it was formally "given" in the Old Testament, because when some tried to gather manna on the Sabbath, six weeks before the Ten Commandments were delivered on Sinai, God asked, "How long refuse ye to keep my commandments, my statutes, and my laws?" Exodus 16. In Genesis 26:5 God testified that "Abraham obeyed my voice, and kept my charge, my commandments, my statutes, and my laws." This was stated hundreds of years before Sinai.

Scriptural support for this all-in-one-general-purpose law position also includes such verses as:

Numbers 15:16 *"One law and one custom* for you and your stranger"
Galatians 5:3 "I am a debtor to keep the *whole law*"
Galatians 3:10 "continue in *all things* written in the book of the law"
Nehemiah 9:14 "You *made known to them Your holy Sabbath*, and commanded them precepts, statutes and laws *by the hand of Moses*"

Some have placed great significance in the words "made known" here to suggest that the Sabbath was not known before Moses made it known. In Ezekiel 20:5 God says, I "made myself known unto them in the land of Egypt." Surely this does not mean that before He made Himself known to the Hebrews in the land of Egypt God had no existence!

It appears that God had to repeatedly make known His Sabbath to Israel. He tested their fidelity to it with manna for forty years; He personally spoke the Sabbath commandment from Sinai; He personally wrote it with His own finger; He reminded them in the ceremonial and civil laws and repeatedly they "greatly polluted" His Sabbaths from the very start of their wilderness wanderings (Eze. 20:13). Not only because of their lack of faith in Caleb and Joshua's report were they prevented from entering the promised land after the spies returned from their reconnaissance mission, but "because they despised my judgments, and walked not in my statues, but polluted my Sabbaths" (Eze. 20:15, 16).

Finally, just before the next generation was to enter Canaan, Moses, now 120 years old, in his final month of life, rehearsed the history of their Exodus. His words are recorded in the book of Deuteronomy (*deuter* second, *nomos* law) where the Ten Commandments are recorded a second time. This time the significance of the fourth commandment changes from its focus on creation in the Exodus 20 version with man, in the image of God, resting like his Creator:

> "Keep the Sabbath day, to sanctify it, as the Lord thy God commanded thee. Six days thou shalt labor and do all thy work: But the seventh day is the Sabbath of the Lord thy God: in it thou shalt not do any work, thou, nor thy son, nor thy daughter, nor thy man-servant, nor thy maid-servant, nor thine ox, nor thine ass, nor any of thy cattle, nor thy stranger that is within thy gates; that thy man-servant and thy maid-servant may rest as well as thou. And remember that thou was a servant in the land of Egypt, and that the Lord thy God brought thee out thence through a mighty hand and by a stretched-out arm: therefore the Lord thy God commanded thee to keep the Sabbath day." Deuteronomy 5:12-15

Notice Moses refers to the original delivery of this commandment by saying they should keep it "as the Lord thy God hath commanded." God had already given the commandment in spoken and written form, this was a second rendition by Moses. Some have taken this version as proof that the Sabbath was given to the Jews at the time of the Exodus as a sign of their release from slavery. But God gave the Israelites another memorial of that event: Passover and the Feast of Unleavened Bread.

The redemption from Egypt is also given as the reason to be merciful to strangers, orphans and widows in a parallel passage from the same book:

> "Thou shalt not pervert the judgment of the stranger, nor of the fatherless; nor take a widow's raiment to pledge; but thou shalt remember that thou was a bondman in Egypt, and the Lord thy God redeemed thee thence; therefore I command thee to do this thing."
> Deuteronomy 24:17,18

If the Sabbath didn't exist before the Exodus, then God's expectation of compassion and humanitarian care for the disadvantaged was not required before that event either. And if the Sabbath is only Jewish, then kindness to the needy and helpless is also only a Jewish obligation. Logic and common sense demand that God is speaking universally to the human family in both of these and all other precepts of His law.

If the Sabbath was an Exodus festival, introduced by Moses with a manufactured creation linkage, then the reliability of all Mosaic literature would be seriously questioned. Instead, the Sabbath has many and multiple aspects of significance that will continue to dawn on the progressive consciousness of man over generations of contemplation on its divine origin, worth and purpose.

The Sabbath, in addition to its symbolic ties to creation and our Creator, in Deuteronomy becomes an emblem of liberation, freedom and release—originally for physical Israel liberated from the tyranny of Egypt, but now for spiritual Israel set free from the bonds of sin by our *Redeemer* at Calvary, and soon for the saints of God when they will at last be released from the curse of death at the dawn of the seventh millennium. No wonder James calls the Ten Commandments "the law of liberty" (James 2:12). By keeping them, we remain free of the devil's enslavement to this world. Bacchiocchi draws the following comparison:

> The 4th commandment in Exodus enjoins remembrance
> on the basis of **God's creative acts**.
> The 4th commandment in Deuteronomy is invoked
> on the basis of **God's deliverance**.

Does this change of Sabbath significance in Deuteronomy portend a future change in the day of worship? Is this a shift or an addition?

Sabbath Synergy
Sabbath is a multi-dimensional concept to be sure, and each individual quality synergistically enhances the whole. It's creative roots do not deny its redemptive value nor its future eternal application, just as God Himself is the One who was, is and is yet to come. His role as man's Redeemer does not dispense with His right to also be our Creator, nor His future title of the returning King of kings. Creation and Exodus speak of holiness in God's image *and* liberation from sin.

2. Ceremonial-Sacrificial Law

Objections to keeping "the law" invariably focus on the impracticality or inconvenience of practicing a Kosher diet or the unreasonableness of enforcing the harsh death penalties proscribed for adultery and Sabbath-breaking. While the civil regulations and dietary-sanitary laws continue to have validity and value in our present world, the ceremonial laws that specified all the detailed regulations for preparing and sacrificing a vast array of animals (meat), meal, and drink offerings are no longer relevant now that the ultimate sacrifice has been made by Christ for us.

The sacrificial system (and the ceremonial law concerning it) was "added because of transgression" Gal. 3:19. Transgression can only exist because a law also does. The law that was added would have to be subsequent to God's eternal moral law which is an expression of His own character. As soon as man sinned there was a Saviour. Jesus stepped into Adam's place, promised to take his penalty and a sacrifice was made for Adam right there in Eden's garden. Then this sacrificial ritual was practiced by every patriarch and throughout the

Old Testament "till the Seed should come," (Gal. 3:19) the Lamb of God who came to shed His blood for our atonement, to redeem us from the penalty of sin. Sacrifices are now no longer needed. In this all Christians agree.

Those same offerings and sacrifices are described in 2 Chron. 8:12,13: "Then Solomon offered burnt offerings unto the Lord... offering according to the commandment of Moses."

What were the commandment of Moses?
Lev, 7:1, "Likewise this is the law of *the trespass offering*."
verse 11, "And this is the law of *the sacrifice of peace offerings*."
verse 37, "This is the law of *the burnt offering, of the meat offering, and of the sin offering, and of the trespass offering*, and of the consecrations, and of the sacrifice of *the peace offerings*."
These were the laws regulating the sacrificial system.

These commandments, that dealt with sacrificial offerings within the law of Moses, were that part of the old-covenant sacrificial system which was "added... till the Seed should come" and then taken away by "the offering of the body of Jesus Christ" Heb. 10:10.

He Takes Away the First

Christ Himself says in Hebrews 10:9 "Lo, I come to do thy will, O God." Then the writer of Hebrews continues, "He takes away the first, that he may establish the second." What is Christ taking away? Surely not God's law, for verse 9 is actually quoting Psalm 40:7,8 which continues with the prophetic Messianic statement "...yea, thy law is within my heart." The law within the heart of Christ is directly tied to the second or new covenant that was to be established.

This explains why Hebrews 10:6 also quotes Jeremiah 31:33:

> "This is the covenant that I will make... I will put my laws into their hearts, and in their minds will I write them."

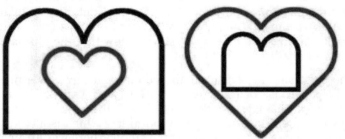

While Israel put their heart into the law,   God puts the law in our heart.

Same law, just a different location.

This law, embodied in the ten commandments, was magnified by Christ (Isaiah 42:21) as He transferred its precepts from external tables of stone to internalized tables of flesh, exemplified in His own life (He "tabernacled in the flesh," John 1:14) and empowered in the lives of all who trust in Him ("to them gave He power to become the sons of God," John 1:12).

Then what did Christ take away in the first or old covenant? The answer is given in Hebrews 10:1 the "sacrifices which they offered year by year." That's why they "ceased to be offered" verse 2. That's why "when he came into the world, he said, Sacrifice and offering you would not... in burnt offerings and sacrifices for sin you have had no pleasure." Verses 5,6.

Earthly priests "offering often times the same sacrifices" "can never take away sins" but Christ "offered one sacrifice for sins for ever." Verses 11,12. It is the sacrifices and their system of endless repetition that Christ took away, abolished and brought to an end with the sacrifice of His "own body on the tree."

When Jesus died, the temple services on earth were forever ended. Daniel had been given advanced notice of this climactic event by the angel Gabriel. The Messiah's death, in the middle of the last prophetic week, would cause the sacrificial system to cease.
See Appendix A for further details.

"And after threescore and two weeks shall Messiah be cut off, but not for himself... And he shall confirm the covenant with many for one week: and in the midst of the week he shall cause the sacrifice and oblation to cease." Daniel 9:26, 27

Keep One Keep All

The early Fathers adopted the notion of a Mosaic origin and exclusive Jewish ownership of the Sabbath to shame or at least challenge those who were defending the continued obligation to observe the Sabbath commandment. Lumping all law, Divine Commandments and Mosaic regulations, into one tidy package effectively consigns all Old Testament law to the Jewish dispensation. If you accept that the Old Covenant no longer exists then the Sabbath along with the other nine commandments can be thrown out together as well.

The implication, then, is that law-abiding New Testament believers must recognize the binding obligation to follow *all* the stipulations and requirements of the Old Testament law. If the seventh day is specified for the fourth commandment then the seventh month festivals and the seventh year land rest should also be observed. Realization of this principal has, in fact, lead some Christian groups to include at least the annual feasts as part of their worship experience. The practice, however, has been criticized as an arbitrary pick-and-choose approach. But there is evidence that for many years New Testament believes continued to observe them as demonstrated in the life and example of Paul.

Paradoxically, those who criticize a selective choice of Biblical practices, appear themselves to exercise a similar partiality in the application of law in the New Testament. There is no dispute over the validity and value of the Ten Commandments for Christians today as long as the fourth commandment is liberalized to mean one day of the week, typically the first, instead of the seventh as specified. Rationalization for this is based on the alleged implicit examples of first day observance by the apostles and Christ Himself. Yet the appeal to comparable examples of Sabbath observance demonstrated on a significantly greater number of occasions by the same individuals is surprisingly denied as invalid. But

> "He that despised Moses' law died without mercy under two or three witnesses: of how much sorer punishment, suppose you, shall he be thought worthy, who has trodden under foot the Son of God, and has counted the blood of the covenant, wherewith he was sanctified, an unholy thing, and has insulted the Spirit of grace?" Heb 10:29,29.

End of the Theocracy

The prospect of reinstituting death by stoning for convictions of marital infidelity and Sabbath misdemeanors appears unacceptable in our modern society. Religious freedom and the "separation of Church and state" has resulted in the discontinuation of capital punishment for religious infractions: blasphemy, idolatry and desecration of holy days. And rightly so. No human government can enforce the observance of the first four commandments without sacrificing freedom of conscience.   Likewise, no society can safely ignore enforcing the last six commandments without sacrificing the stability and moral integrity of civilization itself.

But governmental rule in our current world is no longer a form of Theocracy—direct rule by God—as was the case during the Old Testament era when prophets and judges carried out the judgments of God. Nevertheless, the divine penalties are still in force, and ultimately will be meted out to the whore of Revelation 17 and her apostate daughters for adultery with the world, for blasphemy against Jehovah, for the murder of His saints, and for desecrating the Fourth Commandment (Ezekiel 22:26, 31).

3. The End of the Law

Israel finally caught on to the idea that obedience to the Law was a good thing. It allowed God to protect and bless them. It saved them from becoming slaves to idolatry. After their return from exile, they focused on keeping the law to a fault. Paul observed "that they have a zeal of God, but not according to knowledge" Romans 10:2. Without fully understanding how God provided salvation through His Son, they became very zealous "going about to establish their own righteousness" verse 3, by legalistically following the letter of the law without understanding its spirit. Paul noted that this was doomed to failure "for Christ is the *end of the law* for [the purpose of attaining] righteousness to everyone that believeth," verse 4.

"End" has various and different meanings in Greek. James 5:11 uses a similar expression:

> "You have heard of the patience of Job, and have seen the end of the Lord; that the Lord is very pitiful, and of tender mercy."

Certainly the Lord has not come to an end. But what is *the end result* of the Lord's dealing with Job? In *the end*, the Lord showed mercy. In Romans 10:4 Paul is demonstrating the purpose of the law, what it "leads to," its final goal and what are its "end results."

"I had not known sin, but by the law." Romans 7:7. How would we know what sin is without the law? Is the law our problem?

Get Rid of the Mirror?

The law only displays the standard and exposes our failure to meet it. James compares the law to a mirror (James 1 :23-25). It shows us the spots and blemishes in our lives. So is the problem with the mirror? Is the solution to break the mirror? get rid of it? Will that make us clean again? The law cannot dispense righteousness; it cannot make us clean. That's not its purpose. Those who think they can look good to God by polishing up to the law are making a big mistake. Christ put an *end* to using the law in that manner.

The Law in Romans

The book of Romans traces the place of God's law in the new covenant. Paul certainly did not consider it abolished.

Chapter 2: Gentiles have a law written in their hearts (2:14, 15)
        But Jews are no better (2:23)
        Though they have the written law, the oracles of God (3:2)
Chapter 3: for all have sinned. (3:23)
        The law speaks to those who are under it,
        and all the world is guilty. (3:19)
        The law cannot save, only condemn. (3:20)
        So justification, comes only by Christ's death. (3:24, 25)
        "Do we then make void the law?
        No. We establish it." (3:31)

How? By accepting God's gifts.
the gift of forgiveness for our sins
        (offences against the law)
and the gift of righteousness
        (perfect obedience to the law).
And both gifts,

      forgiveness-justification   and   righteousness-sanctification

are provided in recognition and honor of God's good and perfect standard, the rule of life for all—Jews, Gentiles, and Christians.

Law Abiding Examples

James, the brother of Jesus, quoting two precepts from the Ten Commandments, argued for the integrity of the entire law:

> "For whosoever shall keep the whole law, yet offend in one point, he is guilty of all. For he that said do not commit adultery said also do not kill." James 2:10-12

Paul quoted the Ten Commandments in summarizing the concept of Loving our neighbor:

> "For this, Thou shalt not commit adultery, Thou shalt not kill, Thou shalt not steal, Thou shalt not bear false witness, Thou shalt not covet; and if there be any other commandment, it is briefly comprehended in this saying, namely, Thou shalt love thy neighbour as thyself." Romans 13:9.

Jesus quoted the Ten Commandments in defining this same idea:

> "Thou knowest the commandments, 'Do not commit adultery, Do not kill, Do not steal, Do not bear false witness, Honour thy Father and thy mother... sell all that thou hast, and distribute unto the poor... and come follow me." Luke 18:20,22

Paul believed everything written in the law and the prophets
    (Acts 24:14)
He did nothing "against the law of the Jews [or] the temple"
    (Acts 25:8; 28:17).
He lived "in observance of the law," and practiced ritual purification
    (Acts 21:24-26).
Jesus "as his manner was" (Luke 4:16)
    attended synagogue on the Sabbath.
Paul "as was his custom" (Acts 17:2)
    met regularly on the Sabbath in synagogues or open air
    with the Jews and Gentiles (Acts 13:14; 15:21; 17:2; Acts
    13:42, 44; 16:13; 18:4).

Jesus a Legalist?

Some explain that Christ only kept the Sabbath as a legalist! They claim that He only 'went along' with Sabbath observance in order to merely fulfill the law. At the end of His life He could honestly say, "Technically, I didn't break any of the commandments. I just kept them so I could do away with them." Such faulty reasoning leads to the real possibility that His perfectly obedient life can actually be used as an *excuse* to discount anything Jesus ever said or did. What percentage of His words or deeds are we to discard? This reasoning has no basis in scripture, it is only an attempt to ignore the example that Jesus has given both during His life as the Son of Man and in the beginning as the Creator of Man.

Law and Grace
A New Commandment

Just hours before His death, Jesus gathered the disciples around Him and gave them His parting words. "Peace I give unto you, Love one another even as I have loved you, Happy are you if you do them, that your joy might be full" and "a new commandment give I unto you that you love one another."

Did Christ suggest that He was scrapping the Ten Words of God, the Decalogue of Sinai, the great commandments which He had faithfully kept throughout His life? Was His new commandment really new? But more importantly, was it a substitute and replacement? Was He offering an alternate path to salvation? Was He merely affirming the sentiments of a modern song that says "All You Need is Love?"

Paul did say that "love is the fulfilling of the law" Romans 13:10. It fills full all legal requirements. Love as the motivation for keeping the law by no means eliminates it, but rather renders our observance acceptable and makes our actions reflect the Love of God that constrains us to keep it. 2 Corinthians 5:14.

This truth was rediscovered by Calvin and his followers during the reformation as they recognized in the Old Testament law a guide to Christ *and* holy living. "The law became increasingly important to prepare for grace, as a guide for grace, and to achieve assurance of grace." John H. Primus, *Holy Time: Moderate Puritanism and the Sabbath* (Macon, Georgia: Mercer University Press, 1989), p. 117

The Law of Christ
Jesus said,

> "If you keep my commandments, you shall abide in my love; even as I have kept my Father's commandments and abide in His love." John 15:10.

> "Observe all things whatsoever I have commanded you," Matthew 28:20.

> "Thou knowest the commandments, 'Do not commit adultery, Do not kill, Do not steal, Do not bear false witness, Honour thy Father and thy mother...'" Luke 18:20,22

Jesus indeed summarized the law in terms of love: "Love the Lord thy God with all thy heart and with all thy soul and with all thy mind. This is the first and great commandment" and the second is "love thy neighbor as thyself" Matthew 22:37, 39. But He also went on to say in the next verse that "on these two commandments hang all the law and the prophets."

The First and Great Commandment

"Thou shalt love the Lord thy God with all thy heart, and with all thy soul, and with all thy mind. This is the first and great commandment." Matthew 22:37, 38.

The first and greatest commandment is to love God with all our hearts, minds and souls. This describes the first four commandments which deal with *who* and *how* we worship:

1. Worship God **exclusively**, without any substitutes.
2. Worship God **directly,** without distracting images/saints.
3. Worship God **reverently**, without dishonoring His name.
4. Worship God **Creator** of all things by resting with Him.

The Second Commandment

"And the second is like unto it, Thou shalt love thy neighbor as thyself. On these two commandments hang all the law and the prophets." Matthew 22:39, 40.

The second commandment is to love our fellow man as ourselves. This describes the last six commandments which offer respect to:

5. heritage, **honor** your parents.
6. physical life, be **kind**.
7. marital relationships, be **pure**.
8. property, be **honest**.
9. truth and integrity, be **truthful**.
10. ownership, be **content**.

Law and the Gospel

A proper understanding of God's initiative and Man's response to the Everlasting Gospel is vital to a proper view of how God's Law should be regarded by the believer.

Is the Law our ticket to heaven? Or is it a condemning standard?
Is it our friend or our enemy?
Does it lead us to Christ or stand against us?
Did Christ win us through His Law? Or did He destroy it for us?

At the end of time, three prevailing views of the gospel will compete for the attention of the world's masses. Paul warned that there were other such gospels:

> "But though we, or an angel from heaven, preach any other gospel unto you than that which we have preached unto you, let him be accursed. As we said before, so say I now again, If any man preach any other gospel unto you than that ye have received, let him be accursed." Gal. 1:8-9

What are the other gospels?

Pagan religions have always viewed the path to salvation as being man's quest for God, forever attempting to satisfy the demands of an exacting deity. Salvation is granted to those who can be good enough. Followers of this gospel are legalists who depend on keeping a law.

During the long period of the Dark Ages, the Christian church developed a version of the gospel that viewed man turning to God, doing the best he could and then God meeting him half way and making up the difference. This gospel also depends, at least partially, on good works and legalism.

Discovery of God's amazing grace by the Reformers, as originally taught by the apostles, sparked a revolution in theology. Salvation was seen as a gift given freely by God and initiated by Him. God goes seeking after man "while we were yet sinners." There is nothing that man can do to earn salvation. This is the gospel of righteousness by faith alone.

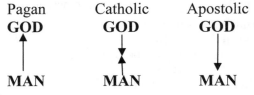

The New Testament Law

To really understand the role and purpose of the Decalogue within the New Testament, we must understand Christ's role as our New Covenant High Priest in the heavenly temple. "There is one mediator between God and man, even the man Christ Jesus" 1 Tim. 2:5. What is Christ's work as our mediator?

Jesus Our Mercy Seat Mediator

Above the ark was the mercy seat and above that was the Shechinah glory: the visible presence of God. The mercy seat or propitiation, was where the blood was sprinkled on the Day of Atonement as a symbol of a life sacrificed for each sinner's sin. Paul tells us that Jesus was "set forth to be a propitiation through faith in his Blood" Romans 3:25. John confirms this. "He is the propitiation for our sins, and not for ours only, but also for the sins of the whole world" 1 John 2:2. Jesus stood between us and the Law; He took our sins, our guilt, our death sentence and at the same time shielded us from the condemnation of the Law, dying in our place that we might live.

If the Law could have been changed or retired, dismissed or abolished, then Jesus died for no reason at all. For "where there is no law, there is no sin" Romans 5:12. Sin a problem? Then get rid of the Law. This is just what many Christians believe God did to solve the sin problem. When they enter the divine court of justice and are asked, "How do you plead?" they will say, "Your Honour, I am innocent because there is no law against the sins you listed; it was repealed at the Cross. You can't judge me. All things are now lawful!"

But the Judge will answer, "I came not to destroy the law (Matthew 5:17). I did not make void the law through faith (Romans 3:31). Sin is still the transgression of the law (1 John 3:4). The law hasn't changed, only the way in which men obtain grace." In fact, grace is meaningless without law.

The Law Establishes Grace
How does the law "establish grace?" Romans 3:31.
First, God judges us by His law.
Romans 8:2 speaks of 2 laws:
> the "law of sin and death" and
> the "law of the spirit of life"
Before Him, we receive either grace (forgiveness, justification, life)
> or punishment (condemnation, death).
>> We can accept the charges and take the penalty ourselves
>> or we can plead for mercy or grace
>> and allow a Substitute to take the penalty for us.
The Judge can aquit us from the charges made by the law against us
> only if Someone else takes the penalty.

Write Off
Many have the impression that God simply "writes off" the debt.
Such "cheap grace" allegedly eliminates the penalty altogether—
> no one has to pay for it.
> The Law doesn't really mean what it says.
> Sin isn't really so bad.
> God simply winks at it.

Real Grace
The Bible describes only one way to obtain grace.
> The guilty one must admit to the charges; (1 John 1:9)
> he must show remorse (Peter went out and wept)
> and express a desire to change his lawless attitude (repent);
> he must acknowledge the authority of the law (Romans 7)
> and the justice of his sentence.
Then he can plead for mercy on the basis of the Substitute
> who paid the penalty for him.
Mercy does not ignore the Law, it merely shifts the blame.
Yes, for *us* there is now no condemnation, no more guilt,
> no debt, no penalty, no shame, no pain—
> *our* sins are erased, blotted out, and removed.
> Because our Substitute has taken it all upon Himself.
> We don't suffer; but He does.

The law remains enforced; justice is satisfied—
>> not because the Law has been repealed,
>> but because the pentaly has been paid in full.

Under Grace

Now, the Judge can legally extend grace on behalf of the court,
>> pardon the plaintiff of his indictment
>> and release him of all charges.
>> He is no longer under the law, but under grace. Rom. 6:14.
>> He is not under the penalty of the law
>> but he is still under its authority and obligation.

In fact, he is now *double* obliged to uphold the law.
>> First, because the law's authority remains binding upon him
>> and secondly, in honor and respect for his Benefactor.
>> He is indebted to the One who paid his debt.
>> Paul says we are now "servants" of God,
>> obedient to His commands and commandments;
>> we are not simply set free to do whatever we please.

No Longer Under a Schoolmaster

"Wherefore the law was our schoolmaster to bring us unto Christ, that we might be justified by faith. But after that faith is come, we are no longer under a schoolmaster." Galatians 3:24, 25.

After faith in the Substitute is fully realized, we are no longer motivated simply because "the law says so." I view the law differently now; it has become a very personal thing because it directly affected my Defender. Being "under the law" is only the Law's view of me, not my view of the law.

Above the Law

Anyone who thinks he can get acquitted without payment of debt
>> and ignore the authority of law is viewed by the court as
>> an arrogant abuser of the legal system
>> who acts as if he is *above* the law
>> and has a license to break it with impunity.
>> Such a person will not receive grace.

The Bible calls this attempt to illegally obtain grace "lawlessness."
So, God does not repeal His law in order to acquit the sinner;
He upholds the law by paying the penalty Himself.

Even God "spared not His own Son" Romans 8:32.
Oh, how He wanted to. But He couldn't.
Jesus pleaded, "O my Father, if it be possible, let this cup pass from me" Matthew 26:39. But it wasn't. There was no other way.

Headache: Failed Promises

The Old Covenant was inadequate, not because of any fault in the Ten Commandments, the standard upon which it was based, but because of two glaring inadequacies. The first was the poor promises of the people, and second: animals were only proxy-substitutes for the Real Sacrifice to come. The promises failed because the *people* tried to obey the Law in human strength alone. And animals were not a permanent solution "for it is not possible that the blood of bulls and of goats should take away sins." Hebrews 10:4.

The promises originally made by Israel were not as good "because they continued not in my covenant" Hebrews 8:9. They didn't keep the promise they made twice: to do "all the words which the Lord has said" Exodus 19:8; 24:3.

Before Moses returned with the signed contract in duplicate (two tables of stone), the Israelites already broke their terms of the agreement. Part 1 Sections 1, 2 and 4 were contractually negated by the party of the second part. To wit: they put another god before them (a golden calf), they bowed down and worshipped the graven image, and established their own substitute day of worship.

> "Aaron made a proclamation, and said, Tomorrow is a feast to the Lord. And they rose up early on the morrow, and offered burnt offerings, and brought peace offerings: and the people sat down to eat and to drink, and rose up to play" Exodus 32:5, 6.

There was nothing wrong with the Everlasting Covenant based on God's commitment to ultimately provide the perfect Sacrifice and shed His blood to meet the just requirements of His own Law. But the reciprocal promises of the cosignatories quickly proved faulty. God then promised once again to redo the contract, not because the Old Covenant was faulty but "for finding fault with them," (Heb. 8:8) the people and their empty promises. This time, instead of putting His law in a golden box, obscured within a high-security restricted access enclosure, He promised to "put [His] laws into their mind, and write them in their hearts." Jeramiah 31:33; Hebrews 8:10. Same Law; new location.

Better Contract

Both the Mosaic Covenant and the Messianic Covenant were written documents. They were not merely verbal agreements. Both covenants had a written law. But the New Covenant is better because, instead of being written on stone, it is written on our hearts. Only God can do that. It's quite clear that Israel couldn't. They didn't last 40 days after promising "All that He has said we will do."

New Contract Initiation

In comparison, the New Covenant was ratified and activated by Jesus Christ at the time of His death (Heb. 12:24; 13:20; Matt. 26:28) "neither by the blood of goats and calves, but by His own blood" (Heb. 9:12). This immediately invalidated the earthly temple and all its sacrificial services. But the new covenant only went into effect the moment Christ died and not a moment before. "For a testament [covenant] is of force after men are dead: otherwise it is of no strength at all while the testator lives" Hebrews 9:17.

Last Will and Testament: Sealed

"Though it be but a man's covenant, yet if it be confirmed, no man disannuls, or adds thereto" Galatians 3:15. This means that after the death of Christ, nothing could be added to or taken away from the new covenant. Any changes that our Saviour would make in His New Testament church would have to be instituted before His death. This is why Jesus introduced the Lord's Supper on Thursday night *before* He died—so that it could be included under the new covenant provisions. Matthew 26:28.

All who believe that Christ ordered this change from Saturday to Sunday maintain that it was instituted "At the resurrection of Jesus." But that is two days too late. It could not be a part of the new covenant at that time. Nothing could be added after the death of Jesus, the Testator, when He cried out, "It is finished." Making a change in the Sabbath *after* His death would be trying to add to an already closed, confirmed and completed will. That would never fly in probate court.

But when Jesus declared, "It is finished" (John 19:30) "the veil of the temple was rent in twain from the top to the bottom" (Matt. 27:51) signaling the event taking place in the Real Temple that hung on the cross. Christ's humanity was suddenly exposed to His divinity. Jesus experienced what every sinner must experience: complete separation from the life sustaining power of His Father and exposure to the sin annihilating effect of His glory. There was now no need to offer further animal sacrifices, no need to rely on an earthly priesthood, no further use of an earthly temple—the Real Temple had just been destroyed. And in three days He would raise it up again.

The Perfect Sacrifice

Christ's mission had been a complete success. His perfect, sinless life was accepted as the perfect sacrifice for every trusting sinner. Now sinners had "a great high priest that is passed into the heavens, Jesus the Son of God" Hebrews 4:14. Now they could come directly, personally, and "boldly unto the throne of grace" (verse 16) whose foundation is "righteousness and truth," "mercy and judgment".

What does our High Priest do now that the sacrifice has been made? He still ministers in the sanctuary of heaven. But what is His ministry? Christians are now under the New Covenant, yet Paul reminds us that "both Jews and Gentiles... [are still] all under sin" Romans 3:9. He drives home our desperate need for salvation: "There is none righteous, no not one" verse 10; "For all have sinned and come short of the glory of God" verse 23. Does this change once we are saved? Are we then free from temptation, free from sin? If so, then repentance, confession, God's forgiveness and grace are no longer needed. Without sin in our lives, the law becomes immaterial "for where no law is, there is no transgression" Romans 4:15.

From Condemnation to Justification
Through faith in Christ's sacrifice and our confession of sin and repentance to turn away from it, we are justified back into acceptance with God and He treats me "just-as-if-I'd" never sinned. "There is therefore now no condemnation" (Romans 8:1) from our breaking the law—not because the law no longer exists, but because Christ "in the likeness of sinful flesh, and for sin, condemned sin in the flesh: that the righteousness of the *law* might be *fulfilled in us*" verses 3, 4. He allowed the law to condemn *our* sin in *His* flesh that the righteousness of *His* law might be filled-full within *us*.

> "For he hath made him to be sin for us, who knew no sin:
> that we might be made the righteousness of God in him"
> 2 Corinthians 5:21

As John Wesley liked to say, "What a marvelous exchange!"
Praise God for His unspeakable Gift.

Heading and Motivation
Jesus, at the head of the line, provides the most effective motivation for following Him and His commands: a response of gratitude and love for His great gift of eternal life by taking our sins and dying our death. Certainly we wish to please Him, to honor Him, to follow Him, bearing our own cross of self-denial, a living sacrifice, in His steps, who showed us the Way through the example of His sinless life. "I have given you an example that you should do as I have done to you." John 13:15.

Jesus did not insist that His disciples follow Him. He merely gave the invitation, "Follow Me." Jesus did not insist that His listeners stop their weary labor. He simply invited them to "come unto Me... and I will give you rest." Matthew 11:28.

- We are not saved by just faith, but obedient faith in Christ.
- We are not saved by just obedience, but faithful obedience in Him.

Our focus, while living the Christian life, is not on the law, but the Lawgiver. Keeping His commandments entitles us to nothing, but abiding in Him entitles us to every gift of the Spirit: grace, forgiveness, repentance, the robe of righteousness, justification, sanctification—they're all the gift of God. He "begins the work in us" and He will "bring it to completion" Philippians 1:6.

Yet how can we remain "safe in the arms of Jesus" without forsaking evil? Jesus came to save us *from* our sins (Matt. 1:21), not *in* our sins. Only through faith in the promise of His Spirit living in us, "the hope of glory," willing and doing of His good pleasure, can we experience any change from stubborn rebellion to loving obedience; from a life of empty powerless independence apart from God to the relief of surrendering our own efforts to the indwelling Spirit of God in whose "presence is fullness of joy" and "pleasures for evermore" Ps. 16:11.

There must be a change in deportment and demeanor, behavior and conduct, attitude and conversation, thinking and motivation when a believer is born again into a new creature, when old things pass away, and everything is new. Jesus said you can tell a person "by their fruits." And the fruits of the Spirit are in harmony with the standard of His law.

> "But the fruit of the Spirit is love, joy, peace, longsuffering, gentleness, goodness, faith, meekness, temperance: *against* such there is no law." Galatians 5:22.

But there *is* a law *against* all the sins in the previous two verses:

> "Adultery, fornication, uncleanness, lasciviousness, idolatry, witchcraft, hatred, variance, emulations, wrath, strife, seditions, heresies, envyings, murders, drunkenness, revelings, and such like... they which do such things shall not inherit the kingdom of God." Galatians 5:19-21

It is the Law that will keep the lost out of heaven even under the New Covenant.

It is the Law, fulfilled in the life of Jesus, embodied in His love, written in the heart, producing the fruits of the Spirit that brings peace and harmony with God.

> "Great peace have they which love thy law:
> and nothing shall offend them." Psalm 119:165

The Head

"Come unto Me, all you that labor and are heavy-laden, and I will give you rest... and you shall find rest unto your souls." Matt. 11:28

Examination of the head begins with a cursory evaluation of its gross external structure noting shape, deformaties and connection to the neck. This latter point, though usually taken for granted, is a legitamate consideration in special cases. Anencephaly (a congenital finding) and decapitation (an acquired condition) are significant physical details of the head exam that must be properly documented when observed.

When the head is detached from the body, viability for both parts becomes immediately jeopardized. Survival is, without exception, never possible. The head is in control of the body. You never want to lose it.

One Dr. Beaurieux recorded his interaction with a freshly severed head during a guillotine execution on June 28, 1905. He noted that the victim, named Languille, opened his eyes in response to calling his name for up to 25 seconds post beheading. This is a surpisingly long but unfortantely short time when considering the possibility of intervention in such cases. There has been general success in the surgical repair of amputated limbs. But the prospect of successful head reattachment is dismally bleak.

Paul entertained the idea of how various members might fair in isolation from the body. Jesus emphasized the vital connection between vine and branches. He is the head; we are the body. He is our example; we follow in His steps.

One of Christ's primary purposes in coming to this world was to live the law as a human being. He was the second Adam, doing what Adam could have done but chose not to, remaining loyal and faithful, while "in all things" being "made like unto his brethren;" He was "in all points tempted like as we are, yet without sin." Hebrews 2:17; 4:15.

> "I delight to do thy will, O my God: yea, thy law is within my heart"
> Psalm 40:8

This prophetic Psalm was written 1,000 years before Christ, yet it foretold exactly how Jesus would fulfill the New Covenant promise. God, speaking through Jeremiah, said

> "I will make a new covenant with the house of Israel, and with the house of Judah...I will put my law in their inward parts, and write it in their hearts." Jeremiah 31:31, 33

Christ not only came to establish the New Covenant, He *was* the New Covenant. This is why the writer of Hebrews quotes Psalm 40 when describing how Christ was a better sacrifice and a better priest than those that were part of the "Old Covenant."

Confirmation from Headquarters

Another and older name for the covenant is **testament** as in "last will and testament," "Old Testament," and "New Testament." At the last supper, Jesus "took the cup, gave thanks, and gave it to them" saying, This is my blood of the new testament, which is shed for many for the remission of sins" or as the Amplified Bible says, "the new covenant which *ratifies* the agreement" (Matthew 26:27,28).

Daniel, some 600 years earlier, had alluded to this very event when he spoke of "the Prince of the covenant" who would "*confirm* the covenant with many" (Daniel 11:22; 9:27). Daniel also indicated that this covenant prince would be "broken" following the rule of "a raiser of taxes." Of course, it was Jesus, "the Prince of Peace," the "Prince of princes," and "Messiah the Prince" (Daniel 9:6; 8:25; 9:25) who began His life during the reign of Caesar Augustus when he decreed "that all the world should be taxed" (Luke 2:1). Thirty years later Jesus began His ministry by proclaiming "The time is fulfilled" (Mark 1:15), the very time prophesied by Daniel.

3½ years later, "in the midst of the week," Jesus "confirmed the covenant," and "ratified the agreement." What agreement? Which covenant? Paul refers to it as "the covenant, that was *confirmed* before of God in Christ" (Galatians 3:17). Christ confirmed the original covenant, the same one that had been made before with Adam, Abraham and Moses.

To Adam and Eve God promised "the Seed of the woman;" Gen 3:15
To Abraham God promised to "provide Himself a lamb;" Gen 22:8
To Moses God promised to give the blood "to make atonement for your souls" Leviticus 17:11.

Head Master
Christ confirmed the covenant by becoming the Seed (Gal. 3:16) of the woman in the fullness of time (Gal. 4:4), presenting Himself to John who identified Him as the Lamb of God, and shedding His "blood of the new testament, which is shed for many for the remission of sins" (Matt. 26:28). He confirmed the covenant by keeping His promises. As a result He has earned the right to be "the mediator of a better covenant, which was established upon better promises" Hebrews 8:6.

Jesus and His Day
The Lord of the Sabbath had much to show and tell about the day He created. When Christ finally came to pay our little world a personal visit, He made each Sabbath an unforgettable day to remember for many of His suffering children. To these, the Sabbath became a wonderfully personal memorial of the day when God touched them. Who else could put an end to pain? Who could remove the burden of sin, or restore the dead and dying to life and love like the One who made all things?

Every Bible student knows that Jesus kept the Sabbath "as His custom was" every seventh day Saturday of His life. Luke recounts the very Sabbath on which Jesus announced the purpose of His mission as Messiah.

"And he came to Nazareth, where he had been brought up: and, as his custom was, he went into the synagogue on the Sabbath day, and stood up for to read. And there was delivered unto him the book of the prophet Esaias. And when he had opened the book, he found the place where it was written, The Spirit of the Lord is upon me, because he hath anointed me **to preach the gospel to the poor; he hath sent me to heal the brokenhearted, to preach deliverance to the captives, and recovering of sight to the blind, to set at liberty them that are bruised**, To preach the acceptable year of the Lord." Luke 4:16-19

The Anointed Messiah

Christ selected Isaiah 61 as His reading because it spoke of being "anointed" with the spirit. He was anointed at His baptism with the visible symbol of the Holy Spirit as John saw the form of a dove light above His head. Jesus was in effect stating that He was the Messiah since the word Messiah in Hebrew and Christ in Greek both mean "the anointed one."   And here Jesus was describing His mission in terms of Sabbath language: liberation of captives, release of prisoners, and proclamation of the acceptable year.

Sabbath Miracles: Liberation, Deliverance, Release

Jesus performed many of His most dramatic miracles on the Sabbath. What was His intent in deliberately choosing Sabbath? Some interpret these Sabbath healings, as did the Pharisees, an intentional denial of the Sabbath obligation—breaking the law as a sign that the law was no longer binding. But was He releasing men from bondage to Sabbath-keeping or from bondage to sin and suffering so that true Sabbath observance could be fully realized?

Jesus deliberately chose the Sabbath to directly demonstrate its primary redemptive purpose of release from work and bondage to sin. Right after proclaiming His Messianic mission to "deliver the captives" and "liberate the bruised," He gives spiritual healing to a demon-possessed man right in the middle of a Sabbath service (Luke 4:16-21); He restores Peter's mother-in-law the same day so she could "serve them" (Luke 4:39). Jesus especially enjoyed healing the chronic cases on the Sabbath. Christ performed seven recorded acts of healing on the Sabbath. And every one was for a chronic long-term, incurable case. He healed the man crippled for 38 years at the pool of Bethesda (John 5), and the man born blind from birth (John 9). Later, when He healed the woman with a crippled back on the Sabbath, He explained:

"Ought not this woman, being a daughter of Abraham, whom Satan hath bound, lo, these eighteen years, be **loosed from this bond on the Sabbath day**?" Luke 13:16

He then tells her she is "freed" from her infirmity and chides the Jews for their objection since they "untie" their livestock on the Sabbath. Satan binds us, through sin, to a life of pain and regret, suffering and disappointment, hard labor in the prison of sin. Sabbath, of all days, is the most appropriate for restoring health, delivering trapped sinners, and redeeming bruised spirits.

Sabbatical Years

The Sabbath release also extended to the sabbatical years.

> "At the end of every seven years, in the solemnity of **the year of release**, in the feast of tabernacles...thou shalt read this law before all Israel in their hearing." Deuteronomy 31:10

> "At the end of every seven years thou shalt make a release." This included debts that were still outstanding. Creditors were not allowed to "exact it of his neighbor or of his brother; because it is called **the Lord's release**." Exodus 15:1

Exodus 21:1 describes the law of the Hebrew slave. If an Israelite landed on hard financial times, he could pay off his debt by working as a bonded slave for seven years. At the end of the seven years he was free to leave—debt free, but with only the shirt on his back. Any relationships formed during his term of service, including the product of those relationships such as a wife and children, remained the landlord's possession. The slave was free to go, but wife and children would have to stay behind—unless. There was only one way he could keep his family: become a servant for life.

"I love my wife and my children," he would tell his master. "I can't bear the thought of leaving them!" Then a very special and unique ceremony was performed. The master would take the freeman to a doorpost and pierce his earlobe with an awl as a sign that this man was a "lifer," permanently casting his lot with the woman and children he came to love.

What a beautiful picture of Jesus and His love for the Church, His bride and children. At the end of His mission He was free to return home to His Father. But He said, "I can't simply abandon my family; I love them too much!" Then He was pierced—not just His ear, but His hands, His feet, His side. These scars will ever remain a sign that He is tied to us with a bond of love for life and eternity.

Acceptable Year of the Lord

The Nazarean congregation anxiously waited for Christ to read the next phrase: "the day of vengeance of our God." But Jesus stopped after proclaiming the acceptable year of the Lord. It is not coincidental that it was in fact a sabbatical year of release when Jesus spoke these words a few months after His baptism. AD 27 was 69 x 7 years after the beginning of the command to rebuild Jerusalem made by Artexerxes in 457 BC. And 457 was a Jubilee-Sabbatical year. This is established by the fact that it occurs on the 5th Jubilee anniversary of Hezekiah's deliverance in 702 BC.

```
702                  457                          27      34
 BC                   BC  ◄─────── 69 weeks ──────► AD
 └──── 5 Jubilees ────┴──────── 10 Jubilees ──────────┘
```

1 Jubilee = 49 (7 x 7) years
5 Jubilees = 5 x 49 = 245 years   10 Jubilees = 10 x 49 = 490 years
702 - 245 = 457   490 − 457 + 1 (no zero year) = 34 AD

Jesus, aware of the deep significance of that exceptionally acceptable year, announced "The time is at hand." Mark 1:15. See Appendix B.

Sabbath Dialogs

"Jesus spent little time... defining sin," Des Cummings, Jr. reminds us. "He spent most of His time demonstrating love... When Jesus came to save the world, He found that humans had taken possession of His day... They had a negative approach to a positive day."

Jesus' Approach	**Pharisees' Approach**
A day for love	A day for law
A day to fully live	A day simply to endure
Focused on delight	Focused on duty
Emphasized doing good	Emphasized avoiding evil

Jesus engaged the clergy in several discussions about the Sabbath. In every instance, the debate was sparked by His intentional acts of healing on the weekly day of rest. The current view of Sabbath-keeping did not provide for the practice of disease elimination, physical restoration or curative healing. Jesus defended His actions by appealing to the original purpose of the Sabbath: rest from labor, and by extension, rest from sin.

The Yoke of Rest

Paul used the metaphor of working for sin when he said "the wages of sin is death" Romans 3:23. And so does Christ when He invites "all ye who labor and are heavy laden" to come to Him, Lord of Sabbath release, because He promises to "give you rest." Matthew 11:28.

> Take my yoke upon you, and learn of me; for I am meek and lowly in heart: and ye shall find **rest** unto your souls. For my yoke is easy, and my burden is light. Matthew 11:29, 30

Once again, Christ presents a paradox of contrasting ideas. He offers an easy yoke that brings rest; a burden that is light. What is the yoke? What is the burden? Not the sterile legal demands of obedience alone (whether to a foreign nation Jer. 2:20 or the practice of circumcision Acts 15:10; Gal 5:1), but the acceptance of Christ as our Saviour, our Redeemer. He does what the law by itself cannot do—He removes our burden of condemnation and guilt by condemning our sins in His own flesh (Romans 8:1-3); He makes us holy on His holy day by fulfilling the righteousness of the law in us as we walk after the Spirit (verse 4).

In the Greek Septuagint translation of the Old Testament, the Hebrew term for "release" (*deror*) used in the Leviticus 25 account of Jubilee and Sabbatical years, is translated as *aphesis*—the word that is used in the New Testament for "forgiveness." This is why Jesus said in the Lord's Prayer's phrase "forgive us our debts" (Matt 6:12) "as we forgive our debtors." The Sabbath, Sabbath years, and the Sabbath of Sabbaths all speak of release from financial debt, liberation from social injustice, and redemption from the bondage and burden of sin. That this is what Jesus had in mind is clearly indicated by what happened next.

Crop Cops

It is more than coincidental that the very next verse begins the famous encounter between Christ and the Legal Eagles, the crop cops, self-proclaimed guardians of the holy day, as He and the disciples walk through a field on the Sabbath.

These holy day vigilantes were very acquainted with all the nit-picking rules for proper Sabbath-keeping that had been embellished by Rabbis for hundreds of years. These miserable misdemeanors included:

Unfastening a button, scraping shoes (except with the back side of a knife blade), wiping a wound, applying a dressing to a wound, applying medicinal alcohol (except orally as part of a meal), moving a sheaf (unless in contact with a spoon), allowing milk to curdle, carrying anything that weighed more than a dried fig, carrying handkerchiefs (except within the city walls), carrying needles or ribbons (unless firmly attached to your clothing), working to save the life of a person (unless it was a Jew), giving comfort to the sick, giving cheer to the sorrowful.

It was equally unlawful to travel more than 2,000 cubits (except from home to home, even a miniature sham dwelling constructed for the very purpose of circumventing this rule), eat an egg laid on the Sabbath (unless the hen is also eaten that day), carrying a body (unless it is alive), taking a shower (although bathing or swimming was OK), erasing one large letter and replacing it with two smaller ones (replacing it with the same sized larger letter was permissible).

And rubbing heads of wheat between your fingers (threshing), bruising the grains (grinding) or tossing them in your palm (winnowing). It was this rule that drew the scorn of Christ's critics.

Jesus defends their conduct by appealing to the work of the priests on the Sabbath, the busiest day of the week for them, with no compensation provided on an alternate day (thus supporting an "every-seventh-day" observance rather than merely "one-day-in-seven"). He quotes Hosea 6:6, applying it as He did earlier (Mark 2:27) in teaching that the purpose of Sabbath is "mercy" (redemptive work directed toward man) rather than "sacrifice" (religious duty directed toward God). And again He concludes that "the Son of Man is Lord of the Sabbath." Matt. 12:8. It is His day.

It is only right that He should be able to relieve hunger, and thirst, aching hearts and crippled limbs, blind eyes and deaf ears on the day He created. Why? Because "One greater than the temple is here."

Jesus was charged with breaking the Sabbath, not for stealing, when He allowed His disciples to pluck and eat grain while they walked through someone else's field. He was accused of healing chronic, non-emergent cases. Repeatedly!

> "And He said to them, 'The Sabbath was made for man, and not man for the Sabbath. Therefore the Son of Man is also Lord of the Sabbath.'" Mark 2:27, 28

Precedent was established by the fact that man's creation preceded the Sabbath. Woman was made for man because she was created *after* Adam. Paul makes this very point:

> "Neither was the man created for the woman; but the woman for the man." 1 Corinthians 11:9

Likewise, the Sabbath was made for man because it was created *after* man. In a related discourse, Jesus connected marriage to the time of creation as well when He said, "from the beginning it was not so." Matt 19:8. Both marriage and Sabbath can be traced to their origins at creation; both are fundamental to the benefit of mankind.

The Sabbath was made for man, but it was not made by man. It was not the work of any priest, prophet, church or council. Jesus said the Sabbath, the Lord's own day, was the Creator's thoughtful gift to man, ανφροποσ, *mankind,* not just to the Jews, but for the entire human race. And He provided it to be a blessing, not a burden. He sought to disencumber the Sabbath of all Pharisaical rigor and divest it of all human additions.

Furthermore, He claimed to be its Lord, Owner and Master. But His Lordship is protective not tyrannical. Only a petty humanistic spirit can imagine the Lord of the Sabbath "doing with it whatever He wants—change it if He wants, get rid of it if He wants to." The self-righteous critics in Christ's day behaved exactly like that. They fulfilled their plan to abolish the Lord of the Sabbath one Friday afternoon and then hurried home to keep His day.

A loving Creator made the world; He made man and He made the Sabbath. And He showed by example and verbal instruction *how* to keep it, not *whether* to keep it. Though He had a perfect opportunity to explain its irrelevance, or its obsolescence He gives no such indication that men need no longer keep it.

Matthew 5:18,19

> "Think not that I am come to destroy the law, or the prophets: I am not come to destroy, but to fulfill. For verily I say unto you, Till heaven and earth pass, one jot or one tittle shall in no wise pass from the law, till all be fulfilled."

Till All Be Fulfilled

Jesus here states that no part of the law would be eliminated until all of it be fulfilled, as long as there is earth beneath our feet and sky above our heads.

Has "all" been fulfilled? Is there any part yet to be fulfilled? The sacrifices for sin offerings were fulfilled by Christ's sacrifice on the cross. The spring feasts (Passover, Unleavened Bread, Wave Sheaf, Pentecost) pointed directly to the Messiah (His sacrificial death, burial, resurrection and ascension) and were fulfilled at the time of the crucifixion and shortly after. But the fall feasts (Trumpets, Atonement, Tabernacles), though initiated in some aspects (Judgment warnings, Pre-advent Investigative Judgment), have not yet been fulfilled in their entirety.

Has God, our Creator, changed His mind about the Sabbath? The weekly Sabbath is a foreshadow of the millennium. Although some believe that this time period has come, it has still to be fulfilled.

The entering into the Promised Land of Canaan and God's resting on the seventh day were both foreshadows of something to come. God worked for six days in creating heaven and earth, then rested on the seventh day, thus creating the Sabbath. Recorded history of mankind is now about six thousand years. God has promised one thousand years when Satan, bound to a bottomless pit, cannot tempt mankind. Thus, the Sabbath is representative of the Millennium. Is Satan still in the business of tempting? Does he still wreak havoc on our planet?

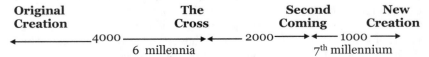

Isaiah, the gospel prophet said, "He will magnify the law, and make it honourable" Isaiah 42:21. Christ respected the law. He had much to say about our obligation to keep it. But His focus was on the underlying purpose of the law, it's value to us as a guide to life and conduct. After declaring His intent to "fulfill" the law, He lists how He would "fill it full" of meaning and expand its application to real life situations that involved the commandments dealing with killing and hatred, adultery and divorce, lying and loving.

Matthew 5:21-48 is the prime example of Christ as Interpreter of the Torah. In these verses He demonstrates the contrast between the prevailing traditional understanding of what the Law *requires* with a new and fresh concept of what God *desires*. He gave several examples to clarify and explain the true meaning of the law. These statements of Christ expanded on the spirit of the law, they did not replace the letter of the law, but rather built on it, "not to nullify or modify...but to clarify and reveal its deeper meaning." [Bacchiocchi, *Crossfire*, Chapter 3, Part 2B]

But Jesus also had much to say about the perverted understanding of the law, the rabbinical traditions that were being promoted by the legalistic leaders of the day.

> "Woe to you, scribes and Pharisees, hypocrites! For you pay tithe of mint and anise and cummin, and have neglected the weightier [matters] of the law: justice and mercy and faith. These you ought to have done, without leaving the others undone." Matthew 23:23

Jesus commended the Pharisees' attention to detail. "These you ought to have done."   But He rebukes them for their misdirected motives—doing the right things for the wrong reasons. Today, many think that all we need to concern ourselves with is justice, mercy and faith, because Jesus had to emphasize this aspect so much. Certainly these are important, but Christ also said, "Do not neglect the other points." Jesus kept His Father's commandments as our example. (John 8:55, 1 Peter 2:21-22).

Jesus persistently struggled to correct the entrenched, distorted Sabbath traditions of the Pharisees. At every opportunity He tried to free His day from the mountain of burdens that had been heaped upon it. How unfair for modern Pharisees to suggest that Christ's effort in rescuing the Sabbath from man-made restrictions is evidence that He disregarded it! To construe Christ's work of Sabbath restoration as proof of its abrogation, that He intentionally violated the fourth commandment to demonstrate its obsolescence is to echo the Pharisees of old: "This man is not of God, because he keeps not the Sabbath day" John 9:16.

Fulfill

"Fulfill" cannot mean "abolish" without destroying the internal logic of Christ's statement. Consider the text if it did express this meaning:

> "I have not come to destroy the law but to abolish it."

Such a remark is senseless double-talk. Then what does fulfill mean? This word is first used to describe Rebekah's delivery readiness.
"when her days to be delivered were fulfilled" Genesis 25:24.
Next, Jacob claims Rachel because he has fulfilled his obligation.
"Give me my wife, for my days are fulfilled." Genesis 29:21.

Fulfilling time, then, means to complete the specified time period.

But although the time is past, the object for which they were waiting is now reality—it has finally arrived. That which was fulfilled has even greater meaning and significance now that it is fulfilled.

Solomon blessed God for keeping His promise to build a temple. "...fulfilled it with Thine hand as it is this day." 1 Kings 8:24. The promised is not abolished but confirmed, it is kept.

Scripture is fulfilled. Matthew 26:53, Mark 14:48, Luke 4:21.
God fulfills prophecy. Ezra 1:1, Daniel 4:33, Matthew 1:22.
God fulfills His own word. Lamentations 2:17.
Obviously, fulfilling here means "to keep, to confirm."

Joy is fulfilled. John 3:29; cf. 17:13; Philippians 2:1.
Paul and Barnabas fulfilled their ministry. Acts 12:25.
Paul asks the Colossians to fulfill his ministry. Colossians 4:17.
David fulfilled the will of God. Acts 13:22. He didn't do away with it.
Christ fulfills the righteousness of the law in us. Romans 8:4.
Love fulfills the law. Romans 13:8. Love is keeping the law.

We are not to fulfill the lust of the flesh. Galatians 5:16.
In the past we fulfilled the desires of the flesh. Ephesians 2:2.
We no longer keep, confirm, observe fleshly desires.

It must be concluded that Christ was not announcing the *end*, the termination of the law and prophets, but rather their final prophetic *realization* as exemplified in His own life. The law and prophets were to continue, to live on in the life of Christ and His followers.

Sabbath Flight

> "Pray that your flight be not in the winter nor on the Sabbath day"
> Matthew 24:20

Jesus was giving a prophetic warning to His followers concerning the destruction of Jerusalem which was yet 40 years in the future. This indicates that Jesus foresaw no change in the Sabbath after His ascension.

Some have suggested that this is because Jesus didn't want His followers to get stuck inside Jerusalem during the Roman siege since He knew that those pesky Jews would have the city gates closed on the Sabbath. Nehemiah, after all, initiated this practice to stop the Jews from carrying on commercial activities on the seventh day. But Jesus said "Let those who are in Judea flee to the mountains." Not just Jerusalem.

From Garden to Garden

Jesus told John at His baptism, that it was necessary for them "to fulfill all righteousness" Matthew 3:15. It is truly amazing how many aspects of the Old Testament symbolism really *were* fulfilled in the details of His life. This is especially evident during the events of Passover weekend. Even in death He honored the Sabbath.

Not only did Christ keep the Sabbath after creating the Garden of Eden but also after visiting the Garden of Gethsemane.

- In Eden, He created life with His breath.
  At Calvary, He redeemed life with His blood.

- From a finished Garden of Eden He pronounced "It is very good."
  From Gethsemane He went to Calvary and said "It is finished."

- From Eden, He finished His work and entered into Sabbath rest.
  From Calvary, He finished His work, and entered into Sabbath rest.

"Both in the Garden and at the Cross, God completes His work on Friday." "In both cases the universe needed to stop and spend time absorbing God's love" (Cummings, Jr. p. 16). "Stop and know that I am God." Psalm 46:10. Then, late Friday afternoon, on the day we now call Good Friday, Joseph of Arimathea placed the body of our Lord in his own unused tomb. The rest is history.

Spring Feasts Fulfilled

Jesus perfectly fulfilled the prophetic symbolism of the spring feasts at His death. The Passover festival began on the 10th day of Nisan, the first month of the Jewish liturgical year. On this day the Passover lamb was selected. Traditionally, this has been placed on Palm Sunday when Jesus was selected as Messiah by the people as they paraded Him with shouts of Hosanna into the city of Jerusalem.

It was to be a perfect sacrifice "without spot or blemish." Jesus is our sinless Lamb. "Who of you convictes me of sin?" He asked. Pilate examined Him and announced, "I find no fault in him."

Then on the 14th of Nisan, in the evening, the lamb was slain and its blood was painted along the sides and over the lentil of the front door in every dwelling. This produced the shape of the Hebrew letter *het*, which is the eighth letter of the Hebrew alphabet. It was symbolic of circumcision because it was performed on the eighth day, and hence implied a separation, a fence, and even life. The sign of the blood indicated the inhabitants were separated by circumcision in a covenant with God. Only those who were circumcised could partake of Passover.

In the year that Christ was crucified, Passover fell on either a Thursday or a Friday depending on how one interpreted the instructions given in Exodus, Leviticus and Deuteronomy. The choice of which day to observe was then and is now the cause of much discussion and debate. The traditional dating aligns Good Friday and Resurrection Sunday as is diagrammed in the following table:

Nisan First Month	13	14	15	16
	THU	FRI	SAT	SUN
	Last Supper	Passover Crucifixion	Unleavened Bread	Wave Sheaf
		Good Friday	Holy convocation	First Fruits

GOOD FRIDAY
Nisan 14 "The Lord's Passover" Leviticus 23:5
"That day was the preparation, and the Sabbath drew on" Luke 23:54.

SATURDAY SABBATH
Nisan 15 First day of Feast of Unleavened Bread
They "rested the Sabbath day according to the commandment" Luke 23:56
"Seven days you must eat unleavened bread. In the first day you shall have a holy convocation: you shall do no menial work therein." Leviticus 23:6,7.
"That Sabbath was a high day" John 19:31.

EASTER SUNDAY
Nisan 16 Feast of Firstfruits or Wave Sheaf
"Very early in the morning the first *day* of the week" Mark 16:1.
"bring a sheaf of the first fruits of your harvest" Leviticus 23:10.
"on the morrow after the Sabbath the priest shall wave it" Lev. 23:15.

Today, many refer to the preparation day as Good Friday. Christ was slain at the time of the evening sacrifice "at the ninth hour" (Matthew 27:46), about 3 PM. With sunset only 2-3 hours away, many preparations had to be quickly made to remove and prepare His body for burial in Joseph's tomb before the Sabbath.

High Sabbath
The day following Passover was the start of a week-long festival called the Feast of Unleavened Bread. The first and last days of this feast were designated as rest days or ceremonial sabbaths. That year the first and last days of the feast would fall on Saturday and the following Friday. Thus when Christ died, the Creator rested in the tomb on a seventh day Sabbath, the day He blessed and sanctified and rested at creation, which that particular year was also the first rest day of the Feast of Unleavened Bread. This made it a double-Sabbath and it was recognized as having special significance by John

in his gospel. The Jews, concerned about leaving victims "upon the cross on the Sabbath day" went to Pilate to see about taking them down "because it was the preparation" and "that Sabbath day was a high day" John 19:31. The Greek word for "high" in this verse is *megas*, this particular sabbath was a Mega Sabbath.

Though the Festival of Unleavened Bread was originally specified to last seven days, in later years an extra day was added because of the additional time it took to reach outlying communities. This practice is still observed by Orthodox and Conservative Jews who extend the feast to a full eight days, whereas Reform Jews keep the original seven day feast. Either way, the first day of unleavened bread apparently coincided with the Passover since unleavened bread was eaten then as well.

> "Now the first day of the feast of unleavened bread the disciples came to Jesus, saying unto him, Where wilt thou that we prepare for thee to eat the Passover?" Matthew 26:17-19

Alternative Dates

Dissatisfaction with the traditional arrangement comes from making it fit the important 10th day selection of the lamb with the Triumphal Entry of Christ on Palm Sunday and His statement that "the Son of man," like Jonah, would be "in the heart of the earth" for "three days and three nights."

10	11	12	13	14	15	16
MON	TUE	WED	THU	FRI	SAT	SUN
			Last Supper	Passover Crucifixion	Unleavened Bread sabbath	Wave Sheaf resurrection

As you can see, the 10th day would have fallen on Monday of Passion Week not Sunday, as many would like to favor. On this day, Jesus cleansed the temple the second time, calling it this time "My house." Matt. 21:13. He also cursed the fruitless fig tree on this day. Though all eyes in Jerusalem had been on Him the day before, it was on Monday, the 10th that the Lamb restored the temple in preparation of His sacrifice and pronounced doom on the nation that would reject the Real Passover.

Matthew, Mark and Luke place the Passover that Jesus kept on Thursday night. John's gospel, however, says the Jews were planning to celebrate Passover on the night following the crucifixion. This apparent discrepancy illustrates the controversy over dating that existed at the time of Christ. It all had to do with how Leviticus 23:15

should be understood. This text specified when the Feast of Firstfruits was to occur. The conservative Pharisees believed "the sabbath" preceding Firstfruits-Wave Sheaf was the "holy convocation" annual sabbath that fell on the first day of Unleavened Bread. But the liberal and ruling Sadducees believed that "the morrow after the sabbath" referred to the day following the seventh day weekly Sabbath that would occur sometime during the week long feast of unleavened bread.

Three Days and Three Nights
More recently, some have noted that a period from Friday evening to early Sunday morning is only two nights and little more than one full day. This doesn't appear to fulfill the "three days and three nights" that Christ specified on one occasion Matt, 12:40. The most popular attempt to reconcile this has been to propose a Wednesday crucifixion and a late Saturday resurrection.

11	12	13	14	15	16	17	18
SUN	MON	TUE	WED	THU	FRI	SAT	SUN
		Last Supper	Passover Crucifixion	Unleavened Bread sabbath			Wave Sheaf

Jesus mentioned this three day period many times:
"in three days" Matt. 26:61; 27:40; Mark 14:58; John 2:19-21.
"after three days" Matt. 27:63; Mark 8:31.
"on the third day" Matt. 16:21; 17:23; 27:64; Luke 9:22; 24:21, 46.

Only once, when quoting Jonah 1:17, did He use the phrase "three days and three nights" Matt. 12:40. But Jesus explained His most common expression, "on the third day," when He sent a message to Herod:

> "Go and tell that fox, Behold I cast out devils and I do cures to day and to morrow, and the third day I shall be perfected. Nevertheless I must walk to day, and to morrow, and the day following: for it cannot be that a prophet perish out of Jerusalem." Luke 13:32, 33.

He was clearly speaking of His death, which must not only take place in Jerusalem, but on "the third day." His formula applied the commonly used "inclusive time reckoning" method. For example, see Genesis 42:17-19, 1 Kings 12:5, 12 and 2 Chron. 10:5, 12. He was in effect saying:

"today"	the day of the crucifixion, Passover
"tomorrow"	the day after, Unleavened Bread
"third day"	the resurrection, Firstfruits

When was the third day? Scripture consistently is clear and united: "the first day of the week" Matt. 28:1. Cleopus and his companion told Jesus "that same day" (Luke 24:1, 13) that "To day is the third day since these things were done" verse 21. Jesus confirmed this when He later appeared in the upper room and said that it was necessary for Him "to rise from the dead the third day" verse 46. Paul agreed that "He rose again the third day according to the scriptures." 1 Corinthians 15:4.

Joseph put his brothers into custody for three days and then went in to see them "on the third day" Gen 42:17. Esther asked her people to fast with her "neither eat nor drink three days, night or day." Then "on the third day" she went in before the king. Esther 4:16-5:1. These examples all illustrate the inclusive reckoning of time by the Hebrews. Any part of three days was considered to be three days and even three nights.

Sabbath Rest in the Tomb

According to Jewish time reckoning, the Sabbath arrived at sundown Friday and lasted until sundown Saturday. Christ's followers rested that Sabbath along with their crucified Saviour. Clearly there was no indication that Christ had informed His disciples that His Sabbath had changed days.

After His death on the cross, Jesus rested the entire Sabbath (from sundown Friday to sundown Saturday) in the grave. **He rested** after His work of **creation** (John 1:3) and **He rested** after completing His work of **redemption**. His followers did the same "according to the commandment" Luke 23:56.

Resurrection Sunday also coincided that year with the Festival of the Firstfruits of the barley harvest. Barley matured early and enough would be available by the time of Passover to cut and present to the Priest who would then "wave it before the Lord" as a token of the greater wheat harvest to come. Paul pointed out the fulfillment of this in the experience of Jesus when he wrote to the Corinthians about Christ's resurrection:

> "But now is Christ risen from the dead, and become the first fruits of them that slept... every man in his own order: Christ the first fruits: afterward they that are Christ's at his coming."
> 1 Corinthians 15:20,23

This Feast of Firstfruits was also called the Festival of Weeks, because it marked the beginning of a seven week interval between the start of the barley harvest and the start of the wheat harvest.

> "And you shall count unto you from the morrow after the Sabbath, from the day that you brought the sheaf of the wave offering: seven Sabbaths shall be complete: even unto the morrow after the seventh Sabbath shall you number fifty days." Leviticus 23:15, 16

Fifty days later, another token cutting of wheat would be performed but this time it would be baked with leaven into two loaves of bread to be "waved" before the Lord. This 50th day was also a special event celebrated with many animal sacrifices (7 lambs, a bullock, 2 rams, a kid plus 2 more lambs). It later became known as Pentecost. The very first Pentecost occurred approximately seven weeks after the Exodus when the children of Israel reached Mount Sinai. This may explain the Jewish tradition of staying up all night on the eve of Shavuot and reading the Torah (the Law) on Pentecost.

An interesting use of the Greek phrase *mia sabbaton* for "First of weeks" might also be considered. All lexicons indicate that this is an ambiguous construction that has multiple possible meanings. With an attempt to make the expression clear in English, most translations have inserted the word "day" so as to read "First *day* of the week."

But the possibility is entertained by some that this might have referred to the ***first day of the seven week period of time*** between the barley and wheat Firstfruit festivals. This is certainly a minority position, although recognized Greek authorities support it.

Communion Sabbath
The Lord's Supper, communion cup, breaking bread are distinctly Christian terms for decidedly Jewish rituals. And what we observe as New Testament believers is remarkably similar in many ways to the original service conducted by ancient Israel.

God instructed the Hebrew slaves in Egypt to choose a lamb and keep it bound until the 14th day of the first month which began the appearance of the new moon. The lamb was then slain "at evening" and its blood collected, and painted with hyssop over the door of their dwellings. The lamb's body was then prepared and eaten with unleavened bread and bitter herbs that night. At midnight the protecting hand of God saved the first born males of each obedient family from the destroying angel that night, the night they left Egypt, free from bondage, redeemed from death.

Moses had instructed all adult Israelite males to convene in Jerusalem three times a year to commemorate the annual feasts.

Passover was the first. It was closely associated with two sister festivals: the feast of unleavened bread and the feast of the First Fruits. The day following Passover was the first day of the feast of unleavened bread. It was designated as a "holy convocation" a day of rest or "a sabbath." Since Passover was set by the lunar cycles, occuring 14 days after the first new moon following the spring equinox, this sabbath could land on any day of the fixed weekly cycle. Only infrequently did it coincide with the seventh day Sabbath. Two days following Passover was the feast of the First Fruits, when a handfull of barley shoots were cut and waved in the air by the priest as a pledge to God for His blessing of the greater harvest to come.

Three Day Shadow
These three consecutive days were a shadow of things to come; they pointed forward to the coming Messiah and His great sacrifice for His people, when they would through faith eat His sinless body (free of any leaven) internalizing His righteousness and then witness the First Fruits being raised as a token of the great harvest of believers.

Details for the observance of Passover are given in Exodus 12:1-28, Leviticus 23:4-8, Numbers 9:1-14, Deuteronomy 16:1-8. But the New Testament also makes considerable reference to this important ritual. Jesus faithfully kept Passover every year starting when He was twelve. Scripture records the very first Passover that Christ attended when He reached the age for bar-mizpah (Luke 2:41). Thereafter He could go up with the other men to Jerusalem.

Passover, like the other Jewish festivals, was rich in Messianic symbolism. And the young Christ witnessing this event for the first time identified with every aspect He saw: the priests inspecting each family's sacrificial lamb for flaws and blemishes (symbols of sin which the Messiah must not have), sacrificing the innocent victim, collecting and applying its blood, removing all leaven from their house, eating the unleavened bread, and watching the priest raise the young barley sheaves high into the air as the people rejoiced in loud celebration.

First Communion Last Supper
As Jesus approached the weeks before His death He made His way to Jerusalem in anticipation of keeping Passover with His disciples. The story is given in Matthew 26, Mark 14, Luke 22. He told them where to go to secure a meeting room for their Pascal meal. As they assembled around the table, Jesus took and then broke the round loaves of bread and distributed them to the disciples bidding them to eat it in remembrance of His broken body; He took the cup and invited them to drink it with Him as a symbol of His spilt blood.

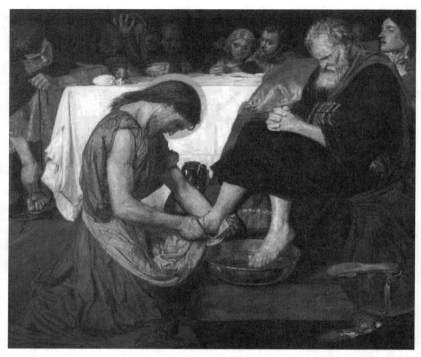

Every Passover held tremendous significance and meaning for Christ. But this one was most important. He could not have kept these festivals in merely a legalistic fashion, just simply to comply with the requirements of the law. No, no. "With desire I have desired to eat this Passover with you before I suffer," He told the anxious disciples. "For I say unto you, I will not any more eat thereof, until it be fulfilled in the kingdom of God." Luke 22:15-16.

These words thrilled the hearts of the twelve men gathered around Him. Now, they were certain, He was going to establish the kingdom of God! Finally, He was going to assert Himself as Israel's Messiah and deliver them from the despicable Roman curse. But again they misunderstood.

Jesus was the Living Torah (John 1:14), the Living Law with its precepts written in His heart. He is the Chief Cornerstone, and under His direction we too are also lively stones, living Torahs because we are under the New Covenant, with the Law in our hearts. Hebrews 8:10. Jesus is the Great Light, and He gives His light to us the lesser lights to reflect His loving character. John 1:5-9.

The symbolic meaning of the Sabbath marriage bond between creature and Creator is strongly expressed in Christ's garden prayer:

> "Holy Father, keep through thine own name those whom thou hast given me, that they may be one as we are... That they all may be one as thou, Father, art in me, and I in thee that they also may be one in us...that they may be one, even as we are one... that they may be made perfect in one. John 17:11, 21-23.

Jesus prayed for communion union. The Sabbath is the answer to His request for it unites us with God in the domain of time.

When Jesus kept Passover with his disciples, an event that is commonly called the "Last Supper," was this the last Passover for his followers? Certainly not! The first Christian church was composed of Jewish Believers in Jerusalem, and it is certain that they celebrated the festivals that now contained so many precious truths concerning their beloved Saviour. In Acts 12:1-4 we are told that there was persecution of this church during *"the days of unleavened bread,"* and the soldiers intended to bring Peter up to the people *"after the Passover"* [King James Version mistranslates the Greek word *pascha* πασχα as Easter.]

See Appendix H for details on the Apostolic Confessions
See Appendix C for additional notes on the Passover

"Sabbath defines love in a perfect world"
"Redemption defines love in an imperfect world"

"Sabbath reveals the meaning of life"
"Redemption reveals the means to life"
Des Cummings, Jr.

Mental Status Exam

Jesus awoke from death "on the third day" after His death. Intense study continues even yet concerning the timing and significance of that sentinel event. Not just the physiology of sleep, but the activation of wakefulness is uniquely manifested in the resurrection phenomenon. Evaluation of the mental status includes an assessment of the patient's

- Orientation to person, place and time
- Short and long-term memory
- Judgment and Insight
- Mood and Affect

Can you recognize a familiar face? Do you know where you are? What year it is? What month? Today's date? Answers to such questions indicate just how oriented a patient is to their surroundings. Knowing where we are in Scripture, what the circumstances are, the time and context provide the proper orientation.

The first day of the week is mentioned several times in the New Testament as the documented day of Christ's resurrection. In addition there are a couple of additional scriptures suggesting the possibility that a communion service might be associated with that day.

Thursday, the day of the Last Supper, or Friday, the day of the crucifixion, are not celebrated weekly. Paradoxically the events that are linked to those days are the source of the symbols that have become the focus of modern Sunday observance. What is the basis of selecting Sunday as the day of worship and, according to some, even rest?

Orientation: The First First of the Week
The first day of the week is mentioned only eight times in the New Testament—(Matt. 28:1; Mark 16:2, 9; Luke 24:1; John 20:1, 19; Acts 20:7; 1 Cor. 16:2). Six of these refer to the same day: resurrection Sunday.

Matt 28:1	The Marys came to the sepulcher
Mark 16:2	The Marys and Salome came to the sepulcher
Mark 16:9	Jesus appeared to Mary
Luke 24:1	The women came to the sepulcher
John 20:1	Mary Magdalene came to the sepulcher
John 20:19	Jesus appeared that day at evening to the disciples

Following is a review of these six passages.

> "In the end of the Sabbath, as it began to dawn toward the first [day] of the week, came Mary Magdalene and the other Mary to see the sepulcher." Matt. 28:1.

Sabbath Memory
The followers of Christ, remembering their Example, waited until the Sabbath ended before returning to the sepulcher. Sabbath observers would naturally wait until after sunset and the Sabbath closing ceremonies before venturing out to resume the work related duties of embalming a dead body. The prevailing Jewish regulations on Sabbath travel in Christ's time limited the length of an excursion to only 2/3 miles. Since Mary Magdalene lived in Bethany, a distance of 2 miles from Jerusalem, she would have spent the Sabbath in

Bethany. For practical purposes this would require further waiting until daylight.

> "And when the sabbath was past, Mary Magdalene, and Mary [the *mother*] of James, and Salome, had bought sweet spices, that they might come and anoint him. And very early in the morning, the first [*day*] of the week, they came unto the sepulcher at the rising of the sun." Mark 16:1

This text indicates that the women bought the embalming spices after the Sabbath was over. Once again, a recognition of the sacred hours is demonstrated. Their waiting until Sunday's daybreak likewise demonstrates that they regarded it as simply another work day rather than a new day of worship. In addition, neither of these scriptures include any comment regarding a change in the Sabbath.

Others interpret these verses differently, taking into consideration the fact that the word "day" is a supplied word. This would make the literal reading of the phrase become: "the first of the week." This, in itself, does not change the basic meaning since Sunday is still the first of the week, but could also apply to Monday or even Tuesday.

However, a second observation is then made by superficial students: the word translated "week" and "Sabbath" is the same Greek word *sabbaton* (σαββατων). This is clearly seen in this segment of Greek text from Matthew 28:1:

Οψε   δε   σαββατων,   τη   επιφωτκονση   εις   μιαν   σαββατων
Opse   de   sabbaton   ta   epiphotkonsa   eis   mian   sabbaton
Late   but   of-sabbaths   at-the   drawing-on   toward   one   of-sabbaths

Those unfamiliar with Greek conclude that the gospel writer is calling Sunday a Sabbath as proof that the day of worship was changed after the cross.

Other novice interpreters again point out that the word "day" is added in our English translations and also noticing the word σαββατον in both positions, translate it as "Sabbath" in both instances and come up with:

> "After the end of the [Jewish] Sabbaths, at the beginning of the first of the [New Christian] Sabbaths"

However, *sabbaton* by itself, isolated from its context is an ambiguous word with a potential for multiple meanings. It can be translated "Sabbath," "sabbaths," "a sabbath day of rest," or "week." Greek grammar uses inflected endings and syntax to determine which meaning is applied. In this instance both occurrences have the same endings, but the second is preceded by a numerical adjective *mian* meaning "first."

Greek Grammar 101

Let's consider the endings first and then we'll look at syntax. There are five noun cases in Greek: nominative, genitive, dative, accusative, and vocative. Each case is indicated by a distinctive form in the terminal ending of the noun. Adjectives must agree with the nouns they are modifying in gender, number, and case; and this also is indicated by their own set of endings. Thus *Sabbaton* with its −on ending is in the genitive case which denotes the sense of ownership or possession.

The genitive case in English is conveyed by the possessive apostrophe or the word "of." For example, "The house's front" is equivalent to "the front of the house."

Now we can put all the pieces together:
- *sabbaton* is neuter gender, pleural number and genitive case.
- *mian* is feminine gender, singular number and accusative case.

But *mian* cannot modify *sabbaton* as these two words do not agree in gender, number or case.   If an adjective cannot agree with an expressed noun it must do so with an implied one.

Sabbaton in its meaning of "week" can agree if we use the division of a week, the day, as the implied noun of agreement. The Greek word for day is *hemera*. In its singular number and accusative case it is *hemeran* which now makes agreement with *mian* complete: "*mian* [*hemeran*] *sabbaton*." Thus the English equivalent of *mian sabbaton* ("first *day* of the week") is strictly accurate.

Sabbath Syntax

Syntax deals with word order and relationships imposed by the sequence of words in a sentence. Although English readers tend to apply the term Sabbath to a particular day of the week (because we utilize specific names for each day), New Testament Greek used numbers together with *sabbaton* (as a general concept indicating a "sabbatical period") to convey different days of the week.

For example, "one of the *sabbaton*, two of the *sabbaton*," etc. Thus *mian* (one) preceding *sabbaton* means "day one of the week." But *sabbaton* without this numerical adjective means "sabbath day of rest." Cruden's Concordance, Bloomfield's Greek N.T., Nevins' "Biblical Antiquities," and Young's Concordance all cite the same effect.

There is another Greek word, *hebdomas*, which means "week," but this word is not used in the New Testament. The word "week" in the New Testament is always derived from *sabbaton*.

The word οψε is translated as "end" in the KJV only here in the New Testament. It is also translated as "late" or "after." Strong's Greek Dictionary renders this entry (3976) as "late in the day; after the close of the day: (at) even, in the end." The same word is used in Mark 13:35 where it designates the first watch of the night: from sunset to about 9:00 P.M. The conventional interpretation, therefore, is that the women came to the tomb late, after the close of the day, in the evening of the Saturday Sabbath which was at the beginning of the first day of the week.

The Greek word επιφωτκονση, "to grow light," "to dawn," is confirmed by the other parallel gospel accounts. In the spring months at Palastinian latitudes morning twilight would begin about 4:00 A.M. and sunrise would occur at about 5:30.

Prototype Sabbath

The remaining "first day of the week" passages use exactly the same Greek construction except for possibly this one:

> Mark 16:9 "Now when [*Jesus*] was risen early the first [*day*] of the week, he appeared first to Mary Magdalene, out of whom he had cast seven devils."

Some manuscripts make a sudden change in this verse, from the standard *mian sabbaton* in verse 1 to *prote sabbatou* from *protos*, meaning first in a series, foremost, leading, most important, chief, principal, from which our word "prototype" comes, and *sabbatou* is now in the singular form of Sabbath.

But there is a difference between early and later Greek manuscripts used for Bible translation. The oldest sources such as Codex Sinaiticus or Vaticanus, both of which date from the 4th century, end the book of Mark at 16:8, while later sources contain additional verses. Even early century contemporaries were aware of the controversial nature of these manuscripts. Eusebius who lived at that time proclaimed that the "accurate" manuscripts ended the book of Mark at verse 8. Jerome, living in the early 5th century, stated that "nearly all" manuscripts in his day lacked the additional 12 verses. Nevertheless, he included them in his famous Latin Vulgate translation.

The difference between the usual *mian sabbaton* and *prote sabbatou* are cited by those who favor the Codex Vaticanus as an inspired revelation of a "new Sabbath." The same difference is used by proponents of Codex Sinaiticus as proof that the extra verses were added by someone other than Mark. In fact, the phrase *prote sabbatou* appears nowhere else in the Greek New Testament Scriptures. Other atypical non-Markian constructions are found in these 12 verses: *meta de tauta, husteron, ho men oun* and *ekeinoi de*.

The oldest copies of Mark's gospel (Codex Sinaiticus-manuscript Aleph and Vaticanus-manuscript B) end at Mark 16:8. The New International Version notes this in its forward with the comment that *"The most reliable early manuscripts and other ancient witnesses do not have Mark 16:9-20."* On the other hand, it must be noted that only these two manuscripts omit the verses whereas at least 618 later sources include them.

Much has been said about the apparently "abrupt" ending at verse 8. But the critical consensus is that the extra verses are a spurious addition. Whether this was intended by Mark (doubted), accidentally lost or destroyed (certainly possible), or intentionally destroyed is still disputed. An intentional addendum is speculated to have been motivated by an unknown scribe because the original ending didn't agree with those provided by the other synoptics and might discredit the confidence in the Scriptures. But this also seems unlikely since Mark already differs with Matthew in the number of women who came to the tomb. Later manuscripts provide either a short ending that quickly wraps up the story, or a longer ending consisting of the 12 verses which are included in KJV without comment and in other versions usually with a footnote.

In summary, it appears that this section of Mark 16:9-20 was restored at a later date using the endings of the other three gospels as sources.

See Appendix I for additional material on Mark 16.

Judgement and Insight
Judgement involves the ability to make correct decisions and draw appropriate conclusions under varying situations. Insight is the ability to comprehend and understand the condition and state of one's immediate environment. What were the conditions surrounding the resurrection and what conclusions can we make?

Christ's appearance to Mary Magdalene on the first day of the week was not understood by the community of believers as constituting a significant change in the weekly Sabbath. There is no documented statement of Jesus or apostles to support such a conclusion. Scripture merely records that the disciples rested along with their Master that Sabbath "according to the commandment" and then resumed their embalming efforts the following day.

> Luke 24:1 "Now upon the first [*day*] of the week, very early in the morning, they came unto the sepulcher bringing the spices which they had prepared, and certain [*others*] with them."

> John 20:1 "The first [*day*] of the week cometh Mary Magdalene early, when it was yet dark, unto the sepulcher..."

John's account coincides with the others and still there is no mention of changing the Sabbath to a different day of worship because of the resurrection. But, clearly, Jesus had already risen and left the tomb well before sunrise perhaps even sometime Saturday night, since according to Jewish reckoning the first day began at sunset Saturday. This raises the question as to why Christendom today conducts Easter *sunrise* services. [See Social History]

There is no evidence that Christ had instructed His followers to embrace a new day of worship and certainly not one of rest prior to His crucifixion. They demonstrated judgement and insight consistent with their understanding of the Sabbath commandment.

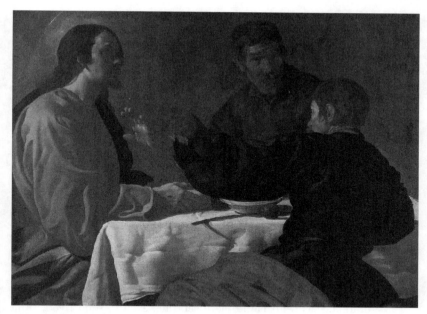

Emmaus Mood

Thus far all the texts mentioning the first day of the week deal with the events of resurrection morning. The next event of resurrection Sunday involved the walk to Emmaus when Jesus appeared to Cleopas and his companion. This account is recorded with considerable detail in Luke 24:13-35. Their discussion confirms the previous events by commenting that "today is the third day since these things (the crucifixion) were done" (verse 21), and that the women "were early at the sepulcher," (verse 22).

But the important discussion is in verses 25-27 where Jesus chides them for not believing what the prophets said about the Messiah's suffering, and then proceeds to expound to them "in all the scriptures the things concerning himself." They later exclaim after Jesus disappears, "Did not our heart burn within us, while he talked with us by the way, and while *he opened to us the scriptures*?" (verse 32).

What was the subject of this personal Bible study by Jesus? "All that the prophets have spoken: Ought not Christ to have suffered these things, and to enter into his glory." (verses 25,26). Did this include a change in the day of worship? No mention of it appears in these texts. The focus is on the realization in Christ's death of the prophetic scriptures foretelling His redemptive sacrifice. The mood was one of burning excitement is witnessing the fulfillment of prophecy!

Sunday Evening
After traveling part of the 7-mile hike (far more than a Sabbath day's journey) from Jerusalem to Emmaus with these two disciples, Jesus accepts their offer to join them for supper because the day was "far spent." It was getting dark. The day was ending. Monday evening was upon them. Then at supper, Jesus reveals Himself, their eyes are opened and He vanishes. Meanwhile, back at the upper room...

> "Afterward he appeared unto the eleven as they sat at meat, and upbraided them with their unbelief and hardness of heart, because they believed not them which had seen him after he was risen." Mark 16:14

The disciples, not believing the women's report that Christ was alive, were still hiding and huddled together when Jesus appeared.

> "Then the same day at evening, being the first [day] of the week, when the doors were shut where the disciples were assembled for fear of the Jews, came Jesus and stood in the midst, and saith unto them, Peace [be] unto you. And when he had so said, he showed unto them [his] hands and his side. Then were the disciples glad, when they saw the Lord. Then said Jesus to them again, Peace [be] unto you: as [my] Father hath sent me, even so send I you. And when he had said this, he breathed on [them], and saith unto them, Receive [ye] the Holy Ghost: Whosoever sins ye remit, they are remitted unto them; [and] whosoever [sins] ye retain, they are retained." John 20:19

This occasion might have been a 'secret' meeting held to change the Sabbath to Sunday. But we are not told this. The passage merely says Jesus came and stood among them. The disciples, holed up in a locked room, were hiding from the Jews in fear that they might be next. Suddenly, Jesus stood in their midst. This would have been the perfect time to set them straight and now tell them that there had been a change in the Sabbath to the first day of the week. But there is no mention of anything to that effect. A week later (actually, eight days and another Monday or even Tuesday evening), when Thomas had doubts about a risen Jesus, the Saviour returned, but again said nothing about worshipping on the first day of the week.

> "And after eight days again his disciples were within, and Thomas with them; then came Jesus, the doors being shut, and stood in the midst, and said, Peace be unto you." John 20:26

Sunday sabbath supporters maintain that Jesus intentionally selected the first day of the week to appear to the disciples as His personal confirmation that this was now His new Sabbath. This assumption cannot be a conclusion for the following reasons:

1. Christ's meetings after His resurrection occurred on various days. This second meeting does not identify it as taking place specifically on the first day of the week, but rather "after eight days."

2. Other scriptural references to events separated by one week are said to happen "after seven days." 1 Chron. 9:25; 2 Kings 11:5.

3. A similar expression is used to designate the time between Christ's statement regarding those who would live to see the kingdom of God and His transfiguration. Matthew 17 and Mark 9 both specify "after six days." Luke says that it took place "about eight days after" He made the statement. Luke 9:28.

4. The purpose of Christ's second appearance is clearly for the benefit of Thomas. Considering that the first appearance to the eleven was in the evening, following the events of the first day, Jewish reckoning (evening precedes morning) would have placed the meeting on early Monday. Eight days later would be counted as Monday or perhaps even Tuesday.

5. The next meeting was a fishing trip on no specified day. And His last appearance was on a Thursday, the day of His ascension.

6. Even the day of Pentecost is not identified with certainty as having occurred on the first day of the week. The interpretation of the phrase "on the morrow after the sabbath" in Leviticus is and has been controversial for millennia.

Obviously, Christ was not giving His new church any mysterious signal concerning a particular day by appearing when He did.

Oriented to Person, Place and Time
Orientation to time is an important component of the mental status examination. Attention to all the information and time clues surrounding the resurrection of Jesus confirm only the prophetic significance of the living Christ. The evening meal in Emmaus and the later night time appearance back in Jerusalem set the mood. Mood and affect are two aspects of our exam that indicate the integrity and appropriateness of the patient's psyche.

> "And when he had so said, he shewed unto them his hands and his side. Then were the disciples glad, when they saw the LORD." John 20:20

Notice the use of the word "*glad*" in verse 20. This is a description of the Disciples' affect, their emotional state.

Glad Day: Affect

Now compare Psalm 118:24 "This is the day the Lord has made; we will rejoice and be *glad* in it." The resurrection was the day when the despondent, discouraged disciples had their sadness turned into joy. Does this verify the sanctity of Sunday? Here is Psalm 118 in context:

> 20 This gate of the LORD, into which the righteous shall enter.
> 21 I will praise thee: for thou hast heard me,
>   and art become my salvation.
> 22 The stone which the builders refused
>   is become the head stone of the corner.
> 23 This is the LORD'S doing; it is marvelous in our eyes.
> 24 This is the day which the LORD hath made;
>   we will rejoice and be glad in it.

The rejected stone becomes the Cornerstone. Those that witness this marvelous event rejoice and are glad.

This Messianic prophecy of Christ the Cornerstone is quoted six times in the New Testament (in Matt. 21:42, Mark 12:10, Luke 20:17 by Christ Himself; and in Acts 4:11, Ephesians 2:20, 1 Peter 2:6 by Paul and Peter). Those who see a connection to the resurrection and a prophetic reference to Sunday as "the day which the LORD has made" point to the contrast between the Stone's rejection and God's response to the rejection: raising Christ from the dead. This is based on the assumption that Jesus became the Cornerstone because of and at the time of His resurrection. But when did Christ become the Cornerstone, the Head of His living body, the church?

According to this Psalm it was when He ascended on high, when He became the chief Cornerstone in Zion above, elect and precious. According to Ephesians 2:20 it was when Christ chose His disciples: for God "gave Him to be head over all things to the church," "built on the foundation of the apostles and prophets, Jesus Christ Himself being the Chief Cornerstone." According to 1 Peter 2:4-7 where He is described as "a living stone, rejected indeed by men, but chosen by God and precious," it was when He was rejected by the Jews before Pilate when they cried, "We have no king but Caesar!" The conclusion must be that there was no definite time when Christ became the cornerstone, His title was only progressively strengthened.

When the Psalmist said, "This is the day... we will be glad," he was referring to the Messiah's "day," the time when God would enter our world and secure our salvation. Jesus, Himself, used this same expression when He said, "Abraham rejoiced to see my *day*; he saw it and was *glad*." John 8:56.

This proposal (that Christ became the cornerstone at His resurrection) is supported by further assumptions:
- the work of redemption supercedes the work of creation.
- Christ didn't complete His redemptive work
  until the resurrection.

Redemption or Resurrection
So, now let's review our list of assumptions. Without explicit scriptural support, many philosophical speculations have been made concerning the "New Christian Sabbath" of the New Testament:

1. Christ finished His redemptive work by raising from the dead
2. Christ sanctified the first day by His resurrection on that day
3. He blessed the first day by sending the Holy Spirit on Pentecost
4. While Israel kept the seventh day as works of the Law
5. Christians enter the true rest from their works on the first day
6. Sunday celebrates the New Creation, Redemption and Grace
7. The first day is now a memorial to our New Creation in Christ

When spoken with authority, and when heard often enough, these statements have come to take on the ring of truth to many Christians. But are they supported by Scripture?

Is Christ's redemptive work finished?
Is this earth redeemed from the curse of sin?
Is the Church redeemed from the curse of death?
Has the resurrection of the saints already taken place?
On what day, then, can we say redemption was finished?
On which day should we honor the great act of redemption?
Can we commemorate a completed redemption before it is finished?

Should not the day on which the price for our redemption was paid mark the pinnacle of divine achievement and take precedence over every other day? To raise His Son back to life was easily the most natural act for the Father to do; He was just waiting for the first chance to call Him forth on the third day. But to stand back and allow His Son to innocently die for a rebel race was the most difficult decision for both Father and Son to make. That day, the day of the cross, is without a doubt the greatest event in all of redemptive history, beyond all comparison the most memorable of days.

But the question of which of these days is most worthy of being the Lord's Day is really immaterial. Both redemption and resurrection already have their own memorials appointed by Christ *before* His death.

Communion Commemorates Redemption
The Lord's Supper was established "the same night in which He was betrayed" to commemorate His crucifixion death for us. "This do in remembrance of me," He said, for "you do show the Lord's *death* till He come." 1 Corinthians 11:23-26.

Baptism Commemorates Resurrection
Furthermore, Baptism is given to the church that we might experience for ourselves not only our Master's death as we plunge into that watery grave and are "buried with Him in baptism," but His resurrection as we rise from the waters to "walk in newness of life." Rom 6:3-5; Col 2:12. Baptism is the "divinely authorized memorial of the resurrection." J.N. Andrews, *History of the Sabbath*, Chap. 10.

"It was the resurrection of the Saviour,
    and not the day of the resurrection...
It was the death of the redeemer,
    and not the day of His death,
that was worthy of commemoration."
                    J.N. Andrews, *ibid.*

The Lord's Supper, the Sabbath, and Baptism are three institutions that were established at the time of a significant divine event in Redemptive history. But it is baptism, not the Sunday, which Paul uses to symbolize the death, burial and resurrection of Christ. (Romans 6:3,4; Colossians 2:12). Only because baptism has been changed from immersion into sprinkling has the need for a resurrection memorial been made to seem necessary.

Changing the Day

"With God all things are possible." Mark 10:26; Luke 1:37; Matt 19:26. But there is a limit to what He will do because "God cannot lie." Num. 23:19; Titus 1:2. Men may speculate that God can change His own law if He wants to. But truth demands that the God of truth remain consistent with His law of truth. Isa. 65:16; Psalm 119:142, 151. If the Law of God were changed to something else, would it still be true? And if the Law-giver changed it would He still be the God of truth?

Summary of Sunday Texts in the Gospels

- Gospel writers make a careful distinction
  between describing the Sabbath and the first day of the week.
- The first day of the week is never identified by a sacred title
- The seventh day is consistently called the Sabbath
- Christ is never said to have rested on the first day of the week
- The first day is never said to have received a blessing
- Christ never mentions the first day of the week
- No command to observe the first day of the week is recorded

> "Taken separately, perhaps, and even all together, these passages seem scarcely adequate to prove that the dedication of the first day of the week to the purposes above mentioned was a matter of apostolic institution, or even of apostolic practice." *Smith's Dictionary of the Bible*, Article "The Lord's Day" Page 356.

The Original

Let's examine once again the essential points of the original Sabbath commandment:

> "Remember the Sabbath day to keep it holy.
> Six days shalt thou labor and do all thy work, but
> The seventh day is the Sabbath of the Lord thy God.
> In it thou shalt not do any work...
> For in six days the Lord made heaven and earth...
> And rested the seventh day, blessed the Sabbath day
> and hallowed it."

If the Sabbath has been changed to the first day, the commandment should then read as follows:

> "Remember the Sabbath day to keep it holy.
> Six days shalt thou labor and do all thy work, but
> The **first** day is the Sabbath of the Lord thy God.
> In it thou shalt not do any work...
> For in six days the Lord made heaven and earth...
> And rested the **first** day, blessed the Sabbath day and hallowed it."

But now the truth of God has been changed into a lie. Romans 1:25. There is no scripture reporting that God rested on the first day of the week. There is none stating that He blessed it or pronounced it holy. For this version of the commandment to be true, Christ would have had to accomplish His work of human redemption in the six days prior to His resurrection, and He would have had to rest on the first day from His work of redemption. But since He didn't, we need to make a further change:

> "Remember the Sabbath day to keep it holy.
> The **first** day is the Sabbath of the Lord thy God.
> For **on that day He rose from the dead.**
> Wherefore the Lord blessed the **first** day and hallowed it."

This is a much more concise and direct commandment and would perfectly meet the need of all who are looking for Biblical support of Sunday observance. Does such a version of the fourth commandment exist? Early Catholic versions came close. They pretty much chopped most of the original text out leaving only the first line. But then they also completely eliminated the second commandment (thus allowing the adoration of images), and then divided the tenth commandment in order to maintain a total of ten. God foretold that a power would arise that would "think to change times and laws." Dan 7:25. They would think they could change them. But it would be just as easy to change the day of Christ's crucifixion to some other day, as some propose, like "Good Wednesday."

So, as we have seen,
Jesus did not weaken the Sabbath by His teaching,
He did not abrogate it by His death, and
He did not change it by His resurrection.

The Eighth Day

The argument arose during the early Gnostic heresy of the first century that Sunday is the new Sabbath because it is the eighth day. Since Christ's name in Greek *Xristos* has a numeric value of 888, the eight trinity was said to give special importance to this number as the first in a new cycle of seven. 8 souls were saved from the flood to begin the new postdiluvian world. The 8th day was designated for circumcision and dedication, the sign of rebirth. Thus, it was given the meaning of "a new beginning" sharing the qualities of "one" and "first."

The eighth day mentioned in the Levitical instructions for observing the annual feasts was seized as an opportunity to make the first day Sunday the new "sabbath day." See also, Leviticus 9:1-2.

The text, however, is referring to the Feast of Tabernacles, the seventh annual festival which was observed for seven days and followed with a final "holy convocation" rest day.

> "And he read in the book of the law of GOD day by day, from the first day till the last, and they kept the solemnity seven days, and in the eighth day a solemn assembly according to the manner." Nehemiah 8:18

Other references to the eighth day include:

> Aaron and his sons were consecrated for seven days.
> On the 8th day they offered sacrifices and the Lord appeared.
> Leviticus 14:23, lepers bring offerings for cleansing on 8th day.
> Leviticus 15:14-15, 29-30, unclean discharges cleansed 7 days, offering made on the 8th.
> Numbers 6:10-11, Nazarite cleansed 7 days, 8th day offering.
> Leviticus 22:27, new born livestock only sacrificed on 8th day.

> Leviticus 23:36-39, Feast of Tabernacles 7 days; 8th day finale.
> Numbers 29:35, Feast of Tabernacles 7 days and 8th day finale.
> Ezekiel 43:27 Altar and priests consecrated 7 days, 8th day onward they begin to offer sacrifices on the altar.

The Ninth Day
But the eighth day was not the only figure used. In Leviticus 23:32 Moses said the Day of Atonement "shall be unto you a sabbath of rest, and you shall afflict your souls: in the ninth day of the month at even, from even unto even, shall you celebrate your Sabbath." Here is an instance where the 9th day is specified as the sunset beginning of observance for the following 10th day of Atonement. These eighth and ninth days were ceremonial sabbaths connected with the sacrificial system. They could occur on any day of the week as the new moons varied from month to month and year to year.

In contrast, the seventh-day weekly Sabbath of God's creative and redemptive rest is uniquely fixed in the divine calendar. Every week we are oriented to Person, place and time.

Deep Tendon Reflexes

DTR's (deep tendon reflexes) are commonly tested as part of the musculoskeletal system examination though they belong equally within the neurological exam. The familiar reflex hammer is used to tap large tendons as they approach their bony insertions near the major joints. As the tendon is struck, it is ever so slightly stretched along with specialized nerve fibers embedded deep within the tendon called stretch receptors. When stretched these sensors send miniature electrical signals that travel along the nerve cell until it reaches interconnections in the spine. There a reflex arc is created by sending an echoing signal back again to the area where the tendon was located. This time, however, the message is directed to a muscle attached to the tendon causing it to contract. The result: a typical "knee-jerk" reaction.

Testing Deep Tendon Reflexes measures both the nerve pathways and the muscles they serve. This combination test verifies the integrity of two systems at the same time. When all the connections are intact, the reflexes are considered to be normal. Damaged nerves or spinal connections will result in a diminished or absent muscular response known as areflexia. Sabbath reflexes can be tested in a similar manner. The Master action should result in a corresponding disciple reaction.

Communication is the key to good reflexes. How does the physical activity of Sabbath keepers in the early apostolic church measure up? Our physical examination will now focus on Sabbath actions and reactions in the New Testament period.

Sabbath Acts
Abundant reference to Sabbath observance was continually made both immediately following the Cross (Luke 23:56; 24:1) and throughout the chronicled Acts of the Apostles covering 8 chapters and 23 years.

Christian Gentiles met on the Sabbath day (Acts 13:42) and they were said to be living "under grace" (verse 43).

Paul in Harmony
Even after being accused of teaching the law's demise, Paul the apostle said to Felix that He kept the commandments:

> "But this I confess unto you, that after the Way which they call heresy, so worship I the God of my fathers, believing all things which are written in the law and in the prophets." Acts 24:14

And to Festus he testified that he had offended in nothing. "Neither against the law of the Jews, neither against the temple, nor yet against Caesar, have I offended anything at all" Acts 25:8.

To make such a statement Paul must have been either keeping the Sabbath or deceiving himself and others. He plainly said that he didn't teach anything other than what the "Old Testament" writers taught:

> "Therefore, having obtained help from God, I continue unto this day, witnessing both to small and great, saying none other things than those which the prophets and Moses did say should come: that Christ should suffer, and that He should be the first that should rise from the dead, and should show light unto the [Jewish] people, and to the Gentiles." Acts 26:22, 23

It is remarkable what Paul did *not* include in this summary of what Christ accomplished. He did not add "...and abolish the law, especially the Sabbath." There is no record clearly stating this in Scripture. Such a momentous event as doing away with the Sabbath should be heavily prophesied in the Old Testament and explicitly documented in the New.

But God does not deal any differently with the Jews than He does with the Gentiles.

> "There is neither Jew nor Greek, there is neither slave nor free, there is neither male nor female; for you are all one in the Jesus Christ." Galatians 3:28

How can anyone say that Jesus has one standard for a particular race of people and a different standard for another? Normal reflexes are dependable and predictable. While God's Word is sharper than any two-edged sword, His law is not double sided. Would Paul do one thing and preach another? Did he preach that the Sabbath had been abolished and then keep it himself? Would He call the Galatians (some of whom were Jewish) "foolish" for observing the Sabbath and then hypocritically observe it himself?

Only One Olive Tree
Paul teaches the continuity of the Church, the called out ones, from its birth at the Exodus (Stephen called it the Church in the Wilderness. Acts 7:38) unto its consummation as the final Church of the redeemed (called the Church of the Firstborn. Heb. 12:23). He uses the example of an olive tree, (Romans 11) its trunk a figure of Abraham, father of the faithful and the patriarchs that followed; its original branches representing the Hebrew kingdom of priests (Ex. 19:6). But the branches were broken off when they rejected the Root of Jesse, the True Vine, the Messiah. Then wild olive branches were

grafted in from Gentile stock, to become the New Testament Church, also called a kingdom of priests (1 Peter 2:9).

The foundation, the root stock, is unchanged. The Church is still an olive tree. In the Garden of Eden there was a tree of life. In the New Jerusalem there will be the same tree of life. In the ark of the covenant was a copy of the same law, the same Ten Commandments, that exist in the ark of the covenant in the heavenly temple. Moses saw the original pattern (Exodus 25:9; Hebrews 8:5). John saw it open at the end of time (Revelation 11:19). The same law, the same tree, the same church.

Sabbath Reactions
Throughout the book of Acts, there is abundant evidence that the new Christian believers continued to adhere to the Jewish religious calendar. The Christians were primarily "believing Jews" (Acts 21:10). Their "conversion" to Christianity was not a rejection of their Judaic religious heritage. Rather it was an enhancement and augmentation of their Messianic hope. Consequently, they continued to structure their life around the established sequence of festivals and Sabbaths. The truth of this is supported by the absence of any disputes or accusations by the Jews that Christians were violating the Sabbath day of worship. Rather, the repeated and frequent mention of the Sabbath as the accepted day of worship and Bible study indicates the common use of the seventh day by both Jews and Christians during the apostolic period.

> "Now when they had passed through Amphipolis and Apollonia, they came to Thessalonica, where was a synagogue of the Jews. And Paul, as his manner was, went in unto them, and three Sabbath days reasoned with them out of the Scriptures, opening and alleging, that Christ must needs have suffered, and risen again from the dead; and that this Jesus, whom I preach unto you is Christ. And some of them believed; and consorted with Paul and Silas; and of the devout Greeks a great multitude, and of the chief women, not a few." Acts 17:1-4

Here Paul attends a Sabbath service composed of both Jews and Greeks. The Scripture explains that this was Paul's habitual custom. It was also the custom of Jesus as we have already noted.

> "And He came to Nazareth, where He had been brought up: and as His custom was, He went into the synagogue on the Sabbath day, and stood up for to read." Luke 4:16

So Paul's manner and Christ's custom were the same. Even 22 years after His death and resurrection the disciples were still attending Sabbath services. In no place do we see Paul or any other disciple teaching them that they should come back the next day for a 'first day of the week' service. But they went to three Sabbath services where there were both Jews and Greeks present.

The doctrine that claims the Jews have their day (the 7th) and that the Gentiles have their day (the 1st) is foreign to scripture. Some would argue that Paul was at the synagogue only because that is where he would find a ready audience—not to observe the Sabbath. Evidence is offered in Paul's comment that "to the Jews" he became a Jew so as to win them to Christ.

> "For though I be free from all men, yet have I made myself servant unto all, that I might gain the more. And unto the Jews I became as a Jew, that I might gain the Jews; to them that are under the law, as under the law, that I might gain them that are under the law; To them that are without law, as without law, (being not without law to God, but under the law to Christ) that I might gain them that are without law. To the weak became I as weak, that I might gain the weak: I am made all things to all men, that I might by all means save some." 1 Cor. 9:19-22.

Is Paul being devious or just hypocritical?
Neither, he is being sensitive and respectful to the customs, practices and beliefs of others. He does not wish to offend anyone. This passage does not clearly identify the differences between Paul's behavior or conduct and that of those he is seeking to gain. But in the context of the previous chapter where he advised the believers in Corinth to be sensitive about the issue of eating food offered to idols,

there is no indication that Sabbath observance was to be included in the realm of the weak or those under the law.

Luke records another instance of Sabbath in the life of Paul:

> "Now when Paul and his company loosed from Paphos, they came to Perga in Pamphylia: and John departing from them returned to Jerusalem. But when they departed from Perga, they came to Antioch in Pisidia, and went into the synagogue on the sabbath day, and sat down. And after the reading of the law and the prophets the rulers of the synagogue sent unto them, saying, You men and brethren, if you have any word of exhortation for the people, say on." Acts 13:13-15.

In AD 45, Paul and the other disciples came to the Synagogue in Antioch to attend the Sabbath Service. There he is invited to speak. His message is very similar to the one Stephen made: a history of God's people, their Exodus, the judges and kings. And then, with the coming of the Messiah, his death and resurrection, he makes his appeal:

> "Men and brethren, children of the stock of Abraham, and whosoever among you fears God, to you is the word of this salvation sent. For they that dwell at Jerusalem, and their rulers, because they knew him not, nor yet the voices of the prophets which are read every sabbath day, they have fulfilled them in condemning him." Verses 26, 27.

His point? Every Sabbath the scriptural writings of the prophets are read to the people. And these prophets spoke about Jesus and His rejection. In condemning Christ the Jews fulfilled the prophet's word.

At the end of his sermon, the Gentiles were quite interested.

> "And when the Jews were gone out of the synagogue, the Gentiles besought that these words might be preached to them the next sabbath." Acts 13:42

Here is a perfect opportunity for Paul to inform these Gentiles "Hey, just come back tomorrow, we keep the Sabbath on the first day now!" But nothing like that is ever said.

> "Now when the congregation had broken up, many of the Jews and devout proselytes followed Paul and Barnabas, who, speaking to them, persuaded them to continue in the grace of God. On the next Sabbath almost the whole city came together to hear the word of God." Acts 13:43,44

This is the fifth time that the disciples attended a Sabbath service as they "continued in grace." And once again, the seventh day is called "the Sabbath" the day sanctified by God at creation.

The Jerusalem Council
Acts 15:1-2, 14-21

All Christians in the original, first generation church came either from Judaism or heathenism. They were championed by either Peter, the apostle to the circumcised Jews, or Paul, the apostle to the uncircumcised Gentiles. This was the beginning of division and debate within the church, the struggle between old school and new school, high church and low church, authority versus freedom, conservative or progressive. As complementary co-existing perspectives, these two factions provided a healthy balance to the growth of Christianity. But when they each gravitated to extreme positions, they became exclusive, polarized and contradictory forces. Exclusive Jewish Christianity became rigid and legalistic; exclusive Gentile Christianity became mystical and superstitious. (Philip Schaff, *History of the Christian Church*, Chapter V)

Jewish converts, the initial core constituency of the infant church in Jerusalem, naturally desired to remain true and faithful to their religious heritage in adhering to the sacred instructions of the Torah, the writings of Moses, the commemorative festivals, the rules of conduct, eating, drinking, fasting and feasting, and even the rite of circumcision. It was this, more than any other feature of Judaism, that was viewed offensive by a world of Gentiles who were otherwise attracted to the Christ of Christianity.

Peter was shown in vision that uncircumcised Gentiles were not "unclean" and he promptly baptized Cornelius to demonstrate his understanding of this important truth. But "certain men," Jewish Christians from the old guard and former Pharisees, traveled all the way from Judea to Antioch as missionaries preaching that Paul's Gentile converts must be circumcised according to "the custom of Moses" in order to be saved (Acts 15:1). They were armed with the mighty Pentateuch, the historical fact of Christ's own circumcision and even the undeniable fact that even the apostles were circumcised. This small but intensely active group caused a serious uproar. "They were baptized with water, but not with the Holy Spirit. They were Christians in name, but narrow-minded and narrow-hearted Jews in fact." (*ibid* Schaff).

These ultra-orthodox fanatics feared Paul as a loose cannon, a dangerous rebel, that filled them with both jealousy and prejudice.

If the wholesale conversion of Gentiles was not checked, the purity of the church would be soiled, not to mention the shift in power, from the Jews in Jerusalem to the Gentiles in Antioch, would leave them powerless. The church in AD 51, only twenty years after its founding, was on the verge of blowing up. Decisive action was demanded and both centers called for a conference at Jerusalem to break the impasse.

Antioch sent Paul and Barnabas to represent the Gentile converts, but Paul also took Titus as exhibit A of what God could do in the life of an uncircumcised Greek. Luke, of course, accompanied Paul and provides the formal minutes of the meeting which addressed two issues:
> 1. The relation between the Jewish and Gentile apostles,
> 2. The relation between Jewish and Gentile Christians.

Paul recorded the final and complete settlement of point number one in his letter to the Galatians. Luke recorded the partial and temporary settlement of point number two in his Acts of the Apostles.

Paul convinced the leaders of the Jewish Church (Peter, James and John) that his fabulous success among the Gentiles was divine evidence of his ordination as the apostle to the uncircumcised.

But point two dominated the debate with sharp arguments and intense feelings on both sides. The legalists demanded that Titus undergo circumcision; Paul fiercely objected and won. Paul did later circumcise Timothy, but as a Jew, not Gentile, and voluntarily in order to further his acceptance among the Jews who claimed him as the son of a Jewish mother. Thus Paul refused to yield to false brethren, but always accommodated weak ones, becoming a Jew to the Jews and a Gentile to the Gentiles in order to save them both. And this was the issue: salvation without circumcision. The entire body of Mosaic law was not being contested, only this one single issue.

The immediate context of Acts 15 deals not with the law in general, but specifically with *circumcision* (15:1, 5, 9). The legalists cited the stipulation of Exodus 12:48: No stranger (Gentile) could partake of Passover unless he was first circumcised. Precedence for this was set long before Moses. When Jacob's daughter Dinah was raped by Shechem the Hivite, her angry brothers persuaded all the men of Shechem to submit to adult circumcision before allowing Dinah to marry him. When these Gentiles were good and sore "on the third day" the sons of Jacob marched in and slaughtered the helpless convalescents.

While the Jews had the advantage of infant circumcision on the eighth day, the Gentiles faced the pain and agony of adult circumcision. Peter's statement in Acts 15:10-11 should be under-stood with this in mind:

> "Now therefore why do you make trial of God by putting *a yoke upon the neck* of the disciples which neither our fathers nor we have been *able to bear*?"

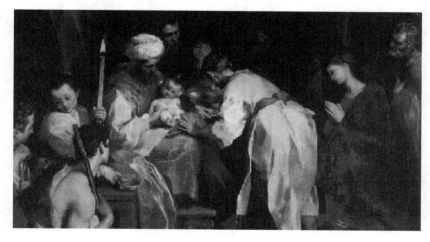

What was the yoke that the patriarchs and Jews were unable to bear? Paul used much the same language in Galatians 5:1 where he called circumcision "the yoke of bondage." Earlier in chapter 2, he described the controversy between himself and Peter over the issue of circumcision (verses 8,9). Circumcision, an ethnic symbol of Jewish identity, especially adult circumcision, would be a *very* understandable burden!

But would the Sabbath, the Sabbath that Christ observed, a day of release from spiritual and physical burdens, a day of restoration, renewal and re-creation—now freed by Christ's example from numerous petty prohibitions—would the Sabbath be a yoke of burden on believing Jews and Gentile converts?

These were God-fearing Gentiles who had been instructed in the Jewish faith (Acts 10:2; 11:19-20; 13:43, 44; 14:1). The custom of Sabbath-keeping had been accepted by many Gentiles. The Jews even influenced the Romans to adopt the seven-day week instead of their eight-day market week (*nundinum*). When this took place just before the Christian era, the Romans made Saturday the most important day of the week for resting and banqueting. Because of this, it would not have been necessary for the council to legislate Sabbath keeping for the Gentiles.

James, who appears to have presided over the meeting, gives this decision:

> "Wherefore my sentence is, that we trouble not them, which from among *the Gentiles are turned to God:* But that we write unto them, that they abstain from pollutions of idols, and from fornication, and from things strangled, and from blood. For *Moses* of old time *has in every city them that preach him,* being read in the synagogues every Sabbath day." Acts 15:19-21

This passage may be interpreted in two ways:

- The Gentiles that are turned to God will hear the words of Moses read to them in the synagogues every Sabbath day and should therefore be familiar with at least these four Mosaic laws.

or

- God-fearing Gentiles should respect at least these four laws of Moses because they are taught every Sabbath by those that preach Moses and will be offended if the Gentiles don't keep them.

Some have seen this episode where only four specific regulations (idolatry, fornication, strangled livestock and blood) are imposed on Gentile converts as proof that the rest of the Old Testament law, including Sabbath keeping, are therefore no longer binding upon Christians. "The council's final court of appeal," they say, "is not Moses and the law (which are not mentioned in the letter) but the Spirit" (Acts 15:28).

Actually, Moses *is* mentioned as the very reason these four ritual laws were chosen because they were the ones which "sojourners and strangers" were expected to observe. These laws are listed in Leviticus 17-18.

Another attempt to lump the Sabbath in with the laws of Moses goes something like this:

> "Instead of requiring Gentile Christians to keep the entire law of Moses, the conference only required them to abstain from blood, strangled things, idolatry and fornication. This was relatively lenient compared to the stringent requirements being preached in the synagogues. The Sabbath was part of the law of Moses, just as much as circumcision was, but nothing was said to make the Sabbath an exception."

By placing the Sabbath and circumcision within the law of Moses, the assumption is made that if circumcision is identified as an unbearable yoke, the Sabbath must also be considered an obsolete Mosaic burden. But both circumcision and the Sabbath are only inherited covenant signs that predate the Mosaic law by hundreds and thousands of years.

In the end, the council endorsed James' proposal *because* of his appeal to Mosaic authority: "For from early generations Moses has had in every city those who preach him, for he is read every Sabbath in the synagogues." Acts 15:21.

They did not exempt the Gentiles from the observance of the whole Law, but only from the law of circumcision.

> "The apostolic decree enjoins Gentiles to keep the law, and they keep that part of the law required for them to live together with Jews. It is not lawful to impose upon Gentiles more than Moses himself demanded. It is false to speak of the Gentiles as free from the law. The church, on the contrary, delivers the law to the Gentiles as Gentiles. Thus Luke succeeds in showing complete adherence to the law."   Jacob Jervell, professor of New Testament at the University of Oslo, *The Unknown Paul: Essays on Luke-Acts and Early Christian History*, Augsburg Press, 1984, 190 pp. *Paul: Rabbi and Apostle, The Theology of the Acts of the Apostle*, Cambridge University Press 1996, 142 pp.

This is in harmony with Isaiah's view of the "foreigner" who keeps the Sabbath and "does not profane it and holds fast my covenant." The prophet says that God would accept these persons as His people "for my house shall be called a house of prayer for all peoples" Isaiah 56:6-7.

Passover Meal for Jews and Gentiles

These four laws were recommended in order not to offend Jewish Christians. The first two prohibitions were moral in nature, not ritualistic, by respecting the 2nd and 7th Commandments.

> Point 1—Refusing food offered to *heathen deities*
> Point 2—Abstaining from *fornication* (adultery)

The last two dealt with dietary laws established at the time flesh food was first introduced to the human race (Genesis 9:4) and later reaffirmed by Moses. Leviticus 3:17; 7:26; 17:10; 19:26.

> Point 3—Abstaining from *things strangled* and
> Point 4—Abstaining from *blood*

Emphasis on the dietary laws was to ensure that both Jews and Gentiles would be able to meet together for Passover and all the other festivals that involve food, including the regular weekly Shabbat. The Gentiles had to observe the essential elements of a Kosher diet, so that they could do their fair share of the work, preparing the food for the communal meals.

Many other laws of Moses were *not* discussed. Tithing, marriage and divorce, capital punishment, animal care, education of children, care of widows, orphans and the poor, laws regarding property, husband-wife relations, etiquette, gossip, weights and measures, usury, clean and unclean flesh, agriculture, land sabbaths, annual feasts, and the Ten Commandments were never mentioned. It is clear that the debate was focused on the single issue of Gentile circumcision.

To allow Sabbath "breaking" would be inconsistent with a desire to keep peace among the Jewish Christians. This peace survived for decades as the Jewish Christians continued to identify themselves with the Temple rituals (Acts 20:16; 21:18-26; 18:19). The New Testament church was not viewed by the apostles as simply a "new" Israel arising out of a rejected "old" Israel, but as a "restored" Israel according to God's promise. The original olive tree continued; only new branches were grafted in (Romans 11). James quoted Amos 9:11 to prove that Gentile conversions were a fulfillment of the prophecy concerning a restored Israel that maintained its observance of the seventh-day Sabbath (Acts 15:16-18).

Acts 16, 17 and 18 are evidence that the Council's decision in chapter 15 did *not* involve the Sabbath since Paul continued to seek out and worship with believers, even Gentile believers, on that day.

> "Therefore, sailing from Troas, we ran a straight course to Samothrace, and the next [day] came to Neapolis, and from there to Philippi, which is the foremost city of that part of Macedonia, a colony. And we were staying in that city for some days. And **on the Sabbath day** we went out of the city to the riverside, where prayer was **customarily** made; and we sat down and spoke to the women who met [there]." Acts 16:11-13 (NKJV)

It was the custom of the Jews of that day for the rabbi to close the synagogue if there were not a quorum of at least 10 men to show up for the Sabbath meeting. This could very well be why there were women meeting by the riverside for prayer. It is less likely that they were meeting there because the city didn't have a synagogue. Furthermore, the next verse tells of Lydia from Thyratira, "who worshipped God." This strongly suggests that she, like Cornelius "who was a worshipper of God" was a Gentile believer. Nevertheless, we see that Paul and the rest of his group sought for a place to meet on the Sabbath and they found one. Again, "the Sabbath Day" was used "customarily" for prayer and the gathering of believers.

> "After these things Paul departed from Athens, and came to Corinth; And found a certain Jew named Aquila, born in Pontus, lately come from Italy, with his wife Priscilla; (because that Claudius had commanded all Jews to depart from Rome:) and came unto them. And because he was of the same craft, **he abode with them, and wrought** [worked]: for by their occupation they were tentmakers. And he reasoned in the synagogue every sabbath, and persuaded the Jews and the Greeks." Acts 18:1-4

Here Paul worked as a tentmaker—but not on the Sabbath. And once again we see that both Jews and Greeks are in the synagogue on the Sabbath. Paul attended the Sabbath services with them. The interesting thing about this verse is that Paul was reportedly there *every* Sabbath persuading both Jews *and* Greeks. Persuading them about what? That Jesus of Nazareth was the Christ, the promised Messiah.

> "And when Silas and Timotheus were come from Macedonia, Paul was pressed in the spirit, and testified to the Jews **that Jesus was Christ**. And when they opposed themselves, and blasphemed, he shook his raiment, and said unto them, Your blood be upon your own heads; I am clean; from henceforth I will go unto the Gentiles. And he departed thence, and entered into a certain man's house, named Justus, one that worshipped God, whose house joined hard to the synagogue. And Crispus, the chief ruler of the synagogue,

believed on the Lord with all his house; and many of the
Corinthians hearing believed, and were baptized...And he continued
there a year and six months, teaching the word of God among
them." Acts 18:5-9,11

If they were reasoning with the Jews about deserting the Sabbath of
the Lord, tremendous debate and opposition would have been
recorded in the book of Acts. But Sabbath observance is rarely a topic
of discussion. And when resistance is encountered it is always in
regard to Christ's Messiaship.

Paul was there a year and six months. With 52 Sabbaths in a year
plus 26 Sabbaths in the following six months Paul met with the
Corinthians a total of 78 Sabbaths.

Paul's Festive Life
Besides Sabbath observance, Luke records a number of other annual
festivals which the apostle kept. Acts 18:21 describes Paul's voyage
from Ephesus in order to "keep this feast that comes in Jerusalem."
This trip occurred at the end of his second missionary journey.
Though Luke doesn't specify which feast it was, his generalized
reference is considered by most as indicating the biggest feast of the
year, Passover.

During Paul's third journey he spent three years at Ephesus (Acts
19:10, 20:31). There, he wrote his first letter to the Corinthians telling
them of his desire to see them soon, but that he would stay at
Ephesus until Pentecost (1 Cor 16:5-8). Then he left for Macedonia
and Greece where he stayed in Corinth for three months. Returning
back through Macedonia, he stopped at Berea and Thessalonica (Acts
20:1-4). Next, he traveled on to Philippi where he celebrated
Passover and the days of Unleavened Bread. After spending a week at
Troas (Acts 20:6), he hurried on to Jerusalem in order to make it in
time for Pentecost Acts 20:13-16.

Acts 27:9 reports that Paul kept "the fast," translation: the most
important fast of the year—Yom Kippur. Paul, at this time a prisoner
on his way to Rome, was able to observe the Day of Atonement
because it simply involved not eating or drinking.

From this brief sketch of Paul's journeys, the busy apostle seems to
have organized his life around the Hebrew festivals. Pentecost at
Ephesus, Passover the following year at Philippi, then Pentecost
again in Jerusalem. This not only suggests but establishes the fact
that the early Christian church continued to observe these feasts.

Pauline Passovers

In addition to the Passover that Christ kept with His disciples on the night before His death, there are several other references in the New Testament that suggest a possible association between the New Passover ceremony. They are based on the link between the act of Jesus at the Last Supper of "breaking bread." In fact, this practice was very common.

> "And all that believed were together, and had all things common, and sold their possessions and goods, and parted them to all *men*, as every man had need. And they, continuing **daily** with one accord in the temple, and **breaking bread from house to house**, did eat their meat with gladness and singleness of heart, praising God and having favor with all the people. And the Lord added to the church daily as should be saved." Acts 2:44-47

According to this scripture, breaking bread was commonly performed on a daily basis. It was one of the customs in those days to eat their 'daily bread.' Even in Jesus' prayer He said "Give us this day our daily bread."

Paul wrote his first letter to the Corinthians while he was in Ephesus, and, as already noted, mentioned his intention to stay in Ephesus until Pentecost. There are seven weeks from Passover to Pentecost, and he says so much about Passover, it seems likely he might have actually written the letter during the Festival.

> "Your glorying is not good. Know ye not that a little leaven leaveneth the whole lump? Purge out therefore the old leaven, that ye may be a new lump, as ye are unleavened. For even Christ our Passover is sacrificed for us: therefore let us keep the feast, not with old leaven, neither with the leaven of malice and wickedness; but with the unleavened bread of sincerity and truth." 1 Cor 5:6-8

Paul is giving them a direct command to observe Passover, and he even tells them what it means. The Israelites ate unleavened bread the night they left Egypt because they had to leave in a hurry. There was no time to wait for a regular batch of dough to rise. The traditional Jewish teaching is that yeast leavening symbolizes pride: being puffed up. When Israel left Egypt there was nothing for them to boast about. They had not secured their release through their own military might. They were indebted to the miraculous intervention of God alone.

Getting rid of the leaven means getting rid of our pride. When Paul wrote his letter sometime around 58 AD, the Jews in Jerusalem were still conducting sacrifices at the temple. It would not be destroyed for another 12 years. So Paul tells his readers that Christ is their

Passover sacrifice. There is now no need for an animal sacrifice, but they should still celebrate Passover.

> "The cup of blessing which we bless, is it not the communion of the blood of Christ? The bread which we break, is it not the communion of the body of Christ? For we being many are one bread, and one body, for we are all partakers of that one bread." 1 Corinthians 10:16

Here is another reference to the Passover meal that Jesus had with his disciples before his crucifixion. During this traditional meal there are four toasts: the cup of sanctification, deliverance, redemption, and praise.

It was the third toast, the cup of redemption, that Jesus offered as a symbol of His blood "of the new testament which is shed for many for the remission of sins" Matthew 26:28. Here Paul refers to it as the "*cup of blessing*" because we are blessed by Christ's redemption for us. Paul may also be referring to two of the other Passover cups in 1 Corinthians 1:30 when he speaks of "*sanctification and redemption*".

> "For I received of the Lord that which also I delivered unto you, that the Lord Jesus the same night in which he was betrayed took bread: and when he had given thanks, he brake it, and said, Take, eat: this is my body, which is broken for you: this do in remembrance of me. After the same manner also he took the cup, when he had supped, saying, This cup is the new testament in my blood: this do ye, as oft as ye drink it, in remembrance of me. For as often as ye eat this bread, and drink this cup, ye do show **the Lord's death** till he come." 1 Cor. 11:23-26

Claims that Paul and the other apostles observed the Lord's Supper on Sunday from the earliest times are contradicted by the teaching of the apostles themselves.

1. Paul is surprisingly silent about any reference to or mention of the Lord's Day in his lengthy instruction to the Corinthians regarding the Passover Celebration.
2. Four times Paul says "when you come together" (1 Corinthians 11:18, 20, 33, 34) specifying an indeterminate time.
3. Paul missed a perfect opportunity to address the timing and sacred nature of the Lord's Supper especially if Christ had set an example Himself or even commanded that His Communion service be conducted on His "Holy" First Day.
4. Paul only refers to Sunday in Hebrew terminology: "first day of the week" never as the "Lord's Day."

In contrast, we see repeated episodes of Paul's faithful Sabbath observance and participation in the traditional annual feasts. One occasion, however, is recorded of a "first day" meeting that involved "breaking bread." But before discussing this event in detail, let's once again review its immediate context.

After spending 78 Sabbaths in Corinth, Paul sailed from Philippi after the days of unleavened bread (Passover, Acts 20:6) intending to arrive at Jerusalem by the feast of Pentecost. On his way to Jerusalem to keep this feast, Paul spends a week at Troas. This visit is the only documented meeting by Christians that occurred on or close to the first day of the week in the New Testament other than the crucifixion weekend. Let's examine this episode closely.

Bread Breaking Sunday
Acts 20:6,7

> "And we sailed away from Philippi after the days of unleavened bread, and came unto them to Troas in five days; where we abode seven days. And upon the first [day] of the week, when the disciples came together to break bread, Paul preached unto them, ready to depart on the morrow; and continued his speech until midnight."

This is the scripture most quoted by those who believe the Sabbath day was changed. It is the only occasion recorded in the New Testament that even comes close to identifying a religious meeting conducted on the first day of the week, and only because Sunday happens to be very close to Saturday.

All scholars agree that the phrase "first of the week" (in this case τη μια των σαββατων) here means Sunday, the first day of the week. Greek manuscripts by Erasmus, Stephens, Beta, Mill, Griesbach, Scholz, Lachmann, Tischendorf, Tregelles, Alford, Green, Wordsworth, Westcott and Hort, Weiss, Nestlé, Von Soden, Kilpatrick, Tasker (N.E.B. Greek), and Aland and Metzger, all have precisely the same reading. And the Greek lexicons of Thayer, Abbot Smith, S. G. Green, and Arndt and Gingrich all report that while the literal meaning is "the first of the sabbaths," the Greek plural was used during New Testament times to signify "week." On this all agree.

However, there are differences of opinion on whether this evening meeting at Troas occurred on the night preceding Sunday or the one following it.

Here's how a number of translations deal with this phrase:

Saturday – Today's English Version, Barclay's Version,
　　　　New English Bible, Jerusalem Bible, Ronald Knox
from 6 pm Saturday to 6pm Sunday – Souter's Pocket Lexicon
　　　　of the Greek NT
first day after the Sabbath – Geneva Bible
day after the Sabbath – Schonfield
one of the Sabbath days – Great Bible, Bishop's Bible,
　　　　Concordant Idiomatic Version, Kingdom interlinear
one of the Sabbath – Concordant and Marshall RSV Interlinear
first of the Sabbath(s) – Rheims, Wilson Interlinear, Ferrar Fenton
first of the week – Young, Rotherham
morrow after the Sabbath day – Tyndale Bible
Sunday – Living Bible, Beck

Saturday Night

A Saturday night meeting is adopted by several Bible translations as shown above. In these translations the "first day of the week" phrase is replaced by "Saturday," based on the premise that Luke was using the Jewish method of reckoning. This is indicated in the Greek by use of the word *sabbaton*, a very typical derivative from the Hebrew *shabbat*. If Luke had intended to specify the first day of the week by a non-Jewish designation, he would most likely have used the prevailing expression *dies solis*—day of the sun.

Historical evidence does indicate that this form of reckoning continued for centuries among the Christian community. This account was recorded by Luke at least 30 years after the crucifixion of Christ. It is amazing that Luke did not refer to it by a sacred title, like "the Lord's day," if Sunday was in fact regarded as such by the apostles following the resurrection. There is the likelihood that Luke, Gentile or not, would have used this in his narrative. Instead, he merely mentions the first day of the week in the conventional Hebrew terminology.

Taking this approach the disciples met on Saturday evening after the conclusion of the Sabbath closing ceremonies which involved the lighting of candles. This harmonizes with Luke's mention of the "many lights in the upper chamber," verse 8. Another reason for the lights might have been an effort on Luke's part to provide an explanation as to why Eutychus became drowsy: all that heat and smoke generated by the oil-fed lamps could well have been a contributing factor in the etiology of his fateful fall. Following the Sabbath closing service, which included a meal, Paul delivered an after-dinner-talk as the esteemed visiting speaker that lasting until midnight. Then, beginning at daybreak, Paul spent most of Sunday walking some twenty miles to Assos.

Sunday Night

Other interpretations appeal to the fact that Luke, a Gentile, would be writing "for the use of Gentile Christians in all ages" and consequently would not use the Jewish method of reckoning, but the Roman system which begins the day at midnight. In fact, the term "midnight" is explicitly used in this text. Furthermore, John also refers to Sunday night as "the first day of the week" in John 20:19. This is the position taken by Bishop Christopher Wordsworth, poet William's nephew, in his 1856 *Commentary on the Whole Bible*:

> "Here we see an example of the disciples gathering together on the first day of the week. There is no mention of a Sabbath being observed in this verse. Nowhere [in the English translation] is this day called "The Sabbath." In fact, we know that Paul was ready to depart the next day. According to verse 7." Comment supplied.

Assuming this meeting took place Sunday night, the next day would have been Monday when Paul and his party set sail for Mitylene (Acts 20:13, 14). The following day (Tuesday) they would have arrived opposite Chios (verse 15). The next day (Wednesday) they would have passed Samos (verse 15), then by Thursday they would have arrived at Miletus (verse 15). There, the elders from the church at Ephesus met Paul and he preached to them (Acts 20:16-36). Here is recorded a Christian service that was held on a Thursday. Just because a religious service is recorded to have occurred on a Sunday, a Thursday, or any other day does not qualify that day to become a replacement for the seventh-day Sabbath, the day of regular Christian worship and rest in the apostolic church. (Edwin R. Gane, *Bible Studies*, 1997).

Breaking Bread

This occasion also mentions that the disciples came together to 'break bread.' Though opinions differ, most conclude that this constituted a special communion service. But notice that the actual "breaking of bread" didn't occur until after midnight:

> "When he therefore was come up again, and had broken bread, and eaten, and talked a long while, even til break of day, so he departed." Acts 20:11

Furthermore, only Paul is reported to have broken the bread and eaten. There is no mention of a blessing or distribution of the bread. There is no record of cup or wine. No prayers, no scripture reading.

With only one instance of a first day meeting involving the breaking of bread, the question remains unanswered as to whether this represents the usual and customary practice of Christians at the time or merely a single isolated incidental event.

Eutychus Drops Out of Church

If it was an isolated occurance, the reason for its inclusion in Luke's record is Eutychus. The absence of other first-day meetings during Paul's extensive travels indicates that there was nothing particular or significant about the day of the week in this case that merits its mention by Luke. The traumatic (and apparently lethal) fall of a young man and his miraculous resuscitation are what makes this occasion noteworthy.

While it cannot be absolutely confirmed that this Scripture in Acts 20 is a Sabbath day observance, history records the fact that it was decades after the death of the apostles before the Sabbath of Scripture was substituted for the observance of the first day of the week [See Doctor's Orders].

Collection Sunday
1 Corinthians 16:1

> "Now concerning the collection for the saints, as I have given orders to the churches of Galatia, so you must do also: 2 On the first day of the week let each one of you lay something aside, storing up as he may prosper, that there be no collections when I come."

Acts 11:28-30 and Romans 15:26 relate the plight of the church members in Jerusalem. The region was suffering from a great famine, and the believers were in serious need of food and supplies. Paul asked the brethren to prepare a collection of food and clothing on the first day of the week. He would come by and pick up their contribution, and bring it to the needy in Jerusalem.

It was the time consuming gathering of foodstuffs and clothing for the needy which the Corinthians were to do for transporting to Jerusalem. Now notice: Paul is not telling the people to "rest and worship"—but to work at preparing for his collection.

More important is Paul's use of the Jewish time references for "the first of the week" *kata mian sabbaton,* or literally "the first [day] from Sabbath". This typical Hebrew expression is once again a clear indication that the apostle had not abandoned the Jewish religious calendar even though the significance of festival events and holy days were modified by the Messiah's coming. If Paul, like Luke, had intended to specify the first day of the week by a non-Jewish designation, he would again have used the Gentile expression *dies solis*—day of the sun.

> "The references to time in Paul's First Epistle to the Corinthians exclusively reflect the adoption of a Jewish calendar. Even in a place like Corinth, Paul speaks of the first day from Sabbath (*kata mian sabbaton*; 1 Cor 16:2), and not of the day of the sun. He builds an

elaborate argument based upon the festival of Passover and unleavened bread (1 Cor 5:6-8) in order to exhort the Corinthians, 'Let us keep the festival' (1 Cor 5:6-8). Although the temporal references in Paul's letters are sparse, 1 Corinthians provides strong evidence for the Pauline adoption of the Jewish practice that marked time by festivals and Sabbaths." *"Pagan and Judeo-Christian Time-Keeping Schemes in Galatians 4:10 and Colossians 2:16,"* Troy Martin in *New Testament Studies 42*, 1996, pp 108, 109.

Nor does the Greek text support the notion of bringing an offering to a worship service. The word 'day' in the King James is in italics. This was used by the translators to indicate that this word is not in the ancient manuscripts. "Day" has been added because the translators assumed that Paul meant Sunday. Rather than reading "the first day of the week" we should be literally reading "the first of the week." Some have pointed out that this suggests a more general rather than specific time reference. Paul could have been referring to Sunday, Monday or even Tuesday and still have been the first part of the week.

The contributions, Bacchiocchi observes, were to be set aside
- *Periodically*   "on the first day of every week"
- *Personally*   "each of you"
- *Privately*   "by himself in store" and
- *proportionately* "as he may prosper"

This was good financial, budgetary advice. Paul's first of the week fundraising plan was also a matter of priority. Setting aside contributions at the beginning of the week would allow the donors to budget their remaining funds responsibly. Waiting until the end of the week (after all their resources were spent) might compromise the size of their gift. Paul was also being sensitive to some donors who might be embarrassed to present a meager offering in public.

Sabbath Rest in Hebrews
The book of Hebrews appeals to the continuity of God's message, His redemptive ministry, His cleansing atonement and His Sabbath rest from the Old to the New Testament dispensation. That is,
God's message to man (the same God who spoke through the fathers of old also spoke by His Son. Hebrews 1:1-2),
God's redemptive ministry (from the earthly sanctuary to the one in heaven. Hebrews 7-10),
God's cleansing atonement (from the ancient Day of Atonement when Israel waited for the High Priest's return from the Most Holy place, to our waiting for Christ's return from the heavenly Temple),
God's rest (from the rest of creation, to the rest of redemption).

The epistle to the Hebrews compares the legacy of God's leading in the past to the new intimate relationship He now has with His people through Jesus, the living, undying High Priest of the Real Temple. Chapters 3 and 4 contrast the experience of Israel entering the Promised Land under Joshua and their failed mission to find God's intended "rest" for them with the renewed opportunity to achieve His goal through Jesus Who is better than the angels, better than Moses, better than Aaron, better than the Levite priests.

First day commentators like to distinguish the rest here in Hebrews 4 as a promise rather than a precept; that it is not commanded like the old testament Sabbath but rather offered as a benefit of the New covenant. If this is so, then why is the imperative urgently repeated to enter into His rest at the possible risk of forfeiting it? The rest mentioned in this passage is not the weekly Sabbath, yet the weekly Sabbath is employed by the writer to illustrate its potential yet missed realization on progressively grander scales: Israel under Moses, Joshua and then David. Each period of opportunity went unfulfilled because of "unbelief" resulting in disobedience. The emphasis in these two chapters is not primarilly on the Sabbath, but on the importance of keeping the faith, persevering, being diligent.

Hebrews chapter 4 contains the translated word "rest" a total of nine times. All but one of these are variations of the same Greek word (*katapausis*) which means a rest from labor. The exception is found in verse 9: Therefore a *sabbatismos* (Sabbath-keeping, derived from *sabbaton*) *apoleipetai* is left over or remains for the people of God. This is the only occurrence of *sabbatismos* in the New Testament. As the dove of Noah kept returning because it found no place to "rest," so the dove of the Holy Spirit longs with anticipation to find a place of rest among the remnant seed of the Woman. It is not just physical rest, but the true spiritual rest from sin to be found only in Jesus. Still, this final rest can be experienced now by loyal Sabbath-keeping.

As the Sabbath continued to be a significant part of the life and experience of the Christian community well into the second century, it continues to be an important model for the spiritual survival and support of God's people living in these end times as they anticipate and prepare for the ultimate rest in His very presence. The action initiated by God in the beginning continued then, as it does now, as a reflexive response within His New Testament Church.

Below is a comparative analysis of a wide variety of translations (and paraphrases) demonstrating the various expressions used to render verses 8 and 9 of chapter 4.

Hebrews 4: 8

For if...
Jesus –KJV, Darby, Douay-Rheims, Inspired, Jesus, Douay-Rheims, Inspired, Bethel
Joshua –Beck, Amplified, Concordant Literal, Concordant Literal, RSV, Living Bible, Lamsa [the son of Nun], Noli, Worrell
Y'hoshua—Complete Jewish
had given them rest—KJV, Amplified, Complete Jewish, RSV, Inspired, Lamsa, Bethel, Worrell
had given this rest—Douay-Rheims, Noli **[to our forefathers]**
causes them to stop—Concordant Literal
brought them into rest—Darby
led them into the land of Israel—Living Bible
he—KJV, Amplified, Concordant Literal, Darby, Duoay-Rheims, Inspired, Lamsa, Bethel, Worrell
God—Beck, Amplified, Complete Jewish, RSV, The Message
the Lord—Noli
would not — (all), Duoay-Rheims **[never]**
afterward—KJV, Amplified, Darby, Duoay-Rheims, Inspired, Lamsa, Bethel, Worrell
after these things—Concordant Literal
later—Beck, Noli [much later date], RSV
have spoken of—KJV, Beck, Complete Jewish, Concordant Literal, Darby, Duoay-Rheims, RSV, Inspired, Lamsa, Bethel, Worrell
speak about—Amplified
keep renewing the appointment—The Message
another day—KJV, Beck, Amplified, Complete Jewish, Concordant Literal, Darby, Duoay-Rheims, RSV, Inspired, Lamsa, Bethel, Worrell
new place of rest—Living Bible
"Today"—Noli, The Message

The majority of translations recognize that the spelling in Hebrew is actually Joshua who lead ancient Israel into the promised land. Because they never experienced the spiritual rest which God intended, God through David later repeated the offer for the people of his time, his "day," to enter into His rest again—"Today."

The opportunity to enter God's spiritual rest from sin is still available. The Sabbath reaches its greatest fulfillment and offers its greatest blessing when God's people realize the true rest in Christ. Thus, the educational value of the Sabbath is not lost even after the great sacrifice of Jesus. This was recognized by the early apostolic church community as they continued to observe the Sabbath in acknowledgment of Christ's act of redemption at the cross.

Hebrews 4: 9

Therefore—KJV, LBP, NASV, Noli
So—AAT, Amplified, CJB, Inspired, Living Bible, SGAT
Hence—EBR, **Consequently**—CLNT,
But God has promised us—CEV, **a promise**—SGAT
the hope of—NNT
there remains—KJV, CJB, Darby, Inspired, NASV
there is still—AAT, Amplified, MNT, NJB [**must be**], SGAT [**must**]
there is left over—EBR,
there is waiting—Living Bible, Amplified, NSNT
it is the duty to keep the sabbath—LBP
a rest—KJV, Inspired, **the rest**—NCV
a sabbath of rest—AAT, SGAT
a sabbath rest—MNT, NASV
a today of sabbath rest—NSNT
a seventh-day rest—New Jerusalem Bible
a Sabbath-keeping—CJB, EBR,
a sabbatism—CLNT, Darby
a Sabbath when we will rest—CEV,
a full and complete Sabbath rest—Amplified,
a full complete rest—Living Bible
a heavenly rest—NNT
even though it has not yet come—CEV,
is reserved—Amplified, MNT, NJB, **is left**—CLNT
is still coming—NCV, **is still there**—NNT
to—KJV, Darby, Inspired
for—AAT, Amplified, CJB, CLNT, EBR, Living Bible, MNT, NASV, NCV, NJB, NNT, SGAT
the people of God—KJV, CLNT, Darby, EBR, Inspired, Living Bible, MNT, NASV, NNT
God's people—Amplified, CJB, NCV, NJB, NSNT, SGAT

God does not get weary (Isaiah 40:28). In this, man is unlike God. We need to rest this physical body on the Sabbath. But this day is especially a time when God nurtures what He has created by offering a time of spiritual rest.

Because of His action we respond with a natural and predictable reaction. This human response is a built-in, innate reflex.
[See Appendix D]

Eyes, Ears and Mouth

What do you see? How well do you see? Can you hear this? Repeat after me. The special senses of sight and hearing, the miracle of articulated speech, these are the portals to the soul. What we think, what we perceive, what we wish to convey, come to us and proceed from us through these avenues.

Our examination must include the ENT organs of special sense.

What is said about the Sabbath by those who saw and heard Christ?
"We are eyewitnesses," Peter affirms.
"I saw Him on the Damascus road," Paul confesses.
Surely they would know the diagnosis.

Nailed to the Cross
The words of Paul to the Colossians have been a source of debate for centuries. No other single text has been more argued.

> "And you, being dead in your sins and the uncircumcision of your flesh, has He resurrected together with Him, having forgiven you all trespasses; blotting out the handwriting of ordinances that was against us, which was contrary to us, and took it out of the way, nailing it to His cross." Colossians 2:14 KJV margin.

Colossae was in central Asia, today's Turkey, situated in the Lycus valley along with its sister city, Laodicea, only 10 miles away. Both communities shared similar spiritual struggles in keeping their eyes and focus on Christ as the one and only Source of their salvation and worth before God. What, then, was nailed to the cross?

Gnostic Teachings
The Colossian Christians were tempted to consider a number of competing teachings and practices that included a preoccupation with certain Greek Gnostic "mysteries," "wisdom," secret "knowledge" and cosmic powers (Col. 1:26,27; 2:3), based on an obsession with angelic beings that were supposedly organized into various orders (Col. 1:6) to serve as intermediaries between God and man, dispensing salvation and deserving adoration, even worship. The promise was that attention to these matters would bring the adherents into a "fuller" religious experience. This was coupled with an extreme fixation on legalistic ceremonies, physical deprivations, taboos, rituals and even abasement of the body. Matter was evil, so inflicting pain and suffering on one's body would bring salvation. This is still practiced today by Hindus who walk on coals of fire or lie on beds of nails, and even Christians in Catholic countries who

practice flagellation, fasting and other forms of self-torture while carrying crosses, climbing steps, making pilgrimages, performing penance and so forth.

Verse 8 in chapter 2 sets the tone for Paul's present instruction: "Beware lest any man rob you through philosophy and vain deceit after the traditions of men." Verse 22 summarizes the focus of his concern: "the commandments and doctrines of men." The terminology used here clearly identifies. Gnostic minutiae served only to detract the attention of the Colossians from the role of Christ as their Creator, Sustainer, Mediator and Emancipator in whom "the fullness" of the Godhead *did* dwell.

Sins Forgiven

The immediate context (Colossians 2:12) is dealing with our "burial baptism" with Christ, dying to sin and the subsequent resurrection to a new life cleansed from sin. Paul then discusses the forgiveness of sins. It is at this point in his discourse that he uses a phrase which occurs nowhere else in Scripture: *chierographon*. It is translated variously as "handwriting of ordinances" (KJV), "certificate of debt" (NASB), "bond written in ordinances" (RV), "with its legal demands" (RSV).

Blotted Out

He then states that Christ blotted this bond out, He took it out of the way, by nailing it to His cross (Col. 2:14). Was this the law including the Ten Commandments of God? Was it abolished at Calvary? Or are the hand-written ordinances those ceremonial regulations dealing with the sacrificial system which ceased at Christ's death? "the statutes and the ordinances by the hand of Moses" 2 Chronicles 33:8; "this book of the law" that was placed "beside the ark of the covenant...that it may be there for a witness against you" Deut. 31:26. Or was this "certificate of debt" the record of our sins and the burden of our guilt that Christ took to the cross in His own body? 1 Peter 2:24.

Chierographon, then, has three possibilities:
- All Law
  (10 Commandments, ceremonial, civil, sanitary, dietary)
- Sacrificial-ceremonial Law
- Sin-debt

We will now explore each of these three possibilities in order.

Law Defined

Interestingly, the word Law (*nomos*) does not even appear in the epistle to the Colossians. This is recognized by many modern scholars:

> "...in the whole of the epistle the word law is not used at all. Not only that, but the whole significance of the law, which appears unavoidable for Paul when he presents his gospel, is completely absent." Eduard Lohse, *A Commentary on the Epistles to the Colossians and to Philemon* (Philadelphia, 1971), p. 116.

> The law "plays no role at all." Herold Weiss, "The Law in the Epistle to the Colossians," *The Catholic Biblical Quarterly* 34 [1972]: 311.

> "...that this passage cannot be interpreted as stating that the Mosaic law itself was 'wiped out' in the death of Christ." Douglas R. De Lacey, "The Sabbath/Sunday Question and the Law in the Pauline Corpus," *From Sabbath to Lord's Day. A Biblical, Historical, and Theological Investigation*, ed. Donald A. Carson (Grand Rapids, 1982), p. 173.

Likewise, efforts to dissect the law into only one type (ceremonial or moral) is not easily done in this passage. Jesus appears to have considered the entire body of scripture as the Law. He even included the Psalms in the Law. In John 10:34, "Jesus answered them, Is it not written in your law, I said, Ye are gods?" There He quotes Psalm 82:6.

Since the Spirit of Christ was in the prophets. (I Peter 1:10, 11) and David was a prophet (Acts 2:29, 30), Christ expressed His own will in the book of Psalms (part of the Law), "All His commandments are sure. They stand fast forever and ever, and are done in truth and uprightness" Psalm 111:7-8.

In His Sermon on the Mount Jesus refers to all Scripture by using the common division of law and prophets: "Think not that I am come to destroy the law, or the prophets: I am not come to destroy, but to fulfill." He affirmed the same thought in John 10:35 by stating "The scripture cannot be broken."

Law or No Law

Certain groups have attempted through appeal to Paul's statements to retire or eliminate either portions of the Law or the entire Law altogether. Sunday Sabbatarians wish to disqualify the Fourth Commandment or if that won't work, then get rid of them all. Saturday Sabbatarians wish to nullify the ceremonial portions of the Law as proof that the annual festivals and their related sabbaths rather than the weekly Sabbath of the Lord are the ones intended in this passage.

At one end of the legal spectrum there are the legalists, supporting and enforcing the law for personal gain and public shame—modern Pharisees cling to rules and regulations, carefully doing all the right things for the wrong reasons. They live a cold legalistic existence, devoid of warmth and assurance, full of criticism and uncertainty. The Old Covenant failed because of legalism and many a New Testament church has withered under its critical, condemning spirit.

And in the other corner, at the opposite extreme, weighing in with no law at all, we have the antinomians. Free from legal demands, no longer under the law, these believe—period. "Jesus kept the law so I don't have to," is their mission statement. The fruit of their gospel has reaped the harvest of our current lawless society with its unbridled immorality. Adolph Korble said, "While legalism is killing its thousands, antinomianism is killing its tens of thousands." Abolishing the law of God as a standard of behavior and moral conduct is no less dangerous than legalistically enforcing it upon others or depending on it ourselves as the means of our salvation. Both lawlessness and legalism are unbiblical extremes.

But did Christ "make void the law" at the cross? Even just a part of it? Paul has already answered that rhetorical question when he wrote, "God forbid! We establish the law." Romans 3:31. "What shall we say then? Shall we continue in sin (breaking the law), that grace (unmerited pardon) may abound? God forbid!" Romans 6:1. Trivializing God's law trivializes sin. Doing so turns the power of the gospel and the magnitude of its deliverance from death and bondage into a simple sentimental story that leads to spiritual mediocrity and ultimately to spiritual apathy and even anarchy.

Many commentaters observe that Paul uses the word "law" over 100 times in his letters to various churches. He refers to it as:

- the Mosaic Law (Gal. 4:21; Rom. 7:22, 25; 1 Cor. 9:9),
- the whole Old Testament (1 Cor. 14:21; Rom. 3:19, 21),
- the will of God in the heart of Gentiles (Rom. 2:14-15),
- principles of conduct (Romans 3:27),
- evil inclinations (Romans 7:21),
- the Holy Spirit's leading (Romans 8:2),
- and God personified (Rom. 3:19; 4:15; 1 Cor. 9:8).

...but not once does he use the word "law" in his letter to the Colossians.

Paul's Ambivalence

Paul also appears ambivalent about the law:
In Ephesians 2:15 the law is "abolished" by Christ,
    but in Romans 3:31 "we establish" the law through faith.
In Romans 7:5 "we are discharged from the law,"
    but in verse 12 "the commandment is holy, just, good."
In Romans 10:4 "Christ is the end of the law,"
    but in Romans 8:3-4 the "the law might be fulfilled in us."
In Romans 2:28 "justified by faith apart from works of the law,"
    but in 1 Cor 7:19 it's "keeping the commandments of God."
In 2 Cor 3:7 law is "the dispensation of death,"
    but in Romans 3:2 law is part of the "oracles of God."

Some have tried to resolve the problem by appealing to a contextual application of the law's purpose:

> When the context concerns **salvation** and **justification**,
>   Paul declares the law useless. *Eg.* Galatians 2:21
>   You can't be saved by keeping the law.

> But when the context concerns **conduct** and **sanctification**,
>   He affirms the law has value and worth. *Eg.* Romans 7:12
>   The Law is a good standard for living.

If you look at Paul's comments on the merits of keeping the law as a means of earning salvation you might get the following picture:
    Before Christ we "were kept under the law." Gal. 3:23
    This law, engraven in stones is "abolished." 2 Corinthians 3
    Christ took it "out of the way" Col. 2:14
    Now, we "are not under the law." Rom. 6:14, Gal. 5:18
    "You also are become dead to the law" Rom. 7:4
    "We are delivered from the law." Rom. 7:6
    "Christ is the end of the law." Rom. 10:4

On the other hand, because of Christ's sacrifice for us:
    The enmity against God and His law is slain. Eph. 2:16
    "We establish the law." Rom. 3:31
    We are "subject to the law of God." Rom. 8:7,8
    We "delight in the law of God." Rom. 7:22

Many commentators conclude that Paul is schizophrenic. He seems to teach Jewish Christians to keep the law and then free Gentile Christians from any obligation to it. But in recent years, some have changed their tune. Dutch Reform scholar Peter Tomson, (*Paul and the Jewish Law,* Van Gorcum & Company, Assen, Netherlands, 1990) identified several common but erroneous ideas about the apostle to the Gentiles:

1. Paul attacked the Jewish law, and
2. Paul taught the law no longer had any practical application in the Christian's life.

Tomson discovered that these ideas first appear in church literature during the Reformation when Bible study revealed truths in conflict with traditional beliefs such as seventh-day and first-day observance.

The problem arises when attempts are made to lump all references to law into one bucket rather than recognize (as we did in the examination of the Heart) the distinction between God's eternal law and the temporary regulations of a sacrificial system that were "added... till" Christ should come and end all sacrifices. Galations 3:19. While the permanent moral code is Man's "standard for living" it is not replaced, but rather vindicated by the coming of the "living Standard."

Against Us

So why are these ordinances against us? Why are they contrary to us? Only when we are guilty, only when we stand as sinners before the law, does it condemn us. "And the commandment, which was ordained to life, I found to be unto death... That sin by the commandment might become exceeding sinful." Romans 7:10, 13. God ordained that His Law should give life. "Love the Lord your God, walk in His ways, and keep His commandments and His statutes and His judgments, that you may live and multiply" Deut. 30:16. "But if your heart turns away, so that you will not hear, but shall be drawn away, and worship other gods... you shall surely perish" verses 17, 18.

Returning to Colossians 2, notice that there are actually two parallel expressions in this passage:

- "canceling the bond" (verse 14) and
- "forgiving all our trespasses" (verse 13)

The action is one. Everyone has sinned. "For all have sinned, and come short of the glory of God" Romans 3:23. And "whosoever commits sin transgresses also the law: for sin is the transgression of the law" I John 3:4. Therefore "death passed upon all men for that all have sinned" Romans 5:12 and "the wages of sin is death" Romans 6:23.

We have broken God's Law. Satan, the prosecuting attorney, presents the legal indictment of our crime to the Judge. The sentence is eternal separation from the Life giver, the second death. We may either accept the sentence or accept the gift of God's Son to take our penalty and die in our place.

Christ, taking our sins upon Himself, removed the record of our guilt, blotting out the death warrant with our name on it, canceling the debt, paying the ultimate price with His own life, by letting them nail His innocent body bearing our sins to the cross. "Our old self was crucified with Him." Romans 6:5.

It is the character of God that stands in condemnation against sin and those who commit it. The prophet Micah foretold the second coming of Christ and the judgment scene to follow in just this way:

> "Hear, all ye people; hearken, O earth, and all that therein is: and let the Lord God be witness against you, the Lord from his holy temple." Micah 1:2

This is why Christ, in cleansing the temple, was so effective. He stood as a sinless witness against the polluted condition of His Father's house. The guilty fled, condemned by His very presence. He is indeed the "faithful witness," the Law personified. Revelation 1:4.

Enmity in Ephesians 2:15

The passage in Colossians 2:14 is very similar to the language Paul uses in Ephesians 2:15 where Christ brings peace between man and God by "abolishing the enmity, even the law of commandments in ordinances." God had placed "enmity between [Satan's] seed and [the woman's] seed" when man fell (Gen. 3:15). Paul said that "the carnal mind is at enmity with God" Rom 8:7. There is a hostility caused by sin because "your iniquities have separated between you and your God" Isaiah 59:2.

When man sinned He was separated from God by his sin. This created a carnal hostility or enmity between God and man:

$$\text{God} \longleftarrow \text{sin} \longrightarrow \text{Man}$$

Part of God's solution was to separate man from his sin by putting enmity between man and the devil. Remember, the Seed is Christ:

Serpent's Seed	**Enmity**	Woman's Seed
(Sin)		(Saviour)

Enmity or animosity (which literally means "against law" from the Greek *ante+nomia*) is the force that opposes rule and authority. We can have animosity against the Devil or against God. God put enmity between us and the Serpent to counteract the enmity that sin places between us and God.

God	**Sin**	Man	**Enmity**	Satan

Before the Gentiles came to Christ they were separated from God and all His blessings by their sinful nature. There was also a very real physical barrier (a four-foot high middle wall of partition) that the Jews built within the temple to limit Gentiles to their own court and keep them a "safe" distance from the holy places:

Gentiles	**Jews**
Children of wrath Eph 2:2,3	Children of God
Uncircumcised vs 11	Circumcised
Without Christ vs 12	Had Messiah
Aliens vs 12	Commonwealth of Israel
Strangers vs 12	Covenants of Promise
No Hope vs 12	Hope of salvation
Without God vs 12	Worshiped God
Far off vs 13	Made nigh

Middle Wall of Partition
Enmity-Sin
Broken down, made one

The broader context of this passage in Ephesians is dealing with the separation, the alienation of the Gentile world—not just from the Jewish nation—but from God! Paul then contrasts this past situation with the present condition resulting from Christ's sacrifice. When Christ died, the middle wall was broken down, the veil was torn top to bottom, the sacrificial system came to an end and all of God's children, Jews and Gentiles—were now united as brothers, fellow believers, members of the same body in Christ. And the Law?

What ended at the cross, in regards to the Law, was its condemnation, its *enmity*, directed at lawbreakers. "There is now no condemnation" for us, Paul declares in Romans 8:1. The law remains, it still has the ability to condemn sin, but Christ takes our sins upon Himself and the condemnation aimed at us is directed to Him. "God has done what the law...could not do." He sent "his own Son in the likeness of sinful flesh...in order that the just requirement of the law might be fulfilled in us." Rom 8:3-4. It was the condemnation of our sins by the law that was nailed to the cross in the body of Christ.

> "Christ died for **our sins** according to the scriptures"
> 1 Corinthians 15:3.

Peter agrees:

> "Who his own self **bare our sins in his own body on the tree**, that we, being dead to sins, should live unto righteousness: by whose stripes you were healed." 1 Peter 2:24
> "The Lord has laid on him the iniquity of us all" Isa 53:6.
> "So Christ was once offered to bear the sins of many" Heb 9:28

Paul in Colossians is talking about forgiveness of sins (2:13); of dying to those sins (2:12); of putting off the body of the sins through Christ (2:11). Our sins have been forgiven, Jesus has taken our death warrant with all its condemnation and our sins upon Himself to the cross. He is the "faithful witness" (Rev. 1:5) that was nailed to the tree. Now both Jews and Gentiles became one: Christians. Now both could "delight in the law of God after the inward man" Romans 7:22. The enmity, the hostility against God and His law was slain (Ephesians 2:16).

Now He could "give them one heart, and I will put a **new spirit** within you; and I will take the stony heart out of their flesh, and will give them an heart of flesh" Ezekiel 11:19. Why? "That they may walk in my statutes, and keep My ordinances, and do them." Verse 20. No longer hostile, no longer carnally minded, now they *can* be "subject to the law of God" and "please God" Romans 8:7, 8.

Therefore

Verse 16 is a transition point in Chapter 2. Notice how it is introduced: "Therefore, Consequently, Then..." It is here that Paul concludes:

> "Let no man therefore judge you in meat, or in drink, or in respect of a holy day, or of the new moon, or of the Sabbath [*days*]: which are a shadow of things to come: but the body [*is*] of Christ."
> Colossians 2:16, 17

This verse has produced more commentary and debate than any other passage on the Sabbath. Recent translations have attempted to make this ambiguous passage more clear by adding additional comments that are not found in the original text. Here are several examples:

> "From now onwards never let anyone else decide what you should eat or drink or whether you are to observe the annual festivals, new moons, or sabbaths. These are only pale reflections of what was coming, the reality of Christ." **Jerusalem Bible**

> "So don't let anyone criticize you for what you eat or drink, or for not celebrating Jewish holidays and feasts or new moon ceremonies or Sabbaths. For these were only temporary rules that ended when Christ came. They were only a shadow of the real thing— of Christ." **Living Bible**

> "In view of these tremendous facts, don't let anyone worry you by criticizing what you eat or drink, or what holy days you ought to observe, or bothering you over new moons or Sabbaths. All these things have at most only a symbolic value: the solid fact is Christ." **The Phillips Bible**

For comparison, here is a word-by-word reading of the Greek text:

Μη ουν   τις υμας   κρινετω εν βρωσει και
Not therefore anyone you   let judge in   eating   and

εν ποσει η εν μερει   εορτης η νεομηνιας η
in drinking or in respect of feast or of new moon or

σαββατων   α   εστιν σκια   των μελλοντων
of sabbaths which are   shadow of   coming things

το δε σωμα του Χριστου.
but the body   of   Christ.

(*The Interlinear Greek-English New Testament*, following the Nestle Greek Text by Alfred Marshall, Samuel Bagster and Sons, LTD, London 1960)

Notice all the padding that has been added by these newer versions: "tremendous facts, from now onwards, never, Jewish, at most, only temporary, ended, was, were." Actually, the Living Bible and Phillips are not translations, but paraphrases and take considerable liberty with their choice of wording.

Also notice that the Greek version of the text ends with the phrase σωμα του Χριστου, *soma tou Cristou*, "the body of Christ" not "the body is Christ." To express the equation "body is Christ" the Greek verb *esti* "to be" would have been used as can be seen in the phrase "which are a shadow." The original construction does not contain the verb "is"—only the possessive "of." The KJV indicates this fact by using an italicized font. This is quite important to a correct understanding of this passage as we shall later see.

But first, in analyzing this passage we find there are four parts:
1. Judgment of believers
2. Religious practices
3. Shadow and coming things
4. Body of Christ

Let no man judge you
Don't allow anyone to upset you, point a finger at you, criticize you, saying you are in error. Several Bible versions render the Judgment component in various ways:

An American Translation (Beck) –
Then **nobody shall say you are wrong** …
Barclay New Testament –
You must not therefore **let anyone criticize you** …
Noli New Testament –
Consequently, **no one can call you to account** …
Williams New Testament –
Stop letting anyone pass judgment on you…

For eating and drinking and keeping holy days? Or for *not* observing these religious rituals? The Greek is ambiguous in this regard. There is no explicit indication as to whether the criticism is leveled because of keeping or not keeping the listed practices. The usual assumption is that the Colossian believers need not be concerned about outside efforts to make them feel guilty for *not* observing these religious holy days and rituals. Yet, the wording is actually neutral as to whether it pertains to keeping or not keeping.

And who is judging and criticizing the believers in Colossae? Are they:

> **Judaizers** harassing Christians for *not* keeping feasts and Sabbaths,
> **Jewish believers** critical of Gentile members for *not* following the
>   holy days in the manner and detail that they proscribe,
> **Gentiles** harassing Christians for keeping Jewish festivals, or
> **Gentiles** pushing Christians to also accept pagan holidays?

1. Some regard this admonition as evidence that Paul considered the Sabbath as an antiquated Jewish ceremony of no pertinence to New Testament Christians. They understand the judges to be Judaizers.

2. Others believe only the ceremonial sabbaths related to the annual feast days listed in Leviticus 23 were being urged by Jewish believers.

3. Still others see Paul actually defending the Hebrew religious calendar and of those who still observe it against Gentile critics.

> "In the context of Colossians, the command to keep festival, new moon, and Sabbath is not based on the Torah according to which Israel received the Sabbath as a sign of her election from among the nations. Rather the sacred days must be kept for the sake of 'the elements of the universe' who direct the course of the stars and also prescribe minutely the order of the calendar" Eduard Lohse, *A Commentary on the Epistles to the Colossians and to Philemon* (Philadelphia, 1971), p. 155.

Judaizers and Their Sabbath Shadows

Together, these verses are popularly interpreted to demonstrate Paul's dismissal of the Jewish system including its distinctive Sabbath, replaced now with the reality of Christ. This position is reflected in those translations that render the timing of the shadows in a past tense. Those in support of this position observe that this is the only mention of the word "Sabbath" in all the epistles of Paul and note that even then it is "only to speak of it as a 'shadow'." So strong is the conviction that this is the correct interpretation that alternative views are regarded as simply "efforts...to 'retranslate' Paul" and "make him say something he does not say." They conclude that this passage is "powerfully against the obligation of Sabbath-keeping."

What kind of religious practice is Paul referring to here? There seems to be two parts. The first involved food and beverage behavior:

meat or drink – King James Version, Douay-Rheims Bible, Inspired Version, Sacred Scriptures Bethel Edition
eat or drink – American Translation (Beck), Smith-Goodspeed, Barclay NT, Contemporary English Version, Living Bible, Norlie's Simplified NT
eat and drink – Cassirer NT, New Evangelical Translation.
food and drink – Amplified Bible, Authentic NT, Holy Bible in Modern English, Noli NT
eating and drinking – Complete Jewish Bible, Interlinear Bible, Restoration of Original Sacred Name Bible, Williams NT

Fellowship Meals

The phrase εν μερει, *en merei* "in respect" might be better translated "in part." This has suggested to a number of commentators that the following list of holy days should be limited to that part dealing with "eating and drinking." This may refer to the communal fellowship meals that were commonly shared by the early Christian church and likely targets for Gnostic critics who would rather fast than feast. Such an interpretation would then read like this:

> "Don't let any man judge you for the eating and drinking [in your fellowship meals] or that portion of the Holy Day festivities [where you eat and drink]."

This interpretation is promoted by contemporary evangelical commentators as well:

> "The 'judgment' seems to be criticism of the Christians' present practice, apparently of eating and drinking and enjoying Jewish festivals [God's festivals (Lev 23:2,4)], in contrast to those whose watchword was 'do not handle, do not taste, do not even touch' (Col. 2:21)." *Dictionary of Paul and His Letters*, InterVarsity Press, 1993, p.403, Douglas R. de Lacey, Ph.D, University of Cambridge, England.

> "This essay provides evidence that the Pauline community at Colossae, not the opponents, practiced the temporal schemes outlined by Col 2:16... This investigation into the function of the list in Col 2:16 indicates that the Colossian Christians, not their critics, participate in a religious calendar that includes festivals, new moons, and Sabbaths." Troy Martin, *New Testament Studies journal*, Spring, 1996, article: "Pagan and Judeo-Christian Time-keeping Schemes in Galatians 4:10 and Colossians 2:16," p.107.

"The most natural way of taking the rest of the passage is not that he [the ascetic judge] also imposes a ritual of feast days, but rather that he objects to certain elements of such observation." Contra Hunter, Archibald M., "The Letter of Paul to the Colossians," Vol. 22 *The Layman's Bible Commentary*, John Knox Press, 1959; page 133.

Sacrificial Feast Days

Another possible reference in this phrase could be to the meat and drink *offerings* that were a part of the Old Testament sacrificial system. This would make the following triad of "days" pertain to the specified sacrificial feast days. The "sabbaths," therefore, would not pertain to the weekly seventh-day Sabbath. Some have suggested that Paul would have used *broma* and *poma* if he wanted to indicate this particular meaning.

Yet, the same language is used in Ezekiel 45 where an oblation is offered by "all the people of the land" for the prince.

"And it shall be the prince's part to give burnt offerings and meat offerings and drink offerings, the feasts and in the new moon and in the sabbath in all the solemnities in the house of Israel." Verses 16-17.

Such a parallel description is strong support for Paul's reference to activities regarding the sacrificial system. These offerings and feasts were regulated around the lunar phases making them completely disconnected from a fixed week day occurance. For example,

- **Passover sabbaths** fell on the 14th day following the new moon of the first month.
- **Feast of Trumpet sabbaths** landed on the first day of the seventh month, also synchronized by lunar phases.
- **Day of Atonement** sabbaths always occured ten days later.
- **Feast of Tabernacles** had two sabbaths on the 15th and 23rd day of the seventh month.

These special days all had symbolic significance concerning various aspects of the sacrificial system and all pointed forward to their ultimate fulfillment in the death of Christ.

Ritualistic Feasting and Fasting

Other possible interpretations are that the eating and drinking may refer to ritualistic feasting and fasting of the kind referred to in Romans 14:1-6. Or they may refer to concerns about food that had been offered to idols (1 Corinthains 8).

Mosaic Dietary Restrictions

There is yet another group of commentators that believe Paul is here referring to the "clean and unclean" distinctions that are placed on foods by the Mosaic dietary regulations. But knowing the nature of the Gnostic position on abstinence, fasting and the avoidance of anything that might bring pleasure, it is clear that the Levitical food classification was *not* on their agenda.

> "The question is not altogether between lawful and unlawful food, but between eating and drinking or abstinence. Asceticism rather than ritual cleanness is in his mind. The Law is not ascetic in its character, its prohibitions of meats rest on the view that they are unclean, and drinks are not forbidden, save in exceptional cases, and then not for ascetic reasons" *Expositor's Greek Testament*, by W. Robertson Smith, vol. 3, p 530.

Furthermore, if the proposition is being entertained that Paul is here sanctioning the annulment of Leviticus 11, the historical basis of "clean and unclean" foods should be considered.   The Mosaic covenant regulations regarding unclean foods were inherited from the covenant with Noah made at the flood. Genesis 6, 8. Therefore, condemning the perversion of a precept should not negate the original precept.

Holy Day Trio
Here's how various translations interpret these particular days:

holyday – KJV, Inspired Version
festival – Beck, Authentic NT, Barclay NT, Cassirer NT
feast – Restoration of Original Sacred Name Bible
a feast day – Amplified Bible, Sacred Scriptures Bethel Edition
feast days – Norlie's Simplified NT
annual feasts – Smith-Goodspeed, Williams NT
festival day – Douay-Rheims, New Evangelical
Jewish festival – Complete Jewish Bible
Jewish holidays and feasts – Living Bible
any other festival – Contemporary English

new moon – KJV, Amplified Bible, Authentic, Barclay, Contemporary English, Cassirer NT, Interlinear Bible, Holy Bible in Modern English, Douay-Rheims, Restoration of Original Sacred Name Bible
new moons – Norlie's Simplified NT
new moon ceremonies – Living Bible
first day of the month – Beck
first day of a month – New Evangelical
monthly feasts – Smith-Goodspeed, Williams NT
Rosh-Chodesh – Complete Jewish Bible

sabbath *days* – KJV
Sabbath days – New Evangelical
sabbaths – Barclay NT, Holy Bible in Modern English, Interlinear Bible,
Norlie's Simplified NT, Williams NT
Sabbaths – Living Bible, Smith-Goodspeed
the sabbaths – Douay-Rheims
the sabbath days - Inspired Version
sabbath – Authentic NT, Restoration of Original Sacred Name
a sabbath – Sacred Scriptures Bethel Edition
a Sabbath – Beck, Amplified Bible, Cassirer NT
the Sabbath – Contemporary English
Shabbat – Complete Jewish Bible

Notice the variations in translating *sabbaton*. Some are singular with an indefinite pronoun (a sabbath), some definite (the Sabbath), some pleural. A few commentators attribute significance to this by arguing for or against identifying the weekly seventh-day Sabbath in this passage. The rationale is that if singular then the implication points to the specific weekly seventh-day of rest; whereas if plural the reference is to the many ceremonial feast day sabbaths that occurred throughout the year. But this is not supported by the usage of this

Greek term. Bacchiocchi claims that the Septuagint always employs the specific compound term *sabbata sabbaton* for ceremonial sabbaths, never the single word *sabbaton* alone. However, he cites evidence that *sabbaton* is used not only for the seventh day Sabbath but the entire seven day week as a whole. Thus the three terms form a logical and progressive sequence of religious days:

Feast day	**New Moon**	**Sabbath(s)**
Yearly	Monthly	Weekly

Sacrificial Sabbaths

This formula, in either the same or reverse order, is used in various Scriptures dealing with *offerings* and *sacrifices*:

- **1 Chron. 23:31** "burnt offerings unto the Lord in the sabbaths, in the new moons, and on the set feasts"
- **2 Chron. 2:4** offerings "on the sabbaths, and on the new moons, and on the solemn feasts of the Lord." See also 2 Chron. 8:12,13.
- **2 Chron. 31:3** "burnt offerings for the sabbaths, and for the new moons, and for the set feasts"
- **Neh. 10:33** "the continual burnt offering, of the sabbaths, of the new moons, and for the set feasts"
- **Eze. 45:17** "offerings in the feasts, and in the new moons, and in the sabbaths"

This association confirms the link between the ceremonial rest days and the sacrificial system by consistently using the weekly, monthly, yearly designation. Special attention to this fact is made in 2 Chronicles:

> "Then Solomon offered burnt offerings unto the LORD on the altar of the LORD, which he had built before the porch, Even after a certain rate every day, offering according to the commandment of Moses, on the **sabbaths, and on the new moons, and on the solemn feasts**, three times in the year, even **in the feast of unleavened bread, and in the feast of weeks, and in the feast of tabernacles.**" 2 Chronicles 8:12, 13.

Again, the weekly-monthly-yearly sequence is cited and then explained. These days applied to the three annual ceremonial festivals when all males had to appear before the Lord in Jerusalem.

These ceremonial sabbaths associated with the Old Testament feasts were undeniably symbolic "shadows of things to come" (verse 17). A list of the annual feasts and their associated rest days or "festival sabbaths" is shown here:

The Feasts of the Lord - Leviticus 23

Shadow	FIRST MONTH			Fulfillment
Passover lamb selected	10th		Monday	Cleansing Temple
	11th		Tuesday	
	12th		Wednesday	
	13th		Thursday	Lord's Supper
Passover	14th		**Friday**	Lord's Passover slain
Unleavened Bread	15th	1	**Saturday**	a **sabbath** + Sabbath
Wave Sheaf	16th	2	**Sunday**	Resurrection
"on the morrow	17th	3	Monday	
after the sabbath"	18th	4	Tuesday	"Festival of Freedom"
Lev. 23:11	19th	5	Wednesday	
	20th	6	Thursday	
	21st	7	Friday	a **sabbath**

(1st & 7th days of Unleavened Bread are festival sabbaths, Lev. 23:7,8)

Pentecost	6th	50	Sunday	a **sabbath**
Wave Loaves	(50th day after Wave Sheaf is a festival sabbath)			

SEVENTH MONTH
(First month of second 6-month semester)

Feast of Trumpets	1st		Tuesday	a **sabbath**
Day of Atonement	10th		Thursday	a **sabbath**
Feast of Tabernacles	15th	1	Tuesday	a **sabbath**
	16th	2	Wednesday	
	17th	3	Thursday	
	18th	4	Friday	
	19th	5	Saturday	
	20th	6	Sunday	
	21st	7	Monday	
	22nd	8	Tuesday	a **sabbath**

(1st and 8th days of Tabernacles are festival sabbaths Lev. 23:39)

"These are the feasts of the Lord which you shall proclaim to be holy convocations..." Leviticus 23:37   "...***beside*** the Sabbaths of the Lord." verse 38. This distinction is evidenced by the fact that these ceremonial sabbaths fell on various days of the week whereas the Sabbaths of the Lord were exclusively observed on the seventh day. Notice there are seven ceremonial annual sabbaths:

1. first day of unleavened bread (Lev. 23:7).
2. last day of unleavened bread (Lev. 23:8).
3. feast of weeks, 50 days after unleavened bread (Lev. 23:21).
4. feast of trumpets (Lev. 23:24, 25).
5. day of atonement (Lev. 23:27-32).
6. first day of tabernacles (Lev. 23:35).
7. last day of tabernacles (Lev. 23:36).

The days of the week used in the first month example above were those that occurred in the year that Jesus died, but would change from year to year. The days used in the seventh month are merely typical and would also change from year to year and could begin on any day of the week.

Redundancy

Others maintain that this trio of terms always indicate weekly, monthly and yearly events. These three terms are considered to be a progressive and sequential designation of all Old Testament sacred times found within the Jewish religious calendar: *annual* feasts, *monthly* new moons, and the *weekly* sabbath. Advocates of this position argue that the term 'Feast day' already includes yearly ceremonial Sabbaths. Making 'Sabbath' refer to annual festivals is "a needless repetition" (Church of God Seventh Day, *Bible Advocate*, May 1982, p.13). But as can be demonstrated in the chart above, there were three annual festival periods (First Month, Pentecost, Seventh Month. See Ex. 23:14) and seven annual holy convocation sabbaths. The two are separate and distinct.

The three annual festival periods are named by the Hebrew word *chag* which means a pilgrimage festival and appears in Leviticus 23:6, 34, 39, 41; Numbers 28:27; 29:12. The seven annual holy convocations are described using the Hebrew word *mo'ed*, an appointed meeting, in Leviticus 23:2, 4, 37, etc.

Hosea and Isaiah

Those who believe the seventh-day Sabbath was a temporary obligation placed on the Jewish people conclude that Paul in Colossians 2 is recognizing the fulfillment of Hosea's prophecy:

> "I will cause all her mirth to cease, *her* feast days, *her* new moons, and *her* sabbaths, and all *her* solemn feasts" Hosea 2:11.

And Isaiah's:

> "Bring no more vain oblations; incense is an abomination unto me; the new moons and sabbaths, the calling of assemblies, I cannot away with; it is iniquity, even the solemn meeting. *Your* new moons and *your* appointed feasts my soul hateth." Isaiah 1:13, 14

However, the context of each of these passages needs to be carefully considered. Isaiah begins with an appeal to "Hear the word of the Lord, you rulers of Sodom: give ear unto the law of our God, you people of Gomorrah." Verse 10. Why does Isaiah address "the daughter of Zion," the people of the southern kingdom of Judah in such derogatory terms as the infamous cities of the plain? Because they were behaving like them. Consider verse 4: "Ah sinful nation, a people laden with iniquity, a seed of evildoers, children that are corrupters: they have forsaken the Lord."

The same applies to the context of Hosea, prophet to the northern kingdom of Israel. These ten break-away tribes had remained rebellious in their counterfeit version of Jehovah worship. They made their own festivals, their own holy days, their own New Moons, their own sabbaths. Notice these are called "her" holy days. And Isaiah says they are "your" feasts. Neither prophet is speaking to conditions in the new covenant, nor predicting the demise of God's Sabbath day.

Matthew 15:3-9, not Colossians 2, is the fulfillment of Isaiah 1:13:

> "Well did Isaiah prophesy of you, saying, This people draws near to me with their mouth, and honor me with their lips; but their heart is far from me. In **vain** they worship me, teaching for doctrines the **commandments of men**."

Isaiah also prophesied of wayward northern Israel, of their destruction and exile, that God would re-gather them, that the Messiah would be born to their nation, (chapter 53) and die for their sins, and that *He* would make a new covenant with them, even the everlasting covenant of mercy (55:3), and extend it also to "the sons of the stranger that join themselves to the Lord, to serve him, and to love the name of the Lord, to be his servants, every one that keeps the Sabbath from polluting it, and takes hold of my covenant" (56:6).

Babel's Best of Both
An unusual hybrid position is promoted by Frances Nigel Lee which combines acceptance of the weekly seventh-day Sabbath as a Creation ordinance and institution that has permanence and obligation upon all of mankind, while also recognizing a temporary Mosaic seventh-day sabbath that was provided only for the Jewish nation. Both coexisted during the period of time stretching from the Exodus to the Cross.

Thus, according to this view, the Sabbath concept was:

- Promulgated by the 4th Commandment,
- Distinguished from the 4th Commandment, and
- Independent of the 4th Commandment

This allows Lee to dismiss the seventh-day Sabbath of the Jews while relying on the Edenic seventh-day Sabbath of Adam, Noah and Abraham to provide a strangely incredible endorsement for the continued obligation of a "New Testament" first-day sabbath.

Lunar Weeks

While most authors debating on both sides of the weekly Sabbath agree that the seven-day weekly cycle has continued uninterrupted since the original creation week, there is one group that maintains an original lunar week dictated the timing of the seventh-day. Evidence for a primal lunar-based seven-day calendar is produced from the Fifth Tablet of the Semitic Story of Creation 12-18:

> "[The moon] he caused to shine, ruling the night:
> He set him then as a creature of the night,
>   to make known the days.
> Monthly unfailing, he provided him with a tiara.
> At the beginning of the month then, appearing in the land,
> The horns shine forth to make known the seasons.
> On the seventh day the tiara perfecting,
> A sa[bath] shalt thou then encounter mid-[month]ly."
> (*Hastings Encyclopedia*, on Sabbath: Babylonian)

Aristobulus is reported to have identified the seventh-day as a holy day in relation to the beginning of the month:

> "Homer and Hesiod let us know, what they learned out of our books, that the seventh day was a holy day. Thus, says Hesiod: There is the first day of the month, and the fourth, and the seventh, that holy day." (quoted by Eusebius in his *Praep. Evang.* 13:12,13)

These writers, who identify the Shawui Calendar of Sons Aumen Israel, distinguish the current fixed seven-day week from what they consider to be the original lunar week, also consisting of seven days, but which was rigidly synchronized to the phases of the moon. This would make the days of the week variable in certain months in order to maintain step with the moon. It is this set of holy days and sabbaths, based on the lunar phases, that Paul, in their opinion, is discrediting in Colossians 2. They read this passage as follows:

> "Let no man judge you for eating and drinking or in part of an holyday, or of the new Moon, or of the sabbaton (of the lunar week cycle)."

Because Paul did not accept the lunar-based Sabbaths, but rather followed a fixed 7-day weekly Sabbath, the Nazarenes regarded his writings as "bad advice and heretical doctrine." This group traces the fixed consecutive day week to the power and influence of Rome, whose practices and customs were resisted by the Essene-Nazarene culture centered in Jerusalem until about 135 AD.

Rome's Fixation

It is of historical interest that Rome has continued to vigorously oppose any attempts to disrupt the fixed seven-day weekly cycle. This was first demonstrated during the 16th century calendar reform. Sometimes it is thought that the change from the Julian to the Greorian calendar in the Middle Ages must have altered the weekdays as we know them. But it didn't.

The calendar reform of 1582 was established by Pope Gregory XIII because the Julian method for calculating leap years had moved the date of the vernal equinox from March 21 in 325 AD to March 11 by 1582. This was important to the Catholic church because Easter was observed by Catholics on the first Sunday after the first full moon occurring after the vernal equinox. So Easter was gradually creeping farther and farther (earlier and earlier) away from the time of year set by the Council of Nicea in 325 AD.

Finally, 90 years after Columbus sailed for the Americas, the time came to correct the problem. Pope Gregory XIII decreed that Thursday October 4, 1582 would be followed not by the 5th but by Friday October 15, 1582. He jumped the calendar 10 days numerically (at the same time changed the year's start from April 1 to January 1), but did not change the weekly cycle. Those who continued to celebrate New Year's Day on April 1st were called "Fools of April." But so this correction would be maintained, the pope then decreed that leap years would occur whenever the year was divisible by four, and centennial years would be leap years that were divisible by 400. During a leap year, one day is added to the month of February, as a correction.

SUN	MON	TUE	WED	THU	FRI	SAT
	1	2	3	4	15	16
17	18	19	20	21	22	23
24	25	26	27	28	29	30
31						

Italy, Spain and Portugal accepted the new calendar at once. Part of Germany took the plunge a year later but the rest of the Germans held out until 1700 when the Dutch and Scandinavians accepted it. England and the American colonies switched to the Gregorian calendar in 1752. Turkey in 1917, Russia in 1918, Serbia in 1919 and finally Greece, the last modern nation to adopt the new calendar, did so in 1923. But during these 300 plus years, the days of the week were never altered, only calendar dates.

The French were a notable exception, when for a period of 14 years (1792-1806) a ten day week was adopted. The French Revolutionary or Republican Calendar was introduced 24 November 1793 and discarded 1 January 1806. It consisted of 12 months of 30 days followed by 5 or 6 extra days. Each month had three 10-day weeks. The 10th day was a day of rest. But the unpopular calendar was short-lived because of the excessively long work week.

During the 1890's when the thirteen month Calendar Reform movement was popular, the Vatican intensely defended the current calendar for liturgical reasons. The thirteen month calendar attracted the attention of many industrialized nations because it produced a predictable and consistent 28 day month with every week beginning with Sunday and every week ending with Saturday. But thirteen 28-day months produced only 364 days, and to keep the weeks in rigid day order, a "null day" had to be added to keep the year in synch with the 365 day solar year. The null day would be called "world day," and would therefore throw the sequence of the week days off each succeeding year.

Rome objected again when the Thirteen Month calendar of Auguste Comte was revived in the early 1900's. Though the League of the International Fixed Calendar, the International Chamber of Commerce in London and the League of Nations promoted the new calendar and even set the date of its inauguration as 1 January 1933, Pope Pius XI warned that the break in the successive seven-day week would create "chaos and calamity." Leading newspapers (*London Times*, October 13, 1931 and *New York Times,* December 16, 1934) took up the cause of Rome and the preservation of the sacred unbroken seven-day week.

Pope Pius XII repeated the declaration of Rome's opposition to any calendar that included "universal days." Vatican II Ecumenical Council affirmed this same position in 1962. As of the beginning of the 21st century, the Gregorian calendar continues to prevail world-wide.

Things to Come

There is yet another way to view the shadow. Instead of referring to the listed religious practices, some have identified the judgement and criticism under which the believers at Colossae suffered. This judging was only the beginning. With prophetic vision, Paul could see more to come. This would make the verse read as follows:

> "Let no one judge you (which is a shadow of things to come) but the body of Christ on how you eat, drink, observe various days"

Critical opposition to matters of faith and practice, judgment of religious days and worship service, in Paul's day were but a taste of what was yet to come, a foreshadow of the future when the Church would dictate the conscience of believers, telling them when to worship, when to fast, how to pray, whom to pray to, what kind of penance to perform, how many steps to climb, what pilgrimages to make, what you could read and what you couldn't and countless other superstitious and unbiblical requirements on the threat of excommunication and loss of salvation.

Paul's message to the assaulted believes in Colossae was one of encouragement and assurance. Let no one judge your eternal destiny; let no religious organization enforce a man-made holy day upon you; let no ecclesiastical body accuse you for following the instruction, example and command of God.

His readers may have been accosted for their manner of worship, but it was only the beginning. As Paul later wrote to the Thessalonian believers, the mystery of iniquity was only in its infancy. The day would yet come when the Beast would call the entire world to worship its counterfeit image on pain of death. Their present trouble was only a shadow of things to come.

A Shadow

If the explanatory phrase in Colossians 2:17, "which are a shadow of things to come" has, as the antecedent of "which," the eating, drinking and observation of holy days, then a significant difference results in whether these practices are described by Paul as being currently applicable and active (30 years after the cross) or as being past practices that were now no longer in vogue.

Notice there is some difference among the translations in how the verb tenses are rendered. While the majority favor a present-future tense transition between shadow and things, a few cast them in a past-present tense:

PRESENT
are – KJV, Amplified Bible, Barlay, Contemporary English, Complete Jewish Bible, Douay-Rheims, Interlinear Bible, Inspired Version, New Evangelical Translation, Restoration of Original Sacred Name Bible, Sacred Scriptures Bethel Edition
being – Cassirer New Testament
represent – Authentic New Testament

The Greek word translated "are" in the KJV is *esti* (Strong's Concordance Dictionary #2076), is the third person singular present indicative of Strong's #1510: *eimi* "to be, to exist, to happen, to be present." Other Greek scholars also agree that *esti* in Colossians 2:17 is in the Present Indicative Active tense "The present indicative asserts something which is occurring while the speaker is making the statement." Spiros Zodhiates, *The Complete Word Study New Testament*, Col.2:17, p.663, and grammatical notations at p.869, PRESENT INDICATIVE, point 82.

That these feasts and holy days are regarded as still important shadows of good things yet to come at the time that Paul was writing is so confusing to some translators that they appear obligated to help Paul explain himself by switching the verb tense to the past time frame:

PAST
have been – Beck
was all – Smith-Goodspeed
were – Holy Bible in Modern English, Living Bible, Noli, Williams

A few versions even add modifying words to emphasize insignificance:

only – Amplified Bible, Authentic, Contemporary English, Living Bible, Noli New Testament, Smith-Goodspeed
no more than - Barclay New Testament, Cassirer New Testament
but – Williams New Testament

a shadow – KJV, Beck, Authentic NT, Contemporary English, Complete Jewish Bible, Douay-Rheims, Interlinear Bible, Inspired Version, New Evangelical Translation, Restoration of Original Sacred Name, Sacred Scriptures Bethel Edition
the shadow – Amplified Bible, Barclay NT, Smith-Goodspeed, Williams
shadows – Living Bible
a pale foreshadowing – Cassirer NT
a forecast of the future – Holy Bible in Modern English
symbols – Noli NT
of
things to come – KJV, Authentic NT, Barclay NT, Douay-Rheims, Inspired Version, New Evangelical Translation, Restoration of Original Sacred Name, Sacred Scriptures Bethel Edition
things that are to come – Amplified Bible
things that are coming – Complete Jewish Bible
coming things – Beck, Interlinear Bible,
what was to come – Contemporary English, Cassirer NT
what was coming – Williams NT
the real thing – Living Bible
future realities – Noli NT
something that was to follow – Smith-Goodspeed

And a couple throw in additional interpretive comments:
have symbolic value – Amplified Bible
temporary rules that ended when Christ came – Living Bible

William Richardson believes that Paul is using "shadow" to contrast the empty, Christ-less sabbath services that had dominated the church in Colossae with the real, full-bodied, Christ-centered Sabbath that Paul was so well known to practice week after week. *Ministry Magazine*, May 1997, William Richardson.

How were these days a shadow or symbol and what did they symbolize? Let's compare each symbolic feast with both its past commemorative event and future reality:

Symbol	Type and Antitype
Passover	Redemption of firstborn at the Egyptian Exodus
	Redemption by our **Firstborn** at Calvary
Unleavened Bread	Meal at midnight during the Egyptian Exodus
	Sinless **Bread of Life** rests in tomb
Wave Sheaf	Presentation of first fruits in spring harvest
	Presentation of the **First Fruit** at His resurrection
Pentecost	God comes down with fire and power at Sinai
	Holy Spirit comes down in Acts 2 as the Early Rain
Trumpets	Preparation for Yom Kippur judgment day
	Reformation prepares Church for judgment
Atonement	Sanctuary cleansed, scapegoat banished
	Heavenly Temple cleansed, **Satan** banished
Tabernacles	Final harvest celebration in ancient Israel
	Final harvest celebration in **heaven:** Later Rain

The annual festivals are both commemorative and prophetic. But although they are reminders of divine events in the past, if Paul is here identifying these symbols as shadows, then he is certainly emphasizng their prophetic aspect in doing so by calling them "shadows," symbols or types of future events in the plan of God.

Atonement in Hebrews

These prophetic feasts show up throughout the New Testament. The book of Hebrews particularly focuses on the Day of Atonement and how it now applied to the Christian believer, how the purification of the earthly sanctuary explained Christ's new role as High Priest in purifying the heavenly sanctuary as well as the living temples of His earthly children. Thus the Old Testament festivals took on an enhanced significance and offered a more meaningful experience to the young Christian church.

Considerable evidence points to the fact that the apostolic church adopted a Christian version of the Old Testament religious calendar.

"The rich liturgical material of the Corinthian epistles, which is closely connected with a gospel tradition, makes it perfectly evident that a Christianized form of the Hebrew Calendar was then in existence, so that it would have been possible and even quite natural for Mark to have arranged his gospel for the liturgical year with a view to having it read in the churches. This Christianized Calendar was of course merely a simplified form of the Hebrew Calendar as used by Jewish Christians in Palestine where the whole Christian tradition had received its primitive form." Philip Carrington, *the Primitive Christian Calendar* (Cambridge University Press, 1952), p. 43

More Feasts
John's gospel contains an account of all three Passovers during Christ's ministry. John also contains additional references to the Feast of Tabernacles in chapters 7 and 8 where Christ applies the principal symbols of this feast (water and light) to Himself. Jesus stood up on the last day of the feast and made the invitation, "If any man thirst let him come unto me."

A beautiful parallel exists in the book of Esther where Ahasurerus celebrates with 127 of his provincial governors for 180 days. At the end of this 6 month period of time, he holds "a feast" for *seven* days. On the *seventh* or last day of the feast the king, in front of his *seven* chamberlains and *seven* princes, calls for the Queen to appear before him wearing her royal crown because he desires to display her beauty before the people. But Queen Vashti refuses. Then the king pronounces her doom: "let her estate be taken away and given to another more worthy."

The beautiful Queen symbolizes the church, God's people, who in Christ's day also refused to respond to the King's invitation to come to His Son's wedding feast. Jesus said their kingdom would be taken away and given to another—the same order pronounced by Ahasurerus. It is most interesting that it is exactly 180 days from the Exodus (15 Nisan) in the first month to the feast of tabernacles or Ingathering on the 15th day of the seventh-month.

Feasts in Revelation
The strongest evidence for the continued observance and acceptance of the annual feasts by the New Testament Church, however, is found in John's Revelation. Some have pointed to evidence for the Spring Feasts (especially Passover) in the earlier chapters where the Lamb which was slain stands before the Father's throne in chapter 4. However, it is the Autumn Feasts that receive the most convincing representation.

"The overall structure of the book of Revelation may be seen to follow the sweep of salvation history as set forth in the OT festival typology. The general outline of Revelation appears to progress sequentially through the OT festivals."

"Striking is the evidence that the book of Revelation appears to be patterned also after the annual feasts of the Jewish year." Jon Paulien, "Seals and Trumpets: Some Current Discussions," Richard M. Davidson, "Sanctuary Typology," *Symposium on Revelation*, Frank B. Holbrook, ed., (Silver Springs, Maryland, 1992, Biblical Research Institute, General Conference of Seventh-day Adventists), vol. 1, pp. 121, 191.

The **Feast of Trumpets** is well represented by the first six trumpets of chapters 8 and 9 where God's redemptive judgment are initiated. The **Day of Atonement** is then introduced by the seventh trumpet and the opening of the most holy place and the exposure of the ark of the testament in Revelation 11:19 but climaxes in chapter 19 at the second coming when God executes His punitive judgment on sinners and His vindictive judgment for the saved.

Finally, the **Feast of Tabernacles** is featured in the last two chapters where God "tabernacles" with His people (Rev. 21:3) and the principal symbols of water and light appear in the "water of life" and in God and the Lamb who are the "light" of the city. This theme, mingled with Passover imagery, is also evident in Revelation chapter 7:9-17 where a great multitude who "came out of great tribulation" (an exodus from spiritual Egypt), praise God and the Lamb while carrying palm branches, protected by God (as was ancient Israel by the pillar of cloud) so that they thirst no more and suffer no heat.

"There can be no hesitation about the predominant paschal character of the vision, and yet St. John cannot restrain himself from looking beyond Passover to the feast of Tabernacles." Austin Farrer, *A Rebirth of Images. The Making of St. John's Apocalypse* (Glouchester, Massachussetts, 1970), pp. 114-115.

It was this recognition that led the early church to transform the Hebrew calendar into one that had even more meaning for the followers of Christ. The feasts, thus, continued to be celebrated only now with greater significance, meaning and importance to the Christian believers.

Body of Christ
Next, we must consider either
- the shadowy symbols are contrasted with the body, or
- the body contrasts with those who were criticizing them

This last position is indicated by those versions honest enough to show they added the verb "is" or leave it out altogether:

but – KJV, AB, CEV, CJB, Douay-Rheims, HBME, Interlinear, Inspired, NET, Bethel
and of which – Authentic NT
whereas – ROSN
the
body [is] – KJV, Douay-Rheims, Interlinear,
body – Bethel
body is – CJB, Inspired, ROSN
body itself is – NET
reality – AB, Barclay NT, Williams
the proper reality is – Cassirer NT
substance – Amplified Bible, HBME
solid fact, the body of it – Amplified Bible
sum total of these realities is – Smith-Goodspeed
one foreshadowed is – Norlie's
of Christ – KJV, Douay-Reims, Interlinear
belongs to Christ – Amplified Bible, Barclay NT, HBME, Williams
found in Christ – Smith-Goodspeed
Christ – Norlie's
Christ is the substance – Authentic NT
Christ is real – CEV
Christ himself – Living Bible
the Messiah – CJB
of the Messiah – ROSN, Bethel
to be found nowhere but in Christ – Cassirer NT

With the verb added, the meaning becomes:
> "Religious practices are only shadows, but the reality is Christ"

Without the verb (which is how the Greek literally reads):
> "Let no one judge you on your religious practices
> but the body of Christ"

This recognizes that the interjected comment regarding the subject of criticism is parenthetical. Thus the entire passage in Paul's original sequence would be diagramed as follows:

> "Let no one judge you on how you eat, drink, observe various days (which are symbols of the future) but the body of Christ"

The grammatically equivalent reading could also be shown as:

> "Let no one but the body of Christ judge you on your religious practices (which are symbols of the future)"

Placing the verb *is* between "body" and "Christ" has no precedent in New Testament Greek texts. Paul uses the same phrase elsewhere in this epistle to the Colossians (1:18; 1:24; 2:17,19; 3:15) where it is translated "body of Christ," the Church.

The phrase, "body of Christ" is *soma tou Christou,* which appears also in 1 Cor. 12:27, "Now you are the body of Christ." The Church, the body of believers, is the community that should concern us—not those "living in the world" (Col. 2:20) "vainly puffed up" with a "fleshly mind" (verse 18) promoting "philosophy and vain deceit after the tradition of men" and "the rudiments of the world" (verse 8).

Paul does not say the festivals or new moons or sabbaths are shadows of Christ. They are shadows of things yet to come. He does not say Christ is the "substance" of the sabbaths, new moons, but rather "the body of Christ." The word is "body." *Soma* means "the body, a sound whole, servants."

Shadow Gone Body Here
A popular reading of this verse is that the shadow is replaced by the body or the real thing, the substance:

> "Paul explicitly refers to the Sabbath as a shadow of Christ, which is no longer binding since the substance (Christ) has come." *Is the Sabbath Binding on Christians Today?* by John MacArthur (cf. 1 Chronicles 23:31; 2 Chronicles 2:4, 31:3; Ezekiel 45:17; Hosea 2:11)

The problem is that *soma* is never translated "substance" elsewhere. All other eight occurrences of *soma* in Colossians are translated as

* The human body (Col. 2:11,23, cf. Rom. 7:24),
* The human body of Jesus (Col. 1:22; 2:9, an adverbial form) and
* The corporate *body of Christ*, the Church (1:18,24; 2:19; 3:15).

Throughout the entire New Testament *soma* is translated only as

* A literal physical body (usually human) or
* The corporeal *body of Christ*, i.e. the Church.

The Greek word *soma* (*Strong's* #4983) is translated "body" 144 times in the KJV, as well as "bodily" once in 2 Cor. 10:10, and once as "slave" in Rev.18:13. The NIV uses "reality" for *soma* only once: this verse in Colossians 2:17; all other occurrences in the NIV it is rendered "body/bodies." Only two verses later the NIV translates *soma* as "body." Again, there appears to be a prevalent and strong desire to make this passage an exception to the consistent position of the New Testament writers.

The context highly suggests that the body of Christ refers to the body of believers. They will follow Christ's rule and authority for He is the head of all rule and authority (Col. 2:10). They will not be subject to the elementary spirits (Col. 2:8), which bring in things that "seem to promote rigor of devotion" (Col. 2:23), "but are not according to Christ" (Col. 2:8). Instead the true "body" of Christ will be subject to Christ. The whole issue will be over whether we worship Christ and make him our head, or follow a counterfeit spirit. This is the final issue in Revelation 13 and 14: who and when and why we worship.

Commandments of Men
Remember, the Colossians had been significantly influenced by pagan philosophies which promoted a religion of severity, devoid of joy. To this Paul gave warning:

> "Beware lest anyone cheat you through philosophy and empty deceit, according to **the tradition of men**, according to the basic **principles of the world**, and not according to Christ." Colossians 2:8

> "Therefore, if you died with Christ from the basic principles of the world, why, as though living in the world, do you subject yourselves to regulations—'Do not touch, do not taste, do not handle,' which all concern things which perish with the using—according to the commandments and doctrines of men? These things indeed have an appearance of wisdom in self-imposed religion, false humility, and neglect of the body." Colossians 2:20-23

In other words, Paul might be saying "You need not be bothered by the attitude of the Colossian society toward your practices and way of life in the church. Do not worry about what the people in the community think about you because you enjoy dining together in Christian fellowship and in celebrating various religious festivals."

Using the fifth commandment as an example Jesus also commented about human tradition in Matthew 15:3,6,9:

> "In vain they worship me, teaching for doctrines the command-ments of men...Why do you transgress the commandment of God by

your tradition...making of none effect the commandment of God by
your tradition?"

The conflict here is between the commandments of men and those of
God. When a man-made liturgy is coerced upon the laity, when
dogma are pronounced by ecclesiastical or secular authority, when
prescribed religious practice is mandated by The Church or the world
in an effort to dominate and control—"Let no man judge you."

Thus the shadows are referring to a perversion of the days and not
the days themselves.

> "The Pauline community at Colossae, not the opponents, practiced
> the temporal schemes outlined by Col. 2:16... This investigation into
> the function of the list in Col. 2:16 indicates that the Colossian
> Christians, not their critics, participate in a religious calendar that
> includes festivals, new moons, and Sabbaths." Troy Martin, "Pagan
> and Judeo-Christian Time-keeping Schemes in Galatians 4:10 and
> Colossians 2:16," *New Testament Studies* 42, 1996, p. 111.

> "Colossians 2:17 suggests that the practices mentioned in 2:16 are
> those of the Colossian Christians and not the opponents...Although
> the observance of *neomenia* [new moon] is less certain, early
> Christians observe both feasts and sabbaths." Troy Martin, "But Let
> Everyone Discern the Body of Christ (Colossians 2:17)," *Journal of
> Biblical Literature* 114/2 (1995), p. 255.

Verse 18-23 is even clearer on this. Paul is encouraging his listeners to
resist the efforts of would-be authoritarians to pressure them into
perverted forms of worship:

> "Let no man beguile you of your reward in a voluntary humility
> [penance] and worshiping of angels, intruding into those things
> which he has not seen [praying to saints]." "If you are dead with
> Christ to the rudiments of the world, why as though living in the
> world, are you subject to ordinances (Touch not; taste not; handle
> not; which all are to perish with the using:) after the
> commandments and doctrines of men? Which things have indeed a
> show of wisdom in will-worship, and humility, and neglecting of the
> body [fasting on Lent]..." Colossians 2:18-23

Paul is not advocating the dismissal of God's Sabbath, but is making
a clear and precise warning against attempts to replace the
commandments of God with "the commandments and doctrines of
men." In this, Paul is in complete agreement with Peter: "we must
obey God rather than men" Acts 5:29.

Hebrew Shadows

In addition, the same contrast of "shadow" and "body" is used in the book of Hebrews:

> "For **the law** having *a **shadow** of good things to come* and not the very image of the things, can never with those **sacrifices** which they offered year by year continually make the comers thereunto perfect" Hebrews 10:1.

This time it's "those sacrifices" of the law that are a shadow. What law? The one that deals with "those sacrifices"—the ceremonial sacrificial laws. That's why the contrasting "body of Jesus Christ" is described in the language of sacrifice in verse 10:

> "We are sanctified through the offering of the body of Jesus Christ once for all." Hebrews 10:10.

Similarly in Hebrews 8:5 Christ's priesthood is compared with the earthly Mosaic priests "who serve unto the **example and shadow** of heavenly things." Once Christ has come, the earthly priests are no longer needed: Christ is now our "high priest of **good things to come**" Hebrews 9:11 "Who is set on the right hand of the throne of the Majesty in the heavens." Hebrews 8:1.   Once Christ died, sacrifices were no longer needed.

Ironically, the same Church that claims the right to change the law of God and His holy day of rest also claims the right to forgive sins, to establish an earthly priesthood that continues to sacrifice our Saviour (after first creating Him!) as a bloodless victim in the daily mass.

> "The priest has the power of the keys, or the power of delivering sinners from hell, of making them worthy of paradise and of changing them from the slaves of Satan into the children of God. And God himself is obliged to abide by the judgment of his priests, and either not to pardon or to pardon, according as they refuse or give absolution,...The sentence of the priest precedes, and God subscribes to it, write St. Peter Damian. St John Chrysosom concludes" The Sovereign Master of the universe only follows the servant by confirming in heaven all that the latter decides upon earth." *Dignity and Duties of the Priest* by St. Alphonsus De Liguari p. 27-28, Imprimatur+ Patritius Cardinalis Hayes, Archipiscopus Neo-Eboracensis, 24 March 1927.

Not only do they, being a man, make themselves God, they make themselves *above* God. John 10:33.

Conclusion

All things were created by Him and for Him (Colossians 1:17).
It took a Creator to create us; the same Creator can "recreate" us.
The Sabbath reminds us that we have not created ourselves,
we cannot redeem ourselves, therefore we must fully trust in Him.

He is the head of the body, the church (Col. 1:18).
Christ is the head of the body, we are the joints and bands
  receiving nourishment from Him, knit together (Col. 2:19).

Don't be deceived with enticing words (Col. 2:4).
Beware of human philosophy and tradition or worldly principles
  stoicheia "elements," spirits and stellar deities
  that are deceitfully promoted (Col. 2:8).
You are complete in Him
  in whom all the powers of Deity dwell (2:10).
You are circumcised in Christ, putting off the sins of the flesh (2:11).
You are buried with him in baptism,
  being dead in your sins (2:12,13).
You are risen with Him from the dead
  having forgiven you all trespasses (Col. 2:12,13).
Erasing the bond of debt and ordinances of sacrifice,
  standing against all sinners and contrary to both Jew and Gentile,
taking it out of the way
  so that "sacrifice and oblation cease" Dan. 9:27,
nailing it to His cross (2:14) along with our sins in His body 1 Pet.
2:24.

Jesus died for our sins, and we have been forgiven. Ceremonial, ritualistic observances that foreshadowed His sacrificial and mediatorial ministries have served their purpose and no Christian should allow anyone else to make them feel guilty for not keeping these sacrificially related observances.

Let no one disqualify you insisting on self-abasement (acts of penance) and worship of spirit beings, (praying to saints and venerating Mary) (Col. 2:18) which have an appearance of wisdom in promoting rigor of devotion and self-abasement (Col. 2:23) but which all are to perish according to human precepts and doctrines (Col. 2:22) .

We need not subject ourselves to the regulations of the elemental spirits of the universe (Col. 2:20). We seek the things which are from above. (Col. 3:1).

"There is no reason, therefore, for Christians to feel incomplete and to seek the help of inferior mediators since Christ has provided complete redemption and forgiveness." Bacchiocchi, *Crossfire*, Chapter 6, Part 1.

On the other hand, God's Holy Days remind us of past, present and future truths concerning the role and station of Jesus Christ. They will continue to be intensely meaningful and relevant days as long as the facts of creation, the Exodus, the cross, the resurrection, the second coming, the millennium and eternity remain in our memories. Those who would advocate their abandonment as obsolete ceremonial laws, and who teach that the privilege to observe them is no longer required of Christians are indeed to be pitied and will be called least in the kingdom of heaven (Mat. 5:19).

"There is no intimation here that the Sabbath was done away, or that its moral use was superseded by the introduction of Christianity. I have shown elsewhere that, Remember the Sabbath day, to keep it holy, is a command of perpetual obligation, and can never be superseded but by the final termination of time. As it is a type of that rest which remains for the people of God, of an eternity of bliss, it must continue in full force till that eternity arrives; for no type ever ceases till the antitype be come. Besides, it is not clear that the apostle refers at all to the Sabbath in this place, whether Jewish or Christian; his sabbaton, of Sabbaths or weeks, most probably refers to their feasts of weeks, of which much has been said in the notes on the Pentateuch." *Adam Clarke's Commentary of the Bible*, 185 1 Edition, on Colossians 2:16.

" 'Or of the Sabbath days.' The word 'Sabbath' in the Old Testament is applied not only to the seventh day, but to all the days of holy rest that were observed by the Hebrews, and particularly to the beginning and close of their great festivals. There is, doubtless, reference to those days in this place, as the word is used in the plural number, and the apostle does not refer particularly to the Sabbath properly so called. There is no evidence from this passage that he would teach that there was no obligation to observe any holy time, for there is not the slightest reason to believe that he meant to teach that one of the ten commandments had ceased to he binding on mankind. If he had used the word in the singular number, 'the Sabbath,' it would then, of course, have been clear that he meant to teach that that commandment had ceased to be binding, and that a Sabbath was no longer to be observed. But the use of the term in the plural number, and the connection, show that he had his eye on the great number of days which were observed by the Hebrews as festivals, as a part of their ceremonial and typical law, and not to the moral law, or the ten commandments. No part of the moral law—no one of the ten commandments—could be spoken of as 'a shadow of good things to come.' These commandments are, from

the nature of moral law, of perpetual and universal obligation."
Albert Barnes Commentary, Edition of 1850, pp. 306, 307.

The word "ordinances" in Colossians 2:14 is Strong's Concordance No. 1378, *dogma*. It is a civil, ceremonial or ecclesiastical law, also translated "decree." In each of the five places where this Greek word *dogma* is used, it refers to human rules and regulations:

> Luke 2:1: "And it came to pass in those days, that there went out a decree [*dogma*] from Caesar Augustus, that all the world should be taxed."

> Acts 16:4: "And as they went through the cities, they delivered them the decrees [*dogma*] for to keep, that were ordained of the apostles and elders which were at Jerusalem."

> Acts 17:7: "Whom Jason has received: and these all do contrary to the decrees [*dogma*] of Caesar, saying that there is another king."

> Ephesians 2:15: "Having abolished in his flesh the enmity, [even] the law of commandments [contained] in ordinances [*dogma*]; for to make in himself of twain one new man, [so] making peace."

Finally, we must compare this single exceptional text which alone identifies the Sabbath in a possible negative context with the nearly 150 other Scriptural references to the seventh-day Sabbath which clearly support its continued observance post-Calvary. As Ford concluded, we have the option of judging the 150 texts by this one or this one by the 150. "The verse no more wipes out all Sabbath-keeping than it wipes out all eating and drinking." Desmond Ford, "Is the Seventh-day Sabbath Christian?" July-Aug edition of *Adventist Today* 1996.

Yoke of Bondage: Galatians 4:9-10

Another example in which Paul expresses his frustration with his Gentile converts is found in Galatians 4. The members there had returned to certain practices which Paul describes as "weak and beggarly elements." He says they were again "in bondage" to them.

> "Stand fast therefore in the liberty wherewith Christ has made us free, and be not entangled again with the yoke of bondage" Gal. 5:1.

But is this bondage to Mosaic ordinances or bondage to paganism? Verse 10 is the key. Here Paul defines these practices as observances of "days and months and seasons and years."

The church in Galatia was composed primarily of Gentiles; the males were physically uncircumcised (Galatians 5:2; 6:12-13). They lived in a society which had a history of worshipping pagan deities. For example, when Paul was in Lystra, a city in the province of Galatia, God healed a crippled man (Acts 14:8-18). Supposing Barnabas and Paul to be gods, they called them Zeus and Hermes (verse 12).

The major thrust of the Galatian epistle is to put them "back on track" because someone had been teaching "a different gospel," a perversion of the gospel of Christ (Galatians 1:6-7). Two possibilities must be considered. The Galatians had returned to

1. The observance of the **Old Testament holy days**.
2. The observance of their former **pagan holidays**.

Holy Days

Those who believe that Paul's admonition is directed against the observance of the Old Testament feasts and holy days note that Paul's emphasis in his letter is on justification by faith. False teachers in Galatia taught that Christians were justified by doing physical works. Paul emphasized that we are justified by faith in the sacrifice of Jesus Christ, "by the works of the law no flesh shall be justified." (Galatians 2:15-16)

One of the "works of the law" that the false teachers insisted on was circumcision (Galatians 5:2-3, 11). Paul says the false teachers themselves did not keep the law (Galatians 6:13). Evidently, the false teachings practiced a licentious lifestyle (Galatians 5:13-21). Evidence indicates that the false teachers were teaching a blend of Judaism and Gnosticism, the philosophy that considered everything physical as evil. Does this sound familiar? It's exactly the same situation Paul was dealing with in the Colossian church.

Holidays

Those who regard the "days, months and years" as time elements referring to the pagan calendar argue that Paul would never refer to God's holy days as "weak and beggarly elements." They note that Paul honored and revered God's law (Romans 7:12, 14, 16). Besides, he taught the Corinthians to observe Passover and the Days of Unleavened Bread (1 Corinthians 5:7-8).

Secondly, an analysis of the Greek word forms indicate that this list in Galatians is typical of secular time reckoning.

> "Paul is worried that he has labored for the Galatians in vain since they have returned to their former pagan life as evidenced by their renewed preconversion reckoning of time. Because of its association with idolatry

and false deities, marking time according to this pagan scheme is tantamount to rejecting Paul's Gospel and the one and only true God it proclaims (Gal. 4:8-9)... A comparison of these lists demonstrates that the Gentile conversion to Paul's gospel involves rejection of idolatrous pagan temporal schemes in favor of the Jewish liturgical calendar." Troy Martin, "But Let Everyone Discern the Body of Christ (Colossians 2:17)," *Journal of Biblical Literature* 114/2 (1995), pp. 117, 119.

Prior to the coming of Christ, "when ye [Galatians] knew not God," (verse 8) both Jews and Gentiles were "in bondage under the elements of the world" (verse 3) and "observed times." The word "elements" is the Greek *stoicheion*.

"But now after you have known God, or rather are known by God, how is it that you turn again to the **weak and beggarly elements**, to which you desire again to be in bondage?" Galatians 4:9.

The "weak and beggarly elements" were demon-inspired, idolatrous practices. "Elements" here is the same word, *stoicheion*, translated "elements" in verse 3. An extension of *stoicheion* can refer to the heavenly bodies that regulate the calendar and are associated with pagan festivals.

"When thou art come into the land which the LORD thy God giveth thee, thou shalt not learn to do after the abominations of those nations. There shall not be found among you any one that maketh his son or his daughter to pass through the fire, or that useth divination, or **an observer of times**, or an enchanter, or a witch, or a charmer, or a consulter with familiar spirits, or a wizard, or a necromancer. For all that do these things are an abomination unto the LORD." Deuteronomy 18:9-13.

Leviticus 19:26 and Deut. 18:10, 14 instructed Israel not to observe "times," the heathen practice of divination often associated with movements of the heavenly bodies. Today, we call this astrology and superstitious regard for certain dates like the solstices and Friday the thirteenth.

The Galatians had begun to return to their former slavish, sinful practices. The time elements in this verse, "days, months, seasons and years," were the pagan, idolatrous festivals and observances that the Galatian Gentiles had observed before their conversion. This included various superstitious holidays connected to the worship of pagan deities.

Chrysostom in the 4th century documented this practice:

"...many were superstitiously addicted to divination... in the celebration of these 'times' (they) set up lamps in market place, and crown their doors with garlands." Bingham's *Antiquities of the Christian Church*, pp. 1123, 1124.

This is similar to the numerous unchristian holidays observed in our time such as Christmas, Easter, Valentine's Day, Halloween and any other days that originated from the worship of pagan gods.

Regarding Days in Romans 14

"Him that is weak in the faith receive ye, but not to doubtful disputations. For one believeth that he may eat all things: another, who is weak, eateth herbs. Let not him that eateth despise him that eateth not; and let not him which eateth not judge him that eateth: for God hath received him. Who art thou that judgest another man's servant? to his own master he standeth or falleth. Yea, he shall be holden up: for God is able to make him stand. One man esteemeth one day above another: another esteemeth every day alike. Let every man be fully persuaded in his own mind. He that regardeth the day, regardeth it unto the Lord; and he that regardeth not the day, to the Lord he doth not regard it. He that eateth, eateth to the Lord, for he giveth God thanks; and he that eateth not, to the Lord he eateth not, and giveth God thanks." Romans 14:1-6 KJV

This passage appears to many as another example of Paul's indifference or even disregard for the Sabbath. The assumption that weak believers cling to Sabbath observance while the strong believers can safely ignore such a crutch is just that: an assumption. Paul is only speaking about whether particular days of the week or throughout the year should be considered more important than other days and whether there are times when we should avoid eating certain foods. He does not identify the day as the Sabbath or that it even involves worship.

Paul is discussing differences of opinion, "doubtful disputes" between those who are strong and weak in faith, not between those in and out of the faith. God accepts both groups and "is able to make him stand." The practices followed by the weak believers are not mentioned in the Mosaic Law. Nowhere in the books of Moses is strict vegetarianism, abstinence from fermented wine (except for those under the Nazarite vow), or specified fast days prescribed. Likewise, the strong believers who "eat anything" and treat "all days alike" are simply showing their freedom from certain restrictive beliefs and superstitious scruples not the Law of Moses. Here Paul calls the food "common" (Greek *koinos*), quite a different word from that used in Leviticus 11 to describe "unclean" food (*akathartos*). He uses the same term in 1 Cor. 8:1-13 in his discussion on food offered to idols.

On the other hand, Paul is not here advocating that Christians may now eat anything that crawls. Just two chapters earlier he appealed to his "brothers and sisters, by the mercies of God, to present your bodies as a living sacrifice, holy and acceptable to God, which is your spiritual worship." Rom 12:1. This is consistent with his admonition to respect the health of their body temples: "Do you not know that you are God's temple and that God's Spirit dwells in you? If anyone destroys God's temple, God will destroy that person. For God's temple is holy, and you are that temple." 1 Cor. 3:16, 17. The issue here was not a matter of health.

Similarly, some argue that Paul is not dealing with moral duty when he comes to the issue of certain days. Some of the believers felt that it was necessary to abstain from certain foods on certain days. Paul summarizes this in 1 Cor. 8:10-13. It is well known that the Essenes, a Jewish subculture, were scrupulous in their observance of fast days and, at times, the avoidance of meat and wine.

The *Didache*, a contemporary document, featured a controversy over fast days. "Your fasts must not be identical with those of the hypocrites. They fast on Mondays and Thursdays; but you should fast on Wednesdays and Fridays." The "hypocrites" refers to the Jews who had rejected Christ as the Messiah but still fasted "twice a week" as Jesus confirmed when telling His parable of the hypocritical Pharisee and the humble Publican (Luke 18:12). The debate over fasting was frequently encountered by Christ during His encounters with the Jewish leaders (Matt. 6:16-18; 9:14, 15; Mark 2:18; Luke 5:33-35).

After devoting 21 verses to the subject of feeding and fasting, Paul spends only two verses on the superstitious observance of certain days and what to eat or not to eat on them.

Finally, Paul only advises the believer "who observes the day" to "observe it in honor of the Lord." He does *not* tell those who refrain from fasting or in eating to do so in honor of the Lord. This is very significant. Paul does not endorse or even encourage those who treat all days the same; he only acknowledges their right to do so if they choose.

Ministration
of Death

In 2 Corinthians chapter 3 Paul presents a study in contrast and comparison of the old and new covenants. He declares that the believers in Corinth are real, live, walking sermons, "epistles of Christ," living examples of the New Covenant in action. God had prophesied through Jeremiah that He would make a New Covenant "with the house of Israel" (Jer 31:31), when He would finally realize the internalization of His character within the lives of His people. He would at last write His law upon their hearts. Here Paul uses this very imagery:

> "You are manifestly declared to be the epistle of Christ ministered by us, written not with ink, but with the Spirit of the living God; not in **tables of stone,** but in fleshy **tables of the heart**." 2 Cor. 3:3.

Law in the Heart
The Decalogue in stone was of no benefit until written on the living heart of man. Deut. 6:6; Ezekiel 11:19-20; 36:26; Hebrews 8:8-10. God doesn't want just "compliance" but "reliance" upon Him and His indwelling presence, His Spirit.

Paul next compares the "letter" of the law, with the "spirit" of the law:

> "[God] also has made us able ministers of the new testament; not of the letter, but of the spirit: for the **letter kills**, but the **spirit gives life**." 2 Cor. 3:6.

This theme is addressed elsewhere by Paul. In Romans 7 he identifies the old letter with the Ten Commandments.

> "We should serve in **newness of spirit**, and not in the **oldness of the letter**. What shall we say then? Is the law sin? God forbid. Nay, I had not known sin, but by the law: for I had not known lust, except the law had said, Thou shalt not covet." Romans 7:6,7

Earlier in Romans, he again compares the inward circumcision of the heart or the spirit of the law, with the outward circumcision of the flesh or the letter of the law.

> "For he is not a Jew, which is one outwardly; neither is that circumcision, which is outward in the flesh: But he is a Jew, which

is one inwardly; and **circumcision is that of the heart, in the spirit, and not in the letter**." Romans 2:25-29.

Letter or the Spirit

It's Attitude

The difference here is one of attitude:

> keeping the law because you *have* to (the letter of the law
versus
> keeping the law because you *want* to (the spirit of the law).

Those who follow merely the letter of the law without being transformed by God's Spirit have only a "form of godliness without the power thereof" 2 Timothy 3:5.

Then Paul gets specific by stressing that the spirit of the law is an **"enhancement"** *to* and not a **"replacement"** *of* the letter of the law.

> God has made us able ministers of the New Testament;
> not of the (external, outward, formal) **letter**,
> but of the (internalized, personal) **spirit**;
> for **the letter** (powerless form of godliness) **kills**,
> but **the spirit gives life**" (to a living religious experience)
> 2 Corinthians 3:6 (parenthetical comments added)

Jesus affirmed this in the New Covenant when He conducted His famous *magnification* of the Law in Matthew 5. There He *builds* on the original letter; He does not discard it. Instead of doing only the least-you-could-do, Christ presented the most-you-should-do.

Now begins the contrast between the two ministrations:

> "But if the **ministration of death**, written and engraven in stones, was glorious, so that the children of Israel could not steadfastly behold the face of Moses for the **glory of his countenance**; which glory was to be done away: How shall not the **ministration of the spirit** be rather glorious? For if the **ministration of condemnation** be glory, much more does the **ministration of righteousness** exceed in glory. For even that which was made glorious had no glory in this respect, by reason of the glory that excels. For if that which is done away was glorious, much more that which remains is glorious." Verses 7-11.

Notice:

> The Ministration of Death, in stones, was glorious.
> The glory on the face of Moses was done away.
> Ministration of the spirit was rather glorious.

Ministration of condemnation is glory.
Ministration of righteousness exceeds in glory.

The ceremonial sacrifices (ministration of death and condemnation) had great significance in representing the wonderful truths concerning the coming Messiah. Abel was a type of Christ—innocent and obedient; Isaac was a type of Christ—the willing, only begotten son of a miracle birth. All Sacrifices were a type of Christ. Sacrificial lambs must be spotless, without blemish, just as the sinless Jesus died for sinners. These examples and symbols of Christ were glorious lessons to the world from God. But without faith in the Lamb to come, the sacrificial system was just a lifeless ministration of death.

Unavoidable Sacrifice of God Himself

Law Done Away?
Some conclude from these verses that the Ten Commandment Law of God was "done away." Certainly, the ministration of death (that sacrificial system requiring an endless slaughter of innocent animals) and the ministration of condemnation (the ceremonial laws that required all these sacrifices) *was* done away! But notice: even that incomplete, temporary system was still glorious. It still spoke of hope in a coming Messiah, the sacrifice of God Himself, a sacrifice that was unavoidable because the Law could *not* be abolished. In agony Christ pleaded, "O my Father, if it be possible, let this cup pass from me" (Matthew 26:39). But it wasn't possible; there was no other way.

> **If the law is abolished, there is no more sin.**
> **No one will be lost; everyone will be saved.**
> **The cross was unnecessary.**
> **John 3:16 is meaningless**.
> **Paul's missionary journeys were not necessary**, and
> **Being religious is just a waste of energy**.

Paul concludes with the account of Moses' veil in 2 Cor. 3:13, 14:

> "...the children of Israel could not steadfastly look to the end of that which is **abolished**: but their minds were blinded: for until this day remaineth the same veil untaken away in the reading of the old testament; which *veil* is done away in Christ."

Their Eyes Were Opened
Reading the Old Testament without seeing Christ in all the symbols, in all the sacrifices and feasts and holy days, is like reading it with a

veil over your face. When Jesus "expounded unto them in all the scriptures the things concerning himself" (Luke 24:27), "their eyes were opened and they knew him" (verse 31).

"Then [we] are changed into the same image from glory to glory" 2 Corinthians 3:18.

The Veil
The Dividing Wall
The Separation

What was abolished?

As the glory on Moses' face faded away, so the Mosaic system of sacrifices would fade once the One to whom they all pointed came and died. But the glory of the stones would never fade away. Christ was *the* Stone. So what was made void? What was taken away? What was abolished? The veil, the dividing wall, the separation. The glory of Christ was hidden behind a veil of symbols, rites, and ceremonies. The written word was finally reaffirmed by the living Word when He came to dwell among us.

"The Word was made flesh and dwelt among us,"
"And we beheld His glory" John 1:14

From the stones to the Stone

The ministration of death is "done away" whenever the ministration of the spirit takes over in the experience of a Christian. Life before the new birth, trying to be good enough to please God, is like "looking through a glass dimly," and catching only a glimpse of God's glorious plan to save us. But as new creatures God's Spirit opens wide an unobstructed view "with open face beholding as in a glass the glory of the Lord," in all His gospel splendor. This is the experience of conversion as we are "changed into the same image," restored once again into the image of God, "from glory [of the stones] to glory [of the Stone], even as by the Spirit of the Lord" 2 Corinthians 3:18; Genesis 1:27.

"Where there is knowledge, it will pass away." 1 Corinthians 13:8
"In times past God spoke by the prophets" Hebrews 1:1
"You have heard it said..." Matthew 5:21.
"In these latter days God spoke by His Son" Hebrews 1:2
"But I say unto you..." Matthew 5:22
"And that Rock was Christ" 1 Corinthians 10:4

Pattern or the Person

The Jews kept looking to the *pattern* instead of the *Person*. They were preoccupied with the rituals instead of the Redeemer. And when the Messiah came, they continued to be absorbed in the symbols instead of the Saviour. And even though the sacrificial shadows came to an end, the coming of Christ "in the fullness of time" was not the *termination* of the Law but its *realization*.

Paul said in Gal. 5:11 "if I still preach circumcision..." suggesting that at one time he *did* preach circumcision as necessary for salvation. But Paul changed his view of salvation after his conversion. Then he identified with the experience of Abraham who became the father of the faithful *before* he was circumcised.

In the same way a Christian is not saved by being baptized, but we seek baptism as a witness to the experience of salvation that has already taken place in our heart. Circumcision continues to function in the New Testament as an inherited symbol of a permanent commitment. But now it is a circumcision "of the heart" through baptism rather than the flesh. The law continues to be respected in the New Testament as the basis of God's government and the standard of Christian conduct. But now it is written on the believers "heart" rather than on slabs of stone.

Likewise, the Sabbath continued to be observed on the seventh day in the New Testament as a pledge of allegiance to the Creator God of Heaven. But now it had new and added significance. Now, the day that was sanctificied in Eden to commemorate the end of creation by the Word in His role as Creator, was honored by the same Word resting in the tomb at the end of a sacrificial life in His role as Redeemer.

Eyes, Ears and Mouth

Eye witnesses maintaining visual contact, directly in the line of sight, who saw the whole thing with their own eyes—what more could you want? They heard the Lord with their own ears and reported what they heard. Up close and personal, the apostles had a front row seat to watch the events of early AD. They were in a prime position to see and hear the first century saga. As a result, they provide the clearest, most accurate account of conditions prevailing in the earliest years of the Christian church. Their perspective may be challenged by our remote point of view but it cannot be denied.

Doctor's Orders

The use of force in medical practice is not rare. Posey belts, restraints, "leathers," straight jackets, and even chemical restraints like sedatives and tranquilizers are common tools to insure compliance with the doctor's orders. Electroshock has been used to change people's minds. Aversion therapy inflicts painful stimuli as an adjunct to persuasion. Patients who pose a risk to themselves or society may be quarantined, isolated or even worse—hospitalized. Strict bed rest is frequently a mandatory order imposed on those uncooperative patients who threaten to buck the system, ignore the established schedule and deliver on their own time table.

History records similar tactics in the control of Sabbath behavior. A review of past medical records can be most enlightening.

Strict Bed Rest

Exclusive thinking and coercive behavior has appeared on both sides of the Sabbath-Sunday issue. Well known are the many "Blue Laws" enforcing Sunday sanctity and we have already reviewed many Church Canons invoked against Sabbath observance. On the other side of the fence, Sabbath keepers have also dished out their share of legal langor.

As the Gentile Christians began to call themselves the "New Israel" many in the Jewish rabbinical community began to teach that the Sabbath was made for the Jews only and not for anyone else (Midr. Exodus 31.12 [109b]; Exodus Rab. 25.11; Deut. Rab. 1.21). By the mid 3rd century Rabbi Simeon b. Laqish was even promoting the idea that a Gentile who kept the Sabbath "deserves death" (Sanh. 58b).

> "The Christians under the Catholic Church and the Jews under the Talmudic Rabbis have made Sunday keeping synonymous with Christian identity and Sabbath-keeping synonymous with Jewish identity respectively. The Rabbinic Jews, the papacy and the 'new covenant' theologians do make strange bedfellows indeed." Sidney Davis, "Universality of the Sabbath," *The Sabbath Sentinel*, JF 2001

This period between the 2nd and 5th century saw an intense effort on the part of Rome to suppress Sabbath celebration through imposed fasting and promote Sunday popularity through joyful feasting. A steady sequence of influential popes and prelates spoke and wrote in favor of this trend:

Bishop Callistus (AD 217-222),
Hippolytus (c. AD.170-236),
Pope Sylvester (AD 314-335),
Pope Innocent I (AD 401-417), and
Augustine (AD 354-430).

About a century later Pope Gregory encouraged the people of Rome to "expiate on the day of our Lord's resurrection what was remissly done for the six days before." At the same time he condemned those who advocated the observance of both Sabbath and Sunday as preachers of Antichrist. A thousand years later William Twisse commented that the Pope was referring to both seventh-day and first-day observers (Peter Heylyn's *History of the Sabbath,* Part 2, Chapter 5, Section 1; Morer's *Dialogues on the Lord's Day,* p. 282). The Papacy's intolerance toward the Sabbath, even when joined with the observance of Sunday, was unyielding. But notice: there were still Sabbath keepers in Rome even at this late date.

Council of Elivira 305 AD

Eighty-one canons were passed by this council which was held in Elvira, Spain about 305 AD. It is notable because of the reference it makes to many of the prevailing conditions in the church of Spain at the time. Canon 26 indicates that the observance of the seventh day was commonly practiced. "As to fasting every Sabbath: Resolved, that the error be corrected of fasting every Sabbath." A. Mansi, *Sacrorum Conciliorum Nova et Amplissima Collectio,* vol 2, p. 10.

This was in direct opposition to Rome's policy of enforcing Sabbath as a fast day. Pope Sylvester (314-335) was first to order the Sabbath fast upon all churches, and Pope Innocent (402-417) made it a binding law.

> "Innocentius did ordaine the Saturday or Sabbath to be always fasted." Peter Heylyn, *History of the Sabbath,* Part 2, Ch. 2, London, 1636, p. 44.

Rome intended to make the seventh day less desirable. Elvira reversed this decision because the early church of Spain kept the Sabbath in harmony with the "Valdenses" who taught them. These were the people known as the *Vaudois* in French, *Valdesi* in Italian, from the Latin, *vallis,* from which come our word "valleys." The people of the Piedmont and the Pyrenees who kept the Sabbath lived in these valleys. It is interesting that in this region of northeastern Spain near the city of Barcelona is a town called Sabadell where the people were first called "Sabbatati." Some have suggested that the town's name derived from "dell of the Sabbath keepers." Robinson, *Ecclesiastical Researches,* p. 299.

The First Sunday Law, 321 AD

Constantine wrote the very first Sunday law in March of 321 AD:

> "On the Venerable Day of the Sun let the magistrates and people residing in cities rest, and let all workshops be closed. In the country, however, persons engaged in agriculture may freely and lawfully continue their pursuits; because it often happens that another day is not so suitable for grain-sowing or for vine-planting; lest by neglecting the proper moment for such operations the bounty should be lost; given the 7th day of March [321 A.D.], Crispus and Constantine being consuls each of them for the second time." Codex Justinianus, lib. 3, tit. 12, 3; translated in Philip Schaff, D.D., *History of the Christian Church*, Vol. 3 of 7, 5th edition 1902, p.380, note 1.

> "This is the 'parent' Sunday law making it a day of rest and release from labor. For from this day to the present there have been decrees about the observance of Sunday which have profoundly influenced European and American society. When the Church became a part of State under the Christian emperors Sunday observance was enforced by civil statutes and later, when the Empire was past, the Church in the hands of the papacy, enforced it by ecclesiastical, and also influenced it by civil enactments." Walter Woodburn Hyde, *Paganism to Christianity in the Roman Empire,* University of Pennsylvania Press, 1946, p. 261.

> "This legislation by Constantine probably bore no relation to Christianity; it appears, on the contrary, that the emperor, in his capacity of Pontifex Maximus, was only adding the day of the Sun, the worship of which was then firmly established in the Roman Empire, to the other ferial days of the sacred calendar...What began, however, as a pagan ordinance, ended as a Christian regulation; and a long series of imperial decrees, during the fourth, fifth, and sixth centuries, enjoined with increasing stringency abstinence from labour on Sunday." Hutton Webster, *Rest Days,* pp. 122-123, 270, 1916, The MacMillan Company.

> "Constantine's decree marked the beginning of a long, though intermittent series of imperial decrees in support of Sunday rest." Vincent J. Kelly, *Forbidden Sunday and Feast-Day Occupations,* 1943, p.29.

335 AD Persia

During the reign of Shapur II (335-375AD) Christians in Persia were persecuted for their Sabbath keeping on the seventh day:

> "They despise our sun-god. Did not Zoroaster, the sainted founder of our divine beliefs, institute Sunday one thousand years ago in honour of the sun and supplant the Sabbath of the Old Testament. Yet these Christians have divine services on Saturday." O'Leary, *The Syriac Church and Fathers*, pp. 83-84.

386 AD Constantine

"By a law of the year 386, those older changes effected by the emperor Constantine were more rigorously enforced, and in general, civil transactions of every kind on Sunday were strictly forbidden." Neander's *Church History*, Vol. II, page 300, edition 1852

425 AD Theodosius the Younger

"In the year 425, the exhibition of spectacles on Sunday and on the principal feast-days of the Christians was forbidden, in order that the devotion of the faithful might be free from all disturbance." "In this way the church received help from the state for the furtherance of her ends... But had it not been for that confusion of spiritual and secular interests, had it not been for the vast number of mere outward conversions thus brought about, she would have needed no such help." *Ibid*, pp. 300, 301

538 AD Synod of Aureliani

"The emperors after Constantine made Sunday observance more stringent but in no case was their legislation based on the Old Testament... At the Third Synod of Aureliani [Orleans] in 538 rural work was forbidden but the restriction against preparing meals and similar work on Sunday was regarded as a superstition. After Justinian's death in 565 various epistolae decretals were passed by the popes about Sunday." Walter Woodburn Hyde, *Paganism to Christianity in the Roman Empire*, 1946, p. 261.

560 AD India

"The famous Jesuit, Francais Xavier, called for the Inquisition, which was set up in Goa, India, in 560, to check the 'Jewish wickedness' (Sabbath-keeping)." Adeney, *The Greek and Eastern Churches*, New York, 1908, pp. 527,528.

602 AD Pope Gregory I

Gregory issued a bull against the practice of keeping Sabbath in the city of Rome.

"Gregory, bishop by the grace of God to his well-beloved sons, the Roman citizens: It has come to me that certain men of perverse spirit have disseminated among you things depraved and opposed to the holy faith, so that they forbid anything to be done on the day of the Sabbath. What shall I call them except preachers of anti-Christ." Pope Gregory I, 590-604 AD, *Epistles b. 13:11*

791 Council of Friaul

This council was convened in northern Italy and again commanded all Christians to observe the Lord's Day (Canon 13). "Further when speaking of that Sabbath which the Jews observe, the last day of the week, which also all peasants observe." A. Mansi, *Sacrorum Conciliorum Nova et Amplissima Collectio*, vol. 13, p. 852.

800 Charlemagne in France

"We decree...that servile works should not be done on the Lord's day...that is, that neither should men do field work, either in cultivating the vineyards or by plowing in the fields, by cutting or drying hay, or by placing a fence, or by making clearings in the woods or felling trees or working on stones or constructing houses or working in the garden; neither should they come together to decide public matters nor be engaged in the hunt....Women may not do any textile work not cut out clothes nor sew nor make garments....But let them come together from all sides to church to the solemnities of the mass, and let them praise God for all things which he does for us on that day." *Historical Chronicles of Germany*, Sec. 2, Vol. I, 22 General admonition, 789, M. Martio 23, page 61, par.81

886 Ireland's Law of Sunday

The first Sunday Law in Ireland appeared in the *Cain Domnaig* that is based on the "Epistle of Christ" an alleged document that was claimed to have fallen from heaven onto the altar of St. Peter in Rome around 590 AD. Lacking scriptural support for Sunday, the miraculous document appeared to bolster the Church's position. The Epistle purports to be written by the very hand of Christ and begins by listing many fabulous calamities occurring as punishment to those who did work on Sunday:

a woman who washed her hair on the Lord's day went bald; a man who chopped wood on Sunday could not release his hands from the axe handle; another man digging with a spade was horrified as the handle caught on fire. The document then heaps curses on Sunday breakers:

"'Whoever shall not keep Sunday', said the heavenly Father, 'within its proper boundaries, his soul shall not attain Heaven, neither shall he see me in the Kingdom of Heaven, nor the archangels, nor the Apostles.'"

" 'I swear,' saith the abbot of Rome, 'by the might of God the Father, and by Christ's Cross, that this is no invention of mine, and no fiction or fable; but it is from God the Father this Epistle was sent unto the altar of Peter in Rome of Latium to make Sunday holy'....The curse of every person on all who shall break this law of Sunday." "Now, even if this wonderful command for keeping Sunday holy had not come from Jesus Christ himself out of Heaven, the day should be sacred, venerable, perfect, and honoured, on account of all the many miracles that have happened thereon."

"Therefore, it is through these commands that God has enjoined Sunday to be kept holy, for God's own hand has written that command to men, lest they should do either work or servile labour on Sunday."

J.G. O'Keefe, "The Law of Sunday—The Epistle of Jesus," Eriu III. 2 (1907) p. 195, 203, 197, 101.

1054   Greek Church

In 1054 when the Greek patriarch, Michael Cerulanius, attacked the Roman Church on its decretal requiring all to fast on the Sabbath, pope Humbert sent three legates to Constantinople with countercharges:

> "Because you observe the Sabbath with the Jews and the Lord's Day with us, you seem to imitate with such observances the sect of Nazarenes who in this manner accept Christianity in order that they be not obliged to leave Judaism." Migne, *Patralogia Latina*, vol. 145, p. 506; Hergentroether, Photius, vol. 3, p. 746.s

Unable to bring the Greek Church into subjection, he excommunicated it. Thus began the Great Schism between the East and West division of Christianity..

Waldensian Crusades

Pope Urban II issued a bull denouncing "heresy" among the people of the valleys. There, a century before Peter Waldo, was Peter de Bruys, born in the French Alps and began to stir the Waldensian believers beginning in 1104. The effect he had on the people was so enduring that 500 years later a bishop of the Church of England was still referring to Sabbath keepers as Petrobrusians.   White, Bishop of Eli, *A Treatise on the Sabbath Day*, p. 8 found in Fisher, *Tracts on the Sabbath*.

> "For centuries evangelical bodies, especially the Waldenses, were called Insabbati or Ensavates, that is Insabbatati, because of Sabbath keeping.   'Many took this position,' says Ussher. The learned Jesuit, Jacob Gretzer, about 1600, recognized that the Waldenses, the Albigenses, and the Insabbatati were different names for the same people." Wilkinson, Benjamin G., *Truth Triumphant*, p. 237; Gretzer, *Praeloquia in Triadem Scriptorum Contra Valdensium Sectium*, found in *Maxima Bibliotheca Veterum Patrum*, vol. 24, pp. 1521, 1522.

The Waldensian influence was remarkably widespread:

> "This sect, says Nangis, were infinit in number; appeared, says Rainerus, in nearly every country; multiplied, says Sanderus, through all lands; infected, says Caesarius, a thousand cities; and spread their contagion, says Ciaconius, through almost the whole Latin world. Scarcely any region, says Gretzer, remained free and untainted from this pestilence. The Waldensians, says Popliner, spread, not only through France, but also through nearly all the European coasts, and appear in Gaul, Spain, England, Scotland, Italy, Germany, Bohemia, Szony, Poland, and Lithuania....Their

number, according to Benedict, was prodigious in France, England, Piedmont, Sicily, Calabria, Poland, Bohemia, Saxony, Pomerania, Germany, Livonia, Sarmatia, Constantinople, Philadelphia, and Bulgaria." Edgar, *The Variations of Popery*, pp. 51, 52.

1147 Evangelicals

When Bernard of Clairaux wrote about these "evangelicals" in 1147, he called them

> "Apostolicals, giving as his reason for so naming them that no one could trace them back to the name of any particular founder. He admitted that the Arians had Arius for a founder; that the Manichaeans had Mani (or Manes); and the Sabellians had Sabellius; the Eunomians had Eunomius; and the Nestorians had Nestorius." *Truth Triumphant* p. 240; Bernard of Clairaux, Sermon 66, on the Canticles, found in Eales, *The Works of St. Bernard*, vol. 4, pp. 388, 400-403.

Ultimately, persecution came to the faithful Waldenses. The king of Aragon became the tool of the church in 1194 to decree their expulsion:

> "We command you in imitation of our ancestors and in obedience to the ordinances of the church, that heretics, to wit, Waldenses, Insabbathi and those who call themselves the poor of Lyons and all other heretics should be expelled away from the face of God and from all Catholics and ordered to depart from our kingdom." Marianae, Praefatio in Lucam Tudensem, found in *Maxima Bibliotheca Veterum Patrum*, vol. 25, p. 190.

1229 France

Laws against Sabbath-keepers were made by the French Council of Toulouse in 1229. "Canon 3: The lords of the different districts shall have the villas, houses, and woods diligently searched, and the hiding-places of the heretics destroyed. Canon 14: Lay members are not allowed to possess the books of either the Old or the New Testaments." Hefele. 5, 981, 962

1442 Eugene IV

"It [the Roman Church] firmly believes, professes, and teaches that the matter pertaining to the law of the Old Testament, of the Mosaic law... after our Lord's coming had been signified by them, ceased... but after the promulgation of the Gospel it asserts that they cannot be observed without the loss of eternal salvation."

"All, therefore, who after that time observe circumcision and the Sabbath and the other requirements of the law, it declares alien to the Christian faith and not in the least fit to participate in eternal salvation, unless someday they recover from these errors." Pope Eugene IV, Papal Bull Cantate Domino, dated February 4th, 1442, from the Thirtieth Edition of Henry Denzinger's *Enchiridion Symbolorum*, published by B. Herder Book Co., Copyright 1957, p. 228

1503 Moscow Executions

"The accused (Sabbath-keepers) were summoned; they openly acknowledged the new faith, and defended the same. The most prominent of them,...were condemned to death, and burned publicly in cages, at Moscow, Dec 17.1503." H. Sternberfi, *Geschichte der Juden.*

In England Sunday laws existed in some form since the 7th century. But it was Edward VI's Act of Uniformity (of religion) in 1551 that marked the beginning of serious ecclesiastical censure and fines imposed by a series of statutes that were not repealed until 1846. This marked the era of the Puritan persecution and their flight to America.

1500-1600 Puritans

After Henry VIII split away from Roman Catholicism and formed his own state church, there were those within the new Anglican community who wanted even further reform. These followers of Calvin called themselves Puritans. They believed that the Old Testament law was an important guide to New Testament Christians. They held to the Protestant creed of *Sola Scriptura*, "the Bible only" in matters of faith and doctrine and desired to return to first century apostolic standards. The Anglican State Church, led by the monarchy, clung to church tradition and justified Sunday worship on the basis of church authority. Puritans, while keeping the same day, appealed to the Biblical Fourth Commandment.

John Hooper published his *Declaration of the Ten Holy Commandments* in 1548 arguing that while God established the Sabbath at the time of creation He changed it from the seventh to the first day after raising Christ from the dead on resurrection Sunday. "This Sunday that we observe is not the commandment of men," he claimed.

1544 Norway

In Norway, during this same time, the royal throne pronounced warning and threats against would be Sabbath keepers. "Some of you, contrary to the warning, keep Saturday. You ought to be severely punished. Whoever is found keeping Saturday, must pay a fine of ten marks." *History of King Christian the Third* (of Norway 1544AD), Niels Krag and S. Stephanius.

1583 Sunday Disaster

In 1578 John Stockwood delivered a stern warning in his sermon at St Paul's Cross that the judgments of God would fall on Sabbath-breakers. He even named Paris Garden as the likely recipient of divine retribution. This popular venue for blood sports was indeed struck with disaster only five years later on a Sunday, January 13, 1583. While cheering on a fight between a bear and a pack of dogs a crowded upper gallery collapsed injuring many and killing seven. Suddenly there was a public outcry for legislation to ensure better observance of the Lord's Day. For decades Parliament debated a series of Sabbatarian bills as the nation clamored for Sabbath reform.

In 1596 Nicholas Bounde published *The Doctrine of the Sabbath*. His dogmatic Cambridge roots argued fiercely that the Sabbath was rooted in God's law not church tradition. The church taught that the Sabbath commandment was both moral and ceremonial. To keep one day in seven was moral and permanently binding on all men from creation, but keeping the seventh day was ceremonial and temporarily imposed on the Jews alone. But now Bounde claimed that the fourth commandment was entirely moral—denying any ceremonial quality in it at all! His arguments for the seventh day commandment were so intense it took him 15 pages of persuasion to get it back to supporting the first day. (John H. Primus, *Holy Time: Moderate Puritanism and the Sabbath* [Macon, Georgia: Mercer University Press, 1989], 76)

The establishment responded by labeling those who wanted to use the Jewish law for their defense of keeping Sabbath as anti-Christian. They were forced to take the position that the Bible established no particular day. "The Lord's day was enjoined by civil and ecclesiastical constitutions." According to them, it could just as well be called the Queen's day as the Lord's day or the Sabbath.

1604 Ethiopia

In Ethiopia, 1604 AD, the Jesuits influenced King Zadenghel to propose to submit to the Papacy "Prohibiting all his subjects, upon severe penalties, to observe, Saturday any longer." Gedde's *Church History of Eithiopia* p. 311 and also in Gibbon's *Decline and Fall* chapter 47.

1607 Sabbatary Christians

In 1607 John Sprint published his *Propositions Tending to Prove the Necessary Uses of the Christian Sabbath*. For the first time, Sprint refers to "sabbatary Christians" who kept the seventh day because they believed in the perpetuity of God's law from creation and that it was still binding on Jews *and* Christians. Some believe he might have been referring to the Anabaptists in Germany who were expelled from the Holy Roman Empire in the 1590s. Others conclude that the Sabbatarian fervor that gripped England had produced a reform within the Puritans themselves as they concluded that the seventh-day was the original and still binding Lord's day.

> In the reign of Elizabeth, it occurred to many conscientious and independent thinkers (as it had previously done to some Protestants in Bohemia), that the Fourth Commandment required of them the observance, not of the first, but of the specified *seventh* day of the week, and a strict bodily rest as a service then due to God.... The former class became numerous enough to make a considerable figure for more than a century in England under the title of "Sabbatarians"—a word now exchanged for the less ambiguous appellation of "Seventh-day Baptists." *Chamber's Encyclopædia,* vol. VIII [London: W. and R. Chambers, 1881], 402.

1610 First "Blue Laws" in America

The Puritans came to the New World in search of religious freedom. Ironically they were just as intolerant of religious offenders when they became the ruling party. The theocratic New Haven colony like other Puritan colonies of New England had rigid laws prohibiting Sabbath breaking, domestic abuses, drunkenness, and dress code infractions. The Sunday laws became known as "blue laws" after the blue paper on which they were printed. The Connecticut Dominion Law included these restrictions on Sunday activities:

> No one shall cross a river on the Sabbath but authorized clergymen.
> No one shall travel, cook victuals, make beds, sweep houses, cut hair,
>   or shave on the Sabbath Day.
> No one shall kiss his or her children on the Sabbath or feasting days.

When Lord De La Warr became the Puritan governor in Virginia in 1610, he enacted strict "Sabbath" (Sunday) laws in the colony.

> "Every man and woman shall repair in the morning to the divine service and sermons preached upon the Sabbath day, and in the afternoon to divine service, and catechizing, upon pain for the first fault to lose their provision and the allowance for the whole week following; for the second, to lose the said allowance and also be whipped; and for the third to suffer death." *Articles, Laws, and Orders, Divine, Politique, and Martial, for the Colony in Virginia*: first established by Sir Thomas Gates, Knight, Lieutenant-General, the 24th of May, 1610 in *For the Colony in Virginea Brintannia, Lawes Divine,* Morall and Martiall, & c, in Peter Force, *Tracts and Other Papers Relating Principally to the Colonies in North America,* 1844 edition, Vol. 3, No. 2, p.11.

Revolving pillory as public punishment

1618 English Sabbatarians

John Traske was ordained an Anglican priest but introduced to the seventh-day Sabbath by the independant study of one of his own disciples, Hamlet Jackson. Traske went on to embrace the Levitical festivals and dietary laws earning him the charge of turning the Majesty's subjects into Jews. He was arrested in 1618 for teaching people to observe the Sabbath, whipped on his way to the public pillory to which he was nailed by one ear, branded on his forehead with the letter I for Jew, released and then whipped again on his way to a second pillory where the other ear was nailed. Following this ordeal he was fined 1000 pounds and thrown into jail. Such were the severe measures taken to supress Sabbath observance in Puritan England, an indication of how threatening the practice was to the establishment. [Henry E.I. Phillips, "An Early Stuart Judaizing Sect," *Transactions of the Jewish Historical Society of England,* vol xv, 66].

1637 Boston Bible Study

In November of 1637, Anne Hutchinson a Boston mother of fourteen children, after holding religious meetings in her home where she proved by Scripture that Christian faith does not merely consist of mechanical works, was convicted of heresy by the Massachusets court and evicted from the colony. Though the Sabbath was not at issue, the spirit of religious intolerance in early colonial America is well demonstrated.

Stocks retrained hands and feet of criminals and offenders

1656 No Sunday Kissing

"Captain Kemble, of Boston, was, in 1656, set for two hours in the public stocks, for his 'lewd and unseemly behavior,' which consisted in kissing his wife 'publicquely' " on Sunday morning at the front door of their home after returning from a three-year ocean voyage.

A man who, having fallen into the creek while on his way to church, had returned home to dry his only suit of clothes, was found guilty and "publicly whipped." Other draconian laws prohibited anyone from walking, driving, or riding horseback on Sunday, unless going to church or to the cemetery. Stringent Sunday laws held the colonies in a tight Puritan grip. Freedom of individual conscience was not a consideration.

1670 William Penn's Trial

Arriving at the Quaker meeting house on Gracechurch Street, London, August 14, 1670, William Penn was met by soldiers barring the entrance. So Penn preached in the street. This landed him in court for "disturbance of the peace."

The trial began on September 1. Penn defended himself. When he asked what law his indictment was based on, the Recorded said, "Upon the Common-Law."

"Where is the Common-Law?" inquired Penn.

He was told that no one knew where it was. Co-defendant William Meade spoke of the Quaker desire for peace and quiet. The chief judge then suggested, "You ought to have your tongue cut out."

The jury of twelve men returned a verdict of "not guilty" to the charge of unlawful assembly. The disappointed court then threatened them with fines and possibly even torture if they did not cooperate with a guilty verdict. But the jury would not yield, "Nor will we ever do it!" their foreman shouted.

The court threatened to keep the jury "lock'd up, without Meat, Drink, Fire, and Tobacco" until they returned the desired verdict. But they repeatedly returned with the same report five times. Penn finally pleaded, "What hope is there of ever having Justice done, when juries are threatened, and their verdicts rejected?"

The judge ordered the guards to "Stop his mouth; Jailer, bring fetters and stake him to the ground." At this point the court recorder entered into the official trial record: "Till now, I never understood the reason of the policy and prudence of the Spaniards, in suffering the Inquisition among them: And certainly it will never be well with us, till something like unto the Spanish Inquisition be in England." Britain, in his opinion, had way too much civil liberty.

In the end the jury, Penn and Meade were heavily fined and jailed until the fines were entirely paid.

1682 Pennsylvania Colony

William Penn decided to flee the tyrannical religious laws of England and sail to the New World with other Christians. But even in the American colonies religious intolerance persisted. When Cotton Mather received news of his coming he sent a letter to John Higginson informing him that the ship was carrying "100 or more of the heretics and malignants called Quakers, with W. Penn, who is the chief scamp at the head of them." Mather went on to describe the plan concocted by the General Court to have the brig Porpoise waylay Penn's ship, the Welcome, near Cape Cod and sell the "whole lot to Barbados, where slaves fetch good prices in rum and sugar, and we shall not only do the Lord great good by punishing the wicked, but we shall make great good for His minister and people."

William Penn managed to elude the Porpoise and go on to establish the colony of Pennsylvania as a haven for the Quakers. But others of their faith, such as Mary Dyer who was hanged in Boston, were severely persecuted merely because their religious beliefs were different. State law legalized such treatment explaining that the "cursed sect of the Quakers" should be "sentenced to banishment upon pain of death."

1664 Rhode Island Colony

Roger Williams, the "father of religious liberty," opened his small colony of Rhode Island to all no matter what faith they might practice. Williams believed that all men should worship God according to the dictates of their own consciences. Back in England he had seen first hand the atrocities of the Star Chamber. He later wrote of the shocking treatment given to Alexander Leighton, a popular Scottish physician and pastor who ministered not only to the spiritual but physical needs of the people. He did not agree, however, with the doctrines of the state religion. This crime sentenced him to life imprisonment, a fine of 10,000 pounds, and facial disfigurement —his ears were cut off, nose slit, and face branded with a hot iron.

In 1664, Stephen Mumford, a Sabbath keeper, came to New England. He founded in 1671 the first Sabbath keeping church in America—in Rhode Island. Soon the report reached England that the Rhode Island colony was no longer keeping Sunday. In reply to this, Roger Williams wrote a letter on June 22, 1670, in which he both denied this accusation, and mentioned that there was no Scripture for "abolishing the seventh day."

"You know yourselves do not keep the seventh day," he remarked. His was the only colony that at the time had tolerance of Sabbath keepers. "The Divine institution of a day of rest from ordinary occupations and of religious worship, transferred by the authority of the Church from the Sabbath, the last day, to Sunday, the first day of the week, has always been revered in this country, has entered into our legislation and customs, and is one of the most patient signs that we are a Christian people."... You know that all England itself (after the formality of morning and evening prayer) play away their Sabbath. 2d. You know yourselves do not keep the Sabbath, that is the seventh day, &c."... Thus also all the Romanists confess, saying, viz.: that there is no express scripture, first, for infants' baptism; nor, second, for abolishing the seventh day, and instituting of the eighth day worship, but that it is at the church's pleasure." *Roger Williams, Letter to Major John Mason of Connecticut, June 22, 1670, in Letters of Roger Williams, in Publications of the Narragansett Club, 1st series, vol. 6, 1874 ed., pp. 333, 346-347.*

1653 Death Penalty

"Whosoever shall profane the Lord's day, or any part of it, either by sinful servile work, or by unlawful sport, recreation, or otherwise, whether willfully, or in a careless neglect, shall be duly punished by fine, imprisonment, or corporally according to the nature, and measure of the sin, and offence. But if the Court upon examination, by clear, and satisfying evidence find That the sin was proudly, presumptuously, & with a high hand committed against the known command and authority of the blessed God, such a person therein despising and reproaching the Lord, shall be put to death, That all others may feare and shun such provoking Rebellious courses." (*Seventeenth century Colonial Sunday Law, quoted in Charles J. Hoadly, Records of the Colony or Jurisdiction of New Haven, From May, 1653, to the Union, Together With the New Haven Code of 1656, p. 605 1858 edition*).

1676 Charles II

"For the better observation and keeping holy the Lord's day, commonly called Sunday: be it enacted...that all the laws enacted and in force concerning the observation of the day and repairing to the church thereon, be carefully put in execution; and that all and every person and persons whatsoever shall on every Lord's day apply themselves to the observation of the same, by exercising themselves thereon in the duties of piety and true religion publicly and privately." *Revised Statutes of England From 1235 - 1685 A.D.* (London, 1870), pages 799, 780; cited in *A Critical History of Sunday Legislation*, by A. H. Lewis, D.D., pages 108, 109.

1763 The Basic English Sunday Law

"Be it enacted ... that all and every Person and Persons whatsoever, shall on every Lord's Day apply themselves to the Observation of the same, by exercising themselves thereon in the Duties of Piety and true Religion, publickly and privately; (4) and that no... Person whatsoever, shall do or exercise any worldly Labour, Business, or Work of their ordinary Callings, upon the Lord's Day, or any Part thereof (Works of Necessity and Charity only excepted;... (6) and that no Person or Persons whatsoever, shall publickly cry, shew forth, or expose to Sale, any Wares, Merchandizes, Fruit, Herbs, Goods or Chattels whatsoever." *29 Charles II, chap. 7, in [British] Statutes at Large (1763), Vol. 3, p. 388 [This law of the 29th year of Charles II, valid in England for nearly two centuries, became the model for many American colonial laws, and hence of our State Sunday laws]*.

1774 Canadian Lord's Day Act

In Quebec in 1774, and in Upper Canada in 1792 this Act made it unlawful "to do or exercise any worldly labour, business or work of one's ordinary calling." This exact same language still appears in Canada's current Lord's Day Act.

1789 George Washington

The first President of the United States narrowly missed being fined and imprisoned for traveling to the capitol to take office after his election in 1789. But the new country would quickly insure religious liberty for all.

1791 The First Amendment

At last, religious freedom came to America, as on November 3, 1791, the First Ten Amendments to the United States Constitution became part of the law of the land. The first sentence of the First Amendment guaranteed that a man's religion henceforth would be secure in America.

"Congress shall make no law respecting an establishment of religion, or pro-hibiting the free exercise thereof; or abridging the freedom of speech, or of the press; or the right of the people peaceably to assemble, and to petition the Government for a redress of grievances." *First Amendment to the Constitution of the United States of America, in United States Code, 1958 edition, p. xlvi.*

Several years later, Thomas Jefferson made this comment:

> "I contemplate with sovereign reverence that act of the whole American people which declares that their legislature should 'make no law respecting an establishment of religion or prohibiting the free exercise thereof,' thus building a wall of separation between church and state."

Because of this legal document, the martyrdoms and bloody persecutions of the Dark Ages could not come to America. We were declared safe from the Inquisition of Spain and the massacre of the Huguenots, the slaughter of the Waldenses and the Tower of London, the "holy" wars and the rack, the screw and the stake, the fines and the imprisonments and the executions.

Your personal liberties depend on these Ten Amendments to our Constitution. Never let them be taken from you by the enactment of religious laws in America—no matter what the pretext.

Patrick Henry wrote the original draft of the First Amendment, using the words, "fullest toleration in the exercise of religion." But James Madison was determined that nothing other than "free exercise" should be written here. And he told us why: A state which could "tolerate" could also prohibit. We call these Ten Amendments, the "Bill of Rights." The freedoms you enjoy every day of your life in your home and as you walk the streets, are dependent on that Bill of Rights.

"With only a few technical restrictions, an American can organize a church, teach or preach religion, conduct a religious school, found a religious hospital and publish and distribute literature about his faith without being molested. All these religious freedoms must be extended impartially to all churches or religious schools without discrimination.

"Those freedoms seem common place enough to most Americans; we tend to take them for granted. Yet they represent one of history's greatest cultural achievements. They distinguish the American way of life in matters of religion from that of many other nations which consider themselves democratic." Paul Blanshard, *God and Man in Washington,* 1960, p. 58.

"It is a monstrous paradox, that God's children should persecute God's children, and that they that hope to live eternally together with Christ Jesus in the heavens, should not suffer each other to live in this common air together, &c. I am informed it was the speech of an honourable knight of the parliament: 'What! Christ persecute Christ in New England?' " Roger Williams, *The Bloudy Tenent of Persecution,* 1848 ed., p. 370.

"When a religion is good, I conceive that it will support itself; and, when it cannot support itself, and God does not take care to support it, so that its professors are obliged to call for help of the civil power, it is a sign, I apprehend, of its being a bad one." *The Writings of Benjamin Franklin, Letter to Dr. Price, October 9, 1780,* Smyth's edition, volume 8, page 154.

"It was under a solemn consciousness of the dangers from ecclesiastical ambition, the bigotry of spiritual pride and the intolerance of sects, thus exemplified in our domestic, as well as our foreign annals, that it was deemed advisable to exclude from the national government all power to act upon the subject." Joseph Story, *Commentaries on the Constitution of the United States,* bk. 3 chap. 44, p. 702, sec. 992, 1833 edition. [Joseph Story (1779-1845), was a jurist and U.S. Supreme Court justice for 34 years, a foremost American legal writer, and a United States Congressman.]

1823 America separates Religion from Government

"Religion is essentially distinct from civil Government, and exempt from its cognizance... a connection between them is injurious to both." James Madison, Letter to Edward Everett, March 19, 1823, in *Letters and Other Writings of James Madison*, Vol. 3 , p. 307.

1829

A petition was presented to Congress to suspend postal service on Sundays because "observance of Sunday was connected with the civil interests of the government." Senator Richard M. Johnson opposed it stating that the function of Government was to protect all citizens "in the enjoyment of their religious as well as civil rights, and not to determine for any whether they shall esteem one day above another."

The House Committee on the Post Office and Post Roads was commissioned to study the question. In its official report the committee observed that throughout the history of the Christian church, that as soon as Christians were

> "...clothed with political power, [they] lost the meek spirit which their creed inculcated, and began to inflict on other religions, and on dissenting sects of their own religion, persecutions more aggravated than those which their own apostles had endured. The ten persecutions of pagan emperors were exceeded in atrocity by the massacres and murders perpetrated by Christian hands; and in vain shall we examine the records of imperial tyranny for an engine of cruelty equal to the holy Inquisition. Every religious sect, however meek its origin, commenced the work of persecution as soon as it acquired political power."

The report reasoned that if such a Federal Sunday law was adopted making it is sinful to carry letters, "it must be equally sinful for individuals to write, carry, receive, or read them." The House Report warned that ultimately laws would be established to suppress travel on the Lord's Day; newspapers would be unavailable because printing, delivering, and reading them would be illegal. Eventually even conversations would be limited to religious topics only.

This analysis by Congress of the religious and Sunday law controversy in 1829 effectively stifled further threats to religious liberty until 1888 when another bid for national Sunday-observance legislation once again surfaced.

1854

Donahoe v Richard (1854) 38 Me. 379, 61 AD 258, 273 (Appleton, J) "Under American Constitutions, the law may not enforce religious observances. But a state may establish a day of rest as a civil institution."

1855 Every State in the Union

Robert Baird wrote in 1855 that "there was no subject on which American Christians were more happily united than that of the proper observance of the Sabbath [i.e., Sunday]. He found that every state in the Union had made laws in favor of proper observance of the Lord's Day, because the whole economy proceeded on the principle that America was a Christian country and because the courts had pronounced Christianity to be 'part and parcel of the laws of the Land.' He said that he uttered the language of every American Christian when he said: 'Woe to America when it ceases to be a Sabbath respecting land.' " (George M. Stephenson, *The Puritan Heritage* [New York: MacMillan Co., 1952], 181)

1858

Ex parte Newman (1858) 9 Cal. 502, 520 (Field, J, dissenting) "There is no nation, possessing any degree of civilization, where the rule is not observed, either from the sanctions of law or the sanctions of religion."

"If it were now to be decided as to whether the seventh or the first day should be observed as the weekly sabbath, ere could scarcely be doubt as to the required answer [the seventh day]. But the almost uniform practice of Christian peoples for more than sixteen centuries cannot be lightly ignored. It must be presumed that the early Christians, in observing the first rather than the seventh day, were actuated by some reason or reasons which to them seemed good and sufficient, if only to distinguish themselves from the Jews and afford some public evidence that Christianity was not merely a new Jewish sect."

1868

In 1868 the Fourteenth Amendment became the law of the land, and it greatly strengthened the power of the First Amendment, by requiring that State laws guarantee certain basic freedoms to the individual.

> "No State shall make or enforce any law which shall abridge the privileges or immunities of citizens of the United States; nor shall any State deprive any person of life, liberty, or property, without due process of law; nor deny to any person within its jurisdiction the equal protection of the laws."

1872 John Wesley

"Condemn no man for not thinking as you think: Let every one enjoy the full and free liberty of thinking for himself: Let every man use his own judgment, since every man must give an account of himself to God. Abhor every approach, in any kind or degree, to the spirit of persecution. If you cannot reason or persuade a man into the truth, never attempt to force him into it. If love will not compel him to come in, leave him to God, the Judge of all." John Wesley, *Advice to the People Called Methodists,* in his Works, 1872 ed., Vol. 8, p. 357.

1872 Supreme Court Justice John Welch

"Government is an organization for particular purposes. It is not almighty, and we are not to look to it for everything. The great bulk of human affairs and human interests is left by any free government to individual enterprise and individual action. Religion is eminently one of those interests, lying outside the true and legitimate province of government." Justice John Welch, in Board of Education of Cincinnati v. Minor et al (1872-1878), *23 Ohio State Reports 253.* [John Welch, LL.D. (1805-1891) was a judge on the Supreme Court of Ohio].

1887

At the 1887 convention of the National Reform Association, Dr. David McAllister stated, "Those who oppose this work now will discover, when the religious amendment [a National Sunday Law] is made to the Constitution, that if they do not see fit to fall in with the majority, they must abide the consequences, or seek some more congenial clime." He received the full support of the delegates. Completely forgotten was the observation of Benjamin Franklin made a century earlier.

1888 National Sunday Law

Senate Bill 2983 of 1888 was sponsored by New Hampshire's Senator Blair as a "Lord's Day" measure "To Promote Its Observance as a Day of Religious Worship." The bill was supported by numerous religious organizations calling for a ban on "secular work, labor, or business" in interstate commerce, transportation, postal service, military musters and drills, that would "interfere with or disturb the people in the enjoyment of the first day of the week, ... or its observance as a day of religious worship." It also condemned "any play, game, or amusement, or recreation" on the day.

Many ministers testified on its behalf before the Senate Committee on Education and Labor. It died in committee. But over the next 50 years Congress considered nearly a hundred similar measures.

With the arrival of the Twentieth Century, Sunday legislation changed tactics. From religious laws "in protection of the Lord's Day," they became civil laws "in protection of the rights of the workingman." Their proponents declared them to be "a legitimate exercise of the police power of the State."

1891 Pope Leo XII

In the Encyclical *Rerum Novarum* (1891) Pope Leo XII called upon civil governments to provide "Sunday rest as a worker's right which the State must guarantee."

1895 Sunday Criminals

A partial review of court records reveals that in a one year period between 1895 and 1896, over seventy-five American citizens were convicted of Sunday law offenses, sentenced after fines to jails, chain gangs, etc., and served a total of 1,144 days. The famous abolitionist William Lloyd Garrison spoke on behalf of the blue laws, "If you do not obey me, I will put my hands into your pocket, and take out as much as I please in the shape of a fine or if I find nothing there, I will put you in prison; or if you resist enough to require it, I will shoot you dead... Passing a law, forbidding me or you to do on a particular day, what is in itself right... is nothing better than sheer usurpation." "The Sabbath, as now recognized and enforced, is one of the main pillars of Priestcraft and Superstition." *Life,* Vol. iii p. 224.

1898 National Blue Law

In 1898 one New Hampshire Senator introduced to Congress a national blue law "...to secure to the people the enjoyment of the first day of the week, commonly known as the Lord's Day, as a day of rest, and to promote its observance as a day of religious worship." The Bill failed to pass following stiff opposition by seventh-day Sabbath observers.

1914

42 Wash. L. Rep, (1914) 770 (Bernard) "Sunday laws are enacted, so that we, and all others, may have the benefit of rest and quiet, and an opportunity for worship, and religious reading and meditation, at least one day out of seven."

Southern Baptist Judson Taylor, *The Sabbatic Question:*
"In every case [in the New Testament] the obligation [to obey] is left with the enlightened conscience, —and any effort to coerce men by statutory enactment is repudiated by all liberty loving states... If they do not [honor God], nothing is gained for Him or for them by legal compulsion.

"On the baseless assumption that the seventh day, set apart and established in the law [of God], has been in some way superseded by the first day, recognized in the gospel, a good deal of hurtful legislation has been enacted on the pretext of sanctifying the Sabbath and honoring God. Men who really do know better are willing to wrest the Scriptures and appeal to popular ignorance in order to gain a point. Such conduct is unworthy of any good cause.

"This error had its origin in the iniquitous union of church and state, and is a relic of that oppressive system. Early Christians never confounded the Sabbath and the Lord's Day. For five hundred years after Christ the distinction between the two, so clearly marked in the Scriptures, was strictly maintained.

"In any form Sunday legislation is either religious or secular. If religious, it violates the principle of separation between church and state. If secular, it tends to secularize the Lord's Day and to obliterate the distinction between the righteous and the wicked by having the same human rule for each. In either case it works mischief, and ought to be expunged from the statute books of every enlightened state." (Joseph Judson Taylor, *The Sabbatic Question*, pp. 51-52, 67, 1914 edition, Fleming H. Revel Company) [Dr. Taylor (1885-1930) was vice-president of the Home Mission Board for the Southern Baptist Convention].

1924
A New Jersey court invoking a 1798 blue law ruled it illegal to play a phonograph or listen to the radio on Sunday if it presented "music for the sake of merriment." In Pennsylvania, the "Pittsburgh Sabbath Association" had the Pittsburgh Symphony Orchestra arrested for performing a concert on Sunday.

1925
The United States Supreme Court decreed that laws enacted by state and local governments were subject to the First Amendment through the provisions of the Fourteenth Amendment (Gitlow v. New York, 268 U.S. 652, 1925).

1929
People v Mantel (1929) 134 NY Misc Rep 529, 236 NYS 122 (Turk, j), "The cessation from all secular employment on Sunday is one of the earliest observances of the Christian world...Sunday means a Calendar day, which consists of 24 hours, and commences and ends at midnight."

1932
A Washington County, Virginia deputy sheriff arrested two women, one a crippled mother who walked with crutches—for washing clothes in their homes on Sunday.   The year prior, a policeman

arrested a boy for kicking a football on Sunday in a Philadelphia suburb. When the father protested, the... policeman shot and killed the man.

1934
46 Va. St. Bar Proceedings (1934) 199 (Hunter) "Sunday laws are not based on the Fourth Commandment"

1943
The Supreme Court confirmed that the freedom of religion guaranteed by the First Amendment also applies to the states through the Fourteenth Amendment (Thornhill v. Alabama, 310 U.S. 88, 1940; Cantwell v. Connecticut, 310 U.S. 296, 1940; Douglas v. Jeannette, 319 U.S. 157, 1943; Murdock v. Pennsylvania, 319 U.S. 105, 1943).   H. B. Clark, *Biblical Law: "Being a test of the statutes, ordinances, and judgments established in the Holy Bible – with many allusions to secular laws: ancient, medieval and modern – documented to the Scriptures, judicial decisions and legal literature."* BinFords & Mort, Portland, Oregon, 1943.

1947
"The 'establishment of religion' clause of the First Amendment means at least this: Neither a state nor the Federal Government can set up a church. Neither can pass laws which aid one religion, aid all religions, or prefer one religion over another. Neither can force nor influence a person to go to or remain away from church against his will or force him to profess a belief or disbelief in any religion. No person can be punished for entertaining or professing religious beliefs or disbeliefs, for church attendance or non-attendance. No tax in any amount, large or small, can be levied to support any religious institutions, whatever they may be called, or whatever form they may adopt to teach or practice religion. Neither a state nor the Federal Government can, openly or secretly, participate in the affairs of any religious organizations or groups and vice versa. In the words of Jefferson, the clause against establishment of religion by law was intended to erect 'a **wall of separation** between Church and State.' " *United States Supreme Court, Everson v. Board of Education, 330, U.S. 1, pp. 15-16 (February 10, 1947).*

1948 Supreme Court Justice Felix Frankfurter
"**Separation means separation**, not something less. Jefferson's metaphor in describing the relation between Church and State speaks of a 'wall of separation,' not of a fine line easily overstepped... 'The great American principle of eternal separation'—Elihu Root's phrase bears repetition—is one of the vital reliances of our Constitutional system for assuring unities among our people stronger than our diversities. It is the Court's duty to enforce this principle in

its full integrity." From concurring opinion of Justice Felix Frankfurter in McCollum v. Board of Education, 333 U.S. 203 (March 1948).

1960 JFK

1960 was an especially important year to the Sabbath-Sunday debate in America. John Fitzgerald Kennedy was elected as the first Catholic president of the United States. Hopes swelled among Sunday promoters; fears grew among Sabbath defenders. Significantly, that same year crucial landmark decisions were enter-tained by the Supreme Court on the issue of Sunday Law constitutionality.

1960 Violation of Church-State Separation the Issue in Sunday Law Enactments

"Often the Protestants who argue most militantly against government aid to church-sponsored institutions, such as parochial schools, see no contradiction of the principle of separation of church and state in their advocacy of blue laws—Sunday closing laws— which are in the last analysis nothing but the legislation of what such Protestants take to be Christian morality." (Ronal Goetz, *An Eschatological Manifesto*, in *The Christian Century*, 76 (November 2, 1960), 1274).

In 1961, the Supreme Court finally decided on two lower court cases challenging the constitutionality of Sunday closing laws. After a lengthy analysis of the origins and nature of Sunday laws the Supreme Court acknowledged that Sunday laws have a religious origin, quoting from various state and colonial laws that referred to the "Lord's Day," prohibitions against "profaning the Sabbath" and other obviously religious language. Justice Douglas dissenting in McGowan v. Maryland, stated: "The Court picks and chooses language from various decisions to bolster its conclusion that these Sunday laws in the modern setting are 'civil regulations.' No matter how much is written, no matter what is said, the parentage of these laws is the Fourth Commandment; and they serve and satisfy the religious predispositions of our Christian communities... It seems to me plain that by these laws the States compel one, under sanction of law, to refrain from work or recreation on Sunday because of the majority's religious views about that day."

But the Court concluded that the motivation behind Sunday laws in the 1960s had changed to that of protecting workers' rights. Thus, in the majority opinion, current Sunday Laws are not guilty of establishing religious doctrine or belief.

Amazingly, the Court also managed to rule that Sunday laws do not violate the Equal Protection Clause nor the Free Exercise of Religion Clause of the Constitution (Braunfeld v. Brown). The decision also was not unanimous. Justices Stewart and Brennan dissented to the Braunfeld opinion. Justice Steward wrote, "I think the impact of this [Sunday] law upon these appellants grossly violates their constitutional right to the free exercise of their religion."

The detailed opinions of these dissenting justices are presented here because of the valuable arguments they contain.

1960 Supreme Court Justice William O. Douglas:

"The question is not whether one day out of seven can be imposed by a State as a day of rest. The question is not whether Sunday can by force of custom and habit be retained as a day of rest. The question is whether a State can impose criminal sanctions on those who, unlike the Christian majority that makes up our society, worship on a different day or do not share the religious scruples of the majority.

"The fact that a State, and not the Federal Government, has promulgated these Sunday laws does not change the scope of the power asserted. For the classic view is that the First Amendment should be applied to the States with the same firmness as it is enforced against the Federal Government." *See Lovell v. Griffin, 303 U.S. 444, 450; Minersville District v. Gobitis, 310 U.S. 586, 593; Murdock v. Pennsylvania, 319 U.S. 105, 108; Board of Education v. Barnette, 319 U.S. 624, 639; Staub v. City of Baxley, 355 U.S. 313, 321; Talley v. California, 362 U.S. 60.* The most explicit statement perhaps was in *Board of Education v. Barnette, supra, 639.*

"I do not see how a State can make protesting citizens refrain from doing innocent acts on Sunday because the doing of those acts offends sentiments of their Christian neighbors.

"The institutions of our society are founded on the belief that there is an authority higher than the authority of the State; that there is a moral law which the State is powerless to alter; that the individual possesses rights, conferred by the Creator, which government must respect. The Declaration of Independence stated the now familiar theme: 'We hold these Truths to be self-evident, that all Men are created equal, that they are endowed by their Creator with certain unalienable Rights, that among these are Life, Liberty, and the Pursuit of Happiness.'

"But those who fashioned the Constitution decided that if and when God is to be served, His service will not be motivated by coercive measures of government. 'Congress shall make no law respecting an establishment of religion, or prohibiting the free exercise thereof'— such is the command of the First Amendment made applicable to the State by reason of the Due Process Clause of the Fourteenth. This means, as I understand it, that if a religious leaven is to be worked into the affairs of our people, it is to be done by individuals and groups, not by the Government. This necessarily weakens his choosing of his own religion; second, that the State may not require anyone to practice a religion or any religion; and third, that the State cannot compel one so to conduct himself as not to offend the religious scruples of another. The idea, as I understand it, was to limit the power of government to act in religious matters (*Board of Education v. Barnette, supra; McCollum v. Board of Education, 333 U.S. 203*), not to limit the freedom of religious men to act religiously nor to restrict the freedom of atheists or agnostics.

"The First Amendment commands government to have no interest in theology or ritual;... On matters of this kind government must be neutral... Certainly the 'free exercise' clause does not require that everyone embrace the theology of some church or of some faith, or observe the religious practices of any majority or minority sect... The 'establishment' clause protects citizens also against any law which selects any religious custom, practice, or ritual, puts the force of government behind it, and fines, imprisons, or otherwise penalizes a person for not observing it. The Government could not join forces with one religious group and decree a universal and symbolic circumcision. Nor could it require all children to be baptized or give tax exemptions only to those whose children were baptized.

"This religious influence has extended far, far back of the First and Fourteenth Amendments. Every Sunday School student knows the Fourth Commandment:

> 'Remember the sabbath day, to keep it holy. Six days shalt thou labour, and do all thy work: But the seventh day is the sabbath of the Lord thy God: In it, thou shalt not do any work, thou, nor thy son, nor thy daughter, thy manservant, nor thy maidservant, nor thy cattle, nor thy stranger that is within thy gates: For in six days the Lord made heaven and earth.' —*Exodus 20:8-11*

396 Sabbath Diagnosis ❼

"This religious mandate for observance of the Seventh Day became, under Emperor Constantine, a mandate for observance of the First Day...The history was accurately summarized a century ago by Chief Justice Terry of the Supreme Court of California in *Ex parte Newman, 9 Cal. 502, 509:*

"The truth is, however much it may be disguised, that this one day of rest is a purely religious idea. Derived from the Sabbatical institutions of the ancient Hebrew, it has been adopted into all the creeds of succeeding religious sects throughout the civilized world; and whether it be the Friday of the Mohammedan, the Saturday of the Israelite, or the Sunday of the Christian, it is alike fixed in the affections of its followers..."

"That case involved the validity of a Sunday law under a provision of the California Constitution guaranteeing the 'free exercise' of religion. *California Constitution, 1849, Art. 1, sect. 4.* Justice Burnett stated why he concluded that the Sunday law, there sought on Sunday, infringed California's constitution.

" 'The fact that the Christian voluntarily keeps holy the first day of the week, does not authorize the Legislature to make that observance compulsory. The Legislature can not compel the citizen to do that which the Constitution leaves him free to do or omit, at his election. The act violates as much the religious freedom of the Christian as of the Jew. Because the conscientious views of the Christian compel him to keep Sunday as a Sabbath, he has the right to object, when the Legislature invades his freedom of religious worship, and assumes the power to compel him to do that which he has the right to omit if he pleases. The principle is the same, whether the act of the Legislature compels us to do that which we wish to do, or not to do...

" '**Under the Constitution of this State, the Legislature can not** pass any act, the legitimate effect of which is forcibly to establish any merely religious truth, or enforce any merely religious observances. The Legislature has no power over such a subject. When, therefore, the citizen is sought to be compelled by the Legislature to do any affirmative religious act, or to refrain from doing anything, because it violates simply a religious principle or observance—**the act is unconstitutional.**'

"**The State can of course require one day of rest a week**: one day when every shop or factory is closed. Quite a few States make that requirement. Then the 'day of rest' becomes purely and simply a health measure. But the Sunday laws operate differently. They force minorities to obey the majority's religious feelings of what is due and proper for a Christian community; they provide a coercive spur... Can there be any doubt that Christians, now aligned vigorously in favor of these laws, would be as strongly opposed if they were prosecuted under a Moslem law that forbade them from engaging in secular activities on days that violated Moslem scruples?" *William O. Douglas, United States Supreme Court, in McGowan v. Maryland, U.S. Supreme Court, October Term, 1960 (May 29, 1961), 366 U.S., 420, at pp. 561-581.*

1960 Supreme Court Justice William J. Brennan

"The Court has demonstrated the public need for a weekly surcease from worldly labor, and set forth the considerations of convenience which have led the Commonwealth of Pennsylvania to fix Sunday as the time for that respite. I would approach this case differently, from the point of view of the individuals whose liberty is—concededly—curtailed by these enactments, For the values of the First Amendment, as embodied in the Fourteenth, look primarily towards the preservation of personal liberty, rather than towards the fulfillment of collective goals.

"The appellants are small retail merchants, faithful practitioners of the Orthodox Jewish faith. They allege—and the allegation must be taken as true, since the case comes to us on a motion to dismiss the complaint—that '...one who does not observe the Sabbath [by refraining from labor on the Seventh day]... cannot be an Orthodox Jew.'... The issue in this case—and we do not understand either appellees or the Court to contend otherwise—is whether a State may put an individual to a choice between his business and his religion. The Court today holds that it may. But I dissent, believing that such a law prohibits the free exercise of religion.

"The first question to be resolved, however is somewhat broader than the facts of this case. That question concerns the appropriate standard of constitutional adjudication in cases in which a statute is assertedly in conflict with the First Amendment, whether that limitation applies of its own force, or as absorbed through the less definite words of the Fourteenth Amendment. The Court in such cases is not confined to the narrow inquiry whether the challenged law is rationally related to some legitimate legislative end. Nor is the case decided by a finding that the State's interest is substantial and important, as well as rationally justifiable. This canon of adjudication was clearly stated by Mr. Justice Jackson, speaking for the Court in *West Virginia State Board of Education v. Barnette, 319 U.S. 624, 639 (1943)*:

'In weighing arguments of the parties it is important to distinguish between the due process of the Fourteenth Amendment as an instrument for transmitting the principles of the First Amendment, and those cases in which it is applied for its own sake. The test of legislation which collides with the Fourteenth Amendment, because it also collides with the principles of the First—which is much more definite than the test when only the Fourteenth is involved. Much of the vagueness of the due process clause disappears when the specific prohibitions of the First become its standard. The right of a State to regulate, for example, a public utility may well include, so far as the due process test is concerned, power to impose all of the restrictions which a legislature may have a 'rational basis' for adopting. But freedoms of speech and of press, of assembly, and of worship may not be infringed on such slender grounds. They are susceptible of restriction only to prevent grave and immediate danger to interests which the State may lawfully protect. It is important to note that while it is the Fourteenth Amendment which bears directly upon the State it is the more specific limiting principles of the First Amendment that finally govern this case.'

"This exacting standard has been consistently applied by this Court as the test of legislation under all clauses of the First Amendment, not only those specifically dealing with freedom of speech and of the press. For religious freedom—the freedom to believe and to practice different and, it may be, foreign creeds—has classically been one of the highest values of our society. *See, e. g., Murdock v. Pennsylvania, 319 U.S. 105, 115 (1943); Jones v. City of Opelika, 319 U.S. 103 (1943); Martin v. City of Struthers, 319 U.S. 141 (1943); Follett v. Town of McCormick, 321 U.S. 573 (1944); Marsh v. Alabama, 326 U.S. 501, 510 (1946).* Even the most concentrated and fully articulated attack on this high standard has seemingly admitted its validity in principle, while deploring some incidental phraseology. *See Kovacs v. Cooper, 336 U.S. 77, 89, 95-96 (1949) [concurring opinion]; but cf. Ullmann v. United States, 350 U.S. 422 (1956).* The honored place of religious freedom in our constitutional hierarchy, suggested long ago by the argument of counsel in *Permoli v. Municipality No. 1 of the City of New Orleans, 3 How. 598, 600 (1845),* and foreshadowed by a prescient footnote in *United States v, Carolene Products Co., 304 U.S. 144, 152, n. 4 (1938),* must now be taken to be settled. Or at least so it appeared until today. For in this case the Court seems to say, without so much as a deferential nod towards that high place which we have accorded religious freedom in the past, that any substantial state interest will justify encroachments on religious practice, at least if those encroachments are cloaked in the guise of some nonreligious public purpose.

"Admittedly, these laws do not compel overt affirmation of a repugnant belief, as in *Barnette*, nor do they prohibit outright any of appellants' religious practices, as did the federal law upheld in *Reynolds v. United States, 98 U.S. 145 (1878)*, cited by the Court. That is, the laws do not say that appellants must work on Saturday. But their effect is that appellants may not simultaneously practice their religion and their trade, without being hampered by a substantial competitive disadvantage. Their effect is that no one may at one and the same time be an Orthodox Jew and compete effectively with his Sunday-observing fellow tradesmen. This clog upon the exercise of religion, this state-imposed burden on Orthodox Judaism, has exactly the same economic effect as a tax levied upon the sale of religious literature. And yet, such a tax, when applied in the form of an excise or license fee, was held invalid in *Follett v. Town of McCormick, supra.* All this the Court, as I read its opinion, concedes.

"What then is the compelling state interest which impels the Commonwealth of Pennsylvania to impede appellants' freedom of worship? What overbalancing need is so weighty in the constitutional scale that it justifies this substantial, though indirect, limitation of appellants' freedom? It is not the desire to stamp out a practice deeply abhorred by society, such as polygamy, as in *Reynolds*, for the custom of resting one day a week is universally honored, as the Court has amply shown. Nor is it the State's traditional protection of children, as in *Prince v. Massachusetts, 321 U.S. 158 (1944)*, for appellants are reasoning and fully autonomous adults. It is not even the interest in seeing that everyone rest one day a week, for appellants' religion requires that they take such a rest. It is the mere convenience of having everyone rest on the same day. It is to defend this interest that the Court holds that a State need not follow the alternative route of granting an exemption for those who in good faith observe a day of rest other than Sunday.

"It is true, I suppose, that the granting of such an exemption would make Sundays a little noisier, and the task of police and prosecutor a little more difficult. It is also true that a majority—21—of the 34 States which have general Sunday regulations have exemptions of this kind. We are not told that those States are significantly noisier, or that their police are significantly more burdened, than Pennsylvania's. Even England, not under the compulsion of a written constitution, but simply influenced by considerations of fairness, has such an exemption for some activities. The Court conjures up several difficulties with such a system which seem to me more fanciful than real.... However widespread the complaint, it is legally baseless, and the State's reliance upon it cannot withstand a First Amendment claim.

"In fine, the Court, in my view, has exalted administrative convenience to a constitutional level high enough to justify making one's religion economically disadvantageous. The Court would justify this result on the ground that the effect on religion, though substantial, is indirect. The Court forgets, I think, a warning uttered during the congressional discussion of the First Amendment itself: '...the rights of conscience are, in their nature, of peculiar delicacy, and will little bear the gentlest touch of governmental hand...." (William J. Brenner, *Dissenting opinion in Braunfeld v. Brown,* U.S. Supreme Court, October Term, 1960 (May 29, 1961), 366 U.S. 599, at pp. 610-616) *[Justice Potter Stewart joined in this dissent].*

1961 Maryland Sunday Closing Laws Constitutional
The U. S. Supreme Court decision in *McGowan v. Maryland,* 366 U. S. 420 (1961) upheld Maryland's Sunday Closing Laws as not violating the Federal Constitution because Sunday has become secularized in American society. That "the day is one of relaxation rather than religion."

1985
"All Americans would do well to petition the President and the Congress to make a Federal law—an amendment to the Constitution if need be—to re-establish the Sabbath [meaning Sunday here] as a national Day of Rest." *Catholic Twin Circle,* August 25, 1985, Article "Sacking Sunday."

1994
"In respecting religious liberty and the common good of all, Christians should seek recognition of Sundays and the Church's holy days as legal holidays." *Catechism of the Catholic Church,* 1994, p. 585.

Sunday Common Ground
Regardless of the historical tension between Catholics and Protestants, both agree on Sunday sanctity. Since the fourth century the majority of Christians have observed Sunday. The mother Roman Church claims responsibility and authority for changing the worship day from the apostolic seventh-day Sabbath. This has been the Church's official position since the Reformation.

Even Protestant scholars agree that Rome made the change contrary to the teaching of Scripture. But in recent years the Vatican has changed tactics. The appeal to Church authority has been played down and a surprising switch to Biblical support is now being presented—just the same as the traditional Protestant position.

Sunday is thus becoming a bridge to reconciliation between Protestants and Catholics. The issues of pro-life anti-abortion and Sunday observance now form the foundation of a new alliance between the Roman Church and evangelical Protestantism. Over half of all Americans ascribe to and identify with this joint platform.

The 'Man of the Year' Pope John-Paul II has become an icon of moral stability, worshipped by massive crowds wherever he goes, identified as a major architect of communism's downfall, courted by politicians and religious leaders as the last hope for international peace.

John-Paul has served notice of his priority to restore Sunday observance and mass attendance through civil legislation when he published in May, 1998 his pastoral letter *Dies Domini*—the Day of the Lord.

In Catholic *Canon Law,* attending Sunday mass is a 'grave obligation' and non-attendance is considered a sin. But in *Dies Domini* the Pope not only urges Christians to come back to Church and fill up the pews but "strive to ensure that civil legislation respects their duty to keep Sunday holy." It does not matter that only God can 'make something holy' because the pope claims to be God on earth.

Deis Domini 1998
Detroit News, July 7

"In a day when computer modems are never fast enough and no one seems to have enough time for a full night's rest, Pope John Paul II is issuing a stern warning to Catholics that they should set aside Sunday for worship— not errands or their free time. "This really is an extraordinary move," said Jay McNally, executive director of Call to Holiness, a Metro Detroit lay group that promotes traditional Catholic teachings. "This appears to be the strongest words the Pope has issued. Period."

"The pontiff used his weekly address Sunday from his window over St. Peter's Square to urge church members to make time to keep the Sabbath holy. And today, the Vatican is expected to issue an Apostolic letter from the pope further stressing the Third Commandment. Apostolic letters are incorporated into church rules.

"Sundays have come to be 'felt and lived only as a weekend,' John Paul lamented Sunday. 'It (should be) the weekly day in which the church celebrates the resurrection of Christ. In obedience to the Third Commandment, Sunday must be sanctified, above all, by participation in Holy Mass.'

"In his letter, the pope goes on to say a violator should be 'punished as a heretic,' said McNally, who read an unofficial English translation of the letter on a Vatican web site. "...Though the pope's letter is directed at Catholics, his concerns reach beyond the Vatican and into other religions." *Detroit News on July 7, 1998.*

Legislation, of course, is written by the civil authorities. Addressing some 15,000 public officials from around the world in November 2000 Pope John Paul told the political leaders that they must conform civil laws and policies to God's objective moral law as interpreted by Rome. Soviet Union president Mikhail Gorbachev responded by challenging the assembly with their marching orders for the twenty-first century: to unite morality with politics.

The *Christian Coalition of America* also wants to see Sunday protected. A surprising number of Roman Catholics are members of the Protestant based *Coalition*. A grass-roots ground swell for Sunday laws is very likely to succeed in the US given the nature of politicians to protect the security of their positions regardless of the moral, ethical, legal or constitutional implications.

"The Pope has power to change times, to abrogate (change) laws, and to dispense with all things, even the precepts of Christ."

"The Pope has authority and has often exercised it, to dispense with the command of Christ." Lucius Ferraris, *Ecclesiastical Dictionary, Decretal, de Tranlatic Episcop*, 1755.

1990 Supreme Court
In 1990 the Supreme Court decided Employment Division v. Smith. Once again the High Court confirmed its 1961 position. Justice Scalia writing for the majority opinion used Sunday laws as an example of the types of laws that impact on people's ability to practice their faith but that are nevertheless constitutional. He stated: "Subsequent decisions have consistently held that the right of free exercise does not relieve an individual of the obligation to comply with a 'valid and neutral law of general applicability'... In Braunfeld v. Brown,... we upheld Sunday-closing laws against the claim that they burdened the religious practices of persons whose religions compelled them to refrain from work on other days."

State laws controlling recreational activities on Sunday, though frequently not enforced, are still on the books in many states. They cover a large number of sports events including shooting, hunting, card playing or racing, football, tennis, golf, theatrical events, circuses, shows, basketball, hockey, skating, field contests, bowling, motion pictures, wrestling, swimming, opera, soccer, auto racing, plays, ballet, acrobatic feats, and polo.

On any given Sunday a significant number of Americans could once again be arrested as "criminals for a day"—simply for doing something on Sunday which would be perfectly legal any other day. In South Dakota, for example, baseball is not only forbidden, but any citizen that advertises it or owns the ball park it is held in, is liable for criminal action. In Maine, inn holders are faced with threatened punishment for the "crimes" of their guests who spend Sunday "idly at play or doing any secular business."

Some of the phrases used on the state law books within the past few years are listed here:

Arkansas:	"Sabbath-breaking", "Christian Sabbath."
Colorado:	"Sabbath day."
Delaware:	"worldly activity."
Florida:	"proper observance of the Sabbath."
Maryland:	"Sabbath day."
Massachusetts:	"Lord's Day" and "secular business."
Michigan:	"secular business."
Minnesota:	"breaks the Sabbath."
New York:	"Sabbath breaking."
North Carolina:	"Lord's day."
North Dakota:	"Sabbath breaking."
Oklahoma:	"Sabbath breaking."
Pennsylvania:	"worldly employment."
Rhode Island:	"breakers of the Sabbath."
South Carolina:	"Sabbath day" and "worldly labor."
South Dakota:	"Sabbath breaking" and "worldly uses."
Tennessee:	"work on the Sabbath."
Vermont:	"secular business."
Washington:	"observance of the Sabbath."
West Virginia:	"On a Sabbath day."
Wyoming:	"desecration of the Sabbath day."

Thirty years (1960-1990) has not changed the Supreme Court's position. It reconfirmed that such laws are still constitutional. The only reason they are not being enforced and nationalized is that currently the US public simply does not favor Sunday laws. Americans like to spend their Sundays in recreation, shopping in the malls, doing their own thing. Some states have even declared their Sunday closing laws as unconstitutional. One state concluded "Sunday as a day of rest has crashed with today's technological advances and the busy lives in which we all find ourselves immersed."

But when the public mood changes, however, Sunday laws can be enforced with criminal penalties without any resistance from the courts.

2001 Petition
The following appeal was authored by Diana Hardman of Beale AFB, CA. It was originally addressed to such notables as Dianne Feinstein, Gray Davis, and Dick Cheney. It was posted as a petition running from 7/30/2001 – 1/1/2002.

> "...I believe that the government should step in and make Sunday a day of rest where all businesses must be closed. Everything must be closed on Sundays, including all gas stations, grocery stores, department stores, small business, and large businesses. We need a day when people are forced to spend time with their families. I believe that this world would be a better place if people would spend more time with their families and less time working. TV is another obstacle in families spending time together. But that's another issue. I would like to see a new law in government in the near future to force all businesses to be closed on Sundays so that nobody has to work on the Sabbath."

ISO Seventh Day Sunday
The International Standards Organization has officially designated Monday as the first day of the week under ISO 8601:1988(E).

5.4 Combinations of date and time of day representations
    3.0 Terms and Definitions
    3.17 Week Calendar
    "A seven day period within a calendar year, starting on Monday and identified by the ordinal number within a year..."

European countries, such as Denmark, Norway and Sweden have adopted Monday as the first day of the week.

In the US ANSI (X3.30) and NIST (FIPS 4-1) are standards organizations that also have adopted ISO 8601. However, calendars have continued to position Sunday as the first day of the week.

Catholic World News posted this article on Dec 19, 2002:
Italian religious and political leaders have been caught up in a heated debate about the observance of the Sabbath.

The European Union has set up the policy that every member-state must have one day of rest during the week. But the policy explicitly states that the designated day need not be Sunday, since a nation's government under "religious pluralism" might choose another day.

In Italy, the designation of Sunday as a "day of rest" was first set in 1993. That policy was changed in 2000, however, when—in order to grant more flexibility for employers—the nation required only that every employer produce workers with a 24-hour rest period each week. But by August 2003, under the new European policy, Italy will again be required to fix a certain "day of rest."

Corriere della Sera, Bishop Giancarlo Bregantini—who heads a committee dealing with social issues for the Italian bishops' conference—...said that any move away from the Sunday rest would be "a perverse act."

Worship Showdown

Such efforts have surfaced periodically and are indicative of the prevailing mood that prophecy depicts will be demonstrated during the final events in eschatological history. Revelation 13 describes a renewed (revived) interest in things religious at the end of time.

"All the world wondered after the beast. And they worshiped the dragon...and they worshiped the beast...And all that dwell upon the earth shall worship him." Rev. 13:3,4,8.

Recognition of God's Creatorship has always been the basis for His worship. *"O come, let us worship and bow down: let us kneel before the Lord our Maker."* Psalm 95:6. *"Thou art worthy, O Lord, to receive glory and honor and power: for Thou hast created all things."* Rev. 4:11. But Revelation 13 describes a competing power seeking worship.

The "great dragon, that old serpent, called the Devil and Satan" (Rev. 12:9) has since the very beginning aspired to be the object of worship. *"I will ascend into heaven, I will exalt my throne above the stars of God: I will sit also upon the mount of the congregation...I will ascend above the heights of the clouds: I will be like the most High!"* (Isa 14:13,14). *"All these things will I give you, if you will fall down and worship me,"* was his offer to Jesus (Matt. 4:9). Finally, at the end of time, he will achieve his goal of world-wide hero worship, idolized by the masses, exalting *"himself above all that is called God, or that is worshiped; so that he as God sits in the temple of God, showing himself that he is God."* (2 Thess 2:4).

The Lord's Day showdown will be a critical factor in this last act in the drama. The final messages of warning to this world begin with an invitation to reverence God, give glory to Him, and worship Him who rose from the dead on the first day of the week? No. *"Worship Him who made heaven, and earth, and the sea."* Revelation 14:6. Worship the Creator on the Creator's day, the Lord's day.

Associated with the issue of enforced, legislated worship is an ominous threat to any would-be dissidents: *"...and cause that as many as would not worship the image of the beast should be killed"* Rev. 13:15.

It is clearly shown that at the end there will be two forces prescribing worship to the inhabitants of Earth. A major faction will appear to draw allegiance from nearly every person on the planet to worship the beast and his image at the pain of death. But a small number patiently maintain their loyalty, not to the earth's political party boss, but to its Creator. *"Here is the patience of the saints: here are they that keep the commandments of God, and the faith of Jesus."* Rev. 14:12.

At the same time "Mary" plans to lead her people back to the keeping what she calls "My Commandments":

> "In those days there will be one Shepherd and one Faith, that of the Roman Catholic Church, which I established when I walked visibly on the earth... My sons and My daughters will keep My Commandments." Ted and Maureen Flynn, *Thunder of Justice*, 1993, ISBN: 096343070X, p. 354.

A key feature of "Mary's" message focuses on the Sabbath:

> "This is where we see many of the root causes of our problems: it is in the commandment of 'KEEPING THE SABBATH HOLY.' In the Old Testament, not honoring this day was punishable by death... There is widespread abuse all throughout the Christian culture concerning the Sabbath... we have lost God" *Ibid*, p. 389.

But the Sabbath mentioned here is Sunday not the Sabbath of the Bible. This is not surprising when we consider that these are the words of an "apparition," a "familiar spirit" who endorses the institution of her creation. She also predicts that

> "After three days of darkness Saint Peter and Saint Paul, having come down from Heaven, shall preach in the whole world and designate a new Pope. A great light will flash from their bodies and will settle upon the cardinal who is to become Pope. Christianity then, will spread throughout the world." *Ibid*, p. 353.

These messages are a prelude to prophetic fulfillment. Paul warned that "such are false apostles, deceitful workers transforming themselves into the apostles of Christ. And no marvel; for Satan himself is transformed into an angel of light." 2 Cor. 11:13,14. No marvel, indeed. It is no mystery why the Sabbath debate is once again intensifying. The celestial message of the first angel can even now be heard loud and clear.

Progress Notes

Chronological Review of the Patient's Course

40th Century BC
Creation Sabbath

"Thus the heavens and the earth were finished, and all the host of them. And on the seventh day God ended his work which he made; and he rested on the seventh day from all his work which he had made. And God blessed the seventh day, and sanctified it: because that in it he had rested from all his work which God created and made." Genesis 2:1-3.

"For in six days the LORD made heaven and earth, the sea, and all that in them is, and rested the seventh day: wherefore the LORD blessed the sabbath day, and hallowed it." Exodus 20:11.

Worship the Creator

"The 24 elders fall down before him that sat on the throne, and worship him that liveth for ever and ever, and cast their crowns before the throne, saying, Thou art worthy, O Lord, to receive glory and honor and power: for thou hast created all things, and for thy pleasure they are and were created." Revelation 4:10, 11.

"O come, let us worship and bow down: let us kneel before the Lord our maker" Psalm 95:6.

"He has made His wonderful works to be remembered" Psalm 111:4.

28th Century BC
Enoch, the Seventh

"And Enoch also, the seventh from Adam, prophesied of these, saying, Behold, the Lord cometh with ten thousands of his saints." Judges 1:14 [*Even the Sabbath patriarch exhibited a Messianic significance in the subject of his prophecy and focused on the event that will epitomize Sabbath rest and restoration.*]

25th Century BC
Noah, 10th Patriarch

Noah, whose name means "rest," waits six days inside the ark. On the seventh day the flood rains began to fall. Genesis 7:4, 10, 11.

The Ark comes to "rest" on Mount Ararat on exactly the 21st week anniversary of entering the Ark. Genesis 8:4.

Noah releases a raven and three doves on the 36th-39th week anniversaries. Genesis 8:6-12.

Noah removes the covering from the ark on the 43rd Sabbath anniversary of entering. Genesis 8:13.

Noah and seven others leave the ark on exactly the 52nd weekly Sabbath anniversary of entering the ark. Genesis 8:14.

18th Century BC
Abraham, 20th Patriarch
Abraham gave seven ewe lambs to Abimelech in a covenant for the well he dug at Beersheba. Genesis 21:28-31.

16th Century BC
Jacob served seven years for each of his two wives. Gen. 29:20, 27. Jacob fulfilled a week of marriage festivities for each wife. Gen. 29:21. Laban spent seven days chasing after Jacob. Gen. 31:23-24.

Joseph's familiarity with the Sabbath week enables him to correctly interpret Pharaoh's dream of seven pairs of cow and corn. Gen. 31:23-24.

Jacob recognizes in Issachar, his seventh son, one who appreciated the blessing of rest. Gen 49:14, 15.
Egypt mourns for Jacob seventy days. Gen. 50:3.
Joseph mourns an additional seven days. Gen. 50:10.

14th Century BC
Exodus
"for six days you shall do your work and labour, but on the seventh day you shall rest, and shall not perform any work: thus shall you do in all the days, as the king and Moses the son of Bathia have commanded." *Book of Jasher* 70:41-51. M.M. Noah and A.S. Gould, New York, 1840.

Pharaoh charged Moses, "You make them rest from their burdens!" Exodus 5:5.

Land Sabbath in Caanan
"When you come into the land which I give you, then shall the land keep a sabbath unto the Lord. Six years you shall sow your field, and six years you shall prune your vineyard, and gather in its fruits; but in the seventh year shall be a sabbath of rest unto the land...you shall neither sow your field nor prune your vineyard." Leviticus 25:2.
"And you shall hallow the fiftieth year and proclaim liberty throughout all the land: it shall be a jubilee unto you." Leviticus 25:10.

"Then I will command my blessing upon you in the sixth year, and it shall bring forth fruit for three years." Leviticus 25:21.

Samson celebrated his marriage seven days. Judges 14:15, 17, 18.

10th Century BC
Samuel instructs Saul to wait for him seven days. 1 Samuel 10:8.
Samuel again asks Saul to wait seven days. 1 Samuel 13:8.
Men of Jabesh Gilead mourn at Saul's death for seven days. 1 Sam. 31:13.

Solomon, "a man of rest," (1 Chron 22:9) dedicated the finished temple in the seventh month, followed by a seven day feast (2 Chron 7:8) and kept the dedication of the altar another seven days, "and the feast seven days." Verse 9.

7th Century BC
"And this shall be a sign unto thee, Ye shall eat this year such as groweth of itself; and the second year that which springeth of the same: and in the third year sow ye, and reap, and plant vineyards, and eat the fruit thereof."   Isaiah 37:30   *[Sennecharib, king of Assyria, is defeated during a Sabbatical-Jubilee year in 702 BC]*

6th Century BC
"Blessed is the man that does this, and the son of man that layeth hold on it; that keepeth the Sabbath." Isaiah 56:2.

Nebuchadnezzar destroyed Solomon's temple and took captives to Babylon in 586 BC "to fulfill the word of the Lord by the mouth of Jeremiah, until the land had enjoyed her sabbaths: for as long as she lay desolate she kept sabbath, to fulfill 70 years." 2 Chronicles 36:21.

1st Century AD
Jesus
"And he came to Nazareth, where he had been brought up: and, as his custom was, he went into the synagogue on the Sabbath day, and stood up to read." Luke 4:16.

"The Spirit of the Lord is upon me, because he has anointed me to preach the gospel to the poor; he has sent me to heal the broken-hearted, to preach deliverance to the captives and recovering of sight to the blind, **to** set at liberty them that are bruised, to preach the acceptable year of the Lord." Luke 4:16, Isaiah 61:1,2.; cf Leviticus 25:10.

"And, behold, one came and said unto him, Good Master, what good thing shall I do that I may have eternal life? And he said unto him, if thou wilt enter into life, keep the commandments." Matthew 19:16,17.

"The Sabbath was made for man. Therefore the son of man is Lord also of the Sabbath." Mark 2:27, 28.

"But pray ye that your flight be not in winter, neither on the Sabbath day." Matthew 24, 20. This flight took place in 70 AD, 40 years after the Cross.

His Followers
"And they returned, and prepared spices and ointments and rested the Sabbath day according to the commandment." Luke 23:56.

Paul
"And Paul, as his manner was went in unto them, and three Sabbath days reasoned with them out of the Scriptures" Acts 17:2.

Gentiles
"And when the Jews were gone out of the synagogue, the Gentiles besought that these words might be preached to them the next Sabbath... And the next Sabbath came almost the whole city together to hear the Word of God." Acts 13:42, 44.

Here we find Gentiles in a Gentile city gathering on the Sabbath. This was not a synagogue meeting. The Bible does not say it is the "old Jewish Sabbath that was passed away," but the Book of Acts some 30 years after the Crucifixion, calls it "the next Sabbath."

John
"I was in the Spirit on the Lord's day." Revelation 1:10.
Mark 2:28, Isa.58:13, Ex.20:10, Clearly show the Sabbath to be the Lord's day.

Josephus
"Moses says that in just six days the world and all that is therein was made. And that the seventh day was a rest and a release from the labour of such operations. WHENCE it is that we celebrate a rest from our labour on that day, and call it the Sabbath; which word denotes rest in the Hebrew tongue." Josephus, *Antiquities of the Jews,* Book 1, Chapter 1, Section 1.

"There is not any city of the Grecians, nor any of the Barbarians, nor any nation whatsoever, whither our custom of resting on the seventh day hath not come." Works of Flavius Josephus (Winston editor) Book 2, par. 40.

PHILO
Declares **the seventh day to be a festival**, not of this or of that city, but **of the universe**. M'Clatchie, "*Notes and Queries on China and Japa*" (edited by Dennys), 1867, Vol. 4, No. 7, 8, p. 99.

Early Primitive Christians

"The primitive Christians had a great veneration for the Sabbath, and spent the day in devotion and sermons. And it is not to be doubted but they derived this practice from the Apostles themselves, as appears by several Scriptures to the purpose." *Dialogues on the Lord's Day*, p. 189. London: 1701, By Dr. T.H. Morer (A Church of England divine).

"...The Sabbath was a strong tie which united them with the life of the whole people, and in keeping the Sabbath holy they followed not only the example but also the command of Jesus." *Geschichte des Sonntags*, pp.13, 14.

2nd Century

"The Gentile Christians observed also the Sabbath," Gieseler's *Church History*, Vol.1, ch. 2, par. 30, 93.

"The primitive Christians did keep the Sabbath of the Jews;...therefore the Christians, for a long time together, did keep their conventions upon the Sabbath, in which some portions of the law were read: and this continued till the time of the Laodicean council." *The Whole Works of Jeremy Taylor*, Vol. IX, p. 416 (R. Heber's Edition, Vol XII, p. 416).

"It is certain that the ancient Sabbath did remain and was observed (together with the celebration of the Lord's day) by the Christians of the East Church, above three hundred years after our Saviour's death." Edward Brerewood, *A Learned Treatise of the Sabbath*, 1630, p. 77.

3rd, 4th Century

"From the apostles' time until the council of Laodicea, which was about the year 364, the holy observance of the Jews' Sabbath continued, as may be proved out of many authors: yea, notwithstanding the decree of the council against it." *Sunday a Sabbath*. John Ley, p.163. London: 1640.

"Thou shalt observe the Sabbath, on account of Him who ceased from His work of creation, but ceased not from His work of providence: it is a rest for meditation of the law, not for idleness of the hands." *The Anti-Nicene Fathers*, Vol 7, p. 413. From *Constitutions of the Holy Apostles*, a document of the 3rd and 4th Centuries.

"The seventh-day Sabbath was... solemnised by Christ, the Apostles, and primitive Christians, till the Laodicean Council did in manner quite abolish the observations of it." William Pryrine, *Dissertation on the Lord's Day*, 1633, p. 163.

EGYPT (OXYRHYNCHUS PAPYRUS) (200-250 A.D.)

"Except ye make the sabbath a real sabbath (sabbatize the Sabbath, Greek), ye shall not see the Father." *The oxyrhynchus Papyri*, pt,1, p.3, Logion 2, verso 4-11 (London Offices of the Egypt Exploration Fund, 1898).

AFRICA (ALEXANDRIA) ORIGEN

"After the festival of the unceasing sacrifice (the crucifixion) is put the second festival of the Sabbath, and it is fitting for whoever is righteous among the saints to keep also the festival of the Sabbath. There remaineth therefore a sabbatismus, that is, a keeping of the Sabbath, to the people of God (Hebrews 4:9)." *Homily on Numbers 23*, par.4, in Migne, *Patrologia Graeca*, Vol. 12,cols. 749, 750.

PALESTINE to INDIA (CHURCH OF THE EAST)

"As early as A.D. 225 there existed large bishoprics or conferences of the Church of the East (Sabbath-keeping) stretching from Palestine to India." A. Mingana, *The Early Spread of Christianity in India*. Manchester: 1926, Vol. 10, p. 460.

INDIA (BUDDHIST CONTROVERSY), 220 A.D.)

"The Kushan Dynasty of North India called a famous council of Buddhist priests at Vaisalia to bring uniformity among the Buddhist monks on the observance of their weekly Sabbath. Some had been so impressed by the writings of the Old Testament that they had begun to keep holy the Sabbath." Arthur Lloyd, *The Creed of Half Japan: the Historical Sketches of Japanese Buddhism*, Smith, Elder and Co. London: 1911, p. 23.

ITALY and the EAST 4th Century

"It was the practice generally of the Easterne Churches; and some churches of the west...For in the Church of Millaine (Milan);...it seems the Saturday was held in a farre esteeme... Not that the Easterne Churches, or any of the rest which observed that day, were inclined to Iudaisme (Judaism); but that they came together on the Sabbath day, to worship Iesus (Jesus) Christ the Lord of the Sabbath." Peter Heylyn, *History of the Sabbath*. (original spelling retained), Part 2, par. 5, pp.73, 74. London: 1636.

ORIENT and most of the WORLD

"The ancient Christians were very careful in the observance of Saturday, or the seventh day...It is plain that all the Oriental churches, and the greatest part of the world, observed the Sabbath as a festival...Athanasius likewise tells us that they held religious assembles on the Sabbath, not because they were infected with Judaism, but to worship Jesus, the Lord of the Sabbath, Epiphanius says the same." *Antiquities of the Christian Church*, Vol.II Book XX, chap. 3, sec.1, 66. 1137,1138.

ABYSSINIA (Ethiopia)

"In the last half of that century St. Ambrose of Milan stated officially that the Abyssinian bishop, Museus, had 'traveled almost everywhere in the country of the Seres' (China). For more than seventeen centuries the Abyssinian Church continued to sanctify Saturday as the holy day of the fourth commandment." Ambrose, *DeMoribus, Brachmanorium Opera Ominia,* 1132, found in Migne, *Patrologia Latima,* Vol.17, pp.1131,1132.

ARABIA, PERSIA, INDIA, CHINA

"Mingana proves that in 370 A.D. Abyssinian Christianity (a Sabbath keeping church) was so popular that its famous director, Musacus, travelled extensively in the East promoting the church in Arabia, Persia, India and China." Benjamin George Wilkinson, *Truth Triumphanat: The Church in the Wilderness,* 1944, p.308, fn 27.

ITALY-MILAN

"Ambrose, the celebrated bishop of Milan, said that when he was in Milan he observed Saturday, but when in Rome observed Sunday. This gave rise to the proverb, 'When you are in Rome, do as Rome does.'" Peter Heylyn, *The History of the Sabbath* (1612).

SPAIN-COUNCIL ELVIRA (A.D.305)

Canon 26 of the Council of Elvira reveals that the Church of Spain at that time kept Saturday, the seventh day. "As to fasting every Sabbath: Resolved, that the error be corrected of fasting every Sabbath." This resolution of the council is in direct opposition to the policy the church at Rome had inaugurated, that of commanding Sabbath as a fast day in order to humiliate it and make it detestable.

In north-eastern Spain near the city of Barcelona is a city called Sabadell, in a district originally inhabited by a people called both "Valldenses" and "Sabbatati."

PERSIA – A.D. 335-375

(40 years of persecution under Shapur II)
The popular complaint against the Christians: "They despise our sun god, they have divine services on Saturday, they desecrate the sacred earth by burying their dead in it." *Truth Triumphant,* p.170.

"They despise our sun-god. Did not Zorcaster, the sainted founder of our divine beliefs, institute Sunday one thousand years ago in honour of the sun and supplant the Sabbath of the Old Testament. Yet these

Christians have divine services on Saturday." O'Leary, *The Syriac Church and Fathers*, pp.83, 84.

COUNCIL LAODICEA – A.D.365
"Canon 16. On Saturday the Gospels and other portions of the Scripture shall be read aloud."
"Canon 29. Christians shall not Judaize and be idle on Saturday, but shall work on that day; but the Lord's day they shall especially honor, and as being Christians, shall, if possible, do no work on that day." Bishop Hefele's *Councils*, Vol. 2, b. 6.

5TH CENTURY
Alexandria and Rome
"For although almost all churches throughout the world celebrated the sacred mysteries (the Lord's Supper) on the Sabbath of every week, yet the Christians of Alexandria and at Rome, on account of some ancient tradition, refuse to do this." The footnote which accompanies the foregoing quotation explains the use of the word "Sabbath." It says: "That is, upon the Saturday. It should be observed, that Sunday is never called 'the Sabbath' by the ancient Fathers and historians." Socrates, *Ecclesiastical History*, Book 5, chap. 22, p. 289.

CONSTANTINOPLE
"The people of Constantinople, and almost everywhere, assemble together on the Sabbath, as well as on the first day of the week, which custom is never observed at Rome or at Alexandria." Socrates, *Ecclesiastical History*, Book 7, chap.19.

AUGUSTINE, BISHOP OF HIPPO (NORTH AFRICA)
Augustine wrote that the Sabbath was observed in his day "in the greater part of the Christian world," and his testimony in this respect is all the more valuable because he himself was an earnest and consistent Sunday-keeper. See *Nicene and Post-Nicene Fathers*, 1st Series, Vol.1, pp. 353, 354.

POPE INNOCENT (402-417)
Pope Sylvester (314-335) was the first to order the churches to fast on Saturday, and Pope Innocent (402-417) made it a binding law in the churches that obeyed him, (In order to bring the Sabbath into disfavour.) "Innocentius did ordain the Saturday or Sabbath to be always fasted." Dr. Peter Heylyn, *History of the Sabbath*, Part 2, p. 44.

Down even to the fifth century the observance of the Jewish Sabbath was continued in the Christian church. *Ancient Christianity Exemplified*, Lyman Coleman, ch. 26, sec. 2, p. 527.

In Jerome's day (420 A.D.) the devoutest Christians did ordinary work on Sunday. *Treatise of the Sabbath Day*, by Dr. White, Lord Bishop of Ely, p. 219.

FRANCE

"Wherefore, except Vespers and Nocturns, there are no public services among them in the day except on Saturday (Sabbath) and Sunday." John Cassian, A French monk, *Institutes*, Book 3, ch. 2.

AFRICA

"Augustine deplored the fact that in two neighbouring churches in Africa one observes the seventh-day Sabbath, another fasted on it." Peter Heylyn, *The History of the Sabbath*. p. 416.

SPAIN (400 A.D.)

"Ambrose sanctified the seventh day as the Sabbath (as he himself says). Ambrose had great influence in Spain, which was also observing the Saturday Sabbath." *Truth Triumphant*, p. 68.

SIDONIUS

(King Theodoric of the Goths, AD 454-526)
"It is a fact that it was formerly the custom in the East to keep the Sabbath in the same manner as the Lord's day and to hold sacred assemblies: while on the other hand, the people of the West, contending for the Lord's day have neglected the celebration of the Sabbath." *Apollinaries Sidonli Epistolae*, lib.1, 2; Migne, 57.

CHURCH OF THE EAST

"Mingana proves that in 410 Isaac, supreme director of the Church of the East, held a world council—stimulated, some think, by the trip of Musacus—attended by eastern delegates from forty grand metropolitan divisions. In 411 he appointed a metropolitan director for China. These churches were sanctifying the seventh day."

EGYPT

"There are several cities and villages in Egypt where, contrary to the usage established elsewhere, the people meet together on Sabbath evenings, and, although they have dined previously, partake of the mysteries." Sozomen. *Ecclesiastical History* Book 7, ch. 119.

6TH CENTURY
SCOTTISH CHURCH

"In this latter instance they seemed to have followed a custom of which we find traces in the early monastic church of Ireland by which they held Saturday to be the Sabbath on which they rested from all their labours." W.T. Skene, *Adamnan Life of St. Columba 1874*, p.96.

IRELAND
"We seem to see here an allusion to the custom, observed in the early monastic Church of Ireland, of keeping the day of rest on Saturday, or the Sabbath." Bellesheim, *History of the Catholic Church in Scotland*, Vol.1, p. 86, (Catholic historian).

SCOTLAND-COLULMBA
"Having continued his labours in Scotland thirty-four years, he clearly and openly foretold his death, and on Saturday, the month of June, said to his disciple Diermit: 'This day is called the Sabbath, that is the rest day, and such will it truly be to me; for it will put an end to my labours.'" *Butler's Lives of the Saints*, Vol.1, A.D. 597, art. "St. Columba" p. 762.

COLUMBA
The editor of the best biography of Colulmba says in a footnote: "Our Saturday. The custom to call the Lord's day Sabbath did not commence until a thousand years later." Adamnan's *Life of Columba* (Dublin, 1857), p. 230.

7TH – 8TH CENTURY
SCOTLAND AND IRELAND
"It seems to have been customary in the Celtic churches of early times, in Ireland as well as Scotland, to keep Saturday, the Jewish Sabbath, as a day of rest from labour. They obeyed the fourth commandment literally upon the seventh day of week." Professor James C. Moffatt, D.D., Professor of Church History at Princeton *The Church in Scotland*, p.140.

"The Celts used a Latin Bible unlike the Vulgate (R.C.) and kept Saturday as a day of rest, with special religious services on Sunday." Flick, *The Rise of Mediaeval Church*, p. 237.

ROME
Gregory I (A.D. 590-640) declared that when anti-Christ should come he would keep Saturday as the Sabbath.

"Gregory, bishop by the grace of God to his well-beloved sons, the Roman citizens: It has come to me that certain men of perverse spirit have disseminated among you things depraved and opposed to the holy faith, so that they forbid anything to be done on the day of the Sabbath. What shall I call them except preachers of anti-Christ?" *Nicene and Post- Nicene Fathers*, Second Series, *Epistles of Gregory I*, Volume or Book XIII (13), epistle 1.

This official pronouncement against the citizens of Rome was made because the Christian believers there rested and worshipped on the Sabbath.

COUNCIL OF FRIAUL, ITALY — A.D. 791 (CANON 13)
"We command all Christians to observe the Lord's day to be held not in honour of the past Sabbath, but on account of that holy night of the first of the week called the Lord's day. When speaking of that Sabbath which the Jews observe, the last day of the week, and which also our peasants observe." A. Mansi, *Sacrorum Consilorum Nova et Ampilissiren Collectio*, Vol. 13, p. 851.

PERSIA AND MESOPOTAMIA
"The hills of Persia and the valleys of the Tigris and Euphrates reechoed their songs of praise. They reaped their harvests and paid their tithes. They repaired to their churches on the Sabbath day for the worship of God." "Realencyclopaedie fur Protestatische and Krche," *The Book of ser Marco Polo*, Vol.2, art. *Nestorianer*; also *Yule*, p. 409.

INDIA, CHINA, PERSIA, ETC
"Widespread and enduring was the observance of the seventh-day Sabbath among the believers of the Church of the East and the St. Thomas Christians of India, who never were connected with Rome. It also was maintained among those bodies which broke off from Rome after the Council of Chalcedon namely, the Abyssinians, the Jacobites, the Maronites, and the Armenians," Schaff-Herzog, *The New Encyclopedia of Religious Knowledge*, art. "Nestorians"; also *Realencyclopaedie fur Protestantische Theologie und Kirche*, art. "Nestorianer."

COUNCIL OF LIFTINAE, BELGIUM — A.D.745
(Attended by Pope Boniface)
"The third allocution of this council warns against the observance of the Sabbath, referring to the decree of the council of Laodicea." Dr. Hefele, *Counciliengfesch*, 3, 512, sec. 362

CHINA — A.D.781
In A.D. 781 the famous China Monument was inscribed in marble to tell of the growth of Christianity in China at that time. The inscription, consisting of 763 words, was unearthed in 1625 near the city of Changan and now stands in the "Forest of Tablets," Changan. The following extract from the stone shows that the Sabbath was observed:

"On the seventh day we offer sacrifices, after having purified our hearts, and received absolution for our sins. This religion, so perfect and so excellent, is difficult to name, but it enlightens darkness by its brilliant precepts." M. l'Abbe Huc, *Christianity in China, Tartary and Thibet*, London: 1857, Vol. I, ch. 2, pp. 48, 49.

BULGARIA

"Bulgaria in the early season of its evangelization had been taught that no work should be performed on the Sabbath." *Responsa Nicolai Papae I* and *Con-Consulta Bulllllgarorum, Responsum 10*, found in *Mansi, Sacrorum Concilorum Nova et Amplissima Colectio*, Vol. 15; p. 406; also Hefele, *Conciliengeschicte*, Vol.4, sec. 478

Pope Nicholas I, in answer to a letter from Bogaris, ruling prince of Bulgaria:
> "Ques. 6-Bathing is allowed on Sunday.
> Ques. 10-One is to cease from work on Sunday, but not also on the Sabbath." Hefele, *Councils* 4, 346- 352, sec. 478

The Bulgarians had been accustomed to rest on the Sabbath. Pope Nicholas wrote against the practice.

CONSTANTINOPLE

Photuus, Patriarch of Constantinople (in a counter-synod that deposed Pope Nicolas), accused the Roman Papacy: "Against the canons, they induced the Bulgarians to fast on the Sabbath." Photius, vonKard, *Hergenrother*, 1, 643

Note: The Papacy had always tried to bring the seventh-day Sabbath into disrepute by insisting that all should fast on that day. In this manner she sought to turn people towards Sunday, the first day, the day that Rome had adopted.

ATHINGIANS

Cardinal Hergenrother says that they stood in intimate relation with Emperor Michael II (821-829) and testifies that they observed the Sabbath. *Kirchengeschichte*, 1, 527

INDIA, ABYSSINIA

"Widespread and enduring was the observance of the seventh-day Sabbath among the believers of the Church of the East and the St. Thomas Christians of India. It was also maintained by the Abyssinians."

AMERICAS

The Los Lunas Commandments Stone is etched in New Mexico by an unknown artisan in Phonecian-like Hebrew Script.

BULGARIA

"Pope Nicholas I, in the ninth century, sent the ruling prince of

Bulgaria a long document saying in it that one is to cease from work on Sunday, but not on the Sabbath. The head of the Greek Church, offended at the interference of the Papacy, declared the Pope excommunicated." *Truth Triumphant*, p. 232

SCOTLAND
"They worked on Sunday, but kept Saturday in a Sabbatical manner." Andrew Lang, *A history of Scotland from the Roman Occupation*, Vol. I, p.96.

CHURCH OF THE EAST – Kurdistan
"The Nestorians eat no pork and keep the Sabbath. They believe in neither auricular confession nor purgatory." Schaff-Herzog, *The New Encyclopaedia of Religious Knowledge,* art. "Nestorians."

WALDENSES
"And because they observed no other day of rest but the Sabbath days, they called them Insabathas, as much as to say, as they observed no Sabbath." Luther's *Fore-Runners* (original spelling), PP. 7, 8.

Roman Catholic writers trying to make Rome the only apostolic church and all others as simply later novelties, suggest that the Waldenses originated with Peter Waldo of the twelfth century. But historians deny such a claim.

"Some Protestants, on this occasion, have fallen into the snare that was set for them...It is absolutely false, that these churches were ever found by Peter Waldo... it is a pure forgery." Dr. Peter Allix, *Ancient Church of Piedmont*, pp.192, Oxford: 1821.

"It is not true, that Waldo gave this name to the inhabitants of the valleys: they were called Waldenses, or Vaudes, before his time, from the valleys in which they dwelt." *Ibid*, p. 182.

Others state that Peter "was called Valdus, or Waldo, because he received his religious notions from the inhabitants of the valleys." *History of the Christian Church*, William Jones, Vol II, p.2.

9TH – 11TH CENTURY
SCOTLAND
"They held that Saturday was properly the Sabbath on which they abstained from work." Skene, *Celtic Scotland*, Vol. 2, p. 350.
"They worked on Sunday, but kept Saturday in a sabbatical manner...These things Margaret abolished." *A History of Scotland from the Roman Occupation*, Vol.1, p. 96.

"It was another custom of theirs to neglect the reverence due to the Lord's day, by devoting themselves to every kind of worldly business upon it, just as they did upon other days. That this was contrary to the law, she (Queen Margaret) proved to them as well by reason as by authority. 'Let us venerate the Lord's day,' said she, 'because of the resurrection of our Lord, which happened upon that day, and let us no longer do servile works upon it; bearing in mind that upon this day we were redeemed from the slavery of the devil. The blessed Pope Gregory affirms the same.' " *Life of Saint Margaret*, Turgot, p. 49 (British Museum Library)

"Her next point was that they did not duly reverence the Lord's day, but in this latter instance they seemed to have followed a custom of which we find traces in the early Church of Ireland, by which they held Saturday to be the Sabbath on which they rested from all their labours." Skene, *Celtic Scotland*, Vol.2, p. 349.

SCOTLAND AND IRELAND
"T. Ratcliffe Barnett, in his book on the fervent Catholic queen of Scotland who in 1060 was first to attempt the ruin of Columba's brethren, writes: 'In this matter the Scots had perhaps kept up the traditional usage of the ancient Irish Church which observed Saturday instead of Sunday as the day of rest.' " Barnett, *Margaret of Scotland: Queen and Saint*, p.97.

COUNCIL OF CLERMONT
"During the first crusade, Pope Urban II decreed at the council of Clermont (A.D.1095) that the Sabbath be set aside in honour of the Virgin Mary." Heyden, *History of the Sabbath*, p.672.

CONSTANTINOPLE
"Because you observe the Sabbath with the Jews and the Lord's Day with us, you seem to imitate with such observance the sect of Nazarenes." Migne, *Patrologia Latina*, Vol. 145, p.506; also Hergenroether, *Photius*, Vol. 3, p.746. (The Nazarenes were a Christian denomination.)

GREEK CHURCH 1054 Schism
"The observance of Saturday is, as everyone knows, the subject of a bitter dispute between the Greeks and the Latins." Neale, *A History of the Holy Eastern Church*, Vol 1, p. 731. (Referring to the separation of the Greek Church from the Latin in 1054)

12TH – 13TH CENTURY
LOMBARDY
"Traces of Sabbath-keepers are found in the times of Gregory I,

Gregory VII, and in the twelfth century in Lombardy." *Strong's Cyclopaedia*, 1, 660.

WALDENSES

"Robinson gives an account of some of the Waldenses of the Alps, who were called Sabbati, Sabbatati, Insabbatati, but more frequently Inzabbatati. 'One says they were so named from the Hebrew word Sabbath, because they kept the Saturday for the Lord's day.' " *General History of the Baptist Denomination*, Vol.II, P. 413.

SPAIN (Alphonse of Aragon)

"Alphonse, king of Aragon, etc., to all archbishops, bishops and to all others... 'We command you that heretics, to wit, Waldenses and Insabbathi, should be expelled away from the face of God and from all Catholics and ordered to depart from our kingdom.'" Marianse, *Praefatio in Lucam Tudensem*, found in *Macima Gibliotheca Veterum Patrum*, Vol.25, p.190.

HUNGARY FRANCE, ENGLAND, ITALY, GERMANY.

(Referring to the Sabbath- keeping Pasagini)

"The spread of heresy at this time is almost incredible. From Bulgaria to the Ebro, from northern France to the Tiber, everywhere we meet them. Whole countries are infested, like Hungary and southern France; they abound in many other countries, in Germany, in Italy, in the Netherlands and even in England they put forth their efforts." Dr. Hahn, *Gesch. der Ketzer*. 1, 13, 14.

WALDENSES

"Among the documents. we have by the same peoples, an explanation of the Ten Commandments dated by Boyer 1120. Observance of the Sabbath by ceasing from worldly labours, is enjoined." Blair, *History of the Waldenses*, Vol.1, p. 220

WALES

"There is much evidence that the Sabbath prevailed in Wales university until AD 1115, when the first Roman bishop was seated at St. David's. The old Welsh Sabbath-keeping churches did not even then altogether bow the knee to Rome, but fled to their hiding places." Lewis, *Seventh Day Baptists in Europe and America*, Vol.1, p.29

FRANCE

"For twenty years Peter de Bruys stirred southern France. He especially emphasized a day of worship that was recognized at that time among the Celtic churches of the British Isles, among the Paulicians, and in the great Church of the East namely, the seventh day of the fourth commandment."

PASAGAINI/PASSAGII

"Not a few, but many know what are the errors of those who are called Pasaagini... First, they teach that we should obey the Sabbath. Furthermore, to increase their error, they condemn and reject all the church Fathers, and the whole Roman Church." Bonacursus quoted in D'Achery, *Spicilegium* I,f.211-214; Muratory, *Antiq. med. aevi.*5, f.152, Hahn, 3, 209.

"On down through history, groups have appeared on the scene who recognized the need to observe God's Holy Days. During the 12th and 13th centuries a sect known as the Passagii were the most concrete example of Judaic-Christianity to come on the scene. They believed the Mosaic Law should be observed and held to the literal view of the Old Testament. They kept the holy days and the dietary laws, but not the sacrificial system. They accepted the New Testament and made it their aim to harmonize the old and new dispensations. They kept the Sabbath along with other Sabbatarian groups in Hungary and in other lands. They were also located in southern France." Louis Israel Newman, *Jewish Influence on Christian Reform Movements*, 255–284.

WALDENSES

"They say that the blessed Pope Sylvester was the Antichrist of whom mention is made in the Epistles of St. Paul as having been the son of perdition. [They also say] that the keeping of the Sabbath ought to take place." *Ecclesiastical History of the Ancient Churches of Piedmont*, p.169

FRANCE (Waldenses)

To destroy completely these heretics Pope Innocent III sent Dominican inquisitors into France, and also crusaders, promising "a plenary remission of all sins, to those who took on them the crusade... against the Albigenses." *Catholic Encyclopaedia*, Vol. XII, art. "Raymond VI," p. 670

"The inquisitors... [declare] that the sign of a Vaudois, deemed worthy of death, was that he followed Christ and sought to obey the commandments of God." H.C.Les, *History of the Inquisition of the Middle Ages*, vol.1

Thousands of God's people were tortured to death by the Inquisition, buried alive, burned to death, or hacked to pieces by the crusaders. While devastating the city of Biterre the soldiers asked the Catholic leaders how they should know who were heretics; "Slay them all, for the Lord knows who is His." *History of the Inquisition*, pp.96.

FRANCE-KING LOUIS IX,1229
Published the statute "Cupientes" in which he charges himself to clear southern France from heretics as the Sabbath-keepers were called.

WALDENSES OF FRANCE
"The heresy of the Vaudois, or poor people of Lyons, is of great antiquity, for some say that it has been continued down ever since the time of Pope Sylvester; and others, ever since that of the apostles." Reinerus Sacho, *The Roman Inquisitor*, writing about 1230

FRANCE – Council Toulouse, 1229
Canons against Sabbath-keepers:
"Canon 3.. The lords of the different districts shall have the villas, houses and woods diligently searched, and the hiding-places of the heretics destroyed."
"Canon 14. Lay members are not allowed to possess the books of either the Old or the New Testaments." Hefele, 5, 931, 962.

EUROPE
"The Paulicians, Petrobusinas, Passaginians, Waldenses, Insabbatati were great Sabbath-keeping bodies of Europe down to 1250 AD."

PASAGINIANS
Dr. Hahn says that if the Pasaginians referred to the 4th Commandment to support the Sabbath, the Roman priests answered, "The Sabbath symbolised the eternal rest of the saints."

MONGOLIA
"The Mongolian conquest did not injure the Church of the East. (Sabbath-keeping.) On the contrary, a number of the Mongolian princes and a larger number of Mongolian queens were members of this church."

14TH – 15TH CENTURY
WALDENSES
"That we are to worship one only God, who is able to help us, and not the Saints departed; that we ought to keep holy the Sabbath day." Luther, *Fore-runners*, p. 38.

INSABBATI
"For centuries evangelical bodies, especially the Waldenses, were called Insabbati because of Sabbath-keeping." Gui, Manueld, *Inquisiteur*.

BOHEMIA, 1310 (Modern Czechoslovakia)
"In 1310, two hundred years before Luther's theses, the Bohemian brethren constituted one fourth of the population of Bohemia, and that they were in touch with the Waldenses who abounded in Austria, Lombardy,. Bohemia, north Germany, Thuringia, Brandenburg, and Moravia. Erasmus pointed out how strictly Bohemian Waldenses kept the seventh day Sabbath." Armitage, *A History of the Baptists*, p.313; Cox, *The Literature of the Sabbath Question*, vol. 2, pp. 201-202.

NORWAY
Then, too, in the "Catechism" that was used during the fourteenth century, the Sabbath commandment read thus; "Thou shalt not forget to keep the seventh day." This is quoted from *Documents and Studies Concerning the History of the Lutheran Catechism in the Nordish Churches*, p.89. Christiania 1893.
"Also the priests have caused the people to keep Saturdays as Sundays." *Theological Periodicals for the Evangelical Lutheran Church in Norway*, Vol.1, p.184 Oslo.

ENGLAND, HOLLAND, BOHEMIA
"We wrote of the Sabbatarians in Bohemia, Transylvania, England and Holland between 1250 and 1600 A.D." *Truth Triumphant*, Wilkinson, p.309.

BOHEMIA
"Erasmus testifies that even as late as about 1500 these Bohemians not only kept the seventh day scrupulously, but also were called Sabbatarians." Cox, *The Literature of the Sabbath Question*, Vol.2, pp.201, 202 *Truth Triumphant*, p.264.

NORWAY
(Church Council held at Bergin, August 22,1435)
"The first matter concerned a keeping holy of Saturday. It had come to the ear of the archbishop that people in different places of the kingdom had ventured the keeping holy of Saturday. It is strictly forbidden—it is stated—in the Church Law, for any one to keep or to adopt holy-days, outside of those which the pope, archbishop, or bishops appoint." *The History of the Norwegian Church under Catholicism*, R. Keyser, Vol.II, p. 488. Oslo: 1858

1435 Catholic Provincial Council at Bergin
"We are informed that some people in different districts of the kingdom, have adopted and observed Saturday-keeping. It is severely forbidden—in holy church canon—one and all to observe days excepting those which the holy Pope archbishop, or the bishops command. Saturday-keeping must under no circumstances be

permitted hereafter further than the church canon commands. Therefore, we counsel all the friends of God throughout all Norway who want to be obedient towards the holy church to let this evil of Saturday-keeping alone; and the rest we forbid under penalty of severe church punishment to keep Saturday holy." Dip. Norveg., 7, 397.

NORWAY, 1436
(Church Conference at Oslo)
"It is forbidden under the same penalty to keep Saturday holy by refraining from labour." *History of the Norwegian Church*, p.401.

FRANCE - Waldenses
"Louis XII, King of France (1498-1515), being informed by the enemies of the Waldense inhabiting a part of the province of Province, that several heinous crimes were laid to their account, sent the Master of Requests, and a certain doctor of the Sorbonne, to make inquiry into this matter. On their return they reported that they had visited all the parishes, but could not discover any traces of those crimes with which they were charged. On the contrary, they kept the Sabbath day, observed the ordinance of baptism, according to the primitive church, instructed their children in the articles of the Christian faith, and the commandments of God. The King having heard the report of his commissioners, said with an oath that they were better men than himself or his people." *History of the Christian Church*, Vol.II, pp. 71, 72, third edition. London: 1818.

ENGLAND
"In the reign of Elizabeth, it occurred to many conscientious and independent thinkers (as it previously had done to some Protestants in Bohemia) that the fourth commandment required of them the observance, not of the first, but of the specified 'seventh' day of the week." *Chamber's Cyclopaedia*, article "*Sabbath*," Vol. 8, p. 462, 1537.

RUSSIA (Council, Noscow, 1593)
"The accused [Sabbath-keepers] were summoned; they openly acknowledged the new faith, and defended the same. The most eminent of them, the secretary of state, Kuritzyn, Ivan Maximow, Kassian, archimandrite of the Fury Monastery of Novgorod, were condemned to death, and burned publicly in cages, at Moscow; Dec. 17,1503." H.Sternberfi, *Geschichte der Juden* (Leipsig, 1873), pp.117-122.

SWEDEN
"This zeal for Saturday-keeping continued for a long time: even little things which might strengthen the practice of keeping Saturday were

punished." Bishop Anjou, *Svenska Kirkans Historia* after Motetthiers, Upsala

LICHENSTEIN FAMILY
(estates in Austria, Bohemia, Morovia, Hungary. Lichenstein in the Rhine Valley wasn't their country until the end of the 7th century). "The Sabbatarians teach that the outward Sabbath, i.e. Saturday, still must be observed, They say that Sunday is the Pope's invention." Wolfgang Capito, *Refutation of Sabbath*, published 1599.

BOHEMIA (the Bohemian Brethren)
Dr. R. Cox says: "I find from a passage in Erasmus that at the early period of the Reformation when he wrote, there were Sabbatarians in Bohemia, who not only kept the seventh day, but were said to be...scrupulous in resting on it." Cox, *Literature of the Sabbath Question*, Vol. II, pp. 201, 202.

GERMANY
Dr. Esk (while refuting the Reformers) "The church has transferred the observance from Saturday to Sunday by virtue of her own power, without Scripture." Dr. Esk's *Enchiridion*, 1533, pp.78,79.

PRINCES OF LICHTENSTEIN (Europe)
"About the year 1520 many of these Sabbath-keepers found shelter on the estate of Lord Leonhardt of Lichtensein held to the observance of the true Sabbath." J.N.Andrews, *History of the Sabbath*, p. 649, ed.

INDIA
"The famous Jesuit, Francis Xavier, called for the Inquisition, which was set up in Goa, India, in 1560, to check the 'Jewish wickedness' (Sabbath-keeping)." Adeney, *The Greek and Eastern Churches*, p.527, 528.

NORWAY – 1544
"Some of you, contrary to the warning, keep Saturday. You ought to be severely punished. Whoever shall be found keeping Saturday, must pay a fine of ten marks." *History of King Christian the Third*, Niels Krag and S. Stephanius.

AUSTRIA
"Sabatarians now exist in Austria." Luther, *Lectures on Genesis*, AD 1523-27.

ABYSSINIA – A.D. 1534
(Abyssinian legate at court of Lisbon) "It is not therefore, in imitation of the Jews, but in obedience to Christ and His holy apostles, that we observe the day." Gedde's *Church History of Ethiopia*, pp. 87,8

DR. MARTIN LUTHER

"God blessed the Sabbath and sanctified it to Himself. God willed that this command concerning the Sabbath should remain. He willed that on the seventh day the word should be preached." *Commentary on Genesis*, Vol.1, pp.138-140

BAPTISTS

"Some have suffered torture because they would not rest when others kept Sunday, for they declared it to be the holiday and law of Antichrist." Sebastian Frank (A.D. 1536)

FINLAND – Dec. 6,1554

(King Gustavus Vasa I, of Sweden's letter to the people of Finland) "Some time ago we heard that some people in Finland had fallen into a great error and observed the seventh day, called Saturday." State Library at Helsingfors, *Reichsregister, Vom J.*, 1554, Teil B.B. leaf 1120, pp.175-180a

SWITZERLAND

"The observance of the Sabbath is a part of the moral law. It has been kept holy since the beginning of the world." R. Hospinian, 1592

HOLLAND, GERMANY

Barbara of Thiers, who was executed in 1529, declared:
"God has commanded us to rest on the seventh day." Another martyr, Christina Tolingerin, is mentioned thus: "Concerning holy days and Sundays, she said: 'In six days the Lord made the world, on the seventh day He rested. The other holy days have been instituted by popes, cardinals, and archbishops.'" *Martyrology of the Churches of Christ*, commonly called Baptists, during the era of the Reformation, from the Dutch of T.J. Van Bright, London, 1850,1, pp.113-4.

17TH – 18TH CENTURY
ENGLAND-1618

"At last for teaching only five days in the week, and resting upon Saturday she was carried to the new prison in Maiden Lane, a place then appointed for the restraint of several other persons of different opinions from the Church of England. Mrs. Traske lay fifteen or sixteen years a prisoner for her opinion about the Saturday Sabbath." Pagitt's *Heresiography*. p.196

ENGLAND – 1668

"Here in England are about nine or ten churches that keep the Sabbath, besides many scattered disciples, who have eminently preserved." *Stennet's letters*, 1668 and 1670. Cox, Sab.,1, 268

HUNGARY, RUMANIA

"But as they rejected Sunday and rested on the Sabbath, Prince Sigmond Bathory ordered their persecution. Pechi advanced to position of chancellor of state and next in line to the throne of Transylvania. He studied his Bible, and composed a number of hymns, mostly in honour of the Sabbath. Pechi was arrested and died in 1640." *Stennet's letters*, 1668 and 1670. Cox, Sab.,1, 268

SWEDEN, FINLAND

"We can trace these opinions over almost the whole extent of Sweden of that day—from Finland and northern Sweden." "In the district of Upsala the farmers kept Saturday in place of Sunday. About the year 1625 this religious tendency became so pronounced in these countries that not only large numbers of the common people began to keep Saturday as the rest day, but even many priests did the same." *History of the Swedish Church*, Vol.I, p.256

MUSCOVIT RUSSIAN CHURCH

"They solemnize Saturday (the old Sabbath)." Samuel Purchase, *His Pilgrims*. Vol. I, p. 350

INDIA (Jacobites)-1625

"They kept Saturday holy. They have solemn service on Saturdays." Pilgrimmes, Part 2, p.1269

AMERICA – 1664

"Stephen Mumford, the first Sabbath-keeper in America came from London in 1664." *History of the Seventh-day Baptist General Conference* by Jas. Bailey, pp. 237, 238

AMERICA – 1671 (Seventh-day Baptists)

"Broke from Baptist Church in order to keep Sabbath." See Bailey's History, pp. 9,10

ENGLAND

Charles I,1647 (when querying the Parliament Commissioners) "For it will not be found in Scripture where Saturday is no longer to be kept, or turned into the Sunday wherefore it must be the Church's authority that changed the one and instituted the other." Cox, *Sabbath Laws*, p.333

ENGLAND – John Milton

"It will surely be far safer to observe the seventh day, according to express commandment of God, than on the authority of mere human conjecture to adopt the first." *Sabbath Literature* 2, 46-54.

ENGLAND

"Upon the publication of the 'Book of Sports' in 1618 a violent controversy arose among English divines on two points: first, whether the Sabbath of the fourth commandment was in force; and, secondly, on what ground the first day of the week was entitled to be observed as 'the Sabbath.' " Haydns *Dictionary of Dates*, art. "Sabbatarians" p.602.

ETHIOPIA – 1604
Jesuits tried to induce the Abyssinian church to accept Roman Catholicism. They influenced King Zadenghel to propose to submit to the Papacy (AD 1604). "Prohibiting all his subjects, upon severe penalties, to observe Saturday any longer." Gedde, *Church History of Ethiopia*. p.311, also Gibbon *Decline and Fall*, ch. 47.

BOHEMIA, MORAVIA, SWITZERLAND, GERMANY
"One of the counsellors and lords of the court was John Gerendi, head of the Sabbatarians, a people who did not keep Sunday, but Saturday." Lamy, *The History of Socinianism*. p. 60.

ENGLAND
The inscription on the monument over the grave of Dr. Peter Chamberlain, physician to King James and Queen Anne, King Charles I and Queen Katherine says that Dr. Chamberlain was "a Christian keeping the commandment of God and the faith of Jesus, being baptised about the year 1648, and keeping the seventh day for the Sabbath above thirty-two years."

ABYSSINIA
"The Jacobites assembled on the Sabbath day, before the Domical day, in the temple, and kept that day, as do also the Abyssinians as we have seen from the confession of their faith by the Ethiopian king Claudius." Abundacnus, *Historia Jacobatarum*, p.118-9.

RUMANIA, 1760 (YUGOSLAVIA, CZECHOSLOVAKIA)
"Joseph II's edict of tolerance did not apply to the Sabbatarians, some of whom again lost all of their possessions." Jahrgang 2, 254.

"Catholic priests aided by soldiers forcing them to accept Romanism nominally, and compelling the remainder to labour on the Sabbath and to attend church on Sunday—these were the methods employed for two hundred fifty years to turn the Sabbatarians."

GERMANY – Tennhardt of Nuremberg
"He holds strictly to the doctrine of the Sabbath, because it is one of the ten commandments." Bengel's *Leban und Wirken*, Burk, p.579.
He himself says: "It cannot be shown that Sunday has taken the place of the Sabbath (P.366). the Lord God has sanctified the last day of the week. Antichrist, on the other hand, has appointed the first day of the week." Ki Auszug aus Tennhardt's *Schriften*, P.49 (printed 1712).

BOHEMIA, MORAVIA (Czechoslovakia).
Their history from 1635 to 1867 is thus described by Adolf Dux: "The condition of the Sabbatarians was dreadful. Their books and writings had to be delivered to the Karlsburg Consistory to becomes the spoils of flames." Aus Ungarn, pp. 289-291. Leipzig, 1850.

HOLLAND, GERMANY
"Dr. Cornelius stated of East Friesland, that when Baptists were numerous, "Sunday and holidays were not observed," (they were Sabbath-keepers). *Der Anteil Ostfrieslands* and Ref. Muenster, 1852, pp l29, 34.

MORAVIA – Count Zinzendorf
In 1738 Zinzendorf wrote of his keeping the Sabbath thus: "That I have employed the Sabbath for rest many years already, and our Sunday for the proclamation of the gospel." *Budingsche Sammlung*, Sec. 8, p. 224. Leipzig, 1742.

AMERICA, 1741
Moravian Brethren (after Zinzendorf arrived from Europe). "As a special instance it deserves to be noticed that he is resolved with the church at Bethlehem to observe the seventh day as rest day." Ibid., pp. 5, 1421, 1422

But before Zinzendorf and the Moravians at Bethlehem thus began the observance of the Sabbath and prospered, there was a small body of German Sabbath-keepers in Pennsylvania. See Rupp's *History of Religious Denominations in the United States*, pp.109- 123.

19TH CENTURY – RUSSIA
"But the majority moved to the Crimea and the Caucasus, where they remain true to their doctrine in spite of persecution until this present time. The people call them Subotniki, or Sabbatarians." Sternberg, *Geschichte der Juden in Polen*, p.124

CHINA
"At this time Hung prohibited the use of opium, and even tobacco, and all intoxicating drinks, and the Sabbath was religiously observed." *The Ti-Ping Revolution*, by Llin-Le, and officer among them, Vol. 1, pp.36-48, 84
"The seventh day is most religiously and strictly observed. The Taiping Sabbath is kept upon our Saturday." P. 319

CHINA
"The Taipings when asked why they observed the seventh day Sabbath, replied that it was, first, because the Bible taught it, and,

second, because their ancestors observed it as a day of worship." *A Critical History of the Sabbath and the Sunday.*

INDIA, PERSIA

"Besides, they maintain the solemn observance of Christian worship throughout our Empire, on the seventh day." *Christian Researches in Asia*, p.143

DENMARK

"This agitation was not without its effect. Pastor M.A. Sommer began observing the seventh day, and wrote in his church paper. "Indovet Kristendom" No.5,1875 an impressive article about the true Sabbath. In a letter to Elder John G.Matteson, he says:

"Among the Baptists here in Denmark there is a great agitation regarding the Sabbath commandment..However, I am probably the only preacher in Denmark who stands so near to the Adventists and who for many years has proclaimed Christ's second coming." *Advent Tidente*, May, 1875

SWEDEN (Baptists)

"We will now endeavour to show that the sanctification of the Sabbath has its foundation and its origin in a law which God at creation itself established for the whole world, and as a consequence thereof is binding on all men in all ages." *Evangelisten* (The Evangelist). Stockholm, May 30 to August 15,1863 (organ of the Swedish Baptist Church)

ALASKA, 1800s

A northwestern Inupiat named Maniilaq and other First Nation Eskimos "rested on the Sabbath, which was understood to be Saturday." When asked why he rested that day, Maniilaq "replied that he lived by the commandments of his grandfather."

AMERICA, 1840s

A spectacular resurgence of seventh day Sabbath keeping erupted in 19th century America. Many recognize a prophetic significance in this phenomenon as a fulfillment of Revelation 12 and 13. "The earth opened up its mouth" giving refuge to Pilgrims and birth to a second beast nation while the first is wounded. Five predominant groups have emerged.

Seventh Day Baptists

Seventh Day Baptists currently number only about 5,000 in the United States, but have many more members worldwide. They are loosely organized under a local church structure from their headquarters in Janesville, Wisconsin. Their magazine, *The Sabbath Recorder*, has been published continually since 1844. SDB's are Baptists first, Sabbath-keepers second and consequently feel more comfortable around Sunday Baptists then SDA's or Church of God members. They have undergone doctrinal changes over the years, from a non-Trinitarian to a Trinitarian position, and from avoiding Christmas and Easter to full participation. Their observance of the Sabbath is similar to Sunday-keepers observance of Sunday: go to Church and then pursue their own interests.

Australian Seventh Day Baptists are much more conservative than their American counterparts. This is commonly observed in other groups as well. With the moral decay of the United States, Sabbath-keepers in other parts of the world are becoming more strict.

In general, Seventh Day Baptists are interesting people, fiercely independent minded, and open to others of differing opinions. They are not dogmatic. They are not worried if their members hold different points of view. They believe in the individual's right to have the personal teaching of the Holy Spirit.

Seventh-day Adventists

In 1844 Seventh-day Adventists arose and had spread to nearly all parts of the world by the close of the 19th Century. Their name is derived from their teaching of the seventh-day Sabbath and the Advent of Jesus. The church was officially organized in the early 1860s and by 1874 their work was established in Europe, 1885 Australasia, 1887 South Africa, 1888 Asia, 1888 South America. Seventh-day Adventists uphold the same Sabbath that Jesus and His followers kept. The sacred Torch of Truth was not extinguished through the long centuries. Adventists are working today in nearly 1000 languages of earth and have over 27,000 churches. With over ten million members around the globe the Seventh-day Adventists dwarf all other Messianic Sabbath-keeping groups combined.

The church is governed through a representative system of Elders elected locally, paid pastors and then advancing from local conferences to regional unions under global divisions administered by a general conference headquartered in Washington D.C. The SDA statement of doctrine has 27 points, which begins with a recognition of the Holy Bible as the written Word of God, the Trinity, belief that God created the earth in six days, that man is mortal and that Christ is our Saviour, that the Sabbath is to be observed, and Christians are to live exemplary lives, that marriage and family are sacred institutions, and that Christ will return soon to establish His kingdom. SDA's promote their church's teaching by radio and television programs such as *Voice of Prophecy*, *It is Written*, *Amazing Facts*, through literature such as *Signs of the Times*, *Liberty*, etc., and public seminars. Their services open with Sabbath schools for various age groups, followed by singing, mission report, Bible lesson study, and a sermon. SDA's often sponsor church schools, from elementary, secondary academies, colleges, and universities with professional schools of medicine, dentistry, nursing, etc. Most non-SDA Sabbath keepers can agree with many of the SDA doctrines and programs. Attending a SDA service, especially the Sabbath school, is an uplifting experience.

Church of God, Seventh Day

Previously known as "Church of God, Adventist" or "Church of God Seventh Day" or simply COG7, this group of churches also spawned from the Adventist movement launched by William Miller, who predicted the end of the world in 1844. While having similar roots to Seventh-day Adventists, the Church of God people never joined the Battle Creek, Michigan, SDA organization and during the late 1850s they parted company.

Five major groups are headquartered in Denver, Colorado; Meridian, Idaho; Caldwell, Idaho; Salem, West Virginia; and Jerusalem, Israel. The groups are decentralized without a central hierarchy. They believe in the millennium reign on earth, not in Heaven; are non-Trinitarian; and believe that Christmas and Easter are pagan holidays. They publish magazines and literature promoting their beliefs, but generally do not use mass media such as television and radio. In the United States, they are barely holding their own; however, in foreign fields, they are growing. COG7 churches looking to Caldwell, Idaho, and Jerusalem generally observe the annual festivals. The Denver Group is more tightly organized than the other major COG7 groups, but is organized upon state conference lines similar to that of SDA's. It publishes *The Bible Advocate* magazine, which has been circulated since 1863.

COG7 services are open and friendly to newcomers. Their Sabbath schools are lively and interesting. The small size of most of their churches make them very attractive for fellowship. The Denver Group sponsors a boarding high school in Owosso, Michigan. Annual or bi-annual camp meetings are held in conjunction with election of church officers.

Worldwide Church of God and Related Groups

Founded in the 1930s by COG7 minister, Herbert W. Armstrong, a one-time SDA, the Worldwide Church of God developed primarily through radio and television ministries. By the early 1950s, the Radio Church of God, as it was then known, developed a strong central hierarchical government. Membership grew to over 100,000 at its peak. For many years services were open only to members or minister-approved invited guests. *The Plain Truth* magazine and *The*

World Tomorrow broadcast became known to millions around the world. Herbert Armstrong, and his son Garner Ted Armstrong, became household words. In 1968, the church's name was changed from Radio to Worldwide Church of God.

Ten major doctrinal differences exist between "Church of God" groups and Seventh-day Adventists: (1) the Trinity, (2) Ellen G. White, (3) going to Heaven, (4) the "Investigative Judgment," (5) name of the Church, (6) vegetarianism, (7) military service, (8) time element of the crucifixion and resurrection, (9) observance of Easter and quarterly communion, (10) moral issues such as homosexuality, abortion, and alcohol.

Today the WCG is only a shadow of its former self. About 10,000 members and hundreds of ministers left in 1974 over church government, Pentecost, and other doctrinal issues. To stem the exodus, Armstrong conceded to a number of doctrinal changes espoused by the dissidents while remaining his rigid stance on a strong central church government.

 It is possible that today there are about 200,000 people or more who were once associated with the Worldwide Church of God. The trend in the WCG grouping of Sabbath-keepers, unfortunately, is toward more fractionalization. Church of God, The Eternal, The Bible Sabbath Association, and a number of other groups have developed.

Assemblies of Yahweh

Sacred Name believers insist on the exclusive usage of the Hebrew names, Yahweh and Yahshua but have much in common with more conservative ex-Worldwide groups. Jacob Meyer of Bethel, Pennsylvania, leads the largest group, the Assemblies of Yahweh. Its *Sacred Name Broadcaster* magazine and radio program have popularized the doctrine that we should use the Hebrew names for the deity. Yahweh's New Covenant Assembly, of Kingdom City, Missouri, publishes *YNCA Light*, among the most professional and interesting of all Sabbath-keeping publications.

Generally, Sacred Name believers are scrupulous in their observance of the Sabbath and food laws. They are avid Bible students and most keep the annual Holy Days. But since it is offensive for Sacred Name believers to hear the terms "God" and "Jesus" in prayers, songs, and Scripture citations, they avoid association with other Sabbath keepers. They have their own Bibles and tend to constantly "harp" on the Sacred Name doctrine in person and in their literature.

Adapted from Richard C. Nickels
The Bible Sabbath Association, Gillette, Wyoming.

Testimonies of Sabbath Keepers

The Sabbath is "a symbol of God's presence in time and an assurance that he is still with us. It sets us free from slavery to things, which are forgeries of happiness, and reminds us of what life is all about. It is a sheltered island of rest and refreshment in the tempestuous ocean of time where we can pause to get our bearings. It sets us free from the tyranny of the mad rush of modern life and gives us a taste of eternity." Raymon Cottrell, editorial, *Adventist Today* July-August, 1996.

"As the new century dawns, the practice of Sabbath keeping may be a gift waiting to be unwrapped, a confirmation that we are not without help in shaping the renewing ways of life for which we long. This practice stands at the heart of Judaism, but it is also available to Christians." Dorothy C. Bass, *Christianity Today*, September 1, 1997

Appendix A
Synchronize Your Clocks

Genesis 1 lists three primary cosmic clocks established at creation:
Earth day: 23 hours, 56 minutes and 4 seconds
Lunar month: 29 days, 12 hours, 44 minutes and 3 seconds
Solar year: 365 days, 5 hours, 48 minutes and 46 seconds

A third non-astronomical clock was started on the last day of creation:
The Week: 7 days, linked only to the Creator's schedule

Four additional clocks were introduced at the Exodus:
Week of weeks: 7 weeks, 49 days, one pentecost
Week of months: 7 months, one festival year
Week of years: 7 years, one sabbatical interval
Week of sabbaticals: 7 sabbaticals, 49 years, one jubilee interval

These were synchronized with the original primary clocks so that
1. the year began with the first month of the Spring Equinox
   when the sun rose due east and set due west
   with a day containing equal amounts of light and dark
2. the month began with the appearance of the new moon phase
   when the "dark" moon is in conjunction between earth and sun
3. the day began at sundown (dark phase first)
   following the "evening and the morning" formula at creation

The nation of Israel was born at the Exodus. The 9th plague of darkness lasted three days to demonstrate its supernatural nature and discredit the initial explainations that it was just a moonless new moon night. But God said, "One more plague will I bring upon Pharaoh." Then He announced, "This month shall be unto you the beginning of months: it shall be the first month of the year to you." Exodus 12:2. Two weeks late, at full moon, Israel left Egpyt, slaves no more, released, their inheritance restored in grand jubilee style.

Israel's first week as a nation began with the Passover. That night they began to eat unleavened bread for seven days. The first and seventh days were to be "holy convocations" in which they were to do "no manner of work" Exodus 12:16. Indeed, the following day they were no longer slaves, but gathered from the Egyptians "jewels of gold" and silver and clothing—they took up an offering. Then they traveled "three days into the wilderness" as Moses had repeatedly requested (Exodus 3:18; 5:3; 8:27) camping at Succoth, Etham and Pihahiroth (Exodus 13:20; 14:2). They had reached the Red Sea by the middle of the week.

As Christ defeated Satan "in the midst of the week (Dan. 9:27), so Israel crossed "through the midst of the sea" and watched as "the Lord overthrew the Egyptians in the midst of the sea" Exodus 14:16, 27. Then they traveled "three days" (Exodus 15:22) to Marah where, on their sixth day out of Egypt, the bitter waters were made sweet when "the Lord showed [Moses] a tree" which he cast into the waters, even as Christ, "a green tree" (Luke 23:31) was sacrificed on Friday, the sixth day, to give us sweet salvation as He drank the bitter cup of death. They then arrived at Elim on the seventh day where there were 12 wells (one for each tribe) and 70 palm trees—a symbol of Sabbath abundance and sanctification (Psalm 1:3).

The year began in the Spring as did other major redemptive events:
- 40 years after the Exodus Joshua entered Canaan, in the Spring, crossing the Jordan on the "tenth day of the first month" Joshua 4:19.
- Ezra "began to go up" from Babylon to Jerusalem with the command of Artexerxes to rebuild Jerusalem in fulfillment of Daniel's 70 week (10 jubilee) prophecy "on the first day of the first month" (Ezra 7:9) or New Year's day, in the Spring of 457 BC, first year of the 1st week.
- Jesus died in the Spring on Passover in the midst of the 70th week.

The Exodus, and the very first Passover, was a prophetic, dated, on-time event that was in synch with God's time-table. It took place in the Spring. An interesting pattern based on synchronous 7-year cycles can be seen to mark important jubilee events such as Sennecharib's invasion (702BC), the Babylonian Exodus (457BC), the 70th week of Daniel 9 (27AD) and the rise of the little horn (538AD). Each sabbatical interval, can be described as a week of years labeled like a week of days:

Sun	Mon	Tue	Wed	Thu	Fri	Sat	Week
702BC	701	700	699	698	697	696	-20th
457BC	456	455	454	453	452	451	1st
27AD	28	29	30	31	32	33	70th
538	539	540	541	542	543	544	143rd
1791	1792	1793	1794	1795	1796	1797*	180th

*Pope taken captive February 15, 1798 at the very end of the Spring-to-Spring year 1797, the 1260th year of the 3½ times, 42 month, 1260 day prophecy.

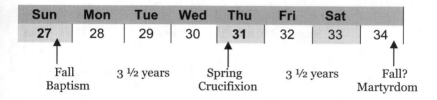

Sun	Mon	Tue	Wed	Thu	Fri	Sat
27	28	29	30	31	32	33	34

Fall Baptism   3 ½ years   Spring Crucifixion   3 ½ years   Fall? Martyrdom

This represents the usual Fall-based years producing the exact mathematical 3½ year spacing that places the crucifixion in early AD 31. However, the placement of the Crucifixion on a "Thursday" year spoils the "midst of the week" reference in Daniel 9:27. The "Wednesday" year AD 30 satisfies this middle day position *and* published lunar data:

Vernal Spring Equinoxes

Julian Date	Time	Day
AD 28 Mar 22	10am	Mon
29 Mar 22	4 pm	Tue
30 Mar 22	10pm	Wed
31 Mar 23	3 am	Fri
32 Mar 22	9 am	Sat

> Data obtained from the U.S. Naval Observatory and NASA web sites. Time is Universal, GMT.
>
> http://aa.usno.navy.mil/data/docs
> http://sunearth.gfc.nasa.gov/eclipse/phase

New Moon

Julian Date	Time	Day
AD 28 Apr 13	14:06	Tue
29 Apr 2	17:24	Sat
30 Mar 22	17:42	Wed
31 Apr 10	11:29	Tue
32 Mar 29	19:57	Sat

Full Moon

Julian Date	Time	Day
April 27	12:35	Tuesday
April 17	02:41	Sunday
April 6	19:38	Thursday
April 25	19:56	Wednesday
April 14	08:57	Monday

Only two years during the 70th week are possible candidates for a Friday crucifixion on the 14th or 15th day after the first new moon on or after the Spring equinox.

AD 28	Sun	Mon	Tue	Wed	Thu	Fri	Sat
New Moon			13	14	15	16	17
	18	19	20	21	22	23	24
Full Moon	25	26	27	28	29	30	31

AD 29	Sun	Mon	Tue	Wed	Thu	Fri	Sat
New Moon							2
	3	4	5	6	7	8	9
	10	11	12	13	14	15	16
Full Moon	17						

AD 30	Sun	Mon	Tue	Wed	Thu	Fri	Sat
New Moon				22	23a	24c	25a
	26	27	28	29	30	31	1
Full Moon	2	3	4	5	6p	7	8p

AD 31	Sun	Mon	Tue	Wed	Thu	Fri	Sat
New Moon			10a	11	12	13	14a
	15	16	17	18	19	20	21
Full Moon	22	23	24p	25	26	27	28p

AD 32	Sun	Mon	Tue	Wed	Thu	Fri	Sat
New Moon							29
	30	31	1	2	3	4	5
	6	7	8	9	10	11	12
Full Moon	13	14	15				

AD 31 Nisan 1 on Saturday April 14, if crescent reckoning is used.
  Nisan 15 (Passover) April 28
  Nisan 1 on Tuesday April 10, if new moon reckoning used.
  Nisan 15 (Passover) April 24 (Tuesday, too early)

AD 30 Nisan 1 on Thursday March 23, if new moon reckoning is used.
  Jerusalem timing is 4 hours later than GMT puting conjunction
  Wednesday afternoon actually after sundown on Thursday.
  Same adjustment applies for years AD 29 and 32.
  Nisan 15 (Passover) April 6 (Thursday, Christ kept)
  Nisan 1 Saturday March 25, if crescent reckoning is used.
  Nisan 15 (Passover) April 8 (Saturday, Jews kept)

Whether the crucifixion year was AD 30 or 31 does not deny the fact that in the first century there were two methods in use for setting the start of each lunar month: visual sighting of the new moon (a dark, moonless night) or the first visible new crescent moon. Israel had been originally instructed to use the new moon method after their Exodus from Egypt. But after their return from Babylon, they adopted that nation's crescent moon method, still employed by arab nations today.

This explains why the gospels report two different Passovers during the crucifixion week. Jesus and his disciples kept Passover after sundown Thursday (early Friday evening) in accordance with the new moon reckoning system originally established by God. The Jewish leaders and the rest of the nation, using the crescent moon method, followed a schedule a day later that year resulting in a Saturday Passover and referred to in John's gospel account as a "High Sabbath."

At the first advent the nation observed a different Passover day than the one kept by Christ. In parallel fashion the world at the second advent will be worshipping on a different day than the one originaly established by God.

Appendix B
The Jubilee Connection

70 Land Sabbaths

The 70 year Babylonian captivity is based on the total number of land sabbaths that were never kept by the divided kingdoms of northern Israel and southern Judah. Ezekiel 4:5,6 details the significant time periods for which these 70 rest years were derived. Ezekiel was instructed to lay on his left side for 390 days (representing the duration of the northern kingdom's apostasy) and on his right side for 40 days (representing the duration of the southern kingdom's apostasy). This totaled 430 days but actually symbolized 430 years "according to the number of the days ...each day for a year."

> 390 years of northern kingdom apostasy
> +40 years of southern kingdom apostasy
> ―――――――――
> 430 years total
>
> $430 \div 7$ = 61.4 sabbatical rest years
> $430 \div 49$ = +8.8 jubilee rest years
> ―――――――――
> 70 total land rest years

A more precise explanation offered by Larry Wilson and F. J. de Waal recognizes the fact that jubilee years were separate from sabbatical years—occurring on the year following the 7th sabbatical year making it not only the 50th year but also the 1st year of the next sabbatical cycle. Thus, there are actually eight land rest years in a 49 year jubilee cycle.

> ...1234567123456712345671234567123456712345671234567...
>   1   2   3   4   5   6   7   8
>
> **430 / 49 = 8** whole jubilee cycles plus a fraction
> **8 x 49 = 392** years in exactly 8 whole jubilee cycles
> or **8 x 8 = 64** land sabbaths
> **430-392=38** years remaining (the fraction)
> **38 / 7 = 5** land sabbaths in the fraction
> **plus 1** more for the jubilee year beginning the partial cycle
> So, 64 + 6 lands sabbaths in fraction = **70 land sabbaths**

70 Week Landmarks

The 49 year interval (7 sabbatical years) between jubilee years appears to have been unappreciated by early church pioneers. Although occasional reference to the 70 week prophecy is made to the fact that this 490 year period is equivalent to 10 jubilees, it is not commonly applied to the other pivotal landmarks of the Great Advent Awakening eschatology of the early 19th century. But in recent years a new awareness has surfaced that there exists an exact 49 year multiple between the *end* of the 70 weeks (33 AD) and the *end* of the 1260 year/42 month/3½ times period (1797 AD). The math is demonstrated as:

$$36 \times 49 = 1764 + 33 = 1797$$

Exactly 36 jubilees extend from the *end* of the Jewish nation's probationary time period (marked by the martyrdom of Stephan) and the *end* of the apostate medieval church's period of domination (identified by Napoleon's seizure of the papal states, abduction of pope Pius VI and his deportation to France inflicting "a deadly wound" Revelation 13:3) on February 15, 1798 just days before the beginning of the 1798th Spring-to-Spring year. This was the *very* end of the 1260th year.

> "The Papacy was extinct: not a vestige of existence remained; and among all the Roman Catholic powers not a finger was stirred in its defense. The Eternal City had no longer prince or pontiff; its bishop was dying captive in foreign lands." *Rome: From the Fall of the Western Empire*, George Trevor. pp. 439, 440. London: 1868.

Both dates marked *terminations* and both occurred here on *earth*.

But, there's more. Another jubilee connection exists. From the beginning of Christ's first apartment Holy Place ministration after His ascension in 30/31 AD to the beginning of His second apartment Most Holy Place ministry on the day of Atonement in 1844 is also exactly 37 jubilee intervals, 1844 being the 50th Jubilee year. Again, here's the math:

$$37 \times 49 = 1813 + 30 = 1843 + 1 \text{ (Jubilee)} = 1844$$

Both are *commencement* dates and both take place in *heaven*.

These mathematical relationships appear to be far more than mere coincidence. The fact that they were *not* noted or publicized during the early years of the Advent Movement is also highly significant. The conviction that these dates were correct was based, at the time, on firm Biblical exegesis and historical application. That these dates are now appreciated to be strategically linked to Jubilee time periods only strengthens and affirms their reliability. Many have fallen prey to doubt regarding these specific dates as the result of critical attacks on them both from within and without the church over the past decades. But this simple realization of their Jubilee connection confirms confidence in their Divine origin and destiny.

	Begin					Begin
	Heaven ◄───────── 30 + 1813 (**37** x 49) = 1843 ─────────► Heaven					
	Holy Place					Most Holy
27	**30**	**33** ◄──── 33 + 1764 (**36** x 49) = 1797 ───►		**1798**		**1844**
	Cross	End			End	
		Earth			Earth	
		Stephen			Papacy	

These dates have been individually recognized for their prophetic and apocalyptic significance since the Great Advent Awakening in the late 18th century. But their jubilee connection has only recently been appreciated. This sequence of awareness and insight instills confidence in the validity of the dates, not as contrived to justify human opinion, but divinely appointed with mathematical precision and significance.

Exodus Jubilee
Sabbath chronology can be identified in other Biblical events such as those surrounding the Exodus and entrance into the Promised Land. Some have appealed to the obvious nature of the Exodus as not only the basis of the Jubilee but a fulfillment as well. Release from slavery and ultimate inheritance of the Promised Land have inspired many thinkers to look for a jubilee connection with the Exodus event.

There appears to be an entire constellation of time periods that converge on the very *day* that Israel left Egypt. The comment in Exodus 12:17, 41 and 51 that God brought His people out "on the selfsame day" exactly 430 years after His original promise to Abraham speaks to the significance of that historic occasion. These 430 years of faithful Divine commitment are in bold contrast to the 430 years of Israel's faithless apostasy; both are rich in sabbatical and jubilee meaning.

Again, to the day, after spending exactly 40 years in the wilderness, they entered Canaan on the 16th day of their 41st year (Joshua 5:11). Israel's first full year in the Promised Land was a Sabbatical year just as Adam and Eve's first full day in Eden also was a Sabbath.

Another time period has been identified with probationary time for people under God's curse. 414 years appears in connection with several important events in redemptive history. Following God's curse of the earth at Adam's fall, exactly four 414 time periods end with the Flood. Noah then curses Canaan, his grandson, and the clock starts ticking on a period of exactly two 414 intervals and expires on the actual conquest of Canaan, the land and its inhabitants, fulfilling the prophetic judgment. Counting the patriarchal ages in the book of Genesis has been performed by every curious Bible reader. There is, within the Mosaic record, clues to several interesting time periods with sabbatical significance.

The Promised Land Jubilee

The ground was cursed at the fall Genesis 3:17.

Adam	was 130	when	Seth was born	in the year	130
Seth	105		Enos		235
Enos	90		Cainan		325
Cainan	70		Mahalaleel		395
Mahalaleel	65		Jared		460
Jared	162		Enoch		622
Enoch	65		Methusalah		687
Methuselah	187		Lamech		874
Lamech	182		Noah		1056
Noah	500		Shem, Ham, Japheth		1556
Noah	502		Shem		1558
Noah	600		**Flood** destroyed the earth		1656
			After 4 x **414** year periods		
Noah's Curse	604		1 year flood + 3 years to fruit		1660

Genesis 11 continues the chronology:

Shem	100		Arphaxad, 2 years after Flood	1658
Arphaxad	35		Salah	1693
Salah	30		Eber	1723
Eber	34		Peleg	1757
Peleg	30		Reu	1787
Reu	32		Serug	1819
Serug	30		Nahor	1849
Nahor	29		Terah	1878
Terah	70		Abram	1948
Abram	70		Covenant Promise made	2018
			2018 + **430** = 2448 Exodus	
Abram	75	Gen 12:4	Departed from Haran	2023
Abram	86		Ismael Gen 16:16. 2048-14=	2034
			begins Egypt's grace period	
			2034 + **414** = 2448 Exodus	
Abram	100		Isaac born (Ishmael 14)	2048
			2048 + **400** =2448 Exodus	
Isaac	60		Jacob, Esau	2108
Jacob	130		Entered Egypt Gen 47:8,9	2238
Moses born	130 yrs after Jacob entred Egypt Jasher 67:11			2368
Moses	80		**Exodus**	**2448**
12 spies sent			2 years after Exodus	2450
			Conquest of Canaan	
			on 50th Jubilee	
			49 x 50 = 2450	

Lamech called his son "Noah, saying, This same shall *comfort* us concerning our work and toil of our hands, because of the ground which the LORD has cursed" Genesis 5:29. However, the name Noah actually means "rest." Further clarification is provided by the book of Jasher 4:13 which explains that Noah was a nickname supplied by grandfather Methuselah. Lamech had originally named his son Menachem which indeed does mean "comfort." This additional information further explains the connection between the flood, Noah's watershed call to fame, and Eden's curse. The significant 414 divisor for the 1656 AM date appears to be associated with time periods under God's curse.

Two of these 414 time spans (828 years) connects Noah's curse of Canaan in 1660 with the actual conquest of Canaan in 2488 which turned out to be 38 years after the potential entry into the Promised Land in 2450, the 50th jubilee from Creation. Noah's curse is dated four years after the flood's date (1656) by accounting for the exactly one year duration of Noah's confinement within the ark plus three years to yield a sufficient grape harvest to produce wine and intoxication. Jesus allowed three years for fruit to be expected on the fig tree in Luke 13:4.

Abram's Promise was 430 years before Exodus. Gal. 3:17; Ex. 12:41.
Ishmael was born 414 years before the Exodus.
Isaac was born 400 years before the Exodus.
 All three of these time periods intersect with the 2448 Exodus date.

In Genesis 15:13-16 God said, "Thy seed shall be...afflicted 400 years." The affliction began with Ishmael who was half-Egyptian. Gen. 21:9, Gal. 4:29. Thus, there were 60+130=190 years of affliction before entering Egypt. Then the seed stayed another 210 years in Egypt (130+80). God said they would "return in the fourth generation." 1 Chronicles 6:1-3 lists them: Levi, Kohath, Amram, Moses. Jochebed is reported to have given birth to Moses at a miraculous 130 years of age in both the book of Jasher 67:11 and the second century AD Jewish haggadah Sotah. An alternate interpretation is that she gave birth to Moses 130 years after Jacob's entry into Egypt and that she was not born during the trip to Egypt but quite some time afterwards as noted in Numbers 26:57. Josephus in his *Antiquities*, XIV.xv.2 evenly divides the 430 years into 215 during Abraham's Canaan sojourn and 215 for the Egyptian residence.

However you divide the pie, the import values of 430, 414 and 400 are unquestionably important Scriptural data.

Appendix C
Additional Notes on Passover

The Passover Ordinance
Exodus 23:18; 34:25 God called it "My sacrifice"
Exodus 12:14,17,24 "an ordinance forever"
Exodus 12:43 "the ordinance of the Passover"
Exodus 13:10 "this ordinance from year to year"
One of 3 annual feasts 2 Chron. 8:13, Deut. 16:16

Passover Preparation
Passover Lamb selected 10th day of 1st month
This was 4 days before Passover, thought by some to represent
one day for each generation Israel was in Egypt. Gen. 15:16.
Firstborn male of the first year, without blemish
Representing Christ, perfect in character, in the prime of His life.
The Lamb of God was without spot or blemish. John 1:29, 1 Pet. 1:19.
Abel brought the firstling of his flock. Genesis 4:2-4.
Each month began with a **new moon.** (not a crescent moon)
"He appointed the moon for seasons." Psalm 104:19.
The moon is a symbol of God's covenant with David. Psalm 89:37

"Sanctify yourselves, prepare your brethren." 2 Chron. 25:6.
If not sanctified sufficiently they can't keep it. 2 Chron. 30:3.
All leaven was collected by candlelight and removed from the house.
Jesus prepared His disciples by washing their feet. John 13:2-17.
Strangers couldn't eat it. Exodus 12:43.
Only circumcised males could participate. Exodus 12:48.
Those defiled by touching a dead body could not keep it. Num. 9:6.
But they may keep Passover on the 14th day of the second month.
Num. 9:11; 2 Chron. 30:2,3

No Passover was kept during wilderness wandering (after the second
one) because no circumcision was conducted during that period.
Israel was circumcised a second time by Joshua before entering Canaan.
Joshua 5:2-10.

Full Moon
Passover was kept on the evening of **14th day** of 1st month:
Lev. 23:5, Num. 28:16, Joshua 5:10, 2 Chron. 35:1, Ezra 6:19.
This was always a **Full moon** indicating that God's deliverance is full
and complete, and evidence of God's protection. Deut. 33:14.

Lamb was killed **"at even**, at the going down of the sun." Deut. 16:5,6;
Lev. 23:5. "Kill it in the evening." Exodus 12:6.
"eat the flesh in that night." Exodus 12:8. Eaten **at even.** Num. 9:11.

Day of Atonement began on the 9th day of the seventh month at even
(*ba erev*) Lev. 23:32, Actually this was the beginning of the 10th day.
"When the even was come, He sat down with the twelve," Matt. 26:20.
Hebrew is literally "between the evenings" (*ben ha erebim*) Ex. 12:6.
In Exodus 16:12 this same phrase is used to indicate when the quail
began to roost, in other words, at dusk.
Lamps of the sanctuary were lit "between the evenings" Exodus 30:8.

14...... death		15.......		16..............	
dusk | dawn		**dusk** dawn		**dusk** dawn	
lamb passover plundering		Exodus at night			
unleavened "morrow went out"					
P A S S O V E R		U N L E A V E N E D	B R E A D ----------------		
		S A B B A T H	M O R R O W		
		Holy Convocation			
F R I D A Y ---------------------		S A T U R D A Y -------------	S U N D A Y -----------		
Last Supper mob	crucifixion	rest all day Sabbath	resurrection		
Gethsemene trial		to tomb	"wave sheaf"		
		"Manna ceased"			
		"morrow ate old corn"			
		"I am the bread of life"			
		"unless the corn die"			

"in the first month, **on** the 14th day of the month at even [*ba erev*], you
shall eat unleavened bread until the 21st day of the month at even"
Exodus 12:18. This would be at the end of the 14th day.
"In the 14th day of the first month at even is the Lord's Passover"
Lev. 23:5

Christ is our Passover. 1 Cor. 5:7-8 First day of Unleavened Bread
Thursday "when they killed the Passover" the upper room was secured.
Matt. 26:17, Mark 14:12, Luke 22:7, Eze. 45:21; Mark 14:1
"The Lord Jesus the same night in which He was betrayed took bread"
1 Cor. 11:23 He may very well have been taken captive at midnight

The Lamb must be sacrificed outside the gates. So was Jesus.
At the place where God chooses to place His name. Deut. 16:5,6
Ultimately it was centered in Jerusalem. 2 Chron. 30:1; 35:1.
Not a bone of the lamb was to be broken Exodus 12:46; Num. 9:12 cf
John 19:36

But the sacrifice of the lamb, though sufficient for all, was not enough.
Sacrifice was the means of salvation. Yet the blood must be applied.
Both were necessary. Both saved the firstborn from death.

Sacrifice of the firstling saved the rest of the herd,
it was a propitiation where God supplied the blood. Leviticus 17:11.
Circumcision was a sacrificial rite where Man supplied the blood.
Blood collected and applied to door posts with hyssop. Exodus 12:22.
Hyssop used in purification Num. 19:6, Psalm 51:7

and ratification. Hebrews 9:19.   Blood was sprinkled. Romans 3:23.

But that wasn't enough. The flesh had to be eaten. John 6:51.
The cross of Christ, symbol of His death and spilled blood, reminds us of His past provision for our salvation. But that is not enough. We must allow Him to sustain our life through partaking of His Communion, eating His flesh symbolically in the unleavened bread, drinking His blood symbolically in the fruit of the vine.

Passover Meal
Lamb eaten in one house, without breaking a bone. Exodus 12:3, 46.
Christ was crucified but not a bone of his body was broken. Psalm 22:17.
The lamb was roasted with fire, not eaten raw or "sodden" with water. Exodus 12:8,9.
It was eaten with unleavened bread and bitter herbs. Numbers 9:11.
in haste, while standing with their shoes on, staff in hand, ready to go. Exodus 12:11. Nothing was to be left untill the morning. Exodus 34:25.
Anything left over burned with fire. Exodus 12:10.
Refusal to keep it: cut off from the people. Numbers 9:13.

We must have the mark of the Lamb's blood.
Bread is Christ's flesh, wine His blood. Luke 22:19-20; Jesus is the "bread of life" John 6:35; Matt. 26:26-28. Jesus was born in Bethlehem, "the house of bread." He changed the ceremony giving it greater meaning, but He didn't change the day—it already had tremendous significance.

Passover Night
Angel of Death passed at midnight. First born were either saved or slain. "Pharaoh rose up in the night...and called for Moses and Aaron by night" Exodus 12:30,31. A future Great Passover will yet bring judgment on all false religions. Josephus *Antiquities of the Jews*, V, iii "The Passover of which Egypt was a type and Jerusalem an example, is yet to come." Heb 10:26-31, Revelation 18:1-5. Spiritual Babylon will yet receive her 7 last plagues.

At daybreak of 14th Israelites left Goshen
and began moving to Rameses, 5-7 miles away
spoiling the Egyptians on their way. Exod 12:33-36.
"the people took their dough before it was leavened." Exodus 12:33-36.
"They departed from Rameses ...on the 15th day." Num. 33:3.
"on the morrow after the Passover [they] went out." Num. 33:3.
"the Lord your God brought you forth out of Egypt by night" Deut. 16:1.
in the light of a full moon and God's pillar of fire.
But "None of you shall go out ... until the morning." Exodus 12:22.
Israel left Rameses on 15th day on morrow after Passover. Num. 33:3.
"in the sight of all the Egyptians" Num. 33:3.

Morrow After Passover

"in the 15th day of this month is the feast" Num. 28:16.
"seven days shall unleavened bread be eaten." Num. 28:17; Eze. 45:21.
Some Jews kept Passover Friday: John 18:28, 19:14.
Rabbinical Jews place "morrow after sabbath" as Nisan 16, the day after
the annual sabbath, the first day of unleavened bread. Lev. 23:10-14.
Samaritans and Sadducees placed it as the day following the seventh-
day Sabbath whenever it occurred during the week of unleavened bread.
They called the 14th Passover one of the days of unleavened bread,
making it 8 in total.

Whenever this day was (though in the year of Christ's death the annual
sabbath and the seventh-day Sabbath both fell on the same day), the
wave sheaf of barley was lifted up before God as a token of the first fruits
of the barley harvest. Jesus is the First Fruits of them that died.
1 Corinthians 15:20.

Unleavened bread, "bread of affliction." Deut. 16:3.
Unleavened bread is "sincerity and truth." 1 Corinthians 5:8.

Leaven is "false doctrine." Matt. 16:6,12; Mark 8:15.
"hypocrisy." Luke 12:1.   "greed and injustice." Matt. 23:14.
"false zeal." verse 15.   Wrong estimate of spiritual values. Matt. 16:22.
lack of mercy and faith. verse 23.   vain puntiliousness. verse 24.
intolerance. verse 29-33.   Cruelty. verse 34-36.
Skepticism. Matt. 22:23.   Flattery, worldliness. verse 16-21.
"malice and wickedness." 1 Corinthians 5:8.

Israel was baptized in crossing the Red Sea on last sabbath of the feast.

The first day of unleavened bread was "an holy convocation, no manner
of servile work." Num. 28:17.
Burnt offering 2 young bullocks, 1 ram, 7 lambs of first year without
blemish. Num. 28:17-24.
"after this manner throughout the seven days." Num. 28:17-24.
On "the morrow" after Passover, they ate "the old corn of the land."
This included unleavened cakes. The "selfsame day" the manna ceased.
Joshua 5:10-12.

Other Important Passovers

Solomon's Passover. 2 Chron. 8:13.
Hezekiah's Passover followed by Feast of Unleavened Bread seven days
with great gladness, making confession, then kept it another seven days.
2 Chron. 30:1-27.
Josiah's Passover and Unleavened Bread seven days. 2 Kings 23:21-23.
Ezra's Passover and Unleavened Bread seven days. Ezra 6:20-22.
Jesus kept Passover as a young child. Luke 2:41-43.

Jesus kept 3 Passovers recorded in John 2:13,23; 6:4; 11:55-57.
Jesus died on His last Passover. John 12:1.

It was Christ's Last Passover Supper; He would not eat it again until His disciples were once again with Him "in the kingdom." Luke 22:15-16.
Passover is still a shadow of things to come.
We continue to keep it "till He come" 1 Corinthians 11:26.
Christians are waiting for deliverance from this world of sin
"As birds flying so will the Lord of hosts defend Jerusalem; defending also He will deliver it; and passing over He will preserve it." Isaiah 31:5.

Prisoner were customarily released at Passover. John 18:39.

Paul kept Passover; He "kept the ordinances" 1 Cor. 11:1-2, Acts 20:6.
"after the days of Unleavened Bread" "we abode seven days."

Symbols continued:
Bread and Wine. Matt. 26:26-30; Mark 14:22-25; Luke 22:19-20.
Abraham feasted with bread and wine with Melchizedek. Gen. 14:18.
Abraham made cakes and dressed calf for Christ. Gen. 18:6-8.
Each cake was made with 3 measures of fine meal.
"three tenth deals of flour for bullock." Num. 28:17-24.
"Woman hid [leaven] in three measures of meal."
Matt. 13:33; Luke 13:21.
Lot prepared a feast with unleavened bread for angels. Gen. 19:3.

The Feasts in Our Lives
Each Christian experiences the feasts in their pilgrimage of faith. We all begin with *Passover* when we accept Christ as our sacrifice and paint His blood over the door of our hearts. Amazingly, many are satisfied to stop at Passover and never make the journey on to *Pentecost*. Those who do reach Sinai, hear the voice of God thundering His will and are baptized by the fire of His Spirit. But if we don't travel on we will stay in the wilderness. Manna may be nice, but God wants us to reach the promised land, to cross the Jordan, respond to the *Trumpet*'s call, to conquer the enemy, to be at-one with our Holy God through His *Atonement* and rest in the joy of His final harvest where we can *Tabernacle* with Him at last.

The final Feast of Tabernacles is the 7th feast, occurring in the 7th month and lasts for 7 days. It is filled with the number seven to indicate the spiritual completeness of this event. It is the second coming, it is the final redemption, it is the final rest. Like the holy of holies was in space to the holy place, so this seventh feast is the Sabbath of Sabbaths, it is the festival of festivals hosted by the Lord of lords in person for His children. It is the grand climax of God's redemption.

Appendix D
Circaseptans and Chronobiology

The Clocks of Life
Biologists have long known of the circadian ("about a day") intervals that influence many functions and processes in living organisms. Daily wake-sleep cycles keep our body's digestive, neural and hormonal systems synchronized with the light-dark phases of our earth's 24-hour rotational frequency. Body temperature, blood pressure and even cell division are all locked into the circadian beat of life. But recent discoveries have identified additional rhythms involving shorter and longer time periods.

Ultradian	<24 hours	Heartbeat, brain waves, energy levels.
Circadian	≈24 hours	Temperature, blood pressure, sleep.
Circaseptan	≈7 days	Infections, organ transplant rejection.
Circatrigintan	≈28 days	Menstruation.
Circannual	≈365 days	Seasonal depression, libido.

Most fascinating is the finding that the circaseptan biological week is found in a wide spectrum of life forms ranging from humans to single celled bacteria and algae. Observations since ancient times have repeatedly cited a 7-day period (or multiple) for the incubation period for many common infections. Hippocrates and Galen (from the 2nd and 3rd centuries BC) and Avicenna in the middle ages (980-1037AD) recorded fever peaks and onset of symptoms at consistent 7-day intervals.

Franz Halberg, head of the Chronobiology Laboratories at the University of Minnesota, has published extensively on this very topic since the 1950s. His presentation at the 1994 Medtronic Chronobiology Seminar (*Introduction to Chronobiology Variability: from foe to friend, of mice and men*) identified circaseptan and circasemiseptan (3 ½ day cycles) to be especially associated with variations in malignant tumor growth patterns, regeneration of kidney tissue following nephrectomy, rejection episodes after kidney transplants, urinary 17-ketosteroid excretion, blood pressures of term babies (with an even stronger association with very pre-term babies), sudden infant death syndrome incidence, and sudden death of adults from myocardial infarction and stroke demonstrating a stable, generalized worldwide pattern that traverses cultures and continents.

Halberg believes that these circseptan 7-day rhythms an innate "feature of nature, not only culture" and that they demonstrate "the genetic basis" of these rhythms. This is intriguing. Could it be that the built-in clocks of all living things share a common structural mechanism written into the genetic code of all DNA?

Dr. Sang Lee, physician director of the New Life Institute on the web at www.newlifein.org, has developed this idea into a comprehensive field of study he calls Biotheology. Advances in molecular biology since the discovery of DNA's double-helix structure by Watson and Crick (and their deciphering of the tri-base amino acid sequences from complimentary base-pairing of the genetic code) now enhance our understanding of certain Biblical statements. For example, 2 Corinthians 3:3, "you are the epistle of Christ, written not with ink, but with the Spirit of the living God; not in tables of stone, but in fleshy tables of the heart." And Jeremiah 31:33 where God promises to write His law on our hearts. Christ, the Creator, has written His will into the very genes that control the ebb and flow of our metabolic pathways and the pulse of life.

Fluctuations in the levels of immune globulins, hormones, enzymes and a multitude of other intracellular molecules appear to be hard-coded into our DNA gene sequences, forming an ancient message, written long ago when life on this planet entered the realm of time; when the seven-day interval for life was initialized by its Programmer at the end of creation week.

> "The compounds coordinating a time structure—proteins, steroids, and amino-acid derivatives—provide for the scheduling of interactions among membrane, cytoplasmic, and nuclear events in a network involving rhythmic enzyme reactions and other intracellular mechanisms. The **integrated temporal features** of the processes of induction, repression, transcription, and translation **of gene expression** remain to be mapped." Franz Halberg, "Quo Vadis Basic and Clinical Chronobiology: Promise for Health Maintenance," *American Journal of Anatomy* 168:543-594 (1983), p. 545.

The 7-day clock of life continues to amaze and inspire.

> "These circaseptan, or about weekly, rhythms are one of the major surprises turned up by modern chronobiology. Fifteen years ago, few scientists would have expected that seven-day biological cycles would prove to be so widespread and so long established in the living world. They are of very ancient origin, appearing in primitive one-celled organisms, and are thought to be present even in bacteria, the simplest form of life now existing." Jeremy Campbell, *Winston Churchill's Afternoon Nap,* (New York: Simon and Schuster, 1986), p. 75.

Appendix E
The Epistle of Ignatius to the Magnesians

"In the sixteenth century, fifteen letters were brought out from beneath the mantle of a hoary antiquity, and offered to the world as the productions of the pastor of Antioch. Scholars refused to receive them on the terms required, and forthwith eight of them were admitted to be forgeries. In the seventeenth century, the seven remaining letters, in a somewhat altered form, again came forth from obscurity, and claimed to be the works of Ignatius. Again discerning critics refused to acknowledge their pretensions; but curiosity was roused by this second apparition, and many expressed an earnest desire to obtain a sight of the real epistles. Greece, Syria, Palestine, and Egypt, were ransacked in search of them, and at length three letters are found. The discovery creates general gratulation; it is confessed that four of the epistles so lately asserted to be genuine, are apocryphal; and it is boldly said that the three now forthcoming are above challenge. But truth still refuses to be compromised, and sternly disowns these claimants for her approbation. The internal evidence of these three epistles abundantly attests that, like the last three books of the Sibyl, they are only the last shifts of a grave imposture." Killen, *The Ancient Church*, pp. 413, 414.

"It is no mean proof of the sagacity of the great Calvin, that, upwards of three hundred years ago, he passed a sweeping sentence of condemnation on these Ignatian epistles." Killen, p. 427.

"Every one at all conversant with such matters is aware that the works of Ignatius have been more interpolated and corrupted than those of any other of the ancient fathers; and also that some writings have been attributed to him which are wholly spurious." Domville, Sir William, *Examination of the Six Tests*, p. 237.

"If any of the writings attributed to those who are called apostolical fathers, as Ignatius, teacher at Antioch, Polycarp, at Smyrna, Barnabas, who was half a Jew, and Hermas, who was brother to Pius, teacher at Rome, if any of these be genuine, of which there is great reason to doubt, they only prove the piety and illiteracy of the good men. Some are worse, and the best not better, than the godly epistles of the lower sort of Baptists and Quakers in the time of the civil war in England. Barnabas and Hermas both mention baptism; but both of these books are contemptible reveries of wild and irregular geniuses." Robinson, *Ecclesiastical Researches*, chap. vi. pp. 50, 51, ed. 1792.

Kitto's Cyclopedia presents the original Greek text of Ignatius and observes that the word 'day' (not present in the Greek, but supplied in the English) is entirely a matter of conjecture:

"We must here notice one other passage... as bearing on the subject of the Lord's day, though it certainly contains no mention of it. It occurs in the epistle of Ignatius to the Magnesians (about A.D. 100.) The whole passage is confessedly obscure, and the text may be corrupt... The passage is as follows:

> *Ei oun oi en palaiois pragmasin anastraphentes eis kainoteta elpidos elthon-meketi sabbatixontes, alla kata kuriaken xoen xontes-(en e kai e xoe emon aneteilen oi autou, etc.)* (*Ignatius ad Magnesios*, sect. 9.)

"Now many commentators assume (on what ground does not appear), that after *kuriaken* [Lord's] the word *emeran* [day] is to be understood... Let us now look at the passage simply as it stands. The defect of the sentence is the want of a substantive to which *autou* can refer. This defect, so far from being remedied, is rendered still more glaring by the introduction of *emera*. Now if we take *kuriake xon* as simply 'the life of the Lord,' having a more personal meaning, it certainly goes nearer to supplying the substantive to *autou*...Thus upon the whole the meaning might be given thus:

"If those who lived under the old dispensation have come to the newness of hope, no longer keeping sabbaths, but living according to our Lord's life (in which, as it were, our life has risen again through him, &c.)...

"On this view the passages does not refer at all to the Lord's day; but even on the opposite supposition it can not be regarded as affording any positive evidence to the early use of the term 'Lord's day' (for which it is often cited), since the material word *emera* [day] is purely conjectural." Kitto, John, *Cyclopedia of Biblical Literature*, London, 1862, art. Lord's day.

Morer, a clergy in the church of England, agrees with Kitto.

"If therefore they who were well versed in the works of ancient days came to newness of hope, not sabbatizing, but living according to the dominical life, &c. . . . The Medicean copy, the best and most like that of Eusebius, leaves no scruple, because *xoen* is expressed and determines the word dominical to the person of Christ, and not to the day of his resurrection." Morer, Thomas M., *Dialogues on the Lord's Day*, London, 1701, pp. 206, 207.

Sir Domville further observes that the passage does not even discuss religious observance:

"Judging therefore by the tenor of the epistle itself, the literal translation of the passage in discussion, 'no longer observing sabbaths, but living according to the Lord's life,' appears to give its true and proper meaning; and if this be so, Ingatius, whom Mr. Gurney [author of *History, Authority, and Use, of the Sabbath*] puts forward as a material witness to prove the observance of the Lord's day in the beginning of the second century, fails to prove any such fact, it appearing on a thorough examination of his testimony that he does not even mention the Lord's day, nor in any way allude to the religious observance of it, whether by that name or by any other." Domville, *Examination of the Six Texts*, pp. 250, 251.

The Epistle of Barnabas

"The writings of the so-called Apostolic Fathers are, alas! come down to us, for the most part, in a very uncertain condition; partly, because in early times writings were counterfeited, under the name of these venerable men of the church, in order to propagate certain opinions or principles; ... We should here, in the first place, have to name Bamabas, the well known fellow traveler of St. Paul, if a letter, which was first known in the second century, in the Alexandrian church, under his name, and which bore the inscription of a Catholic epistle, was really his composition. But it is impossible that we should acknowledge this epistle to belong to that Barnabis who was worthy to be the companion of the apostolic labors of St. Paul, and had received his name from the power of his animated discourses in the churches. We find, also, nothing to induce us to believe the author of the Epistle was desirous of being considered Barnabas. But since its spirit and its mode of conception corresponded to the Alexandrian taste, it may have happened, that as the author's name was unknown, and persons were desirous of giving it authority, a report was spread abroad in Alexandria, that Barnabas was the author." Neander, Wilhelm August Johann, *History of the Christian Church of the First Three Centuries,*, London, 1831 (Rose's translation from the German edition, Hamburg, 1826) p. 407, 408.

"That a man by the name of Barnabas wrote this epistle I doubt not; that the chosen associate of Paul wrote it, I with many others must doubt." Gurney, Joseph John, *History, Authority, and Use of the Sabbath,* 1831, p. 86.

"The tract known as the Epistle of Barnabas was probably composed in A.D. 135. It is the production apparently of a convert from Judaism who took special pleasure in allegorical interpretation of Scripture." Killen, William. D., Professor of Ecclesiastical History, to the General Assembly of the Presbyterian church of Ireland, *The Ancient Church*, 1883, pp. 367, 368.

"The letter still extant, which was known as that of Barnabas even in the second century, cannot be defended as genuine." Hackett, Horatio B., *Commentary on Acts*, Kregel Publications; ISBN: 0825427487, p. 251.

"It is a great injury to him to apprehend the epistle, which goes by his name, to be his." Milner, Joseph. *The History of the Church of Christ.* 5 vol. London: Luke Hansard & Sons, 1819, century 1, chap. xv.

"The epistle of Barnabas, bearing the honored name of the companion of Paul in his missionary labors, is evidently spurious. It abounds in fabulous narratives, mystic, allegorical interpretations of the Old Testament, and fanciful conceits, and is generally agreed by the learned to be of no authority." Coleman, Lyman, *Ancient Christianity Exemplified, 1852*, chap. i. sect. 2.

"The so-called epistle of Barnabas, probably a forgery of the second century." Kitto, *Cyclopedia of Biblical Literature*, article *Lord's day*, tenth ed. 1858.

"But the epistle was not written by Barnabas; it was not merely unworthy of him, it would be a disgrace to him, and what is of much more consequence, it would be a disgrace to the Christian religion, as being the production of one of the authorized teachers of that religion in the times of the apostles, which circumstance would seriously damage the evidence of its divine origin. Not being the epistle of Barnabas, the document is, as regards the Sabbath question, nothing more than the testimony of some unknown writer to the practice of Sunday observance by some Christians of some unknown community, at some uncertain period of the Christian era, with no sufficient ground for believing that period to have been the first century." Domville, Sir Willam, *The Sabbath, or an Examination of the Six Texts commonly adduced from the New Testament in proof of a Christian Sabbath*, 1849, p. 233.

Even Eusebius, the earliest of church historians, regards the epistle of Barnabas to be a forgery:

"Among the spurious must be numbered both the books called, 'The Acts of Paul,' and that called, 'Pastor,' and 'The Revelation of Peter.' Besides these the books called 'The Epistle of Barnabas,' and what are called, 'The Institutions of the Apostles.'" *Ecclesiastical History*, Book iii. chap. xxv.

Some have pointed to what they consider as "absurd content" the following passage:

"Neither shalt thou eat of the hyena: that is, again, be not an adulterer; nor a corrupter of others; neither be like to such. And wherefore so? Because that creature every year changes its kind, and is sometimes male, and sometimes female." *Epistle of Barnabas*, 9:8. In some editions it is chap. 10.

Actually, hyenas (as well as spider monkeys) actually do manifest an external form of hermaphroditic sexual confusion. More thorough research of this biological phenomenon would spare the unwitting embarrassment that other commentators have fallen into. This does not, however, constitute a defense of the otherwise apocryphal epistle.

Though it is the only writing purporting to come from the first century except the New Testament, in which the first day is even referred to, yet it furnishes no credible support for Sunday observance. Instead, the weight of evidence indicts this forgery to a later date of 130-135 AD.

So, the epistles ascribed to Barnabas and Ignatius were forgeries, the Didache is too indefinite and Pliny's letter is only relative if the word day can be interpolated into the document. This conclusion was embraced by the historian Neander:

"The festival of Sunday, like all other festivals, was always only a human ordinance, and it was far from the intentions of the apostles to establish a divine command in this respect, far from them, and from the early apostolic church, to transfer the laws of the Sabbath to Sunday." *Neander's Church History*, translated by H. J. Rose, p. 186.

Torrey's *Neander*, vol. i. p. 295, 1852 edition, a later translation (which may have been "corrected" by the knowing hand of censorship), does not contain the statement included in Rose's earlier version. But neither does he deny it elsewhere in any of his writing. Mosheim, prominent historian that he is, appears to discard objectivity altogether and follow the party line:

> "The Christians of this century, assembled for the worship of God, and for their advancement in piety, on the first day of the week, the day on which Christ reassumed his life: for that this day was set apart for religious worship, by the apostles themselves, and that, after the example of the church of Jerusalem, it was generally observed, we have unexceptionable testimony." Murdock's Mosheim, cent. 1, part ii. chap. iv. sec. 4.

Appendix F
Historical Review of Catholic Comments Concerning Sunday

Monsignor Louis Segur, *Plain Talk About the Protestantism of Today* (1868), p. 213
"The observance of Sunday by the Protestants is an homage they pay, in spite of themselves, to the authority of the [Catholic] church."

John Gilmary Shea, American Catholic Quarterly Review, January, 1883.
"Protestantism, In discarding the authority of the (Roman Catholic) Church, has no good reasons for its Sunday theory, and ought logically to keep Saturday as the Sabbath."

J. O'Keefe, Catholic Mirror, July 3, 1987
"The Jew is rational; he obeys his teacher, the Bible, pointing to the command, 'Keep holy the Sabbath;' the Catholic is ever rational, he obeys the teacher [the Church] appointed him by Christ; but the Protestant obeys neither God nor his teacher, the Bible."

The Catholic Mirror, official publication of James Cardinal Gibbons, Sept. 23, 1893.
"The Catholic Church, . . . by virtue of her divine mission, changed the day from Saturday to Sunday."

The Catholic National, July, 1895.
"The Pope is not only the representative of Jesus Christ, but he is Jesus Christ Himself, hidden under veil of flesh."

The Catholic Press, Sydney, Australia, August, 1900.
"Sunday is a Catholic Institution, and its claims to observance can be defended only on Catholic principles. . . .From beginning to end of Scripture there is not a single passage that warrants the transfer of weekly public worship from the last day of the week to the first."

Priest Brady, in an address, reported in the Elizabeth, N.J. "News", March 18, 1903.
"It is well to remind the Presbyterians, Baptists, Methodists, and all other Christians, that the Bible does not support them anywhere in their observance of Sunday. Sunday is an institution of the Roman Catholic Church, and those who observe the day observe a commandment of the Catholic Church."

Daniel Ferres, ed., *Manual of Christian Doctrine* (1916), p.67.
Also in Henry Tuberville, *An Abridgment of the Christian Doctrine* (1833 approbation), p.58
"Question: How prove you that the Church hath power to command feasts and holy days?"

"Answer: By the very act of changing the Sabbath into Sunday, which Protestants allow of, and therefore they fondly contradict themselves, by keeping Sunday strictly, and breaking most other feasts commanded by the same Church."

Albert Smith, chancellor of the Archdiocese of Baltimore, replying for Cardinal Gibbons in a letter, February 10, 1920.

"If Protestants would follow the Bible, they should worship God on the Sabbath Day. In keeping the Sunday, they are following a law of the Catholic Church."

Martin J. Scott, *Things Catholics Are Asked About* (1927),p. 136.

"Nowhere in the Bible is it stated that worship should be changed from Saturday to Sunday .... Now the Church ... instituted, by God's authority, Sunday as the day of worship. This same Church, by the same divine authority, taught the doctrine of Purgatory long before the Bible was made. We have, therefore, the same authority for Purgatory as we have for Sunday."

John Laux, *A Course in Religion for Catholic High Schools and Academies* (1936), vol. 1, P. 51.

"Some theologians have held that God likewise directly determined the Sunday as the day of worship in the New Law, that He Himself has explicitly substituted the Sunday for the Sabbath. But this theory is now entirely abandoned. It is now commonly held that God simply gave His Church the power to set aside whatever day or days she would deem suitable as Holy Days. The Church chose Sunday, the first day of the week, and in the course of time added other days as holy days."

The Catholic Universe Bulletin, August 14, 1942, page 4.

"The Church changed the observance of the Sabbath to Sunday by right of the divine, infallible authority given to her by her founder, Jesus Christ. The Protestant claiming the Bible to be the only guide of faith, has no warrant for observing Sunday. In this matter the Seventh-day Adventist is the only consistent Protestant."

Catholic Virginian Oct. 3, 1947, p. 9, art. "To Tell You the Truth."

"For example, nowhere in the Bible do we find that Christ or the Apostles ordered that the Sabbath be changed from Saturday to Sunday. We have the commandment of God given to Moses to keep holy the Sabbath day, that is the 7th day of the week, Saturday. Today most Christians keep Sunday because it has been revealed to us by the[Roman Catholic] church outside the Bible."

Our Sunday Visitor, February 5, 1950.

"Protestants. . .accept Sunday rather than Saturday as the day for public worship after the Catholic Church made the change. . .But the Protestant mind does not seem to realize that . . in observing the Sunday, they are accepting the authority of the spokesman for the church, the Pope."

Peter Geiermann, C.S.S.R., *The Converts Catechism of Catholic Doctrine* **(1957), p. 50.**
"Question: Which is the Sabbath day?
Answer: Saturday is the Sabbath day.
Question: Why do we observe Sunday instead of Saturday?
Answer. We observe Sunday instead of Saturday because the Catholic Church transferred the solemnity from Saturday to Sunday."

S.D. Moana, Storia della Domenica, 1969, pages 366-367.
"Not the Creator of the Universe, In Geneses 2:1-3, —but the Catholic Church "can claim the honor of having granted man a pause to his work every seven days."

Peter R. Kraemer, Catholic Church Extension Society (1975),Chicago, Illinois.
"Regarding the change from the observance of the Jewish Sabbath to the Christian Sunday, I wish to draw your attention to the facts:
1) That Protestants, who accept the Bible as the only rule of faith and religion, should by all means go back to the observance of the Sabbath. The fact that they do not, but on the contrary observe the Sunday, stultifies them in the eyes of every thinking man.

2) We Catholics do not accept the Bible as the only rule of faith. Besides the Bible we have the living Church, the authority of the Church, as a rule to guide us. We say, this Church, instituted by Christ to teach and guide man through life, has the right to change the ceremonial laws of the Old Testament and hence, we accept her change of the Sabbath to Sunday. We frankly say, yes, the Church made this change, made this law, as she made many other laws, for instance, the Friday abstinence, the unmarried priesthood, the laws concerning mixed marriages, the regulation of Catholic marriages and a thousand other laws.

It is always somewhat laughable, to see the Protestant churches, in pulpit and legislation, demand the observance of Sunday, of which there is nothing in their Bible."

Fr. Leo Broderick, Saint Catherine Catholic Church *Sentinel,* **Algonac, Michigan, May 21, 1995.**
"Perhaps the boldest thing, the most revolutionary change the Church ever did, happened in the first century. The holy day, the Sabbath, was changed from Saturday to Sunday. 'The Day of the Lord' (dies Dominica) was chosen, not from any directions noted in the Scriptures, but from the Church's sense of its own power. The day of resurrection, the day of Pentecost, fifty days later, came on the first day of the week. So this would be the new Sabbath. People who think that the Scriptures should be the sole authority, should logically become 7th Day Adventists, and keep Saturday holy."

It is quite clear that the Catholic position regarding the seventh day Sabbath has been unbending for over 400 years. Pleased to embarrass the Protestant world with their illogical departure from Biblical doctrine, the Roman Church has until very recent years continued to ridicule "the estranged brethren" in this matter.

Father O'Brien, *The Faith of Millions*, 1974.

"Let me address myself to my dear non-Catholic reader. You believe that the Bible alone is a safe guide in religious matters. You also believe that one of the fundamental duties enjoined upon you by your Christian faith is that of Sunday observance. But where does the Bible speak of such an obligation? I have read the Bible from the first verse of Genesis to the last verse of Revelation and have found no reference to the duty of sanctifying the Sunday. The day mentioned in the Bible is not the Sunday, the first day of the week, but the Saturday, the last day of the week."

Catholic Press, Sydney, Australia, August, 1900.

"Sunday is a Catholic institution, and its claim to observance can be defended only on Catholic principles . . From beginning to end of Scripture there is not a single passage that warrants the transfer of weekly public worship from the last day of the week to the first."

John Gilmary Shea, American Catholic *Quarterly Review*, January 1883.

"Protestantism, in discarding the authority of the [Roman Catholic] Church, has no good reason for its Sunday theory, and ought logically to keep Saturday as the Sabbath."

Priest Brady, in an address, reported in the Elizabeth, N.J. News of March 18, 1903.

"It is well to remind the Presbyterians, Baptists, Methodists, and all other Christians that the Bible does not support them anywhere in their observance of Sunday. Sunday is an institution of the Roman Catholic Church, and those who observe the day observe a commandment of the Catholic Church."

The Catholic Mirror, December 23, 1893.

"Reason and common sense demand the acceptance of one or the other of these two alternatives: either Protestantism and the keeping holy of Saturday or Catholicity and the keeping holy of Sunday. Compromise is impossible."

Vincent J. Kelly, *Forbidden Sunday and Feast-Day Occupations*, p. 2.

"God simply gave His [Catholic] Church the power to set aside whatever day or days she would deem suitable as Holy Days. The Church chose Sunday, the first day of the week, and in the course of time added other days, as holy days."

Our Sunday Visitor, February 5, 1950.

"Protestants...accept Sunday rather than Saturday as the day for public worship after the Catholic Church made the change....But the Protestant mind does not seem to realize that...in observing the Sunday, they are accepting the authority of the spokesman for the church, the Pope."

S. C. Mosna, Storia della Domenica, 1969, pp. 366-367.
"We hold upon this earth the place of God Almighty."—Pope Leo XIII, in an Encyclical Letter, dated June 20, 1894.

"Not the Creator of Universe, in Genesis 2:1-3,—but the Catholic Church can claim the honor of having granted man a pause to his work every seven days."

The Catholic National, July 1895.
"The Pope is not only the representative of Jesus Christ, but he is Jesus Christ, hidden under veil of flesh."

Albert Smith, Chancellor of the Archdiocese of Baltimore, replying for the Cardinal, in a letter dated February 10, 1920.
"If Protestants would follow the Bible, they should worship God on the Sabbath Day. In keeping the Sunday they are following a law of the Catholic Church."

A Decree of the Council of Trent, quoted in Philippe Labbe and Gabriel Cossart, "The Most Holy Councils," col. 1167.
"We define that the Holy Apostolic See (the Vatican) and the Roman Pontiff hold the primacy over the whole world."

Monsignor Louis Segur, Plain Talk About the Protestantism of Today, p. 213.
"It was the Catholic Church which, by the authority of Jesus Christ, has transferred this rest [from the Bible Sabbath] to the Sunday...Thus the observance of Sunday by the Protestants is an homage they pay, in spite of themselves, to the authority of the [Catholic] Church."

Peter Geiermann, CSSR, A Doctrinal Catechism, 1957 edition, p. 50.
"We observe Sunday instead of Saturday because the Catholic Church transferred the solemnity from Saturday to Sunday."

The Brotherhood of St. Paul, "The Clifton tracts," Volume 4, tract 4, p. 15.
"We Catholics, then, have precisely the same authority for keeping Sunday holy instead of Saturday as we have for every other article of our creed, namely, the authority of the Church...whereas you who are Protestants have really no authority for it whatever; for there is no authority for it [Sunday sacredness] in the Bible, and you will not allow that there can be authority for it anywhere else."

Appendix G
Selected
DECLARATIONS OF THE COUNCIL OF TRENT

FOURTH SESSION: DECREE CONCERNING THE CANONICAL SCRIPTURES: "If anyone does not accept as sacred and canonical the aforesaid books in their entirety and with all their parts [the 66 books of the Bible plus 12 apocryphal books, being two of Paralipomenon, two of Esdras, Tobias, Judith, Wisdom, Ecclesiasticus, Baruch, Sophonias, two of Macabees], as they have been accustomed to be read in the Catholic Church and as they are contained in the old Latin Vulgate Edition, and knowingly and deliberately rejects the aforesaid traditions, LET HIM BE ANATHEMA."

SIXTH SESSION, CANONS CONCERNING JUSTIFICATION: "If anyone says that justifying faith is nothing else than confidence in divine mercy, which remits sins for Christ's sake, or that it is this confidence alone that justifies us, LET HIM BE ANATHEMA" (Canons Concerning Justification, Canon 12).

"If anyone says that the justice received is not preserved and also not increased before God through good works, but that those works are merely the fruits and signs of justification obtained, but not the cause of its increase, LET HIM BE ANATHEMA" (Canon 24).

"If anyone says that the Catholic doctrine of justification as set forth by the holy council in the present decree, derogates in some respect from the glory of God or the merits of our Lord Jesus Christ, and does not rather illustrate the truth of our faith and no less the glory of God and of Christ Jesus, LET HIM BE ANATHEMA" (Canon 33).

SEVENTH SESSION, CANONS ON BAPTISM: "If anyone says that in the Roman Church, which is the mother and mistress of all churches, there is not the true doctrine concerning the sacrament of baptism, LET HIM BE ANATHEMA" (Canon 3).

"If anyone says that baptism is optional, that is, not necessary for salvation, LET HIM BE ANATHEMA" (Canon 5).

"If anyone says that children, because they have not the act of believing, are not after having received baptism to be numbered among the faithful, and that for this reason are to be rebaptized when they have reached the years of discretion; or that it is better that the baptism of such be omitted than that, while not believing by their own act, they should be baptized in the faith of the Church alone, LET HIM BE ANATHEMA" (Canon 13).

SEVENTH SESSION, CANONS ON CONFIRMATON: "If anyone says that the confirmation of those baptized is an empty ceremony and not a true and proper sacrament; or that of old it was nothing more than a sort of instruction, whereby those approaching adolescence gave an account of their faith to the Church, LET HIM BE ANATHEMA" (Canon 1).

THIRTEENTH SESSION, CANONS ON THE MOST HOLY SACRAMENT OF THE EUCHARIST: "If anyone denies that in the sacrament of the most Holy Eucharist are contained truly, really and substantially the body and blood together with the soul and divinity of our Lord Jesus Christ, and consequently the whole Christ, but says that He is in it only as in a sign, or figure or force, LET HIM BE ANATHEMA" (Canon 1).

"If anyone says that Christ received in the Eucharist is received spiritually only and not also sacramentally and really, LET HIM BE ANATHEMA" (Canon 8).

FOURTEENTH SESSION, CANONS CONCERNING THE MOST HOLY SACRAMENT OF PENANCE: "If anyone says that in the Catholic Church penance is not truly and properly a sacrament instituted by Christ the Lord for reconciling the faithful of God as often as they fall into sin after baptism, LET HIM BE ANATHEMA" (Canon 1).

"If anyone denies that sacramental confession was instituted by divine law or is necessary to salvation; or says that the manner of confessing secretly to a priest alone, which the Catholic Church has always observed from the beginning and still observes, is at variance with the institution and command of Christ and is a human contrivance, LET HIM BE ANATHEMA" (Canon 7).

"If anyone says that the confession of all sins as it is observed in the Church is impossible and is a human tradition to be abolished by pious people; or that each and all of the faithful of Christ or either sex are not bound thereto once a year in accordance with the constitution of the great Lateran Council, and that for this reason the faithful of Christ are to be persuaded not to confess during Lent, LET HIM BE ANATHEMA" (Canons Concerning the Most Holy Sacrament of Penance, Canon 8).

"If anyone says that God always pardons the whole penalty together with the guilt and that the satisfaction of penitents is nothing else than the faith by which they perceive that Christ has satisfied for them, LET HIM BE ANATHEMA" (Canon 8).

TWENTY-SECOND SESSION, CANONS ON THE SACRI-FICE OF THE MASS: "If anyone says that in the mass a true and real sacrifice is not offered to God; or that to be offered is nothing else than that Christ is given to us to eat, LET HIM BE ANATHEMA" (Canon 1).

"If anyone says that by those words, Do this for a commemoration of me, Christ did not institute the Apostles priests; or did not ordain that they and other priests should offer His own body and blood, LET HIM BE ANATHEMA" (Canon 2).

"If anyone says that the sacrifice of the mass is one only of praise and thanksgiving; or that it is a mere commemoration of the sacrifice consummated on the cross but not a propitiatory one; or that it profits him only who receives, and ought not to be offered for the living and the dead, for sins, punishments, satisfactions, and other necessities, LET HIM BE ANATHEMA" (Canon 3).

"If anyone says that it is a deception to celebrate masses in honor of the saints and in order to obtain their intercession with God, as the Church intends, LET HIM BE ANATHEMA" (Canon 5).

TWENTY-THIRD SESSION, CANONS ON THE SACRAMENT OF ORDER: "If anyone says that there is not in the New Testament a visible and external priesthood, or that there is no power of consecrating and offering the true body and blood of the Lord and of forgiving and retaining sins, but only the office and bare ministry of preaching the Gospel; or that those who do not preach are not priests at all, LET HIM BE ANATHEMA" (Canon 1).

"If anyone says that the bishops who are chosen by the authority of the Roman pontiff are not true and legitimate bishops, but merely human deception, LET HIM BE ANATHEMA" (Canon 8).

TWENTY-FIFTH SESSION, DECREE ON PURGATORY: "Since the Catholic Church, instructed by the Holy Ghost, has, following the sacred writings and the ancient tradition of the Fathers, taught in sacred councils and very recently in this ecumenical council that there is a purgatory, and that the souls there detained are aided by the suffrages of the faithful and chiefly by the acceptable sacrifice of the altar, the holy council commands the bishops that they strive diligently to the end that the sound doctrine of purgatory, transmitted by the Fathers and sacred councils, be believed and maintained by the faithful of Christ, and be everywhere taught and preached."

**TWENTY-FIFTH SESSION, ON THE INVOCATION, VENERA-
TION, AND RELICS OF SAINTS, AND ON SACRED IMAGES:**
"The holy council commands all bishops and others who hold the office
of teaching and have charge of the cura animarum, that in accordance
with the usage of the Catholic and Apostolic Church, received from the
primitive times of the Christian religion, and with the unanimous
teaching of the holy Fathers and the decrees of sacred councils, they
above all instruct the faithful diligently in matters relating to
intercession and invocation of the saints, the veneration of relics, and
the legitimate use of images, teaching them that the saints who reign
together with Christ offer up their prayers to God for men, that it is good
and beneficial suppliantly to invoke them and to have recourse to their
prayers, assistance and support in order to obtain favors from God
through His Son, Jesus Christ our Lord, who alone is our redeemer and
savior; and that they think impiously who deny that the saints who
enjoy eternal happiness in heaven are to be invoked, or who assert that
they do not pray for men, or that our invocation of them to pray for each
of us individually is idolatry, or that it is opposed to the word of God and
inconsistent with the honor of the one mediator of God and men, Jesus
Christ, or that it is foolish to pray vocally or mentally to those who reign
in heaven."

Appendix H

The
ANTI-NICENE FATHERS
translations of
The Writings of the Fathers down to a.d. 325
The Rev. Alexander Roberts, D.D.,
and
James Donaldson, LL.D.,
EDITORS
AMERICAN REPRINT OF THE EDINBURGH EDITION
revised and chronologically arranged,
with brief prefaces and occasional notes
by
A. Cleveland Coxe, D.D.
T&T CLARK
Edinburgh
Wm. B. Eerdmans publishing company
Grand Rapids, Michigan

Apostolic Constitutions

Dated in the 4ᵗʰ century, they claim to be the writings of the original apostles, but their authenticity has been denied since the 7ᵗʰ century. Yet, they are valuable in giving a picture of what issues were being discussed in the 300's AD. The following excerpts are taken from the *Apostolic Constitutions*, Anti-nicean Fathers, Book VII.

Book V
When to observe Passover

XVII. "Do not you yourselves compute, but **keep it when your brethren of the circumcision do** so: **keep it together with them**; and if they err in their computation, be not you concerned. Keep your nights of watching in the middle of the days of unleavened bread. And **when the Jews are feasting, do you fast** and wail over them, because an the day of their feast they crucified Christ; and **while they are lamenting and eating unleavened bread in bitterness, do you feast**."

XVIII. Do you therefore fast on the days of the passover, beginning from the second day of the week **until the preparation, and the Sabbath**, six days, making use of only bread, and salt, and herbs, and water for your drink; but do you abstain on these days from wine and flesh, for they are days of lamentation and not of feasting. Do ye who are **able fast the day of the preparation and the Sabbath-day entirely**, tasting nothing till the cock-crowing of the night; but if any one is not able to join them both together, at least let him **observe the Sabbath-day**; for the Lord says somewhere, speaking of Himself: 'When the bridegroom shall be taken away from them, in those days shall they fast.'

XIX. Wherefore we exhort you to fast on those days, as **we also fasted till the evening, when He was taken away from us**; but on the rest of the days, before the day of the preparation, let every one eat at the ninth hour, or at the evening, or as every one is able. But from the even of the fifth day till cock-crowing break your fast when it is daybreak of **the first day of the week, which is the Lord's day.**

For this reason do you also, now the Lord is risen, offer your sacrifice, concerning which He made a constitution by us, saying, 'Do this for a remembrance of me;' and thenceforward leave off your fasting, and rejoice, and keep a festival, because Jesus Christ, the pledge of our resurrection, is risen from the dead. And let this be an everlasting ordinance till the consummation of the world, until the Lord come. For to Jews the Lord is still dead, but to Christians He is risen: to the former, by their unbelief; to the latter, by their full assurance of faith. For the hope in Him is immortal and eternal life. ***After eight days let there be another feast observed*** *with honour, the eighth day itself, on which He gave me Thomas, who was hard of belief, full assurance, by showing me the print of the nails, and the wound made in His side by the spear. And again,* ***from the first Lord's day count forty days****, from the Lord's day till the fifth day of the week, and celebrate the feast of the ascension of the Lord, whereon He finished all His dispensation and constitution."*

"We enjoin you to fast every fourth day of the week, and every day of the preparation, and the surplusage of your fast bestow upon the needy; ***every Sabbath-day*** *excepting one, and* ***every Lord's day****, hold your solemn assemblies, and rejoice: for he will be guilty of sin who fasts on the Lord's day, being the day of the resurrection, or during the time of Pentecost, or, in general, who is sad on a festival day to the Lord. For on them we ought to rejoice, and not to mourn." Section XX*

Book VI
XIX. He nowhere has dissolved the law, as Simon pretends, but fulfilled it; for He says: 'One iota, or one tittle, shall not pass from the law until all be fulfilled.' For says He, 'I come not to dissolve the law, but to fulfil it.' For **Moses himself**, who was at once the lawgiver, and the high priest, and the prophet, and the king, **and Elijah**, the zealous follower of the prophets, **were present at our Lord's transfiguration** in the mountain,[109] and witnesses of His incarnation and of His sufferings, as the

intimate friends of Christ, but **not as enemies and strangers**. Whence it is demonstrated that the law is good and holy, as also the prophets.

XXII. If, therefore, before His coming He sought for 'a clean heart and a contrite spirit' more than sacrifices, much **rather would He abrogate those sacrifices, I mean those by blood, when He came. Yet He so abrogated them as that He first fulfilled them.** For He was both circumcised, and sprinkled, and offered sacrifices and whole burnt-offerings, and made use of the rest of their customs. And **He that was the Lawgiver became Himself the fulfilling of the law; not taking away the law of nature, but abrogating those additional laws** that were afterwards introduced, although not all of them neither.

XXIII. For **He did not take away the law of nature, but confirmed it**. For He that said in the law, **'The Lord thy God is one Lord;'** the same says in the Gospel, 'That they might know Thee, the only true God.' And He that said, **'Thou shalt love thy neighhour as thyself,'** says in the Gospel, renewing the same precept, 'A new commandment I give unto you, that ye love one another.' He who then **forbade murder**, does now forbid causeless anger. He that **forbade adultery**, does now forbid all unlawful lust. He that **forbade stealing**, now pronounces him most happy who supplies those that are in want out of his own labours. He that **forbade hatred**, now pronounces him blessed that loves his enemies. He that **forbade revenge**, now commands long-suffering; not as if just revenge were an unrighteous thing, but because long-suffering is more excellent. Nor did He make laws to root out our natural passions, but only to forbid the excess of them. He who had commanded to honour our parents, was Himself subject to them. He who had commanded to **keep the Sabbath, by resting thereon for the sake of meditating on the laws**, has **now commanded us to consider of the law of creation**, and of providence **every day**, and to return thanks to God, **He abrogated circumcision** when He had Himself fulfilled it. For He it was 'to whom the inheritance was reserved, who was the expectation of the nations.' He who made a law for swearing rightly, and forbade perjury, has now charged us not to swear at all. **He has in several ways changed baptism, sacrifice, the priesthood, and the divine service,** which was confined to one place: for **instead of daily baptisms, He has given only one**, which is that into His death. **Instead of one tribe,** He has appointed that **out of every nation** the best should be ordained for the priesthood; and that not their bodies should be examined for blemishes, but their religion and their lives. **Instead of a bloody sacrifice**, He has appointed that reasonable and **unbloody mystical one of His body and blood**, which is performed to represent the death of the Lord by **symbols**. Instead of the divine service **confined to one place**, He has commanded and appointed that He should be glorified from sunrising to sunsetting in every place of His dominion. **He did not therefore take away the law from us**, but the bonds. For concerning the law Moses says: 'Thou shalt meditate on the word which I command thee, sitting in thine house, and rising up, and walking in the way.' And David says: 'His delight is in the law of the Lord, and in His law will he meditate day and night.' For **everywhere would he have us subject to His laws**, but not transgressors of them. For says He: 'Blessed are the undefiled in the way, who walk in the law of the Lord. Blessed are they that search out His testimonies; with their whole heart shall they seek Him.' And again: 'Blessed are we, O Israel, because those things that are pleasing to God are known to us.' And the Lord says: 'If ye know these things, happy are ye if ye do them.' "

Book VII
XXIII. But do you either fast the entire five days, or on the fourth day of the week, and on the day of the Preparation, because on the fourth day the condemnation went out against the Lord, Judas then promising to betray Him for money; and you must fast on the day of the Preparation, because on that day the Lord suffered the death of the cross under Pontius Pilate. But **keep the Sabbath, and the Lord's day festival; because the former is the memorial of the creation, and the latter of the resurrection**. But there is one only Sabbath to be observed by you in the whole year, which is that of our Lord's burial, on which men ought to keep a fast, but not a festival.

These excerpts indicate that there was no antinomian teachings by these alleged apostles. But they made a distinction between the law of God which remains, and the "added" laws of sacrifice which are "abrogated" by Christ's sacrifice. The co-existing observation of both a seventh day Sabbath and a first day resurrection festival called the Lord's day is also evident.

Victorinus
Bishop of Petau, who flourished towards the end of the third century. [He died in the persecution A.D. 304.] For the text and full annotations, see Routh, iii. 451-483.

On the Creation of the World
On this day also, on account of the passion of the Lord Jesus Christ, we make either a station to God, or a fast. On the seventh day He rested from all His works, and blessed it, and sanctified it. On the former day we are accustomed to fast rigorously, that on the Lord's day we may go forth to our bread with giving of thanks. And let the *parasceve* become a rigorous fast, lest we should appear to observe any Sabbath with the Jews, which Christ Himself, the Lord of the Sabbath, says by His prophets that "His soul hateth;" (Isa 1:13,14) which Sabbath He in His body abolished, although, nevertheless, He had formerly Himself commanded Moses that circumcision should not pass over the eighth day, which day very frequently happens on the Sabbath, as we read written in the Gospel.[7] (John 7:22) Moses, foreseeing the hardness of that people, on the Sabbath raised up his hands, therefore, and thus *figuratively* fastened himself to a

cross. And in the battle they were sought for by the foreigners on the Sabbath-day, that they might be taken captive, and, as if by the very strictness of the law, might be fashioned to the avoidance of its teaching.

Jesus also, the son of Nave, the successor of Moses, himself broke the Sabbath-day; for on the Sabbath-day he commanded the children of Israel[11] to go round the walls of the city of Jericho with trumpets, and declare war against the aliens. Matthias[12] also, prince of Judah, broke the Sabbath; for he slew the prefect of Antiochus the king of Syria on the Sabbath, and subdued the foreigners by pursuing them. And in Matthew we read, that it is written Isaiah also and the rest of his colleagues broke the Sabbath[13] -that that true and just Sabbath should be observed in the seventh millenary of years. Wherefore to those seven days the Lord attributed to each a thousand years; for thus went the warning: "In Thine eyes, O Lord, a thousand years are as one day."[14] Therefore in the eyes of the Lord each thousand of years is ordained, for I find that the Lord's eyes are seven.[15] Wherefore, as I have narrated, that true Sabbath will be in the seventh millenary of years, when Christ with His elect shall reign.

Clement reasons that the first day has mystical importance because:

"on the same day on which the dragon seduced Eve, the angel Gabriel brought the glad tidings to the Virgin Mary; that on the same day the Holy Spirit overflowed the Virgin Mary, on which He made light; that on that day He was incarnate in flesh, in which He made the land and water; that on the same day He was put to the breast, on which He made the stars; that on the same day He was circumcised,[43] on which the land and water brought forth their offspring; that on the same day He was incarnated, on which He formed man out of the ground; that on the same day Christ was born, on which He formed man; that on that day He suffered, on which Adam fell; that on the same day He rose again from the dead, on which He created light? He, moreover, consummates His humanity in the number seven: of His nativity, His infancy, His boyhood, His youth, His young-manhood, His mature age, His death.

Appendix I
More on Mark 16

Four endings to Mark's gospel were in common circulation at the time of the early Christian church. This is found by a comparison of the Major NT manuscripts (from www.holyspiritinfo.net):

1. **B (Codex Vaticanus).** 350 AD. missing Revelation, Heb 11:14 to the end of Heb and 1 & 2 Timothy. It has been in the Vatican library since 1481.

2. **Aleph (Codex Sinaiticus)** 375 AD. A complete NT (with the exception of Mark 16:9-20). This was found by Tischendorf, a Bible archeologist, at St. Catherine's Monastery on Mt. Sinai Tischendorf took shelter in St. Catherine's one night to get out of the rain. There he observed a monk starting a fire with pieces of parchment from a box. On closer inspection he found in the box a bound copy of the NT. It looked very old to him and he asked if he could look at it. He spent all night reading it by candle light. The manuscript is now in the Imperial Library at St. Petersburg.

3. **A (Codex Alexandrinus)** 425 AD. Lacks Mt 1:1 - 25:6, 2 chapters from John and 8 chapters in II Corinthians. Found in Alexandria Egypt. It was a gift to Charles I, king of England, in 1627 and in 1757 it was presented to the Royal Library and now is in the British Museum.

4. **C (Ephraemi Rescriptus)** 450 AD. Originally it contained the entire N.T. but now about half of each book is missing. It contains 145 of 238 pages of the NT. It came to Italy from the East in the 16th century then to France with Catherine de' Medici and now is in the Bibliotheque Nationale, Paris. A monk by the name of St. Ephraem needed something to write his sermons on. He had an old manuscript of the NT on vellum. He scraped the letters off the pages and wrote his sermons over the original. It was not until the invention of the x-ray machine that the original writing underneath could be clearly read.

5. **D (Codex Bezae)** 475-550 AD. This is a parallel manuscript. It is written in two languages: Greek and Latin. Currently it is in the University of Cambridge library. Theodore Beza was a French scholar associated with John Calvin while working on the Geneva Bible. From 1565 to 1604 AD Beza published nine editions of the Greek New Testament, all of which were based on the text of Stephanus. During this time he had in his possession this manuscript. He made very little use of it, being

ignorant of its age and value. It contains the Gospels and the book Acts.

6. **33 (a minuscule)** 9th century. It is sometimes referred to as "the queen of the cursives" because by examining the text it is obvious to textual critics that it was copied from a very early manuscript. It is very close to MS B.

7. **W (Codex Washingtonensis)** 450 AD. Is in the Smithsonian. Contains portions of the Gospels.

There are many other important manuscripts in Greek that contain various parts of the NT. Also found are manuscripts of the NT translated into other languages. These are known as versions. The earliest were in Latin. There are 8,000 of these in Latin and 1,000 in other languages. Also important are the "patristic" writings of early Church fathers where they quote from Scripture.

For example, Irenaeus in 180 AD quoted from Mark 16:19 in his book *Against Heresies*. "Also towards the conclusion of his Gospel, Mark says; So then, after the Lord Jesus had spoken to them, He was received up into heaven, and sits on the right hand of God."

Tatian's *Diatessaron*, which is a harmony of the four Gospels written around 175 AD contains Mark 16:9-20.

Textus Receptus
In 1520 an English scholar named Erasmus collected all the manuscripts he could find (8 late date Miniscules) and compiled what became known (after a revision by Stephanus based on additional manuscripts) as the Textus Receptus. It was translated into English and became the source for the King James Bible.

Through the centuries scholars have repeated Erasmus' work as more manuscripts have become available. Two scholars from Cambridge, Westcott and Hort, spent 26 years studying all the manuscripts and produced the *Westcott and Hort Greek* text in 1881. This was the source text for the Revised Version and others.

The argument that Mark 16:17 is not in the original Greek comes from the fact that it is missing from manuscripts Aleph and B. It is also missing from manuscript 304 from the 12th century, the Old Latin codex Bobiensis, the Sinaitic Syriac manuscript, from the two oldest Georgian manuscripts and from about 100 Armenian manuscripts. It is in manuscripts A,C,W,D, and MS 33 as well as many others.

Mark 16 in manuscript B
The scribe of manuscript B finished Mk. 16:8 near the bottom of a column then left the next column entirely blank. It is the only blank

column in the entire manuscript. This blank space may indicate that the copyist was reading from a torn or otherwise damaged manuscript and left a space hoping to supply the ending later from another source. The empty column after verse 8 is large enough to contain the last 12 verses. This large blank space testifies loudly to the fact that the scribe of B knew that Mark 16 did not end at verse 8. (See John Darby's translation of the New Testament, 3rd rev. ed. introductory notes, p. 3).

Mark 16 in manuscript Aleph "The leaf containing the omission is one of 6 leaves in Aleph that were not done by the hand that produced the rest of the manuscript." (*A Historical Introduction to the Books of the New Testament*, George Salmon. p. 142). Tischendorf, who discovered manuscript Aleph, was the first to notice this. (*Handbook to the Textural Criticism of the New Testament*, Frederic G. Kenyon, p. 66).

A corrector later inserted these 6 leaves outright. Whatever the correctors reason might have been, the fact is that these replacement leaves renders it impossible to say that manuscript Aleph in the original hand did not contain Mark 19:9-20.

The last section of Mark contains letters more spread out than else where in the manuscript. And the last column of Mark contains a blank space before Luke starts. George Salmon says: "This (spread out printing) suggests that the page as originally written must have contained something of considerable length which was omitted in the substituted copy. Unless some precaution were taken, an omission of the kind would leave a tell-tale blank [as there is in manuscript B]. But by spreading out his writing the scribe was enabled to carry over 37 letters to a new column, the rest of which could be left blank without attracting notice, since it was the conclusion of a Gospel." (*A Historical Introduction to the Books of the New Testament*, p. 147).

The remainder of the column is left blank as mentioned earlier. Salmon concludes; "I do not think these... phenomena can be reasonably explained in any other way than that the leaf, as originally copied, had contained the disputed verses; and that the corrector, regarding these as not a genuine part of the Gospel, canceled the leaf, recopying it in such a way as to cover the gap left by the erasure. It follows that the archetype of Aleph had contained the disputed verses." (*Ibid.*, pp 147, 148) An archetype is the source manuscript that this one was copied from.

Internal evidence
If Mark ended with chapter 16:8 the conclusion of his gospel would read: "And they went out quickly, and fled from the sepulcher; for they trembled and were amazed; neither said they any thing to any man; for they were afraid." This would be a rather disappointing ending.

Jamieson, Fausset, and Brown Commentary remarks: "That so carefully constructed a narrative as that of this Gospel terminated with the words, 'for they were afraid'... is what one wonders that *any* can bring themselves to believe."

There is some debate on whether or not some of the fragments found in the Dead Sea scrolls are from parts of the New Testament or not. In an article about the Dead Sea scrolls published in 1972 by the Evangelical Foundation, 1716 Spruce St., Philadelphia, Pa titled "Why All the Fuss" there is an explanation of the work by Dr. O'Callaghan whereby he concludes that some of the fragments come from I Timothy (1), Mark (4 fragments), James (1), Romans (1), Acts (1) and 2 Peter (1).

Manuscript 304 is not typical. It contains the gospels of Matthew and Mark with commentary interspersed with the text. There is a lengthy commentary section following Mark 16:8 which ends abruptly before completing the narrative. Most likely the end of this manuscript has been lost.

Other manuscripts containing verses 9-20 contain scribal notes stating that older Greek copies lacked the passage. In other manuscripts this section is marked with asterisks or obeli, the convential signs used by copyists to indicate a spurious addition has been made to the document. (Correspondence from John J. Grosboll).

Reference Sources

I have collected the material in this case study from many valuable sources and relied on the professional opinion of numerous consultants.   Only a few concepts are original with me. Though many sources are credited within the text, I have attempted to list all sources here. CGH

Alföldi, Andreas (Andrew). *The Conversion of Constantine and Pagan Rome.* Oxford, 1948 and 1969.

Allen, Joel, *The Sabbath: Saturday or Sunday,* Cornerstone Publishing, 1994, 59 pages

Allix, Peter, *The Ecclesiastical History of the Ancient Churches of Piedmont and of the Albigenses,* Clarendon Press, Oxford, England, 1821, 2 vols., 643 pages.

Andreasen, ML, *A Day from Eden,* Review & Herald Publishing Association, 1951, 64 pages
___*God's Holy Day,* RHPA, 1949, 118 pages
___*The Sabbath—Which Day and Why?,* TEACH Services, 2003, 255 pages.

Andreasen, Niels-Erik A, *Old Testament Sabbath,* Society of Biblical Literature, 1972, 301 pages

Andrews, John Nevins, *History of the Sabbath and the First Day of the Week,* Steam Press of the SDA Publishing Association, 1873, 536 pages; with Conradi, LR, 1912 4th edition 864 pages, 815 pages. 1998 reprint by TEACH Services, Brushton, New York.

Appel, Dan M, *A Bridge Across Time,* RHPA, 1996, 125 pages

Thomas Aquinas, *Summa Theologica,* New York, 1947, Part I-II.

Armstrong, Herbert W, *Which Day is the Christian Sabbath?* Worldwide Church of God, 1976, 108 pages

Arnold, Dr. Philip, "Little Known History of Sabbatarians (Taiping, China)," audio cassette.

Ashton, Ned S, *The Bible Sabbath,* RHPA, 1960, 32 pages

Augustine, *Confessions* 13, 24, 25, Nicene and Post-Nicene Fathers of the Christian Church (Grand Rapids, 1979), vol. 1.

Authoritative Quotations on the Sabbath, compilation, VOP, 1961, 31 pages

Bacchiocchi, Samuele, *Anti-Judaism and the Origin of Sunday,* Pontifical Gregorian University Press, 1975, 141 pages.
___*Divine Rest for Human Restlessness,* Biblical Perspectives, 1980, 319 pages
___*From Sabbath to Sunday, A Historical Investigation of the Rise of Sunday Observance in Early Christianity,* Pontifical Gregorian University Press, 1977, 372 pages.
___*God's Festivals in Scripture and History,* Biblical Perspectives,
___*Rest for Modern Man—The Sabbath for Today,* SPA, 1976, 32 pages
___*The Sabbath in the New Testament*, Biblical Perspectives, 1985, 275 pages.
___*The Sabbath Under Crossfire*, Biblical Perspectives, 1998, 303 pages.

Ball, Bryan W, *The Seventh-Day Men, Sabbatarians and Sabbatarianism in England and Wales, 1600-1800,* Clarendon Press, Oxford, England, 1994, 402 pages.

Baltger, K. *The Covenant Formularv in Old Testament, Senersh and Early Christian Writings*, tr. David E. Green, Philadelphia: Fortress, 1971.

Barber, Randy, *The Lord's Day,* The Quiet Hour, 1984, 87 pages

Barnes, Albert, *Commentary*, Edition of 1850.

Barnhouse, Donald Grey, *The Christian and the Sabbath*, Evangelical Foundation, Inc, 1958, 50 pages.

Barnett, T. Ratcliffe, *Margaret of Scotland: Queen and Saint*

Barth, Karl, *Church Dogmatics,* ET, Edinburgh, 1956, vol. 3, part 2.

Baynes, Norman, H., *Constantine the Great and the Christian Church*, London, 1934.

Beckwith, Robert T, Wilfrid Stott,*This is the Day,* 1978.

Bellesheim, *History of the Catholic Church of Scotland*

Bingham, Joseph, M.A, *Antiquities of the Christian Church.*

Bollman, Calvin P, *Sunday—Origin of its Observance in the Chrisitan Church*, RHPA, 1924, 30 pages

Dietrich Bonhoeffer, *Creation and Fall. A Theological Interpretation of Genesis 1-3,* New York, 1964.

Bourdeau, Daniel T, *Refutation of 44 Objections Against the Ancient Sabbath,* Steam Press of the SDA Pub Assoc, 1876, 87 pages
___*The Ancient Sabbath,* Review & Herald Publishing Association, 1887, 86 pages.

Bradford, Charles E, *Sabbath Roots: The African Connection*, L Brown and Sons Printing, Inc, 1999, 234 pages.

Branson, Roy, editor, *Festival of the Sabbath,* Association of Adventist Forums, 1985, 127 pages

Buchanan, George Wesley; "Worship, Feasts and Ceremonies in the Early Jewish-Christian Church," *New Testament Studies* 26, 1980.

Buck, *Theological Dictionary*

Burckhardt, Jacob, *The Age of Constantine the Great*, Pantheon Books Inc., New York, 1949.

Butler, George Ide, *The Change of the Sabbath, Was it by Divine or Human Authority?,* Southern Publishing Association, Nashville, Tennessee, 1889, 218 pages; 1904, 196 pages

Canright, Dudley Marvin, *The Morality of the Sabbath,* Steam Press of the SDA Pub Assoc, 1875, 96 pages

Carlow, George, *Defense of the Sabbath,* Leaves of Autmn Books, Inc, 1982, 168 pages

Carrington, Philip, Archbishop of Quebec, T*he Primitive Christian Calendar,* Cambridge University Press, 1952.

Casebolt, DE, *Saturday or Sunday,* Southern Publishing Association, 1978, 63 pages

Catholic Encylcopedia, article "Ten Commandments"

Chaikin, Miriam, *The Seventh Day: Story of the Jewish Sabbath*, Doubleday & Company, Inc, 1980, 47 pages

Clarke, Adam, *Commentary of the Bible*, 1851 Edition.

Clement of Alexandria, *The Miscellanies*, Book 6, chapter 16. Ante-Nicene Christian Library.

Cline, Donald, "The Los Lunas Stone," *Epigraphic Society Occasional Publications* **10** (1982, part 10), 68-73.

Cohen, Richard, *Sunday in the Sixties*, Public Affairs, 1962, 28 pages

Coleman, *Ancient Christianity Exemplified*

Coltheart, JF, *Sabbath of God Through the Centuries*, Leaves of Autumn, 1978/1990, 28 pages

Conybeare, Fred C., translator and editor, *The Key of Truth, a Manual of the Paulician Church of Armenia*, Clarendon Press, Oxford, England, 1898, photocopy, 397 pages.

Coon, Glen A & Ethel, *Lovely Lord of the Lord's Day*, PPPA, 1976, 192 pages.

Cottrell, Roy Franklin, *The True Sabbath*, SPA, 1942, 96 pages.

Coulter, Robert, "*The Story of the Church of God (Seventh Day)*," Bible Advocate Press, Denver, Colorado, 58 pages.

Cox, Robert, *The Literature of the Sabbath Question, Vol. II*, Maclachlan and Stewart, London, 1865, 500 pages.

Crews, Joe, *Why God Said Remember*, Amazing Facts, 1980, 28 pages.

Cummings, Des, Jr, *Original Love*, Hart Books, 2001.

Davidson, Richard M, *A Love Song for the Sabbath*, RHPA, 1988, 128 pages.
___ "Sanctuary Typology," *Symposium on Revelation*, Frank B. Holbrook, ed., (Silver Springs, Maryland, 1992, Biblical Research Institute, General Conference of Seventh-day Adventists), vol. 1.

Davis, J, *History of the Welsh Baptists*, D.M. Hogan, Pittsburgh, 1835, 204 pages.

Davis, Tamar, *General History of the Sabbatarian Churches*, Lindsay and Blakiston, Philadelphia, 1851, 255 pages.

De Haan, MR, *Who Changed the Sabbath?* Radio Bible Class, 1950, 32 pages.

De Lacey, Douglas R, "The Sabbath/Sunday Question and the Law in the Pauline Corpus," *From Sabbath to Lord's Day. A Biblical, Historical, and Theological Investigation*, ed. Donald A. Carson, Grand Rapids, 1982.
___*Dictionary of Paul and His Letters*, InterVarsity Press, 1993, University of Cambridge, England.

De Liguari, St. Alphonsus, *Dignity and Duties of the Priest*, Imprimatur 1927.

Deal, David Allen, *Discovery of Ancient America*, 1st ed., Kherem La Yah Press, Irvine CA, 1984.

Domville, Sir Willam, *The Sabbath, or an Examination of the Six Texts commonly adduced from the New Testament in proof of a Christian Sabbath*, 1849.

Dugger, Andrew N. and Dodd, Clarence O., A History of the True Church Traced From 33 A.D. to Date, Third Edition, 1972 (original edition, 1936), Giving & Sharing reprint, 1996, 106 pp., Earle, Alice Morse, *The Sabbath in Puritan New England*, Charles Scribner's Sons, 1892, 335 pages.

Edwards, Tilden, *Sabbath Time—Understanding and Practice for Christians*, Upper Room Books, 1992, 148 pages.

Ellis, Peter Berresford, *Celtic Inheritance,* Dorset Press, N.Y. 1992

Eusebius Pamphilius, Bishop of Caesarea (260 — 340), *Preparation for the Gospel, Proof of the Gospel, Ecclesiastical History, Life of Constantine, Oration to Constantine*, etc., etc. Hendrickson ed. Grand Rapids, Baker Book House, 1981, 500 pages.

Everson, Charles T, *Which Day of the Week Did Christ Sanctify Bless & Keep?* RHPA, 1950, 63 pages.
Faber, George Stanley, *The History of the Ancient Vallenses and Albigenses*, R.B. Seely and W. Burnside, London, 1838, 596 pages.

Farrer, Austin; *A Rebirth of Images. The Making of St. John's Apocalypse,* Glouchester, Massachussetts, 1970.

Fell, Barry, "Ancient Punctuation and the Los Lunas Text," *Epigraphic Society Occasional Publicatons* 13, 1985.

Finley, Mark A, *The Almost Forgotten Day,* Concerned Group, Inc., 1988, 145 pages.

Finn, James. *The Jews in China,* B. Wertheim, London, 1843

Fleming, Robert, *The Rise and Fall of the Papacy,* 1696

Fletcher, EB, *The National Book on the Sabbath,* Bailey & Noyes, 1861

Flick, A.C, *The Rise of the Medieval Church*

Ford Desmond, *The Forgotten Day,* Desmond Ford Publications, 1981, 318 pages.

Fuller, EQ, *The Two Sabbaths,* Poe & Hitchcock, 1864, 101 pages.

Gane, Edwin R, *How, When and Why was the Sabbath Changed from Saturday to Sunday,* November, 1997.

Gardner, Laurence, *Bloodline Of The Holy Grail, "The Stone Of Destiny,"* Element Books, 1996.

Gibbon, Edward, *The Decline And Fall Of The Roman Empire.* An Abridgement by D M Low. Penguin Great Britain, 1963.

Gilfallan, James, *The Sabbath Viewed in the Light of Reason,* American Tract Society, 1862.

Ginzberg, Louis, *Legends of the Jews,* Philadelphia, 1946, vol. 5.

Goldstein, Clifford, *A Pause for Pease,* PPPA, 1992, 126 pages, 1993 5th printing

Gordon, Cyrus, "Diffusion of Near East Culture in Antiquity and in Byzantine Times," *Orient* 30-31, 1995.

Grant R. Jeffrey, The Astonishing Pattern of Sevens in Genesis "The Signature of God" Frontier Research Publications, Inc. (1996), p.230-237

Grant, Miles, *Sabbath,* , A.E.Bloom Pub., 1924
___*The True Sabbath—Which Day Shall We Keep?* Advent Christian
    Publication Society, 1874, 104 pages

Grosboll, John J, *How to Keep the Sabbath,* Steps to Life, Inc, 1991, 25
    pages (and personal correspondence).

Gurney, Joseph John, *History, Authority, and Use of the Sabbath*, 1831,
    p. 86.

Hackett, Horatio B, *Commentary on Acts*, Kregel Publications; ISBN:
    0825427487, p. 251.

Halsberghe, Gaston, H., *The Cult of Sol Invictus*, E.J. Brill, Leiden, The
    Netherlands, 1972.

Hardinge, Leslie, *The Celtic Church in Britain,* TEACH Services,
    Brushton, New York, 1995 reprint of 1972 edition, 265 pages.

Hawkins, Yisrayl, *The Sabbath—Every Question Answered*, The House
    of Yahweh, 1992, 596 pages

Haynes, Carlyle B, *Calendar Changes Threatens Religion*, Religious
    Liberty Association, 1944, 23 pages
___*From Sabbath to Sunday*, RHPA, 1928, 128 pages
___*The Christian Sabbath,* SPA, 1916, 128 pages

Hefele, Charles Joseph, *A History of the Councils of the Church,*
    Edinburgh: Clark, 1896.

Herbert, Dwight P, *Saturday, Sunday & Salvation*, PPPA, 1980, 63
    pages

Heschel, Abraham Joshua; *The Sabbath: its meaning for modern man*,
    Farrar, Straus and Giroux, New York, 1951.

Hey, Wilf, "Sabbatarianism in British History," audio cassette.

Heylyn, Peter, *The History of the Sabbath*, The Second Edition,
    Revised. London, 1636.

Hisop, Alexander, "The Two Babylons," 1907, London. Reprinted
    TEACH Services, 352 pages.

Holbrook, Frank B., ed., "Sanctuary Typology," *Symposium on Revelation*, Silver Springs, Maryland, 1992, Biblical Research Institute, General Conference of Seventh-day Adventists, vol. 1.

Holland, Kenneth J, *The Magnificent Seventh*, VOP, 1970, 32 pages, 64 pages

___*This Day is Yours*, SPA, 1969, 192 pages

___*Those Sabbath Hours*, SPA, 1966, 214 pages

___*What's Holy About Saturday?* Adventist Information Service, 1975, 11 pages.

Hunter, Archibald M., "The Letter of Paul to the Colossians", Vol. 22 *The Layman's Bible Commentary*, John Knox Press, 1959.

Hurlbut, Jesse Lyman, *The Story of the Christian Church*, Zondervan, 1986 (1918, 1933, 1954), 254 pages.

Iraenus *Against Heresies*, Book V.

Jerome, *Die dominica Paschae homilia* , Corpus Christianorum Series Latina.

Jewett, Paul K, *The Lord's Day*, 1971.

Johns, Warren L, *Dateline, Sunday, USA*, PPPA, 1967, 252 pages

Johnsen, Carsten, *Day of Destiny—Mystery of the Seventh Day*, Untold Story Publishers, 1982, 163 pages

Johnson, O Q, *Sabbath Sunday & Friday in the Light of the Bible*, Walla Walla College Press, 1922, 60 pages

Jones, Alonzo Trevier, *Christ and the Pharisees or Christ Faithfulness in Sabbath*, International Religious Liberty Association, 1980, 33 pages

___*The Abiding Sabbath and the Lord's Day*, Leaves of Autumn Books, 1898, 173 pages

Jones, William, *The History of the Christian Church, from the Birth of Christ, to the XVIII Century, including the very interesting account of the Waldenses and Albigenses,* fifth edition, in 2 vols., Paternoster Row, London, 1826, 1,048 pages.

Jordan, James B, Basileans lectures, 1990, from Great Christian Books.

Josephus, *Antiquities of the Jews,* Book 1.

Jowett, George F, *The Drama of the Lost Disciples,* Covenant Publishing Co., Ltd, London, 251 pages.

Justin, *The First Apology of Justin,* chapter 67. Ante-Nicene Christian Library.

Katz, David S, *Sabbath and Sectarianism in Seventeenth-Century England,* E.J. Brill, New York, 1988, 224 pages.

Kaye, *Ecclesiastical History of the Second and Third Centuries, Illustrated from the writings of Tertullian,* p. 388. London, 1845

Kee, Alistair, *Constantine Versus Christ: The Triumph of Ideology,* SCM Press, London, 1982.

Kelly, Ronald D., *Now Revealed, The True History of the Early Christian Church,* 81 pages.

Kiesz, John, *A History of the Sabbath & Sunday,* The Bible Sabbath Association, Fairview, Oklahoma, 1992, 64 pages.

Killen, William. D., Professor of Ecclesiastical History, to the General Assembly of the Presbyterian church of Ireland, *The Ancient Church,* 1883

Kitto, John, *Cyclopedia of Biblical Literature,* London, 1862

Kohn, Samuel, *The Sabbatarians in Transylvania,* translated by Thomas McElwain and Bonne Brook, edited and forward by Wade Cox, Christian Churches of God reprint, 1998, 311 pages.

Kubo, Sakae, *God Meets Man,* SPA, 1978, 160 pages

Kuyper, Abraham, *Tractaat van den Sabbath (Treatise on the Sabbath),* Wormser, Amsterdam, 1890.

Lang, Andrew, *A History of Scotland*

Lardner, *Credibility of the Gospel History,* Vol. 2, pp. 292, 293. London, 1847.

Lee, Frances Nigel, , Th.D., Ph.D., D.Min., S.T.D., D.R.E., D.Ed., D.Hum., D.Jur., D.C.L., D.Litsft., D.Phil. Professor of Systematic Theology and Caldwell-Morrow Lecturer in Church History at

Queensland Presbyterian Theological College, Brisbane, Australia. *The Everlasting Covenant Sabbath*, doctoral thesis.

Leigh, Richard; Michael Biagent & Henry Lincoln, *The Messianic Legacy,* Dell Publishing, 1986

Leonard, Phillip M., and William R. McGlone, "An Epigraphic Hoax on Trial in New Mexico," *Epigraphic Society Occasional Publications* 17, 1988.

Lewis, *Seventh Day Baptists in Europe and America*

Lewish, AH(Rev), *Sunday Laws, Past and Present,* Chautauqua Herald, 1881, 14 pages

Lidzbarski, Mark, Letter Chart in Appendix to Wilhelm Gesenius and Emil Kautzsch, *Hebräische Grammatik*, 27th ed., Leipzig, 1902.

Liechty, Daniel, *Andreas Fischer and the Sabbatarian Anabaptists, An Early Reformation Episode in East Central Europe*, Studies in Anabaptist and Mennonite History No. 29, Herald Press, Scottdale, Pennsylvania, 1988, 166 pages.
___*Sabbatarianism in the 16th Centry*, Andrews University, 1993, 94 pages.

Lincoln, A. T.; "From Sabbath to Lord's Day: A Biblical and Theological Perspective," in *From Sabbath to Lord's Day; A Biblical, Historical, and Theological Investigation*, ed. Donald A. Carson, Grand Rapids, 1982.

Littlejoh, Wolcott R, *Constitutional Amendment; Or, The Sunday, The Sabbath,* SDA Pub Assoc, Steam Press of the, 1873, 384 pages.

Loewen, Marvin E, *Accused of Sabbath-Breaking*, GC of SDAs, tract, 1963, 11 pages.

Logan, Maurice S., *Sabbath Theology: A Reply to Those who Insist that Saturday is the Only True Sabbath Day.* Lord's Day Alliance of the United States, New York, 1913, 451 pages.

Lohse, Eduard, *A Commentary on the Epistles to the Colossians and to Philemon,* Philadelphia, 1971.

Lord's Day as Catholic, Readers Information Service, 1960, 7 pages

MacArthur, John, *Is the Sabbath Binding on Christians Today?*

MacMullen, Ramsey, *Constantine*, The Dial Press, New York, 1969.

Main, Arthur Elwin, *Bible Studies on the Sabbath Question*, American Sabbath Tract Society, 1910, 80 pages

Manrick, DC, *The Day God Rested*, Amazing Facts, Inc, 1990, 76 pages

Martin, E. L. *Secrets of Golgatha*, ASK Publications, Portland, Oregon, 2000.

Martin, Troy, Professor at Saint Xavier University in Chicago, "But Let Everyone Discern the Body of Christ (Colossians 2:17)," *Journal of Biblical Literature* 114/2, 1995.

___"Pagan and Judeo-Christian Time-keeping Schemes in Galatians 4:10 and Colossians 2:16," *New Testament Studies Journal* 42, Spring 1996.

Maslin, Simeon J, *The Sabbath Eve Seder,* Janowski, Max, Seder Erev Shabbat, 1974, 56 pages

McBirnie, William Steuart, *The Search for the Twelve Apostles*, 312 pages.

McGlone, William R., Phillip M. Leonard, James L. Guthrie, Rollin W. Gillespie, and James P. Whittall, Jr., *Ancient American Inscriptions: Plow Marks or History?* Early Sites Research Society, Sutton MA, 1993.

Melanchthon, *On Christian Doctrine, Lou Communes 1555*, Clyde L. Manschreck, ed. and trans., Grand Rapids, 1965.

Mendenhall, G.E., *Law and covenant in Israel, the Ancient Near East,* Pittsburgh: The Biblical Colloquium, 1955.

Milner, Joseph. *The History of the Church of Christ.* 5 vol. London: Luke Hansard & Sons, 1819, century 1.

Moffat, *The Church in Scotland*

Moore, Marvin, *Prescription for Reconciliation*, RHPA, 1982, 30 pages

Moorehouse, George E, "The Los Lunas Inscriptions: A Geological Study," *Epigraphic Society Occasional Publicatons*, 13, 1985.

Morer, Thomas M., *Dialogues on the Lord's Day*, London, 1701

Morgan, Kevin, *Sabbath Rest*, TEACH Services, 2002, 101 pages

Morton, Eliza H, *The Sabbath Question,* Eliza H. Morton pub, 1916, 135
    pages
Mosheim, *Ecclesiastical History*, century 1.

Nathan,K.S., PhD, *The Time and Second Coming of the Lord of the
    Sabbath,* 1988, 120 pages

Neander, Wilhelm August Johann, *History of the Christian Church of
    the First Three Centuries,,* London, 1831 (Rose's translation from
    the German edition, Hamburg, 1826).

Nelson, Gregory P, *A Touch of Heaven,* PPPA, 1999, 192 pages

Nickels, Richard C, *History of the Seventh Day Church of God*, Volume
    I, third ed., Volume II,186 pages.
___*Six Papers on the History of the Church of God*, second edition,
    Giving & Sharing, Neck City, Missouri, 1993, 354 pages. (Six
    sections include: "Sabbatarian Baptists in England,"
    "Sabbatarian Baptists in America," "The Adventist Movement:
    Its Relationship to the Seventh Day Church of God," "Sabbath
    Adventists: 1844-1863," "The Remnant of Israel: An Analysis of
    G.G. Rupert and His Independent Church of God (Seventh Day)
    Movement, 1915-1929," and "History of the Church of God
    (Seventh Day)" by John Kiesz.)

Odom, Robert Leo, *How Did Sunday Get its Name?* Souther Publishing
    Association, 1947, 32 pages
___*Sabbath and Sunday in Early Christianity*, Review and Herald
    Publishing Association, Washington D.C., 1977, 304 pages.

O'Keefe, Rev J O, *Rome's Arraignment of Sabbath-Breakers,* LMN
    Publishing, 16 pages

O'Leary *The Syriac Church and Fathers*

Olson, S. Gusten, *The Apostasy of the Lost Century*, Stedman Printers,
    Norway, 223 pages.

One Hundred Bible Facts on the Sabbath Question, RHPA, 1950, 4
    pages

Origin, Twenty-Third Homily on Numbers, Tome ii, *Patrologia Græca.*

Parise, Frank. *The Book of Calendars*, New York: Facts on File, Inc.

Paulien, Jon; "Seals and Trumpets: Some Current Discussions," *Symposium on Revelation*, Frank B. Holbrook, ed., Silver Springs, Maryland, 1992, Biblical Research Institute, General Conference of Seventh-day Adventists, vol. 1.
___ "The Role of the Hebrew Cultus, Sanctuary, and the Temple in the Plot and Structure of the Book of Revelation," *Andrews University Seminary Studies*, vol. 33, 1995.

Perrin, Jean Paul, *History of the Ancient Christians inhabiting the Valleys of the Alps: The Waldenses, The Albigenses, The Vaudois,* Griffith and Simon, Philadelphia, 1847, 475 pages.

Philo, *The Life of Moses* (De Vita Mosis) LCL.

Pickle, Bob, *A Response to the Video: Seventh-day Adventism, The Spirit Behind the Church.* Pickle Publishing Company, Halstad, Mn, 2002.

Pinkoski, Jim, *Truth About the Sabbath,* Amazing Facts, Inc, 1988, 56 pages.

Pliny the Younger, *Letters,* book 10, Letter 96. Loeb ed., vol. 2.

Prescott, WW, *Christ and the Sabbath,* Milepost Tracts and Books, 1989, 33 pages.

Primus, John H. *Holy Time: Moderate Puritanism and the Sabbath,* Macon, Georgia: Mercer University Press, 1989.

Pro or Con—Sabbath Question in a Nutshell, American Sabbath Tract Society, 1980.

Pummer, Reinhard, "How to Tell a Samaritan Synagogue from a Jewish Synagogue," *Biblical Archaeology Review*, vol. 24 #3, May/June 1998, pp. 24-35.
___ *The Samaritans*, E.J. Brill, Leiden, 1987.

Purvis, J.D., *The Samaritan Pentateuch and the Origin of the Samaritan Sect* Harvard Semitic Monographs, vol. 2. Harvard University Press, 1968.

Ratzlaff, Dale, *Sabbath in Crisis*, Life Assurance Ministries, 1990, 345 pages.

Rawlinson, Sir Henry, *Rest Days: A Study in Early Law and Morality.* New York: The MacMillan Company. 1916.

Reid, G Edward, *Sunday's Coming!* RHPA, 1996, 251 pages

Remember the Sabbath Day to Keep it Holy, G C Ministerial Association, 1980, 16 pages

Richards, Sr, HMS, *The Sabbath Christ Made*, PPPA, 1963, 8 pages

Ringgold, James T, *The Legal Sunday: It's History and Character*, International Religious Liberty Assoc, 1894, 252 pages
___*The Law of Sunday*, pp. 265-267.

Roberts, Brigham H, *The Lord's Day*, Church of Latter-Day Saints, 1972, 14 pages.

Robinson, *Ecclesiastical Researches*, chap. vi. 1792.

Rome's Challenge, *Catholic Mirror*, 1900, 32 pages.

Sabbath—Symbol of God's Rulership, SPA Tract, 1980, 16 pages.

Sabbath & Sanctuary Conference, compilation, SDA Church, 1998, 19 pages.

Sabbath and Festival Prayer Book, Rabbinical Assembly of America, 1957, 396 pages.

Sanford, Don A, *A Choosing People: The History of Seventh Day Baptists,* Broadman Press, Nashville, TN, 448 pages.

Sayce, A.H, *The Higher Criticism and the Monuments*, 1895.

Schaff, Philip, *History of the Church*, 1864.

Schaff-Herzog Encyclopaedia of Religious Knowledge.

Scriven, Charles, *Jubilee of the World,* SPA, 1978, 32 pages

Shuler, John Lewis, *God's Everlasting Sign,* SPA, 1972, 124 pages

Sidonius, *Apollinaris Sidonii Epistolæ.*

Sidonius, *Apollinaris Sidonii Epistolæ*.

Skupin, Michael, "The Los Lunas Errata," *Epigraphic Society Occasional Publications* 18 (1989), 249-52.

Smith, Hugh, *History of the Christian Church*, 1837.

Smith, W. Robertson, *Expositor's Greek Testament*, vol. 3.

Smith, Uriah, *A Word for the Sabbath: or False Theories Exposed*, Steam Press of the SDA Pub Assoc, 1875, 64 pages.
___*The Sabbath*, Steam Press of the SDA Publishing Association, 1875, 64 pages.

Smith's Dictionary of the Bible, Article "The Lord's Day" Page 356.

Socrates' Ecclesiastical History, Book 6, Chapter 8, *The Nicene and Post-Nicene Fathers*, Volume 3.

Sozomen, *Ecclesiastical History*, Book 1, chap. 8, 450 AD.

Spalding, Arthur Whitefield, *The Blessed Sabbath*, Review & Herald Publishing Association, 1940, 40 pages
___*The Sabbath and the Sabbath Day*, Pacific Press Publishing Association, 1937, 79 pages.

Spayd, LW, *Embracing Two Covenants and the Sabbath*, PPPA, 1898, 224 pages.

Stanley, "Eastern Church" lecture 5.

Stewart, Prince Michael, *The Forgotten Monarchy of Scotland*, Element Books, 1998.

Stonebreaker, Jay, "A Decipherment of the Los Lunas Decalogue Inscription," *Epigraphic Society Occasional Publications* **10** (1982, part 1), 74-81.

Strand, Kenneth A, *How Sunday Became the Popular Day of Worship*, These Times, 18 pages.
___*The Sabbath in Scripture and History* (Washington, DC.: Review and Herald, 1982).

Straw, Walter E, *Origin of Sunday Observance*, RHPA, 1939, 118 pages.

Tabor, James D. "An Ancient Hebrew Inscription in New Mexico: Fact or Fraud?" *United Israel Bulletin* Vol. 52, Summer 1997, pp. 1-3.

Tertullian, *Apology*, sect. 2.

Teske, Jacob M, *The Lord's Day and a National Sunday Law*, Cornerstone Publishing, 1995, 96 pages.

The Anti-Nicene Fathers, translations of *The Writings of the Fathers down to a.d. 325*, Alexander Roberts, D.D, and James Donaldson, LL.D, EDITORS, T&T CLARK, Edinburgh, Wm. B. Eerdmans publishing company, Grand Rapids, Michigan

The Apocrypha and Pseudepigrapha of the Old Testament (Oxford: Clarendon Press, 1913)

The Book of Jasher, M.M. Noah and A.S. Gould, New York, 1840.

The Epistle of Barnabas, Staniforth, M (Translator) 1968. Early Christian Writings. Penguin, Great Britain. Tatford, F A 1947. Paperback edition 1969. Prophecy's Last Word, Pickering & Inglis, Great Britain.

The Israel of the Alps, the story of the Waldenses, 85-minute VHS video, filmed in the Alps, LLT Productions, Angwin, California.

The Oxyrhynchus Papyri, Pt. 1, p. 3, Logion 2, verso 4-11, London: Offices of the Egyptian Exploration Fund, 1898.

The Sabbath—Sign of God's Power: Past and Present, Westworth, W.A., publisher unknown, 1914, 96 pages.

Thomson, Thomas, *A History of the Scottish People from the Earliest Times*, Gresham Publishing Co., London, 1887

Thurmon, Roy B, *The Sabbath Today,* Southern Publishing Association, 1962, 92 pages.

Torrey, R A,DD, *Ought Christians to Keep the Sabbath?* Fleming H Revell Company, 1899, 44 pages.

Tucker, Julius L, *Another Look at the Christian Sabbath*, The Quiet Hour, 1977, 99 pages.
___*When God Said "Remember",* The Quiet Hour, 1996, 19 pages.

Tucker, Laverne E, *A Day for Freedom*, The Quiet Hour, 1991, 58 pages.

Twisse, William (1578-1646), *Morality of the Fourth Commandments Still in Force to Binde Christians delivered by way of Answer to the translator of Doctor Prideaux his Lecture, Concerning the Doctrine of the Sabbath*, London, 1641, pp. 56, 57.

Underwood, L. Lyle, "The Los Lunas Inscription," *Epigraphic Society Occasional Publications* 10 (1982, part 1), 57-67.

Vandeman, George E, *A Day to Remember*, PPPA, 1965, 103 pages.

Van Dolson, Leo R; Spangler, J Robert, *The Case Against Saturday Blue Laws*, SPA, 1977, 32 pages.

Waggoner, Ellet Joseph, *Can We Keep the Sabbath?* LMN Publications, 1988, 12 pages.

Waggoner, Joseph Harvey, "A Review of a Series of Discourses Delivered by N. Fillio, in Battle Creek, Mich, March 13th, to April, 4th, 1857 on the Sabbath Question," Review and Herald, Battle Creek, 1857. 64 pages.
___*Nature and Obligation of the Sabbath of the Fourth Commandment*, PPPA, 1890, 92 pages

Walker, Allen, *The Law and the Sabbath*, Evangelist Allen Walker, 198 pages

Webster, William, *The Church of Rome at the Bar of History*, Banner of Truth Trust, Edinburgh, Scotland, 1997, 244 pages.

Weiss, Herold, "The Law in the Epistle to the Colossians," *The Catholic Biblical Quarterly* 34 [1972]: 311.

Wenham, Gordon J, *Word Biblical Commentary: Genesis 1-15*, Waco, Texas: Word Books, 1987.

Wesley, John, *Sermon 95*.

What About the Sabbath? RHPA, 1930 15 pages

White, James; Smith, Uriah, *The Biblical Institute*, 1878 reprint 2000 by TEACH Services, 352 pages

Wilcox, Milton Charles, *Is Sunday the Sabbath?* PPPA, 1894, 8 pages
___*The Lord's Day—The Test of the Ages,* PPPA, 1931, 96 pages.

Wilder, T.E. *The Seventh Day: Against Humanistic Biblical Interpretation,* Contra Mundum No. 1, Fall 1992.

Wilkinson, Benjamin George, *Truth Triumphant—The Church in the Wilderness,* PhD, PPPA, 1944, reprint 1994 TEACH Services, 424 pages.

Wilson, Larry W., *Daniel Unlocked for the Final Generation,* Wake Up America, Inc., 2003.

Wood, Kenneth H, *From God with Love,* Ellen G White Estate, Inc, 2000, 23 pages
Word of God or Traditions of Men? American Sabbath Tract Society, 1981, tract.

Wylie, J.A, *History of the Waldenses,* 1882, reprint TEACH Services 2001, 206 pages.

Yeates, *East Indian Church History*

Yost, Frank H, *The Early Christian Sabbath,* PPPA, 1947, 96 pages

Zodhiates, Spiros, *The Complete Word Study New Testament.*

Photo and Art Credits

We'd love to send you a free catalog of titles we publish
or even hear your thoughts, reactions, criticism,
about things you did or didn't like about this
or any other book we publish.

Just write or call us at:

TEACH Services, Inc.
Brushton, New York 12916
1-800/367-1844

www.tsibooks.com